THIRD EDITION

CASES IN LEADERSHIP

THE IVEY CASEBOOK SERIES

A SAGE Publications Series

Series Editor

Paul W. Beamish
Richard Ivey School of Business
Western University

Books in This Series

CASES IN ALLIANCE MANAGEMENT
Building Successful Alliances
Edited by Jean-Louis Schaan and Micheál J. Kelly

CASES IN BUSINESS ETHICS
Edited by David J. Sharp

CASES IN ENTREPRENEURSHIP
The Venture Creation Process
Edited by Eric A. Morse and Ronald K. Mitchell

CASES IN GENDER AND DIVERSITY IN ORGANIZATIONS
Edited by Alison M. Konrad

CASES IN LEADERSHIP (Third Edition)
Edited by W. Glenn Rowe and Laura Guerrero

CASES IN MARKETING MANAGEMENT
Edited by Kenneth E. Clow and Donald Baack

CASES IN OPERATIONS MANAGEMENT
Building Customer Value Through World-Class Operations
Edited by Robert D. Klassen and Larry J. Menor

CASES IN ORGANIZATIONAL BEHAVIOR
Edited by Gerard H. Seijts

CASES IN THE ENVIRONMENT OF BUSINESS
International Perspectives
Edited by David W. Conklin

INTRODUCTION TO NONPROFIT MANAGEMENT
Text and Cases
Edited by W. Glenn Rowe and Mary Conway Dato-on

MERGERS AND ACQUISITIONS
Text and Cases
Edited by Kevin K. Boeh and Paul W. Beamish

THIRD EDITION

CASES IN LEADERSHIP

W. GLENN ROWE
Richard Ivey School of Business
Western University

LAURA GUERRERO
University of Texas, El Paso

Los Angeles | London | New Delhi
Singapore | Washington DC

Los Angeles | London | New Delhi
Singapore | Washington DC

FOR INFORMATION:

SAGE Publications, Inc.

2455 Teller Road

Thousand Oaks, California 91320

E-mail: order@sagepub.com

SAGE Publications Ltd.

1 Oliver's Yard

55 City Road

London EC1Y 1SP

United Kingdom

SAGE Publications India Pvt. Ltd.

B 1/I 1 Mohan Cooperative Industrial Area

Mathura Road, New Delhi 110 044

India

SAGE Publications Asia-Pacific Pte. Ltd.

3 Church Street

#10-04 Samsung Hub

Singapore 049483

The Ivey cases have been prepared solely to provide material for class discussion. The authors do not intend to illustrate either effective or ineffective handling of managerial situations. The authors do not intend to provide legal, tax, accounting, or other professional advice. Such advice should be obtained from a qualified professional. The authors may have disguised certain names and other identifying information to protect confidentiality.

Richard Ivey School of Business Foundation prohibits any form of reproduction, storage, or transmittal without its written permission. Reproduction of this material is not covered under authorization by any reproduction rights organization. To order copies or request permission to reproduce materials, contact Ivey Publishing, c/o Richard Ivey School of Business Foundation, Western University, London, Ontario, Canada, N6A 3K7; phone (519) 661-3208; fax (519) 661-3882; e-mail cases@ivey.uwo.ca.

Printed in the United States of America

Library of Congress Cataloging-in-Publication Data

Cases in leadership / editors, W. Glenn Rowe, Laura Guerrero. — 3rd ed.

p. cm.
ISBN 978-1-4522-3497-7 (pbk.)

1. Leadership—Case studies. 2. Management—Case studies. I. Rowe, W. Glenn. II. Guerrero, Laura.

HD57.7.C372 2013
658.4′092—dc23   2011053502

This book is printed on acid-free paper.

Acquisitions Editor: Patricia Quinlin

Editorial Assistant: Katie Guarino

Production Editor: Laureen Gleason

Copy Editor: Lana Todorovic-Arndt

Typesetter: C&M Digitals (P) Ltd.

Proofreader: Stefanie Storholt

Cover Designer: Candice Harman

Marketing Manager: Liz Thornton

Permissions Editor: Adele Hutchinson

12 13 14 15 16 10 9 8 7 6 5 4 3 2 1

Contents

Introduction to the SAGE-Ivey Casebook Series

As the title of this series suggests, these books all draw from the Ivey Business School's case collection. Ivey has long had the world's second largest collection of decision-oriented, field-based business cases. Well over 1 million copies of Ivey cases are studied every year. There are more than 3,000 cases in Ivey's current collection, with more than 8,000 in the total collection. Each year approximately 200 new titles are registered at Ivey Publishing (www.iveycases.com), and a similar number are retired. Nearly all Ivey cases have teaching notes available to qualified instructors. The cases included in this volume are all from the current collection.

The vision for the original series was a result of conversations I had with SAGE's then senior editor, the late Al Bruckner, starting in September 2002. Over the subsequent months, we were able to shape a model for the books in the series that we felt would meet a market need. Each volume in the original series contained text and cases. Some text was deemed essential in order to provide a basic overview of the particular field and to place the selected cases in an appropriate context. We made a conscious decision to not include hundreds of pages of text material in each volume in recognition of the fact that many professors prefer to supplement basic text material with readings or lectures customized to their interests and to those of their students.

In early 2010, Lisa Shaw, then senior executive editor at SAGE, contacted me about extending our publishing partnership. This present volume is a result.

The editors of the books in this new series are all highly qualified experts in their respective fields. I was delighted when each agreed to prepare a volume. We very much welcome your comments on this book.

Paul W. Beamish
Series Editor and Director, Ivey Publishing

Preface

The purpose of this leadership casebook is to expose MBA, undergraduate business students, and students in other areas of study to cases that help them gain a better understanding of leadership. It is expected that this understanding will better enable them to be effective leader/managers and to more effectively lead their organizations given the opportunities and challenges they will face throughout their careers. This casebook may be used alone or serve as a supplement to a leadership textbook such as Northouse's (2013) *Leadership: Theory and Practice* (6th ed.). The cases selected for this casebook describe complex leadership issues that require the attention of the decision maker in the case.

In addition, the cases will generate much discussion in the classroom as students grapple with difficult real-world decisions that have grabbed the attention of real-world managers already. The casebook contains 32 cases (21 of which are new to this edition) from Ivey Publishing and 16 readings (seven of which are new to this edition) related to leadership issues from the *Ivey Business Journal*. In addition, we have added a new chapter on servant leadership in accordance with the new chapter in Northouse (2013). Each chapter begins with a quotation (all of which are new) from a real-world CEO/former CEO or recognized leadership expert selected to introduce the concepts and theories in that chapter. For each chapter, we briefly summarize leadership concepts and theories and describe the relevance of the issues/problems in the case. As a whole, the cases provide students with the opportunity to practice and hone several skills. Some of these skills are the ability to analyze, to make decisions, to apply lessons learned, and to plan and engage in oral communication.

Kotter (1998) argued that business organizations are overmanaged and underled. Mintzberg (1998) suggested that as organizations become more diversified, those in leadership positions rely more on managerial skills and less on leadership skills. Others have argued that large, overdiversified business organizations will result in those with leadership skills only exercising managerial skills, because they will use their leadership energy to fight the system or they will leave the organization (Rowe, 2001; Rowe & Hossein Nejad, 2009). All these scenarios leave many organizations without strategic or visionary leadership and with only managerial leadership. This casebook is designed to help students grapple with leadership issues so that they can more effectively exercise leadership as well as exercise effective managerial skills. Leading is different from managing (Kotter, 1998; Mintzberg, 1998; Rowe, 2001; Rowe & Hossein Nejad, 2009; Zaleznik, 1977), and most, if not all, business schools teach their undergraduate and graduate students to be effective managers. Few business schools do as well at giving their students the opportunity to develop leadership skills. This casebook is designed to help leadership professors facilitate a discussion on leadership concepts among business students and to engage students in that discussion.

The cases are selected for their integrative issues. These include globalization, diversity, ethical dilemmas, and motivation. These issues will surface in several cases and are not emphasized in only one case. There is opportunity for professors to refer to previous cases and to integrate learning from one case into another case. Of course, all of the cases have leadership implications—whether they concern leading within the organization, leading teams, and/or leading oneself.

⊠ References

Kotter, J. P. (1998). What leaders really do. In *Harvard Business Review on leadership* (pp. 37–60). Boston, MA: Harvard Business School Press.

Mintzberg, H. (1998). Retrospective commentary on the manager's job: Folklore and fact. In *Harvard Business Review on leadership* (pp. 29–32). Boston, MA: Harvard Business School Press.

Northouse, P. G. (2013). *Leadership: Theory and practice* (6th ed.). Thousand Oaks, CA: Sage.

Rowe, W. G. (2001). Creating wealth in organizations: The role of strategic leadership. *Academy of Management Executive*, 15, 81–94.

Rowe, G., & Hossein Nejad, M. (2009). Strategic leadership: Short-term stability and long-term viability, *Ivey Business Journal*, 1–9.

Zaleznik, A. (1977). Managers and leaders: Are they different? *Harvard Business Review*, 55, 67–78.

Acknowledgments

We want to acknowledge and thank all of those involved in the writing of this book. First, we want to thank the staff at Ivey Publishing, the case writers, and the *Ivey Business Journal* authors, without whom this casebook would not have been possible. Second, this project would not have happened without the initiative, encouragement, and support of Paul Beamish and the late Al Bruckner. Without Al's support and encouragement, this book would not have been written. Third, Mayan White and Lisa Shaw displayed the nicest ability to encourage us to get done what needed to be done when it needed to be done. Finally, Lana Arndt did a wonderful job as our copy editor—thank you.

To Fay, Gillian, and Ryan—I love you and I am so proud of you.

—Glenn Rowe

To Alec, Julian, and Andy—thank you for inspiring me.

—Laura Guerrero

Leadership

What Is It?

I dream, I test my dreams against my beliefs, I dare to take risks, and I execute my vision to make those dreams come true

—Walt Disney[1]

Peter Northouse (2013) defines leadership as "a process whereby an individual influences a group of individuals to achieve a common goal" (p. 5). Gary Yukl (2010) defines leadership as "the proc ss of influencing others to understand and agree about what needs to be done and how to do it, and the process of facilitating individual and collective efforts to accomplish shared objectives" (p. 8). Mark van Vugt and Anjana Ahuja (2011) define leadership as "a process of social influence to attain shared goals" (p. 24). These definitions suggest several components central to the phenomenon of leadership. Some of them are as follows: (a) Leadership is a process, (b) leadership involves influencing others, (c) leadership happens within the context of a group, (d) leadership involves goal attainment, and (e) these goals are shared by leaders and their followers. The very act of defining leadership as a process suggests that leadership is not a characteristic or trait with which only a few certain people are endowed at birth. Defining leadership as a process means that leadership is a transactional event that happens between leaders and their followers.

Viewing leadership as a process means that leaders affect and are affected by their followers either positively or negatively. It stresses that leadership is a two-way, interactive event between leaders and followers rather than a linear, one-way event in which the leader affects the followers but not vice versa. Defining leadership as a process makes it available to everyone—not just a select few who *are*

---

[1]Believed to have been said by Walt Disney as stated in B. Capodagli and L. Jackson (2007, p. 1).

born with it. More important, it means that leadership is not restricted to just the one person in a group who has formal position power (i.e., the formally appointed leader).

Leadership is about influence—the ability to influence your subordinates, your peers, and your bosses in a work or organizational context. Without influence, it is impossible to be a leader. Of course, having influence means that there is a greater need on the part of leaders to exercise their influence ethically (more on this in Chapter 15).

Leadership operates in groups. This means that leadership is about influencing a group of people who are engaged in a common goal or purpose. This can be an Executive MBA program in a business school with a staff of six, a naval ship with a ship's company of 300 (a destroyer) or 6,000 (an aircraft carrier), or a multinational enterprise such as Starbucks with more than 16,800 stores operating in 48 countries and in excess of 137,000 partners (employees) as of December 2010. This definition of leadership precludes the inclusion of leadership training programs that teach people to lead themselves.

Leadership includes the achievement of goals. Therefore, leadership is about directing a group of people toward the accomplishment of a task or the reaching of an endpoint through various ethical means. Leaders direct their energies and the energies of their followers to the achievement of something together—for example, hockey coaches working with their players to win a championship, to win their conference, to have a winning (better than 0.500) season, or to have a better won–lost percentage than last season. Thus, leadership occurs in, as well as affects, contexts where people are moving in the direction of a goal.

Leaders and followers share objectives. Leadership means that leaders work with their followers to achieve objectives that they all share. Establishing shared objectives that leaders and followers can coalesce around is difficult but worth the effort. Leaders who are willing to expend time and effort in determining appropriate goals will find these goals achieved more effectively and easily if followers and leaders work together. Leader-imposed goals are generally harder and less effectively achieved than goals developed together.

In this casebook, those who exercise leadership will be referred to as leaders, while those toward whom leadership is exercised will be referred to as followers. Both are required for there to be a leadership process. Within this process, both leaders and followers have an ethical responsibility to attend to the needs and concerns of each other; however, because this casebook is about leadership, we will focus more on the ethical responsibility of leaders toward their followers. Finally, it needs to be said that leaders are not better than followers, nor are they above followers. On the contrary, leaders and followers are intertwined in a way that requires them to be understood in their relationship with each other and as a collective body of two or more people (Burns, 1978; DuBrin, 2010; Hollander, 1992).

In the previous paragraphs, leadership has been defined and the definitional aspects of leadership have been discussed. In the next few paragraphs, several other issues related to the nature of leadership will be discussed: how trait leadership is different from leadership as a process, how emergent and appointed leadership are different, and how coercion, power, and management are different from leadership.

⬚ Trait Versus Process

Statements such as "She is a born leader" and "He was born to lead" imply a perspective toward leadership that is trait based. Yukl (2010) states that the trait approach "emphasizes leaders' attributes such as personality, motives, values, and skills. Underlying this approach was the assumption that some people are natural leaders, endowed with certain traits not possessed by other people" (p. 13). This is very different from describing leadership as a process. In essence, the trait viewpoint suggests that leadership is inherent in a few select people and that leadership is restricted to only those few who have special talents with which they are born (Yukl, 2010). Some examples of traits are the ability to speak well, an extroverted personality, or unique physical characteristics such as height (Bryman, 1992). Viewing leadership as a process implies that leadership is a phenomenon that is contextual and suggests that everyone is capable of exercising leadership. This suggests that leadership can be learned and that leadership is observable through what leaders do or how they behave (Daft, 2011; Jago, 1982; Northouse, 2013).

Assigned Versus Emergent

Assigned leadership is the appointment of people to formal positions of authority within an organization. Emergent leadership is the exercise of leadership by one group member because of the manner in which other group members react to him or her. Examples of assigned leadership are general managers of sports teams, vice presidents of universities, plant managers, the CEOs of hospitals, and the executive directors of nonprofit organizations. In some settings, it is possible that the person assigned to a formal leadership position may not be the person to whom others in the group look for leadership.

Emergent leadership is exhibited when others perceive a person to be the most influential member of their group or organization, regardless of the person's assigned formal position. Emergent leadership is exercised when other people in the organization support, accept, and encourage that person's behavior. This way of leading does not occur when a person is appointed to a formal position but emerges over time through positive communication behaviors. It has been suggested that some communication behaviors that explain emergent leadership are verbal involvement, keeping others well informed, asking other group members for their opinions, being firm but not rigid, and the initiation of new and compelling ideas (Fisher, 1974; Northouse, 2013).

The material in this casebook is designed to apply equally to emergent and assigned leadership. This is appropriate since whether a person emerged as a leader or was assigned to be a leader, that person is exercising leadership. Consequently, this casebook uses cases that focus on the leader's "ability to inspire confidence and support among the people who are needed to achieve organizational goals" (DuBrin, 2010, pp. 2–3).

Leadership and Power

Power is related to but different from leadership. It is related to leadership because it is an integral part of the ability to influence others. Power is defined as the potential or capacity to influence others to bring about desired outcomes. We have influence when we can affect others' beliefs, attitudes, and behavior. While there are different kinds of power, in organizations, we consider two kinds of power—position power and personal power. Position power is that power that comes from holding a particular office, position, or rank in an organization (Daft, 2011). A university president has more power than a dean of a business school, but they both have formal power.

Personal power is the capacity to influence that comes from being viewed as knowledgeable and likable by followers. It is power that derives from the interpersonal relationships that leaders develop with followers (Yukl, 2010). We would argue that when leaders have both position and personal power, they should use personal power a vast majority of the time. Overuse of position power may erode the ability of a leader to influence people. Of course, it is important to know when it is most appropriate to use position power and to be able and willing to use it (Daft, 2011).

Power can be two-faced. One face is the use of power within an organization to achieve one's personal goals to the detriment of others in the organization. The other face is that power that works to achieve the collective goals of all members of the organization, sometimes even at the expense of the leader's personal goals.

Leadership and Coercion

Related to power is a specific kind of power called coercion. Coercive leaders use force to cause change. These leaders influence others through the use of penalties, rewards, threats, punishment, and negative reward schedules (Daft, 2011). Coercion is different from leadership, and it is important to distinguish between the two. In this casebook, it is important for you to distinguish between those who are being coercive versus those who are influencing a group of people toward a common goal. Using coercion is counter to influencing others to achieve a shared goal and may have unintended negative consequences (DuBrin, 2010; Yukl, 2010).

Leadership and Management

Leadership is similar to, and different from, management. They both involve influencing people. They both require working with people. Both are concerned with the achievement of common goals. However, leadership and management are different on more dimensions than they are similar.

Zaleznik (1977) believes that managers and leaders are very distinct, and being one precludes being the other. He argues that managers are reactive, and while they are willing to work with people to solve problems, they do so with minimal emotional involvement. On the other hand, leaders are emotionally involved and seek to shape ideas instead of reacting to others' ideas. Managers limit choice, while leaders work to expand the number of alternatives to problems that have plagued an organization for a long period of time. Leaders change people's attitudes, while managers only change their behavior.

Mintzberg (1998) contends that managers lead by using a cerebral face. This face stresses calculation, views an organization as components of a portfolio, and operates with words and numbers of rationality. He suggests that leaders lead by using an insightful face. This face stresses commitment, views organizations with an integrative perspective, and is rooted in the images and feel of integrity. He argues that managers need to be two-faced. They need to simultaneously be managers and leaders.

Kotter (1998) argues that organizations are overmanaged and underled. However, strong leadership with weak management may be even worse. He suggests that organizations need both strong leadership and strong management. Managers are needed to handle complexity by instituting planning and budgeting, organizing and staffing, and controlling and problem solving. Leaders are needed to handle change through setting a direction, aligning people, and motivating and inspiring people. He argues that organizations need people who can do both—they need leader-managers.

Rowe (2001) contends that leaders and managers are different and suggests that one aspect of the difference may be philosophical. Managers believe that the decisions they make are determined for them by the organizations they work for and that the organizations they work for conduct themselves in a manner that is determined by the industry or environment in which they operate. In other words, managers are deterministic in their belief system. Leaders believe that the choices they make will affect their organizations and that their organizations will affect or shape the industries or environments in which they operate. In other words, the belief systems of leaders are more aligned with a philosophical perspective of free will.

Organizations with strong management but weak or no leadership will stifle creativity and innovation and be very bureaucratic. Conversely, an organization with strong leadership and weak or nonexistent management can become involved in change for the sake of change—change that is misdirected or meaningless and has a negative effect on the organization. Bennis and Nanus (1985) expressed the differences between managers and leaders very clearly in their often quoted phrase: "Managers are people who do things right and leaders are people who do the right thing" (p. 221). Implicit in this statement is that organizations need people who do the right thing and who do the "right things right."

References

Bennis, W. G., & Nanus, B. (1985). *Leaders: The strategies for taking charge.* New York, NY: Harper & Row.

Bryman, A. (1992). *Charisma and leadership in organizations.* London, England: Sage.

Burns, J. M. (1978). *Leadership.* New York, NY: Harper & Row.

Capodagli, B., & Jackson, L. (2007). The Disney way (2nd ed.). New York, NY: McGraw-Hill.

Daft, R. L. (2011). *The leadership experience* (5th ed.). Mason, OH: Thomson, South-Western.

DuBrin, A. (2010). *Leadership: Research findings, practice, and skills* (6th ed.). Mason, OH: South-Western/Cengage.

Fisher, B. A. (1974). *Small group decision making: Communication and the group process.* New York, NY: McGraw-Hill.

Hollander, E. P. (1992). Leadership, followership, self, and others. *Leadership Quarterly, 3*(1), 43–54.

Jago, A. G. (1982). Leadership: Perspectives in theory and research. *Management Science, 28*(3), 315–336.

Kotter, J. P. (1998). What leaders really do. In *Harvard Business Review on leadership* (pp. 37–60). Boston, MA: Harvard Business School Press.

Mintzberg, H. (1998). Retrospective commentary on the manager's job: Folklore and fact. In *Harvard Business Review on leadership* (pp. 29–32). Boston, MA: Harvard Business School Press.

Northouse, P. G. (2013). *Leadership: Theory and practice* (6th ed.). Thousand Oaks, CA: Sage.

Rowe, W. G. (2001). Creating wealth in organizations: The role of strategic leadership. *Academy of Management Executive, 15*(1), 81–94.

Vugt, M. van, & Ahuja, A. (2011). *Naturally selected: The evolutionary science of leadership.* New York, NY: HarperBusiness.

Yukl, G. (2010). *Leadership in organizations* (7th ed.). Upper Saddle River, NJ: Pearson-Prentice Hall.

Zaleznik, A. (1977). Managers and leaders: Are they different? *Harvard Business Review, 55,* 67–78.

The Cases

Adcock Ingram: Decisions and Motives That Steer Acquisitions

This case sketches the story of an ambitious and charismatic young business leader, who through value-adding commercial transactions helps a South African pharmaceutical company to grow. In May 2009, he faces his inability to close on a deal when he makes an offer to buy a smaller pharmaceutical company.

Dickinson College: Inspiration for a Leadership Story (In the Vision of a Founding Father)

In January 1999, William Durden became the 27th president of his alma mater, Dickinson College. He quickly realized that for much of the 20th century, Dickinson had lacked a strong sense of organizational purpose. By autumn, Durden had turned to the life and writings of Dr. Benjamin Rush, who had secured the college charter in 1783, as the inspiration for the story. After introducing Durden and the challenges confronting Dickinson, the case describes the early history of the college and the ideas and accomplishments of Rush. It then provides students with a brief overview of the strategic challenges that had surfaced for Dickinson by the mid-1990s. The conclusion indicates that Durden still had to resolve many issues associated with the identity story.

⊠ The Reading

Great Leadership Is Good Leadership

Look into the soul of any great leader and you will find a good leader. But if only that were the case! Some leaders, those who crave and bathe in the spotlight, are in fact not so great. Others, who are highly effective (and modest) and possess the five key characteristics this author describes, are good leaders first and foremost—which is what, in the end, makes them great!

Adcock Ingram: Decisions and Motives That Steer Acquisitions

Charlene C. Lew

Dr. Jonathan Louw's face was drawn, the pressure of the last few weeks clearly visible in his eyes. He had placed R2.125 billion[1] on the table to buy Cipla Medpro South Africa (Ciplamed). With this acquisition, he could secure an impressive share in South Africa's generics medication market and boost the respiratory and central nervous system portfolios of Adcock Ingram, a leading world-class health-care company (see Exhibit 1), as well as ensure a strong position in relation to his competitor Aspen. For Adcock Ingram, the merit of the Ciplamed acquisition was indisputable; still, no matter how compelling the board and analysts' case for value creation may have been, and no matter how strong his personal determination to accelerate the success of Adcock through acquisitions appeared, he now realized that the conclusion of the deal was no longer certain. He could not help

but wonder, "Was there anything more I could have done to ensure that the offer was accepted?"

As Louw turned on the ignition of his car to drive home, his thoughts flashed through his life, the history of Adcock and its victories since 1890. The events of the preceding two years that had set the stage for the board of Adcock to offer Ciplamed a "scheme of arrangement" in April 2009 were foremost in his mind.

⊠ Background

Becoming a Business Leader

Louw began his career as a medical doctor in South Africa. His ambitions soon took him to the United Kingdom, where he was exposed to the National Health Service (NHS). Seeing as many as 150 patients per day in casualty, this period

---

Version: (A) 2010-06-18

[1]Currency is presented in South African rands, unless otherwise noted. US$1 = R9.04 approximately.

instilled in him the ability to work efficiently and the desire to see others do the same. After about a year in this environment, Louw identified a coveted position as anaesthetist at St. Mary's hospital in London. Against all odds and through sheer determination he secured the position to work in this prestigious facility with highly qualified specialists; however, within four years he became restless again. Louw wanted to grow beyond the focused detail of the role of anaesthetist: this led him to return to South Africa to obtain an MBA qualification.

His first commercial job was as a medical advisor at AstraZeneca, where he utilized his skills in the fundamentals of marketing pharmaceutical products, before he moved to Tiger Brands. The period at Tiger Brands, first in the role of new business development and then heading up the Adcock Ingram business, not only developed his deal-making competencies but also equipped him with examples of different management styles. He valued his leaders for working hard and for dedicating their lives to growing the business. Louw also learnt the importance of staying up to date with the detail of the business in order to shape the big picture strategy. The deals he made at Tiger Brands came from opportune timing, the contribution of colleagues and his willingness to make unpopular decisions: one such decision was to go over the head of a local manager to convince an international pharmaceutical company to divest a business that he wanted to buy. Although this temporarily angered the local manager, he secured the acquisition and managed to maintain the relationship.

Louw had been described as a charismatic yet driven, determined and tenacious medical doctor with a ruthless passion for success. Drawing on the influences of his early career, he developed the view of Adcock as "an organism that needs to be lean and mean and muscular and that has to constantly adjust to what is happening around it." Along with this fervour for organizational agility, Louw developed a preference for servant leadership by getting involved

in business operations and striving to serve employees, customers and shareholders; however, continual crises and difficult situations eventually compelled him to adapt the rigour of his leadership style and to hold people accountable for their actions. He reasoned: "Being accountable to shareholders and doing what's right for the business sometimes doesn't go with being liked at all. I will make the hard decisions that are required. That's my role."

His co-workers soon learned that Louw accepted nothing less than high performance from himself and those working for him. Having worked in "life and death situations" and then in this industry that was intensely regulated, perfection was one of his key values. One of his executives commented that his persistent drive for excellence was what brought out the best in some of his employees: "He makes people deliver beyond their own expectations of themselves. When they are prepared to follow, he'll get them to the same level he is on."

Although some found this combined tenacity and introversion disconcerting, he was deeply respected by his colleagues: they were proud of his values, his passion for Adcock and his knowledge of the industry. One of his executives who had worked in the industry for many years said the following about his leadership: "There's no question in my mind that [Louw's] a visionary leader. Given his relative youth, it's surprising just how his vision for the pharmaceutical industry extends beyond what most of us can contemplate. It's almost as if he has a sixth sense."

To reflect on his values, his colleagues spoke about him as being scrupulously honest, truthful and generous in every way. Money did not drive him, nor did personal gain; instead, he valued growth, "planting the seed and watching it turn into something else." Louw's moral standards were very important to him as well, as his words reflected: "Success at work is driven by metrics, but not by achieving it at all cost. If there is a cost to the soul of the organization, I won't walk that path. I'll walk away. I'll walk the path of truth." Louw's experiences had enlarged his vision, shaped his motives and values and adapted his leadership style for the distinct challenges in Adcock Ingram.

Looking Back at Adcock Ingram Under Tiger Brands

The origins of Adcock Ingram lay in a small-town pharmacy in South Africa that opened its doors in 1890. From these humble roots, the company grew through the development of the Ingram's Camphor Cream brand, the establishment of a pharmaceutical manufacturing facility and subsequent relationship with the international company Baxter Healthcare. By 1950, Adcock Ingram was listed on the Johannesburg Stock Exchange (JSE).

Since becoming a division of Tiger Oats Limited (later Tiger Brands) in 1978, Adcock had demonstrated its understanding of the competitive advantage that its acquisition strategy could offer. With Tiger Brands' 50 per cent ownership in Adcock, it was able to secure several value-adding acquisitions almost on an annual basis. In the 1980s, it celebrated acquisitions of 40 per cent of the Critical Care Division of Baxter, the Mer-National division from Dow Chemicals Africa, the final 50 per cent shareholding in Restan Laboratories and Sterling Winthrop's interest in South Africa. The latter deal, in 1988, was particularly valuable as it included highly rewarding over-the-counter brands such as Phipps, Stearns, WetWipes and, especially, the Panado brand.

Adcock Ingram's momentum of acquisitions was maintained in the 1990s: it strengthened its competitiveness with continued vigour in buying Leppin, Laser, Pharmatec, Zurich Pharmaceuticals, Covan Pharmaceuticals and Salters, as well as leading over-the-counter brands in Zimbabwe. A joint venture with the Menarini Group signed in 1994 brought Adcock the Fastum Gel brand. In 1996, Adcock Ingram merged with Premier Pharmaceuticals to become the leading supplier of health care products in South Africa.[2]

In 1999, Adcock Ingram failed to acquire S.A. Druggists Pharmacare (later Aspen Pharmacare). The Competition Commission had ruled against the merger for reasons relating to employment, international competitiveness and empowerment.[3] This was one of the catalysts that raised uncertainty as to how Adcock fit strategically into the Tiger Brands business. Although Adcock's growth seemed certain, the best route with Tiger Brands was unclear; yet, amidst the haziness of their route, the thrust towards ever-improving portfolios of products and pipelines continued with acquisitions beyond 2000.

In 2000, Adcock became a wholly owned subsidiary of Tiger Brands. It was at that point that Louw joined Adcock as New Business Development executive in 2001. In that year, his acquisition of Steri-Lab directly improved Adcock's medical diagnostic business capacity. Showing his prowess in effectively executing acquisitions, Louw took over the leadership of the pharmaceutical business in May 2002, including the over-the-counter, prescription and critical care divisions. Supportive of then chief executive officer (CEO) Mike Norris' diversification strategy, Adcock became known not only for its health-care products, but also for owning leading brands in the home-care market, following Louw's acquisition of Robertsons Homecare the following year. For Louw, this was only the beginning of an impressive array of product and company acquisitions (Parke-Med generics, Organon, distribution rights of Vita-Thion, Abbot Citro-Soda, 74 per cent of the Scientific Group and Donmed Pharmaceuticals) (see Exhibit 2).[4]

[2]Adcock Ingram Milestones, www.adcock.co.za/milestones.aspx, accessed May 9, 2009.

[3]Alex Petersen, "Sekunjalo will continue to court Adcock," *Sunday Independent*, February 7, 1999, p. 3, www.busrep.co.za/index.php?fSectionId=563&fArticleId=62127, accessed April 25, 2010.

[4]Adcock Ingram Milestones, www.adcock.co.za/milestones.aspx, accessed May 9, 2009.

The resulting diversified portfolio aggravated the mismatch with the vision of Tiger Brands. Although Adcock was contributing almost 49 per cent of Tiger Brands' headline earnings by September 2005,[5] Tiger Brands was progressively favouring its fast-moving consumer goods (FMCG) business. It was in this climate that Louw was entrusted with steering Adcock ahead as of April 1, 2006, with Norris retiring shortly afterwards. In the next three years, Tiger Brands limited its investment in Adcock and no further acquisitions were made. This meant that Louw had reached a point in his leadership journey where it became difficult to demonstrate the facet of his leadership that required the execution of strategic deals. By April 2007, Reuters reported that, despite Adcock's profitable compound growth of between 16 and 17 per cent per annum, Tiger Brands was divesting the business in order to focus on their core business of FMCG.[6]

Adcock's Coming of Age

On August 25, 2008, Adcock was unbundled from Tiger Brands and relisted on the JSE.[7] This relisting gave Louw and the new Adcock leadership reason to be enthusiastic but also brought with it the apprehension one may expect from this new self-determination. With this coming of age, Louw purposefully set the direction to engage in acquisitions in the local South African market, with further expansion plans throughout Africa and the world.

As part of its growth strategy—but not limited to this strategy—the newly liberated Adcock would continue with its resolute advances to acquire competence. It had been three years since the last major acquisition, and further acquisitions would not only strengthen Adcock's product portfolio but also cement Louw's leadership and future accomplishments.

An Opportunity for Acquisition

Towards the end of 2008, investors speculated that Ciplamed, a much smaller pharmaceutical firm in the South African market with a focus on generic medications, wished to enlarge its operating capacity either through a joint venture or through contractual activities. Sixteen years prior, an entrepreneur named Jerome Smith bought a struggling pharmaceutical company, and by partnering with the Indian generics manufacturer Cipla, developed it into a strong contender in the South African generics market. Even though Smith had sold the company (then known as Enaleni Pharmaceuticals to public shareholders), he reclaimed the position of CEO within two years. The medium-sized Ciplamed's insistent drive to increase market share was enveloped in the notion of the right to affordable medicine for all; however, by 2008, pressures on Ciplamed included suboptimal manufacturing operations, possible loss of an antiretroviral manufacturing agreement with Aspen and the rumoured threat of a possible South African state-owned and, therefore, tax-funded pharmaceutical competitor that would focus on low-cost antiretroviral products.[8]

Given the limited acquisition opportunities in the South African pharmaceutical market and Louw's enthusiasm for deal making, he had become especially interested in Ciplamed by this

---

[5]"Adcock Ingram se rol by Tiger Brands." *Finweek*, March 16, 2006, p. 6, http://download.fin24.com/DataVendors/Helena/59x58%20Thumbnails/FIN24/Info_Center/PDF's/Adcock%20Ingram.pdf, accessed May 27, 2010.

[6]"Tiger Brands divest from health care," *Reuters*, April 20, 2007, available at www.moneyweb.co.za/mw/view/mw/en/page292520?oid=87291&sn=2009%20Detail, accessed February 13, 2010.

[7]Adcock Ingram Abridged Pre-listing statement (2008), www.koo.co.za/Investor/Downloads/PDFReports/Adock%20article/Abridged%20Pre-Listing%20Announcement.pdf, accessed May 14, 2009.

[8]"Adcock Ingram and Cipla Medpro should be talking," December 12, 2008, www.sharetips.co.za/2008/12/adcock-ingram-and-cipla-medpro-should-be-talking/, accessed May 14, 2009.

time. The commercial rationale for acquiring Ciplamed was clear in Louw's mind. Adcock's strategic focus was aimed firstly at local consolidation, then African expansion and, following that, global reach. In April 2009, a small acquisition of Tender Loving Care launched the re-entry of Adcock into the fast-moving consumer goods market. The supplements and personal care products associated with this acquisition reflected an appetite for a wider health and wellness focus in their product range; however, driven by the strategy for local consolidation, Louw realized that apart from Ciplamed, there were not many other prospects in the South African health-care market. Adcock's phased expansion strategy would make Ciplamed an obvious choice. It was also an opportune time for the acquisition, as Ciplamed's share price was at an all-time low of R2.20.

Louw's experience had taught him that success in the generics business was dependent on optimizing size and scale. The two companies together would be a more credible competitor to Aspen, as the combined Adcock and Ciplamed would come close to reaching the 38 per cent market share that Aspen held in the generics market (see Exhibits 3 and 4). To achieve the same position organically would have taken at least 10 years, not to mention the magnitude of required financial investment. The risk of gaining very little market share with questionable return on investment could also not be excluded. Instead, as a combined entity with Ciplamed, success in the generics market could be achieved through economies of scale (range and availability) and winning the price war game. Together, the firms would be able to reach a larger market and keep costs down. Ciplamed's entrenched position in respiratory and central nervous system medication was also highly desirable, given that Adcock had no presence to speak of in these classes.

Making a Play for Cipla

As a seasoned deal maker, Louw had taken two years to prepare the ground for the deal, beginning in 2007. This included encounters and consultation with the board, his executive team, Adcock and Ciplamed shareholders, analysts, Jerome Smith (CEO of Ciplamed) and Amar Lulla (joint managing director of Cipla India—the key supplier to Ciplamed) as well as legal advisors and a firm of economists for competitor analysis. The decision had been carefully crafted for months, with shareholders' value in mind. It had taken time and calculated effort for board members to align their thinking and for analysts to ascertain an acceptable price for the shares.

To raise interest in the acquisition, Louw had taken various flights to Cape Town for discussions with Smith. After about a year, Louw extended his advances to Lulla, as Cipla India's supplies would strengthen the value of the deal. During this period of courting, Smith's sentiments vacillated, but he also, on numerous occasions, confirmed a deep interest in the deal. Towards the end of this period of preparation, Louw and Smith were making plans and discussing the meeting of the management teams of their various divisions to ensure a smooth transition. Although a date and time for this meeting had been set, Smith withdrew his team at the last minute and never rescheduled the meeting.

Louw remained confident that he had won the support of the Adcock board and shareholders. He believed that the price offered for the shares would be acceptable to Adcock investors and very attractive to Ciplamed shareholders. The Adcock board did not see any real risk in the offer. The only tangible risks were advisors' fees and the cost of raising capital, and comparatively this was nominal. As far as Louw was concerned, all the key players were aligned and he had a fiduciary duty to his shareholders to take action.

In the Adcock boardroom, consensus had been reached on the chosen acquisition and approach. For a listed company, Ciplamed's board would have the supremacy of choice. With their buy-in and their acceptance of the price as fair and just, the legal hurdles to the acquisition would be easily overcome. At face value, following the rules of sound governance and ensuring shareholder value would be the key elements for clinching the deal. The questions remained: How would Smith, Ciplamed's CEO, who for more than sixteen years had built up the firm from its small beginnings, respond to the offer? Would Ciplamed's partner and key supplier support the transitions that the acquisition would bring?

⬜ The Proposal

On April 9, 2009, Adcock made an offer to Ciplamed shareholders of R4.75 per share, or R2.125 billion. The price was robust at a 32 per cent premium to the closing price of the share capital the day before the offer. Adcock's board had decided to announce a potential offer, a "scheme of arrangement." This was an invitation to the board of Ciplamed to come to an agreement on the offer before a joint submission was made to the Competition Commission. Through this collaborative and cooperative approach, Adcock aimed to rule out any hostility and overcome any residual negativity amongst Ciplamed management or shareholders.

Adcock's offer to buy Ciplamed was to be for the entire issued share capital, or failing which, at least a majority share of 51 per cent. Louw and company ultimately intended to delist Ciplamed from the JSE. Alternatively, if they were unable to acquire the full share capital of the firm, Ciplamed's shares would remain listed on the stock exchange with the organization becoming a subsidiary of Adcock.[9]

Benefits All Around: The Case for Acquiring Ciplamed

As primary argument and rationale for the acquisition, Louw's presentations in the media and Stock Exchange News Service (SENS) announcement highlighted the trend of multinationals to

consolidate as a strategy to reduce risk—the risk of a rising number of products with soon-to-expire patents and the risk of declining innovation. Taking the influences in the changing South African pharmaceutical environment and local legislation into account, the basis for the offer was clear. Louw remarked that the only way for both firms to remain competitive would be to adapt to this change. This he put forward as the burning platform and compelling reason to optimize synergies.

Adcock listed many potential benefits for Ciplamed:

1. An improved strategic position and competitiveness against multinationals of the industry in this market;

2. Reduced risk through greater diversification;

3. A stronger and more complementary portfolio of prescription products, over-the-counter products and hospital products;

4. A more balanced exposure to target markets through this stronger portfolio and diversification;

5. Economies of scale and value chain consolidation.

Significantly, this move would also bring about stronger synergies of revenue and greater access to products. Adcock's marketing and distribution capabilities would assist Ciplamed in bringing their strong generics product pipeline to market. Louw emphasized Adcock's experience in FMCG and hospital channels, and promised strong sales, marketing, distribution and branding capabilities. Then, the rest of Africa was also waiting. Adcock's customer base beyond the borders of South Africa would welcome the complementary product offering.

---

[9]Adcock Ingram—Firm Intention Announcement, JSE SENS, April 9, 2009, www.sharenet.co.za, accessed February 13, 2010.

Louw indicated that the benefits would also extend to Ciplamed's key supplier. As Cipla India had greatly invested in research and development and in building their clinical capabilities, these aspects could now be employed beyond Ciplamed's current scope. The South African market would also be exposed to Cipla India's over-the-counter and hospital products. Cipla India would also benefit from a more effective distribution channel, which held the promise of increased sales in South Africa and further sales abroad.[10]

The deal and underlying strategic rationale seemed solid. Certainly, the offer and related benefits were sound, institutional investors from both sides would see the value and, in Louw's mind, the offer would be accepted. According to principles of corporate governance, it was now up to the Ciplamed board to consider the worth and merits of the offer and to respond.

Waiting

The board of Ciplamed did not respond to Adcock.

Instead, on April 9, they released a cautionary announcement to their shareholders: "The board is in the process of convening a meeting to consider, and to take the appropriate advice on the proposal, following which a detailed announcement will be made."[11] In stark contrast to the official silence of their board towards Adcock was the proliferation of communication of staff, shareholders and the media, both publicly and privately. Shortly after the bid was made, there were rumours that Smith had sent an emotive text message to his staff indicating that he did not support the offer.

On Wednesday, April 15, six days after the offer was announced, the *Business Report* indicated that Cipla India was in full support of Adcock's offer for Ciplamed[12]; however, Ciplamed cautioned its shareholders that its board had not yet been able to reach a decision.

The Turning Point

Early indications of a possible rejection of the offer appeared on Friday, April 17, only eight days after the offer was made. Ciplamed issued a second cautionary announcement, now to indicate that they would appoint independent advisors and would establish an independent sub-committee of the board to assist the board in making the decision. They announced that Smith had spoken to his staff to inform them that he opposed the proposed offer as it was then formulated but that he would support the board's process.[13]

On the same day, the media reported that approximately 25.1 per cent of Ciplamed shareholders (representing Kagiso Asset Management and Sweet Sensations) were set against the deal,[14] and that Lulla had stated, "Cipla will not support any such bid and will exercise its options as may be legally advised."[15]

---

[10]Ibid.

[11]Cipla Medpro South Africa Limited—Cautionary Announcement, JSE SENS, April 9, 2009, www.sharenet.co.za, accessed February 13, 2010.

[12]Marc Ashton and Nolulamo Matutu, "Kagiso: no to Adcock's Cipla bid," *www.Fin24.com*, April 15, 2009, www.fin24.com/articles/default/display_article.aspx?ArticleId=1518-24_2501617, accessed February 13, 2010.

[13]Cipla Medpro—Preliminary Response by the Board of Directors of Cipla, JSE SENS, April 17, 2009, www.sharenet.co.za, accessed February 13, 2010.

[14]"Adcock runs into new hurdle in proposed buyout of Cipla," *Business Report*, April 17, 2009, www.busrep.co.za/index.php?fSectionId=552&fArticleId=4938858, accessed May 27, 2010.

[15]Nolulamo Matutu, "Cipla CEO opposes Adcock offer," *www.Fin24.com*, April 17, 2009, www.fin24.com/articles/default/display_print_article.aspx?ArticleId=1518-24_2503168&Type=News, accessed on May 14, 2009.

Louw had been so focused on the merits of the deal that these signs of rejection came as an awful surprise. With the realization of his worst fears, Louw decided to act promptly in an attempt to realign the stakeholders and save the deal. Failing to reach Smith, he decided to call Lulla to find out what was happening. It was three o'clock, Central Africa Time, on the Saturday morning that Louw made the call to Lulla in India. He had to find out why Lulla had said he would not support "a hostile deal." In this early morning conversation, Lulla made it clear that he would not back an offer of which Smith was not in favour.

Could it all have come to this? Louw felt a deep sense of disappointment and confusion. How could he go back to his shareholders with this news? Ciplamed's board had not responded to Adcock and the content of a telephone conversation in the middle of the night would be seen as nothing more than hearsay. Louw realized that he would need the reasons for the rejection in writing and should try to overcome Lulla's wavering. This prompted him to write a letter to Lulla, in which he assured him that the deal would not be optimal without Cipla India and that Adcock remained committed to a successful transaction for all stakeholders, including Cipla India.

On Saturday April 18, the *Economic Times* of India published a shocking quote from Lulla: "The drug-supply agreement allows us to terminate the supply programme if there is a change in the management. We oppose the takeover by Adcock. We will exercise all options, including legal process."[16]

The following Monday, Ciplamed retracted media statements of the preceding Friday that implied that the offer was rejected: "An unapproved and unauthorised statement was erroneously distributed to certain media channels," they publicly announced. It was a "clerical error." This was to stress that their board had not "formally rejected" the proposed offer and that it was still under consideration.[17]

The renewed hope was short-lived for Louw. On the same day, Ciplamed published a portion of a letter that Lulla had allegedly sent to Louw. Although Louw was anticipating a written response from Lulla, he had not yet seen this letter before it went public. An audit of Adcock's network firewall showed that the letter had not reached anyone in the firm, and it only reached Adcock two weeks later. The letter, signed by Lulla on behalf of the board of Cipla India, plainly indicated that they would not support the bid to purchase Ciplamed "now or at any time in the future."[18]

Lulla's letter listed stark reasons for the rejection:

a. Adcock held relations with competitors of Cipla India;

b. They were not convinced that the case for merging the two companies was compelling;

c. It was a matter of relationships: Lulla had personal relationships with individuals in Ciplamed for 14 years. He called these individuals "hard working, committed, passionate and totally noncorporate"; "They have been loyal partners and friends and we see no reason whatsoever to change what has worked for both of us";

---

[16]"Adcock's plan to buy Medpro hits Cipla hurdle," *The Economic Times*, April 18, 2009, http://economictimes.indiatimes.com/news/news-by-industry/healthcare/biotech/pharmaceuticals/Adcocks-plan-to-buy-Medpro-hits-Cipla-hurdle/articleshow/4416519.cms, accessed May 14, 2009.

[17]Cipla Medpro South Africa Limited—Clarification Announcement, JSE SENS, April 20, 2009, www.sharenet.co.za, accessed February 13, 2010.

[18]Cipla Medpro South Africa Limited—An Update on the Unsolicited Potential Offer by Adcock, JSE SENS, May 4, 2009, www.sharenet.co.za, accessed on February 13, 2010.

d. The deal would not benefit Cipla India's shareholders, as their growth would instead come through product innovation.

By this time, the dissonance caused by the rejection from India, coupled with the silence from Ciplamed with no practical recourse, was bearing down on Louw. Despite the pressure, he remained determined to realize the vision for a stronger generics business in Adcock.

Further Rejection

Almost a month after the bid for their company, on May 4, 2009, Ciplamed publicly informed their shareholders of the following:

a. Lulla had rejected the deal, and that in order to ensure sustained growth, they needed continued supplies from Cipla India and access to their intellectual property until September 2025. They warned their shareholders of the implicit consequences of a threat to this relationship. In their words: "[A] transaction or development which could result in the termination of this relationship or lead to a material alteration of the existing agreement between the Company and Cipla India would not be in the best interest of the Company or its shareholders."

b. Twenty-nine per cent of their shareholders did not support the Adcock offer. They stated that their Black Economic Empowerment (BEE) partner's interests had not been taken into consideration. The Ciplamed announcement read: "Sweet Sensations firmly believes that the Potential Offer is unlikely to deliver the performance and returns to shareholders that could be achieved through an

independent Cipla Medpro in partnership with Cipla India, with current management in place. As such, Sweet Sensations is not supportive of the Potential Offer as value would be eroded for the shareholders." (Sweet Sensations held only 18.5 per cent of the issued share capital).[19]

At this point, it seemed that what was determining the outcome of the deal was not the wishes of the majority of shareholders or the independent committee of the board of Ciplamed but rather the motives of the CEO, a key supplier and Ciplamed's BEE partner.

A Matter of Friendship and Pride

The media was awash with speculations about the impending outcome of the deal. By mid-May, Bruce Whitfield, multiple award-winning business journalist quoted Smith saying, "We're extremely close, like brothers—extremely close. We love each other!" This quote was in reference to the relationship between Lulla and Smith. Whitfield's article left the impression that close personal relationships, emotions and vested interest were keeping Ciplamed and Adcock apart. The article also revealed that Smith felt insulted by the offer and that he resolved never to work for Adcock.[20]

The Ultimatum

It was with mounting irritation at not having received an official response from the Ciplamed board that Louw again wrote to Cipla India's directors at the end of May. This time, his letter was more direct, factual and to the point, demanding a decision from India whether they would continue supplies if the offer was accepted. Two days later, Lulla responded in writing:

---

[19]Cipla Medpro South Africa Limited—An Update on the Unsolicited Potential Offer by Adcock, JSE SENS, May 4, 2009, www.sharenet.co.za, accessed February 13, 2010.

[20]Bruce Whitfield, "Gotcha!" *Finweek*, May 14, 2009, p. 25.

It is our considered view that the proposed transaction at face value is not in the best interests either of our business partner in South Africa or that of our company, both presently and into the future. If implemented, the proposal would inevitably lead to an irreparable breakdown of the current good business relationship between our company and Cipla Medpro SA Limited.

For that reason alone, and irrespective of any contractual niceties, we are of the firm view that we cannot, and will not, do business with Adcock Ingram Holdings Limited in South Africa, whether directly or through an entity controlled by it. For that reason, we will not support the proposed transaction. Further, should it be implemented we will do whatever it takes to preserve and further our fundamental business philosophy.[21]

Louw realized that without the continued supplies from India, the key condition for a successful transaction was no longer in place, and therefore the deal no longer made sense.

The Deal Is Off

Louw and the Adcock board found themselves in what they called "an untenable position." The risk of the nature of the relationship between Lulla and Smith had brought them to this junction in the road. Institutional investors, members of the media and interested parties waited in eager anticipation to see Adcock's response. With

their non-negotiable suspensive condition under threat, they would need to change direction.

In a press release on June 2, 2009, Adcock's frustration was palpable: frustration with the Ciplamed board for defaulting on their public duty and their corporate governance obligations by not indicating their opinion of the merits of the offer; disappointment that Cipla India's viewpoints were upheld as the decisive factor; and annoyance with the implied termination right on change of management that was not previously known or mentioned.[22]

The course to take was clear: Adcock decisively withdrew the potential offer. In withdrawing the bid, Adcock demanded clarification on the reasons for the silence of Ciplamed's board. They also solicited an investigation by the JSE into the negative control that Cipla India professed to have over Ciplamed's operations. In response, Ciplamed advised their shareholders that they would answer to "Adcock's announcement and the allegations contained therein in full, in due course."[23] Their public response followed three days later. Ciplamed denied that Adcock had made an offer and that their board was under any obligation to respond to what they termed Adcock's "unilaterally imposed timetable." They were in fact still awaiting the advice of their subcommittee and advisors on the potential offer. As for the nature of the relationship with Cipla India, Ciplamed maintained that it was a long-standing association based on trust and respect. They accused Adcock of being "disingenuous and misleading" to imply that the transaction was withdrawn based on the lack of support from Cipla India. They stated, "In answer to certain incorrect perceptions that have been quoted in the market, Cipla India has no right of termination linked to a change of management of the Company."[24]

[21]Cipla Medpro—Withdrawal of Firm Intention, JSE SENS, June 5, 2009, www.sharenet.co.za, accessed February 13, 2010.

[22]Adcock Ingram—Withdrawal of the Firm Intention, JSE SENS. June 2, 2009, www.sharenet.co.za, accessed February 13, 2010.

[23]Cipla Medpro South Africa Limited—Withdrawal of Cautionary Announcement, JSE SENS, June 2, 2009, www.sharenet.co.za, accessed February 13, 2010.

[24]Cipla Medpro South Africa Limited—Withdrawal of Adcock Offer, JSE SENS, June 5, 2009, www.sharenet.co.za, accessed February 13, 2010.

In the same announcement, they argued, "Cipla India's views on Adcock's undesirability as a potential business partner have been consistent throughout." In support of this statement, they maintained that previously in December 2008, when Adcock officially expressed interest, Adcock had been informed that Cipla India would not support such an offer. They expressed concern that this was not addressed in the potential offer. They viewed Louw's media statements on possible other and "multi source supplies" as ambiguous and contrary to the Ciplamed-Cipla India relationship. Lastly, they contended that there would be competitive issues and implications in the generics market if the transaction had gone ahead.[25]

The *Sunday Times' Business Times* reported afterwards that some Ciplamed shareholders intended to take action against their board, and others demanded an explanation, since as many as 36 per cent of the shareholders had supported the deal. The reporter derisively commented: "Adcock must feel like a suitor who never gets a hot date, let alone reaches the altar."[26]

Further scathing comments followed from Ciplamed leadership. Deputy CEO, Dr. Pieter Potgieter, described Adcock's bid as lacking business protocol and good manners. He accused Adcock of using Cipla India's resistance to the offer as an excuse to direct attention away from the transaction. According to him, Ciplamed had submitted documents to the Competition Commission to show that the proposed acquisition would reduce their competitiveness. Potgieter accused Adcock of using Cipla India's reaction as a smokescreen to distract the public from "Adcock's poor arguments before the Commission."[27] These allegations

were made despite the fact that there had never been a competition filing (as it was only a potential offer), nor did Adcock have to appear or make any arguments before the Competition Commission concerning this deal up to that stage.

✉ **Afterwards**

What Went Wrong?

As the dust settled, Louw reflected upon the proposed offer; in retrospect, it was easier to see what went wrong. "Jerome changed his mind," he thought. "I know he changed his mind. It's nothing more complex than that." He remembered Smith's almost emotional insistence eight months before that the deal should be done. "Lulla also changed his mind." Louw had discussed the deal with Lulla, as the continued supply relationship was part of the rationale for the proposed transaction. Shortly after the offer was made, Lulla was quoted in the *Business Standard* of the Indian press, saying, "This development will not impact us, since we have our own supply arrangements in South Africa and other African countries. If Adcock Ingram is ready to continue with the existing arrangement, we will continue the supplies."[28] Something must have changed his mind.

"We underestimated the power of relationships. That was our mistake," Louw thought. The deal had a very high chance of success commercially. On paper, Cipla India's relationship was a pure contractual supply relationship. The nature of the relationship should have held no potential prejudices towards an acquisition, and legally there was no apparent reason why they should be able to alter the contractual relationship should

[25]Ibid.

[26]Adele Shevel, "Cipla shareholders in pain over bid," *Sunday Times' Business Times*, June 7, 2009, p. 8.

[27]"Adcock steur hom nie aan goeie maniere, sê Cipla," *www.fin24.co.za*, July 4, 2009, www.fin24.com/articles/default/display_article.aspx?ArticleId=_2536041, accessed on January 17, 2010.

[28]P. B. Jayakumar, "Cipla's Africa network gets booster dose," *Business Standard*, April 10, 2009, www.business-standard.com/india/news/cipla/s-africa-network-getsbooster-dose/354633, accessed May 14, 2009.

the management of Ciplamed change. Although contractually there seemed to be no such right, the argument had been enough to upset shareholders. "Jerome played a good game of chess," he reasoned.

Louw also realized that not everybody plays by the same set of rules. Sound governance would have meant that the Ciplamed board should have made the decision in the interest of shareholders, without being influenced by the CEO or supplier. Ciplamed was, in fact, not a private company but a listed company with diverse shareholders. The motives of individuals should not sway a deal. This, Louw learnt, was not always true.

"The strategy was right, maybe the timing was wrong," Louw reflected further. Although previously Adcock would not have had the right corporate structures in place, had the deal been put on the table sooner, events would have likely played out differently.

In Louw's mind there remained a few unanswered questions: "What was Amar Lulla's incentive to withdraw after showing initial appetite for the deal? With such a commercially viable rationale, what possible hold could Smith have had over Lulla and the Ciplamed board? Is Lulla disappointed that the deal never went through? Is there a possibility that the deal will return?"

Exhibit 1   Adcock Ingram Business Overview November 2009

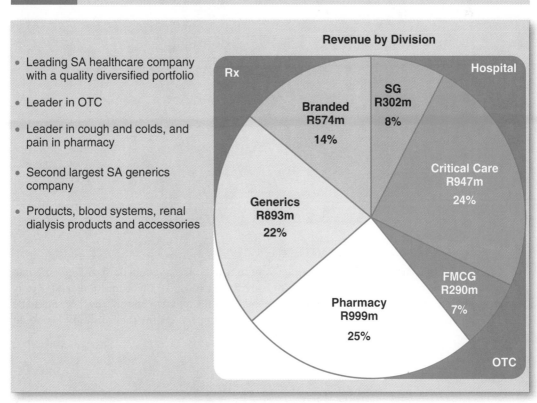

- Leading SA healthcare company with a quality diversified portfolio
- Leader in OTC
- Leader in cough and colds, and pain in pharmacy
- Second largest SA generics company
- Products, blood systems, renal dialysis products and accessories

Revenue by Division

Rx

Branded R574m 14%

SG R302m 8%

Hospital

Critical Care R947m 24%

Generics R893m 22%

Pharmacy R999m 25%

FMCG R290m 7%

OTC

SOURCE: NDTI (September 2009), Adcock Ingram Investor Presentation Group Results for the Period ended 30 September, 2009 (November 24, 2009), www.adcock.co.za/DynamicData/Investors/2009%20Results%20Presentation%20(4).pdf, accessed on January 17, 2010.

Exhibit 2 Some Milestones on Adcock's Journey

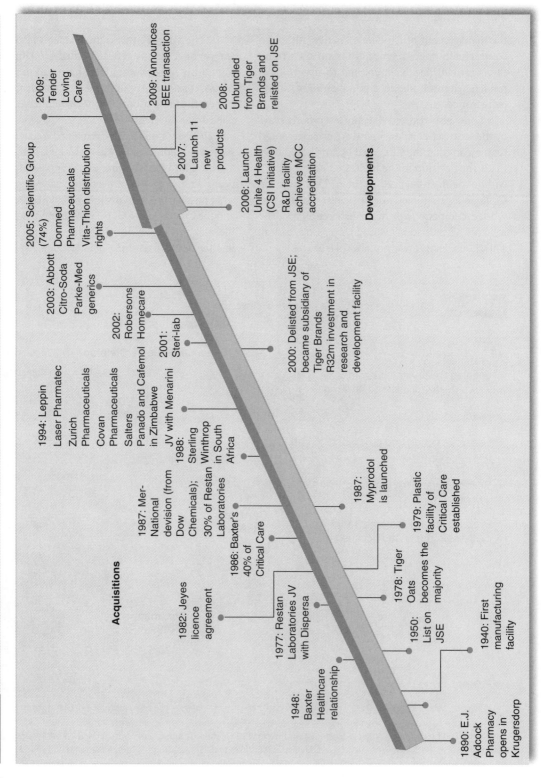

Acquisitions

1890: E.J. Adcock Pharmacy opens in Krugersdorp

1940: First manufacturing facility

1948: Baxter Healthcare relationship

1950: List on JSE

1977: Restan Laboratories JV with Dispersa

1978: Tiger Oats becomes the majority

1979: Plastic facility of Critical Care established

1982: Jeyes licence agreement

1986: Baxter's 40% of Critical Care

1987: Mer-National devision (from Dow Chemicals); 30% of Restan Laboratories

1987: Myprodol is launched

1988: Sterling Winthrop in South Africa

1994: Leppin
Laser Pharmatec
Zurich Pharmaceuticals
Covan Pharmaceuticals
Salters
Panado and Cafemol
JV with Menarini in Zimbabwe

2000: Delisted from JSE; became subsidiary of Tiger Brands R32m investment in research and development facility

2001: Steri-lab

2002: Robersons Homecare

2003: Abbott
Citro-Soda
Parke-Med generics

2005: Scientific Group (74%)
Donmed Pharmaceuticals
Vita-Thion distribution rights

2006: Launch Unite 4 Health (CSI Initiative) R&D facility achieves MCC accreditation

2007: Launch 11 new products

2008: Unbundled from Tiger Brands and relisted on JSE

2009: Tender Loving Care

2009: Announces BEE transaction

Developments

SOURCE: Adapted from Adcock Ingram Milestones, www.adcock.co.za/milestones.aspx, accessed October 21, 2009.

Exhibit 3 Adcock Ingram's Share in the South African Pharmaceutical Market November 2009

Pharmaceutical Market Share

TOTAL MARKET

Value: R 23.7bn
Counting Units (CU): 36bn = 100%

Value: R 2.4bn
Counting Units (CU): 6.8bn = 100%

PRIVATE SECTOR

Value: R 20.4bn = 86%
(Growth: 13.7%)
CU: 24.7bn = 69%
(Growth: 1.0%)

Value: R 2bn = 87% *[10.1%]
(Growth: 8.2%)
CU: 6.2bn = 92% *[25.3%]
(Growth: 0.3%)

PRESCRIPTION

Value: R 14.8bn = 73%
(Growth: 14.9%)
CU: 6.5bn = 26%
(Growth: 3.5%)

Value: R 1.1bn = 52% *[7.3%]
(Growth: 6.6%)
CU: 910m = 15% [14%]
(Growth: –3.7%)

Original R and D products – (Patented and Non-patented original branded > Sch 3)

Value: R 9.9 bn = 67%
(Growth: 12.5%)
CU: 2.3 bn = 35%
(Growth: 3.2%)

Value: R 537 m = 50% *[5.4%]
(Growth: 14.3%)
CU: 380m = 42% *[16.8%]
(Growth: 1.5%)

PUBLIC SECTOR

Value: R 3.4bn = 14%
(Growth: 12.5%)
CU: 11.1bn = 31%
(Growth: 7.7%)

Value: R 298.4m = 13% *[8.8%]
(Growth: 223%)
CU: 573.9m = 8% *[5.2%]
(Growth: –10.8%)

OTC (OVER THE COUNTER)

Value: R 5.5bn = 27%
(Growth: 10.6%)
CU: 18.2bn = 74%
(Growth: 0.2%)

Value: R 983.5m = 48% *[17.8%]
(Growth: 10%)
CU: 5.3bn = 85% *[29.3%]
(Growth: 1.0%)

Generics (Off patented > Sch 3)

Value: R 4.9bn = 33%
(Growth: 20.0%)
CU: 4.2bn = 65%
(Growth: 3.7%)

Value: R 540.6m = 50% *[10.9%]
(Growth: –0.1%)
CU: 530m = 58% *[12.6%]
(Growth: –7.1 %)

South Africa   Adcock Ingram   *Adcock Ingram Market Share

SOURCE: Company files.

| Exhibit 4 | Comparative Share Prices in the South African Market August 2008–May 2009 |

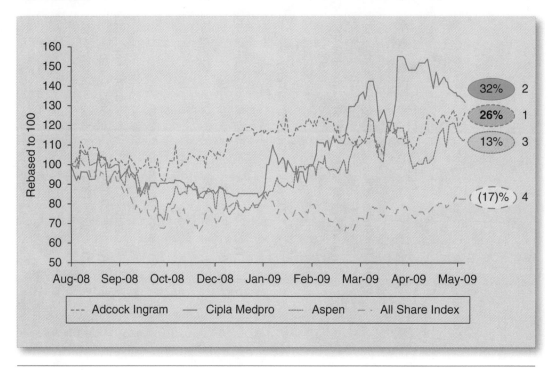

SOURCE: Deutsche Securities (SA) (Pty) Ltd., Adcock Ingram Unaudited Interim Results Presentation for the Period ended March 31, 2009 (June 2, 2009), p. 11, www.adcock.co.za/DynamicData/Investors/2009%20Results%20Presentation%20(7).pdf, accessed May 14, 2009.

Dickinson College: Inspiration for a Leadership Story (In the Vision of a Founding Father)

Michael J. Fratantuono

On a mid-October morning in 1999, William G. (Bill) Durden got up from his desk and looked out his window onto the main green of the campus. Many thoughts filled his mind. The prior January, the board of trustees had named him the 27th president of his alma mater, Dickinson College. In a few weeks, on October 30, during the autumn board meeting,

Version: (A) 2008-04-16

he would be officially instated and deliver his inaugural address.

In both personal and professional terms, the appointment represented a dramatic turn of events. When contacted by the Dickinson search committee in late autumn of 1998, Durden was not initially interested in the position. Yes, he had graduated from Dickinson in 1971, was certainly grateful for the education he had received and was mindful of the opportunities that had flowed from that experience.[1] However, he was serving as the president of a division of the Sylvan Learning Systems, Inc. and the vice-president of academic affairs for the Caliber Learning Network, positions that he found challenging and rewarding. Furthermore, as an alumnus, he had become increasingly angry and frustrated that over the past few decades, the school had not realized its potential; sometimes he had even been embarrassed that the name Dickinson did not command more respect in academic and professional circles. He only agreed to take the job after talks with trustees, alumni, faculty and students convinced him there was a genuine, broad-based desire for fundamental change at the college.[2]

Once he decided to accept and was named by the board, Durden began the process of transition. In the spring, he had visited the college several times. On July 1, at the start of the academic year, he had moved into the president's office in West College, Dickinson's most historically significant building. In the final days of August, as the semester started, he had mingled with students and their families and prepared his convocation speech. Over the past nine months, Durden had uncovered what he regarded as two shortcomings at the college. The first quickly surfaced. For its entire

216-year history, the college had never had a fully articulated strategy. That realization had informed Durden's first major goal: the college would have a strategic plan by the spring of 2000. Towards that end, in the spring of 1999 he had asked the dean and other administrators to invite respected members of the college to serve on a special committee. During the summer, he and the group read more than 1,200 pages of white papers, reports, self-studies, and other documents that had been written in recent years about Dickinson. Informed by that background material, with the start of the semester, the committee began to meet each week to start the process of writing a first draft of a high-level strategic plan, one that would identify a vision and mission, defining attributes, and priorities for the college. Their objective was to complete a first draft by late autumn so that the document could be vetted by faculty, students, administrators and trustees; redrafted over the winter; re-circulated; and then released in final form to the community by the end of the academic year. Later that day, he would be attending another such meeting, participating not as a convener or facilitator, but as a contributor to the conversation. While the work was tough going, the attitude among committee members was upbeat and they had started to make some good progress.

The second shortcoming, more subtle and deeply embedded, involved the culture of the college. For much of the 20th century, the Dickinson community had lacked the sense of organizational pride and purpose one typically encountered at a college with a national reputation for excellence. Previous leaders had been comfortable with the status quo and had not conveyed a sense of urgency with respect to the

---

[1]For example, Durden won a Fulbright Scholarship, studied in Switzerland and Germany, and earned a Ph.D. in German language and literature from Johns Hopkins University. He had stayed on at Johns Hopkins, taught in the German department for 16 years, and had become the executive director of the well known Center for Talented Youth (CTY). He had acted as a consultant and advisor to numerous government agencies, non-profit organizations, and foundations in the field of education. "President William G. Durden, Biography," Dickinson College web site, http://www.dickinson.edu/about/president/bio.html, accessed July 28, 2007.

[2]Bill Durden, "Comments as Guest Lecturer for the Dickinson College course, Financial Transformation of Dickinson College, February 6, 2007," Dickinson College, Carlisle, PA.

internal and external challenges that confronted the school. Dickinson had remained relatively anonymous in the field of higher education, had failed to establish a strong and clear identity—the type of identity that could help distinguish the college from rivals and contribute to the experience of students, the sense of purpose of the faculty, and the affinity of alumni. That insight had come to Durden some two months earlier. During orientation week, he had gone on a day-hike with a group of students, engaged in a lengthy conversation with a rising senior who had earned good grades, and been deeply involved in campus life before spending time abroad during her junior year. The same evening, she sent him an e-mail and confessed that despite all that she had accomplished and experienced, she still did not have a clear sense of what it meant to be a Dickinsonian. That troubled Durden: if such an accomplished student could not explain what a Dickinson education stood for, then who could?[3]

The disturbing, albeit important, exchange with the young lady gave Durden a new purpose. That is, while Durden had—in addition to reading college documents for the special committee—also spent time throughout the summer studying the history of the college, the exchange had prompted him to revisit the circumstances associated with the college being granted a charter from the Assembly of Pennsylvania in 1783. Durden had become particularly intrigued by the life and writings of Dr. Benjamin Rush, the man responsible for founding the college. During a period of American history characterized by dramatic change in political, social, and economic affairs, Rush had articulated a clear and compelling vision for Dickinson. Unfortunately,

in rather short order, those managing college affairs chose to disregard Rush and dismiss some of the central elements of his plan. Soon thereafter, Rush and his vision faded as guiding lights: by the 1900s, new generations of Dickinson faculty and students—including Durden when he was an undergraduate—never heard much at all from old hands about the man, his efforts, or his ideas.

Through his various life experiences, Durden had developed a somewhat non-traditional view about leadership. First, while he was a voracious reader, he did not spend much time with popular books about business management. Instead, he far preferred to read works of literature and visit museums for insights about human nature and group dynamics. Second, he had come to appreciate the power of a leadership story for motivating and channeling the energies of members of an organization. In his various posts, he always asked himself and those around him, "What is our story?" and given the story, "How are we doing?"[4] Durden now wondered, could Rush's vision and the history surrounding the college's origin be translated into a leadership story that informed the strategic plan and helped establish a strong sense of identity among members of the Dickinson community?

⊠ Turbulent Events; Clear Vision (1681–1783)

Early History of Pennsylvania and of Carlisle[5]

William Penn was born in London in 1644 to a family of wealth and status—his father was

---

[3]Bill Durden, "Leadership, Language Study, And Global Sensibility," keynote address delivered at the East Asia Regional Council of Overseas Schools (EARCOS), Ho Chi Minh City, Vietnam, November 2, 2004, http://www.dickinson.edu/about/president/earcos.html.

[4]Bill Durden, comments as guest lecturer, February 6, 2007.

[5]Most of this section is based on information found at the web site of the Pennsylvania Historical and Museum Commission: http://www.phmc.state.pa.us/bah/pahist/quaker.asp, accessed July 2, 2007.

Admiral Sir William Penn. He gradually gravitated to the beliefs of the Society of Friends, or Quakers, then a persecuted sect. Despite his conversion, he retained the trust of the Duke of York (later King James II) and thus good social standing at the King's Court. Given his beliefs, Penn petitioned the Crown for land in the Americas that might serve as a haven for those of all religious persuasions. Ultimately—and at least in part due to an outstanding debt of £16,000 owed to the estate of the admiral, who had passed away in 1670—King Charles II signed the Charter of Pennsylvania, named in honor of the elder Penn, in March of 1681. Later that year, Penn visited the colony and summoned a general assembly. Under the charter, while officials bearing the title lieutenant-governor would represent the interests of the Penn family, the assembly would concentrate on matters of concern to residents.

During the 1700s, immigrants to the colony tended to cluster according to their heritage. English Quakers and Anglicans gathered in the southeast, in and around Philadelphia, which became a vibrant center for commercial, political, and intellectual life. Germans, many among them followers of the Lutheran faith, tended to move to the central part of the colony and take up farming. Scottish and Irish settled further west and were primarily frontiersmen and practitioners of Presbyterianism.

To help shape development, in 1750 the Assembly established Cumberland County, which included all of Pennsylvania west of the Susquehanna River. In 1751, Carlisle, a community of between 500 and 1,000 people, who were mostly of Scottish-Irish descent, was designated as the county seat.[6]

In the 1750s, hostilities broke out between settlers and Indian tribes, and then between the British and the French over lands in the Allegheny Mountains and the Ohio River Valley. Carlisle served as an outpost for royal and provincial militias heading west, a place "where the wagon roads ended and the pack horse trails began."[7] By 1756, when the French and Indian War was officially declared, defenses in Carlisle had been fortified. By 1758, Carlisle was a boom town, with some speculating it might grow into a metropolis.[8]

In the 1750s and 1760s, Carlisle was also witness to a power struggle between two factions of Presbyterians, one that was being waged on a larger scale in congregations, grammar schools, and colleges throughout the colonies. Generally speaking, the Old Side (conservatives) displayed the two defining characteristics of the religion: they organized themselves into a traditional governance structure, under which congregations belonged to presbyteries, and presbyteries to synods; and they accepted traditional Calvinist theology, which asserted that God had to intervene in order for an individual to achieve salvation—essentially, a form of predestination that dismissed the relevance of human volition and self-reliance in shaping one's spiritual destiny. The New Side (progressives) had no quarrel with governance structure, but influenced by the Enlightenment, they saw a greater role for the individual: a person could evaluate scripture, attempt moral self-improvement, and in a moment of transformation be touched by God's grace and experience a personal "revival."[9] In

---

[6]Charles Coleman Sellers provides a nice sketch of the history of Carlisle and the town's most prominent citizens in *Dickinson College: A History*, Wesleyan University Press, Middletown, CT, 1973, chapter 2. A digital version of the book is available at http://chronicles.dickinson.edu/histories/sellers/toc_frame.html.

[7]Ibid, p. 22.

[8]Ibid, p. 22 and p. 31.

[9]D. G. Hart and John R. Muether, "Turning Points in American Presbyterian History Part 3: Old Side versus New Side, 1741–1758," New Horizons, web site of the Orthodox Presbyterian Church, http://www.opc.org/nh.html?article_id=46 and The American Presbyterian Church, History of American Presbyterianism, http://www.americanpresbyterianchurch.org/.htm.

Carlisle, while members of the Old Side maintained a dominant position in the local congregation, advocates of New Side principles established a foothold.

By the late 1760s, a Carlisle minister had begun to offer lessons to the boys living in the town. In 1772, construction of a church, under the leadership of an Old Side clergyman was completed, and it afforded space for regular school lessons. In keeping with the practices found in grammar schools of the day, boys 10 years of age and older studied moral philosophy ("the application of sound doctrine to right living"), Latin, Greek, and other topics. Schools such as this were only a step below and in some cases were an adjunct to the handful of colleges that had been established in the colonies.[10] In 1773, the Assembly granted a deed to a plot of land for a grammar school in Carlisle. Nine of Carlisle's most prominent residents, men who had achieved their status through their military, church, or commercial activities, were named to the school board.[11] While the school was immediately successful, the outbreak of the American Revolutionary War distracted all parties from the task of constructing a schoolhouse. Lessons continued to be held in the Presbyterian Church.

In 1781, the trustees were finally able to initiate construction of a new building. They also were intent on requesting a formal charter from the assembly, a document that would give the school status as a permanent corporation. In 1782, Colonel John Montgomery, one of the trustees, shared news of those developments with Dr. Benjamin Rush. Rush, who believed that an educated citizenry was the key to preserving liberties that had been earned during the American War for Independence, became intrigued—and a bit obsessed—by the prospect of establishing a college in Carlisle.[12] Within a year Rush, in consultation with Montgomery and in conjunction with his compatriot and friend John Dickinson, would see his vision become a reality.

John Dickinson and Benjamin Rush: Founding Fathers of a New Country[13]

John Dickinson was born in 1732 and was raised as a Quaker, on his family's Maryland wheat and tobacco plantation. He received his higher education in London. Upon his return to the colonies, he settled in Philadelphia, began the practice of law, and was elected to the Pennsylvania Assembly. Dickinson became more deeply involved in public affairs when parliament levied the Stamp Act of 1765. Under the pen name A Farmer, he wrote 12 powerful essays that were published in newspapers throughout the colonies. Therein, he criticized the act on the grounds that it contradicted traditional English liberties, citing legal authorities and the works of antiquity to buttress his arguments. He was elected to the First Continental Congress of 1774 and made a significant contribution by drafting declarations in the name of that body. He was also elected to the Second Continental Congress.

---

[10]Charles Coleman Sellers, *Dickinson College: A History*, Wesleyan University Press, Middletown, CT, 1973, p. 3.

[11]James Henry Morgan, *Dickinson College: The History of One Hundred and Fifty Years 1783–1933*, Mount Pleasant Press, Carlisle, PA, 1933, chapter 1. The book is also available in digital form at http://chronicles.dickinson.edu/histories/morgan/chapter_1.html

[12]Charles Coleman Sellers, *Dickinson College: A History*, Wesleyan University Press, Middletown, CT, 1973, chapter 3 provides a history of the grammar school.

[13]This section is based on a range of sources, including the respective entries for Benjamin Rush and John Dickinson found in the Chronicles of Dickinson College, *Encyclopedia Dickinsonia*, http://chronicles.dickinson.edu/encyclo/r/ed_rushB.html and http://chronicles.dickinson.edu/encyclo/d/ed_dickinsonJ.html, as well as a variety of other web sites dealing with John Dickinson, Richard Henry Lee and the Second Continental Congress.

On June 7, 1776, Richard Henry Lee of Virginia introduced a resolution in the Second Congress declaring the union with Great Britain dissolved, proposing the formation of foreign alliances, and suggesting the drafting of a plan of confederation to be submitted to the respective states. Dickinson stood in opposition, believing the colonies should first form a confederation before declaring independence from Great Britain. One month later, on July 4, 1776, Dickinson held to his principles and in an act of moral courage, did not sign the Declaration of Independence. Given Dickinson's opposition to the declaration, he was assigned to a committee to draw up Articles of Confederation. The Congress was unable to reach agreement on the articles until November 17, 1777, at which time the articles were forwarded to each of the thirteen states. The articles were finally approved by a sufficient number to become operative on July 9, 1778.

At the conclusion of the Congress, Dickinson took a position as a colonel in the Continental Army. However, he eventually resigned his commission, due to what he interpreted as a series of insults stemming from the public stance he had taken. While there is a mixed record, some accounts suggest he subsequently served as a private soldier at the Battle of Brandywine. Following that service, he remained centrally involved in political affairs. In 1782, Dickinson was elected president of the Supreme Executive Council of Pennsylvania, a post equivalent to a modern day governor. In 1786 he participated in and was elected president of a convention at Annapolis to revise the Articles of Confederation. The brief session was soon adjourned, in favor of a constitutional convention held in Philadelphia from May to September, 1787. In the latter gathering, Dickinson drafted passages that dealt with the election of and powers for the President of the United States. The constitution was completed in 1787. To promote ratification, Dickinson wrote nine widely read essays under the pen name Fabius. The constitution was adopted in 1788 and took effect in 1789, thereby replacing the Articles of Confederation. While amended over time, it is the oldest, operative, written constitution in the world. Given his patriotic efforts, Dickinson earned a spot in U.S. history as the "Penman of the Revolution."

Benjamin Rush was born in 1745 on a farm near Philadelphia. He was raised in the Calvinist tradition. He earned his bachelor's degree in 1760 from the University of New Jersey (subsequently renamed Princeton), returned to Philadelphia and studied medicine from 1761 until 1766, and then moved abroad and earned a degree in medicine from the University of Edinburgh (Scotland) in June 1768. He returned once again to Philadelphia in 1769 and started a private practice while also serving as the professor of chemistry at the College of Philadelphia. He wrote essays on a range of subjects. His commentary about the emerging crisis between the colonies and Britain brought him into association with men such as John Adams and Thomas Jefferson. When the American Revolutionary War broke out in 1775, Rush joined the Continental Army as a surgeon and physician. In June 1776, he was appointed to the Second Continental Congress. Unlike Dickinson, when the time came, he chose to sign the declaration.

In April 1777, Rush was appointed surgeon-general of the Continental Army. However, he soon became embroiled in a dispute with Dr. William Shippen Jr., director of hospitals for the Continental Army, about medical conditions for the troops. He wrote letters about his concerns to key persons, including Commander in Chief George Washington.[14] When he received no answers, Rush wrote a letter to Patrick Henry: therein, he repeated his concerns and expressed doubts about Washington's leadership.[15] After

---

[14] *Letters of Benjamin Rush*, Princeton University Press, Princeton, NJ, 1951, Volume 1, pp. 180–182.

[15] Ibid, pp. 182–183.

Henry disclosed the contents of the letter to Washington, Rush was asked to appear before a congressional committee. The committee sided with Shippen, prompting Rush to resign his commission. Nonetheless, Rush would not let the matter drop. He continued to write letters to Washington and other leaders, claiming that Shippen was guilty not only of mismanagement, but also of selling supplies intended for patients for his own profit. In one such letter to Nathaniel Greene, he unleashed his scathing wit.

> I find from examining Dr. Shippen's return of the numbers who die in the hospitals that I was mistaken in the accounts I gave of that matter in my letters to you. . . . All I can say in apology for this mistake is that I was deceived by counting the number of coffins that were daily put under ground. From their weight and smell I am persuaded they contained hospital patients in them, and if they were not dead I hope some steps will be taken for the future to prevent and punish the crime of burying Continental soldiers alive.[16]

In January of 1780, Shippen was arrested. In what was regarded as an "irregular trial," which included Shippen wining and dining members of the hearing board, he was acquitted by one vote.[17] Rush eventually repaired his private relationship with Washington; but given that Washington had already started his rise to godlike status at the time of Rush's letter to Patrick Henry, the incident undermined Rush's public reputation for a number of years to come.

Rush returned to his practice in Philadelphia in 1778. In 1780, he began to lecture at the new University of the State of Pennsylvania. In 1783, Rush joined the staff of the Pennsylvania

Hospital. He was relentless in his efforts to help battle the yellow fever epidemics, which repeatedly surfaced in Philadelphia between 1793 and 1800; however, he was excoriated by some contemporaries for his aggressive advocacy and use of purging (bleeding) as proper treatment for the disease. Ultimately, he gained the reputation as a pioneer, credited with writing the first textbook published in the United States in the field of chemistry and the first major treatise on psychiatry. At the time of his death in 1813, he was regarded as the preeminent physician in the United States.

In 1787, Rush briefly reentered politics: he actively advocated ratification of the constitution and was appointed to the ratifying convention for the state. Of greater significance, Rush was an ardent social activist—he helped found the Pennsylvania Society for Promoting the Abolition of Slavery—and a prolific writer, advocating prison reform, abolition of capital punishment, temperance, better treatment of mental illness, universal health care, and a robust system of education. In 1797, he was appointed by President John Adams to be treasurer of the United States Mint, a post he occupied until he passed away.

Rush's Values and World View

Rush was a complex character. He accumulated an enormous breadth of formal knowledge, was a keen observer of everyday events, and was able to engage in either detailed analysis or sweeping generalization. He was a man of principle who would not back down in the face of pressure. At times, he was charming and persuasive, at others, nasty and domineering. While he could be a loyal, devoted, and caring friend, he sometimes abruptly turned on those who did not share his sentiments or opinions, and only later sought reconciliation.

---

[16]Ibid, p. 195.

[17]"William Shippen, Jr.," University of Pennsylvania Archives, http://www.archives.upenn.edu/histy/features/1700s/people/shippen_wm_jr.html, accessed September 23, 2007.

All of Rush's efforts to institute social reforms and promote the cause of education in the new country were informed by his assertion that the struggle for independence was a never ending process, illustrated for example by a public statement he made in 1787.

> There is nothing more common than to confound the terms of American Revolution with those of the late American war. The American war is over; but this is far from being the case with the American Revolution. On the contrary, nothing but the first act of the great drama is closed.[18]

Rush was the type of man who, as the years passed by, could be found arguing positions he had previously rejected—at times he even appeared to be self-contradictory.[19] Despite that tendency, at the most fundamental level he was concerned with two sets of relations: the configuration of social institutions such as family, church, school, and state and the role of the individual within the context of those institutions.

Rush was informed by and contributed to three major intellectual movements of his time. First was the Scottish Enlightenment.[20] The University of Edinburgh, where Rush received his medical training, was an important center of the movement. Like their French counterparts, Scotsmen wrote about the power of the human mind to uncover the logic of natural laws and celebrated the scientific achievements of the 17th century. However, they had an additional point of emphasis: they were concerned that Scotland, which in 1707 had been unified with an economically superior England, risked becoming a poverty-stricken backwater. Thus, men such as David Hume and Adam Smith investigated moral philosophy, history, and political economy in order to better understand the process of economic growth and development, in hope of applying insights and keeping Scotland economically vibrant.

Second, Rush was raised as a Calvinist. He gradually became sympathetic to the teachings of the New Side Presbyterians. The College of New Jersey was decidedly Presbyterian in its affiliation. While at Edinburgh, Rush, acting at the behest of some of the College of New Jersey Trustees, wrote to and visited with the progressive Scottish clergyman John Witherspoon, and convinced Witherspoon and his wife that Witherspoon should accept the presidency of the college. That was a maneuver important in the ongoing struggle being waged at the school between Old Side and New Side factions. Nonetheless, in later years, Rush became frustrated with Presbyterian elders and began to attend services of various Christian faiths. Even later in life, he withdrew to his own private reflections on religious matters.

Third, in terms of political philosophy, Rush's position also changed. In the years preceding the American Revolution, he was radical in his beliefs, calling for an overthrow of existing authority. As the prospect of independence became more certain, Rush became more conservative. For example, in the early 1780s, he asserted that democracy "meant rule by an elite drawn from the whole," with the elite reflecting the influence of God's grace.[21] A few years later, in the debate regarding the need for a bill of rights in the U.S. Constitution, Rush was sympathetic to the conservative views associated with

---

[18]*Letters of Benjamin Rush,* Princeton University Press, Princeton, NJ, 1951, Volume 1, p. lxviii.

[19]Ibid, Introduction.

[20]Department of Economics, New School for Social Research, "Scottish Enlightenment," The History of Economic Thought http://cepa.newschool.edu/het/schools/scottish.htm.

[21]Charles Coleman Sellers, *Dickinson College: A History,* Wesleyan University Press, Middletown, CT, 1973, p. 53.

the Federalist Party of John Adams and stood in opposition to the Democrat-Republicans and Thomas Jefferson, who favored a more egalitarian concept of democracy.

> There can be only two securities for liberty in any government . . . representation and checks. By the first the rights of the people, and by the second the rights of representation, are effectively secured. Every part of a free constitution hangs upon these two points; and these form the two capital features of the proposed Constitution of the United States. Without them, a volume of rights would avail nothing; and with them, a declaration of rights is absurd and unnecessary . . .[22]

In the presidential election of 1796, however, he favored Jefferson, who was defeated by Adams. In the early 1800s, he maintained a steady correspondence with Jefferson, who by that time had been elected president, as well as with Adams.

In 1797, when Rush was seeking the position at the U.S. Mint, Judge Richard Peters, a long time Philadelphia Federalist, was asked by Secretary of State Pickering to provide a written evaluation of Rush. Peters suggested that Rush had made a series of bad political choices over time—he had after all, gravitated to the Democrat-Republicans—and had suffered from the Shippen affair. But he went on to say the following.

> I lament his Want of Stability, for he certainly has great Merit, unshaken Integrity & eminent Talents. . . . I admire his Abilities, lament his Foibles, & with

them all sincerely love him, therefore I cannot but wish him gratified.[23]

Securing a College Charter[24]

Rush imagined that the college in Carlisle would be part of a larger system that also included a handful of colleges located throughout the state and a university in Philadelphia. At the outset, it would be located at the site of the grammar school. He initially asserted that it should be affiliated with one religion—in this case the Presbyterian Church—and that a symbiotic relationship existed between religion and learning.

> Religion is best supported under the patronage of particular societies. Instead of encouraging bigotry, I believe it prevents it by removing young men from those opportunities of controversy which a variety of sects mixed together are apt to create and which are the certain fuel of bigotry. Religion is necessary to correct the effects of learning. Without religion I believe learning does real mischief to the morals and principles of mankind; a mode of worship is necessary to support religion; and education is the surest way of producing a preference and constant attachment to a mode of worship.[25]

Rush soon realized that in order to achieve his objective of founding a college, he would have to win the support of three groups of constituents. First were the leaders of Carlisle, for although Montgomery endorsed the idea, others who were on the board of the grammar school were resistant. Second was the Donegal Presbytery,

---

[22]*Letters of Benjamin Rush*, Princeton University Press, Princeton, NJ, 1951, Volume 1, p. 453.

[23]Ibid, p. 1210.

[24]The following paragraph is based on James Henry Morgan, *Dickinson College: The History of One Hundred and Fifty Years 1783–1933*, Mount Pleasant Press, Carlisle, PA, 1933, chapter 2.

[25]*Letters of Benjamin Rush*, Princeton University Press, Princeton, NJ, 1951, Volume 1, pp. 294–295.

composed of elders from congregations located in communities throughout the region. Third was the Assembly of Pennsylvania. The need to win over the last group led him to retreat from the notion of an exclusive affiliation with the Presbyterian Church and to consider a non-sectarian school, one that could be endorsed by clergymen of other Christian faiths including the Lutherans and could eventually win financial support from the assembly.

Thus, during the first eight months of 1783, Rush adapted four sets of tactics. First, he contacted influential and wealthy friends from Philadelphia to elicit political support and financial commitments for the college. Among those he visited was John Dickinson, who was by that time the president of the Supreme Executive Council of Pennsylvania. Dickinson rejected Rush's first proposal to name the school John and Mary's College after Dickinson and his wife, on grounds that it sounded too much like the College of William and Mary, which had been named for British royalty; however, he gradually warmed to the idea of a college that would bear his family name.[26] Second, Rush wrote letters to those he knew objected to the plan and made his case for a school: it would obviate the need for young men from the Carlisle region to travel to Philadelphia or New Jersey for an education; and it would contribute to the emergence of a new commercial center in Carlisle, thereby raising land prices and creating better economic balance with Philadelphia, which dominated the eastern part of the state.[27] Third, in light of the heavy Scottish-Irish presence in the region, Rush argued that the college would provide a sound educational foundation to young men who

aspired to be ministers in the Presbyterian Church. Fourth, he told those he contacted about the pledges of money and support he had already earned from others and held out the promise of positions on the board of trustees of the college to people representing different professions, religions, and parts of Pennsylvania. As Rush acknowledged, the going was not easy.

> [One group of opponents] accuse us of an attempt to divide the Presbyterians . . . [To some groups] they say our college is to be a nursery . . . of the Old Lights [Old Side]—with the Old Lights they accuse us of a design to spread the enthusiasm of the New Lights [New Side] through the state. . . . In some of their letters and conversations I am considered as a fool and a madman. In others I am considered as a sly, persevering, and dangerous kind of fellow. Almost every epithet of ridicule and resentment in our language has been exhausted upon me in public newspapers and in private cabals since the humble part I have acted in endeavoring to found a college at Carlisle.[28]

Nonetheless, his methods worked. He successfully neutralized critics in Carlisle. In spring of 1783, the Donegal Presbytery endorsed the idea of a college. And, on September 9, 1783, by a margin of only four votes, the General Assembly of Pennsylvania approved the Dickinson College charter, entitled "An act for the establishment of a college at the borough of Carlisle, in the county of Cumberland, in the state of Pennsylvania."[29]

---

[26]Charles Coleman Sellers, *Dickinson College: A History*, Wesleyan University Press, Middletown, CT, 1973, p. 55.

[27]*Letters of Benjamin Rush*, Princeton University Press, Princeton, NJ, 1951, Volume 1, pp. 294–296.

[28]Ibid, pp. 299–300.

[29]A digital copy of the original charter is available at the Chronicles of Dickinson College, http://chronicles.dickinson.edu/archives/charter_orig/. A digital copy of the original plus subsequent amendments through 1966 is available at http://chronicles.dickinson.edu/archives/charter_1966/charter.html#amendments.

The date of the charter fell only six days after the September 3, 1783, signing of the Treaty of Paris, an event that formally ended the American Revolutionary War and included recognition by the United Kingdom and by France of the thirteen colonies as independent states.

Rush's Vision for the New College

Rush's philosophical leanings informed his vision of a Dickinson education. At the third Carlisle meeting of August 1785, Rush shared his "Plan of Education for Dickinson College." The original document, which survived, is filled with notations, suggesting Rush's plan was modified during conversations with other board members. The initial curriculum actually approved by the board included instruction in six major areas of study: (1) philosophy of the mind, moral philosophy and belles lettres (the translation from French is "fine letters" or "fine literature"), economics, and sociology; (2) Greek and Latin; (3) history and chronology; (4) mathematics; (5) English; and (6) natural philosophy (science).

As far as Rush was concerned, the curriculum was not ideal. For example, in his plan, Rush had placed chemistry in the same cluster of courses as mathematics and natural philosophy; but it was lined through. Given that Rush was one of the leading experts in the field in the United States and that he believed that chemistry was fundamental to other sciences and could be applied to fields of practical importance in the new nation, such as agriculture and manufacturing, the omission of chemistry as a stand-alone topic in the initial Dickinson curriculum had to be a source of frustration to him: indeed, the first professor in that field did not arrive at Dickinson until 1810.[30] Furthermore, while Rush believed that history and government were

critical courses, he downplayed the significance of moral philosophy. Finally, despite his low opinion regarding the study of Greek and Latin, he had made a strong concession: in light of the central place those languages held in the education of the times, they should be included in Dickinson's program. But he did expect that modern languages such as French and German should also be taught.[31] However, as was the case with chemistry, the first faculty member who was expert in Spanish, Italian and French did not arrive on the scene until 25 years had passed. It took even longer for a professor of German to come to Dickinson.

Rush's disappointment with the shape of the initial Dickinson curriculum did not stop him from speaking out and staying involved in educational reforms. In 1786, Rush wrote the first version of an essay titled "Upon the spirit of education proper for the College in a Republican State" in which he more clearly and fully articulated his view of the purpose, principles, and content of the education that should be provided at Dickinson College (see Exhibit 1). He asserted that a liberal education should be informed by the core values associated with religious doctrine—especially that of the New Testament—in order to cultivate virtue; in turn, virtue was essential to liberty, and liberty to a republican form of government. An education should promote a sense of homogeneity, civic duty, and patriotism among young men and women who had a critical role to play in shaping the new nation. With respect to the residential experience, students should live with host families rather than in dormitories, in order to learn civility and to develop an appreciation of family values. In terms of life style, students should have a balanced diet, avoid consuming liquor, and be exposed to rigorous physical activity and manual labor, all for the purpose of learning discipline and

---

[30]Charles Coleman Sellers, *Dickinson College: A History*, Wesleyan University Press, Middletown, CT, 1973, Appendix A, pp. 507–508.

[31]Ibid, pp. 81–82.

achieving balance in the conduct of life and affairs. A college should be located in a county seat so that students could leave the classroom, visit the courthouse and witness government in action. The curriculum should not be preoccupied with the classics but instead should include subjects—from history, to contemporary foreign languages such as French and German, to mathematics and chemistry—that were useful, that would help strengthen the intellectual, economic, political, and technical foundations of the new republic.

In "Thoughts on Female Education" written in 1787, he argued that in America, which had fewer class distinctions and a lower prevalence of servants than did England, a woman needed an education so she could be a partner to her husband in managing household property and affairs.[32] In "Observations on the Study of Greek and Latin," written in 1791, Rush posited that because useful knowledge was disseminated in contemporary languages, time spent studying Greek and Latin crowded out topics more relevant to a republic.[33] He also pointed to the instrumental and intrinsic nature of a liberal education.

> The great design of a liberal education is to prepare youth for usefulness here, and happiness hereafter.[34]

Citing rationales similar to those he cited when founding Dickinson, Rush continued to endorse other educational initiatives. For example—and perhaps a reflection of his disappointment about the absence of German language at Dickinson[35]—he helped found in 1787, in Lancaster, Pennsylvania—located only 55 miles from Carlisle—the German College, which was subsequently named Franklin College and even later Franklin and Marshall College. Since instruction would be in English, he believed the school would help German-speaking citizens in that part of the state be more quickly assimilated and eliminate barriers between them and English speaking inhabitants. Meanwhile, he felt that capability in German could be preserved and employed to understand books and articles from the sciences and other fields written in that language. He also believed the school would help unite the Calvinists and Lutherans among the German population.[36]

As another illustration of his thinking, in 1788, Rush publicly advocated a federal university to help prepare youth for civil and professional life, one which students would attend after completing a college education in their respective home states.[37] A promising handful should be deployed to Europe, and others selected to travel the United States, to collect insights on the latest innovations in agriculture, manufacturing, commerce, the art of war, and practical government, in order to report these to their faculty. The purpose of the curriculum for the University was much like that he had proposed for Dickinson College: it should be forward looking and practical in its orientation.

---

[32]Benjamin Rush, "Thoughts Upon Female Education, Accommodated to the Present State of Society, Manners, and Government in the United States of America—July 28, 1787," *Essays Literary, Moral, and Philosophical*, Thomas & Samuel F. Bradford, Philadelphia, 1798, available in digital form at http://deila.dickinson.edu/cdm4/document.php?CISOROOT=/ownwords&CISOPTR=19843.

[33]Benjamin Rush, "Observations on the Study of Latin and Greek Languages, As a Branch of Liberal Education, With Hints of a Plan of Liberal Instruction, Without Them, Accommodated to the Present State of Society, Manners, and Government in the United States—August 24, 1791," *Essays Literary, Moral, and Philosophical*, Thomas & Samuel F. Bradford, Philadelphia, 1798, p. 21, available in digital form at http://deila.dickinson.edu/cdm4/document.php?CISOROOT=/ownwords&CISOPTR=19843.

[34]Ibid, p. 27.

[35]This possibility was suggested by Bill Durden, interview with the case author, October 23, 2007.

[36]*Letters of Benjamin Rush*, Princeton University Press, Princeton, NJ, 1951, Volume 1, pp. 420–429.

[37]Ibid, pp. 491–495.

While the business of doing education in Europe consists in lectures upon the ruins of Palmyra and the antiquities of Herculaneum, or in disputes about Hebrew points, Greek particles, or the accent and quantity of the Roman language, the youth of America will be employed in acquiring those branches of knowledge which increase the conveniences of life, lessen human misery, improve our country, promote population, exalt the human understanding, and establish domestic social, and political happiness.[38]

Rush and Nisbet[39]

On the important question of who should serve as the first headmaster, Rush strongly endorsed a well renowned scholar Dr. Charles Nisbet of Montrose, Scotland, who had completed his studies at Edinburgh in 1754—twelve years prior to the time when Rush started his studies—and was also deeply influenced by the Scottish Enlightenment. Rush had first heard of Nisbet when John Witherspoon, who had initially declined the invitation to become president of the College of New Jersey, had suggested Nisbet as a worthy candidate. At their April 1784 meeting, the board unanimously elected Nisbet the first principal of the college. Following that meeting, John Dickinson, as chairman of the board of trustees, wrote to Nisbet, informing him about the position. Nisbet was not initially eager for the job. Thus, from December 1783 to June 1784, Rush took it upon himself to write letters to Nisbet, describing in enthusiastic if not hyperbolic terms the prospects for the college.

The trustees of Dickinson College are to meet at Carlisle on the 6th of next April to choose a principal for the College. I have taken great pains to direct their attention and votes to you. From the situation and other advantages of that College, it must soon be the first in America. It is the key to our western world.[40]

[T]he public is more filled than ever with expectations from your character. They destine our College to be THE FIRST IN AMERICA under your direction and government. [Rush provided the emphasis in his original letter].[41]

Our prospects ... brighten daily. ... Indeed, Sir, every finger of the hand of Heaven has been visible in our behalf. ... Dickinson College, with Dr. Nisbet at its head, bids fair for being the first literary institution in America.[42]

Rush's repetition of the phrase "first in America" in his series of letters was provocative for it had two possible meanings: Dickinson would become the foremost college in the new country, in terms of quality; and, in light of the date September 9, 1783, coming as it did only six days after the signing of the Treaty of Paris, Dickinson had been the first college to receive a charter in the newly recognized country.

Nisbet ultimately succumbed to Rush's persuasiveness and accepted the post. His first months in America were filled with highs and lows. He arrived with his family in Philadelphia,

---

[38]Ibid, p. 494.

[39]This section is primarily based on James Henry Morgan, *Dickinson College: The History of One Hundred and Fifty Years 1783–1933*, Mount Pleasant Press, Carlisle, PA, 1933, chapter 4.

[40]*Letters of Benjamin Rush*, Princeton University Press, Princeton, NJ, 1951, Volume 1, p. 316.

[41]Ibid, p. 334.

[42]James Henry Morgan, *Dickinson College: The History of One Hundred and Fifty Years 1783–1933*, Mount Pleasant Press, Carlisle, PA, 1933, chapter 1, pp. 31–32.

on June 9, 1785. They stayed with Rush for three weeks before departing for Carlisle on June 30. Rush wrote to a friend, "The more I see of him, the more I love and admire him."[43] Nisbet reached Carlisle on July 4, 1785, took the oath of office the next day, and got to work. Ten days later, July 15, he wrote his first letter to Rush and was somewhat critical of conditions in Carlisle—for example, he pointed to the need for a new building, describing the grammar school as shabby, dirty, and too small to accommodate all the students. Soon thereafter, he and his entire family contracted malaria. He became demoralized, and in August informed Rush that he had experienced a change of heart, would relinquish the position of principal and return to Scotland as soon as feasible.

Perhaps Rush, like an overly protective parent, was offended by Nisbet's early criticism of the college. Perhaps he was disappointed with Nisbet's lack of resolve. Perhaps he was beginning to get a different read on the man. For whatever reason, by the time of the August 9, 1785, board meeting in Carlisle, Rush had soured on Charles Nisbet. He ignored a note delivered to him on Nisbet's behalf and did not visit the Nisbet family, who were still convalescing. Nisbet, at first perplexed, grew angry. In the ensuing years, the relationship between the two men remained strained.

⊠ Glorious Intentions; Disappointing Outcome (1785–1816)

In summer 1785, the board accepted Nisbet's resignation and appointed faculty member Robert Davidson as acting principal for the first year of classes. At the outset, the attributes of the school bore little resemblance to a modern liberal arts college. The school was in session year round, except for one month breaks in October and May, with commencement occurring on the last Wednesday of September. Fees ranged from $15 to $25 per year. The campus consisted of one building, the original Carlisle Grammar School, which had been ceded to the college in 1783. In 1786, the building was enlarged from its original two-story, two-room dimensions. The original faculty consisted of only four professors, including the head of the Grammar School. Enrollment in the classes of 1787 to 1816 fluctuated between zero and 60. Students found it relatively hard to earn an undergraduate degree, as the average number who actually received a diploma during that period was often less than 75 per cent of each class.[44] In terms of scale, Dickinson was typical of the times: for example, in the 1780s, while Columbia College had two professors and some two dozen students, the College of New Jersey had two professors, a provost, and roughly 60 students.[45]

Meanwhile, Nisbet decided he and his family would wait until spring of 1786 to return to Scotland. Over the winter months, the weather cooled, Nisbet and family recovered their health, and he had a change of heart. By February of 1786, he expressed in writing his desire to be reinstated. While Rush was opposed, the Carlisle-based members of the board rallied to the idea and in May of 1786 reelected him as first principal of Dickinson College. His performance as principal was influenced by a range of factors, including his own character traits, the structure in place for governing the college,

---

[43]James Henry Morgan, *Dickinson College: The History of One Hundred and Fifty Years 1783–1933*, Mount Pleasant Press, Carlisle, PA, 1933, p. 34.

[44]Author's computations, based on information found in "Alumni 1787–1900," *Encyclopedia Dickinsonia*, Dickinson Chronicles, http://chronicles.dickinson.edu/encyclo/a/alumni/.

[45]Charles F. Himes, *A Sketch of Dickinson College*, Lane S. Hart, Harrisburg, 1879, chapter 1, p. 3. A digital version of this book is available at the Chronicles of Dickinson College, http://chronicles.dickinson.edu/histories/himes, accessed July 23, 2007.

financial pressures, and efforts to construct the first major building on the college campus.[46]

Nisbet was a relentless worker and generally regarded as a brilliant scholar, a man who possessed deep knowledge about an extraordinary range of subjects. In addition to serving as principal, Nisbet carried a full-time teaching load, responsible for lectures in philosophy of the mind, moral philosophy and belles lettres, economics, and sociology. His lectures—which the students wrote verbatim in their notebooks—were remarkable for their breadth and insights. Nisbet was extremely well liked and admired by his students. Although Nisbet tended to place a higher value on the classics than did Rush, intellectually speaking the two men appeared to be in fundamental agreement about the purpose of a liberal education.[47] Unlike Rush, however, Nisbet remained politically conservative throughout his life. Ultimately, he was not able to sympathize with the dominant values and institutions of the new country, and he regarded himself an outsider in his community.[48]

Throughout his administration, Nisbet—who was quite good at being critical of events but quite ineffective at being persuasive[49]—was constrained by his formal relationship with the board of trustees. Under the original charter, neither the principal nor any faculty member could serve on the board, and by 1786, the board had adopted an even more stringent policy—the principal and faculty were prohibited from attending board meetings.

When the charter for Dickinson was being drafted, Rush had endorsed the idea that the president of the college should be subservient to the board of trustees. He based his opinion on what he had observed at the College of Philadelphia: he believed that a controlling and rigid-minded president had dominated the board to the detriment of the school.[50] Nevertheless, Rush objected to this new development at Dickinson on both philosophical and practical grounds. In a letter written to the trustees in October of 1786, Rush wondered why his plan, which had been agreed by the board in August of 1785, had not been adopted. He was particularly concerned that the behavior of the boys was "irregular" and that the faculty was not imposing discipline.

> . . . I beg leave to recommend that the trustees would exercise a watchful eye over their own authority, and that they would divide the government of the College among every branch of the faculty agreeably to the spirit and letter of our charter. Unless this be the case, the dignity and usefulness of our teachers will be lessened and destroyed, and the republican constitution of the College will be reduced to the despotism of a private school. When our professors cease to be qualified to share in the power of the College, it will be proper to dismiss them, for government and instruction are inseparably connected.[51]

---

[46]This section is based on James Henry Morgan, *Dickinson College: The History of One Hundred and Fifty Years 1783–1933*, Mount Pleasant Press, Carlisle, PA, 1933, chapters 5–10 and on Charles Coleman Sellers, *Dickinson College: A History*, Wesleyan University Press, Middletown, CT, 1973, chapters 5 and 6.

[47]Dickinson College History Professor John Osborne, interview, September 6, 2007, and Dickinson College Archivist Jim Gerencser, interview, September 7, 2007, each suggested that Rush and Nisbet were actually closer in their way of thinking than one might expect, given the tension in their personal relationship.

[48]James Henry Morgan, *Dickinson College: The History of One Hundred and Fifty Years 1783–1933*, Mount Pleasant Press, Carlisle, PA, 1933, p. 66.

[49]Charles Coleman Sellers, *Dickinson College: A History*, Wesleyan University Press, Middletown, CT, 1973, p. 79.

[50]Ibid, pp. 139–140.

[51]*Letters of Benjamin Rush*, Princeton University Press, Princeton, NJ, 1951, Volume 1, p. 397.

However, the situation did not change. Given that making the journey to Carlisle from any of the cities to the east was a difficult undertaking; that seven of the nine Carlisle men who had been on the board of the grammar school were also members of the board of the college; and that only nine people were needed for a quorum, the Carlisle contingent of the board were in a position to dominate college governance and micromanage daily affairs.

In its early history, the endowment of the college never exceeded $20,200, an amount achieved in 1784. Thus, the endowment did not generate large annual returns. Furthermore, the small number of students paying tuition caused the college to experience budget deficits. Given those difficulties, the trustees repeatedly appealed to the assembly for assistance; in turn, the Assembly responded with modest annual grants that averaged about $550 per year. However, budget pressures continued, the college took out loans, and overall debts began to rise.

Furthermore, the college had some difficulties in raising contributions. Rush assigned some of the blame to Nisbet. He believed that when Nisbet announced his decision to retire that first year, and when he continued to publicly complain about the treatment he had received at the hands of Rush and more generally about the state of affairs in America, he did harm to the reputation of the college.[52] By 1799, Rush—who had become a supporter of Jefferson—was even more distressed that Nisbet was expressing pro-federalist sentiments in his classroom, thus undermining the college's ability to raise contributions from Democratic-Republicans.[53]

In 1800, the board voted to reduce Nisbet's salary from $1,200 to $800 per year, to reduce those of the other faculty as well, and to borrow $2,000. In 1801, the board sold stock worth another $2,000. In spring 1802, the board stopped making full payment of faculty salaries. Those developments impacted the morale of Nisbet and his faculty.

Meanwhile, in 1799 the college purchased a seven acre parcel of land on the then-existing western boundary of Carlisle, for $151. The board began to solicit contributions, and on June 20, the cornerstone for a building called New College was set in place. The board hoped construction would be finished by winter, but progress was slow. That fact, along with the college's mounting financial difficulties, fueled speculation that Dickinson would have to close its doors. Finally, in the winter of 1802–1803, New College was receiving final touches: sadly, on February 3, 1803, the building burned to the ground.

In the aftermath of the disaster, the trustees demonstrated their determination. They appealed to the presbytery for financial assistance. They visited Philadelphia, Baltimore, New York and Norfolk to raise funds, and met with success. In Washington DC, they won a personal contribution of $100 from President Thomas Jefferson, as well as contributions from other important political figures. Buoyed by the inflow of funds, the board solicited help from one of the foremost architects and engineers of the time, Benjamin Latrobe, who graciously agreed to contribute a design for a replacement building larger than the first. The new building—which became known in later decades, when other buildings were added to the campus, as West College—would be constructed of limestone with brown sandstone accents and would be multipurpose in nature, providing dormitory, dining hall, chapel, and classroom space for the students and living quarters for the faculty. Once again, Rush had to accept a compromise, as the plan to house students in the building, rather than to have them board with local families, ran counter to his philosophy of education. The corner-stone of the building was laid on

---

[52]*Letters of Benjamin Rush*, Princeton University Press, Princeton, NJ, 1951, Volume 1, p. 537.

[53]Ibid, p. 812.

August 8, 1803. It was first used for academic purposes in November of 1805.

Charles Nisbet died from complications associated with pneumonia on January 18, 1804. While they had been at odds for the better part of 20 years, at the last it appears that Rush and Nisbet managed to find some common ground, judging by a letter Rush wrote to Montgomery when Nisbet died.

> He has carried out of our world an uncommon stock of every kind of knowledge. Few such men have lived and died in any country. I shall long, long remember with pleasure his last visit to Philadelphia, at which time he dined with me in the company [of two friends]. His conversation was unusually instructing and brilliant, and his anecdotes full of original humor and satire.[54]

Following Nisbet's death, the board once again turned to Robert Davidson[55] to serve as acting principal, a position he held for the next five years. While never formally elected as such, he came to be recognized as the second principal of Dickinson College. Financial pressures were a reality throughout Davidson's tenure. Although Davidson was an outstanding churchman, he was not a successful college president. Of note, John Dickinson, still serving as a trustee of the college, died on February 14, 1808.

Davidson was succeeded by Jeremiah Atwater,[56] a Presbyterian who was serving as the first president of Middlebury College when informed of the post at Dickinson. A devout, conservative Presbyterian, he hoped to create a culture at Dickinson based on religious principles and in this sense was in step with Rush. However, upon his arrival, he was aghast at the state of affairs in Carlisle, complaining in correspondence to Rush that the boys were prone to "drunkenness, swearing, lewdness, & dueling" and the faculty did not take responsibility for imposing discipline.[57] Atwater quickly took steps to introduce the type of discipline typical of that found in the colleges of New England.

During Atwater's tenure, financial pressures continued to plague the college, especially given efforts to add dining rooms and other features to the interior of the college building. Given the small scale of the college and the relatively low standard of living at the time, the ongoing construction drained resources, consumed the entire endowment, and forced the college into debt. In light of developments, Rush wrote in 1810 about raising tuition, which he understood would limit access to a liberal education.

> I wish very much the price of tuition be raised in our College. Let a learned education become a luxury in our country. The great increase of wealth among all classes of our citizens will enable them to pay for it with more ease than in former years when wealth was confined chiefly to cities and to the learned professions. Besides, it will check the increasing disproportion of learning to labor in our country. This suggestion is not intended to lessen the diffusion of knowledge by means of reading, writing, and arithmetic. Let those be as common and as cheap as air.

---

[54]Ibid, p. 878.

[55]This section is based on James Henry Morgan, *Dickinson College: The History of One Hundred and Fifty Years 1783–1933*, Mount Pleasant Press, Carlisle, PA, 1933, chapter 14.

[56]This section is based on James Henry Morgan, *Dickinson College: The History of One Hundred and Fifty Years 1783–1933*, Mount Pleasant Press, Carlisle, PA, 1933, chapter 15 and Charles Coleman Sellers, *Dickinson College: A History*, Wesleyan University Press, Middletown, CT, 1973, chapter 7.

[57]James Henry Morgan, *Dickinson College: The History of One Hundred and Fifty Years 1783–1933*, Mount Pleasant Press, Carlisle, PA, 1933, p. 183.

In a republic no man should be a voter or juror without a knowledge of them. They should be a kind of sixth or civil sense. Not so with **learning**. Should it become **universal**, it would be as destructive to civilization as universal barbarism. [Emphasis provided by Rush.][58]

During the first three years of Atwater's term, the number of students at the college nearly tripled. But the War of 1812 had a negative impact on student attendance and graduation rates. As time passed, Atwater became increasingly discouraged by the unyielding financial difficulties and by internal dissention among his faculty. On April 19, 1813, Atwater lost a sympathizer when Benjamin Rush died rather suddenly at his home.

In early 1815, the trustees ordered Atwater and each professor to submit a weekly written report to the secretary of the board that identified all student absences or transgressions. In a corrosive environment of friction among the faculty and hostility between the faculty and the board, that proved to be the last straw. Within the year, Atwater retired from the college, as did the other faculty. The college was in shambles.

In November of 1815 the board elected John McKnight,[59] a professor and member of the board of trustees at Columbia University and influential Presbyterian, to serve as fourth principal of Dickinson. In December 1815, a Dickinson student was killed in a duel. The incident further undermined the college's reputation. In 1816, the board of trustees closed down the college.

Dickinson remained closed for five years, resumed operations in 1822, and then closed its doors again in 1832.

Despite the enormous strains of the first 50 years and the sad circumstances associated with the closing of the college, many of the young men who attended Dickinson during the era 1785 to 1832 went on to highly successful careers. Their number included ministers; college professors and presidents; secondary school teachers and principals; representatives and senators at the state and national level of government; a U.S. president and members of the executive branches of various administrations; military officers; lawyers and judges; physicians; civil servants; and businessmen.[60]

In order to reopen the college yet again, the board of trustees realized they had to end their loose affiliation with the Presbyterian Church and accept the invitation of the Methodist Episcopal Church to establish an alliance. In 1834, the college was reopened. Over the next 130 years, Dickinson experienced eras of growth and decline. The college's fortunes were influenced by external events, such as wars, economic fluctuations, and shifts in social norms. They were also influenced by internal factors, including the governance structure, the culture and the financial health of the college. Finally, they were influenced by the leadership and management abilities of individual presidents and the relationships each man had been able to forge with various constituents. Throughout that period, Dickinson remained a school with a relatively conservative and parochial culture.

In the 1960s, the college began the lengthy process of separation from the Methodist Church. By the 1970s, the college was characterized by a culture based on cooperation and collegiality. In that environment, the faculty greatly enhanced the curriculum, as reflected in more breadth in the foreign languages and opportunities for international education; innovative teaching methods in the sciences; interdisciplinary programs of

---

[58]*Letters of Benjamin Rush*, Princeton University Press, Princeton, NJ, 1951, Volume 1, p. 1053.

[59]This section and the next are based on James Henry Morgan, *Dickinson College: The History of One Hundred and Fifty Years 1783–1933*, Mount Pleasant Press, Carlisle, PA, 1933, chapter 16.

[60]A matrix that describes professions pursued by alumni graduating during the administrations of various presidents is provided in James Henry Morgan, *Dickinson College: The History of One Hundred and Fifty Years 1783–1933*, Mount Pleasant Press, Carlisle, PA, 1933, pp. 396–397.

study; and more faculty-student interaction. Dickinson had an enrollment of approximately 1600 students. By the mid-1990s, the relationship between the Methodist Church and Dickinson was cordial—the church continued to hold approximately $2 million in trust on behalf of the college and conducted its own decennial review of the college's performance. However, the church had no substantive influence on matters related to college policy or strategy.

⊠ Mounting Frustrations

In the early 1980s, the external environment confronting colleges became more challenging: costs of providing an education continued to rise; families were becoming less willing and able to pay higher tuition fees; and the public increasingly questioned the relevance of a liberal arts education. In that competitive environment, Dickinson made two strategic choices. First, given the dominant, egalitarian culture of the 1960s and 1970s, the college did not celebrate the accomplishments of any single department over others and continued to describe itself as a pure liberal arts college. Second, the college opted to award aid to incoming students on a loan-first rather than grant-first basis, and to award less overall aid than other colleges—to illustrate, through the mid-1990s, Dickinson had an average discount rate[61] of 24 per cent, compared to a discount rate of 33 per cent of most rivals.[62] Between 1988 and 1996, applications for first year admissions dropped from 4,438 to 2,829, the acceptance rate rose from 40 per cent to 84 per cent, enrollment dropped from 2,079 to 1,824, and average SAT scores for admitted students dropped from 1,216 to 1,150.

To combat that trend, in the mid-1990s, the college moved to a grant-first aid approach, and

aggressively elevated average aid awards. At one level, the tactic worked. From 1996 to 1999, applications rose from 2,829 to 3,434; the acceptance rate fell from 84 per cent to 64 per cent; and average SAT scores rose from 1,150 to 1,193. At another level, it was a serious mistake. By 1999, the discount rate had risen to 52 per cent, and the college was experiencing an operational deficit of roughly $5 million with an even larger deficit forecasted for the following year. Those deficits could only be covered in the short term by drawing down the endowment and were clearly unsustainable in the long run.

More broadly, there was gnawing concerns among various members of the college community that successive administrations had been ineffective relative to those at rival schools in terms of managing admissions and raising funds. For example, while there were certainly many highly motivated and talented students entering the college, Dickinson remained a school with regional appeal that primarily received applications from students living in the Mid-Atlantic States. By the early 1990s, some among that group regarded Dickinson as a "safety" school rather than as a first choice. Furthermore, while Dickinson prided itself on admitting students who were the first in their family to receive a college education, and while it had good socio-economic diversity, it had very low representation from students of color or from international students. With respect to financial profile, although Dickinson's endowment was experiencing relatively high returns, by the end of 1998, it stood at only $143 million, an amount that did not measure up well to the endowments of other colleges.

Those circumstances prompted Dickinson's Committee on Planning and Budget to release a white paper in the spring of 1996 to the entire faculty. The paper asserted that Dickinson had to develop a "grounding vision."

---

[61]The discount rate states, in percentage terms, the reduction from the full tuition price paid by the average student. To say this in another way, a 24 per cent discount rate implied that Dickinson realized $.76 for each $1.00 of the posted tuition price.

[62]The data included in this paragraph and the next is based on the PowerPoint presentation, "Dickinson College: A Case Study in Financial Transformation," created by Annette S. Parker (Class of 1973), vice-president and treasurer of the college, spring 2007.

Dickinson must be able to show . . . that a liberal education is simultaneously the most humanly fulfilling and ennobling **and** the most practical education. And it must be able to show that the liberal arts education offered **by this college** is superior to one offered elsewhere. (Emphasis included in original.)[63]

In response, college President A. Lee Fritschler formed a task force on the future of the college, consisting of a student and six senior faculty and administrators, to convene in early summer of 1997, for the purpose of identifying problems and proposing general solutions. Their report was released to the faculty, under the cover letter and signature of President Fritschler, on June 18. The telling language contained in the preface echoed the themes of the white paper.

We want Dickinson to be generally recognized as one of the twenty-five most prestigious liberal arts colleges in the United States within the next ten years. . . . [We envision] Dickinson as a living and learning community that embraces change, that regards diversity as an essential feature of an educational community, and that declares liberal education to be the most humanly liberating and practical preparation for citizenship in an interdependent, competitive, culturally-complex world.[64]

The report offered the following diagnosis: "The College's greatest external challenge is visibility, the greatest internal challenge is communication." To address the former, the college had to stop describing itself as a "pure liberal arts college" with "balance across all departments" and start celebrating core competencies, such as "excellence in international education."

To address the latter—which involved concerns that in light of growing difficulties, the administration was becoming insular and less than transparent—steps had to be taken to reopen communication channels among administration, faculty, students and trustees.

In late 1997, President Fritschler indicated to the community he would resign his position in June of 1999. In January of 1998, a search committee was named to find a new president.

The Challenge of Creating an Identity Story

When Bill Durden agreed to be president of Dickinson College, he was aware that the board of trustees wanted to improve the reputation and the financial foundation of the college, but did not have a detailed blue-print on how to proceed; instead, they hoped they could establish high expectations and grant a new president a broad mandate to engineer a transformation. He was aware that the program of study was first-rate and the internal governance system was sound.

Durden also knew that there was an intense desire for change and progress among the faculty and some members of the administration: he had come to appreciate that desire via conversations during the spring and from his extensive review of previously written white papers and self-studies during the summer months.

Of all the documents he had read, a passage included in the 1997 Report of the President's Task Force—"We want Dickinson to be generally recognized as one of the 25 most prestigious liberal arts colleges in the United States within the next ten years"—was most provocative. While he would certainly give it more thought, his initial reaction was that such an externally focused

---

[63]Planning and Budget Committee, April 29, 1996, "A White Paper," Dickinson College internal document, p. 2.

[64]"Report for the President's Task Force on the Future of the College," June 18, 1997, Dickinson College internal document, pp. 1–2.

objective—based on rankings produced by for-profit organizations such as *U.S. News and World Report*—might be a distraction from what he saw as the appropriate areas of concentration: the organizational culture and capabilities and the financial foundation of the college. Furthermore, he believed those rankings were based on a set of flawed metrics that did not properly capture the relative strengths of various institutions, including Dickinson. Finally, he was also troubled by what he saw as an emerging tendency in America to regard higher education as a standardized commodity: he believed that the increased attention being paid by the public to the rankings were a manifestation of that tendency.

Via his various experiences, Durden had come to believe in the power of a leadership story.

He acknowledged that he had been influenced by the work of psychologist and leadership theorist Howard Gardner (see Exhibit 2).[65] Given his general assessment of the situation at Dickinson and prompted by his conversation with the rising senior who had expressed her concerns about what it meant to be a Dickinsonian, Durden had over the past several weeks started to imagine a story based on Rush and the founding of the college that he believed would help create a unique Dickinson identify. But several issues and questions remained unresolved. Durden knew that he had to achieve greater clarity regarding the story's purpose and target audience and its structure and content. He also had to think more about the tactics and timing he would employ in introducing the story to the Dickinson community.

| **Exhibit 1** | Selected Passages From Benjamin Rush, "Of the Mode of Education Proper in a Republic" |

The business of education has acquired a new complexion by the independence of our country....

An education in our own, is to be preferred to an education in a foreign country. The principle of patriotism stands in need of the reinforcement of prejudice . . . formed in the first one and twenty years of our lives.

Our schools of learning, by producing one general, and uniform system of education, will render the mass of the people more homogenous, and thereby fit them more easily for uniform and peaceable government.

The only foundation for a useful education in a republic is to be laid in Religion. Without this there can be no virtue, and without virtue there can be no liberty, and liberty is the object and life of all republican governments....

Next to the duty which young men owe to their Creator, I wish to see a regard to their country, inculcated upon them. [Our student] . . . must love private life, but he must decline no station . . . when called to it by the suffrages of his fellow citizens.... He must avoid neutrality in all questions that divide the state, but he must shun the rage, and acrimony of party spirit.

[To improve students' ability to absorb their lessons] it will be necessary to subject their bodies to physical discipline.... [T]hey should live upon a temperate diet . . . should avoid tasting Spirituous liquors. They should also be accustomed occasionally to work with their hands.... [They should receive guidance on] those great principles in human conduct—sensibility, habit, imitations and association.

[Students should not be crowded] together under one roof for the purpose of education. The practice is . . . unfavorable to the improvements of the mind in useful learning.... [If we require them to separately live in private households] we improve their manners, by subjecting them to those restraints which the difference of age and sex, naturally produce in private families.

---

[65]Bill Durden, interview with case author, August 31, 2007, Dickinson College, Carlisle, PA.

A knowledge of [the American language is essential] . . . to young men intended for the professions of law, physic, or divinity . . . [and] in a state which boasts of the first commercial city in America.

The French and German languages should . . . be . . . taught in all our Colleges. They abound with useful books upon all subjects.

Eloquence . . . is the first accomplishment in a republic . . . We do not extol it too highly when we attribute as much to the power of eloquence as to the sword, in bringing about the American Revolution.

History and Chronology [are important because the] . . . science of government, whether . . . related to constitutions or laws, can only be advanced by a careful selection of facts, [especially those related to the] . . . history of the ancient republics, and the progress of liberty and tyranny in the different states of Europe.

Commerce . . . [is] . . . the best security against the influence of hereditary monopolies of land, and, therefore, the surest protection against aristocracy. I consider its effects as next to those of religion in humanizing mankind, and lastly, I view it as the means of uniting the different nations of the world together by the ties of mutual wants and obligations.

Chemistry by unfolding to us the effects of heat and mixture, enlarges our acquaintance with the wonders of nature and the mysteries of art . . . [and is particularly important] [i]n a young country, where improvements in agriculture and manufactures are so much to be desired.

[T]he general principles of legislation, whether they relate to revenue, or to the preservation of liberty or property . . . [should be examined, and towards this end, a student should] be directed frequently to attend the courts of justice . . . [and for this reason] colleges [should be] established only in county towns.

[T]he prerogatives of the national government . . . [should be studied, including] those laws and forms, which unite the sovereigns of the earth, or separate them from each other.

[W]omen in a republic . . . should be taught the principles of liberty and government; and the obligations of patriotism should be inculcated upon them.

SOURCE: Selected by the case author from Benjamin Rush, "Of the Mode of Education Proper in a Republic," *Essays, Literary, Moral & Philosophical*, Printed by Thomas and Samuel F. Bradford, Philadelphia, 1798, available in digital form at http://deila .dickinson.edu/theirownwords/title/0021.htm, accessed July 23, 2007).

| **Exhibit 2** | Role of a Leader and the Relevance of an Indentity Story |

Leaders are "persons who, by word and/or personal example, markedly influence the behaviors, thoughts, and/or feelings of a significant number of their fellow human beings."

Leaders influence other people either *directly*, through the stories they communicate to others; or *indirectly*, through the ideas they create. Examples of these two types include Winston Churchill, a direct leader who sits at one end of a spectrum, and Albert Einstein, an indirect leader who sits at the other. Other leaders would fall somewhere between those two, with most corporate and political leaders closer to the spot occupied by Churchill, and most artists and researchers closer to the spot occupied by Einstein.

(Continued)

Exhibit 2 (Continued)

Direct leaders achieve their effectiveness in one of two ways: they *relate* stories to others, and they *embody* those stories, thereby serving as an example which inspires others. The ability to embody stories is much more relevant to direct leaders than indirect leaders.

While it may be hard to draw precise lines between categories, leaders can be ranked as *ordinary*, *innovative*, or *visionary*. An "ordinary leader . . . simply relates the traditional story of his or her group as effectively as possible. . . . The innovative leader takes a story that has been latent in the population, or among the members of his or her chosen domain, and brings new attention or a fresh twist to that story. . . . [T]he visionary leader . . . [is not] content to relate a current story or to reactivate a story drawn from a remote or recent past . . . [and therefore] actually creates a new story."

"The ultimate impact of the leader depends most significantly on the particular story that he or she relates or embodies, and the receptions to that story on the part of audiences. . . . [A]udience members come equipped with many stories that have already been told and retold. . . . The stories of the leader . . . must compete with many other extant stories; and if the new stories are to succeed, they must transplant, suppress, complement, or in some measure outweigh the earlier stories, as well as contemporary counterstories."

"[L]eaders present a *dynamic* perspective to their followers: not just a headline or snapshot, but a drama that unfolds over time, in which they—the leader and followers—are the principal characters or heroes. Together, they have embarked on a journey in pursuit of certain goals, and along the way and into the future, they can expect to encounter certain obstacles or resistances that must be overcome. Leaders and audiences traffic in many stories, but the most basic story has to do with issues of *identity*. And so it is the leader who succeeds in conveying a new version of a given group's story who is likely to be effective. Effectiveness here involves fit—the story needs to make sense to audience members at this particular historical moment, in terms of where they have been and where they would like to go."

SOURCE: Howard Gardner, in collaboration with Emma Laskin, *Leading Minds: An Anatomy of Leadership*, Basic Books, a Division of Harper Collins Publishers, New York, NY, 1995.

Great Leadership Is Good Leadership

Jeffrey Gandz

Look into the soul of any great leader and you will find a good leader. But, if only that were the case. Some leaders, those who crave and bathe in the spotlight, are in fact not so great. Others, who are highly effective (and modest) and possess the five key characteristics this author describes, are good leaders first and foremost. Which is what, in the end, makes them great.

Reprint# 9B07TC07

The extraordinarily successful book *From Good to Great*[1] focused attention on the kind of leadership that was required to achieve enduring high performance. While it has been one of the best-selling management books of all time, it tends to focus on the effectiveness dimension of leadership to the virtual exclusion of other important dimensions. In my view, you cannot have truly great leadership without considering the broader challenges that face organizational leaders today. Great leadership must be good leadership too.

The word "good" is an interesting word in the English language because of the many meanings that it has. No more so is this true than when it is used in conjunction with the words "leader" or "leadership." Good leadership can, indeed, refer to *effective* leadership—getting followers to pursue and attain goals. But it can also refer to the *purpose* or goals that leaders pursue and whether those are deemed fitting by the societies within which they operate; it can refer to the *ethics* of leaders—doing the right things in the right ways. It can also refer to the ways in which leaders make followers *feel* good and, indeed, the way they feel about themselves as leaders.

[1]Collins, J. C. (2001). *Good to great: Why some companies make the leap—and others don't.* New York, NY, HarperBusiness.

Good as Effective

It goes without saying that good business leaders must be highly effective in getting people to follow them in pursuit of selected goals. Highly effective leaders

- Recognize and analyze the driving forces in the political, economic, societal and technological environments in which they operate and understand the impact of these forces on their current strategies;
- Develop winning strategies based on sound competitive analysis, understanding buyer-behaviors, building core competencies and selecting the right domains in which to compete that will satisfy the expectations of their shareholders and other stakeholders;
- Execute those strategies brilliantly by involving people in their formulation and implementation;
- Evaluate the execution and results systematically, making strategic adjustments as indicated;
- Beyond this, they continually build for the future by increasing the capabilities of their organizations, divisions, departments, teams and themselves.

Really effective leaders drive for results *now* while *simultaneously* building for the future. It is simply not acceptable to view these as trade-offs, as perhaps used to be done by coaches of perpetually losing sports teams. The performance bar is continually being raised and to be three, four, six percent or more than last year is baked into the expectations that we have of leaders of organizations today.[2]

Much has been written about effective leadership. Suffice it to say that we expect our leaders to work with their followers to develop a compelling future vision; enlist the support of others—inside and outside their organizations—in achieving this vision; energize, enable, and encourage high performance; empower people to act within an agreed-upon vision; and to be exemplars of the values of the organizations they lead. To do this requires both competencies and character. Competencies determine *what* leaders are able to do; character determines what they *will* do, how they will exercise those competencies under various circumstances. Good leaders, especially those who endure, are seldom one-dimensional, simple individuals. They are often complex, contradictory and multi-faceted, especially in how they respond to different situations: confident *and* humble, assertive *and* patient, analytical *and* intuitive, deliberate *and* decisive, principled *and* pragmatic, among others.

Good Purpose

When the character Gordon Gecko uttered his famous phrase "Greed is good" in the movie *Wall Street*, he reflected the view that managers, by single-mindedly pursuing the interests of shareholders, are fulfilling the true purpose of the business entity. The late Milton Friedman, the Nobel Prize winner and high-priest of free-market economics, held that this approach by business produces the most good for the most people since other institutions—government agencies, trade unions, consumer protection associations, etc. —will curb the excesses of business and that the maximum aggregate benefits come from the tension between these forces. Leaders of businesses must then pursue shareholder interests exclusively and should be compensated for so doing. They should eschew the role of social arbiters attempting to balance competing interests, a role with which they are neither charged nor competent to perform. This is not an immoral or amoral argument on the part of Friedman. Indeed, it holds to the precept that the moral action is the one that brings the most good to the most people. Attempts to demonize Friedman for this argument are misguided.

---

[2]Gandz, J. (2005). "The Leadership Role." *Ivey Business Journal* 66(1): 5.

Such a philosophy does not negate the importance of other stakeholders in the business enterprise. Indeed, customers, suppliers, employees, governments—national, regional and local—and the broader societies within which these businesses operate are also very important. Businesses benefit suppliers but also depend on excellent service and quality from those suppliers; they pay wages to employees but depend on their engagement and commitment; they provide value to customers but also benefit from the dependence of customers on them; they provide employment to members of communities but also depend on getting planning permission from a local government when they want to put up a new building; and they pay taxes to governments but also seek subsidies and other protections. But it subordinates their importance to the fundamental primacy of shareholders. They are to be considered only to the extent that they may be instrumental in creating a return to shareholders.

The alternate perspective is that shareholders are but one group of stakeholders in the business enterprise and that there are other stakeholders such as customers, suppliers, employees, community groups, pensioners, etc. to whom the business enterprise has obligations.

These obligations stem from the reciprocal social and moral obligations between the parties. Businesses owe senior employees job security and a rising standard of living because employees who have worked for the organization for many years have been committed and involved in the business; they should not pollute or degrade their environments because they are responsible moral actors in the societies within which they operate; they should not outsource work to countries with poor labor or environmental standards because to do so is morally wrong for employees in those countries since it perpetuates those poor standards while damaging the livelihoods of those on the countries from which products were outsourced; they should not deplete natural resources because it will make the societies in which they operate

unable to sustain economic and social life for generations to come.

Leaders of businesses, as viewed from this perspective, must seek a fitting balance between the interests of various stakeholders both when they coincide and when they differ, constantly seeking "win-win" or compromise resolutions when conflict occurs between stakeholders' interests. If this balance or integration sub-optimizes profit and reduces shareholder value, good business leaders should take the high road of "balance of interests." As leaders, business people cannot avoid the requirement to seek this balance even though—as the protagonists of shareholder primacy point out—they may be ill equipped to do so. They can seek advice, sift arguments, reflect and consider different interests and endeavors to find creative solutions that either satisfy all parties' demands or compromise between them, sub-optimizing shareholder value in favor of some broader, societal contribution.

This debate is ongoing. Sometimes it is trivialized by those who seek to make the case that striving for good purpose is axiomatic with shareholder value creation and that in the long-run business does well by doing good. This negates the reality that by consolidating plants, profits are increased and communities are destroyed; that by pursuing minimally legal environmental compliance, costs are minimized; and that by selling legal products that may be harmful, profits are generated for years or even decades. Recent hard-edged research indicates that the financial returns to corporate social responsibility are dubious but, despite this, there are increasing demands on business leaders to expand their horizons to embrace this ethic.

Ethical Goodness

The excesses of business and business leaders have been a pervasive if not dominant theme in the popular business literature in the last decade, leading not only to new legislation but to a widespread revulsion with the ways in which some managers have been proven to have ripped off shareholders, customers, employees, creditors, and other stakeholders. Unlike the broader issue of corporate social responsibility, this does not address the fundamental purpose of business but, rather, the ways in which business people act. It recognizes that many decisions made by managers and executives benefit some people at the expense of others. Whenever someone may be hurt by an action of management, there is an ethical decision involved.

Business ethicists recognize three distinct forms of unethical behavior.[3] The first of these are actions that are clearly not within the scope of the role. Chief financial officers should not fiddle the books; senior executives should not pad their expense accounts or charge personal expenses to the corporation; corporate directors should not trade stock based on inside information; companies should not conspire to rig bids; defense contractors should not charge unrelated expenses to cost-plus government contracts; and so on. In many cases we have laws and regulations that expressly prohibit these behaviors and, in most cases, breaking laws or evading regulations is *prima facie* unethical.

The second type of unethical action is one that serves the purpose of the role but pushes beyond the types of behavior that society would consider morally right. So, we expect marketers to emphasize the benefits of their products, but they should not lie about the performance of their products or conceal dangers that might be associated with their use; human resource managers should not mislead people about terms and conditions of employment to induce them to accept a job; salespeople should not spread false rumors about the financial health of their competitors in order to deter customers from doing business with them; financial advisors should not tailor their advice to meet their rewards to the detriment of their clients. Clearly, different societies have different tolerance levels

for these behaviors and what is considered ethical in one society might be considered beyond the pale in another.

The third type of unethical action is one that describes something that should be done but which is not done—an act of *omission* rather than commission. These non-actions that many people consider unethical include a failure to recognize the talent that exists in minority groups, failure to give people regular performance reviews and candid feedback that would help them improve, failure to point out to people that their choice of products and services may not be in their best long-term interests, and failure to review a client's financial portfolio to ensure that it is appropriately balanced for their investment objectives. This type of unethical action is often fiercely debated since it clashes with other philosophies such as "buyer-beware," or "you get what you negotiate" that appear to put the onus on the customer, employee, or other party. Unlike the more black-and-white non-role acts, this type of unethical behavior is also more subject to gradations, with some people expecting minimal compliance and others expecting standards of excellence.

When businesses meet or exceed the expectations of the societies within which they operate, they will be free to operate. When they cease to meet those expectations they will be regulated, controlled and, perhaps, even be put out of business.

The issue of what "society" condones and what is right is not trivial. At the extreme, the anti-Semitic laws of National Socialist Germany were both popular and passed by parliament as, indeed, were the anti-apartheid laws of South Africa. Petty bribery—and some that is not so petty—is commonplace in some societies yet frowned upon in others. Some societies protect intellectual property rights whereas others either have no protection or, if a law does exist, may not bother to police it. The extent to which

---

[3]Bird, F. B. and J. Gandz (1991). *Good management: Business ethics in action.* Scarborough, Ont., Prentice-Hall Canada.

something is criminal or not, widely or narrowly accepted, or considered a civil tort may vary widely from place to place.

Quite often, people make an assumption that "if it's widely done, it must be okay!" With this assumption, there would have been very little, if any, progress made over the years to deal with the blatant discrimination against racial minorities, gender-based discrimination, or indeed *any* act of discrimination by a powerful group imposed on a less powerful one. Even if something is widely practiced, people may not think that it is right. For example, while corruption is widespread in business in many parts of the world, it may be expressly forbidden by both legal and moral authorities but, because the powerful can escape the sanctions associated with the disapproval, they may perpetuate the practice.

Feel-Goodness

It's a leap from thinking about "good" as effective, purposive and ethical, to thinking about the importance of making people *feel* good or feeling good about your leadership. Yet it is a critical leap. The sociologist Amitai Etzioni proposed that people comply with leadership if they are *forced* to do so, if they are *paid* to do so or if they are moved by ideas and ideals so that they *want* to do so.[4] When people are forced to follow, they feel alienated; when they are paid to follow, their followership can be bought by others or will cease when the money stops flowing. When they buy into ideas or ideals and when they realize them through effective leadership, then the positive feelings generate their own energy and momentum, and wanting to be led is more likely to result in extraordinary and sustained support for those shared goals. The leaders of slave or mercenary armies were never as durable as those whose armies were fired up by ideals and values.

The great leader described by Jim Collins is one who through "level-5" leadership embraces fierce determination and humility that leads to involvement and commitment by his or her followers.[5] They develop a sense of self-efficacy, of value, of worth. They want to be led by such leaders, not because they are sheep but because they understand that they can achieve their goals through those leaders. And they are prepared to exercise leadership themselves within the umbrella of the organizational leader who makes them feel good about themselves.

None of this is intended to suggest that the good leader should always adjust to the surface wants and desires of those who are to be led. Indeed, panderers generally make poor leaders since they end up promising too much to too many and cannot deliver the goods.

A cynical perspective on leadership suggests that leaders find out which way the parade is heading and scramble to the front of it, or that leaders take people where they really want to go anyway. Some have proposed, judgmentally or paternalistically, that leaders take people not to where they want to go but, rather, to where they really need to be. Perhaps it is more accurate to suggest that great leaders satisfy people's deep needs rather than their surface wants, even if they may not immediately realize their needs.

The ability of leaders to understand their potential followers' needs has been associated with great religious, military, political and, yes, even business leaders. Sometimes this has resulted in great good and sometimes in great evil. Sadly, not all effective leaders who tap into their followers needs and motivate them to action do so with good purpose in mind. Genocides, persecutions, and the unrelenting pursuit of corporate greed

---

[4]Etzioni, A. (1961). *A comparative analysis of complex organizations: On power, involvement, and their correlates.* New York, Free Press of Glencoe.

[5]Collins, J. (2001). "Level 5 leadership: The triumph of humility and fierce resolve." *Harvard Business Review* 79(1): 66–76.

through fraud, misrepresentation, or even callous indifference of the impact of their actions on others have left their scars.

However, the good leader never ignores how his or her followers feel about their leadership. They know that short-term pain must be followed by long-term gain, that efforts must lead to rewards, that sacrifices will be made but not forever. And they nurture their followers through these tough times. They draw on wellsprings of optimism when things are not going well, without losing their grip on reality.

Leadership is also hard work, especially when times are tough, when things are not working the way they were planned and people are beginning to question the credibility of leadership. Often the only thing that leaders have to draw on at those times is their own self-confidence, their sense that they are doing the right things for their people. The borderline between self-confidence and arrogance, between steadfastness and hubris, may be very narrow and the leader treads it all the time. If they are to cope with the stresses and strains of leadership, it is essential that they feel good about what they are doing to make it worth the effort.

The "Good" Leader

There will always be debates about what constitutes good or great leadership in a business context, and each generation will yield its crop of candidates. Creation of shareholder value will always be high among the criteria considered, as indeed it should be. But as societal values embrace broader concerns, as we judge not only what these leaders appear to have achieved but also how they have done it, as we assess leaders not just in terms of their achievements but on their contributions to the societies within which they operate, I suspect that the emphasis will shift toward the goodness of leadership as described in this article as a necessary condition for leadership greatness.

There is an argument to be made that, given a long enough time frame, "Goodness" as I mean it and "Greatness" as suggested by Jim Collins converge into one and the same thing. That may turn out to be the case but there is too much press given to leaders who have yet to achieve either. Perhaps it is we—the public, who look to our business leaders to drive the prosperity of this and future generations—who need to be more restrained in granting this ultimate accolade and granting someone the title a "good leader."

Leadership Trait Approach

There are positive traits like trust, respect, and that sort of thing. You could be a very smart guy but if people can detect that you're not really sincere or heartfelt—that you don't have a basic respect for people—then people will be turned off by you. You might do very well as a one-man entrepreneurial show, but if you want to be a big team leader, it's a different matter. You need positive traits and the absence of negative ones.

—Dr. Victor Fung[1]

Leadership trait research was developed to ascertain why certain people were great leaders. This research led to the development of the "great person" theory as it focused on the inherent characteristics and qualities of leaders who were considered to be great. This research also led to the nature argument, which said that only certain people were born with these traits and, consequently, only those certain people became great leaders. The research focused on finding those traits that discriminated between followers and leaders (Bass, 1990; DuBrin, 2010; Jago, 1982).

Eventually, researchers questioned the universality of leadership traits. It was argued that no one set of traits was appropriate in all situations. This led to the reconceptualization of leadership as relationships among individuals in social situations. Recently, researchers have returned to the trait approach. The nature of this research is different in that it now emphasizes the importance of traits in effective leadership.

Traits are attributes that include aspects such as values, needs, motives, and personality (Yukl, 2010). One very prominent leadership researcher (Stogdill, 1948, 1974) demonstrated that average leaders were different from average group members in several ways. In his first study, Stogdill (1948) identified the following traits: (1) intelligence, (2) alertness, (3) insight, (4) responsibility, (5) initiative, (6) persistence, (7) self-confidence, and (8) sociability. This study also identified that traits and situations intersected in the sense that some traits were more important in some situations if an individual was to be an effective leader (Yukl, 2010). Stogdill's (1974) second study reported on 10 traits

---

[1]Dr. Fung is the Group Chairman of Li & Fung Group, Hong Kong's largest export trading company, and the quote is from Mercer (2009, p. 37).

associated with leadership in a positive way. These were (1) drive for responsibility and task completion, (2) vigor and persistence in pursuit of goals, (3) venturesomeness and originality in problem solving, (4) drive to exercise initiative in social situations, (5) self-confidence and sense of personal identity, (6) willingness to accept consequences of decisions and actions, (7) readiness to absorb personal stress, (8) willingness to tolerate frustration and delay, (9) ability to influence other people's behavior, and (10) the capacity to structure social interaction systems to the goal to be achieved (Northouse, 2013).

Mann (1959) determined that leaders were strong in traits such as (1) intelligence, (2) masculinity, (3) adjustment, (4) dominance, (5) extroversion, and (6) conservatism. He agreed that traits could help differentiate leaders from nonleaders. Lord, DeVader, and Alliger (1986) reviewed Mann's work and concluded that (1) intelligence, (2) masculinity, and (3) dominance are very important traits that people use to distinguish leaders. Kirkpatrick and Locke (1991) argued that leaders and nonleaders differ on six traits: (1) drive, (2) desire to lead, (3) honesty and integrity, (4) self-confidence, (5) cognitive ability, and (6) knowledge of the business. These writers argued for a nurture and nature perspective in that they believed that people can learn these traits, be born with them, or both. Summarizing the traits identified above suggests five that are mentioned most frequently: These are (1) intelligence, (2) self-confidence, (3) determination, (4) integrity, and (5) sociability. It is these five that we will focus on (Northouse, 2013).

Intelligence

Zaccaro, Kemp, and Bader (2004) found that leaders and nonleaders differ in their intellectual ability in that leaders have higher levels of intelligence than nonleaders. Their research suggests that having certain abilities helps one be a better leader—these are strong verbal, perceptual, and reasoning abilities. Conversely, their research also indicates that it may be counterproductive if a leader's intelligence is a lot higher than his or her followers' intelligence (DuBrin, 2010). This situation could lead to an inability to effectively communicate with followers as leaders may be too advanced in their thinking to be accepted and understood by their followers. Intelligence does allow leaders to more effectively develop social judgment and complex problem-solving skills. It also appears to be positively associated with effective leadership (DuBrin, 2010; Northouse, 2013).

Self-Confidence

Self-confidence means that you have a positive perspective on your ability to make judgments, to make decisions, and to develop ideas (Daft, 2011). Self-confidence aids people to develop as leaders (Yukl, 2010). It helps individuals to be assured of their skills, knowledge, abilities, and competencies. It encourages leaders to consider that influencing others is right and appropriate. It allows individuals to believe that their decisions will make a difference. In addition to being self-confident, it is important for a leader to be able to express that confidence to followers; one example of exhibiting self-confidence is being calm, cool, and collected in a crisis situation (DuBrin, 2010).

Determination

Determination is a trait that we like to call "stick-to-it-ive-ness." Others would describe it as having a task orientation—a desire to get the job done. DuBrin (2010) calls it tenacity. Daft (2011) calls it drive and says that it is related to having high energy. Many leaders have this sense of "stick-to-it-ive-ness"—this desire to finish the job and to do it well. Initiative, persistence, dominance, and drive go along with determination. Leaders with determination are willing to be assertive, to be proactive, and to persevere when the going gets tough. Determined leaders will demonstrate a sense of dominance, especially when followers need explicit direction and when there is little or no time to explain the reason for the direction being given.

Integrity

We like to think of integrity as consistency between what you believe, what you think, what you say, and what you do. Integrity is being trustworthy and honest. It is taking responsibility for one's actions and holding fast to strong principles. Followers trust and have confidence in leaders with integrity because these leaders do what they say they will do (Daft, 2011; Yukl, 2010). In the 1990s and 2000s, many political and business leaders abused the trust of their followers; consequently, trust of followers toward their leaders is absent in many organizations (Daft, 2011). This led to cynicism on the part of followers toward leaders in these arenas because many were disappointed in what was believed to be hypocritical behavior on the part of leaders. As those of you reading this casebook become leaders, you can be sure that your followers will demand that you demonstrate integrity in your beliefs, thoughts, words, and actions.

Sociability

Sociability is an important trait for leaders. Leaders who are sociable are more inclined to pursue enjoyable social relationships. They are empathetic to the concerns and needs of others and want the best for them. They exhibit friendliness, courtesy, tactfulness, diplomacy, and an outgoing personality. Their interpersonal skills are above average, and they develop a higher level of cooperation with, and among, their followers (Northouse, 2013).

These five traits are substantive contributors to effective leadership. However, the other traits listed earlier also contribute to effective leadership. Collins (2004) argues that two traits exemplify those with the highest level of leadership—a sense of humility and a steely resolve to get the job done. Their sense of humility means that they accept and take the blame when things go wrong but give others the credit when things go right. Their steely resolve means that they will find a way to go through, over, under, or around obstacles.

The Five-Factor Personality Model

Since the early 1980s, researchers have come to generally agree on five factors that determine an individual's personality. These factors are known as the Big Five and include neuroticism, extraversion, openness or intellect, agreeableness, and conscientiousness or dependability (Judge, Bono, Ilies, & Gerhardt, 2002; Yukl, 2010). Judge et al. (2002) found empirical support for personality traits being associated with effective leadership. In particular, extraversion, conscientiousness, and openness are positively associated with effective leadership, in that order of importance. Neuroticism is ranked third with openness but is negatively associated with effective leadership—in other words, less is better. Finally, agreeableness was only weakly, albeit positively, associated with effective leadership (Northouse, 2013).

☒ Emotional Intelligence

Emotional intelligence combines our affective domain (emotions) with our cognitive domain (thinking) (Yukl, 2010). It is concerned with our understanding of emotions and applying this understanding to the tasks we engage in throughout our lives. Mayer, Salovey, and Caruso (2000) used four components to define emotional intelligence: being aware of one's ability to perceive and express emotions, having the ability to control our own emotions while behaving with integrity and honesty, being empathetic toward others and sensing organizational concerns, and effectively managing our own emotions and those involved in our relationships with other people (DuBrin, 2010. Another researcher (Goleman, 1995, 1998) suggests that emotional intelligence encompasses social and personal competencies, with social competence consisting of empathy, communication, and conflict management, while personal competence involves motivation, conscientiousness, self-regulation, confidence, and self-awareness (Northouse, 2013).

Emotional intelligence is a relatively new concept in leadership trait research. There is debate on how important it is in people's lives, with some arguing that it is very important in success at home, school, and work and others saying that it is somewhat important. It is reasonable to suggest that emotional intelligence is important to effective leadership as leaders with more sensitivity to their own emotions and the effect of their emotions on other individuals should be more effective (Yukl, 2010). DuBrin (2010) says that emotional intelligence is a supplement to cognitive ability and that leader effectiveness needs more than only emotional intelligence. More research is needed to give us a better understanding of the relationship between emotional intelligence and effective leadership.

☒ How Does the Trait Approach Work?

The trait approach to leadership is not relational. It concentrates on leaders with no focus on followers or situations. The trait approach emphasizes that effective leadership is about having leaders with specific traits. Inherent in the trait approach is the suggestion that organizations will have better performance if they put people with specific leadership traits into particular leadership positions. In other words, selecting the right people will improve organizational performance (Northouse, 2013).

☒ References

Bass, B. M. (1990). *Bass and Stogdill's handbook of leadership: A survey of theory and research.* New York, NY: Free Press.

Collins, J. (2004). Level 5 leadership: The triumph of humility and fierce resolve. In *Collection of articles—Best of HBR on leadership: Stealth leadership* (pp. 15–30). Boston, MA: Harvard Business School Press.

Daft, R. L. (2011). *The leadership experience* (5th ed.). Mason, OH: Thomson, South-Western.

DuBrin, A. (2010). *Leadership: Research findings, practice, and skills* (6th ed.). Mason, OH: South-Western/Cengage.

Goleman, D. (1995). *Emotional intelligence.* New York, NY: Bantam.

Goleman, D. (1998). *Working with emotional intelligence.* New York, NY: Bantam.

Jago, A. G. (1982). Leadership: Perspectives in theory and research. *Management Science, 28*(3), 315–336.

Judge, T. A., Bono, J. E., Ilies, R., & Gerhardt, M. V. (2002). Personality and leadership: A qualitative and quantitative review. *Journal of Applied Psychology, 87,* 765–780.

Kirkpatrick, S. A., & Locke, E. A. (1991). Leadership: Do traits matter? *The Executive, 5,* 48–60.

Lord, R. G., DeVader, C. L., & Alliger, G. M. (1986). A meta-analysis of the relation between personality traits and leadership perceptions: An application of validity generalization procedures. *Journal of Applied Psychology, 71,* 402–420.

Mann, R. D. (1959). A review of the relationship between personality and performance in small groups. *Psychological Bulletin, 56,* 241–270.

Mayer, J. D., Salovey, P., & Caruso, D. R. (2000). Models of emotional intelligence. In R. J. Sternberg (Ed.), *Handbook of intelligence* (pp. 396–420). Cambridge, UK: Cambridge University Press.

Mercer (2009). *Creating value through people: Discussions with talent leaders.* Hoboken, NJ: Wiley.

Northouse, P. G. (2013). *Leadership: Theory and practice* (6th ed.). Thousand Oaks, CA: Sage.

Stogdill, R. M. (1948). Personal factors associated with leadership: A survey of the literature. *Journal of Psychology, 25,* 35–71.

Stogdill, R. M. (1974). *Handbook of leadership: A survey of theory and research.* New York, NY: Free Press.

Yukl, G. (2010). *Leadership in organizations* (7th ed.). Upper Saddle River, NJ: Pearson-Prentice Hall.

Zaccaro, S. J., Kemp, C., & Bader, P. (2004). Leader traits and attributes. In J. Antonakis, A. T. Cianciolo, & R. J. Sternberg (Eds.), *The nature of leadership* (pp. 101–124). Thousand Oaks, CA: Sage.

The Cases

A New Executive Director

A newly promoted assistant deputy minister of business and trade must decide which of two candidates to recommend for her previous role as executive director, business and consumer regulation. One candidate is creative, innovative, client focused, and an inspirational and charismatic leader with a history of ruffling some feathers with other departments within the government. The other candidate seems to lack drive and innovativeness but has earned the respect of his team and others within various government departments with whom he has interacted. This appointment is being made at a time of change within the government as it faces severe budgetary pressures and believes that there are opportunities to do many of its traditional functions in new, more cost-effective ways.

The Ciputra Group: Shaping the City in Asia

The Ciputra Group was set up by Mr. Ciputra in the 1980s, after a long entrepreneurial career with a vision to provide a business for his children. The case describes the development of this group, which evolved into a prominent and innovative player in the Indonesian property sector. One of the issues is that Mr. Ciputra is in his late 70s, and a generational change in leadership is imminent. Students are asked to reflect on the most appropriate path toward further development of the business from one led by a charismatic entrepreneur toward a professional family business.

The Reading

The Character of Leadership

Scratch the surface of a true leader, or look beneath his or her personality, and you'll find character. The traits and values that make up the character of a good business leader are, for the most part, similar to those that make up the character of an outstanding citizen. These authors describe the traits and values that make up the character of leadership.

A New Executive Director

Jeffrey Gandz and Elaine Todres

Amanda Chiu, recently appointed assistant deputy minister (ADM) of Business and Trade in the provincial government, was thinking about which of two candidates for her former role as executive director (Business and Consumer Regulation) she should recommend for promotion.

The promotion to ADM was a big one for Chiu, one that would place her firmly on the next step of her career path and could well lead to a deputy's job within the next five years. But she also knew it was an opportunity that would require continued and, indeed, accelerated performance on her part. There was a lot of competition for top jobs within the provincial civil service at a time when budgets were tight; many departments and agencies were downsizing as government was using more and more technology to provide even higher levels of customer service within financially constrained budgets. Chiu would be expected to play a major role in the drive to rationalize and streamline the delivery of services in the future.

At the same time, the economic turbulence of the 2007–2010 period had created major trade tensions, and businesses were demanding more and more government intervention to create "a level playing field" in both interprovincial and international trade while deregulating business and making it easier for businesses to operate in the province. Well-organized consumer groups were pushing for stronger consumer protection legislation; workers and their trade unions were demanding more intervention by the government in safety and workplace issues; the "economic" departments of the government were trying to overhaul everything from minimum-wage laws to pension regulation; and even the social welfare agencies were trying to force businesses to provide everything from child care to protection for work-life balance.

The Business and Consumer Division had to balance a number of competing pressures: three old business regulation statutes that were clearly not synchronized with current government thinking and needed an overhaul but that were sensitive in nature; the public's deepening concern about safety regulation, given a number of highly publicized safety accidents that were directly linked to regulatory agencies that fell within the purview of the division; and a growing sensitivity at the political level about the need to modernize and streamline business regulation without threatening the public interest. The political appointees on the boards of the regulatory agencies also knew how to "end run" any concerns they had and could go right to the top. The provincial premier had announced that his jurisdiction would be "open for business" and was placing a lot of responsibility on the ministry and the executive director to deliver results.

In her previous role as executive director, mainly when she had meetings with the assistant deputy ministers (ADMs) or deputy ministers (DMs) of other departments, Chiu felt that she was the only spokesperson for the concerns of business. There were others around the table who measured their success by the number of pieces of legislation and regulation they had worked on and were taking to the various legislative committees. She often had to bite her tongue to refrain from reminding them that it was business that paid taxes, created jobs and drove the economy of the province.

It was the job of Chiu's department to advocate for the needs of businesses, large and small, but also to lead legislative and regulatory initiatives that would ensure that businesses were

                    Version: (A) 2010-03-22

appropriately "controlled" in the public interest. Chiu had needed to know when to contact the political arm of government and how to interact effectively with the chairpersons and board members of the regulatory bodies. This frequently brought her and her staff into positions of potential conflict with many stakeholder groups and with other branches of government. Chiu's personal skill in handling these conflicts had earned her high praise and rapid promotion. A natural mediator and skillful conflict manager, she had earned the respect of her peers and the confidence of more senior people in the public service.

Chiu clearly recognized that much of her success had come from having a strong management team working for her. She was not a "micro-manager" but generally gave good, clear directions about what needed to be done, and she was always there to help her people perform to the maximum of their potential. While Chiu's staff liked her, they thought she was too much of a compromiser or appeaser, not taking strong enough positions or pushing her staff's recommendations hard enough with other branches of government. Chiu knew that, behind her back, many of her own people wanted her to take a much stronger "pro-business" stance on issues. "That's the difference between being a lower-level staff member and being a senior civil servant," she said. "At the lower levels you see what needs to be done; at the senior levels you work on the art of the possible."

There were, in Chiu's view, two candidates to fill her former job as executive director, but they were as different as any two people could be.

▨ Joanne Fernandez

Joanne Fernandez, 37, was currently the director of Business Field Services in the ministry. A professional engineer by training, she had subsequently graduated from a top-tier MBA program and had been recruited into the government's "high-potentials" pool 12 years ago, having been rapidly promoted to her present position, never staying longer than two years in any one position and always receiving "excellent" or "outstanding" performance assessments. At a recent all-deputies meeting with the deputy minister of the Human Resources Secretariat—in effect, the chief talent officer for the province—Fernandez had been identified as one of "the top 40 under 40" civil servants, those who would likely make up the senior leadership in the civil service in the next decade.

After graduating from her engineering studies, Fernandez joined one of the large civil engineering contractors in their project management division. She soon became bored with the "backroom work"—and requested and received a transfer to a major defence project that was underway in the Arctic. She loved the work there, so much so that when she was promoted to a head office role, she decided to leave the company and go back to university to take her MBA. The head office role was, she said, "too political."

One of the people that Fernandez met during her time in the engineering firm was an economic development officer with the provincial government. He often talked about the work that he did and, in particular, the enjoyment he got from helping companies with some of the real challenges they had in their relationships with government. Fernandez gave this man a call when she was close to finishing her MBA and, armed with an introduction from him, landed an interview with Amanda Chiu for a job with the provincial government. After several more interviews with department officers, Fernandez was hired as an economic development officer. She realized the irony: "I'd left the engineering firm because it was too political, and here I end up working for the government!"

Over the next eight years, in three different, progressively more senior roles, Fernandez built a reputation as a hard-working, successful advocate for the interests of the businesses and business sectors with whom she worked. She developed very strong—some said too strong—relationships with industrial stakeholder and interest groups, and she was often seen in attendance at their meetings. Part of her success was the way she saw her role, which can be seen in this recent address to a group of new recruits:

> I regard any time spent in head office as a waste of time. Your task is to get out there, get close to the clients we serve, get to know how they think about their businesses, their language, their views about us—the government. When you do that, you'll be able to define their legitimate interests with respect to government and differentiate between those and their other attempts to get something for nothing or just get government to line their pockets without any public interest benefits. Once you've done that, then the real issues that you need to push in government circles will be fewer and more supportable. The more time you spend with your clients, the less time you *need* to spend with bureaucrats because your cases will be better.

Such talk was appealing to new recruits in the department, and when Fernandez talked this way during recruitment sessions in universities and colleges, she made a great impression and attracted talent to the department. The director of human resources often referred to Fernandez as "our talent magnet" and was delighted that she found time for these recruiting sessions.

Clients were equally impressed with Fernandez. One chief executive officer of a company in the hospitality industry said:

> Usually there's no love lost between business—especially small businesses—and government people. But when Joanne says "We're from government and we're here to help you," she means it. Don't misunderstand: she's no pushover. If she thinks we have a poor case she'll say so. And you try to pull the wool over her eyes only once—she's got a built-in radar detector that can spot a

phony case a mile away. She is not your typical, anonymous civil servant. She is entrepreneurial and represents our interests brilliantly.

Fernandez's reputation inside the department was mixed. Many felt that she was a breath of fresh air, the kind of manager that could really make a difference. Others—some of whom Amanda Chiu respected—were less enthusiastic. One of her colleagues had expressed it this way.

> The problem with Joanne is that she's so good that she's usually right. But she knows it and she shows it. It's hard to argue with her, and this creates some resentment. When someone *knows* they are right, they sometimes steamroller over others who have some legitimate points to make. As one of my people said just the other day, "I wish I were as certain about anything as Joanne is about everything." Joanne has "sharp elbows"—even if you know she's right, you don't like the way she proves it.

The last two years had been a difficult one for Fernandez. Her elderly mother, already in the early stages of dementia, had been admitted to hospital after a stroke and had tried to return to her own apartment to lead an independent life. Eventually, Fernandez had persuaded her to go into a nursing home. She had taken quite a lot of time off work during this time and had even considered taking an extended leave of absence to look after her mother personally. However, she had not done so, and it appeared, through all the usual metrics, that her work had not suffered at all.

Except for one project. Two years previously, Chiu had asked Fernandez to undertake a study of using technology to reduce the number of field officers that the department deployed. There were 36 in total, reporting through three district supervisors to Fernandez as the department director. Chiu had suggested to Fernandez that, with the right blend of people and new technology, staff numbers might be trimmed by at least one-third. With a more sophisticated website, greater use of teleconferencing and video conferencing and perhaps even some limited kiosk presence in key centres, Chiu sensed that service could be maintained or even enhanced with fewer people.

The study had not been done. Fernandez had contacted the IT department to get briefed on technology possibilities, but then the pressure of both work and the personal distractions with her family got in the way of moving it forward. At the mid-point of the year, Chiu suggested that Fernandez give the task to one of her district supervisors. Fernandez had resisted doing this since she felt that it would be bad for morale to have one of the field supervisors undertake a study that could lead to the redundancy of some of their own field agents. She had assured Chiu that she would be able to complete the study during the second half of the year. But still it was not done. In the end, Chiu got an external consultant to prepare a study, and he concluded that there would be a very marginal payback to greater use of technology and some significant risks in disrupting excellent client-government relationships by even attempting it. Chiu had suspected that Fernandez would have felt that way all along, which was perhaps why she had not pushed to complete the study herself.

⬛ Roger Earnshaw

"When it comes to personality," Chiu observed, "you couldn't have a greater difference than between Joanne Fernandez and Roger Earnshaw. Nor, for that matter, could you have people with more different backgrounds."

Roger Earnshaw, 42, was the son of a small-town college professor and a homemaker in Central Canada. He had been educated at a local high school where he was active in military cadets. After high school, he attended military college, where he earned a degree in economics and political science. He ranked in the top third

of his class, was commissioned as a second lieutenant and served five years in the army, with one tour in Bosnia and a second in Afghanistan where he was wounded twice, recovered from his injuries, and was eventually honorably discharged with the rank of captain.

Earnshaw spoke little about his military service. In fact, he spoke little about himself at all. His personnel file showed that he was married with two children and had been recruited into the government about three months after his discharge from active service. He had served in four different roles since entering government service. His military experience as a logistics officer had been put to use immediately in a key co-ordination role in the agency responsible for infrastructure build, and there he had set up and run a bidding process for public-private partnerships. Recognized as a high potential and given credit for his prior military service, Earnshaw had been rapidly promoted into a management role in the department of health. In that role, he had been given responsibility for the amalgamation of several regional health boards and had developed a reputation as an excellent mediator, able to handle the sometimes-oversized egos of trustees and hospital presidents, as well as the many special interest groups that got involved in these issues.

Earnshaw's annual performance reviews singled out his thoughtful, disciplined approach to all the tasks he undertook. He took direction extremely well and, when left on his own, he demonstrated reasonable initiative and resourcefulness. He blended in well with any team on which he was placed, pulled his weight on the team and was thought of as a good colleague by those who worked with him. As one of his peers said:

> Roger has the ability to say "No" without anyone taking offence. You can be told, quietly but firmly, that the initiative you've been working on for the last year is not going to make it onto the legislative agenda in the foreseeable future but, somehow, because it's Roger that tells you, you don't get mad.

Earnshaw had applied for his current role, director of legislative co-ordination, in an open competition. Interestingly, he had been the only person short-listed for the job who was not a lawyer. When questioned about the suitability of his background for the role, he pointed out that his experience in logistics, his work as a mediator and his record in working diplomatically with lots of special interests had prepared him well for this new role. "Besides which," he had said, "when you've spent time in the military, you've been exposed to more rules and regulations than you'd find in most governments."

In his new role, Earnshaw was responsible for proposing the legislative and regulatory changes that would be required for the department to achieve its goal of promoting provincial business development and trade. There were, of course, limits to what could be included in any government's legislative agenda, but since business and trade meant jobs, and jobs meant votes, he was able to manoeuvre through all the central agencies and see to it that his items were given high priority.

The lawyers in the department at first resented Earnshaw's lack of formal legal training, but after a few months, those sentiments disappeared.

In a way, it's not bad to have a non-lawyer running this department. He doesn't get caught up in the details of drafting—he leaves that to us. He trusts us to do our jobs. What he's great at is spotting where some proposed legislation affecting one area contradicts or complements an initiative coming from elsewhere. And he forces us to use plain language—not a bad thing for us to be forced to do occasionally!

Earnshaw and Fernandez had frequent interactions, and these were nearly always interesting. Fernandez would usually be pushing for changes in laws or regulations for businesses. Earnshaw would invariably listen carefully, ask a few questions, question some assumptions—always respectfully—and would then thank Fernandez for her initiative and say that he needed to give the matter some thought. He would then consult widely with his colleagues, seek external expert opinion, talk with people in other departments and agencies, speak with the political aides to various government ministers. "In due-time," after not-too-long a delay but never quickly, Fernandez would get his very reasoned assessment about the likelihood and timing of getting her initiatives on the legislative agenda and what his recommendation would be should he be asked for his view—which he usually was.

Fernandez could, of course, appeal to higher authority, i.e., Amanda Chiu or even to the deputy minister. Occasionally one of these officers would overturn Earnshaw's judgment, but not very often—just often enough for Fernandez to keep on trying, however.

Chiu had met several times with both Earnshaw and Fernandez over the last two years to discuss their career aspirations. Fernandez had always been quite clear about her ambitions: she wanted to stay in the department, succeed Chiu and eventually become the deputy minister. Her timetable? Five to seven years to become deputy! And if it was not going to happen, she'd move elsewhere. The discussion had usually ended with Chiu encouraging Fernandez but pointing out that she would need to develop her diplomatic skills to a greater degree if she aspired to the deputy's role. Fernandez's usual counter was that her role called for her to be assertive and that, if the situation called for it, she was as able to be as diplomatic as she needed to be.

Earnshaw had seldom asked about promotion or what it took to get ahead. On one occasion, Chiu even suggested that he lacked ambition. His response, when questioned about his aspirations, had been characteristically cool:

I suppose that I get that from having been in the military. You get used to having to put time in working on lower level jobs, some of which aren't all that exciting. I guess you get used to just doing a good job and hoping and expecting that someone will notice and give you an opportunity to take on bigger challenges and responsibilities. I think the same thing happens in business or government—not much point in putting myself forward if the job performance is not there. . . .I just let the performance speak for itself.

While the people that Earnshaw managed always spoke well of him and believed they had benefited from his teaching and coaching, he didn't seem to have the same magnetism as Fernandez. When she went on campus recruiting trips and made presentations, there were crowds of students who came up to her asking questions and trying to impress her; when Earnshaw did recruiting trips, the responses were less enthusiastic—people listened politely but did not seem as eager to engage him in discussion.

People who worked for Earnshaw found him to be a good boss—considerate, caring, willing to spend time with them. Sometimes Chiu wondered whether they had it a little too good—she remembered always feeling stretched and on the edge of having too much to do in too short a time when she had been a supervisor or manager. Maybe Earnshaw's superior organizing skills meant that

his people had an easier time of it. Or maybe he just did not stretch his people far enough.

Amanda Chiu summarized:

The executive director's job is a big step up from being a director of a branch. Apart from a Regulatory Liaison Group, a Policy Unit and Legislative Co-ordination Unit, there is a substantial Research department, an Issues Response Unit with direct access to the minister's office to deal with crises and other serious matters emanating from the ministry or the numerous regulatory agencies, and a Financial Analysis group. All together, there are about 200 people. Not huge as departments go, but a very high proportion of specialized professionals.

The choice that Chiu had to make: Fernandez or Earnshaw? There were no other internal candidates, and the deputy had the authority to make the appointment without going to external candidates from outside the department. Chiu wondered which candidate to recommend. Her recommendation would be just that—a recommendation. But she was sure that it would carry weight with the promotion panel.

The Ciputra Group: Shaping the City in Asia

Marleen Dieleman

"If you have the will, and the spirit, and you have confidence, you follow up with forecast, all will happen." Mr. Ciputra

Mr. Ciputra, founder of the Ciputra Group, looked back on his long career as one of Indonesia's most prominent entrepreneurs. As a developer in the real estate sector, he had provided modern and comfortable spaces for

millions of Indonesians to live, recreate, shop and work. Ciputra's courage, vision and expertise led to extraordinary successes in the 1990s. But the Ciputra Group also went through a particularly difficult period during the Asian Crisis of 1998, a crisis that exposed the vulnerabilities of the Ciputra Group's business model. Ciputra had felt relieved when the last debt

Version: (A) 2009-11-18

restructuring agreement was signed in 2005. Yet, right at the moment when the Ciputra Group was gearing up for a new era of growth, a global economic crisis struck in late 2008. Ciputra, who was now 77 years old and planning to retire, was again forced to reassess the Ciputra Group's strategy. He thought about the appropriate balance between his many ideas for innovative real estate projects and the level of risk the company could manage. The ongoing transfer of leadership toward his children and children-in-law also required his attention. How could the business continue the tradition of entrepreneurship while also building a professionally managed family business group? The Ciputra family needed to work out a comprehensive strategy to prepare the family business for the next decades.

Awakening the Spirit of Entrepreneurship

Ciputra, who, like many Indonesians, went by one name, was born into an ethnic Chinese merchant family in 1931 in Sulawesi, an island in the Indonesian archipelago. During the Pacific War, his father was interned by the Japanese on false charges of spying for the Dutch, and he passed away in prison in 1943, when Ciputra was only 12 years old. Ciputra, now a fatherless child, was raised in poverty, but he was able to continue his schooling after the war. After completing high school, he subsequently went to the famous Institute of Technology Bandung (ITB) in Java, where he studied architecture. His career would be one that showed, as he himself explained, his "spirit of entrepreneurship."

Because the allowance he received from his mother during his university days was not sufficient, he started his first venture as a student in 1957. He established an architecture consulting agency with two friends, Budi Brasali (who passed away in 2006) and Ismail Sofyan. After graduating in 1960, Ciputra decided that, rather than working as a consultant for others, he wanted

to implement his own ideas as a developer. He subsequently managed to convince the then governor of Jakarta, Soemarno, of his talents. His proactive attitude and vision must have played a role in his early success as a young man. The timing was also conducive as Indonesia, formerly a colony of the Netherlands, had become an independent nation, and Sukarno, its first president, had sent most foreign experts away. As a consequence, there were few architects capable of supporting the rapid development of Jakarta. Ciputra was bold and full of ideas and was an ideal candidate to become a major force in shaping Indonesia's capital city.

Ciputra subsequently became the chief executive officer of Pembangunan Jaya, a developer partly owned by the Jakarta provincial government, where he stayed for 35 years and worked closely with several of Jakarta's former governors. In this capacity, he shaped Jakarta, including building or renovating several prominent markets, a recreation park and various housing projects. In exchange for his services, Ciputra received a minority shareholding in the company. Behind his property projects were original and visionary ideas for the future social conditions of Indonesia, for example on how to integrate housing projects with their natural surroundings. Never afraid of problems, Ciputra did not shy away from large-scale projects, despite his young age and the relative lack of experience of Pembangunan Jaya.

Aside from this job, he and his friends also established the Metropolitan Group after graduation, where Ciputra became the president commissioner, a non-executive role in which he actively provided guidance and facilitated the development of this expanding group. Other investors, such as the Salim Group, were also involved in a subsidiary of the Metropolitan Group, which developed the first privately built satellite city of Jakarta. The group also had investments abroad. In 2009, his long-term partner, Ismail Sofyan, was still playing an active role within the Metropolitan Group.

In the 1980s, the three friends, who had hitherto shared their projects, decided that they could now start their own groups once their children grew up. So, when Ciputra's children graduated and returned from their university studies overseas, Ciputra started his own family group, the Ciputra Group, in which his children, children-in-law, wife and brother were active. The new Ciputra Group was created for his children, whom he hoped would grow as professionals and continue his entrepreneurial spirit in the property sector.

In contrast to his fellow entrepreneurs at the time, who diversified into a range of different industries, Ciputra thus became the co-founder of three business groups: the government-linked Pembangunan Jaya Group, the Metropolitan Group, and the Ciputra Group, all of which were active as developers in the real estate sector. Ciputra himself explained that the focus on being a developer was a conscious choice: "There are two options, and both are good. The first is that I have knowhow as an architect, how I can use this knowhow ... to create wealth. The second option is: which is the best business: a, b, c, so I enter this business. Whether or not I have background in that business, I can hire people to do it. The second one is more successful than the first one. You can become successful and very rich, but sometimes you don't love the job. The first one may not be as big as the second one, but you love the job. This is a choice. I chose the first one." Due to this, he earned the nickname "Mr. Developer" in Indonesia.

⊠ The Ciputra Way: Think Big, Look Ahead

Ciputra was considered the pioneer of the Indonesian property sector and was often credited and awarded for his visionary ideas. One of his achievements was to think big. He could see opportunities where others could not. In the late

1960s, while heading Pembangunan Jaya, he transformed a swampland, infested with mosquitoes and monkeys, into the now popular Jakarta seaside, re-positioning Jakarta as a beach city. According to Ciputra: "Every problem is an opportunity. The more difficult the problem, the more opportunity: that is entrepreneurship." Some of his colleagues at Pembangunan Jaya at the time were reluctant to take up the project because of its many problems, but Ciputra simply put the director who voiced objections in charge of the project, because, according to him, the director already understands the problems, and now his task was to overcome them.[1]

When his colleagues were thinking mere buildings, he was thinking new towns. The development of entire satellite cities, or new towns, was a business model that became one of the trademarks of Ciputra, although it was gradually copied by other players in the market. His first project, while still with Pembangunan Jaya, was a project called Bintaro Jaya. Since the 1960s, Jakarta, like many other Asian cities, witnessed a large influx of people from the rural areas (see Exhibit 1). In the decades to come, Indonesia would witness impressive economic growth as well as urbanization, all of which put a strain on the existing infrastructure in Indonesia's capital. According to some estimates, on average 167,000 people were added to Jakarta's population each year between 1961 and 1971,[2] and Jakarta's population growth continued. The Jakarta administration was struggling to find the funds to put in place infrastructure such as roads, sewerage, water and public markets. Given the government's budgetary constraints, several of Jakarta's governors and housing ministers were eager to work with private or semi-private parties in the planning and development of the capital city.

Just like other Asian cities, there were two ways to grow the city: either to increase the density

---

[1]B. Winarno, *Tantangan jadi peluang: Kegagalan dan sukses Pembangunan Jaya selama 25 tahun*, Pustaka Grafiti Press, Jakarta, 1987.

[2]C. Silver, *Planning the megacity: Jakarta in the twentieth century*, Routledge, New York, 2008, p. 92.

in the existing area or to expand the boundaries of the city into the rural areas. The phenomenon of the satellite city was part of the second strategy, namely expanding the city at the fringes. The advantages were numerous. Land in the rural areas was often cheap, and a larger land area could be acquired which offered possibilities for development projects on a larger scale, with more freedom for the architect to design modern living spaces.

In the absence of government services and facilities, developers often built schools, roads and other social and physical infrastructure themselves, paid for through the higher prices of the housing and office real estate. While such infrastructure was often officially the task of the government, the latter frequently lacked the skills or budget to actually construct and maintain it. Especially after 1985, a period of deregulation in Indonesia, the government warmed up to the idea of using the private sector to develop housing and public infrastructure. It was in this vacuum that Ciputra saw commercial opportunities.

With a keen eye for promising new business models, Ciputra moved into these large-scale property projects, and provided middle- and upper-class citizens with living conditions that the government could not provide. Economic development, especially in the era in which the country was led by President Suharto, from 1966–1998, also created a growing middle class, which was willing and able to pay for spacious living in surroundings with privately built facilities. Exhibit 1 gives an overview of some key economic and population indicators in Indonesia.

The inconveniences of living in Jakarta were many. Most inhabitants suffered from polluted air, traffic jams, lack of security, lack of parking space, poor public transport, pavements taken over by vendors and parked cars, regular flooding and poor basic services, such as garbage collection and sewerage. The Ciputra Group targeted the upper middle class for its large-scale property projects, and offered services and facilities beyond what other areas offered, including

healthcare, security, maintained roads and greenery. Middle-class Indonesians were willing to pay for much more pleasant and convenient living conditions. Ciputra's love for the arts also seeped into the projects, as many of his new town developments were marked with sculptures and other art objects, adding to the experience of living in a modern and vibrant city.

As such, the satellite city provided a business model where economies of scale could be employed, and real value could be added to the experience of living in a city. Given that the government was only partially able to provide such basic things as security, clean air and well-maintained roads, developers like Ciputra turned problems into opportunities and provided their own solutions. These projects were naturally also more complex, since they involved the technical skills to design and run larger areas, as well as to manage traffic flows, do flood prevention and master other aspects of urban planning. The projects tended to be carried out in phases and could altogether amount to hundreds of hectares and more than a decade of development, requiring a substantial amount of capital.

Growing the Business in the 1990s

The Ciputra Group developed rapidly into a developer with a broad portfolio of residential and commercial projects. Its activities were a mix of different projects. The group had housing projects in the city centre of Jakarta; it built hotels, and serviced apartments, offices and malls, often in an integrated manner. It also developed large plots of land into new towns at the boundaries of the city. Eventually, the Ciputra Group became known for its large property projects, such as the satellite city CitraLand in Surabaya.

The 1990s were a period of rapid growth in Indonesia as well as Southeast Asia. In 1994, Ciputra floated one of his companies, Ciputra

Development, on the Jakarta Stock Exchange, and it witnessed a very rapid growth, in line with the growth of the Indonesian economy at the time, and a boom in the property sector. Its turnover jumped from around US$50 million in 1992 and 1993 to just under $250 million in 1997, with the number of projects and their scale rapidly increasing. Exhibit 2 gives key indicators for the group's main listed company, Ciputra Development, while Exhibit 3 gives an overview of the company's milestones. Aside from listed companies, the Ciputra Group also owned various other companies.

By 2009, the group was into hotels, offices, malls and entertainment projects, which were spread out over different places in Java, including the larger cities such as Jakarta, Surabaya and Semarang. In Surabaya, the second largest city in the country, the group operated one of its largest projects, CitraLand, a satellite city with more than 1,000 hectares under development. CitraLand was launched in 1993 and was dubbed the "Singapore of Surabaya" with its motto of a green, clean and modern city. The facilities within the area included a golf course, a university (The Ciputra University of Entrepreneurship), various schools, and a water park, in addition to the usual infrastructure and greenery. It also contracted a large group of security guards to supplement the government police. Some of its services were offered against fees from residents. The tap water, which was sold at government-mandated prices to residents, was a money-making venture which the group used to subsidize other services, including maintenance of greenery and security. While the area catered to different customer segments, it was mostly targeted at middle- and upper-income customers.

Increasingly, the group started to use the word "Ciputra" in its projects as part of a strategy to develop the brand. The group believed that it had something unique to offer in the market, which other real estate developers did not. In the words of an executive: "We don't just rely on consultants and architects. We believe that regardless of whom you use as consultant,

the concept should come from us. Because the architect does not understand the commercial aspects of the project, and the consultant does not understand the design. We have the whole picture. We own the concepts." Whereas in the past, the group often used the name Citra ("image" in the Indonesian language), which was confusing because other groups also used that name, now many of the projects were termed "Hotel Ciputra," "Mall Ciputra," and so on.

Ciputra wanted to develop his land bank in the centre of Jakarta's business district into a shopping street lined with shopping malls, modeled after Singapore's Orchard Road. This was an even more ambitious project in terms of its planned budget, which exceeded $3 billion, and was to be developed with various partners over a period of 20 years under the name "Ciputra World Jakarta." In addition to the usual mix of property, Ciputra, who was an avid arts lover and collector, planned to construct the largest fine arts museum in Jakarta as part of the project.

In addition to this, Ciputra started to look abroad and envisioned his group as a multinational company. He had acquired permission from the authorities in Hanoi, Vietnam, to build a large satellite city there encompassing 300 hectares of land between the city centre and the airport. When asked what made the Vietnamese government select him for the project, Ciputra insisted that his concepts were the main reason. "I recommended an international city for Vietnam. At the time the Vietnamese built only less than 10 hectare, but I built more than 100 hectares, and I stretched to the international community. We already have the international school, and the American embassy will be in our project. We have a hospital, houses, condominium, golf course, something like that. It is a joint venture with the local government."

These large projects required advanced technical skills and project management. Ciputra hired professionals and modernized his company, which was often admired for its concepts and its skill in taking on complex projects involving multiple stakeholders. Despite his advanced age, Ciputra was still active in the company as a mentor and was now considered its "creative navigator."

⬚ The Asian Crisis: Exposing the Vulnerabilities

The Asian Crisis started in 1997 in Thailand and quickly spread to other Asian countries, including Indonesia. In addition, the Asian Crisis also caused the demise of the Suharto regime after 32 years in power. As is common in economic cycles, the property sector was among the first and worst hit.

In Indonesia, the Asian Crisis caused a severe depreciation of the local currency, the rupiah, exactly at a time when many companies were borrowing to fund a very rapid pace of expansion. Since, at the time, loans denominated in U.S. dollars were cheaper than in rupiah, most Indonesian companies took out foreign currency loans, and therefore were vulnerable to a depreciation of the currency. This also happened to the Ciputra Group, which had hedged very little of its foreign currency loans, and was faced with ballooning debts, declining income and declining demand for real estate. The group started to post losses each year between 1997 and 2001 (see Exhibit 2).

In May 1998, the economic crisis turned into a political crisis when Suharto was forced to step down amidst severe riots, targeted mostly at the Chinese minority, to which the Ciputra family belonged. Looting, violence and gang rape occurred in Jakarta, and several of the satellite cities with their middle- and upper-class populations, amongst which there were many Indonesians of Chinese origin, were attacked and set to fire.

These circumstances plunged the Ciputra Group into a very dark period. Unable to service its debts, the group was faced with oblivion. Most projects had to be put on hold. Fortunately, the Ciputra projects were not severely damaged

by the May 1998 riots, but the outlook for the group was very dark. Ciputra's son-in-law Harun Hajadi commented later: "I really felt sorry for Ciputra, we thought it was the end of the company. It was all collapsing. He had nothing left to be proud of." However, the Ciputra family was able to solve its many problems and re-negotiate its debts. Harun took the lead in this. He recalled having to go to a difficult meeting of angry debt holders who threw things at him when he told them the Ciputra Group was unable to pay. Despite this, he was able to cope, cut costs, and negotiate with contractors, buyers and debt holders. The Ciputra Group moved to a small office that was originally a marketing office for one of the real estate projects, as it could not afford the rent anymore. The group worked on the principle that people who had pre-paid their houses and apartments should get it delivered, although those who had not fully pre-paid were sometimes paid in kind, such as pieces of land. Most of the contractors were also paid, although some prices were re-negotiated.

Some of the bondholders received equity in the company, and to give them an option to exit their investments, another Ciputra company, Ciputra Surya, was listed on the stock exchange in late December 1998 after negotiations with the stock exchange authorities. Harun recalled: "There is a rule that you can become a public company if you have more than 300 shareholders or something. Usually you list a company through an IPO. Finally we became the first company listed on the Jakarta Stock Exchange without an IPO. We issued the shares for Rupiah 500 par value, on the first day of the listing, the bondholders dumped the shares, and they dropped to Rupiah 100."

The most difficult issue was to deal with the foreign currency loans. In 2005, much later than most other Indonesian companies, the Ciputra Group finally wrapped up the last unresolved debt issues, and the family could sigh with relief. Ciputra, in the meantime, had found consolation in religion, and attributed the narrow escape of the company to God. Finally, after almost eight years of struggle, the Ciputra Group was ready to regain its position as a prominent player in the property market.

New Post-Crisis Strategies

Indonesia was the country in Southeast Asia that was most seriously hit by the Asian Crisis, and took longest to recover. The political regime change that coincided with the economic crisis also changed many of Indonesia's political realities. Almost overnight, the country turned into a large democracy, and the centralized bureaucracy built up by Suharto to maintain his grip on the country was decentralized, giving more autonomy to the provinces, which often differed widely from each other in terms of cultures, languages and provincial economies. Some of the provinces received a fairly large degree of autonomy.

The Asian Crisis had severely weakened the Ciputra Group and had exposed some of the vulnerabilities of its business model. It was active in a very volatile sector—property—which was the first to be hit in the event of an economic crisis. Political stability, an issue in Indonesia, also affected its business as it lowered prices for housing and office space, and reduced hotel occupancy. Compared to surrounding countries, Indonesian real estate prices were still low.

In addition, its focus on ever larger projects had initially seemed beneficial, since the economies of scale such projects offered could help cover more facilities such as healthcare and schools alongside the property projects, which would be paid for by affluent inhabitants eager to live in areas with greater service levels. But the downside of this strategy was that large amounts of capital were tied up in these projects, which typically lasted for a decade.

Also, given their long-term nature and interaction with various authorities, the projects were vulnerable to changes in governments and governments' policies. For example, the governments' inability to maintain or build sufficient roads could cause traffic jams or flooding on the roads to and from the satellite city, making the travel time for inhabitants to and from their offices prohibitively high. Lastly, the group's competitors were also aggressively building satellite cities around Jakarta, thus creating more supply, while the size of the affluent middle class, and thus the demand, was limited.

Many other Indonesian companies were widely diversified, but the Ciputra Group focused on property. As a consequence, other groups could restart the engines earlier after the crisis, because they had cash-generating businesses that were in less volatile economic sectors, for example in food or in mining. The Ciputra Group, because of its dependency on property, did not have the ability to use funds from elsewhere in the group to overcome the downturns.

Therefore, Ciputra had to act. "After the crisis I changed the strategy. I don't build big cities any more. I created a good brand, the Ciputra brand. Although we continue in Java [Indonesia's most populous island], we also explore outside Java. There is potential in the provinces for projects of 25 hectares or more. When we sell the property, we split the income with the landowner. We don't do borrowing. In Jakarta and Java, it is already full, land is difficult to get, so we moved to the other provinces. The provinces achieved a much larger degree of autonomy. The money is now outside Java. We need to expand." Exhibit 4 shows the geographical segment information for Ciputra Development. Indonesian economists estimate that around 70 per cent of all the money that circulates in Indonesia is located in Jakarta, which demonstrates the importance of the capital city in comparison with the many provincial capitals (see also Exhibit 1). Ciputra's son-in-law, Harun, remarked regarding the smaller projects in the provinces that "with our brand name we can capture the entire market. After you launch your real estate, the market is gone. It takes about three years for the market to come back."

The new model was to reduce borrowing by working with landowners and equity partners.

The landowners would share the revenue of the project without contributing anything more than the land they already owned. Harun explained, "We work with the land owner, we contribute our expertise in development. We spend the development costs, the landowner sits nicely, and we share the revenue. We don't share the profits, so if I want to spend on something, say advertisement, it is not a problem because we share the revenue. Usually the landowner does not have ideas. I always tell him, this model is like an autopilot for us already. I spend, but we split the revenue. It works well."

The equity partners also benefited from Ciputra's reluctance to borrow. One of the partners said: "Ciputra needs us. They are too conservative. They are too scared to borrow. I understand it too. Their assets are tied to property, but we have different businesses. Property is always initiating a crisis. Ciputra needs us to grow. If he stays where he is, he cannot grow." With Ciputra supplying the excellence in building, and the partner supplying the money by taking calculated risks where the Ciputra Group was reluctant to take them, the equity partnerships worked for both parties.

An expert in property considered the Ciputra Group a land-based property player, in contrast with what he termed the sky-based players, who sought to accelerate growth and reduce risks through innovative financial structures—something that the Ciputra Group did not get involved in. He commented that the sky-based players often grew faster than the land-based players. Thus, from the perspective of an *avant garde* property player, the Ciputra Group now seemed to opt for a slower and more conservative approach.

Internally, the company sought to stimulate an entrepreneurial spirit. All employees — from directors to administrative staff—were encouraged to develop their sales qualities, and one executive spoke highly of Ciputra's secretary, who had already sold several apartments. The group held competitions between different project teams, and the winning project teams would go abroad on trips together. Ciputra explained that all project staff would be rewarded: "Yes, until servants and security people go there. All go there. One group went to Paris—the Citra Garden team—they chose where they wanted to go. We gave them an extra bonus of 3 to 8 months." Ciputra liked to involve staff at all levels in projects, and he regularly interacted with younger staff members and stimulated them to express their views. All employees looked up to Ciputra, and several insiders remarked that "he is so outstanding."

The Ciputra Group also started to devote more of its attention to projects abroad. According to Ciputra's son-in-law Budiarsa Sastrawinata: "Our way of diversifying is to go abroad. This will help when the storm comes. We do not put all our eggs in the same basket. Also, the large scale means that it is interdisciplinary, e.g., residential, office, etc. so the one will support the other. These will not all go down at the same time. This is how we try to be crisis-resistant."

Many developing countries in Asia did not yet possess the capability to develop real estate on a large scale as the Ciputra Group did, and the leaders thought that this was something they could leverage in other countries that had similarly large populations, upcoming middle classes and growing economies. This added to the group's reputation. A person familiar with the group commented, "Ciputra is a hero in Vietnam. He is a man with vision, he actually built entire cities. While other companies focused on commercial and real estate, Ciputra goes much further. He opened new paths in this business. He has maintained his good reputation in city development, despite the crisis."

In Vietnam, the Ciputra Group could leverage the skills built up in designing satellite cities in Indonesia. A partner of the group commented that "to build a satellite city you need a design team, the internal resources and the technical capabilities. It must be our core business. You need to put in sewerage, urban planning, etc. Ciputra did very well in Indonesia. When they went to Vietnam, he already knew how to do it. They already had a master plan."

⊠ New Generations

Ciputra had four children: the eldest two were daughters, and the youngest two male twins. Because he considered them all talented, the eldest two daughters with their spouses (respectively, Rina Ciputra Sastrawinata and Budiarsa Sastrawinata; and Junita Ciputra and Harun Hajadi) each led one division of the Ciputra Group, while the twins (Cakra and Candra Ciputra) led another. Budiarsa focused on the international projects, including the new town in Vietnam, and had built contacts with officials in that country. Harun, amongst others, ran several large projects in Surabaya, another large city in Indonesia. The twins were mainly active in commercial buildings like offices in Jakarta. Although the official structure of the group and its listed companies did not reflect this, informally the projects were divided amongst the children, who were engaged in subtle competition.

There were differences in style between the children. An executive of the Ciputra Group commented that "Candra is only involved in the strategy, not in the daily operations. Harun is involved in everything, he is more in the details. He also has an architect background, so he is also involved in the design. Budiarsa is in the middle. Candra is more interested in the financial aspects, such as the stock market." The division led by Rina and Budiarsa had become reluctant to borrow after the crisis and tried to avoid this at all costs, instead choosing to work with partners who provided financing and land. Harun, however, thought that this might be too conservative, and took a slightly different approach. As such, within one company, there was a diversity of managerial styles and project preferences. One of the insiders remarked: "Are

the sub-holdings going to go on their own or is it one person that will succeed Ciputra? Sometimes I try to talk about it with the family members. But they say, if Ciputra has not decided, why should we talk about it."

As the children all had the same level of ownership, and there was no legal separation between the different divisions, they equally benefited, irrespective of how much profits their projects contributed. It was Ciputra's vision that his children and children-in-law would work together harmoniously to continue to be a "legend in property." For Ciputra, this was one of the most important goals, since he had started the Ciputra Group primarily as a vehicle for his family. In terms of ownership, the Ciputra family had a holding company, the ownership of which was structured as follows: 15 per cent of the shares for each child, 15 per cent for Ciputra's wife, Dian Sumeler, and 25 per cent for Ciputra. The holding company then held controlling stakes in the listed companies that belonged to the group, while the public held the rest of the shares. Exhibit 5 shows the structure of the different listed companies and their holding structure.

The boards of the listed companies (Ciputra Development, Ciputra Surya, Ciputra Property) were mostly composed of family members, with the minimum seats for independent directors as was required by Indonesian law. In line with Indonesian law, companies had a two-tier board structure with a board of directors that was overseen by a separate board of commissioners. Day-to-day management was in the hands of a team of family members, complemented by professional executives. Exhibit 6 provides a description of the directors and commissioners of Ciputra Development.

Other large competitors hired more professionals on the board of their real estate companies. As such, the Ciputra Group could be seen as an old-fashioned family firm where all top positions were held by family members and where it was difficult to attract sufficient managerial talent. A person close to the group commented: "If you compare LIPPO Group with Ciputra, they are both good. Perhaps Ciputra has the better vision. But for the technical competences he relies too much on his children and sons-in-law. LIPPO has hired the best outsiders, and they have better people. That is why I think that, in the future, the Riady family [who controls LIPPO] will overshadow Ciputra in real estate."

The shortage of talent was all the more constraining as the Ciputra Group moved into projects outside Jakarta. In order to maintain the unique "Ciputra" brand, it was necessary to work not only with local staff in the provinces and abroad, but to develop people who would be familiar with the "Ciputra spirit" and quality levels. However, all the provincial cities had different cultures, and it was sometimes hard to find the right project managers who could work on location.

The Future of the Ciputra Group: Planning for the Family and the Business

Since emerging from its ashes after the Asian Crisis, the Ciputra Group had started to expand again, and it had changed its direction. The company expanded into others cities in Indonesia, mainly capital cities of provinces with big enough populations. As most capital cities outside Java were smaller than capital cities in Java, it was more difficult for the company to develop new large satellite city projects because the markets were small. Furthermore, the group accelerated its internationalization and worked on various large satellite city projects abroad, including in Vietnam, Cambodia and China. Because of the bitter experiences during the crisis, the group tried to avoid large borrowing, instead stepping up its local

and international partnerships, raising capital through the capital market, creating limited partnership funds and leveraging its unique brand.

While the group had slowly restarted from 2001 onward, by the end of the year 2008 it became clear that a global downturn was set to affect property sectors worldwide. Whereas before 2008, the Ciputra Group mapped out a range of strategies, it was not so clear anymore whether all these could be pursued simultaneously in times of crisis. Should the group focus on its large-scale projects abroad and, if yes, how should it divide its attention? On a larger number of smaller regional projects? On town development or on integrated projects within city boundaries? Would the group be overshadowed by its competitors if it maintained its conservative strategy?

It was also clear that each of the informal "divisions" of the company, run by different people, was taking a slightly different direction. What would happen if the company were to miss the inspiration and vision of the founding entrepreneur? Without a new strategy, the family harmony might be lost and diverge into three different approaches to running the business. Anticipating that Ciputra would step back, how was the company going to retain its entrepreneurial flavor, while also moving on towards a more professional structure? How was the group to deal with the dilemma of the requirements of the business and those of the family? Harun Hajadi said that Ciputra "is now thinking about how to leave his legacy, how to ensure that the brand name and image will be extended into the future."

Now was a good time to plan the strategy for the firm and for the family and to strengthen the business for the coming decades. Whereas the group had been designed along the way by the founder, as it grew larger, a more systematic view of the progress of both the business and the family in different stages could support its future development.

| Exhibit 1 | Key Economic and Population Indicators for Indonesia |

Indicator	1970	1980	1990	2000
GNI per capita Purchasing Power Parity (current international $)	n.a.	620	1,440	2,260
Population (million)	120	151	182	211
Urbanization (% of population)	17	22	31	42
Population of Jakarta (million)	3.9	5.9	8.2	8.4
Population of other major cities (million)				
Surabaya	1.5	2	2.5	2.6
Bandung	1.2	1.5	2.0	2.1
Semarang	0.6	1.0	1.2	1.4
Medan	0.6	1.3	1.7	1.9
Palembang	0.6	0.8	1.1	1.4
Malang	0.4	0.5	0.7	0.8

SOURCES: World Bank, World Development Indicators; United Nations, World Urbanization Prospects, 2007 revision.

| Exhibit 2 | Key Financial Indicators for Ciputra Development |

Indicator	1995	1996	1997	1998	1999	2000	2001	2002	2003	2004	2005	2006	2007
Turnover (US$ million)	229	243	121	13	32	32	33	46	68	84	110	127	147
Profits (US$ million)	41	56	−17	−59	−25	−89	−59	84	14	−25	8	61	18
Total Assets (US$ million)	930	1,225	1,203	457	564	573	505	492	546	562	554	552	815
Total Liabilities (US$ million)	626	702	863	409	526	621	608	485	539	587	564	247	403
Gross Profit Margin (%)	52	51	52	46	39	50	58	51	48	49	46	47	44
Return on Assets (%)	4.5	4.6	−1.4	−12.9	−4.3	−15.5	−11.7	17.1	2.6	−4.4	1.5	11.1	2.2
Total Debt to Equity (%)	2.1	1.4	2.5	8.5	14.0	−12.9	−5.9	64.8	83.1	−23.1	−56.0	0.8	1.0

SOURCE: Annual Reports of Ciputra Development.

Exhibit 3	Ciputra Development Milestones

1981	Established under the name of PT Citra Habitat Indonesia
1984	Launched the first residential project, namely CitraGarden (now CitraGarden City), which is located in Cengkareng, West Jakarta.
1993	The first and largest project developed in greater Surabaya, CitraLand City (now CitraRaya), was launched in April. The first commercial project, CitraLand Mall and Hotel (now Ciputra Mall and Hotel) located in Grogol, West Jakarta is opened for public. In the following year, the Company developed a similar project in Semarang.
1994	CitraGrand City (now CitraRaya) Tangerang, which has the largest development area (more than 2,700 hectares), was officially launched. Initial Public Offering (IPO) of 50,000,000 shares and listed on Jakarta Stock Exchange (JSX).
1996	Rights Issue I of 250,000,000 shares. Listed on Surabaya Stock Exchange.
1997–1998	Economic crisis in Indonesia. The Company started to restructure its debts.
1999	PT Ciputra Surya Tbk, a subsidiary, listed in JSX.
2005	The launching of CitraGarden Lampung and CitraGarden Banjarmasin, which marked the beginning of business expansion to outer Java.
2006	The issuance of 2,307,276,912 shares without Pre-emptive Rights regarding debts settlement. Rights Issue II of 2,449,860,570 shares.
2007	IPO of PT Ciputra Property Tbk, a subsidiary. Ciputra World Surabaya, a super block development which consists of shopping center, apartment, office and hotel in Surabaya, was officially launched.

SOURCE: Annual Report of Ciputra Development, 2007.

Exhibit 4	Ciputra Development Geographical Segment Information (% of Revenues)

	2007	2006	2005
Greater Jakarta	38	37	40
Greater Surabaya	49	54	52
Other*	13	9	9

SOURCES: Annual Reports of Ciputra Development, 2005 and 2007.

*Foreign investments are not included in these figures.

Exhibit 5   Ownership Structure of Ciputra's Listed Companies

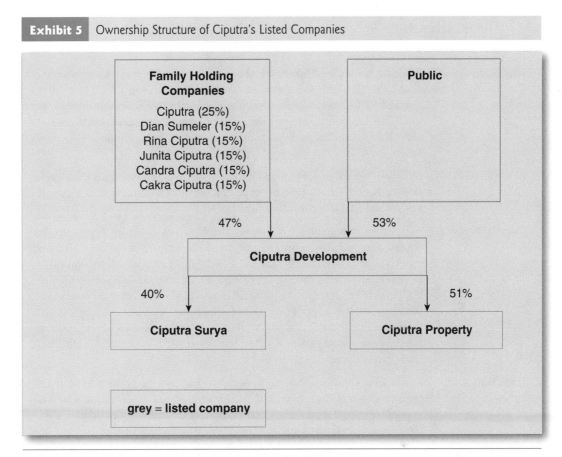

SOURCE: Annual Report of Ciputra Development, 2007, company interviews.

Exhibit 6   Board of Directors and Board of Commissioners of Ciputra Development

Board of Commissioners

Ir. Ciputra   President Commissioner. Ir. Ciputra is the founder and chairman of Ciputra
                   Group. He also founded PT Pembangunan Jaya in 1961 and PT Metropolitan
                   Development in 1971 and currently serves as a Commissioner of the both com-
                   panies. He is actively involved in many social and organization activities, such
                   as Indonesia Architectural Engineers Association, Indonesian Real Estate Asso-
                   ciation, Jaya Raya Foundation, Association of Foundations for the Nation, Ir.
                   Ciputra Educational Foundation and Tarumanagara Foundation. He is often
                   granted awards from both domestic and overseas institutions, the latest was
                   Entrepreneur of the Year 2007, organized by Ernst & Young. Ir. Ciputra earned
                   his bachelor degree in engineering from Bandung Institute of Technology.

(Continued)

Exhibit 6 (Continued)

Dian Sumeler	Wife of Mr. Ciputra. Dian Sumeler has held the position as a Commissioner since 1997. Currently she also serves as a Commissioner of PT Ciputra Surya Tbk and PT Ciputra Property Tbk, the subsidiaries. She is actively involved in social and educational activities through Ir. Ciputra Education Foundation and Citra Kasih Foundation. Dian Sumeler graduated from Surabaya Pharmacy School in 1954.
Bayan Akochi	Brother of Mr. Ciputra. Bayan Akochi has served as a Commissioner since 1993. He has also served as a Director of several subsidiaries, namely PT Cakrawala Respati and PT Lahan Adyabumi since 1991.
Cosmas Batubara	Independent Commissioner. Cosmas Batubara has extensive experience in organization and governmental institutions. He formerly served as a Minister in several governmental periods and a member of parliament. In worldwide organization, he used to serve as the President of International Labour Organization in 1991. Currently he is the Chairman of Cosmas Batubara & Associaties. He has been appointed as the Chairman of the Company's Audit Committee since 2007. Cosmas Batubara graduated from Social and Political Science Faculty and earned his Doctoral degree in the same field, both from University of Indonesia, Jakarta.
Henk Wangitan	Independent Commissioner. Henk Wangitan has held the position as an Independent Commissioner since 2001. He formerly served as a Director, who was responsible in land acquisition. Currently he also serves as a Commissioner of PT Citra Gelombangkencana and as a Director of PT Cikupa Buana.
Widigdo Sukarman	Independent Commissioner. Widigdo Sukarman has excellence experience in banking sector. He formerly served as President Director of Bank Papan Sejahtera and Bank Negara Indonesia 1946 and as a Director of Bank Tabungan Negara. Currently he also serves as a member of Indonesian Bank Supervisory Agency and as a lecturer in several universities. He has also been appointed as an Independent Commissioner of PT Ciputra Property Tbk since 2007. Widigdo Sukarman earned his bachelor degree in economy from Gadjah Mada University, Yogyakarta, his MPA degree from Harvard University, USA, his MBA degree from Boston University, USA and his Doctoral degree in economy from Gadjah Mada University.

Board of Directors

Candra Ciputra	President Director, son of Mr. Ciputra. Has held the position as the President Director since 2002. He has experience of more than 20 years in property business. Currently he also serves as the President Director of PT Ciputra Property Tbk and Vice President Commissioner of PT Metrodata Electronics Tbk. He earned his bachelor degree in finance from the University of San Francisco, USA and an MBA in finance from the Golden Gate University, San Francisco, USA.

Budiarsa Sastrawinata	Son-in-law of Mr. Ciputra. Joined the Company in 1990 and has served as a Director till now. Currently he also serves as the President Commissioner of PT Bintaro Serpong Damai and as a Director of PT Damai Indah Golf. He is also a member of parliament (MPR/DPR) for the 2004–2009 periods. He earned his bachelor degree in civil engineering from Plymouth Polytechnic, UK and an MBA from Prasetya Mulya Management Institute, Jakarta.
Harun Hajadi	Son-in-law of Mr. Ciputra. Has joined the Company since 1988 and has served as a Director since 1990. Currently, he also serves as the President Director of PT Ciputra Surya Tbk and as the Vice Chairman of the Infrastructure, Property and Transportation Committee in Indonesian Issuer Association (AEI). He earned his bachelor of architectural engineering from the University of California, Berkeley, USA and an MBA in finance and real estate from University of Southern California, Los Angeles, USA.
Cakra Ciputra	Son of Mr. Ciputra. Joined the Company since 1990 and was appointed as a Director since then. Currently he also serves as the President Director of PT Ciputra Semarang and as a Director and a Commissioner of several companies within Ciputra Group. He earned his bachelor degree in civil engineering from San Francisco State University, San Francisco, USA.
Rina Ciputra Sastrawinata	Daughter of Mr. Ciputra. Has an experience of more than 20 years as a Director and a Commissioner of several companies within Ciputra Group. She served as the Company's President Director from 1983 to 1990. Currently she also serves as the President Director of Century 21, a company engaged in property brokerage. She earned her Bachelor of Commerce from University of Auckland, New Zealand and an MBA from Claremont Graduate School, Los Angeles, USA.
Junita Ciputra	Daughter of Mr. Ciputra. Has joined the Company since 1988. She used to serve as a Commissioner of the Company in 1996. Currently she also serves as a Commissioner and a Director of several companies within Ciputra Group. She earned her bachelor degree in finance from University of San Francisco, USA and an MBA in finance and real estate from University of Southern California, Los Angeles, USA.
Tulus Santoso Brotiswidjojo	Has served as the Company's Director since 2001. Currently he also serves as the Corporate Secretary. He is actively involved in the Indonesian Real Estate (REI), as the Chairman of Jakarta Region for the 2005-2008 periods and has acted as a member of Finance and Trading Committee in the AEI since 2005. He earned his bachelor degree in accounting from Satya Wacana Christian University, Salatiga and a master in accounting from University of Indonesia, Jakarta.
Tanan Herwandi Antonius	Joined the Company in 1987 and was appointed as a Director in 2003. He has also served as the Vice Chairman of the Indonesian Humanity Habitat Foundation since 2004. He earned his bachelor of civil engineering from Parahyangan Catholic University, Bandung, an MBA from Prasetya Mulya Management Institute, Jakarta and a Master of Science from University College, London, UK.

SOURCE: Annual Report of Ciputra Development, 2007.

The Character of Leadership

James C. Sarros, Brian K. Cooper, and Joseph C. Santora

Scratch the surface of a true leader, or look beneath his or her personality, and you'll find character. The traits and values that make up the character of a good business leader are, for the most part, similar to those that make up the character of an outstanding citizen. These authors describe the traits and values that make up the character of leadership.

I have a dream today . . . I have a dream that my four little children will one day live in a nation where they will not be judged by the color of their skin but by the content of their character. I have a dream today.

Martin Luther King Jr.
Speech on steps of Lincoln
Memorial
Civil Rights March
23 August 1963

Character has come in from the cold. Once the poor cousin of clinical psychology and behavioural studies, character is once again recognized as a critically important component of personality, and therefore, of what makes people tick. Its importance to leadership is considerable.

⊠ Character in Leadership

Not surprisingly, the importance of the character of leadership is making inroads in the business world, Johnson & Johnson (J&J), the major manufacturer of health care products in the United States, views character as a leadership

essential. Former Chairman Ralph Larsen believes that people with character can give a company a significant competitive advantage. The company actively seeks to recruit and be represented by people of exceptional character. Johnson & Johnson's stance is supported by research, which suggests that, in leadership, good character counts. According to Frances Hesselbein, the author and chairman of the Drucker Foundation, leadership that achieves results goes beyond *how to be* and becomes *how to do*; this type of leadership is all about character. So in other words, in order to get things done personally and organizationally, one first needs to get in touch with his or her character.

Leaders with character achieve results that transcend everyday organizational imperatives and outcomes. A study of world leaders over the past 150 years asserts that managers who possess strong character will create a better world for everyone, while leadership generally is vital to the social, moral, economic, and political fabrics of society.

For example, Theresa Gattung is the CEO of Telecom NZ, a New Zealand telecommunications company. Her candour about her vulnerabilities, as well as her philosophy on leadership, has won her the admiration of her male colleagues. She recognizes that good leadership consists more of character than personality:

When I went to management school 20 years ago, I thought it was about personality, desire, determination, and a little bit of technique. I didn't actually realise it was about character, and that struck me more as I have gone along . . . The leaders whom people respect and will follow have the characteristics of

Reprint# 9B07TC10

being themselves, of being passionate about what they are doing, communicating that in a heartfelt way that touches hearts.

However, we often take the character of leadership for granted. We expect good leaders to be strong in character, that is, to have a moral imperative underwrite their actions. These leaders with character have been identified as *authentic* leaders: They are what they believe in; show consistency between their values, ethical reasoning and actions; develop positive psychological states such as confidence, optimism, hope, and resilience in themselves and their associates; and are widely known and respected for their integrity.

Nonetheless, the key attributes of authentic leaders, or leaders with character, remain problematic. To identify these attributes and better understand them, we undertook a study. This paper is based on that study, and in it, we identify the three underlying dimensions of leadership character—universalism, transformation, and benevolence.

We also suggest ways of further enhancing these dimensions and their constituent attributes.

Universalism represents an understanding, appreciation, and tolerance for the welfare of people generally and is a macro perspective approach to work and life. The character attributes of respectfulness, fairness, cooperativeness, and compassion in particular fit best with this definition of universalism.

Transformation is consistent with the concept of transformational leadership as an activity that inspires others in the achievement of long-term, visionary goals. The character attributes of courage and passion best represent this factor. Transformation is a situation-specific process that relies on the competence and self-reliance of the incumbent in their delivery of inspired and values-driven strategic direction for the enterprise.

Benevolence is a micro approach to work and focuses on concern for the welfare of others through one's daily interactions. Selflessness, integrity, and organization loyalty best represent the characteristics of benevolence.

1. Universalism

Universalism is the outward expression of leadership character and is made manifest by respectfulness for others, fairness, cooperativeness, compassion, spiritual respect, and humility.

Respectfulness

Juliana Chugg, the former Managing Director of General Mills Australasia, illustrated respect for her workers by dramatically altering the time employees needed to spend at the workplace by closing the doors at 1pm every Friday. Against the board's advice, this decision allowed the company's executives and factory workers to start their weekends earlier. More importantly, this action resulted in no job losses or salary reductions, no drop in productivity, and no increase in working hours on other days during the week. Chugg, who now heads up General Mills' head office in Minneapolis, Minnesota, is the new face of home baking giant Betty Crocker, a $1 billion business in the US alone. As a relatively young mother in charge of a diverse international company, Chugg understands the need to balance her personal and work demands: "The role of a managing director is not to make all the decisions. It is to get the people who have access to the right information together so that, collectively, they are able to make better decisions than they would on their own." Chugg received the Victorian Businesswoman of the Year award in 2000 for her visionary and caring approach to business.

Fairness

Fairness is treating people equitably and in a just manner. Max De Pree, the former CEO of furniture maker Herman Miller, is guided by a deep concern for others. His approach to life manifests itself in his approach to work and the way in which Herman Miller conducts its business affairs. De Pree believes a corporation is a community of people, all of whom are valued. His main contention is that when you look after your people with care and consideration, they in turn look after you.

Former Chrysler CEO Lee Iacocca was known to say that if you talk to people in their own language and you do it well, they'll say, "God, he said exactly what I was thinking." And when your people begin to respect you, Iacocca claimed "they'll follow you to the death," metaphorically speaking.

Cooperation

The ability to work as a team has been praised as a strategic advantage. Unfortunately, many corporations prevent good teamwork through antiquated organizational structures and protocols. However, creating new office towers with transparent offices, mezzanine floors, and atrium-style meeting places may not necessarily promote a more cooperative workplace. Attitudes need to change also. One way of influencing attitudinal change is by linking individuals' sense of identity with the organization's destiny. The more a leader assists workers in defining their work identities, the greater the chance of encouraging worker commitment and building a cooperative workplace.

Merck, a leading pharmaceutical products and services company in the US, lists its recognition of its employees' diversity and teamwork capacities as one of its core values. It promotes teamwork by providing employees with work that is meaningful in a safe and dynamic workplace. Therefore, building cooperation as an attribute of character requires commitment, possible corporate redesign, and consciousness of client needs, both internal and external.

Compassion

Compassion has deep religious connotations, for it refers to showing concern for the suffering or welfare of others and shows mercy to others. In a company sense, compassion manifests itself when leaders make an effort to understand the needs of their employees and take steps to address those needs and concerns. A compassionate leader takes the Atticus Finch approach (the attorney in Harper Lee's 1962 novel *To Kill a Mockingbird*), which means walking around in another person's shoes and climbing around under their skin, to understand what it looks like from their side of the ledger: "You never understand a person until you consider things from his point of view . . . until you climb into his skin and walk around in it."

Linda Nicholls, chairperson of Australia Post, argues that recent terrorist activities and the spate of corporate collapses around the globe have given rise to widespread social concerns for safety, security, and certainty. Nicholls argues that leaders need to show compassion because of the fears such events have generated and to balance the drive for innovation, risk, and growth with the human need for safety and security.

Peter Sommers, managing director of Merck's Australian division, provides an anecdote that exhibits how compassion for employees takes precedence to work demands:

> We've got stock-take this Thursday. The mother of one of the women who works in our factory, died a few days ago and the funeral is going to be on stock-take day. We only do stock-take once a year; it's a very, very big day. The employee's manager and I have both said, "Well, if the funeral is on stock-take day, then stock-take will have to stop for an hour." It's a very important day, it's a full day, I work a 12-hour day and I'm usually exhausted. But, we will go to our employee's mother's funeral to give support, because we care for our people. They're not just numbers here. Each person is treated as an individual, we know their needs, and we try to cater to some of their wants.

Spiritual Respect

Today's organizations are multidimensional; they provide services and products at an ever-increasing rate and superior quality and achieve these outcomes through a multicultural and diverse workforce. Leaders who respect these differences in workers' backgrounds, cultures, and beliefs help build vibrant and relevant workplaces.

Respect for individual beliefs and customs has a long history. In Athenian society, Plato viewed leadership as "an activity with utility for the polis, the activity of giving direction to the community of citizens in the management of their common affairs, especially with a view to the training and improvement of their souls." The reference to soul suggests that leaders engage the full person and help make him or her a productive and morally strong member of society through their contributions in the workplace.

In recent years, the Track-Type Tractors Division of Caterpillar Inc. has experienced unprecedented improvement across the board by establishing workplace values and making employees feel important in the organization. Jim Despain, vice president of this division, acknowledges that leadership is "about others and not about self. It is about trust and not about power. It is about producing results by creating cultures where people know it's okay to be unique and different, so they willingly take off their masks, express themselves, and do great things." This approach confirms the view that workers can achieve great things with the right type of encouragement and respect.

Humility

Fifth Century BC Chinese Taoist philosopher Lao-Tzu described humility as the capacity to keep yourself from putting the self before others and argued that, in doing so, one can become a leader among men.

Despite broad acknowledgement of its importance, being humble does not sit comfortably with the healthy egos of many executives. Some CEOs operate under the mistaken beliefs that they are infallible and that to admit error or concede a superior point of argument is a weakness. Sometimes a leader becomes a boss to get the job done, and there's not much room for humility when the job demands action.

A recent study of over 2,000 Australian executives revealed that often executives were democratic and collegial at the beginning of the working week but often resorted to authoritarian direction giving at week's end in order to meet deadlines. There was no room for humility in those situations. Humility may be an anachronism in a world recognized by the combat of commerce rather than by cooperative and collegial workplaces. For instance, when managers are asked to apply Benjamin Franklin's (1784) "Moral Virtues" to contemporary society, there is a predictable resistance to Franklin's virtue of humility, which is to "imitate Jesus and Socrates." Today's executives see themselves as more worldly and upbeat than that, regardless of the valuable lessons implicit in the statement.

When we examine humility across cultures, there are compelling differences. For example, Japanese CEOs have been known to resign when their projected company profits fell short of the mark. These businessmen blamed themselves for their company's poor performance. When the world's largest bank, Mizuho Holdings, experienced severe computer breakdowns that delayed business transactions, CEO Terunobu Maeda took swift action. He cut the pay of the employees directly involved in the computer system integration, as well as taking a personal pay cut of 50% for six months. Leaders who shift responsibility back to themselves in good times as well as bad have strength of character that goes beyond standard leadership constructs. These leaders possess the attributes commonly referred to as servant leadership. One of the key elements of this leadership philosophy is humility, or the capacity to commit to your workers as much as you do to the bottom line. The guiding principle of servant leadership is to serve rather than to lead. Serving your workers, being a steward of their efforts, takes a considerable dose of humility and rests on a strong sense of self-identity.

Many western business leaders may reject humility as a desirable or useful attribute in today's fast moving, competitive world. Nonetheless, the common characteristics of company leaders who have achieved outstanding and sustainable financial performance in this dynamic environment include modesty, humility, quietness, and self-effacing behavior. These attributes are indicators of leaders quietly aware of their roles in the overall scheme of things. Humility therefore appears to be about a realistic sense of perspective, an acceptance of one's strengths and weaknesses.

2. Transformation

Transformation is how leaders achieve universal and benevolent outcomes, and is the second main factor of leadership character. Transformational leaders with character have courage, passion, wisdom, competency, and self-discipline in their leadership repertoire.

Courage

From a business perspective, courage is having strong convictions about the strategic objectives of the company and being prepared to harness the minds of workers and company resources to achieve those objectives. There are no second-place getters in this approach to business. Courage is not constrained by fear of the unknown and thrives in the problems and promises of dynamic environments.

Managerial courage includes the willingness to do what is right in the face of risk. With "risk" there is a possibility of failure or loss and no guarantee that everything will turn out fine. Acting with courage may result in unpleasant experiences, yet it is a fundamental ingredient of leadership.

Corporate courage manifests itself in many ways. General Electric (GE) requires law firms on its panels to compete for projects through online, eBay-style auctions, which force competing bids to a financial bottom line that allows for comparability across all contenders who are promoting their wares. This innovative and courageous approach coaxes the best out of competitors. From this perspective, courage is immediate and localized.

Michelle Peluso, the chief executive of Travelocity, a US travel company, exemplifies courage. She knows that being innovative requires risk and facing the possibility of failure. Peluso proposed an innovative business model that she believed would assist Travelocity regain ground lost to the company's key competitors. Peluso's business model, "seamless connectivity," focuses on customer and supplier satisfaction. Implementing the model required an investment in technology and training. Investors expressed concern about the time it would take to implement Peluso's strategy and questioned whether it was the right approach. Peluso was unwavering in the face of mounting ambivalence. She believed that her business model was compatible with the company's philosophy of doing things differently and having a long-term view.

Peluso did not yield to these pressures. Instead, she worked hard to influence investors by developing a strong rapport with employees and encouraging them to be innovative and passionate about their work. She introduced a weekly prize for outstanding and innovative work by staff. She also mentors twenty-five "exceptional" Travelocity employees.

Peluso's courage and conviction appear to have paid off handsomely. Travelocity has recently been certified as an official third-party distributor for the Intercontinental Hotels Group because of its supplier-friendly policies.

Passion

Passion is about energy and deeply committed enthusiasm to producing the best one can. In business, passion is an indicator of a company's guiding principles, its *raison d'etre*, and helps others identify the underlying culture of the organization. Unilever is a top ranking Fortune Global 500 company, with over US$46 billion in revenues, US$7 billion in operating profit, and over 240,000 employees globally. The company is a world leader in ice cream, frozen foods, teas, and the second-largest manufacturer of laundry, skin cleansing and hair-care products. Its corporate slogan, "Your passion. Our strength," represents "total commitment to exceptional standards of performance and productivity, to working together effectively and to a willingness to embrace new ideas and to learn continuously" (Unilever, 2004).

John McFarlane (2003), the CEO of the ANZ bank in Australia, believes that leadership is about choosing to make a difference and that when you reflect on making a difference it must be in areas about which one is passionate. A leader's passion can make a significant difference in the degree to which she inspires others or provides focus and motivation for the organisation.

Leadership guru Warren Bennis thinks passion is inherent in effective leadership: "We are productive when we do what we love to do." For example, toward the end of his seventh year as president of the University of Cincinnati, Bennis was giving a talk at the Harvard School of Education. During question time the dean asked Bennis not if he "enjoyed," but whether he "loved" being president of the University of Cincinnati. Bennis acknowledged that he didn't know but on reflection realized that he did not love the job of president. For Bennis, this realization was a major turning point in his life, as it made him realize that his passion lay in teaching and writing. If passion or love of your work or vocation is missing, then choose another vocation.

Wisdom

Wisdom is the ability to draw on one's knowledge and experience to make well-formed judgments. It also involves the use of one's power and personal authority to implement an effective course of action.

Wisdom underpins major decisions. Former BP CEO John Browne was the first CEO in the oil industry to openly acknowledge the impact the industry was having on the environment and to highlight the ways of reducing green-house gas emissions. Browne advocated a responsible approach to limiting the energy industry's impact on the environment through BP's "Beyond Petroleum" campaign. This approach could have impacted on the company's bottom line, but the wisdom of the decision was that it tapped into the moral conscience of society at the time.

Compare Browne to Lee Raymond, his counterpart at Exxon Mobil. Raymond initially was skeptical about global warming. Consequently, Raymond is said to have become the "energy executive everyone loves to blame for the industry's PR problems." Exxon became the target of a boycott in Europe, which encouraged Raymond to change his stance. Recognizing the positive impact Browne's approach had on BP's corporate image, Exxon Mobil subsequently launched its own green ad campaign.

Competence

Those actively pursuing a career as a leader need to be competent in order to maintain the confidence of others. They need to be expert in something to the extent that their expertise commands the respect of peers and followers. According to the former Australian Governor-General, Sir Ninian Stephens (1997):

> The first and most important ingredient of leadership seems to me to be to possess a rounded and comprehensive knowledge of the subject matter with which you are dealing and about which you want others to act in a particular way.

FedEx's founder and CEO, Fred Smith, exemplifies the power of competence. Awarded *Chief Executive* Magazine's 2004 CEO of the Year prize, Smith was recognised for his ability to take FedEx from being "just an idea to being a great company."

Smith says that his vision for creating FedEx was the result of studying a mathematical discipline called topology. Through this study he realized that if you connected all points on a network through a central hub, the resulting efficiencies could be huge.

For Smith, competence does matter. When asked what it takes to be a leader who creates a company and then builds it up to a $25 billion-a-year business, employing 240,000 employees and contractors, Smith advocates "continual learning and education and the discipline to apply those lessons to your operation." He also advises others to make the time and effort to benchmark and learn the lessons of history.

Self-Discipline

Leaders with self-discipline exercise appropriate personal control over their thoughts and actions and are able to manage and express emotions in constructive ways. They are well organised and able to persist in the face of difficulties. Through self-discipline, leaders engender confidence in their followers that they can be relied upon to make rational and logical decisions. As a consequence, their capacity to influence others often increases. Lao Tzu proposed that through mastering ourselves we find true power.

Author and former CEO of international medical technology company, Medtronics, Bill George (2004) argues that self-discipline is the attribute that converts values into consistent action. George describes his successor at Medtronics, CEO Art Collins, as a highly self-disciplined leader as his ego and emotions don't get in the way of taking appropriate action. Collin's consistency in his disposition, behaviours, and decisions lets employees know where he stands on important issues.

Self-discipline requires the maturity to do what is needed, not always what is desired in the present moment. Amy Brinkley, Chief Risk Officer, Bank of America, exhibits such maturity. Brinkley (2003) includes self-discipline as a key component of her personal equation for success and in order to maintain the right balance between her roles as bank executive, wife, mother, and as a member of her church and community: "I try very hard to be fully in the zone I am in at the moment. I give everything I have at that moment to what I am focusing on. I also abide by my own operating principles like staying away from voice mails and e-mails when I am with my kids and my husband."

As a means of maintaining a balance between professional and personal roles, self-discipline is an important component of effective leadership.

3. Benevolence

The third major dimension of leadership character is benevolence and is associated with loyalty, selflessness, integrity, and honesty.

Loyalty

Leaders who demonstrate organisational loyalty show a deep commitment to building organisational sustainability. Such leaders have been described as having the resolve to do whatever it takes to make a company great irrespective how hard the decisions or how difficult the task.

Take Anne Mulcahy, the CEO of Xerox, as a case in point. Mulcahy has exhibited a deep loyalty to her organisation. When she was asked by the board to take on the role of CEO, Xerox was in financial crises, with a $17.1 billion debt and $154 million in cash. In 2000 the stock fell from $63.69 a share to $4.43.

While Mulcahy had an excellent reputation within Xerox, she had no prior CEO experience. Despite the dire financial position of the company, the board recognized Mulcahy was straightforward, hard-working, disciplined, and fiercely loyal to the company. Mulcahy accepted the CEO role based on a sense of duty and loyalty.

When Xerox's external financial advisors suggested Mulcahy consider filing for bankruptcy, the easier way out, she refused to do so. According to Joe Mancini, Xerox's Director of Corporate Financial Analysis, the company's financial advisors didn't think Mulcahy had the courage to make the painful but necessary changes to save Xerox. But Mulcahy indeed did have what it takes.

In her efforts to achieve what can only be described as an extraordinary corporate turnaround, it is claimed that Mulcahy did not take a single weekend off in two years. Timothy R. Coleman, a senior managing director at the private equity firm, Blackstone, said of Mulcahy at the time: "She was leading by example. Everybody at Xerox knew she was working hard and that she was working hard for them."

Organizational loyalty, as a component of character, means commitment to the idea and ideals of the company as much as it does to the nature of its business.

Selflessness

The character attribute of selflessness requires leaders to put others' interests ahead of their own.

Ping Fu, a founding member of Raindrop Geomagic, a North Carolina-based innovative software company, is a leader who demonstrates a capacity for selflessness. Fu took on the role of CEO in 2001 when the company's viability was threatened. The company was running out of money and the venture capital markets were drying up.

Under Fu's leadership, several cost-cutting initiatives were implemented, which included laying off almost half the company's employees. Those who remained took pay cuts. In her efforts to save the business, Fu loaned the company money in order to pay its workers. She also declined to take a pay check until the company straightened out its financial situation.

Raindrop Geomagic board member Peter Fuss acknowledges Fu's personal sacrifices. He says she invested considerable time and was tenacious in her efforts to rebuild the company.

Integrity

The word integrity comes from the Latin word *integritas*, meaning wholeness, coherence, rightness, or purity. Integrity has been defined as consistency between word and deed or "the perceived degree of congruence between the values expressed by words and those expressed through action."

Integrity is the most often cited element of corporate mission statements. In most cases,

integrity refers to honest representation of a company's values and operating protocols. Texas Instruments (TI) refers to "representing ourselves and our intentions truthfully" as evidence of their integrity. General Electric (GE) identifies integrity as a "worldwide reputation for honest and reliable business conduct." The Gillette Company highlights "mutual respect and ethical behavior" as hallmarks of integrity.

Roger Corbett (2004), the CEO and Managing Director of Woolworths, Australia's largest supermarket chain, consisting of more than 150,000 employees and 1,500 stores, believes integrity is the glue that holds his values and the organization's success together: "The closer you can get the business towards integrity and the further away from cynicism, then that really is a good measure of the effectiveness of your business . . . integrity of purpose and example, of lifestyle and attitude, are probably the most important cultural contributions a leader can make to the business."

Honesty

Honesty is absolutely essential to leadership and character. People value working for leaders they can trust. Lindsay Cane is the Chief Executive Officer of an Australian national sporting body, Netball Australia. Her views on honesty and integrity testify to their important role in building leadership character.

Netball Australia receives public funds and is involved with over a million people nationally. Cane (2004) believes her ability to win the confidence of others is critical to the success of the organization, and relies on her capacity to be honest and direct:

> I think it's really important I be seen as a very sound, honest person with high integrity and I need people to want to do business with me. The capacity to build relationships which relates to trust and listening and respect and empathy, those are very important

things because they absolutely affect sponsorship outcomes, business financial outcomes, what money we get from the government, from corporate Australia, what money we might get in the future from our members.

Successful leaders are open and honest with others, but they also understand that maintaining trust requires them to exercise discretion in how they use and disclose information. They take care to avoid violating confidences and do not carelessly divulge potentially harmful information.

Greg Dooley, the Australian General Manager of international financial services and technology company Computershare, rates honesty as the most important character attribute of leadership: "If you're dishonest as a leader then you've got no chance. As soon as you lose trust you may as well give up the ghost." Dooley differentiates between withholding information and deceiving someone. He acknowledges that being open and honest with people may at times be difficult when you have commercially sensitive information that you can't disclose. However, Dooley argues that appropriately withholding information is critical to Computershare's business: "Clients need to know that they can trust us, that we'll be able to handle that information and deal with it on a needs-to-know basis."

A leader's capacity for honesty can help followers work constructively on solving issues and problems. American leadership development consultant Joan Lloyd (2001) says: "I think most employees today are hungry for some good old-fashioned honesty." Employees prefer to work for leaders who they trust can be honest with them about the reality of their circumstances.

Lloyd argues that the best leaders are respected, in part, because they level with people and tell it like it is.

Future of Leadership With Character

Our study identified three underlying dimensions or factors of leadership character. Universalism represents an understanding, appreciation, and tolerance for the welfare of people generally and is a macro perspective approach to work. Transformation is consistent with the concept of transformational leadership as an activity that inspires others in the achievement of long-term, visionary goals. Transformation is a situation-specific process that relies on the competence and self-reliance of the incumbent in their delivery of inspired and values-driven strategic direction for the enterprise. The third dimension, Benevolence, is a micro approach to work and focuses on concern for the welfare of others through one's daily interactions. As a process, Transformation can be seen as the link between Universalism as the externally-focused manifestation of leadership character and internally-focused Benevolent intentions. We propose that leaders who manifest courage (setting a long-term direction and taking people along without fear) with passion (energy and enthusiasm) are more often associated with outcomes that have external as well as internal benefits and are typical of character-led organizations.

The study on which this article is based was made possible through the generous support of the Australian Institute of Management (Queensland Division).

We appreciate the contributions of Dr. Anne Hartican, research assistant, Monash University, to this study.

3

Leadership Skills Approach

You should focus on trying to optimize what you can do with the skills and talents you've got. The more you're a lifelong learner, and the more intellectually curious you are, the bigger the base of potential you'll have to build on when the opportunity presents itself. It also makes you better at recognizing opportunity.

—Admiral Thad Allen, USCG[1]

In a manner similar to the trait approach, the skills approach to leadership is a leader-centered perspective. The two approaches are different, however. In the trait approach, we focused on personality traits that are considered inherent and relatively stable from birth, whereas in this chapter, we focus on a person's "skills and abilities that can be learned and developed" (Northouse, 2013). Skills suggest what leaders can achieve, whereas traits suggest who they are based on their intrinsic characteristics. The skills approach implies that skills, knowledge, and abilities are required for a leader to be effective. In this chapter, we focus on two studies that defined the skills approach: Katz (1974) and Mumford, Zaccaro, Harding, Jacobs, and Fleishman (2000).

※ Katz's Three-Skills Approach

Katz's (1974) seminal article on the skills approach to leadership suggested that leadership (i.e., effective administration) is based on three skills: technical, human, and conceptual.

---

[1]Allen, T. (2010, p. 79)

Technical Skills

Technical skill is proficiency, based on specific knowledge, in a particular area of work. To have technical skills means that a person is competent and knowledgeable with respect to the activities specific to an organization, the organization's rules and standard operating procedures, and the organization's products and services (Katz, 1974; Yukl, 2012). Technical skill is most important at supervisory levels of management, less important for middle managers, and least important for top managers such as CEOs and senior managers. Finally, technical skill is proficiency in working with *things.*

Human Skills

In contrast to technical skills, human (or interpersonal) skills are proficiency in working with *people* based on a person's knowledge about *people* and how they behave; how they operate in groups; how to communicate effectively with them; and their motives, attitudes, and feelings. They are the skills required to effectively influence superiors, peers, and subordinates in the achievement of organizational goals. These skills enable a leader to influence team or group members to work together to accomplish organizational goals and objectives. Human skill proficiency means that leaders know their thoughts on different issues and, simultaneously, become cognizant of the thoughts of others. Consequently, leaders with higher levels of interpersonal skills are better able to adapt their own ideas to other people's ideas, especially when this will aid in achieving organizational goals more quickly and efficiently. These leaders are more sensitive and empathetic to what motivates others, create an atmosphere of trust for their followers, and take others' needs and motivations into account when deciding what to do to achieve organizational goals. Interpersonal skills are required at all three levels of management: supervisory, middle management, and senior management (Katz, 1974; Yukl, 2012).

Conceptual Skills

Conceptual skills allow you to think through and work with ideas. Leaders with higher levels of conceptual skills are good at thinking through the ideas that form an organization and its vision for the future, expressing these ideas in verbal and written forms, and understanding and expressing the economic principles underlying their organization's effectiveness. These leaders are comfortable asking "what if" or hypothetical questions and working with abstract ideas. Conceptual skills allow leaders to give abstract ideas meaning and to make sense of abstract ideas for their superiors, peers, and subordinates. This skill is most important for top managers, less important for middle managers, and least important for supervisory managers (Northouse, 2013). We would offer one caveat. While conceptual skills are less important at lower levels of management, to be promoted to higher levels of management, it is important to develop and demonstrate this skill at all levels of management (Yukl, 2012). It is a skill that can be learned; consequently. We encourage you to take advantage of every opportunity to develop and the ability to learn conceptually.

Recent research used a four-skill model similar to Katz's that includes interpersonal, cognitive, business, and strategic skills. Results show that although interpersonal and cognitive skills were required more than business and strategic skills for those on the lower levels of management, as leaders climbed the career ladder, higher levels of all four of these leadership skills became necessary (Mumford, Campion, & Morgeson, 2007).

⊠ Leadership Skills Model

This approach suggests that leadership is not just the purview of a few people born with traits that make them effective leaders. The skills approach implies that many people have leadership potential, and if they can learn from their experiences, they can become more effective leaders. This means involvement with activities and/or exposure to people and events leading to an increase in skills, knowledge, and abilities. This model is different from a "what leaders do" approach and focuses on capabilities that make leaders effective (Mumford, Zaccaro, Harding, et al., 2000; Northouse, 2013). The leadership skills approach by Mumford, Zaccaro, Harding, et al. (2000) has five elements: individual attributes, competencies, leadership outcomes, career experiences, and environmental influences.

Competencies are the most important element—the "kingpin"—in this model. Competencies lead to leadership outcomes but themselves are affected by a leader's individual attributes. In addition, the impact of leaders' attributes on leaders' competencies and leaders' competencies on outcomes is dependent on career experiences and environmental influences. In the next few paragraphs, we describe competencies, how attributes affect competencies, and how competencies affect leadership outcomes, and we briefly discuss the impact of career experiences on attributes and competencies and the impact of environmental influences on attributes, competencies, and outcomes.

Leader Competencies

Mumford, Zaccaro, Harding, et al. (2000) identified three competencies that result in effective leadership: problem solving, social judgment, and knowledge. These three work together and separately to affect outcomes.

Problem-Solving Skills

These are creative abilities that leaders bring to unique, vague, "hard to get a handle on" organizational problems. These skills include the following: defining problems and issues that are important, accumulating information related to the problem/issue, developing new ways to comprehend each problem/issue, and developing unique, first-of-its-kind alternatives for solving the problems/issues. Problem-solving skills operate in the context of an organization and its environment and require that leaders be aware of their own capacities and challenges relative to the problem/issue and the organizational context (Mumford, Zaccaro, Connelly, & Marks, 2000). The solutions or alternatives developed to solve problems and issues require that leaders be conscious of the time required to develop and execute solutions—whether the solutions are achieving short-term and/or long-term objectives, whether these objectives are organizational or personal—and the external context such as the industry, national, and international environments (Mumford, Zaccaro, Harding, et al., 2000).

Social Judgment Skills

These are skills that enable leaders to comprehend people and the social systems within which they work, play, and have a social life (e.g., friends and family) (Zaccaro, Mumford, Connelly, Marks, & Gilbert, 2000). Social judgment skills facilitate working with others to lead change, solve problems, and make sense of issues. Mumford and colleagues (Mumford, Zaccaro, Harding, et al., 2000) outlined four elements important to social judgment skills: perspective taking, social perceptiveness, behavioral flexibility, and social performance.

Perspective taking is sensitivity to others' objectives and perspective; it is an empathic perspective to solving problems, and it means that leaders actively seek out knowledge regarding people, their organization's social fabric, and how these two very important areas of knowledge intersect with each other.

Whereas perspective taking is associated with others' attitudes, *social perceptiveness* is about leaders knowing what people will do when confronted with proposed changes. *Behavioral flexibility* means being able to change what one does when confronted with others' attitudes and intended actions based on knowledge gained through perspective taking and social perceptiveness, respectively. Leaders with behavioral flexibility understand that there are many different paths to achieving change and the goals and objectives associated with change.

Social performance means being skilled in several leadership competencies. Some of these are abilities in persuading and communicating in order to convey one's own vision to others in the organization, abilities in mediation that enable the leader to mediate interpersonal conflict related to change and to lessen resistance to change, and abilities in coaching and mentoring by giving subordinates support and direction as they work to achieve organizational objectives and goals.

To summarize, Northouse (2013) stated that

> social judgment skills are about being sensitive to how your ideas fit in with others. Can you understand others and their unique needs and motivations? Are you flexible and can you adapt your own ideas to others? Last, can you work with others even when there are resistance and change? Social judgment skills are the people skills required to advance change in an organization.

Knowledge

Knowledge is the gathering of information and the development of mental structures to organize that information in a meaningful way. These mental structures are called schema, which means a diagrammatic representation or depiction. Knowledgeable leaders have more highly developed and complex schemata that they use to collect and organize data. Knowledge is linked to a leader's problem-solving skills. More knowledgeable leaders are able to consider complex organizational issues and to develop alternative and appropriate strategies for change. Knowledge allows leaders to use prior incidents to constructively plan for and change the future.

Individual Attributes

Mumford and his colleagues (e.g., Mumford, Zaccaro, Harding, et al., 2000) identified four attributes that affect the three leader competencies (problem-solving skills, social judgment skills, and knowledge) and, through these competencies, leader performance.

General Cognitive Ability

Think "perceptual processing, information processing, general reasoning skills, creative and divergent thinking capacities, and memory skills" (Northouse, 2013). This is a brief description of general cognitive ability. This type of intelligence grows as we age to early adulthood but declines as we grow older. General cognitive ability positively affects a leader's ability to acquire knowledge and complex problem-solving skills (Northouse, 2013).

Crystallized Cognitive Ability

Think "intelligence that develops because of experience." As we age and gain more experience, we acquire intelligence—this is crystallized cognitive ability. This type of intelligence remains relatively consistent and generally does not diminish as we age. As our crystallized cognitive ability increases, it positively affects our leadership potential by increasing our social judgment skills, conceptual ability, and problem-solving skills.

Motivation

Motivation affects leadership competencies in several ways. We discuss three ways in which motivation helps in the development of leadership competencies. First, a person must want to lead—there must be a willingness to engage in solving complex organizational issues and problems. Second, leaders must be willing to exert influence—to be willing to be dominant within a group of people. Finally, the leader must be willing to advance the "social good" of the organization (Northouse, 2013; Yukl, 2012).

Personality

This is the fourth attribute positively linked to leadership competencies. Northouse (2013) gives three examples of personality that affect how motivated leaders are able to resolve organizational issues and problems. They are tolerance for ambiguity, openness, and curiosity. Leaders with confidence and adaptability may be helpful in situations of conflict. The skills model suggests that personality traits that aid in developing leader competencies lead to better leader performance (Mumford, Zaccaro, Harding, et al., 2000).

Leadership Outcomes

Individual attributes lead to leader competencies, which lead to leadership outcomes. It is noteworthy that without the development of leader competencies, individual attributes may have little effect on leadership outcomes. This reminds us that the leadership competencies element is the "kingpin" component of the leadership skills model. We discuss two leadership outcomes: effective problem solving and leader performance.

Effective Problem Solving

Mumford and his colleagues (e.g., Mumford, Zaccaro, Harding, et al., 2000) developed the skills model to explain variation in the ability of leaders to solve problems—this makes it a capability model. An effective problem solver develops unique, original, and high-quality solutions to issues and problems. Leaders with higher levels of competencies will be more effective problem solvers.

Performance

This outcome refers to the individual leader's job performance—how well he or she has performed. This is usually evaluated by objective external measures. Better performance leads to better evaluations. Leaders whose performance is better will receive better annual evaluations, larger merit pay increases, and recognition as better leaders. Effective problem solving and leader performance are linked, even though they are separate ways of measuring leadership outcomes.

Career Experiences

Career experiences affect both individual attributes and leadership competencies. We believe that some career assignments may develop a leader's motivation to be a better problem solver or be better at interacting with people. These career assignments may also help increase a leader's crystallized cognitive ability. Of course, this depends on being in assignments that have been progressively more difficult, with long-term problems and issues, and at increasingly higher levels in the organization's hierarchy. Arguing that leaders develop as a result of their career experiences suggests that leaders can learn leadership abilities and are not necessarily born with leadership abilities (Mumford, Zaccaro, Harding, et al., 2000; Northouse, 2013).

Environmental Influences

These are factors that are external to individual attributes, leader competencies, and career experiences and that affect leadership outcomes along with the effect of individual attributes through leadership competencies. We will not discuss particular external influences. However, we acknowledge that they exist and that they may affect a leader's ability to be an effective problem solver. They are factors that are considered beyond the control of the leader. Of course, leaders who use the environment as an excuse for their poor performance may not be allowed to continue in their leadership role/position if external factors are not the real cause of poor performance. Top-tier leaders use the environment with great caution and only when they are sure it is the real reason. One of our favorite sayings is "look in the mirror not out the window."

How Does the Leadership Skills Approach Work?

The leadership skills approach is mainly a descriptive model. This approach allows students of leadership to comprehend what it takes to be an effective leader rather than offering prescriptive ways to be an effective leader.

Katz's (1974) three-skills approach implies that where one is in an organization determines how important each skill is to a leader's effectiveness. The leadership skills approach (Mumford, Zaccaro, Harding, et al., 2000) is a much more complex model of leadership effectiveness that is based on rigorous research conducted on U.S. Army officers who ranged in rank from second lieutenant to colonel. This model suggests that leadership effectiveness as measured by outcomes is a direct result of leader competencies and the indirect result of individual attributes working through leader competencies. Finally, the model contends that career experiences work indirectly to affect leadership outcomes, while environmental influences work indirectly and directly to influence leadership outcomes.

References

Allen, T. (2010). You have to lead from everywhere. *Harvard Business Review, 88*(11), 76–79.

Katz, R. L. (1974, September/October). Skills of an effective administrator. *Harvard Business Review, 52*(5), 90–102.

Mumford, M. D., Zaccaro, S. J., Connelly, M. S., & Marks, M. A. (2000). Leadership skills: Conclusions and future directions. *The Leadership Quarterly, 11*(1), 155–170.

Mumford, M. D., Zaccaro, S. J., Harding, F. D., Jacobs, T., & Fleishman, E. A. (2000). Leadership skills for a changing world: Solving complex problems. *The Leadership Quarterly, 11*(1), 11–35.

Mumford, T. V., Campion, M. A., & Morgeson, F. P. (2007). The leadership skills strataplex: Leadership skill requirements across organizational levels. *Leadership Quarterly, 18*, 154–166.

Northouse, P. G. (2013). *Leadership: Theory and practice* (6th ed.). Thousand Oaks, CA: Sage.

Yukl, G. (2012). *Leadership in organizations* (8th ed.). Upper Saddle River, NJ: Pearson-Prentice Hall.

Zaccaro, S. J., Mumford, M. D., Connelly, M. S., Marks, M. A., & Gilbert, J. A. (2000). Assessment of leader problem-solving capabilities. *The Leadership Quarterly, 11*(1), 37–64.

The Cases

Coaching for Exceptional Performance Workshop

Informal coaching opportunities occur in the course of daily activities. In this workshop, students are provided with ways to improve their responsiveness to these opportunities. The format is a series of sessions in which students and each member of their teams, in turn, play the role of the director of operations for a software products business. Two staff members drop in to see the director, on their initiative, to ask for ideas, help, guidance, or a decision on an issue. The director knows key details about each staff member's background and development needs but does not know in advance what the specific issues or concerns are. It is necessary to explore these issues or concerns before any decision can be made. The students' performances are videotaped and critiqued in terms of identifying each staff member's problem(s); the effectiveness of responses to the immediate problems; and contribution to that staff members' longer-term growth or awareness through coaching.

Performance Coaching: Darcy Gallagher Role

In preparation for a meeting between Darcy Gallagher, sales manager, and his general manager regarding his annual performance review, Darcy has done a self-assessment of his performance. In doing this self-assessment, Darcy has also considered his beliefs about leadership, sensitivity to criticism, and motivators.

The Reading

Train Dogs, Develop Leaders

Leaders can be trained, but highly successful leaders, this author writes, can be developed. The burden is on the organization to develop leaders—to actively involve leaders in recruitment and selection, development, career-move decisions, and other leadership activities. These executives also recruit the best prospects, challenge them constantly, and manage them. Leadership, the author notes, may be the only sustainable advantage today, which is why it should never be left to chance.

——— *Coaching for Exceptional Performance Workshop*[1] ———

Jane Howell

⊠ Overview

The objective of the Coaching for Exceptional Performance Workshop is to improve your responsiveness to informal coaching opportunities that occur in the course of daily activities.

The *format* of the workshop is a series of sessions in which you (and each member of your team in turn) will play the role of Terry Hepburn, the director of operations for the software products business of the Multi Product Manufacturing (MPM) Company. Two of your staff members will drop in to see you, on their initiative, to ask for your ideas, help, guidance or a decision on an issue. You have only six minutes to see each staff member in this informal coaching session since you have to leave for another important meeting at head office.

Terry Hepburn knows key details about each staff member's background and development needs, but does *not* know in advance what the specific issues or concerns are. It will be necessary to explore these issues or concerns before any decision can be made. Depending on the situation, the staff member may be looking for your ideas, guidance or emotional support rather than for an actual decision.

The *quality* of your coaching performance as Terry Hepburn will be critiqued in terms of your identification of each staff member's problem(s); the effectiveness of your responses to the immediate problems; and your contribution to that staff member's longer-term growth or awareness through coaching.

⊠ How the Role Play Works

Every member of your team will play the role of Terry Hepburn in turn. When each person does so, the other team members will play staff roles.

Each of the staff roles is typical of those you might meet in any organization:

- an over-conscientious manager who is very critical of staff and who can't delegate;
- an insecure supervisor who is very reluctant to make decisions and take responsibility;
- a frustrated supervisor whose ambitions have not been taken seriously and who has been passed over for promotion;
- an ambitious and talented analyst who pushes hard for recognition;
- a very competent manager who is eager for promotion;
- a brilliant engineer who lacks interpersonal and conflict resolution skills;
- a dedicated production supervisor who believes manufacturing should be the company's number one priority.

You will also take a turn playing the role of one of these staff members for the purposes of visits to other team members when they are acting as Terry Hepburn. You should play your staff role with conviction and sincerity.

Your facilitator will set up the sequence of coaching interviews and give you further details of the staff character you are to play.

Version: (A) 2010-01-07

[1]This workshop is a revision and extension of the Coaching Workshop prepared by Citicorp.

⊠ Summary

There will be as many 12-minute rounds as there are members on your team.

In one round, you will be Terry Hepburn, director of operations; you will meet with two of your staff members and deal with the issues they bring to you.

In two other rounds, you will be a staff member visiting Terry Hepburn to discuss an issue you have.

⊠ Multi-product Manufacturing (Mpm) Company

An organization chart of the MPM Company can be found in Exhibit 1. A brief description of the job responsibilities and functions follows.

Mickey King	Vice-President, Photo Media, Software and Chemical Group
Terry Hepburn	Director of Operations, Software Products Business

Terry's Staff

Kelsey Scott	Telesales Supervisor: supports all group products (four telesales coordinators and one specialist)
Kim Hughes	Market Development Manager: supports all group products under Mickey King's sector (three analysts, including Pat Cox)
Jody Hickson	Project Sales and Marketing Manager, Software Products Business: two regional sales managers, one marketing supervisor (Chris Parkins), one secretary/assistant
Robin Maynard	Manufacturing Engineering Manager, Software Discs: responsible for technical aspects of manufacturing the product, i.e., quality improvements, cost improvements (five engineers)
Lee Sewell	General Production Supervisor: responsible for all aspects of manufacturing software discs (three shift supervisors and 10 process workers)

Functions

Telesales

- expand sales revenue through selling to C and B accounts in Mickey's group;
- implement special project assignments that expand sales for various businesses

Market Development

- develop new markets and track competitive activity
- liaise with MPM Company's key distributors

Project Management

- responsible for all aspects of marketing and sales of current business and developing new business opportunities

Engineering

- support manufacturing in both day-to-day and long-term troubleshooting with respect to the technical aspects of manufacturing the product, i.e. quality improvements, cost improvements;
- to investigate, recommend and implement modifications to processing equipment

Manufacturing

- manufacture the product, meeting cost, quality and service goals

⬙ What You Already Know About Your Staff Members

Kim Hughes—Market Development Manager, Photo Media, Software & Chemical Group

Kim, age 35, has been employed by MPM Company for 14 years, seven years in the current position. Kim leads a group of three analysts, including Pat.

Kim is meticulous and accurate at administrative tasks, completes assignments on time, and avoids risks at all costs. Kim tends to over-supervise staff members in order to guarantee that their work is perfect. Due to poor delegation skills, lack of rapport with staff members, and drive for perfection, Kim works overtime practically every evening. In your opinion, Kim has peaked as far as promotion potential is concerned.

You assigned Kim to assist your boss, Mickey, on a feasibility study for a new information system to track sales leads.

Pat Cox—Market Analyst for Kim in Market Development

Pat, age 27, joined MPM Company as a market analyst 18 months ago. Pat shows intelligence and initiative, and tries to broaden his/her knowledge of departmental activities. Pat has made several creative procedural recommendations, which have been successfully implemented.

Pat is ambitious and easily bored with routine work. Kim has complained about Pat's careless attention to detail.

Terry believes Pat will be ready for promotion or transfer within six months.

Kelsey Scott—Telesales Supervisor, Photo Media, Software & Chemical Group

Kelsey Scott, age 31, has worked in the manufacturing industry for 10 years, the last six with MPM Company. Kelsey's tenure in the telesales supervisor role is three months. Kelsey's performance as an analyst was adequate, and Kelsey was promoted to the current role as the best of a weak group of candidates.

Kelsey lacks self-confidence, is reluctant to make decisions, and avoids confronting staff with mistakes. Kelsey constantly brings simple problems to *Terry* to solve.

Jody Hickson—Project Sales and Marketing Manager, Software Products Business

Jody Hickson, age 31, joined MPM Company four years ago, and has been in his/her current role for two years. Jody has been designated as a high potential employee. Previously, Jody was an executive account manager at Xerox The Document Company, and has developed a rich network of contacts in the local business community over time. Recently, Jody has been hinting to you at every opportunity that the timing is right for a promotion to a higher-level sales management position.

Chris Parkins—Marketing Supervisor, Software Products Business

Chris Parkins, age 41, has 18 years of marketing experience, 12 years with MPM Company, eight years in the present position. Chris lacks a university education, but is totally familiar with marketing practices. Chris's current performance is satisfactory.

Your major concern about Chris is lack of ambition and creativity. Chris could be marginally effective as a manager although you have serious doubts about Chris's ability and motivation to advance.

Robin Maynard—Manufacturing Engineering Manager, All Products in Mickey's Group

Robin Maynard, age 42, has been with MPM Company for four years, working for Terry in Mickey's businesses. Robin is a brilliant engineer but needs to work on interpersonal skills. Robin has a tendency to be short with people and unable to empathize. Robin views engineering as the most important function in the company and therefore undervalues other colleagues' contributions.

Lee and Robin have difficulty resolving their own disputes and tend to look to higher management for solutions.

Lee Sewell—General Production Supervisor, Software Products Business

Lee, age 38, joined MPM Company 10 years ago and has been in his/her current position for three years. Lee has broad exposure to manufacturing across the company and takes great pride in achieving monthly production and revenue targets. Lee is fastidious about safety and ensures all precautions are taken in the manufacturing process. At times Lee can have too narrow a focus on "process" at the risk of losing sight of costs.

Lee has difficulty with the way engineering prioritizes its projects and feels manufacturing process issues must be first and foremost at all times.

Exhibit 1   Multi Product Manufacturing Company Organization Chart

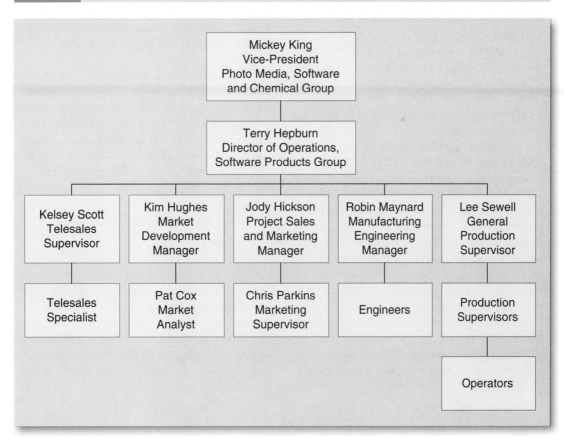

Performance Coaching: Darcy Gallagher Role

Ken Mark

⊠ Background on Darcy Gallagher

Gallagher graduated from the University of Toronto with a bachelor of commerce degree, majoring in marketing, and joined an export-import firm in Toronto. Because of his excellent process-oriented skills, Gallagher immediately had a positive impact on the business performance in his area of responsibility and was rapidly promoted to a supervisory role. After hearing about Gallagher through his informal network, David Elliott, who was a divisional general manager in The Elmwood Group, enticed Gallagher to move to Ottawa and join the company in the retail operation as the assistant sales manager. In this new role, Gallagher was responsible for developing customer relationship management processes that would enable the retail operation's business development managers to establish relationships with local area contractors with the goal of building repeat sales business.

Gallagher reported to the sales manager who, in turn, reported to Elliott. Both the sales manager and Elliott were impressed with Gallagher's accomplishments and rated him as an exceptional performer. Gallagher seemed like a natural fit for the assistant sales manager role because of his data-driven decision-making, his detail orientation, and his ability to learn and adapt processes to a sales environment. Elliott appreciated these skills because they complemented his own; he had joined The Elmwood Group upon graduating from high school and had worked his way up the ranks to become a divisional general manager. Elliott was not considered a stellar performer, but he was viewed as a loyal and dependable senior manager who consistently delivered results.

After three years as assistant sales manager, Gallagher was promoted to sales manager after the incumbent retired. Six months after this promotion, the division's vice-president announced that Gallagher was moving to Windsor to replace another sales manager.

At company functions over that past two years, Gallagher has developed a relationship with the division's vice-president, Thomas Lockie, Elliot's immediate superior. Lockie considered Gallagher to be one of the most promising managers he had ever met, and he made a note to track Gallagher's progress. Gallagher viewed his move to Windsor as a fast-track promotion, initiated because the vice-president wanted to groom Gallagher for bigger challenges within the company.

Gallagher, who is married to a chartered accountant, had purchased a house in Windsor, and he and his wife had become actively involved in the community, joining the private Essex Golf and Country Club and attending many charity and social events. Gallagher was very comfortable with his personal and professional life in Windsor.

⊠ Performance Coaching Discussion

Gallagher is 28 years old and has been in his current role as sales manager in Windsor for one year. During his first four years at Elmwood, he received several salary increases, reflecting his exceptional performance ratings. Gallagher was viewed as a rising star by his previous manager and was part of Elmwood's leadership talent

Version: 2011-03-18

pool. In previous 360-degree reviews, Gallagher gave himself high ratings on virtually every competency, and his former manager matched those ratings on all competencies and even gave Gallagher higher ratings on some.

In the past, Gallagher has received vague feedback about his people skills. David Elliott, the general manager who hired Gallagher, once casually told him that "this [interpersonal relations] is something you have to work on," but Elliott did not elaborate. Gallagher did not take this piece of advice seriously, especially since neither Elliott nor Gallagher believed in the need for "soft skills." In Gallagher's mind, Elmwood mainly values strong results, which can more than compensate for a gap on the "soft" side.

Gallagher's new boss moved to Ottawa nine months ago to accept the position of general manager for a division of The Elmwood Group and has scheduled an annual performance coaching discussion with Gallagher. The general manager asked Gallagher to provide a self-assessment of his performance (see Exhibit 1).

Role and Responsibilities

As sales manager, Gallagher is the point of contact for large accounts, is responsible for developing and implementing sales plans, and manages a diverse group of employees, including an assistant sales manager, business development managers and onsite support staff such as site accountants. He also works closely with the purchasing team to set and update price plans for key accounts, represents the company at industry or building association functions, and is responsible for staying abreast of key indicator trends such as housing starts. Managing and developing employees constitutes a significant component of Gallagher's new role (40 per cent).

Performance

Gallagher is a top-tier employee with exceptional business performance. He has a systematic approach to problem solving and looks for root causes. As a business development manager, Gallagher's accomplishments include developing and implementing a customer relationship management system.

However, Gallagher's direct reports are not pleased with his leadership. After three months at the Windsor location, two of his direct reports asked for transfers to other locations, citing job-related stress. Gallagher considered their departures as "desirable turnover" since in his view they had some difficulties in living up to his high performance expectations. In another instance, two business development managers quietly complained to him that they were missing their children's hockey tournament to deal with a thorny client issue over the weekend. In Gallagher's view, he was an effective delegator who empowered his people to do their jobs.

After the most recent round of 360-degree feedback, Gallagher was seen walking around in a bad mood. His direct reports had rated him below expectations whereas his self ratings were high. In Gallagher's mind, this was just an unfortunate misunderstanding. Gallagher believes that his direct reports, some of whom were peers before his promotion to Windsor, have banded together to undermine his career progress and are jealous of his success.

⬛ Individual Role Preparation

Although you graduated with a marketing degree from the University of Toronto, you have since taken an interest in sales, climbing the ranks at The Elmwood Group (Elmwood). You do not hesitate to show displeasure through the use of facial expressions. Some people have asked you to make more of an effort to contain your emotions, but you believe there is nothing to be gained from timidity. To make an omelette, you've got to break a few eggs, right?

The paradox you face is that while you feel a need to freely dispense advice, you are unable to stomach negative feedback, no matter how constructive it may be. According to your managers, you've always performed well, and that's good enough for you. You like to trust your gut, offering unsolicited advice on a whim. You've been told by your former sales manager that you have a "hard edge," and you have tried to soften it by cracking jokes, especially when you have to ask your employees (whom you see as subordinates, not colleagues) to come into work on weekends. You think of yourself as a three-star general in command of a highly efficient, highly obedient force, and you developed this mental model of an authority figure by watching interviews with business executives on CNN.

Your new general manager has asked you for a self-assessment of your performance. You've provided it (see Exhibit 1), but you don't see the point of this exercise since, in your own opinion, you are clearly head and shoulders above your peers. If something critical is said during the upcoming discussion of your self-assessment, you may look at the new general manager with a look of incredulity. You will say something like, "Why am I listening to this?" You don't believe you need to change. And you believe that as long as Thomas Lockie, the company's vice-president (and your personal mentor), believes you're alright, then you are alright.

As Gallagher, prepare your objectives and your approach for the upcoming performance coaching discussion with your boss. Adopt Gallagher's personality, motivators, and beliefs to credibly portray this role. Gallagher is a confident person who would be highly employable elsewhere and would not hesitate to leave Elmwood if his ego were bruised.

Exhibit 1	Darcy Gallagher's Self-Assessment

Business Knowledge					
General Subject	Competency	Description	Level Attained −	Job Requirement =	Gap
Running the Business	1. **Business Innovator**	Understands developments within own industry. Looks at innovative ways of doing things. Puts new ideas into action.	10	10	0
	2. **Organizes for Alignment**	Aligns individual, departmental, company, and corporate objectives.	5	5	0
	3. **Technologically Inclined**	Understands and uses different technologies and tools to increase productivity and improve efficiency of projects.	5	5	0
Finance	4. **Financial Acumen**	Understands and manages financial objectives of job; can plan and implement cost-efficient initiatives.	10	5	5

Business Knowledge					
General Subject	Competency	Description	Level Attained	_ Job Requirement =	Gap
Marketing & Sales	5. Puts Customers First	Strives to create the most value for the customer (internal and external) that results in mutual long-term success.	10	10	0
	6. Keen Competitive Awareness	Able to identify current and potential competitors and understand their ability to impact our business.	10	10	0
Human Capital	7. Human Capital	Hires and assigns personnel in their area of responsibility to maximize their effectiveness; Effectively develops personnel to maximize their personal growth and contribution to the organization.	10	10	0
	8. Leadership Development	Invests considerable time and resources into planning for the development of the best people for the key roles in the organization (including own role).	10	10	0

Exhibit 2

Leadership Competencies & Skills					
General Subject	Competency	Description	Level Attained	_ Job Requirement =	Gap
Focused Drive	1. Focus	The ability to identify an important goal or vision and to concentrate efforts that support that goal or vision.	10	5	5
	2. Drive	Is motivated to consistently reach high levels of performance.	10	5	5

(Continued)

Exhibit 2	(Continued)

Leadership Competencies & Skills					
General Subject	Competency	Description	Level Attained −	Job Requirement =	Gap
Emotional Intelligence	3. Understanding Others	The ability to use insight and empathy to understand the emotions and thoughts of others.	10	10	0
	4. Emotional Maturity	The ability to control emotions and cope with stress in a way that instills confidence and motivates others.	10	10	0
Trusted Influence	5. Commitment	The ability to earn respect and trust by keeping commitments, leading by example, and recognizing the contributions of others.	10	10	0
	6. Empowerment	The ability to help others reach higher levels of performance through trust, delegation, participation, and coaching.	10	5	5
Conceptual Thinking	7. Innovation	The ability to generate new ideas, products and processes by challenging traditional beliefs and thinking "outside the box."	10	10	0
	8. Big Picture Thinking	The ability to identify and consider the overall impact of a decision or action on other departments, the company or the organization.	10	10	0
Systems Thinking	9. Process Thinking	The ability to design, improve or connect critical work processes to increase performance.	10	5	5

Leadership Competencies & Skills					
General Subject	Competency	Description	Level Attained	− Job Requirement	= Gap
	10. **Mental Discipline**	The ability to follow a logical thought process to a successful conclusion.	10	5	5
Leadership Skills	11. **Leading Change**	The skill of successfully leading others in times of internal or external change.	5	5	0
	12. **Coaching/ Mentoring**	The ability to utilize a comfortable coaching style to improve performance.	10	10	0
	13. **Communication (Written, Oral, Listening)**	The skill of communicating and relating to a broad range of people internally and externally.	5	5	0
	14. **Negotiation**	The skill of arriving at and reaching understandings and agreements with a broad range of people internally and externally.	10	10	0
	15. **Problem Solving**	The ability to recognize and systematically resolve complex problems.	10	5	5

Train Dogs, Develop Leaders

Jeffrey Gandz

There is an old Chinese proverb: "Give a man a fish and he will eat for a day. Teach a man to fish and he will eat for the rest of his life." But what happens when there are no more fish to catch?

That is the limitation with training. Successful training ensures that a person will act predictably in response to a given stimulus. Pavlov trained dogs to respond to bells and the provision of food . . . so well, indeed, that they even salivated when the food

Reprint# 9B02TC02

was not presented. And B. F. Skinner was able to train chickens to behave predictably with a wide variety of different reward ratios.

I am not arguing against training. People need knowledge and skills to develop the competencies required to do their jobs. But what does this have to do with leadership? Organizations need leaders to be able to assess situations that are frequently complex and seldom identical to past situations. Leaders must recognize patterns without assuming that a situation is identical to one they have encountered before. They must be able to use analogies to make inferences and figure out what to do when they encounter new situations. In short, they must use and develop their judgment to the point where it becomes wisdom.

In the pursuit of leadership talent, organizations tend to hire for knowledge, train for skills, develop for judgment—and hope for wisdom. When wisdom does not materialize, they are forced to hire it. Certainly, there is nothing wrong with selective hiring, but organizations should hire to enrich their gene pool, not because their internal reproductive system has failed, as shown in Figure 1.

When organizations look at their leadership pipelines, the demographic facts of life stare them in the face. Through the last two decades, the severe, short-lived recession and painful downsizings of the 1980s taught them how to stay lean. Out went multiple layers, "assistants-to" and the narrow spans of control that allowed leaders to spend time developing people. Senior executives could boast of personally "managing" 20–30 people by e-mail. But "lean" turned into anorexic as organizations starved their people of developmental experiences and the counselling of those who had gone before.

Now organizations have 50-somethings with judgment and wisdom, but their 30-somethings have only skills and knowledge. The question is, can organizations accelerate the development of this leadership talent?

Leadership Can Be Developed

In the unending nature-versus-nurture debate about leadership, I stand firmly in the middle. Leaders are "born," innate leadership talent can be accelerated, but not everyone with skills and

---

Figure 1 Hierarchy of Leadership Development

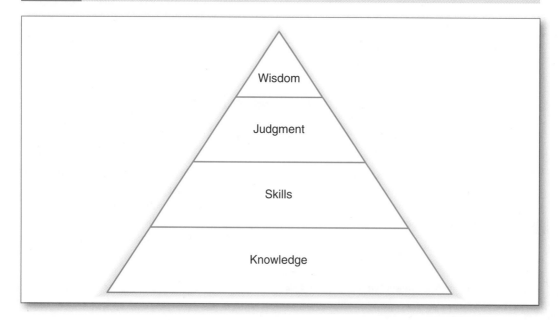

knowledge will develop judgment. The challenge of human resource development is to accelerate the development of high-quality leadership in organizations, increase the yield of mature leaders from the pool of high potentials, and create a pipeline of management talent that delivers leaders where and when they are needed. (While the term *leadership pipeline* has been used by many authors over many years, it is described in greatest detail in *The Leadership Pipeline*, by Ram Charan, Stephen J. Drotter and Jim Noel, Jossey-Bass Publishers, 2001; also, see article "The Leadership Pipeline," by Charan and Drotter, Ivey Business Journal, May/June 2001.) Research in the field of leadership development is not conclusive, but my 25 years of teaching experience leads me to several conclusions:

- It pays to start with excellent talent. This requires the commitment of senior executives because recruiting the very best prospects is both expensive and challenging. Top performers are the best recruiters of top talent.
- It pays to channel high potentials into the "right" experiences. Challenging job assignments and well-designed learning programs encourage individual development.
- Learning does not simply "happen." "Doing" without reflecting does not lead to learning. When learning is combined with "doing"—the concept of action-learning—the loop is effectively closed. This also happens when individuals receive excellent coaching from caring mentors. It does not happen when high potentials are assigned to supervisors who have no interest or skill in leadership development.
- Development must be integrated with personal career management and organizational development. It is pointless and expensive to pour money into developing people who have no leadership challenges.
- There must be "on-" and "off-ramps." Some high potentials are late bloomers.

Others fail to live up to their original promise or decline to commit to their own development.

- High potentials must be managed differently. They are high-maintenance and their development must be accelerated. They require frequent, in-depth, project-based performance reviews and consistent reassurance that they are high-potentials.

The Role of HRD in Leadership Development

Human resource departments play an important role in leadership development, especially in multidimensional businesses or conglomerates. The best organizations view leadership development as a treasury function. They centralize ownership of high-potential leaders and their value to the organization, rather than downloading responsibility to the departments where the high potentials happen to be working

The onus is on the HR Development function to:

Make the connection between corporate and business-unit strategies. When leadership development is disconnected from strategy, the leadership pipeline becomes clogged or sucks air. High potentials leave the organization for lack of opportunities, or the organization struggles to implement strategies without leadership resources

Integrate critical HR systems around the leadership development challenge, as shown in Figure 2. Common flaws in HR development are development without succession planning, information systems that are inadequate for inventorying talent and experiences, and assessment and evaluation systems that make no allowance for talent spotting and deployment.

Manage the development and deployment of the infrastructure of leadership development activities, including assessments, evaluations, programs, courses and career tracking.

Figure 2   Integrated Leadership Development Systems

Advise and consult on individual career plans and developmental moves, working with candidates, supervisors, mentors and top management.

Brief management on developments in leadership thinking.

Seek and evaluate "outside" leadership development resources (e.g., consultants, academics, organizations)

Benchmark development leadership practices against high-performing organizations.

A Commitment to Leadership Development

Some 30 or 40 years ago, everyone assumed that great grapes grew only in selected regions of certain countries and that great wines developed from those grapes as a matter of chance. Vintages that showed promise were left to mature for many years. No longer. As a result of the careful selection, feeding and pruning of vines, yields have increased and maturation periods have decreased. Excellent wines are produced in shorter time frames and in regions of the world previously known only for their "plonk."

It is no accident that some companies have great leadership bench strength and others do not. That is because some companies work at developing leadership. Their senior executives are actively involved in recruitment and selection, development, career-move decisions and other leadership activities. They recruit the best prospects, challenge them constantly manage them centrally and locally, and utilize the "off ramp" when the candidate wants to abandon the fast track or his or her potential does not match the needs of the organization.

In an increasingly competitive and boundaryless world, leadership may be the only sustainable competitive advantage. That is why leadership should never be left to chance.

CHAPTER

4

Leader Style Approach

Leadership used to be all about authority—top-down and personality-driven. Like a hammer. Those days are gone. The world is becoming more and more global. The world, as well as business, has become radically decentralized. We have moved from vertically integrated centers of power and centralized authority to localized constellations of horizontally linked networks, where leadership and authority migrates from station to station and from skill to skill.

—Arkadi Kuhlman[1]

The leadership style approach is different from the trait approach and the skills approach. The trait approach emphasized the personality characteristics of leaders. The skills approach focused on the leader's competencies. The leadership style approach accentuates leader behaviors—in other words, what leaders do and how they act, particularly toward subordinates, in a multitude of situations to change subordinate performance and influence subordinate behavior (Yukl, 2012).

These behaviors can be distilled into two broad types: initiating structure (task behavior) and consideration (relationship behavior). Task behavior makes it easier for group members (subordinates) to accomplish goals and objectives. Relationship behavior makes it easier for group members (subordinates) to feel at ease with the context in which they are operating, with other members of the group, and with who they are themselves. The ultimate objective of the leadership style approach is to help in our understanding of how leaders integrate these two broad conceptualizations of behaviors to positively influence group members in efforts to achieve personal and organizational goals and objectives (Northouse, 2013).

Consequently, we describe three streams of research that focus on task and relationship behaviors and their intersection. The first stream was conducted at the Ohio State University (e.g., Stogdill, 1948) and pursued style research to demonstrate the need to account for more than leaders' traits

---

[1]Kuhlman, A. (2011, p. 3). Arkadi Kuhlman is the founding CEO of ING Direct and author of *The Orange Code*.

(DuBrin, 2010). The second stream was conducted at the University of Michigan (e.g., Likert, 1961, 1967) and examined how leadership happened in small groups. The third stream (Blake & Mouton, 1964, 1978, 1985) researched how leaders used relationship and task behaviors in an organizational context (Yukl, 2012).

The Ohio State Studies

As we see from Table 4.1, the Ohio State University studies found that leader behaviors clustered under two broad categories: initiating structure and consideration (Stogdill, 1974). Characteristics of both are included in Table 4.1.

Table 4.1	Task Behavior and Relationship Behavior	
	Task Behavior	**Relationship Behavior**
Ohio State studies	*Initiating structure* Organizing work Giving work structure Defining role responsibilities Scheduling work activities	*Consideration* Building respect, trust, liking, and camaraderie between followers and leaders
University of Michigan studies	*Production orientation* Stress technical aspects Stress production aspects Workers viewed as way to get work done	*Employee orientation* Workers viewed with a strong human relations aspect Leaders treat workers as human beings, value workers individuality, give attention to workers' needs
Blake and Mouton's grid	*Concern for production* Achieving tasks Making policy decisions Developing new products Optimizing processes Maximizing workload Increasing sales volume	*Concern for people* Attending to people Building commitment and trust Promoting worker personal worth Providing good work conditions Maintaining fair salary/benefits Promoting good social relations

SOURCE: Adapted from *Leadership: Theory and Practice,* Sixth Edition, by Peter Northouse. Copyright © 2013, SAGE Publications, Inc.

These two behaviors were viewed as two separate and different continua. This means that an individual can be high on both, low on both, or high on one and low on the other (Daft, 2011). In addition, these behaviors need to be considered in context as in some situations, high consideration and low initiating structure may be appropriate, whereas in others, the opposite may be appropriate. Being high on both is the best form of leadership, but this is very difficult for many individuals (Daft, 2011; Northouse, 2013).

The University of Michigan Studies

As reported in Table 4.1, this body of research found results similar to the Ohio State studies. Their two broad categories were production orientation and employee orientation. Characteristics of both are included in Table 4.1.

Contrary to the Ohio State studies, initially, these two types of leader behaviors were argued to be on opposite ends of one continuum (Daft, 2011), thus suggesting that leaders high on production orientation had to be low on employee orientation and vice versa. Later, the Michigan researchers came to agree with the Ohio State studies and view the two types of leader behavior as two separate continua. This meant that leaders could be viewed as being able to have high production and employee orientations. Some research viewed this as being valuable for employee satisfaction and employee performance, but most research was inconclusive (Northouse, 2013; Yukl, 2012).

The Blake and Mouton Grid

Blake and Mouton (1964, 1978, 1985) developed their leadership grid to demonstrate that leaders helped organizations achieve their goals through two leader orientations: concern for production and concern for people. These two orientations resemble task behavior and relationship behavior, as shown in Table 4.1. Using the grid, the researchers developed five leadership styles.

The *authority–compliance* style describes leaders who are results driven with little or no concern for people except to organize them in a way that keeps them from interfering with getting the job done. Communication with followers is limited and used only to give instructions regarding the task. These leaders are controlling, hard driving, overpowering, and demanding—not nice people to work for. Some research suggests a higher turnover rate under this style of leadership (Yukl, 2012).

The *country club* style describes leaders with a high concern for people and a low concern for results or production. These leaders focus on meeting people's needs and creating a positive environment in which to work. Turnover rates seem to decrease under these leaders (Yukl, 2012).

Impoverished management describes leaders who have little or no concern for people or for production (Daft, 2011). They do enough to not get fired, but mentally, they have probably already defected from the organization.

The *middle-of-the-road* style describes leaders who have a moderate concern for people and for production (Daft, 2011). These leaders are compromisers who do not push production hard or push to meet the needs of their followers to the maximum limit.

Team management-style leaders emphasize interpersonal relationships and getting results. These leaders help employees focus on and commit to their work and promote teamwork and a high level of participation in work-related decisions by employees. Northouse (2013) suggests that the following phrases describe these leaders: "stimulates participation, acts determined, gets issues into the open, makes priorities clear, follows through, behaves open-mindedly, and enjoys working."

The team management style integrates high concerns for people and for production. It is possible to use a high concern for people and a high concern for production but not in an integrative manner. These leaders switch from the authority–compliance style to the country club style depending on the situation. An example would be the benevolent dictator who acts graciously to get the job done. This style is called *paternalistic/maternalistic,* and leaders who use this style do so because they consider that people are not associated with what it takes to achieve the organization's goals and purposes.

The final style based on the leadership grid is *opportunism.* This refers to a leader who opportunistically uses any combination of the five styles to advance his or her career.

Blake and Mouton (1985) argue that leaders usually have a style that is most dominant and one that is their backup style. Leaders revert to their backup style when the dominant style is not working and they are under a great deal of pressure (Northouse, 2013).

How Does the Leadership Style Work?

This style helps students, practitioners, and academics to assess leadership based on two broad dimensions: task behavior and relationship behavior. It does not tell leaders what to do but describes the major dimensions of what they do in their relationships with their job and their followers. This style suggests to leaders that how they affect followers "occurs through the tasks they perform as well as in the relationships they create" (Northouse, 2013). There may be a situation perspective to the leadership style approach in that some followers may need to be directed more, while others may need to be nurtured and supported more (Yukl, 2012).

References

Blake, R. R., & Mouton, J. S. (1964). *The managerial grid.* Houston, TX: Gulf.

Blake, R. R., & Mouton, J. S. (1978). *The new managerial grid.* Houston, TX: Gulf.

Blake, R. R., & Mouton, J. S. (1985). *The managerial grid III.* Houston, TX: Gulf.

Daft, R. L. (2011). *The leadership experience* (5th ed.). Mason, OH: Thomson, South-Western.

DuBrin, A. (2010). *Leadership: Research findings, practice, and skills* (6th ed.). Mason, OH: South-Western/Cengage.

Kuhlman, A. (2011). *Rock then roll: The secrets of culture-driven leadership.* Canada: Deak & Company Inc.

Likert, R. (1961). *New patterns of management.* New York, NY: McGraw-Hill.

Likert, R. (1967). *The human organization: Its management and value.* New York, NY: McGraw-Hill.

Northouse, P. G. (2013). *Leadership: Theory and practice* (6th ed.). Thousand Oaks, CA: Sage.

Stogdill, R. M. (1948). Personal factors associated with leadership: A survey of the literature. *Journal of Psychology, 25,* 35–71.

Stogdill, R. M. (1974). *Handbook of leadership: A survey of theory and research.* New York, NY: Free Press.

Yukl, G. (2012). *Leadership in organizations* (8th ed.). Upper Saddle River, NJ: Pearson/Prentice Hall.

The Cases

Scarborough YMCA: Getting Back on Track

Tammy MacDonald, the newly appointed general manager of the Scarborough YMCA, was discussing her plan of action with the YMCA Greater Toronto Area's senior leadership team. The Scarborough YMCA had been a perennial underperformer from several perspectives: particularly membership, member satisfaction, and financial perspective. Tammy was determined to turn the Scarborough YMCA around. Several previous general managers had failed to improve the facility, and it continued to lag behind the average YMCA in Canada. Tammy sensed a complacent organization. She had practically grown up in the Scarborough YMCA, and although she had served in several leadership roles in the center, she wondered how she would advocate change now that she was the formal leader of the Scarborough YMCA.

Consultancy Development Organization

The director of Consultancy Development Organization (CDO), a not-for-profit organization that helps develop the consultancy profession in India, needs to respond to CDO's poor morale and specifically to the recent incident with the deputy director of projects. The director's encounter with the deputy director was the latest in a series of frustrating experiences that he has faced since joining CDO the previous year. The director needs to decide whether to resign from CDO or to continue trying to improve the situation.

⊠ The Reading

Navigating Through Leadership Transitions: Making It Past the Twists and Turns

Adaptability is a must-have for a leader. At different points and for different reasons, he or she must change behavior to succeed. This author shares the advice she's given to business leaders.

The Scarborough YMCA: Getting Back on Track

Ken Mark and Gerard Seijts

⊠ Introduction

"I've been at the Scarborough YMCA since the early 1990s," stated Tammy MacDonald, the newly-appointed general manager. On February 12, 2003, MacDonald was discussing her plan of action at the Scarborough YMCA with the YMCA senior leadership team of the Greater Toronto Area. The Scarborough YMCA had been a perennial underperformer from a membership, member satisfaction and financial perspective, and MacDonald vowed to turn the facility around. She explained:

I've volunteered my time, and I've worked in several different roles. During this time, we've seen four different general managers lead the facility through difficult times. I believe my team and I can find a way to close the performance gap in the next two years.

When the meeting was over, MacDonald drove back to Scarborough, Ontario. She was excited by the potential to have a lasting impact on the facility; however, there were several challenges that she needed to address.

   Version: (A) 2010-06-16

Firstly, despite the fact that four general managers had given their best effort in Scarborough, the facility continued to lag behind the average YMCA in the Greater Toronto Area. MacDonald wondered whether the facility had the potential to be competitive on every level with the other YMCAs in Toronto. She sensed that some people in the organization had adopted a complacent mindset: some felt that Scarborough should be judged on a more lenient scale, given that the centre was located in what some would consider a "difficult" neighbourhood. People were not used to setting challenging goals, partly because holding people accountable for their individual performance was not part of the culture at the Scarborough YMCA. People were therefore not used to success!

Secondly, MacDonald thought about the fact that she was an insider at Scarborough: now 31 years of age, she had practically grown up in the Scarborough YMCA. Many staff and volunteers remembered the days when MacDonald worked alongside them as a fellow volunteer when she was in university. Most recently, prior to her promotion to general manager, she had been in charge of membership sales and services. MacDonald had assumed other leadership responsibilities in the centre, including leading teams and taking on change initiatives; however, she sensed that it would be challenging to advocate change now that she was the formal leader. She explained:

> I've been part of the system for more than a decade now. I was in mid-manager roles at Scarborough—I actually played every single position on the Scarborough team; and then I took on a number of senior roles. This is the same system that I'm now tasked with changing. It's tough to sort of grow up within a staff team and then provide leadership to the team. I had to think

about whether the facilities manager, program managers, senior volunteers and the members would respect me in the new leadership role. Will the team support me? Will the team work with me? Do I have the skills and competencies to effectively change the current situation? Because if I was going to come in and just maintain the status quo I would not have been interested in leading Scarborough.

The YMCA

The Young Men's Christian Association was founded in 1844 and the first YMCA in North America got its start in Montreal, Quebec in 1851. The YMCA described its mission, which had not changed from its early days:

> This was the industrial era—a time when major changes in agriculture, manufacturing, production and transportation were taking place. This brought more regimented routines with fixed work shifts along with a clear divide between the hours spent working and those spent at leisure. The YMCA supported people during their leisure time by focusing on their personal growth in spirit, mind and body. The YMCA was interested in putting Christian principles into action, giving people the opportunity to learn, improve themselves, choose a healthy lifestyle and support others. Today, the YMCA's mission still reflects those early day ideals. The YMCA grew up with Canada, changing and introducing programs needed by the communities it served; a practice that continues today.[1]

---

[1] http://www.ymca.ca/en/who-we-are/history.aspx, accessed June 15, 2010.

The YMCA's mission and values are shown in Exhibit 1.

The YMCA had pioneered many social services that were later considered essential to communities; for example, adult education, daycare for children and community outreach. Once the YMCA had demonstrated that it was meeting an unmet need in the community, other providers for these services emerged from the private sector and, in some cases, from government-run programs.

The YMCA priced its services to ensure that they were reasonable and still generated enough profit to be able to reinvest in the support of its overall mission. The YMCA usually conducted an annual funds campaign to help those who could not afford a YMCA experience. Unlike many not-for-profit and charitable organizations, YMCAs tended to operate with minimal grants from the government. To fund the construction of new facilities or launch large-scale programs, YMCAs embarked on fundraising campaigns.

In 2003, the YMCA was a worldwide movement of more than 45 million members from 124 national federations affiliated through the World Alliance of YMCAs.

The Scarborough YMCA

In 1989, the YMCA of the Greater Toronto Area embarked on an expansion phase, increasing the number of health facilities and recreation centres in its region from three to five. The two additional facilities would be located in Mississauga (located in the western part of Toronto) and Scarborough (located in the eastern part of Toronto). In the years before 1989, the Scarborough YMCA had been a summer day camp and offered community education classes.

When the YMCA opened, Scarborough was a rapidly-changing community due to the influx of ethnic minorities into the city. Both immigration and the higher cost of living in downtown Toronto increased the population in the Toronto suburbs. The relatively lower costs of housing in Scarborough attracted lower-income employees and their families. The Scarborough community was a mix of affluent households and lower-income families.

During the planning phase of the two new facilities, a challenge for the Greater Toronto Area YMCA was to find experienced staff who could lead a full-service facility. These staff members would have to build the facility's membership from the ground up, and recruit and maintain a cadre of volunteers. The YMCA leadership seemed to have resolved this issue when most staff positions for Scarborough were filled prior to opening.

Construction of the Scarborough facility had been delayed and cost more than expected: this was because the facility had been designed and built at the same time as Toronto's SkyDome, a massive entertainment complex in downtown Toronto. The SkyDome's construction employed thousands of contractors who would otherwise have been working on other local projects. YMCA management believed that due to the lower quality of subcontractors working on the Scarborough facility, the quality of workmanship was below acceptable standards, leading to problems such as leaking roofs, sub-par electrical wiring and poorly-insulated walls.

Despite these setbacks, the facility opened at 230 Town Centre Court in June 1989, at the corner of Ellesmere and McCowan in Scarborough. It was a full-service facility with 110,000 square feet, offering health, fitness and recreation activities. There were 23 full-time and part-time staff and a growing list of volunteers; however, as a result of cost overruns in the construction phase, Scarborough's opening budget was halved. This meant that promotional activities were cut back drastically, which affected the facility's initial membership drive.

Almost immediately after it was opened, Scarborough started to fall behind expectations for its membership drive. By the second month, the number of members was 30 per cent behind management's expectations; in addition, as compared to the other YMCAs in the Greater Toronto Area, it had 40 per cent more assisted members—individuals who received assistance equal to half of the regular membership fee.

The Scarborough YMCA's first general manager, James Sinclair, struggled throughout this challenging time period. Sinclair was able to work with his staff to put various programs in place, and a volunteer base was slowly being developed; however, due to his time commitments and personal preferences, he had neglected to emphasize the importance of increasing members at the health and fitness centres. In a typical YMCA facility, health and fitness membership revenues accounted for approximately 40 per cent of revenues from members. The gap between revenues and expenses worsened over time. Sinclair resigned as general manager less than a year after the facility opened.

Senior leaders at the Greater Toronto Area YMCA approached Laura Palmer-Korn, the general manager of the West End YMCA, and vice-president of the YMCA's Eastern Region, to step in as Scarborough's next general manager. In September 1990, Palmer-Korn relocated to Scarborough, taking on the role of general manager in addition to her region-wide YMCA responsibilities. She saw a facility that was in need of help from an operational perspective. In a facility designed for 10,000 members, Scarborough had only 3,000 members, approximately 50 per cent of its projected target. About half of the members were in the assisted membership category.

Palmer-Korn drew on her experience as a former manager for health, fitness and recreation to revitalize the department by setting new targets for staff. She scrutinized the membership drive efforts and replaced the incumbent membership director when she discovered that he continued to emphasize assisted memberships over regular, full-fee options.

The biggest challenge Palmer-Korn faced was in reaching out to the culturally-diverse neighbourhoods; for example, there had been no strategy to promote the YMCA to Asian, South Asian and African-populated neighbourhoods. One of Scarborough's main priorities was to make sure that the membership reflected the demographics of the local community.

Over the next seven years, Palmer-Korn divided her time between her regional duties (e.g. overseeing the licensed child care centres in the area, employment services or camping) and being the general manager at Scarborough. Her responsibilities meant that she was travelling at least 50 per cent of the time, thus it was only natural that the execution of ideas suffered, and that details fell through the cracks. An insider to the Scarborough YMCA opined:

> To have a leader that holds additional responsibilities outside of the centre draws their focus and attention away from that centre. When the centre wasn't meeting its targets—or the hopes and dreams that we had for the Scarborough community—that person wasn't given the opportunity to focus the energy and attention that it needed at that time. Frankly, even if the centre was doing well, it is a significant role for a person to play.

By 1997, Palmer-Korn and her staff had boosted membership to the 8,000 range, though about 5,000 members continued to be on the assisted membership level.

Palmer-Korn was promoted to senior vice president of National Initiatives at YMCA Canada. Scarborough saw its third general manager, Janet Johnson, hired at the end of 1997. Johnson came to the position with 25 years of experience at the YMCA.

When Johnson reviewed the state of affairs at Scarborough, she set her sights on improving productivity at the facility. Her review had consisted of meeting with each of the 20 full-time staff members, talking to volunteers and members and analyzing participation reports for each of Scarborough's programs. Johnson scheduled regular meetings with staff to review their goals and objectives. She held staff members accountable for the programs they were running; for example, the program director was expected to be present during peak hours such as evenings and Saturdays—this was the only way, Johnson explained, that leaders at Scarborough could see how their departments were being run.

Johnson set priorities for three, six and nine months out. In addition to the formal, scheduled meetings that she set, Johnson made sure to walk around the facility as much as possible, greeting staff, volunteers and members, and demonstrating her commitment to change at the facility. As was the case with her predecessor, Johnson had to juggle multiple responsibilities: she was in charge of Regional Programs, Childcare and Employment for the Durham Region. Johnson travelled extensively to fulfill those duties.

In 1999, Johnson was picked to become the general manager of the Mississauga YMCA. An external hire, Sarah Biel, was then selected to lead Scarborough. Biel had been vice-president at a provincial government department: she had no prior YMCA experience. A senior executive recalled:

> I think that the thinking at that time was that we had had existing general managers that had floated from one centre to the other, come in to Scarborough to see if they can affect change, and some were having some success, some incremental, some great success for a short period of time, and then things would slip back. I think the perception at that time was that maybe we needed somebody with an outside perspective—somebody with outside experiences that would think outside of the YMCA box that we tend to think in.

Biel was very organized and had high attention to detail. She focused on putting in place reporting and operating systems that were similar to her previous role in government; for example, there would be a process in place to approve increases to budgets or to make changes to a particular program. If a department did not spend its budget for the year, that department's budget would be trimmed for the following year.

Biel saw an organization that was in need of discipline; however, her staff saw the situation from a different perspective. The YMCA had always managed two bottom line priorities at its facilities: mission and margin. Biel had a hard time managing those two priorities when decisions had to be made. Furthermore, her staff found the adherence to process stifling. Morale dropped at Scarborough.

Biel was removed as general manager of Scarborough in 2003, and a replacement was sought. After a search process, the committee hired Tammy MacDonald. MacDonald had been the director of Memberships at Scarborough. When she was hired, Scarborough had 23 full-time staff and over 200 part-time staff and volunteers serving approximately 7,300 members.

A leadership change at the regional level preceded a shift in how the job of general manager was structured. A new layer of management was added to take over the general managers' regional responsibilities. From 2003, general managers would be allowed to devote all of their time on their own facility. Since there had been quite a few changes in leadership at Scarborough, there was a morale issue—people were quite concerned with whom the new general manager would be and what changes he or she would bring to the centre.

Tammy MacDonald

MacDonald started volunteering with Scarborough while she was a student at York University. A Scarborough native, she taught fitness classes and worked as a fundraiser. She had seen how Scarborough had developed over the years. MacDonald recalled:

> As I was from Scarborough, I was familiar with the challenges facing the community and the facility. But the truth was a little more balanced than the news reports would have one believe. Scarborough was not unlike any other small city: there are rich areas and there are parts which are struggling.

> Remember that Scarborough developed into a multi-ethnic community, so you'd have teenagers from a wide variety of backgrounds hanging out around the YMCA. Teenagers are naturally very

energetic and, if they have no other place to go, they'll hang out in the corridors and on the stairs.

Some members, especially those who were older or parents with young children, were extra cautious around these teens. But I knew that most of them were good kids.

As director of Memberships, MacDonald had been focused on tweaking the mix of memberships at Scarborough. She explained:

While young people comprised between 15 per cent and 20 per cent of the community, they made up 40 per cent of the membership at Scarborough. I set out to change this, to attract families and to broaden the mix of members to reflect the community as a whole; for example, the was a need for a family change room—members had been asking us that for the past six years, as the community was becoming a family community. The revenue that we are bringing in from children and youth is less than half of what we would for an adult.

We were fighting against media perceptions of Scarborough being a "bad community"—the fact that we were located close to the teenager hangouts. When prospective new members—a single adult or an adult with children wanting to use the facility as a family—walked into our facility for the first time, their first impression was not always positive. They'd see groups of loud teenagers walking around and being rowdy.

This was because we had open enrollment programs for activities such as basketball and other team sports. When these programs ended, teenagers would spill out into the lobby and sit around the stairs.

There wouldn't be any real issue—only the odd random theft once a month.

But this would be similar to the situation in any other YMCA. To make our members feel safer, Sarah Biel, the former general manager, had hired security staff to sit in the lobby at night. But some believed that the mere presence of security staff was not the right message to send to our membership.

She also observed:

YMCA research suggested that potential members—especially more affluent individuals—choose to join private fitness clubs such as Good Life or Extreme Fitness over the facilities at Scarborough because there was a perception that singles adults didn't belong at the YMCA. Staff and volunteers often felt intimidated by the presence of the teenagers. Staff had not been consistently greeting members or going out of their way to be helpful. There were no formal training programs in place to support a service culture.

For many years, the YMCA had been the only large fitness and recreation facility in town; however, starting in 1997 and 1998, the centre was beginning to see more competition. Members in the community thus had a choice of which club or facility to join. People could choose to go to another club and be offered the same programs. Prospective members would be going out and looking at options, and they would go to a centre and see brand new—and clean—facilities and new equipment.

When members were surveyed on the state of Scarborough, the scores suggested that Scarborough lagged far behind other YMCAs in the country. The results were unambiguous: members reported that they were experiencing poor quality of service (see Exhibit 2).

From a financial perspective, Scarborough had suffered operating deficits—between $500,000 and $750,000 per year—since its opening. The facility generally took in $3.7 million to

$3.9 million in revenue per year. The YMCA was a not-for-profit institution, but the healthier the centre was financially, the more programs it could offer to the community and the more members it could invite to participate.

Scarborough also faced the challenge of deteriorating infrastructure and ageing equipment. There had been little investment into the upkeep of the facility since it was built 13 years previously. Year after year had passed and very little preventative maintenance had taken place. Members were starting to see the wear and tear that the centre was experiencing. Its health and fitness equipment was circa 1990, therefore making it difficult for the facility to compete with private health and fitness clubs: the purchase of new equipment was challenging because Scarborough was running a deficit.

In addition to ageing equipment, Scarborough lacked a formal schedule of fitness programs, a key feature that would be appealing to busy individuals looking to fit exercise time into their daily schedule. Moving from open enrollment to a schedule of programs would require staff to become more organized in their scheduling and more creative in their planning. MacDonald observed:

> We were allowed to be complacent—so therefore we did not necessarily need to have the latest and greatest equipment or programs. There wasn't a real expectation for Scarborough to grow in terms of its membership or to turn around its fiscal situation. Scarborough was always perceived as the poor community, and therefore the poor YMCA. The other YMCAs would contribute to support Scarborough. It was kind of like, "We'll just leave it alone" kind of thing. We had accepted the reputation of being the poor YMCA! I stepped into the role of general manager and wanted to turn things around. I really wanted the Scarborough community, as well as the Scarborough YMCA, to have a better reputation. At that time it

had a reputation for not-so-friendly staff, a youth hangout and not serving the community well, as the focus was predominantly on youth and the young adults. My own personal goal was to turn Scarborough around in two years. There were low expectations for Scarborough—and thus I knew that the goal was a challenging one.

MacDonald Looks Ahead

MacDonald stated:

> Scarborough has great potential to contribute to the association. If some changes are put in place, if membership rises, I can see a point in time when Scarborough starts to contribute margin—in addition to mission—to the association.

When the position for general manager came up, MacDonald had been eager to be considered for the position. It was a step up in terms of responsibilities: a chance for her to demonstrate leadership. She said to herself: "I could really make a change here, and I want to. Scarborough is my home, and I grew up at (the) Scarborough (YMCA), and I really want to have impact in that community and I think I can do this."

She had also met with Steve Boone, the vice-president of Membership, YMCA of the Greater Toronto Area. Boone and MacDonald had a candid discussion in which she told him that she was willing to take on the role of general manager, but that she wanted the autonomy to make changes in organizational staffing and reporting structures. She explained:

> This was important to me because we had never done that since the building opened. So to be able to get his commitment that yes, you can take this on, and yes, you'll have the autonomy to do what you think you'll need to do to effectively make change was important to me. It was evident that some positions were

staffed with the wrong people—some people didn't really have the skills to be in the position they were in; for example, they did not always understand that financial health and fiscal responsibility was part of their role—they did not understand the budget process. Reporting relationships also contributed to ambiguities around ownership and responsibilities for results.

Early in the selection process, she recalled reading the first paragraph of a report on Scarborough:

Scarborough's lower than average income, age and educational status, coupled with its higher than average family size and unemployment rates

make for a unique and satisfying challenge for the leadership team to provide strong hands-on leadership.

"It was the opportunity to make a difference that attracted me to this role," MacDonald explained. "How I start and what I choose to do in my first few weeks will be of great importance." She reached the parking lot at Town Centre. Locking her car, she walked to Scarborough's front entrance, thinking about her plan for the next few months. She wondered what her priorities should be, and what goals she should set for herself. How aggressive should her targets be for turning around the Scarborough YMCA? She was cognizant of the fact that her responsibility was to make sure her colleagues at Scarborough stayed motivated to achieve success, and stayed motivated for the reason that they joined the organization.

Exhibit 1	Mission and Values

YMCA

A Healthy Choice
A Holistic Approach
A Welcoming Place
A Global Perspective
A Leading Charity

Mission

The YMCA is a charitable association dedicated to
the development of people in spirit, mind and body as well as
the improvement of local, national and international
communities.

Core Values

Caring
Honesty
Respect

SOURCE: Company files.

| **Exhibit 2** | Scarborough YMCA Member Survey |

	1999	2000	2002
Overall satisfaction	77	76	71
Value for fee	74	74	69
% certain to renew	44%	50%	43%
Convenience	D	D	D
Cleanliness	C	D	D
Maintenance	C	D	D
Safety	C	C	D
Friendly & welcoming	D	D	D
Emphasizing YMCA core values	B	B	C

Members were asked to rate each facility on a variety of metrics on a scale of 1 to 100, with 100 being extremely satisfied.

The letter grades for other areas have been calculated on a different basis. In each case, comparisons have been made between a specific centre's results and:

- The NATIONAL AVERAGE on the particular measure, and
- The BEST SCORE achieved by any Y in this year's survey

Scores have been translated into grades as follows:

GRADE	SCORE
A+	Within one point of BEST SCORE
A	In between A + and B
B	Plus/minus two points of NATIONAL AVERAGE
C	Three to five points below NATIONAL AVERAGE
D	Six or more points below NATIONAL AVERAGE

SOURCE: Company files.

Consultancy Development Organization

Unnat Kohli and W. Glenn Rowe

It was just after 3 p.m. on Friday, January 4, 2008. Rohit Sharma, director of Consultancy Development Organization, stormed into the office of the deputy director of projects, Mukesh Kumar:

> One of our organization's prestigious members, Krish Industrial Consulting Limited, has complained that it received the information on the Mahanadi Electrical Company proposal from us after the last date for submission. As a result, it has lost the opportunity to participate. Why was it delayed?

Kumar replied:

> It takes time to gather information. We engaged New Infotech Limited to collect the information. They took their time to send the information. We have to follow government rules to get it printed in our newsletter, *Business Opportunities*, and then it is mailed to all members. There are procedures. What can I do if there is a delay? I have to follow these procedures.

"Do we have any plan to reduce the time lag so we can get the information to our members in time for them to use it?" asked Sharma.

"No. We work as the government tells us from time to time," replied Kumar.

Sharma could not believe what he had just heard. This was not the first time that he had felt let down by his employees. He left the room feeling embarrassed and vowing to himself that this latest incident would be the last.

Consultancy Development Organization

In January 1990, Consultancy Development Organization (CDO) was set up by the Indian government in conjunction with the Indian consultancy industry as a not-for-profit body to help develop the Indian consultancy profession. CDO acted as a facilitator by providing information on consulting opportunities, a database on consultants and a platform for policy suggestions and networking. Among its main activities, CDO organized annual conferences and training programs and published a fortnightly publication on business opportunities, which listed CDO's expected consulting assignments.

CDO was based in Chennai (see Exhibit 1) and its membership included 200 individual consultants and 40 consultancy companies. It was headed by a full-time director, Rohit Sharma, who was supported by eight professionals and 20 support staff (see Exhibit 2). The Governing Council (the board) of CDO comprised 20 members, of which two-thirds (14 members) were elected by the general membership and the remaining members were nominated by the government. CDO's chairman was appointed directly by the government for a fixed two-year term. Approximately three-quarters of CDO's annual expenses were met through government grants.

Rohit Sharma

Rohit Sharma joined CDO in October 2007, as a full-time director. He had an MBA from the Indian Institute of Management (IIM) in Ahmedabad, India's premier business school.

Version: (A) 2008-04-18

Prior to joining CDO, Sharma had worked for 20 years in various positions in the industry, consulting both in India and abroad. Sharma had a reputation for being a hard task master and a dynamic, hard-working person with a vision.

Sharma had been appointed to the post of director by the Ministry of Industrial Promotion, which was the nodal government ministry in charge of CDO. Prior to Sharma's appointment, the Ministry of Industrial Promotion had used the CDO director position as a parking place for unwanted government officials, a practice that had led to three directors joining and leaving CDO in the last three years. Nevertheless, Sharma accepted the challenge of leading CDO and turning it into a leading player.

Mukesh Kumar

Mukesh Kumar received an engineering degree from Delhi University. After graduation, he worked as a junior engineer in a government organization. He joined CDO in 1992, as an assistant manager, and had progressed through the ranks to become one of four deputy directors who reported to the director. Kumar was hard working and knowledgeable but lacked ambition and drive. He was currently the deputy director of projects at CDO, the second-most prestigious profile in CDO after the director.

Naresh Chadha

Naresh Chadha, a commerce graduate, had been employed at CDO since its inception in 1990. He was politically well connected and regarded as a hands-on employee. He had worked in various positions in CDO, ranging from administration to marketing, and was currently deputy director of support services. His work included organizing annual conferences and conventions. He reported to the director.

Dheeraj Ahuja and Amit Kachru

Dheeraj Ahuja and Amit Kachru were the other two deputy directors at CDO who reported to Rohit Sharma. They were responsible for human resources and finance, respectively. Prior to joining CDO the previous year, both Ahuja and Kachru had spent their entire careers serving the Indian government in various roles.

Ujwal Nagdeote

Ujwal Nagdeote was the non-executive chairman of CDO, appointed by the government. He was a politically well-connected, knowledgeable and respected figure in the industry. Nagdeote served on the board of a dozen leading Indian companies and played a dormant role in the affairs of CDO.

Organization Culture

CDO had four deputy directors and four assistant directors. The deputy directors reported to the director, and the assistant directors reported to the deputy directors (see Exhibit 2). The director, deputy directors and assistant directors comprised the officer category, and the 20 support staff (personal assistants, secretaries, clerks and peons[1]) comprised the Class II category. Each officer had at least one personal assistant or secretary and one peon. All clerks worked in the administration wing of CDO, where all files were located.

In 1990, when CDO was established, the staff was recruited according to the structure prevalent in government organizations. In the early 1990s, clerks were needed for typing and administrative tasks, and the peons were required to run office errands, such as delivering files, dispatching letters, serving water, and preparing

---

[1]Peons were persons of menial position, such as messengers and servants.

tea and coffee for the officers. However, by 2008, computers were available to all the officers, and coffee and tea machines were common in the office. The clerks and peons did not have enough work; however, they were very difficult to fire, because they had job security, in accordance with the government system.

At all levels of the organization, the salaries were fixed and equal with no variable pay or rewards system. As a result, employees had no incentive to perform. Until Sharma's appointment, no outside appointments had been made for the past 10 years. The culture was not very professional, and government organizations constantly interfered, wanting to use the CDO facilities (such as CDO's office car) and staff for their own purposes. As a result, morale within CDO was poor.

⬡ Rohit Sharma's First Week in Office

When Sharma joined CDO in October 2007, he was greeted by Naresh Chadha and Mukesh Kumar, two of his four direct reports. That week, the attendance was abysmally low. Sharma learned that most of the staff were absent because it was Diwali[2] season. Even though Diwali was five weeks away, some of the employees had taken time off to be with their families and friends. They had scant regard for Sharma, which was reinforced through their absence. Sharma was aghast to see that no one on the administration staff had bothered to fill the water coolers with fresh water or to clear the cupboards in his office.

⬡ National Convention

CDO was organizing the National Convention scheduled for January 15, 2008. For this annual conference, eminent speakers had been invited to address consulting issues and discuss their experiences with the participants, generally the member organizations and individuals and executives from the corporate sector.

On January 4, 2008, Sharma went to the office of Naresh Chadha, the deputy director in charge of the National Convention to inquire about the conference's progress, particularly the number of speakers that had confirmed and the number of participants that had registered.

"We sent letters to the members. Their responses continue until the last date. We have not set any targets. Do not worry. We will have good numbers," replied Chadha, casually sipping his tea and eating pakoras.[3]

Sharma returned to his own office an unhappy person. He was feeling uneasy: there was not much response to show and most activities had been delayed. The annual conference was not expected to be successful. The attitude of most employees was callous and inept. The fiscal year-end on March 31, and he was concerned that CDO's performance would be seen as much below average.

⬡ International Consultancy Congress

International Consultancy Congress was scheduled to be held in London, England, from February 3 to 6, 2008. Sharma thought it would be a good opportunity to interact and network with consultancy organizations in other countries. He considered taking one of his officers with him to boost morale.

According to government rules, any foreign visit had to be approved by the Ministry of Industrial Promotion. Thus, Sharma had sent the proposal for his own participation and that of Naresh Chadha on December 1, 2007.

---

[2]Diwali, the festival of lights, is an important festival celebrated throughout India.

[3]Pakoras are a deep-fried South Asian fritter made by dipping pieces of vegetable in a chickpea flour batter. They are generally eaten as a snack.

After several follow-up attempts, he was informed on January 3, 2008 that the proposal had not been accepted. This rejection had a further demoralizing effect on employees who now thought that Sharma, despite all his talk, was not able to do much.

⊠ Sharma's First Three Months

Sharma realized quickly that employee morale at CDO was very low and was compounded by the absence of career development and low remuneration. The company had no clear strategy or direction. The government grants took care of the salaries of staff and the administrative expenses. Consequently, employees had no motivation to perform or to increase the business.

"How are we expected to facilitate our members?" asked Sharma.

"It is not our concern. In any case, the members pay very little and our salaries are paid by the government. You should not worry so much. Whether you undertake the same or more activities, you will be paid the same salary," advised Kumar.

Sharma faced the choice of continuing on the path of his predecessors (i.e. doing nothing new and having an easy time) or working towards a turnaround strategy for the organization and setting it on a growth path.

⊠ The December 28, 2007 Meeting

Sharma had called a meeting of all officers and staff on Friday, December 28, at 9 a.m. He asked them for ideas for the growth of CDO. Divergent views were expressed:

CDO has been in existence for 18 years and has been doing well. It can continue to function as such.

The government grant received annually is sufficient to pay for the salaries and some activities only.

We are a government controlled organization. We undertake activities as directed by the controlling Ministry of Industrial Promotion.

There is no incentive for extra effort or growth. Following the government pay scales, we get the same salary whether we do the same activities or take up more.

Members of CDO pay very small subscription [membership fee]. They are not interested in any major initiatives, which may lead to their paying more subscription.

Sharma disagreed. He observed that he had joined the organization because he believed it had great potential. Consultancy was fast growing, and India had an edge in the global consultancy field because of a large professionally skilled pool of workers and the relatively low cost of consultants. CDO could greatly help in developing the consultancy profession in the country. He outlined his five-year vision:

- CDO should be fully self-supporting and not dependent on government grants. For this purpose, CDO must increase its income from its own activities by at least five times.
- CDO should function on a non-government pattern and the employees need to be accountable for results.
- CDO should strive for a 10-fold increase in memberships, both individual and corporate. The members must benefit from CDO's activities. They must receive information about a larger number of business opportunities within the country and abroad, online, without delay.
- CDO should help consultants in consultancy exports, through studies, data

collection and providing opportunities for networking.

- CDO should function as facilitator by using its government links for policy intervention to promote the profession.
- CDO should also take up consultancy assignments that can be outsourced to its members, to generate income and to help employ its members.
- Support staff need to be given work responsibility after being trained in new skills that can be useful for the organization.
- Employee morale needs to improve, performance needs to be linked to incentives and promotions need to be introduced.

Some of the executives were enthusiastic but only if these changes could lead to better prospects for themselves. Others expressed apprehension, particularly regarding the operational freedom they would have from the controlling ministry. The Governing Council also had to be consulted for endorsement.

Mahanadi Electrical Proposal Incident

Mahanadi Electrical Company (MEC) was an electricity distribution utility in the eastern state of Orissa (see Exhibit 1), which supplied electricity to about one-fourth of the state. The distribution system was very old, and breakdowns were frequent, as were the failure of transformers and interruptions to the electrical supply. Consumers were unhappy, and the State Electricity Regulation Commission had asked MEC to revamp the distribution system. Accordingly, the company had invited bids for consultancy work, which involved the preparation of a feasibility report for the revamping of the distribution system. This major assignment worth about US$2.5 million, and few consultancy companies had the necessary competency in this field.

Krish Industrial Consulting Limited (KICL), a founding member of CDO and one of the competing companies bidding on the MEC project, was confident of being awarded the assignment and was waiting to receive the information needed to bid for the job. On behalf of CDO, New Infotech Limited (to whom this work was outsourced) was collecting information regarding potential consultancy assignments from tender notices published in newspapers, websites and other sources. This information was then passed to CDO, which published it in a fortnightly newsletter that was mailed to all of its members. The last date for receipt of bids by MEC was December 15, 2007, but KICL received the CDO newsletter with the information on this assignment on January 1, 2008. The CEO of KICL had expressed his disappointment to Sharma regarding the delay.

January 4, 2008 Incident

On January 4, Sharma stormed into the office of Kumar to inquire about the MEC proposal and why it had been delayed. Kumar had been non-apologetic and unfazed that KICL lost the opportunity to participate. He had justified the situation by suggesting he had been following government guidelines.

Sharma could not believe Kumar's lackadaisical attitude. KICL was an important member of CDO, yet Kumar seemed unperturbed by KICL's loss of business because of CDO's delay and ineptness. Kumar's attitude was a clear reflection of the state of affairs in the organization. Sharma left the room very frustrated. Things needed to improve or CDO would lose its elite status as the nodal agency for consultancy in India, and his career would be at stake.

Sharma wondered whether he had made a mistake by accepting the director's position and whether he could do anything to improve the situation at CDO.

Exhibit 1 Map of India

SOURCE: Office of the Registrar General & Census Commissioner, India, "India 2001: State Map." Retrieved from http://www.censusindia.gov.in/maps/State_Maps/maps.htm, accessed April 12, 2008.

Exhibit 2	Organization Chart of Consultancy Development Organization

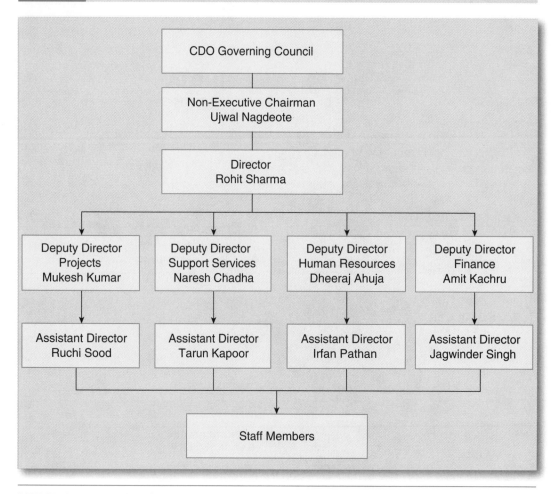

SOURCE: CDO Organization Chart.

Navigating Through Leadership Transitions: Making It Past the Twists and Turns

Christine M. Riordan

Agility and adaptability are mandatory these days, as leaders prepare, manage, and sometimes reinvent themselves in order to navigate the twists, turns, and transitions they must make. Otherwise, making the wrong move could eventually scuttle a once-promising leadership career.

Reprint# 9B08TC04

*All things change; nothing abides. Into
the same river, one cannot step twice.*

—Heraclitus

Many points in our jobs and careers require, even demand, changes in our leadership behaviors, competencies, attitudes, and thinking. How well we navigate these potentially treacherous junctures often determines our ultimate success—or failure—as leaders.

Whether change involves the strategic direction of the corporation, a merger, acquisition or reorganization, the development of a new product line or a shift in the competitive market place, or new bosses or co-workers, leaders must constantly monitor their environment and adjust their leadership skills to match the new demands. This requirement for constant personal modification can be daunting for anyone not agile enough to adapt.

It is imperative that leaders determine how they need to adjust their leadership behaviors and style to navigate the changes surrounding them. This task sounds easy, but it is often very difficult. This article describes tactics leaders can use to reach this goal.

What Happens When Times Change

Sometimes, leaders do not recognize environmental changes or, perhaps more importantly, the need for them to behave differently because of these changes. Leaders will often cling to the past or continue "business as usual." They think that past behaviors that have proven successful will again carry them into the future. While they are correct in many respects, one set and style of behaviors rarely moves a person seamlessly throughout his or her leadership career. At each transition, a leader must be prepared to adopt new and different behaviors to succeed. This ability (or failure) to recognize, navigate, and make personal changes influences the effectiveness of leaders over time.

For example, a woman I will call Barbara, a vice president of operations for a major insurance company, found herself in unfamiliar waters when the business went through a major review process. One result was a restructuring that established a new strategy and accompanying performance goals. Barbara retained her position but had a new boss, new strategic objectives, new performance demands, and new teammates. Her boss now expected Barbara to focus most of her time and energy on being accountable and delivering results.

Over time, however, she had difficulty changing her behavior, attitudes, and thinking to match the new strategy and goals. She was unaccustomed to being personally accountable and the high demands from her new boss. Her supervisor provided feedback during the transition, but after a year of trying to help Barbara, he decided she was not delivering. Further, Barbara did not seem able or willing to make the personal leadership transformations needed to support the new strategic direction and environment, nor was she able to help her subordinates make the transition. While the company rarely fired anyone, Barbara's supervisor eventually let her go. She had worked for the company for 27 years.

Transitions: Potentially Turbulent Waters

If they are to demonstrate and retain their value, leaders must steer their organizations through various transitions. Failure to handle such transitions adequately can result in career disaster. Successful navigation, on the other hand, results in vital lessons learned, greater flexibility and adaptability, and stronger leadership skills. With each transition, leaders must adapt their skills to face the new set of challenges.

Ron Parker, executive vice president of Human Resources at PepsiCo, notes that successful leaders must be "learning agile." "You have to be agile in your approach to complex issues," he says. Parker indicates that corporations need people who can change with the times. "You cannot stay in a steady state in a competitive global environment. That which is not broken today should be broken tomorrow. We look at the entire value chain and are constantly asking ourselves what needs to change." Leaders need to be asking themselves the same questions: How and what do I need to change to keep up with the future and to be of value to this organization?

Leaders commonly face several major types of transitions in their careers. Each of these requires an adjustment in behaviors, capabilities, attitudes, and thinking. Some of these major transitional challenges are described below.

Change in Job/Role. The most common transition for which a leader will need to change is taking on a new role or job. Charan, Drotter, and Noel (May/June 2001, *Ivey Business Journal*) note six passages an individual makes while progressing in leadership roles through an enterprise: from managing self to managing others; to managing other managers; to functional management; to business leadership; to group leadership; and to enterprise leadership.

At each passage, the person must acquire new skills and competencies to make major transitions. The skills that made a leader successful in a previous role are typically not sufficient for the new role.

This need to adapt also comes about in lateral moves, changes in jobs that may occur due to restructuring, reorganizations, or mergers and acquisitions. Additionally, as the leader grows and develops in his/her job, he or she must look for new ways to improve performance and value within that role.

For example, Jason worked in state government as the manager of a department. He was a high achiever and extremely successful in the technical aspects of his job. He developed quite a reputation for his expertise and was proud of it. Jason received a promotion to a management position, in part because of this expertise.

After becoming a manager, Jason networked only with people at his level of seniority and skill. He had a hierarchical mentality but proved ineffective at networking with those above him and neglected to network with those below him. He was also into strictly maintaining the status quo in his unit, even though the entire division was undergoing dramatic changes. He was quick to dismiss new and innovative ideas.

This attitude frustrated many of his subordinates, who saw other work units making dramatic improvements in processes and outcomes. As part of the performance appraisal process, Jason's subordinates completed feedback evaluations on his performance. Each year they became more devastating. It was clear his leadership style was weighing down both him and his work unit. Yet, rather than following the feedback and trying to change, he attributed the negative results to external factors. He blamed his failure on things other than his own behavior. For example, he thought, since the evaluations were given to subordinates right after they had received their raise information, they were angry about their wages and not at Jason.

As the feedback became increasingly worse, Jason stopped socializing and talking casually with his subordinates. He never went to lunch or stopped by subordinates' offices to chat. He became negative and abrasive, and seemed to embody and intensify bad management practices. He became the butt of jokes and gossip among his peers and subordinates. No one took him seriously anymore. Finally, after receiving yet another crushing evaluation from his subordinates, he simply resigned. While Jason had been an excellent individual performer, he had never been able to become a manager of others.

Change in People. Sometimes the people we work with change jobs. Working with different bosses, peers, and subordinates is an important transition and one in which leaders must ride the waves. Learning to interact productively with new people who have diverse ideas, styles, and preferences is a difficult challenge. While learning such lessons seems basic, many leaders fail to navigate people changes—particularly when they get a new boss.

For example, Bob was leading a new product development group in a professional services firm. In one year, his direct boss changed along with the leader one level above. Bob's old boss was very hands off in his leadership style, not asking for much information about the performance of the unit. He also did not spend any time helping Bob succeed.

When the new leadership arrived, it recognized that Bob had been successful in implementing new product lines. However, it also believed that there was room for improvement in both the number of products developed and the way in which he introduced these inside the firm.

To start the unit down the path of improvement, Bob's new boss began asking him for strategic and execution plans for the development department. Rather than taking this request as an opportunity to demonstrate his understanding of how to reshape the development department, Bob felt threatened by these requests and thus resisted any requests for information. His behaviour became adversarial when dealing with any suggestions for change. He longed for the days when his old boss simply left him alone and he was not accountable.

Bob talked negatively about the changes occurring within the firm and about his bosses to others inside and outside of the firm. Bob's bosses and co-workers, of course, became aware of this unconstructive behavior. Bob consequently gained a reputation for being uncooperative, for not being a team player, and as being a person that others did not trust. Bob's new bosses started questioning whether he could run the development department effectively. Eventually, the bosses brought in someone new to run the department; the individual reduced Bob's job scope.

In another example, Tom was a senior vice president at a financial services firm that recently transferred him to a new region within the same corporation. He had two vice presidents reporting to him. Though Tom had been in this role in another region, this was the first time he worked with these particular vice presidents.

After a few months, Tom realized that he was having difficulty connecting and working with one of his vice presidents. Therefore, Tom elicited the advice of an executive coach who helped him understand that there were simple differences of style between Tom and his vice president. They also determined that the other vice president had a style very similar to Tom's, which made that relationship easier to navigate. Rather than trying to change the vice president

to suit his own style, Tom made some simple adjustments in his interactions. Today, his relationships with his two vice presidents are strong. Moreover, he continues to adjust his style slightly to relate to them each more effectively.

Change in the Marketplace. Markets change in many ways and leaders who are effective in transitions pay attention to these market changes. They understand the need to keep abreast of the business, industry, and marketplace trends. They do not take things for granted.

As the director of a major business line for a consumer products firm, Sara had seen her line grow for many years. However, the competitive environment changed, not only in her region but all over the country. She started to see a significant reduction in interest and sales. Rather than look at how the organization had designed or positioned the product relative to the competitive market and changing consumer interests, she poured more money into advertising and marketing.

Yet, sales continued to erode. She blamed the reduction in sales on national trends. Eventually, other leaders in the organization began to take control of the situation. Sarah lost significant amounts of autonomy, as senior leaders began telling her what to do and reduced her responsibilities. Other leaders in the firm restructured and repositioned the business line to respond to the changing consumer interests. Over time, sales began to increase again.

Change in Strategy/Products. Often in response to the competitive environment, firms will look at changing their strategy and/or their product mix. Leaders must adjust their organizational thinking and way of doing business when the enterprise shifts direction. Yet, many leaders have difficulty making this transition.

Leaders who successfully embrace this type of change become the enablers, or the people who help promote, accept, and make the change happen. The organization values these types of leaders because they ensure strategic growth.

On the other hand, it is difficult for the organization when leaders become "open resistors" to the change or actively work against the changes. They may engage in activities such as sabotaging change efforts, promoting to keep things the same, arguing openly against the changes in meetings, or creating coalitions to fight the change effort. They may also become "nay-sayers" or openly criticize the changes and those involved in it. Leaders who are not successfully transitioning may also become "passive resistors" or privately refuse to support the change, though they do no overtly resist the change. However, they also do not do anything to enable the change. Finally, some individuals may be unwary resistors or not be aware that they are resisting the change effort. They simply revert to what they know, which could be old processes, old priorities, and old strategies.

For example, Bill was a vice president of sales for a consumer services and products firm for an entire state. He had hundreds of sales people as well as 35 sales managers. The company decided to roll out a completely new product line as a way to grow business and buffer predicted declines in its traditional lines of business. While the new product line complemented the existing lines, it did represent a major strategic shift that required sales people to acquire a new knowledge base for the products and to learn how to cross sell the products. Additionally, it meant that Bill needed to keep up with sales results, the competition, and the marketplace in three different, but related, lines of business.

Bill had strong relationships with his sales people and managers. He just figured that he could keep doing things the same without making any major adjustments. Over time, sales in the old product lines started to drop while sales in the new product lines became limited. Bill could not figure out a way to turn things around. In short, he could not get out of the mindset of doing business in the same way. He rarely sought out information about the local marketplace, nor did he read industry or company literature that discussed market and strategy changes. Over time and after much coaching, the senior leaders of the firm moved Bill into a less demanding position. He just could not transition into being a strategic leader who focused on new ways of operating.

How Transitions Impact a Leader's Performance

As these and other transition points come up during a leader's tenure, he or she needs to be prepared to advance through them. Perhaps the most common mistake is that the leader does not recognize the critical juncture in the leadership river and, therefore, fails to respond or make the correct turns. Over time, this failure to transition affects the performance of the leader. In a similar situation, the leader may recognize the juncture, but does not know how to respond and change. Performance also suffers. As depicted in the figure below, we can generally categorize a leader's ability to navigate transition points on three levels:

(1) Staying ahead—these leaders have the ability to recognize transition points; this type of leader generally navigates all changes and transition points with ease while maintaining high levels of performance.

(2) Keeping up—these leaders have the ability to recognize the transition points; performance may dip for a slight period as the leader adjusts to the new situation, but the leader is able to respond and bring performance back to peak levels—until the next transition point; over time however, the leader's overall performance is high, leading to success in the role.

(3) Falling behind—these leaders may or may not recognize the transition points; they generally do not know how to respond or choose to not respond; over time, their leadership performance suffers; these leaders are the ones who commonly lose their leadership roles or have their leadership roles reduced.

One should recognize that sometimes there is a fourth level of response. A leader may choose not to navigate a transition point. That is, the leader may decide that he or she does not want to make the transition. This situation could occur for a variety of reasons, including the leader's philosophical disagreement with the changes or her belief that the change will fail with the given resources. Ultimately, this type of leader often decides to move proactively into another situation within the firm or sometimes outside of the firm. As an example, we commonly see very successful founders of entrepreneurial ventures leave the organization they started because they do not want to become the type of leader needed to take the firm to the next level.

For example, Dan was a very successful senior executive with a major indemnity company in the northeast. Brought into the organization to help turn around the performance of the eastern region, Dan thrived in this role for several years. The company, however, decided to change strategy. Dan did not philosophically agree with the changes. Rather than staying with the organization, Dan decided to leave. He knew that he was not the right person to make the next set of changes and felt that he and the firm would be better off with someone else in the role.

Company Responses to Leadership Transitions

It is extremely expensive and disruptive for an organization to see leaders fail or to have leaders who are ill equipped for their positions. As a result, companies are beginning to recognize how critical it is to help their leaders make a transition through the more difficult situations. For example, Burlington Northern Santa Fe Railway offers an executive education class for

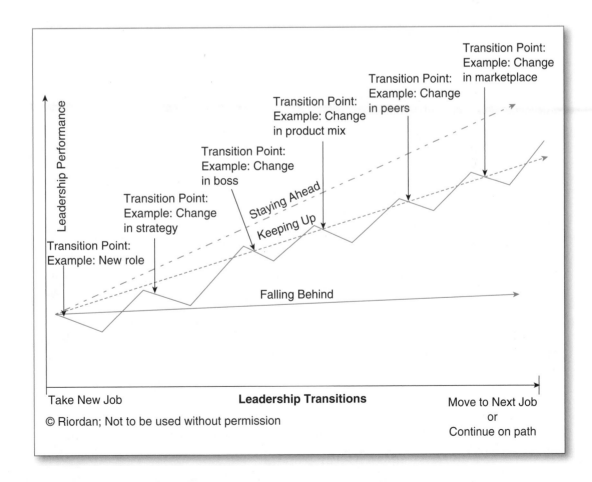

© Riordan; Not to be used without permission

new leaders. This class focuses exclusively on what changes the new leaders need to make in their new roles, how to handle these changes, and what challenges they may face.

In 2003, *The Economist* estimated that organizations were already spending more than $1 billion providing coaches for their employees; it projected that this expenditure would double in two years. This growth in the executive coaching industry is in part due to the increase in companies' recognition that leaders commonly need assistance in managing the transitions and that an external party may help the leaders gain the needed skills, abilities, and fresh perspective.

Individual Transition Skills Needed

While organizations may try to facilitate transitions, navigating transitions is a skill that leaders need to acquire if they do not already possess it.

Successful leaders focus on their ability to navigate changes in the environment and their ability to reinvent themselves to adapt to those changes. Generally, successful navigation and personal reinvention require three things: 1) a change in attitude and thinking; 2) a change in competencies and skills; and 3) a change in behaviors.

Changing one area is not usually sufficient to navigate transitions successfully. For example, Sandra was a successful corporate relations manager for a consumer products company. She had a successful performance results record, worked well with others, and prided herself on being open to developmental feedback. As Sandra moved up and the organization changed, it became obvious that she needed advanced leadership skills and competencies in strategic thinking and positioning, managing change, and project management. Sandra knew she needed to change, and was open to feedback. While her attitude was positive, she had a difficult time acquiring the advanced skills she needed. It took many different types of development activities and continuous feedback for Sandra to develop these skills. Eventually she succeeded, though

her performance suffered a bit while she learned to change her behaviors.

You can ask yourself several questions to determine if you will navigate transitions easily (see box 1 at the end of article). If you answer "No" to any of these questions, you can take several developmental actions to help reinvent yourself and navigate difficult transitions.

Specific Steps

Navigating transitions is not something you do only for the organization. It is something you do for yourself. As such, you need to take charge of developing the skills you need to periodically reinvent and realign yourself with environmental changes.

One key is to dedicate yourself to becoming a student of leadership throughout your career. Study effective leadership practices. Knowledge of what constitutes effective leadership at each stage of your career is fundamental. At each transition point, your perspective on leadership should change as you work to acquire advanced leadership skills and competencies. Acquiring such knowledge can save many errors, reduce learning time, and improve your leadership success.

A second key is to look in the mirror. Your leadership effectiveness begins with you. You need to answer important questions such as how does your leadership style need to change, what roles and responsibilities do others expect you to give them, what type of leader do you want to be, and what type of leader do you need to be at each transition point? Are you a steward for the organization or do you collude with the status quo? Do you need to change your attitude and thinking, your competencies, and/or your behaviors to navigate the transition?

A third key is being open to feedback and coaching—*really* open to feedback and coaching. You should understand that sometimes this feedback is unpleasant, challenges our egos, and simply stings a bit. However, getting one-on-one feedback and advice from a boss, executive coach, or mentor is invaluable. It is important to seek feedback and suggestions for leadership development throughout your career.

As you hit transition points, being open to feedback and coaching may help you adjust faster. Additionally, other people can serve as a sounding board for ideas for leadership development activities targeted towards your specific needs; help identify different types of activities, which will help you practice the skills; and provide valuable coaching or feedback based on observation and interaction with you. Finally, having someone who provides honest feedback can affirm the things that you do well and potentially prevent you from adopting attitudes, thinking and behaviors that may derail your career. A fourth key is recognizing that effective leadership takes lots of practice and reflection. As part of the transition, try doing things differently, but be reflective. If something goes well, reflect on why it went well. If something does not go well, ask why it did not and what can you do differently.

The fifth key is observing and learning from other successful leaders. Observe people who seem to flourish in their leadership roles. It is equally important, though, to learn from people who are not succeeding in their leadership roles. Some of the most powerful learning occurs by observing "what not to do" in a situation.

Finally, make sure that you understand the business, industry, and community in which you operate. Stay current about industry and company trends. Attend conferences and classes, listen to and participate in business conversations, or go back to school for an advanced degree if appropriate. You will only be able to identify transition points if you know what the competitive environment looks like and understand the challenges that the company may be facing.

Outstanding leaders recognize the need to modify their skills, attitudes, and behaviors frequently to smoothly maneuver through their careers and leadership challenges. They also recognize that while they may need assistance along the way, no one else can make the changes for them. They are the only ones who can successfully navigate their own leadership river.

Assessing Your Capability to Navigate Transitions

Evaluate your skill in each of the below competencies to assess your agility to adapt and navigate leadership transitions.

Adaptability and Openness to Change—the ability to respond to new demands and challenges and to maintain a constructive, positive outlook about change.

- Do new challenges excite you and are you willing to tackle them?
- When presented with a change in the organization, do you view it as an opportunity rather than a threat?
- Do you challenge status quo within the organization?

Self-awareness—the ability to recognize when you do not possess the skills/competencies needed to navigate the transition and the ability to recognize that you need to change competencies, behaviors, and/or attitude.

- Do you recognize when you need to gain some new capabilities or change behaviors and/ or attitude?

(Continued)

(Continued)

- Are you willing to learn or seek help when needed?
- Are you willing to admit that you have to change to succeed?
- Do you proactively work on expanding your capabilities/competencies?
- Do you commonly ask yourself, if I were to start this job all over again, what would I need to do differently?

Leadership Maturity—the felt responsibility to make the changes in competencies, behaviors, and attitude needed to support the direction of the organization and to be successful in the role.

- Do you feel that it is important to improve as a leader to help the organization succeed?
- Do you look for ways in which you can be better to help the organization achieve its goals?
- Do you recognize that a change in attitude can result in a change of behavior?
- Do you seek to understand why changes are needed?
- Are you an active steward of the organization and its goals?

Leadership Resilience—the ability to rebound from setbacks and/or changes.

- When things do not go well, do you work to make them better?
- When there is a setback, do you reflect on what happened and look for ways to improve?

Strategic Thinking—the ability to look ahead and behind to determine the best plan for improvement.

- Do you proactively look for ways to improve?
- Do you periodically question your own assumptions, ideas, and thinking?
- Are you able to define the issues or problems clearly to determine appropriate actions?
- Do you focus on the big picture *and* the details in planning how to change?
- Do you periodically conduct a reality test of yourself to see if you are on track?

Business Acumen—developing a deeper understanding of the business so that you understand how the business is changing and why and how you might need to change as a leader.

- Do you proactively seek to know more about the business so that you can help move it in the direction it needs to go?
- Do you pay attention to industry trends, market trends, and strategic shifts that are taking place?
- Do you apply these trends to how you might need to change as a leader?

5

The Situational Approach to Leadership

A leader has to be able to sense what's coming up ahead, to see opportunities that should be the target of action and to identify threats before they materialize. The view has to extend well into the future. Leaders who can only see what they have seen before, whose scope and vision is limited by their past experience, prove to be inadequate in a rapidly changing world. We expect leaders to have their feet on the ground, their eyes on the horizon, and their imaginations beyond it.

—Jeffrey Gandz[1]

Contrary to other theories of leadership that are descriptive, the situational approach to leadership is prescriptive. This leadership approach tells leaders what to do in different situations and what not to do in other situations. It is widely used in leadership development and training and has been refined and revised several times (Blanchard, Zigami, & Nelson, 1993).

The situational leadership theory has two underlying assumptions. First, as situations vary, so must a person's leadership. This means that leaders are able to adapt their styles to different situations. Second, leadership is made up of a directive component and a supportive component, and these two components have to be exercised appropriately based on the context. To assess the appropriate level of each component, it is critical that leaders evaluate their subordinates and determine their level of competence and commitment to a given task or job. Inherent in this latter assumption is that subordinates' levels of competence and commitment may change over time, requiring that leaders change their level of direction and personal support to match these changing needs in their employees. The situational leadership approach suggests that leaders who are more capable of assessing what their subordinates need and changing their own style will be more effective as leaders (DuBrin, 2010).

[1]Gandz, J. (2010, p. 17)

This approach to leadership suggests that understanding situational leadership is best accomplished by discussing the two underlying principles: leadership style and subordinates' level of development (Northouse, 2013).

Leadership Styles and Subordinate Developmental Level

As in Chapter 4, leadership style describes a leader's behavior when he or she tries to influence others. Thus, it includes directive or task behaviors and supportive or relationship behaviors. Examples of both types of behaviors are listed in Table 5.1.

These two groups of behaviors help subordinates to accomplish goals and to be positively encouraged in how they feel about their job, their coworkers, and themselves. Four styles based on being directive and supportive are suggested by the situational leadership approach: directing, coaching, supporting, and delegating. These styles are described, accompanied by brief descriptions of when and why they should be used based on the developmental level exhibited by subordinates with respect to their competencies for and their commitment to getting the job done.

Directing Leadership Style

This style is directive and nonsupportive. Leader communications are focused on getting the job done with little or no communication effort focused on supportive behaviors. The communication effort is one-way and emphasizes instructions that give subordinates direction about what to do and how to do it. This style is associated with close and careful supervision (Northouse, 2013).

Table 5.1 Directive and Supportive Behaviors for Situational Leadership

Directive behaviors aid in goal achievement	Some supportive behaviors are
• by giving directions • by establishing goals • by establishing methods of evaluation • by setting time lines • by defining roles • by showing how to achieve goals	• asking for input • problem solving • praising • sharing information regarding self • listening • job related
In addition, directive behaviors	Supportive behaviors help subordinates to
• clarify what is to be accomplished • clarify how it is to be accomplished • clarify who will accomplish it	• feel comfortable with the situation • feel comfortable with their coworkers • feel comfortable with themselves
Often through one-way communication	Often through two-way communication

SOURCE: Adapted from *Leadership: Theory and Practice*, Sixth Edition, by Peter Northouse. Copyright © 2013, SAGE Publications, Inc.

This style is most appropriate when subordinates are most committed but least competent in what to do and how to do it—when they have a low development level (D1); see the Situational Leadership II model in Northouse (2013). Because they are most committed, the level of leader support can be minimal, while the level of direction has to be high because subordinates are least competent. The reason for the lower level of competence is generally because subordinates are new to the job or task to be accomplished (DuBrin, 2010).

▨ Coaching Leadership Style

This style is highly directive and highly supportive. Communications from the leader to followers focus on getting the job done and on employees' emotional and social needs. Communication is two-way in that leaders communicate to subordinates and encourage input from subordinates. Leaders still decide on what needs to be accomplished and how it will be accomplished (Northouse, 2013).

This style is most appropriate when subordinates have some competence but a lower level of commitment. They are learning their job but losing some of their commitment to and motivation for the job—when they have a moderate development level (D2); see the Situational Leadership II model in Northouse (2013). In this situation, the leader still needs to be directive but also needs to be supportive (DuBrin, 2010).

▨ Supporting Leadership Style

This style is highly supportive but relatively low on direction. The leader focuses on supportive behaviors in his or her communications to subordinates to bring out the skills required to accomplish the task. Subordinates have control over day-to-day operations, but the leader is still available for problem solving if needed. These leaders give deserved recognition to subordinates in a timely manner and support subordinates socially when needed (Northouse, 2013).

This style is most appropriate when subordinates have the required job skills but lack the necessary commitment because they are uncertain whether they have the necessary skills—when they have a moderate developmental level (D3); see the Situational Leadership II model in Northouse (2013). Direction is not required in this situation, but a lot of encouragement is needed to support subordinates in using their well-developed skill sets (DuBrin, 2010).

▨ Delegating Leadership Style

The delegating style is best described as low direction and low support. In this approach, employees have more confidence and motivation when leaders are less directive and less supportive. Leaders agree with subordinates on the result but then back off and allow subordinates to be responsible for accomplishing the desired result. In essence, the leader gives the employees control and avoids any unnecessary social support (Northouse, 2013).

This approach is appropriate when subordinates are very skilled and highly committed—when they have a high developmental level (D4); see the Situational Leadership II model in Northouse (2013). In this situation, giving subordinates more control and less social support is best because of their seasoned skills and motivation to do their best for the organization. Being even a little directive or supportive may cause subordinates to work less skillfully and with less commitment as they sense a lack of trust on the part of their leaders (DuBrin, 2010).

✉ How Does the Situational Approach to Leadership Work?

The key to this approach is to understand that subordinates individually and as a group move along the developmental continuum. This movement could occur from day to day, week to week, or even over longer periods depending on the subordinates and the task to be accomplished. Effective leaders discern where subordinates are and adapt their style appropriately.

Questions that help leaders discern where subordinates are on the developmental continuum are as follows: What job needs to be accomplished? How difficult is the job? Do subordinates have the necessary skills to accomplish the job? Are subordinates sufficiently motivated to start and complete the job? In addition, understanding the directive and supportive behaviors available to leaders will enable them to use the appropriate behaviors depending on the answers to these questions (Northouse, 2013). The trait approach (Chapter 2) and the contingency approach (Chapter 6) suggest that leader style is fixed; the situational approach to leadership suggests that leaders need to behave in a manner that is adaptive and flexible (Yukl, 2012).

✉ References

Blanchard, K., Zigami, D., & Nelson, R. (1993). Situational leadership after 25 years: A retrospective. *Journal of Leadership Studies, 1*(1), 22–36.

DuBrin, A. (2010). *Leadership: Research findings, practice, and skills* (6th ed.). Mason, OH: South-Western/ Cengage.

Gandz, J. (2010). In M. Crossan, J. Gandz, & G. Seijts (Eds.), *Cross-enterprise leadership: Business leadership for the twenty-first century,* (pp. 15–26). Mississauga, Canada: Jossey-Bass.

Northouse, P. G. (2013). *Leadership: Theory and practice* (6th ed.). Thousand Oaks, CA: Sage.

Yukl, G. (2012). *Leadership in organizations* (8th ed.). Upper Saddle River, NJ: Pearson/Prentice Hall.

✉ The Cases

Conflict Management at TKC Consulting

Rao and Naik are two senior executives at TKC Consulting. In a battle of power and egos, they scapegoated an innocent subordinate. Their actions, which were not appropriate for the positions they held, created misunderstanding and confusion, and this had an adverse impact in the organization. The chairman was caught between pointing out their egotistical, power-hungry actions, as this would merely result in a blame game, and addressing the conflict immediately, before it resulted in more casualties within the organization.

A Bomb in Your Pocket? Crisis Leadership at Nokia India (A)

As of 2007, Nokia, the Finnish telecommunications company, was the leading brand in the Indian mobile devices market, capturing market share from well-established players such as Motorola, Ericsson, and Samsung. India was the second-largest market for Nokia, next only to China. In August of 2007, a routine product feedback and defect analysis process identified a defective batch of batteries supplied by a Japanese vendor, Matsushita. Although the defect was not seen as a major safety issue, Nokia was shocked to receive the antagonistic response from the Indian press to the product advisory and the ensuing mayhem that spread quickly through the country. Shivakumar, head of Nokia India, and his team had to act swiftly to preserve the company's hard-earned reputation and market share.

◪ The Reading

Just Ask Leadership: Why Great Managers Always Ask the Right Questions

The smart, aware executive knows that asking questions is more important than having all of the answers. Knowing the right questions to ask is more important than having knowledge of any particular functional area. Almost like leading itself, "asking" has different techniques and styles. Readers will learn which techniques and styles are right and the best fit for them in this article.

Conflict Management at TKC Consulting

V. Padhmanabhan

TKC Consulting was a pioneer in the business of financial brokerage, including share trading and commodities. It also managed dematerialization of shareholders' accounts and distribution business divisions such as insurance, mutual funds, fixed deposits, initial public offerings, etc. The company had been in this business for more than 25 years and ran its operations in India through branches in different cities. However, over time, many employees had left to become entrepreneurs on their own and competed with their former organization. In Tamil Nadu, Southern India, the company operated through 50 branches. The operations in the Tamil Nadu region were managed by Rao, the regional head.

Rao and another senior executive, Naik, were involved in a conflict that looked like it was going to require intervention from the company chairman.

◪ Background

The Company's Style of Operation

At the top of the organizational structure (see Exhibit 1) was the chairman, Mukharjee. Naik,

the country head of the distribution business, and Sam, the country head of the stock-broking business, reported to him. The country head of the distribution business led the country heads of insurance and mutual fund products, who in turn led their respective regional product heads. Each regional product head was allotted a region with a regional headquarters from where they operated their business.

Executives with rich experience and expertise in the product along with a customer base were designated as regional heads. They managed the regional headquarters and were responsible for administering the operations. They acted in an advisory position for regional product heads in their respective regions. Regional product heads achieved business through their various branch heads in their respective regions. Regional product heads reported simultaneously to both country heads of their respective products as well as their regional heads.

Aman

Aman, a 35-year-old management graduate, started his career in the company as a marketing

Version: 2011-03-15

executive in 2004. Because of his commitment and consistent achievement of targets, he was promoted within three years to the level of regional product head of the life and non-life insurances division for the region of Tamil Nadu. He operated from a separate office premises with operation executives assisting him to manage his portfolio smoothly. He reported to regional head Rao and also to the country head of the insurance division.

Rao

Rao, a 52-year-old veteran, who had joined the company as a vice-president, was designated the regional head for the Tamil Nadu region. He had been in the company for more than 15 years and had persevered to establish the company in his region. He expanded the company's operation by opening branches at various cities in his region and built a vast and strong customer network. He acquired strong expertise in the stock-broking business and gained confidence among investors for his strategic fund management skills, showing excellent growth in the business. He followed a conservative style of management towards employees and his operations were cost-effective. He had an authoritarian approach within his region but was never questioned by the top management as he had always proved himself through results.

Naik

Naik joined as an operation executive during the inception of the company and went on to become the head of the Karnataka region. He was also one of the vice-presidents of the company. He developed a strong customer base in his region and had good rapport with customers who made major investments. During periods of low business, he used his customer contacts to do cross selling. His rapport was so strong that he could sell his products over the phone

without stepping out of his office. In terms of performance, Naik always drove his region to achieve excellent growth in the distribution business and to rank as one of the top regions in the country.

Relationship Between Rao and Naik

At one point, Rao and Naik had a misunderstanding over an employee's transfer request. The issue arose after Naik failed to respond to Rao's request for approving the transfer of a female executive from his Tamil Nadu region who had planned to settle down in the Karnataka region after her marriage. Rao felt insulted over this incident.

In terms of career growth in TKC Consulting, both Rao and Naik had an equal chance of promotion to the position of country head of the company. However, when a vacancy for country head of the distribution business arose, luck favored Naik due to his experience in this business. Rao was quite disappointed by this and cast aspersions to his close circle of friends on Naik's ability to manage the responsibilities of country head.

✉ Naik's Branch Visits

Naik, after his succession to the position, made regular visits to different regions all over India. He felt the need to revamp the conservative style of managing the operations, and he revitalized the system. Naik made a series of visits to Rao's region, and every time he visited the region, Rao deputed Aman for various branch visits in Tamil Nadu. As a protocol, whenever Naik planned a visit, he would send an email message to Rao about his plan with a copy to Aman. Naik was impressed by Aman's knowledge about the region and his commitment to the business. Over a period of time, Naik emailed his visit schedule to Aman directly without a copy to Rao, and Aman shared Naik's schedule with Rao by forwarding the email. On one occasion, Rao invited Naik for lunch at his house after he returned from branch visits. Due to an urgent meeting with agents at a local branch, Naik sent a message through his mobile phone to Aman that he could not make it for lunch as he was in the branch meetings. Aman promptly forwarded the message to Rao.

▧ The Start of Crisis

Within a week, Aman received an instruction in his email about a temporary assignment of managing at a different branch a newly launched product which did not belong to his insurance division. The transfer order was from his regional head, Rao. Aman was unable to understand the reason for such a transfer, as the area did not require his presence. Later, Aman perceived that he had been transferred to prevent him from joining the branch visits with Naik. He was deputed for almost two months to manage the new product and in the meantime, there was a slump in the insurance business (his original product division) due to diversion of focus to the new product launch. Although there was a lag in business, Aman was confident of a revival since two more quarters remained to show the overall business for the division. He was also aware that it was common to have the first two quarters show a slump in the overall insurance industry, and that the real business began in the third and fourth quarters of the financial year.

After some time, another blow came through yet another email. Aman was relieved of the life insurance portfolio that he had been taking care of since he had joined and was instructed to manage the non-life insurance portfolio alone. The reason cited was poor performance in the first two quarters. Aman saw the email copied to not just the country product head of insurance and country head of distribution, but also to the chairman. Aman struggled to understand this decision by Rao, his regional head. He also felt that there was no need to send an email to the chairman about his underperformance based on the appraisal of the first two quarters. He felt that the evaluation of his performance was biased, as the insurance business peaked only in the last two quarters of the financial year. The country head of distribution conveyed to Aman his inability to intervene as the issue had been addressed directly to the chairman.

Later, Aman was also instructed to leave his new office premises and return to the premises where Rao was located. He felt that his every movement was closely watched and that he was selectively targeted. Aman found himself reeling in a crisis that was not related to his performance but was instead related to his relationship with his superiors. The crisis tormented him day after day and cost him his happiness. He contemplated quitting, but the whole economy was in a recession with job cuts and lay-offs everywhere, and searching for a new job was difficult. He found himself alienated and at a loss to handle the situation anymore. The crisis took a toll on his performance and cost him his peace of mind at home.

▧ Chairman's Dilemma

The chairman knew that Rao could understandably be upset as he had shown undoubted sincerity and commitment to the organization's growth right from the early years. The chairman also understood that he could not let these veteran heads clash, lest it dent the younger generation's morale. This would hamper the organization's future, besides forcing talented employees to move out. Whenever employees quit, they took customers with them. The chairman felt an intervention was needed to revitalize the situation.

Exhibit 1   Organizational Structure

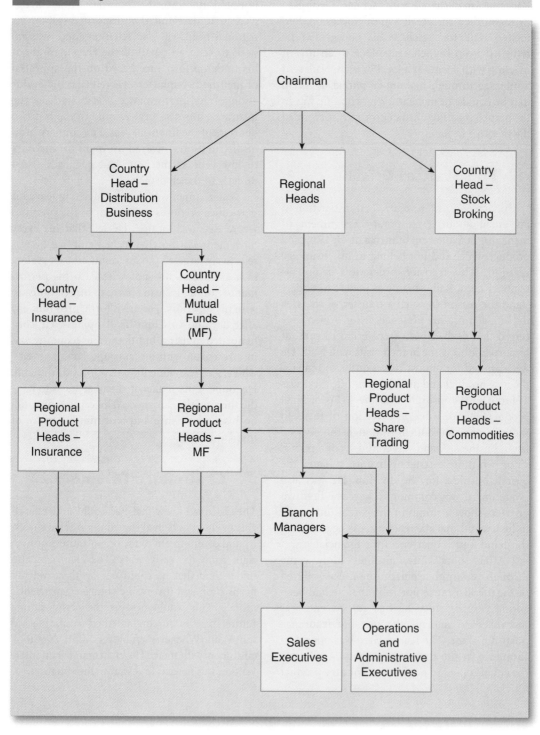

A Bomb in Your Pocket? Crisis Leadership at Nokia India (A)

Hima Bindu, Monidipa Mukherjee, and Charles Dhanaraj

Singapore Airlines flight SQ 408 from Singapore had just landed at the Indira Gandhi International Airport at Delhi. It was past 10:00 p.m. on August 14, 2007, the eve of India's Independence Day. D. Shivakumar, managing director of Nokia India, was cutting short his plans to visit Nokia's headquarters in Finland and was returning to Delhi. Throughout the day, Poonam Kaul, director of communications at Nokia India, had been sending text messages to Shivakumar, keeping him abreast of the developments. Her last message was short but disturbing: "The media is hostile. We have asked the crisis management team to meet tonight."

Indian media had been focusing on a product advisory (see Exhibit 1) that Nokia had issued from its global headquarters in Finland earlier that day. The advisory warned Nokia phone owners that a particular batch of BL-5C batteries, manufactured by Matsushita, a Nokia supplier, was found to be overheating while the phone was being charged. Nokia offered free replacement batteries in the advisory. The Indian media was turning the advisory into a sensational news story, covering incidents of mobile phone explosions in far-flung Indian states. Headlines such as "Are you walking around with a bomb in your pocket?" were flashed on television screens and caused panic among millions of Nokia mobile phone users in India. Much of the media frenzy caught the Nokia management in both India and Finland by surprise. The brand image and market leadership, which Nokia had carefully cultivated in India, were

suddenly under severe threat. Shivakumar was anxious to meet with his team, knowing it was going to be a long night—perhaps one of the most crucial nights of his career.

⊠ Nokia Corporation

Nokia Corporation acquired its name from the Nokianvirta River in Finland. It started as a paper pulp business in 1865 and over the years morphed into a global telecommunications leader. Operating in more than 150 countries around the world, Nokia manufactured mobile devices and telecom equipment, and delivered mobile content services. Globally, it reported net sales of $66.7 billion[1] for 2007, with an operating profit of about €10.46 billion. Nokia's two largest markets, China and India, accounted for 23 per cent and 15 per cent of total revenues, respectively, while Great Britain and Germany accounted for 10 per cent each.[2]

The 1990s were a high-growth period for the cellular industry. Nokia nurtured its brand name through print advertising and pan-European television advertising. Deviating from the industry norms of emphasizing the technical features of the product, Nokia appealed to the emotional benefits of buying a brand-name phone. With an estimated brand value of $33.69 billion, the global branding consultancy, Interbrand, ranked Nokia among the top five "Best Global Brands" in 2007.[3] In spite of a highly competitive market, Nokia had 40 per cent of the global market share in 2007, with

Version: 2011-02-01

[1]All currencies are in US$ unless otherwise stated.

[2]www.nokia.com/about-nokia/financials/key-data/markets, accessed July 2010.

[3]Interbrand survey, www.interbrand.com/best_global_brands.aspx?year=2007 &langid=1000, accessed January 2010.

three of its rivals, Samsung, Motorola and Sony-Ericsson, taking 13.4, 11.9 and nine per cent, respectively. Others, including Korea's LG and Canada's Research In Motion (BlackBerry), held single-digit shares of the market.[4]

Mobile Phone Industry in India

Until the mid-1990s, the Indian telecom industry was served by two public-sector agencies—Bharat Sanchar Nigam Ltd. (BSNL) for domestic services and Videsh Sanchar Nigam Ltd. (VSNL) for international long-distance services. In 1997, the Indian government established the Telecom Regulatory Authority of India (TRAI) and announced a new telecom policy that allowed privately owned operators in the telecom industry. Since 2000, the mobile subscriber base in India had been doubling annually, reaching about 261 million in 2007, overtaking the U.S. market and becoming the second-largest wireless network, next only to China.[5] Ten million new subscribers were being added every month. Mobile tariffs in India were among the lowest in the world. Average (monthly) revenue per use (ARPU), a metric that was used to assess service operators, was estimated at under $3, compared to over $50 in the United States. India used two mobile platforms: GSM (Global System for Mobile communications) with a subscriber base of 192 million, growing at nearly 60 per cent annually, and CDMA (Code Division Multiple Access) with a subscriber base of 68.37 million, growing annually at 53 per cent.[6]

Nokia India Operations

Nokia entered the Indian market in 1995, and within a decade, established itself as a leader. By 2004, Nokia's market share in India was estimated at 70 per cent by a *Wall Street Journal* report, and at 76 per cent by 2006 as reported by several market surveys[7]. Nokia's marketing organization also included more than 500 customer care centres (CCCs) and more than 600 Nokia priority dealers (NPDs) across India (see Exhibit 2). The company had three research and development (R&D) centres in Hyderabad, Bangalore and Mumbai. Nokia opened a manufacturing facility at Chennai, India, in 2006, and in the first 18 months, rolled out 60 million handsets. This facility was expected to emerge as one of Nokia's top three global manufacturing centres. Overall, the company was growing rapidly, with employment increasing from 450 in 2004 to over 10,000 in 2007.

Chronology of a Controversy

The BL-5C was one of 14 battery models used in Nokia products, and featured lithium-ion technology; several suppliers collectively produced more than 300 million units. Matsushita Battery Industrial Co. Ltd. of Japan was one of the battery suppliers. Nokia's batteries were tested against internationally recognized quality standards and Nokia's own stringent quality requirements.

In the summer of 2007, Nokia received a few consumer complaints about BL-5C batteries; the batteries were overheating while charging. Within a month, over 100 complaints were registered globally. In-house analysis of the data suggested that the defects were attributable to a particular batch of batteries manufactured by Matsushita from between December 2005 to

---

[4]TelecomWorldwire, May 28, 2008, www.highbeam.com/doc/1G1-179466910.html, accessed January 2010.

[5]Telecom Regulatory Authority of India Annual Report 2007–2008, pp. 17–19, www.trai.gov.in/annualreport/TRAIAR2007-08E.pdf, accessed January 2010.

[6]TRAI Annual Report, 2007-2008, www.trai.gov.in/annualreport/TRAIAR2007-08E.pdf, accessed January 2010.

[7]India Resource Centre, www.ibef.org/download/inthetopspot.pdf, accessed January 2010.

November 2006. Following standard operating procedures, Nokia's global product management directed its communications team to issue a global product advisory. The global communications and legal team was to liaise with the specific host team of countries where the issue was expected to arise.

August 11, 2007

Kaul received a call at 10:00 a.m. Indian Standard Time (IST) (7:30 a.m. in Finland) from the global headquarters office in Finland regarding the product advisory. Kaul was informed that the advisory was routine and was expected to plainly state the solution to the faulty battery issue. Owners of Nokia phones would input battery numbers at Nokia's website, which would advise the owner if his or her battery was faulty, and if faulty, would also inform the owner about the free battery replacement process. The news about the advisory was to be kept confidential until the formal announcement.

Shivakumar was on his way to the headquarters on the same day and had stopped over at Singapore, Nokia's regional headquarters. At about 1:00 p.m., Kaul called Shivakumar and expressed her concerns about the advisory:

> I was apprehensive that people in India may not differentiate between a product advisory and a product recall. In addition, I was not sure if our customers would be able to go online in order to check if their phone was affected, given that Internet usage is very low in our country. Moreover, India is an open distribution market, as compared to most developed countries, where the business is mainly through the service operator's chain (e.g. Verizon wireless).

While a product recall is a request to return to the maker a batch or an entire production run of a product, usually due to the discovery of

safety issues, an advisory is considered to be routine material information.

August 12, 2007

Throughout the day, Kaul and her team kept close contact with headquarters and Shivakumar. They ensured that all data and facts concerning the incident were in place. Although it was more engaging than a normal day, there was no sense of urgency over the product advisory.

August 13, 2007

The global advisory was to be released at 9:00 a.m. Finnish time the next day. The priority at the India office that day was to finalize the draft of the press release. The India office communications team also developed an action plan to deal with the press that highlighted the difference between a product advisory and a recall in the release to the Indian press.

August 14, 2007

Early that morning, Nokia India issued the product advisory as a press release (see Exhibit 3) to approximately 200 publications and media outlets. Kaul recalled:

> It was a routine press release. But I continued to have the nagging feeling that this might not work in India. I kept Shiv updated periodically. We also decided that he could proceed to Finland as scheduled and that this product advisory did not warrant his presence in Delhi.

As the media was notified, Sudhir Kohli, head, Nokia Care, India, went on conference call with his regional care managers and regional general managers and explained to his team that the defective batteries would not be replaced at the care centres and that customers would be asked to check the Nokia website to learn whether their batteries were defective. Customers had to provide information via the website and would then receive a new battery within 15 days. The Nokia call centres would operate normally with no extended working hours. Kohli described the situation as follows:

> My main goal was to let the care centre managers know that the advisory was a routine one and did not warrant concern. I just wanted to make sure that they all knew that it was simple and routine. But, as I finished the conference call, I was anticipating operational problems.

August 14, 2007—4:00 P.M.

Aaj Tak, a regional media player, was the first to broadcast the news about the battery problem and the advisory, stating the facts in a straight forward, neutral manner. Kaul recalled that, until that time, everything had seemed under control:

> I remember sitting in the office cafeteria watching Aaj Tak and one or two other channels. Suddenly at around 5:00 p.m., Star News started flashing reports about how Nokia phones could potentially explode, headlines screaming in Hindi—"Aap ke jeb mein bomb ho sakta hain" (meaning: There could be a bomb in your pocket). This was coupled with archived television footage of the July 2007 Mumbai train blasts, a railway platform with slippers strewn, kids crying, cycles overturned and all such gory pictured being flashed. That's when it all started.

Within the hour, mobile broadcast vans from Delhi media started gathering outside the Nokia office at Gurgaon. The media wanted a response and were linking the advisory to historical reports of stray blasts of counterfeit

phones/batteries in the past few months. The Nokia battery "blast" was the headline story across all television channels, each news channel adding its own flavour to the story, sensationalizing it further and accelerating panic. It became a fight for television rating points (TRPs) among the channels (see Exhibit 4). Kaul recalled:

> Editors were in no mood to listen to the facts, as everybody wanted to be the first one to report. Fuelling the main stream media frenzy, even regional media outlets picked up the news from prominent Hindi and English channels and added their own insights and interpretations—neatly playing upon emotions.

Devinder Kishore, head of marketing at Nokia India, was assigned as the media spokesperson. He had a one-on-one rapport with the channels, and he could speak fluent Hindi to the vernacular press. The communications team called the heads of every channel and got air time on nearly all of them. Kishore took questions from the media and the public and tried to provide clarifications. Kaul recalled:

> While they [television channels] were carrying our story, they were still showing pictures of the blast. They were not doing anything to help to resolve panic among the customers. In fact, while DK [Kishore] was live on television, he was unaware that the other half of the screen had gory pictures of blasts. Only around 10:30 p.m. the tone of the news was getting neutral, after it became clear to the channels that the company was not shying away but was there, talking and addressing concerns.

Meanwhile, because of the media stories, consumers started thronging the care centres.

Sudhir Kohli, head of Nokia Care knew that a local solution was needed.

> We had customers walking into the care centres asking staff to check their phones and for battery replacements. We neither had the replacement batteries in stock, nor were we advised to exchange across the counter. I felt that we needed a local solution because Indian customers are different; they will not log on to the website to check up and wait.

✉ Management Response

In Singapore, Shivakumar closely watched the day's events in India and was getting worried. He wanted to interact with the press but was advised to keep away, as the crisis team felt it would present a negative and defensive stance from the company if the managing director himself came into the picture. Things were getting out of hand, with customers panicking and hounding every Nokia outlet as the media continued to sensationalize the story. On consultation with the leadership team in India, Shivakumar decided to cancel his Finland trip and return to India. A crisis team was set up (see Exhibit 5). The team knew the next few days would be trying times. By the time Shivakumar landed at Delhi, Kaul and her team had begun to conceptualize advertisements for the next day's newspapers. They also kept a tab on every channel and every report broadcasted. Telephone lines were active and ready, and the team was ready to take calls in order to dispel myths and provide information.

At the same time, the technical team started working on an alternative battery checking and replacement solution. One of the engineers at the Nokia Delhi office suggested a local solution using the short message services (SMS) or texting, which was popular among Indian customers.

Instead of using the Internet, customers could send the battery number to a particular number via SMS. The system would be designed in such a way that customers would instantaneously receive a response advising them whether or not the battery was defective. If defective, the system asked for contact information, which was registered in a global database and activated shipment of a replacement battery.

At around midnight on August 14, Shivakumar finally arrived at Nokia's office and joined the crisis planning meeting that was in progress. He was informed of the developments on the SMS process and the tentative logistics planning. It was clear that they needed many more hands and an immediate supply of new batteries. Local execution was key and that was the message from global teams as well. With all the media frenzy, Nokia's brand image, and its future in India, was at stake. Kaul recalled:

> As happy as I was that Shiv [Shivakumar] was there, I knew that the issue had suddenly become too large for India, and not so much in the other parts of the world. It was as if my fears had come true. I kept thinking that the next day was August 15, a holiday, and this should give us [a] breather and some ground to get our act right.

As Shivakumar listened to his team, several concerns surfaced: How should Nokia prevent false rumours of battery explosion from being linked to the product? How should the company handle irate consumers? How could it quickly control the damage and consolidate the brand image as market leader? What was the implication to Nokia's market share? Could Nokia hold on to the customers and stop losing them to competitors? How should Nokia manage the logistics, particularly dealing with second-tier cities in India? Finally, what would the cost implications be?

Exhibit 1	Excerpts From Nokia's Global Product Advisory

Dear Nokia Customer,

This is a product advisory for the Nokia-branded BL-5C battery manufactured by Matsushita Battery Industrial Co. Ltd. of Japan between December 2005 and November 2006. This product advisory does not apply to any other Nokia battery. Nokia has identified that in very rare cases the affected batteries could potentially experience over heating initiated by a short circuit while charging, causing the battery to dislodge. Nokia is working closely with relevant local authorities to investigate this situation. Nokia has several suppliers for BL-5C batteries that have collectively produced more than 300 million BL-5C batteries. This advisory applies only to the 46 million batteries manufactured by Matsushita between December 2005 and November 2006. There have been approximately 100 incidents of overheating reported globally. No serious injuries or property damage have been reported.

Consumers with a BL-5C battery subject to this advisory should note that all of the approximately 100 incidents have occurred while charging the battery. According to Nokia's knowledge this issue does not affect any other use of the mobile device. Concerned consumers may want to monitor a mobile device while charging that contains a BL-5C battery subject to this product advisory.

While the occurrence in the BL-5C batteries produced by Matsushita in the time-period specified is very rare, for consumers wishing to do so, Nokia and Matsushita offer to replace for free any BL-5C battery subject to this product advisory. "Nokia" and "BL-5C" are printed on the front of the battery. On the back of the battery, the Nokia mark appears at the top, and the battery identification number (consisting of 26 characters) is found at the bottom. If the battery identification number does not contain 26 characters, it is not subject to this product advisory.

If you are interested to know if your battery is part of this product advisory, please follow the two steps below:

1) Switch off your mobile device and check the battery model. If your battery is not a BL-5C model, you are not included in this product advisory and your product will not be replaced.

2) If your battery is a BL-5C model, remove the battery and check the 26-character identification number from the back of the battery. Enter the identification number in the field below and you will be advised if your battery may be replaced.

Top of Form

ENTER HERE THE 26-CHARACTER PRODUCT IDENTIFICATION NUMBER AND PRESS 'SUBMIT' – **Battery identification number:** [   ] | Submit |

SOURCE: Nokia website, http://batteryreplacement.nokia.com/batteryreplacement/en/advisory-2007.html, accessed January 2010.

Exhibit 2   Nokia India Distribution Centres

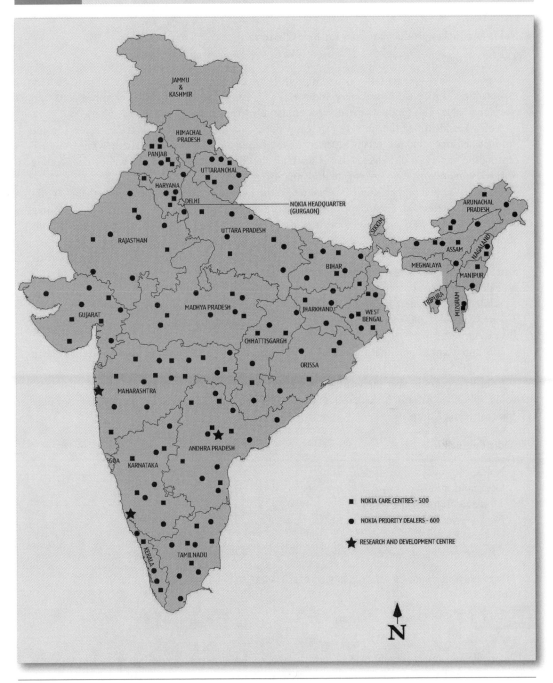

Exhibit 3	Excerpts From Press Release, August 14, 2007

Nokia announces product advisory for BL-5C battery

August 14, 2007

Espoo, Finland—Nokia today issued a product advisory for the Nokia-branded BL-5C battery manufactured by Matsushita Battery Industrial Co., Ltd. of Japan between December 2005 and November 2006. This product advisory does not apply to any other Nokia-branded battery.

Nokia has identified that in very rare cases the Nokia-branded BL-5C batteries subject to the product advisory could potentially experience overheating initiated by a short circuit while charging, causing the battery to dislodge. Nokia is working closely with Matsushita and will be cooperating with relevant authorities to investigate this situation.

Nokia has several suppliers for BL-5C batteries who have collectively produced more than 300 million BL-5C batteries. This advisory applies only to the 46 million batteries manufactured by Matsushita between December 2005 and November 2006, from which there have been approximately 100 incidents of overheating reported globally. No serious injuries or property damage have been reported.

Consumers with a BL-5C battery subject to this advisory should note that all of the approximately 100 incidents have occurred while charging the battery. According to Nokia's knowledge this issue does not affect any other use of the mobile device.

While the occurrences in the BL-5C batteries produced by Matsushita in the time-period specified are very rare, concerned consumers can request a replacement for any BL-5C battery subject to this product advisory.

It is important to note that the BL-5C battery is not used in all Nokia products and that only a portion of the Nokia BL-5C batteries in use are subject to this advisory.

Consumers should visit the website www.nokia.com/batteryreplacement or contact their local Nokia call center. A list of Nokia products that include the BL-5C battery is available at www.nokia.com/batteryreplacement.

Media Enquiries:

Nokia
Communications
Tel. +358 7180 34900
E-mail: press.office@nokia.com
www.nokia.com

SOURCE: Nokia website, http://press.nokia.com/PR/200708/1146281_5.html, accessed January 2010.

Exhibit 4	A Brief Overview of Indian Media

The media and entertainment (M&E) industry was a vibrant part of the Indian economy. Industry revenues were estimated at Rs513 billion in 2007, with an annual growth rate of about 20 per cent. Print media revenues were estimated at 40 per cent of the total industry, with the rest coming from the television industry.

Print Media: Indian print media had a history dating back to the 18th century. The vernacular press had the distinction of bringing out the first major newspaper, *The Bengal Gazette*, in 1780, when India was still under the British rule. It was started by James Augustus Hickey, who is now recognized as the father of the Indian press. The first newspaper in an Indian language (Bengali) was *Samachar Darpan*, which started in 1818. The first Gujarati newspaper, *Bombay Samachar* started in 1822, while the first Hindi newspaper, *Samachar Sudha Varshan*, started in 1854. The 2001 National Census put the literacy rate at 65.38 per cent, and it was estimated that there was one copy of the newspaper available for every 20 Indians. Newspapers and magazines reached out to 222 million readers, with an almost equal readership base in rural and urban areas—making it the world's second-largest market for newspapers. As of 2007, English-language newspapers registered the highest daily circulation with 99 million copies, with Hindi-language papers following closely at 70 million copies. Five regional languages registered a circulation of over 10 million, namely Tamil (30 million), Marathi (22 million), Malayalam (19 million), Telegu (18 million) and Gujarati (13 million).

Broadcast Media: India received its first television broadcast in 1959 in Hindi, and until the market liberalization, Doordarshan, the state-run network, remained the only broadcast channel. International satellite television was introduced in India by CNN through its coverage of the Gulf War in 1991. Within months, Hong Kong-based Star TV started broadcasting five channels into India using the ASIASAT-1 satellite. Subsequent to market liberalization in 1992, the broadcast industry saw the arrival of several international channels via satellite and the rapid emergence of several private Indian broadcasters. As of 2007, there were over 300 channels available via cable, including 30 news channels broadcasting in almost all of India's 22 official languages (see Table 1 for top five channels in English and Hindi). The rapid growth of this industry also exacerbated the rivalry among the channels, often leading to accuracy and objectivity being replaced with sensational strategies to increase TRPs, a measure that influenced the channels' advertisement rates. Over-sensationalism of news was a common feature, especially in the regional divisions where ad-hoc stringers were the sources of news.

Table 1	Top Five Television News Media Channels in English and Hindi		
	English news channels market share of viewership		**Hindi news channels market share of viewership**	
Rank	**Channel name**	**Market share (%)**	**Channel name**	**Market share (%)**
1	NDTV 24 x 7	33.0	Aaj Tak	20.5
2	CNN-IBN	24.0	Star TV	20.0
3	Times Now	23.5	India TV	14.0
4	Headlines	9.0	NDTV	12.5
5	News X	8.0	IBN7	10.0

SOURCES: AdEx India 2007, www.indiantelevision.com/tamadex/y2k7/adexindex.htm;

Industry Edelweiss Research, The India Entertainment and Media Industry, Sustaining Growth, Report 2008, A FICCI-Pricewaterhousecoopers report;

World Association of Newspapers, www.wan-ifra.org;

Census 2001, National Readership Survey, 2007, accessed July 2010.

Exhibit 5 Nokia India Organization Crisis Committee Members (2007) (Members marked with an asterisk)

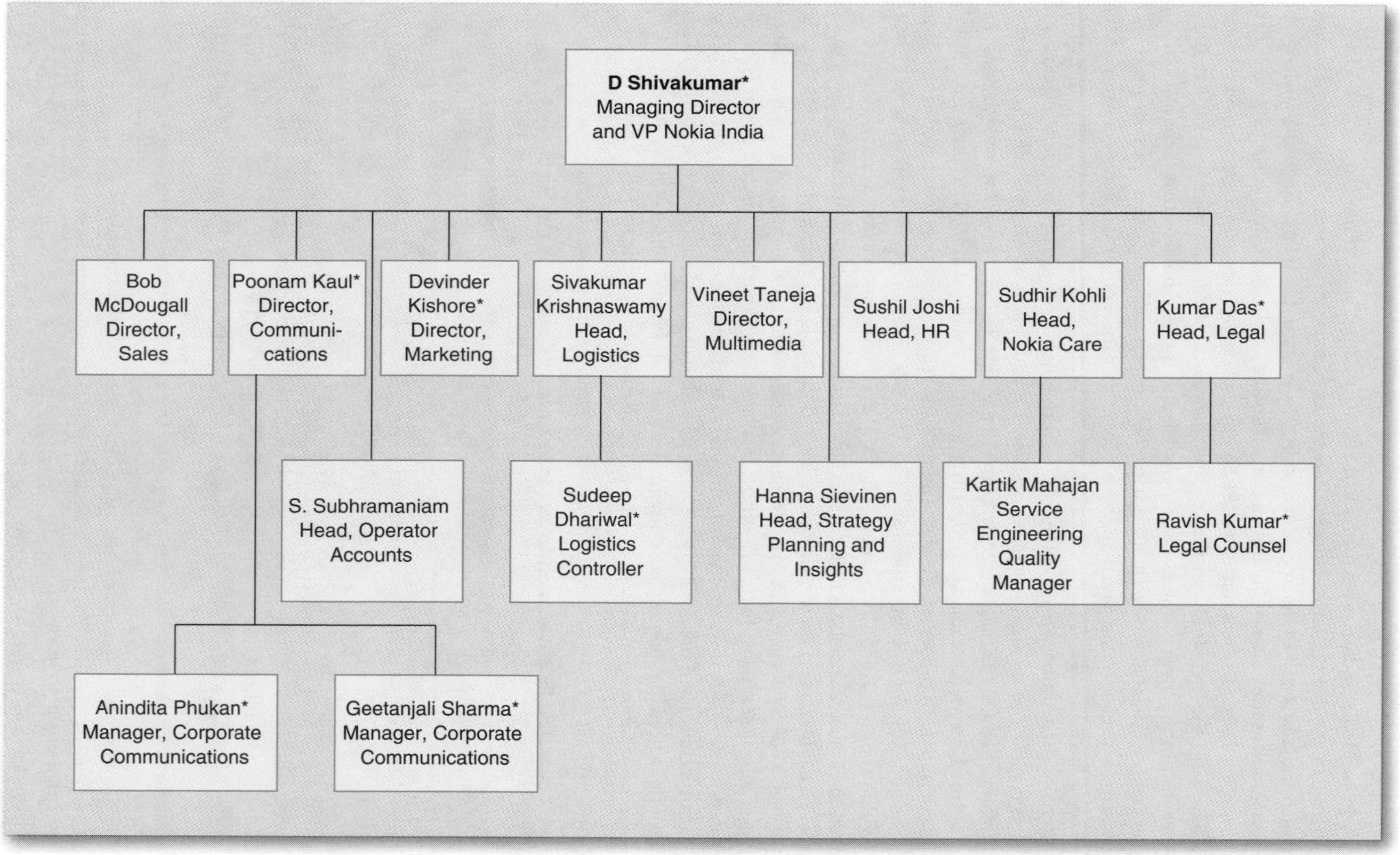

Nokia India Organization Crisis Committee Members chart:

D Shivakumar* — Managing Director and VP Nokia India

- **Bob McDougall** — Director, Sales
- **Poonam Kaul*** — Director, Communications
  - **S. Subhramaniam** — Head, Operator Accounts
    - **Anindita Phukan*** — Manager, Corporate Communications
    - **Geetanjali Sharma*** — Manager, Corporate Communications
- **Devinder Kishore*** — Director, Marketing
- **Sivakumar Krishnaswamy** — Head, Logistics
  - **Sudeep Dhariwal*** — Logistics Controller
- **Vineet Taneja** — Director, Multimedia
  - **Hanna Sievinen** — Head, Strategy Planning and Insights
- **Sushil Joshi** — Head, HR
- **Sudhir Kohli** — Head, Nokia Care
  - **Kartik Mahajan** — Service Engineering Quality Manager
- **Kumar Das*** — Head, Legal
  - **Ravish Kumar*** — Legal Counsel

SOURCE: Company files, Crisis Committee Members, 2007.

Just Ask Leadership: Why Great Managers Always Ask the Right Questions

Gary B. Cohen

The smart, aware executive today is doing something different. He or she is asking questions. Almost like leading itself, "asking" has different techniques and styles. Readers will learn which ones are right and the best fit for them in this article.

Questions Are the Answer

Company leaders today face new and increasingly complex problems. Most of these problems are intractable, if not, in the end, problems without real, lasting solutions. It is an extremely frustrating situation for today's leaders, who are accustomed to finding answers and whose ability to find the right answers got most of them into leadership positions in the first place.

This conundrum leaves leaders with two options: They can try to keep abreast of every issue and make the best possible decision, or they can start to ask more questions.

"Just Ask" Leadership

Business schools don't teach courses on question asking, so leaders typically don't study and analyze questions the way they would a quarterly report or a performance review.

The devaluing of questions can be attributed, in large part, to our educational system. During the first and second industrial revolution, when our educational system was designed, we trained our children to be factory workers. Anything the worker needed to know beyond that education could be learned on the job, from the manager. In turn, the manager was responsible for mentoring, coaching, or developing those employees that showed interest, ability, and tenacity. The worker rarely knew more than their boss

about how the business worked, since the boss had held and succeeded in most key jobs on his or her way up the organization.

The Wharton School of Business opened in 1881 and, with a Masters of Business and Administration, graduates could jump past the factory floor right into management. But even with this development, those at the top of the organization usually had more knowledge than those underneath. The same can't be said now, at least with any degree of certainty. Technology has put knowledge in the hands of anyone with access to a computer (approximately 76 percent of the U.S. population).

In the 21st century, it's not possible for leaders to be know-it-alls, nor is it in their or the organization's best interest to try. Leaders need to ask questions that move others to action and answers.

The employees that work for you today either know more than you do about their job or at least they should know more than you. As you move up the ranks of an organization or migrate up the ranks by job transfer, you will end up leading people that do things you cannot possibly understand. Rather than using a conventional way of getting up to speed, say reading extensively, leaders should use questions to increase others' alignment, engagement, and accountability.

"Just Ask" Leadership isn't simply about asking more questions; it's about asking more and better questions. "Just Ask" leaders are aware of the full range of options, their own question-asking proclivities, and the ways in which they can and ought to trust members of their team.

Moving From Knowing to Not Knowing

One of the most difficult challenges you have as a leader is to accept that you may not know what is right, or best, for most situations. You're accustomed to having the right answers, so it's hard to let go of the answer-providing habit. However, it's also important to recognize how much and how fast things change. Even if you've spent your entire career with the same organization, it was nearly impossible to have kept up with all the changes. There are different players, different scales and different competing environments. The answers you knew to be true or the best might not even be relevant anymore.

Just Ask leaders are comfortable with Not Knowing. When they ask a question, it's because they are genuinely interested in learning the answer—both in how it meets their expectations and how it diverges.

Just Ask leadership is not built around the Socratic Method. Plato suggests that Socrates did not know the answers to the questions he asked. I never bought that argument, nor should you. If you have been using this questioning method at work, please do yourself a favor and stop. Many smart employees can see right through it as just another technique. They do not like playing cat and mouse with you. If you know the answer that you want them to arrive at, tell it to them. Bear in mind, though, that it's generally more advantageous to doubt that you know the answer and to *ask*.

Asking allows others to engage in independent and creative thought. It promotes accountability when your team members are held responsible for their decisions. And your team members will be more engaged in the outcome if they have a hand in decision making. Keep in mind that if you provide the answer (even if it's the best one or the one they would have arrived at eventually), team members might not execute the solution as well as they would if they owned the decision. Exceptional leaders today swallow their egos and ask. That's because exceptional leaders realize that leadership comes from developing others' egos, not their own.

History Is *Not* Always a Good Teacher

What we believe to be the truth is often a product of having a bias. There are five biases that can unduly influence leadership and decision making:

1. **Negative bias:** When you have a negative experience, it has a larger impact on your memory and leads you to believe that certain roads are to be avoided, to a greater degree, than a quantitative analysis would demonstrate.

2. **Frequency bias:** When you hear or see something repeatedly over time, you will be more inclined to believe it.

3. **Recent bias:** When making a decision, something you learned just recently will often carry more weight than information you learned a while ago.

4. **Attachment bias:** Leaders can very easily become overly conservative and avoid making the right decision, simply because they don't want to disrupt the status quo, which they helped achieve.

5. **Escalation bias:** When you start down a path, you look for evidence to support your direction and at your peril, choose to ignore warning signs.

While a "Not Knowing" approach can help eliminate many of these biases, what about the questions themselves? How might our questions be biased?

Four Styles for Asking Questions

In studying questions—the impetus for them and the results they achieved—I identified four distinct question-asking styles: Professor, Judge, Innovator, or Director. When asking a question, leaders generally attempt to gain knowledge or move others to action, expand their perspective or evaluate what is known, and focus on the present or the future.

	Professor	Judge	Innovator	Director
Focus	Knowledge Gaining Perspective Present Time	Knowledge Evaluate Present Time	Action Gaining Perspective Future	Action Evaluate Future
Value of Style	• Gaining knowledge • Expanding insight • Generating ideas • Building broad understanding	• Analyzing and prioritizing ideas • Reaching decisions, agreements, or commitments • Focusing shared understanding	• Exploring new directions • Identifying opportunities • Improving current methods • Innovating solutions • Rallying the team to the cause	• Motivating the team to achieve specific goal or task • Implementing the plan • Focusing to accomplish results
When to Use	• When needing to better understand a situation • When going too fast and jumping too quickly • When exploring new ideas • When promoting creativity • When brainstorming all potential possibilities • When identifying potential factors related to the issue	• When assessing alternatives • When determining priorities • When identifying key themes • When refining ideas • When synthesizing information • When evaluating • When defining options	• When setting direction • When encouraging possibilities • When new behavior is desired • When working around barriers • When pushing beyond status quo • When energizing people to reach further	• When implementing clear goals • When needing to achieve specific results • When identifying next steps (what-who-by when) • When moving the team to act on a plan • When creating a task tension to get action moving
Business Need	• Strategy Building • Negotiation Preparation	• Decision Making • Performance Review/Hiring	• Visioning • Motivating Employees	• Problem Solving • Performance Management
What Happens If Over-Used	• May not reach conclusions (analysis paralysis) • May not initiate plan	• May stifle creative thinking missing best solution • May not get plan implemented	• May change course frequently • May rush to action resulting in more time re-doing ("Ready- Fire-Aim" mentality)	• May implement the wrong things well • May perpetrate outdated processes

(Continued)

(Continued)

	Professor	Judge	Innovator	Director
Negative of Style	• Condescending	• Disapproving	• Abdicate control	• Micro manage
Sample Questions	• What's the goal? • What are your options? • What are the alternative choices being considered? • What's the current reality? • What other approaches have you tried? • Is there another choice that hasn't been considered yet? • How have you taken emotion out of the decision?	• Whose decision is it? • What's the most important consideration here? • Which option makes the most sense to you? • What are the consequences of the choices? • What conclusions have you reached so far? • Are your choices mutually exclusive? • What's the biggest risk? • Are the risks for each alternative manageable? • What decision making process have you used to get to the point you're at now? • Have you weighed the pros and cons of each option? • What is the greatest possible success? • Are you struggling because of things that are knowable (info, facts) or unknowable? • Will others follow you? • What's your biggest fear about making this decision?	• What would you do if time and funds were unlimited? • What is your recommended way forward? • How could I support moving forward on that decision? • Is there anything I can do, add, or absolve you of that will make this easier for you to decide? • What does your gut tell you to do? • What is holding you back from making this decision? • What will the end result be?	• When is a decision due? • Do you understand the key drivers of the outcome for the situation? • If you make the wrong decision is it easily reversible? • Is this close to a 50-50 decision and if so, should we flip a coin? • What needs to happen for that to succeed? • Do you feel you have my support and the support of the rest of the team?

Of course, not all leaders fall perfectly into one of the four categories. You may be a cross between a Judge and a Director or, at times, consider yourself more of a Professor. What matters is that you recognize these shifts and your proclivities and learn how you can address any imbalances.

Knowing your predominant style can help you better frame questions, based upon the task and your goals. If you would categorize yourself as a Professor, for instance, and you're engaging in performance reviews, you ought to put on your Judge hat and ask more Judge-style questions than might not occur to you instinctively.

It's important to know and use questions that will help you and others achieve your respective goals. Bear in mind, though, that the same questions might not work equally well for all team members.

The Seven *C*'s of Trust

Chances are that you don't ask each team member the same set of questions. Based upon their skills and past experience, you customize your questions. Yet you might not be very intentional about the process—since question asking is viewed more as an art than a science.

It pays to vary the wording of questions. If you ask a team member the same questions over and over, you're likely to wind up with the same answers—creating a frustrating cycle for everyone involved.

One of the reasons we avoid asking specific team members certain questions or hardly any questions at all is due to trust. If we don't trust them, what's the point of asking for their input? It's a mistake, though, to think of trust in general terms.

I've identified seven aspects of trust (the 7 *C*'s) that may explain why your relationships with direct reports is either succeeding or failing:

1. Capability: Has the skill and ability to do their job well.

2. Commitment: Has the level of desire and focus toward the team's efforts.

3. Capacity: Has the time, energy, and personal management skills to complete what needs to be done well and on time.

4. Connection: Has the resources to complete the work that needs to be done.

5. Commonality: Shares interests that help build and extend the relationship.

6. Consistency: Has a strong track record of success and acts in a predictable fashion.

7. Character: Has integrity.

Questions will come easily when you trust others. Often the issue of trust has little to do with the follower and more to do with the leader. Here's a way to determine if the problem lies with you: Do all or most of your direct reports share one or more of these 7 *C*'s? The extent to which this commonality exists likely has more to do with how you perceive the world rather than how these traits show up in the world. If this is the case, you will need to work on correcting underlying assumptions.

Trust is essential to Just Ask Leadership. Delve deeply into the level of trust you have with each team member. Work on the *C*'s that they aren't excelling in and commend them for the *C*'s on which you have come to rely.

Good questions generate thought, focus, and action from the listener. They also convey respect. Maybe that's why 95 percent of leaders prefer to be asked questions, rather than be told what to do. And yet, according to a survey I conducted, these same leaders give instructions 58 percent of the time, rather than ask coworkers for their input!

It's time for leaders to practice the type of leadership they most prefer themselves. If you want to lead and motivate others, questions are the answer. Question asking may be an art, but if you approach it as a science, your questions and leadership will improve.

The Contingency Theory of Leadership

A company achieves uncommon excellence by bringing together uncommon people for a common purpose. As [Mohandas Karamchand] Gandhi did, the leader of a company that aspires to excellence must find ways to give the members of his organization a common identity without sacrificing the unique talents, experience and perspectives of individual employees. This requires setting forth clearly defined and significantly challenging goals of obvious high value, securing full organizational buy-in to these goals, and then giving the widest possible latitude to middle managers and their staffs to find or create the best routes to the goals.

—Alan Axelrod[1]

In Chapter 5, we described the situational approach to leadership as an approach that suggested to the leader what to do in different situations. This requires a great deal of flexibility on the part of the leader (Yukl, 2012). In the contingency theory of leadership, it is assumed that the leader's style is relatively stable and needs to be matched with the most appropriate situation for the leader's style (Daft, 2011). Fiedler and Chemers (1974) call contingency theory a leader–match theory. The closer the match between leader style and a particular situation, the more effective the leader will be.

Leadership Styles

As with the theories in Chapters 4 and 5, in contingency theory leadership, styles are broadly described as falling into two categories: task motivated and relationship motivated (DuBrin, 2010). Fiedler (1967) placed these two styles on opposite ends of a continuum and developed a scale he called the Least

---

[1]Axelrod, A. (2010, p. 61)

Preferred Coworker (LPC) scale. When a leader scores high on the LPC, it means that the leader is relationship oriented, whereas being low on the LPC means that the leader is task oriented (Daft, 2011). Task-oriented leaders want to achieve goals. Relationship-oriented leaders want to develop close relationships with their followers (Yukl, 2012).

Situational Variables

The contingency model helps leaders evaluate three variables using a dichotomous measure. In essence, leaders ask three questions: Are the leader–member relations good or poor? Is the task structure high or low? Is the leader's position power strong or weak? Answering these three questions allows leaders to determine what situation they are in and whether their style is a good match for that situation (see Figure 6.1).

Criteria for assessing these three variables are shown in Table 6.1. The variables need to be assessed in the order they are presented in Figure 6.1 and Table 6.1. As these are fairly self-explanatory, we will discuss the intersection of leadership styles with the situations defined by these three variables.

As mentioned, the order of these three variables is important. Leaders should examine leader–member relations, then task structure, and, finally, position power (Yukl, 2012). Good leader–member relations combined with high task structure and strong leader position power (Position 1 in Figure 6.1) is a very favorable situation for leaders. Poor leader–member relations combined with low task structure and weak leader position power (Position 8 in Figure 6.1) is the most unfavorable situation for leaders.

Contingency theory suggests that leaders with a low LPC score (those who are very task motivated) will be most effective in these two situations. In addition, leaders with middle LPC scores will be effective in Position 1 as well as being effective when the situation is assessed as being somewhat less favorable (Positions 2 to 3 in Figure 6.1). Furthermore, leaders with low LPC scores are effective in Positions 2 to 3. Finally, in situations that are moderately favorable to somewhat less favorable (Positions 4 to 7 in Figure 6.1), leaders with a high LPC score (very relationship oriented) will be most effective (DuBrin, 2010).

Figure 6.1 Contingency Model

Leader-Member Relations	Good				Poor			
Task Structure	High Structure		Low Structure		High Structure		Low Structure	
Position Power	Strong Power	Weak Power	Strong Power	Weak Power	Strong Power	Weak Power	Strong Power	Weak Power
Preferred Leadership Style	1	2	3	4	5	6	7	8
	Low LPCs Middle LPCs				High LPCs			Low LPCs

SOURCE: Adapted from Fielder (1967).

Table 6.1	Three Variables in the Contingency Model	
Leader-member relations	*Good*	*Poor*
	Followers	Atmosphere
	• like leader	• unfriendly
	• trust leader	• friction between leader/ followers
	• get along with leader	
		Followers
		• no confidence in leader
		• no loyalty to leader
		• not attracted to leader
Task structure	*High*	*Low*
	Task accomplishment	Task accomplishment
	• requirements clear	• requirements vague and unclear
	• few paths to achieving task	• many paths to achieving task
	• end to task clear	• end to task vague many correct solutions
	• solutions limited	
Leader's position power	*Strong*	*Weak*
	Leader has authority to	Leader has no authority to
	• hire subordinates	• hire subordinates
	• fire subordinates	• fire subordinates
	• promote	• promote
	• give pay raises	• give pay raises

How Does the Contingency Theory of Leadership Work?

The answer to this question is not entirely clear. Why are leaders with low LPC scores best in very favorable and most unfavorable situations? And why are leaders with high LPC scores most effective in situations that are moderately favorable? These are two questions that are still unanswered. Fiedler (1995) has suggested why a mismatch between situation and style may not work. A mismatch leads to anxiety and stress, more stress leads to coping mechanisms developed earlier in a leader's career, and these less developed coping mechanisms lead to bad leader decisions and, consequently, negative task outcomes (Northouse, 2013).

However, while we may not be able to explain why a mismatch between style and situation does not work and a match does work, we can predict whether a leader will be effective in certain situations and not in others. Consequently, you should assess several work-related situations based on the three variables in the contingency model, assess your own leadership style (are you mostly task oriented, relationship oriented, or somewhere in the middle?), and choose the best situation for your leadership style (Daft, 2011).

References

Axelrod, A. (2010). *Gandhi, CEO: 14 principles to guide & inspire modern leaders.* New York, NY: Sterling Publishing.
Daft, R. L. (2011). *The leadership experience* (5th ed.). Mason, OH: Thomson, South-Western.
DuBrin, A. (2010). *Leadership: Research findings, practice, and skills* (6th ed.). Mason, OH: South-Western/Cengage.
Fiedler, F. E. (1967). *A theory of leadership effectiveness.* New York, NY: McGraw-Hill.
Fiedler, F. E. (1995). Reflections by an accidental theorist. *Leadership Quarterly, 6*(4), 453–461.
Fiedler, F. E., & Chemers, M. M. (1974). *Leadership and effective management.* Glenview, IL: Scott, Foresman.
Northouse, P. G. (2013). *Leadership: Theory and practice* (6th ed.). Thousand Oaks, CA: Sage.
Yukl, G. (2012). *Leadership in organizations* (8th ed.). Upper Saddle River, NJ: Pearson/Prentice Hall.

The Cases

New York Bakery (A)

Patrick Blanshard, a technical consultant, has taken on a project to help New York Bakery, an eastern U.S. confectionery company that is under bankruptcy protection. His task is to assess New York Bakery's readiness for the installation of a new payroll system. This readiness includes the willingness of current employees to help even though they believe that this new system could lead to layoffs. If the project is successful, it will help New York Bakery to move through the bankruptcy process. At the end of his first week, Patrick realizes that the job he has undertaken is greater than he imagined. He is realizing that he faces a series of tough decisions that require his immediate attention.

Transkin Income Fund: Leading Entrepreneurial Teams

Garreth Lind, the chief operating officer of Transkin Income Fund (Transkin), faces a very difficult decision. His company provides freight transportation services in Canada and the United States but is suffering in February 2009 because of a sharp fall in demand for transportation services due to the economic crisis. Lind has asked each of his six freight divisions and six support divisions and the corporate division to voluntarily implement a salary rollback. Within 2 months, he had the support of 10 out of Transkin's 12 divisions. However, two of Transkins' most senior vice presidents (who were leading the two most profitable divisions) were indicating reluctance to share the pain. Lind wondered what to do next. Should the two vice presidents be allowed to not participate? Lind wondered what message this would send to those who had indicated they would participate in the rollback. He wondered if there were steps he could follow to gain the commitment of the two vice presidents?

The Reading

Why Emotional Intelligence Is Not Essential for Leadership

It is often argued that leaders need to have emotional intelligence to effectively lead their organizations. In this thought provoking article, the author asks, "Can leaders effectively connect with people if they do not have the innate skills and knowledge to manage their emotions?" The author says yes—even if such a leader is not the archetypal emotionally mature leader but the brash and at times out-of-control type of leader.

New York Bakery (A)

Ken Mark and David Loree

Introduction

Patrick Blanshard approached the airline check-in counter and greeted the attendant. It was July 11, 2009, and Blanshard was on his was to Albany, New York, for an information technology (IT) consulting assignment he had just secured. As this was his most prominent consulting assignment to date, Blanshard wanted to make sure he was well prepared for his trip. He stated:

> New York Bakery (NYB) sounds like a typical large manufacturer whose processes have grown complex after years of acquisitions. My task is to review the IT department's readiness to implement a payroll project. I have been told this is a critical piece that will enable the company on its journey out of bankruptcy—it will finally give the firm a chance to monitor its payroll. Payroll accounts for 35 per cent of the budget! If they don't have a new system in place, they will not be able to secure debtor-in-possession finance to help it restructure. No one will invest in a firm that cannot manage its cash. I have been given two weeks to complete this task and am wondering how I should organize my time to meet my objectives.

Blanshard had been referred to NYB by James Grimaldi, an IT recruiter who was a former executive at NYB. Grimaldi met Blanshard on a previous project for another company involving the installation of an enteprise resource planning software package and had been impressed with his work. Blanshard understood that if he was successful in the NYB project, Grimaldi would likely send more contract work his way. "I have been given a lot of information on NYB so far," said Blanshard, "and from what I can tell, there may be issues I have to manage right off the bat." He continued:

> I am walking into a company that is in the midst of a restructuring as a result of a 2008 bankruptcy filing. The company was already struggling with managing its debt load after a series of three regional acquisitions. Then in late 2008, due to the global economic crisis, the collapse in demand for baked goods drastically reduced sales at NYB, triggering the bankruptcy filing. The net result is that people are afraid for their jobs.

> Worse, I am told that many think this payroll initiative is a way to make redundant a quarter of the IT and human resources personnel. Of course it isn't as reductions in head count will not be so drastic, but I was told that was the general sentiment in both departments. I need to secure the cooperation of these employees and others tasked with implementing the payroll project. My mission is to assess the readiness for change and to estimate if the project will succeed. If there is a chance that this project will succeed, I want to be able to identify the hurdles the company has to overcome to proceed with the implementation.

Blanshard boarded the airplane and sat down in his assigned seat. He would be landing in Albany in about an hour and a half, and he would have a full day to himself before he started work at NYB. He had one meeting scheduled with the IT director for 8:00 a.m. on Monday, July 13; after that, he would be expected to set up his own meetings and manage the rest of this two-week stay.

New York Bakery

Jim Huntington founded NYB in Albany starting with a small bakery in 1913 and grew it to become the largest baker of retail bread and cakes in New York by 1948. Economic growth in the postwar years supported expansion at NYB, and the second generation of Huntingtons took the company public in 1972. By 1990, NYB had 30 bakeries spread out over New York, Massachusetts, North Carolina and South Carolina. It was the largest private label baker of store brand breads and cakes in the Eastern United States. The third generation of Huntingtons continued their company's expansion mainly through acquisitions, doubling the firm's size to $560 million in sales by 2000.

By 2007, NYB employed 20,625 full-time workers in its bakeries, distribution system and customer service. NYB operated two separate headquarters when it outgrew its Albany head office in 2001 as a result of acquisitions. The first location near Madison Avenue in Albany housed the executive office, sales and marketing and customer service. A second building on Broadway Avenue in Rensselaer, New York—across the river from Albany—housed NYB's distribution and logistics, finance, legal and human resources functions. About 90 per cent of employees—largely the non-management personnel—were covered by one of the 250 union contracts that NYB had signed. It was a complex task to manage pay and benefits to meet the agreements in each of these 250 contracts. For the union, pay was an especially sensitive issue: workers would be expecting to be paid on time and be given the benefits they had

negotiated. Any deviation or delay from the contractual agreements was likely to spark wild-cat strikes across the country.

NYB purchased bulk ingredients such as flour, oil and condiments from national suppliers, delivering them to their bakeries on a weekly basis. Bread and sweet goods were baked around the clock, with the majority of production scheduled to be ready at five o'clock every morning. NYB's dedicated trucks delivered these baked goods directly to national retailers on a daily basis, and its sales personnel managed shelf space and implemented in-store promotions such as coupons, stand-alone displays or new product introductions.

There were dozens of competitors in each of NYB's markets: competitors differentiated themselves through product quality, price, customer service for retailers and by brand. In 50 per cent of NYB's retail client locations, NYB products competed directly with the store's in-house bakery. For the past 30 years, NYB had set itself apart from its competitors by trying to be the lowest-cost producer of branded products. It achieved this through economies of scale in purchasing and by focusing regional bakeries on producing long runs of a single product group; for example, in the greater New York area, there were five bakeries producing nothing but whole wheat bread, one bakery producing white bread and two bakeries producing cakes. Grouping production by type reduced equipment changeover time and reduced waste. While the physical product itself was largely undifferentiated, NYB customized the packaging for each confection to meet the needs of local consumers; thus, the packaging for bread produced for a New York-based retailer was slightly different than that produced for a North Carolina-based retailer.

In 2007, with the objective of achieving lower costs and better coordination across the company, NYB attempted to install an enterprise resource planning (ERP) software package. This was a significant decision for the company, as the new software was not just "plug and play." Unlike installing a version of Microsoft Word, the new ERP software had to be customized by department, and even by individual as it had to take into account the specifics outlined in each of NYB's union contracts; for example, calculating a worker's pay in a plant in New York might require a payroll employee or manager to go through 16 separate calculations. Before the software, the nuances, exceptions and changes were handled manually and affected by the input of several hundred people spread out across the country. The objective was to move from a manual, paper-based monitoring and payment system to one that was automated by a single piece of software. For a company of NYB's size and complexity, this was a monumental project.

The installation of the ERP package required all departments to review and revamp their work processes in order to adhere to a standard "best practice" model touted by the software provider. While the potential for efficiency gains seemed possible, internal conflicts began to derail the process; for example, employees in the finance department refused to change the way they managed the monthly budgeting process. The finance managers downloaded spreadsheets e-mailed to them by different business units, assembled the monthly forecast, then disseminated the information via a return e-mail to the heads of each business unit. If an ERP package were in place, finance argued that it would lose control over the process and lessen the interaction it had with business unit managers. The bakeries were reluctant to move to an electronic payroll system in which an employee's pay was directly transferred to his or her own bank account; instead, they insisted that local control over payroll was essential and continued to rely on an old payroll software system to manually print individual cheques.

These and other "exceptions" that had to be written into the software eventually served to bog down the efficiency of the ERP package.

When the package was rolled out as scheduled in July 2007—as promised to public shareholders—operations suddenly ground to a halt. While the system had worked in pre-testing, some additional data issues—due to the many work-arounds written into the system—had crept up. Managers who were used to relying on certain data to inform their daily decision-making scrambled to find alternatives. "We thought the software would solve our problems—we threw our support behind it—and it failed us," lamented one executive in finance.

The resulting confusion led to a disastrous rise in the error rate of orders shipped out, from one per cent to 20 per cent. Some customers who were sent product were not billed; in other cases, duplicate invoices were sent, which became a source of frustration for customers. In August 2007, the ERP package was taken off-line and managers were told to revert to their old ways of doing business; however, the damage had been done. By the end of 2007, an anticipated 10 per cent increase in sales turned into a 25 per cent decrease. NYB suffered its first net loss, $30 million on revenues of $540 million. Customers, frustrated by delays in product delivery, started to find alternatives to NYB.

NYB spent the first six months of 2008 trying to stem the losses, but its situation worsened in the second half of 2008 when the global economic crisis started to have an effect on retail sales. Revenues plunged to $350 million, and NYB was on track for a net loss of $50 million for the year. By August 2008, it had breached its debt covenants. With the threat of creditors breaking up the company, NYB filed for Chapter 11 bankruptcy protection in February 2009. Two hundred staff members—mostly management—were laid off and the rest took part in rotating furloughs (unpaid time off work). Seventy-five per cent of NYB unions agreed to a 10 per cent wage rollback to ensure that no jobs were made redundant.

By May 2009, NYB had found a consortium of private equity firms willing to lend it debtor-in-possession financing in exchange for a controlling share in the firm. As they were concerned about the threat of large-scale redundancies at NYB, employees under 20 union contracts (which had yet to be renewed in 2009) went on strike, disrupting product deliveries and manufacturing schedules.

The sentiment started to change in June 2009, when the new private equity managers announced that NYB stood a strong chance of emerging out of bankruptcy protection without any further layoffs if it was able to recover 50 per cent of the accounts it had lost in the last year. A plan was filed with the bankruptcy court and new management was put in place. As management turned its attention to getting NYB back on the path to recovery, the managers started to divide amongst themselves the task of fixing NYB's different departments. The incoming chief information officer (CIO) reviewed aspects of NYB's information systems: as part of his analysis, he reviewed the IT software license contracts and noticed that the payroll software program being used at NYB's bakeries would no longer be supported in six months.

Despite the company's previous failure with new software, the CIO knew that he had to get new payroll software implemented. Payroll was an especially hot topic at NYB, as almost all employees felt anxiety about their employment status. Even a few hours of delay in receiving cheques was enough to visibly upset many of the front line staff. The inability to manage payroll would be an absolute disaster for NYB, as it would trigger wildcat strikes at the bakeries; labour troubles were the last thing the executive team needed to manage, as they were delicately trying to negotiate a new employment contract with each of the many unions representing NYB's workers.

Realizing that his team was overwhelmed with work and could not devote any additional resources to the assessment of the payroll software project, the CIO reached out to his network of contacts in an attempt to find contract personnel to augment his team's work. One

of his contacts, Jason Grimaldi, referred Patrick Blanshard to the CIO. The CIO agreed to give Blanshard a contract for two weeks to evaluate the readiness for change in the organization with regard to putting in place a new payroll software system. In discussions with Grimaldi, the CIO did not go into the specifics of Blanshard's work program.

Patrick Blanshard

Blanshard had been a soldier in the Canadian Armed Forces for 10 years before going back for his MBA at the Richard Ivey School of Business in 2006. Graduating from the MBA program, Blanshard started a health care technology firm in 2007, to capitalize on the growing need for portable computing in health care. He took a break from his start-up to take this two-week contract with NYB. He was excited about the prospect of working in a high pressure, turnaround situation:

> I'm not here to decide whether NYB will implement the ERP or not. As I understand, I'm just here to take the pulse of the organization and to let the CIO know how likely a payroll software rollout is likely to fare. From what I've heard, the place is a mess: I have no issues about that, but that makes it more difficult for me to get information from employees. They'll know that I'm a consultant. They'll be wary of my motives. How do I get them to cooperate with me in my investigation? The CIO can't force the change because the other departments will just reject it.

Blanshard's airplane touched down in Albany and he stepped off, hailed a taxi and was on his way to the local Marriott Courtyard. He thought about the tense situation he would walk into on Monday. He wondered how he could prepare himself to do the best job possible.

Transkin Income Fund:
Leading Entrepreneurial Teams

Ken Mark, Gerard Seijts, and Jana Seijts

⬚ Introduction

On April 1, 2009, Garreth Lind, chief operating officer of Transkin Income Fund (Transkin), was preparing to respond to an e-mail from Kyle McFadden, a vice-president (VP) of the tank division, one of Transkin's six freight divisions. Following a series of discussions with Lind, McFadden had e-mailed him to say that his team would not participate in a company-wide salary rollback of five per cent that Lind had suggested (see Exhibit 1).

Headquartered in Peterborough, Ontario, Transkin provided freight transportation services in Canada and the United States. In 2009, Transkin had about 1,300 power units (i.e., the vehicle that provides the power to pull the transported load) and 2,300 trailers in operation. The company employed about 1,100 people (company drivers, salaried and hourly staff) and had contracts with over 700 owner-operators, who owned their own power units and provided driving services to Transkin.

In mid-February 2009, in response to a sharp fall in demand for transportation services due to the economic crisis, Lind had suggested that each of his six freight divisions and six support divisions and the corporate division should all implement a salary rollback. Lind believed that a strong message needed to be sent to customers, shareholders, banks, owner-operators, drivers and suppliers that Transkin was being proactive by taking action internally to ride out the crisis.

The recession started in Eastern Canada during the first fiscal quarter of 2008 when Transkin lost its largest customer, representing 30 per cent of the van division's business. The paper industry in particular was hard hit. The recession then moved westward: Ontario and Quebec got hit during the last half of 2008, and Saskatchewan and Alberta were affected during the first quarter of 2009.

Although Lind had indicated that participation in the rollback was voluntary, by the start of April 2009, 10 out of Transkin's 12 divisions had signaled that they would participate in the program, effective immediately. Of the two holdouts, one—McFadden—had left Lind an e-mail on April 1, 2009.

While he waited for his last division to respond, Lind wondered how he should handle McFadden's decision to opt out of the rollback. He much preferred that all 12 service divisions and the corporate division would participate.

⬚ Transkin

Founded in 1985, Transkin was one of Canada's leading providers of freight transportation services. It competed primarily in the truckload market where customers had exclusive use of a trailer that was generally filled to capacity by volume or weight. The truckload market generally encompassed large shipments; for comparison, DHL, FedEx and Canada Post generally competed in the less-than-truckload and parcel freight transportation market, where small parcels were shipped to a central sorting depot, aggregated based on parcel destination and carried to their final destination.

Version: (A) 2009-07-31

Transkin provided various modes of transportation to meet its customers' needs. It transported a wide range of commodities and other products such as steel, salt, aggregates, lime, food and liquid food products, lumber, drywall, cement, waste, aggregates and paper products. The company categorized its services under six specific services: flatbed, van, bulk, tank, logistics and waste (see Exhibit 2).

In addition to its full-time drivers, Transkin utilized the services of about 700 owner-operators, each of whom purchased and maintained their own trucks. The use of owner-operators allowed Transkin to offer its customers equipment availability without requiring the company to commit capital to purchasing power units and hiring drivers. The use of owner-operators also allowed Transkin to quickly increase or decrease its complement of power units in response to changes in economic conditions. While under contract with Transkin, owner-operators had to work exclusively for the company. However, the contract could be terminated by either party at any time. Most owner-operators were compensated by Transkin on a flat rate and/or mileage basis; the drivers were compensated on the same basis. The company made maintenance facilities available to owner-operators at a reasonable cost. The salary rollback that Lind had proposed included only the administrative staff of Transkin since the owner-operators and drivers had already been hit hard by the steep decline in business.

The freight transportation industry was fragmented and consisted of relatively few large companies and many small companies serving various markets. The markets were defined by geographical location, point-to-point service location, target customer industries and the type of service provided, such as van, flatbed, tank or bulk. The smaller carriers generally operated in a highly competitive environment in which the customer could have several available options. Many of the large carriers were independent subsidiaries of larger transportation companies, offering a wide variety of freight services on a national basis.

The company located its terminals—from which power units and trailers were dispatched—close to its customers' operations. Transkin's equipment was kept new to minimize repair costs and downtime. The average fleet age was approximately two years for power units and six years for trailers. Although these pieces of equipment had useful lives of approximately eight and 15 years, respectively, management did not generally retain power units that had been in service for four years or longer.

Carriers competed primarily on price and ability to provide reliable, efficient and safe transportation service. Transkin had grown steadily over the past few years as a result of acquisitions, strong operational systems, equipment strategies (especially the reliance of both full-time drivers and owner-operators), safety standards and policies, and dedication to customer service.

Transkin's 6,000 customers were located in Canada and in the eastern, mid-western and southern United States. The company's business was spread out among its customers, with the 10 largest customers accounting for 27 per cent of total revenue and no individual customer accounting for more than 10 per cent of total revenue. This broad base of customers allowed Transkin to limit its exposure from seasonal fluctuations and, to a certain extent, economic downturns.

About 40 per cent of the total distance travelled by Transkin vehicles was in the United States. As such, border delays could in turn delay shipments at Transkin's expense. As many shipments were time-sensitive, missing a shipment deadline could result in penalties for Transkin. In addition, as with other players in the transportation industry, the price of fuel, insurance costs, interest rates, business cycles and general economic conditions were factors that affected Transkin's results.

In 2008, despite a difficult year for the trucking industry, Transkin earned $30 million in net income on $489 million in revenues from transportation services. The company had 1,064 full-time employees, including 473 drivers,

363 operations personnel and 228 administrative personnel. The company was not unionized. Financial data are included in Exhibit 3.

In addition to delivering a profitable year, in late 2008, management had renewed its interest-only loan for five additional years. This meant that Transkin did not have to repay any principal on its loans until 2013. Lind remarked on the good timing in closing the financing: "If we had not closed the financing in late 2008, our refinancing costs would have gone up by 30 to 40 per cent, not including significant fees." Lenders were demanding higher interest rates and higher loan evaluation fees from potential borrowers, in part to offset the financial crisis that was gripping the United States and Canada. Also, the company ended 2008 with a healthy cash balance of $28 million. At the start of 2009, despite a severe downturn in the economy, Transkin seemed to be in a strong financial position.

Structure

Transkin's operations were managed on a decentralized basis. The company was structured in this manner to foster an entrepreneurial business environment to maximize its profit. Driver dispatch, marketing, driver recruitment and training, equipment management, administration and accounting were performed at the divisional level. Lind had 13 direct reports, each of whom managed the following parts of the business:

1. Flatbed
2. Van
3. Bulk
4. Tank
5. Waste
6. Logistics
7. Environmental services (transportation of regulated products)
8. Special projects
9. Finance
10. Secretary Treasurer
11. Risk and compliance
12. Payroll and benefits
13. Executive assistant

Each division's business model differed in important ways. Lind indicated that each division had a broad scope to make decisions:

Each division is as close to an entrepreneurial company as we can get them. We are structured into six primary operating units—flatbed, waste, logistics, van, bulk and tank—and our head office in Peterborough acts as a resource centre for each of these divisions. In our structure, flatbed operators run the flatbed division; van operators run the van division; and so forth. Each primary operating unit conducts its business differently because of the equipment type and customer demands. For example, running a dump business requires quick analysis and the ability to mobilize resources rapidly. Also, if the price of steel goes up, there would suddenly be huge demand for scrap metal, requiring trucks to ship it.

Each GM has full profit-and-loss responsibility: we hold them accountable for the profit and loss from their divisions as well as the balance sheet. Many people want to run their own business. I ask them if they're really sure about wanting to do this because they'll get the good, the bad and the ugly. Some GMs and VPs call me every other day to discuss ideas. Others call me once a month. If there's anything I can help them with, I will. But they're responsible for their own divisions and there are no excuses. This is my job:

bring me all the excuses you want but I will take them away. I've told my reports that I won't bother them if they deliver the results. The GMs and VPs understand that they "live and die by their decisions." Entrepreneurship is a strategic anchor here at Transkin.

In the beginning, we built up each of the divisions with managers in their early 30s, and have been educating them on both the profit-and-loss and balance sheet side of the business for years. We made sure we hired good comptrollers and taught them to focus on long-term issues. As the company has grown, the number of people reporting to me has gone from four to 17; I recently shifted several reports to Lamar Jenkins, our VP of flatbed operations. The number of people that were reporting to me was getting too large.

In each of the divisions, the general managers (GMs) involved Lind occasionally, for example, when they did not know how to handle a particular problem or if they wanted to shorten the approval process. In order to facilitate regular business updates, the GMs of the six primary operating units paid a visit to headquarters once a month. Some of the GMs were located outside in Peterborough, Windsor, Kitchener and Cornwall. The GM typically brought with him a comptroller and a marketing resource. The visit was an opportunity for Lind and others to stay current on the business issues and discuss the challenges they were facing and how they planned to deal with these issues. While GMs had the leeway to identify investments they hoped to make, all capital expenditures had to be approved by Lind.

The Role of Headquarters

Lind saw headquarters as a resource centre for the company's operating divisions. In addition to having access to the senior management team, headquarters provided other services to the divisions. For example, headquarters was responsible for company payroll processing, accounts payable, disbursements, insurance and claims handling, corporate accounting, as well as hardware and software computer support. Transkin's information systems were controlled from Peterborough as well. Lind explained: "Unlike other firms, we have one software package, not 14 systems that don't talk to each other. As we acquire firms, we convert the new companies over to our own financing and operations systems."

The Business Case for Rolling Back Salaries

The downturn in the economy in late 2008 tested the company. In December 2008, with significant input from his VPs, Lind had developed a budget for 2009 that was well received by the board of directors. Then, between January and February 2009, the economic conditions went from bad to worse, and there was a perceptible slowdown in demand for transportation services. Plants were closing. Customers demanded better rates. There was more competition for new contracts. Lind indicated to his management team that they had to start "tightening the belts."

We need to make a statement, not just to our organization, but to our owner-operators, drivers, suppliers, banks, shareholders and customers. We need to show them that we understand their pain and that we know what they're going through. But do I force this on the organization? Or do I truly give them a choice: here is why we're doing what we're doing, and you have to make a choice. In the end, I decided that participation should be voluntary, again, back to one of the strategic anchors: autonomous business units.

I suggested a salary rollback of five per cent across the board involving every salaried position to show our stakeholders that we have taken a hit. With the payroll at about $33 million, the savings would amount to approximately $1.7 million. The rollback was meant to be company-wide. But I left it to the GMs to figure out how to do it. I offered to put my name beside any memo the VPs and GMs wanted to send out; and I would even sign the letter by myself if the VPs and GMs wanted me to do so.

To ensure that the correct message and tone was conveyed, I hired a professional writer who was a lawyer by training and who specialized in corporate communications. We crafted it in a way that we'd be comfortable with it even if the letter got out to customers, suppliers, competitors and the media.

Lind contacted each of his VPs and GMs individually as opposed to meeting them in a group. The meetings were face-to-face and were held early in the morning, typically over breakfast. Lind explained the rationale for the rollback, pointing out the areas where he could use some input and asking for buy-in. He gave the GMs and VPs some time to make their decision. But most of them offered to implement the cuts immediately. However, Lind faced resistance from two of his 12 VPs.

He understood of course that pushing for a voluntary salary rollback was salient for a number of reasons, in particular given the guiding principles or strategic anchors of the company. The guiding principles of Transkin are shown in Exhibit 4. Was the issue of enough importance that Lind should dictate the rollback to the divisions and thus circumvent a key strategic anchor, i.e., the company's autonomous business units? Or should he let the GMs run their divisions without too much interference from headquarters, even during these very difficult economic times?

✉ Refusing to Participate in the Rollback

The first dissenter, Kyle McFadden of the tank division, insisted that they had already implemented cutbacks in his division . . . until Lind pointed out that the cutbacks had not extended to McFadden's own staff. In an attempt to convey the importance of the rollback, Lind met with McFadden for a second breakfast meeting. During this second meeting, Lind gave McFadden additional information to help him see the significance of the rollback. While the meeting seemed to go smoothly, McFadden followed up with a terse e-mail to Lind outlining why his division would not be contributing. McFadden raised a number of specific concerns:

1. The first quarter is always a slow quarter—therefore, is the rollback the right thing to do at this time? Are we being premature with this tough request? We are a seasonal business.

2. The ask for a rollback sends the wrong message, given what our people have done thus far to help turn things around—people have already made personal sacrifices such as sharing the work between owner-operators and drivers.

3. Do these tough measures affect turnover down the road? Do people believe they have been treated in a fair manner? Will they be loyal when business picks up, or will they jump ship for a little more money from a competitor?

4. Are we opening ourselves up to union issues?

5. I have hard-working people here who do not watch the clock. What will their incentive be to stay and put in hours? Some may believe that, no matter how hard they work, the senior leadership will just take away a slice of their paycheque.

Lind then asked one of McFadden's peers to speak with him. Despite the use of peer pressure, McFadden did not provide Lind with an immediate response.

As Lind gathered his thoughts on McFadden's situation, the "new message" light blinked on his BlackBerry. Lind noticed that it was from Todd Plouffe of the bulk division; Plouffe was the only GM who had not yet responded. Like McFadden, Plouffe also refused to participate in the rollback, citing the fact that his division would hit their budget for 2009. Under Plouffe's leadership, the bulk division had been one of the top performers for Transkin for the past 15 years. Despite the economic slowdown, bulk had just won an $8 million contract in late 2008, beating out a handful of competitors. Plouffe's division had been working flat out to cope with the additional demand.

A factor that complicated the decision to urge Plouffe to get his division to accept the rollback was that his wife had recently passed away. His colleagues had supported him throughout the difficult times. And now Plouffe had to ask them for a wage rollback. Lind could not help but think that a tragic personal circumstance had affected a critical business decision that needed to be taken. Should he be more lenient with Plouffe? What would the insistence on the salary rollback do to the motivation in the bulk division?

Lind realized that the two dissenters were from Transkin's two most profitable divisions; these two individuals were also the most senior VPs. And both divisions had already begun to cut costs in a significant way, for example, in overhead costs. He agreed with McFadden that imposing a rollback would not aid morale. He wondered how he should respond to both dissenters.

| **Exhibit 1** | E-mail From Kyle McFadden to Garreth Lind |

Garreth,

I have been pondering and thinking about the proposed wage rollback, and I am struggling with what to do. On one hand I understand the corporation and what the "big picture" represents, but I have concerns about what this would do to staff and the message it would be sending if I did the rollback. Keep in mind that many people have access to the division financials, and you know what Mark Brewster [Chairman and CEO of Transkin Income Fund] has always said to us. Look at the attachment and tell me what your thoughts are. I have forecasted from our Ops report what the revenues and results are going to be and applied them to our first quarter. I held contribution margin at 30%, which should be no problem given no accidents; overhead I applied absolute dollars from February and company truck loss I applied at the same loss as February. Doing this got me the results you see, which are not that bad. If you added back the $ 136,000 for the NEER hit I took in February, my EBIT for the quarter would have been $ 681,000 @ 6.5 per cent, which is actually better than the last two years, both in absolute dollars and per cent. I know: if my aunt was my uncle! But I think about what you said about how Matt felt and now I am struggling with that. I know we reacted quickly when the downturn came. We cut $ 90,000 per month from overhead, saved money in every other area we could, the biggest being maintenance, shared the work evenly with owners-operators and driving staff to retain them for the spring. We are a seasonal business and have had to deal with

(Continued)

Exhibit 1	(Continued)

the first quarter always being slower, not like other divisions that, when one quarter is usually representative of the ones to follow, they have to react differently. Here are some of the concerns I have.

1. We asked our people to bear with us and share the work, which they have done, so taking a slice of their paycheque again sends the wrong message.

2. Will these good people stay when things get better, or will they jump ship for a little money, given how they have been treated? Look at how low my turnover is. I try to be fair and lenient with my staff when they have needs; on the other hand, when I say "all hands on deck," they know what I mean are there without question.

3. Will they perceive this to be another Brewster grab?

4. Are we opening ourselves up to union issues?

5. Will we have the good people around when we get busier? We are a seasonal business and we always have had to deal with this.

6. I have hard working people here who do not watch the clock. What will their incentive be to stay and put in hours? Or will they say "no matter how hard I work, the company will just take it away anyway," and *then* where are my morale and turnover going?

Do not get me wrong—if my percentages started to drop because of revenue or rates, I'd be the first to react, as I have proven recently and many times in the past.

Kyle

Exhibit 2	Transkin Service Categories

Categories	% of revenue	Markets
Flatbed	27	Shipments on open trailers mainly in Canada and the eastern United States.
Van	26	Shipments in closed vans throughout Canada and the eastern United States.
Bulk	19	Shipments in bulk trailers primarily throughout Ontario, Quebec, and the northeastern United States; ships hazardous waste, scrap material, agricultural products, and aggregate.
Tank	15	Shipments of liquid and dry bulk material in enclosed tank trailers primarily throughout Ontario, Quebec, Alberta and the northeastern United States.
Logistics	8	Services to clients to meet their worldwide shipping requirements.
Waste	5	This division hauls organic and industrial waste in Ontario and Michigan.

Exhibit 3	Transkin Financials

Consolidated Income Statements **(in thousands except for per unit amounts)**		
Years ended December 31	*2008*	*2007*
Revenue	488,832	485,865
Operating expenses	389,737	386,686
Selling, general and administration expenses	42,973	42,798
Foreign exchange loss	3,950	374
Amortization of property and equipment	12,342	12,854
Amortization of intangible assets	3,778	3,881
	36,052	39,272
Net interest expense (income) - long-term	6,281	5,113
- short-term	(531)	(92)
Earnings before Income Taxes	30,302	34,251
Income Tax Provision:		
Current	677	1,129
Future	113	6,897
	790	8,026
Net Earnings and Comprehensive Income	29,512	26,225
Earnings per unit - basic and diluted	1.01	0.91
Weighted average number of units outstanding - basic and diluted	29,122	28,826
Consolidated Balance Sheets (in thousands)		
As at December 31	*2008*	*2007*
Assets		
Current Assets		
Cash and cash equivalents	28,826	18,301
Accounts receivable	49,089	54,599

(Continued)

Exhibit 3	(Continued)

Income taxes recoverable	538	—
Other current assets	6,167	6,021
	84,620	78,921
Note Receivable	538	—
Property and Equipment	106,551	107,295
Intangible Assets	18,905	22,905
Goodwill	63,978	61,478
	274,592	270,599
Liabilities and Unitholders' Equity		
Current Liabilities		
Accounts payable and accrued liabilities	33,215	31,191
Distributions payable	3,087	2,996
Income taxes payable	—	417
Current portion of capital lease obligations	1,823	398
Current portion of long-term debt	—	7,408
	38,125	42,410
Long-Term Debt	83,686	82,071
Capital Lease Obligations	7,518	482
Asset Retirement Obligations	1,036	1,192
Future Income Taxes	15,773	15,660
	146,138	141,815
Unitholders' Equity		
Contributed surplus	834	744
Trust units	127,185	120,660
Retained earnings	435	7,380
	128,454	128,784
	274,592	270,599

SOURCE: Company files.

| **Exhibit 4** | Transkin's Guiding Princples |

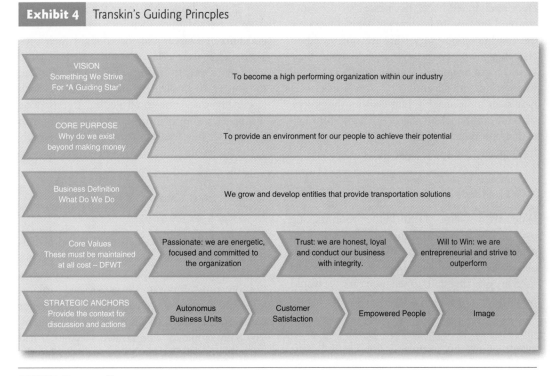

VISION Something We Strive For "A Guiding Star"	To become a high performing organization within our industry			
CORE PURPOSE Why do we exist beyond making money	To provide an environment for our people to achieve their potential			
Business Definition What Do We Do	We grow and develop entities that provide transportation solutions			
Core Values These must be maintained at all cost – DFWT	Passionate: we are energetic, focused and committed to the organization	Trust: we are honest, loyal and conduct our business with integrity.	Will to Win: we are entrepreneurial and strive to outperform	
STRATEGIC ANCHORS Provide the context for discussion and actions	Autonomus Business Units	Customer Satisfaction	Empowered People	Image

SOURCE: Company files.

Why Emotional Intelligence Is Not Essential for Leadership

Mitch McCrimmon

Can a leader who lacks the innate skills and knowledge to manage his or her emotions and connect with people be effective? Yes, says this author, even if such a leader is the brash and at times out-of-control opposite of the archetypal emotionally mature leader. In fact, such a leader, or potential leader, can even be found where an organization would least expect, near the bottom of the organizational chart.

Thanks primarily to Daniel Goleman, it is accepted wisdom that leaders must be emotionally intelligent to be effective. But this notion is not only wrong; it is harmful, especially if it blocks certain people from showing leadership, such as those who might otherwise be great and vitally important leaders. For example, challenging the status quo is usually a preoccupation of many leaders. Yet, dissatisfaction with an existing order is often based on youthful rebelliousness, a condition not normally associated with

    Reprint# 9B09TA05

emotional intelligence. Businesses that require constant innovation to compete depend precisely on youthful innovators who are not afraid to challenge the status quo, even if, in so doing, their style is blunt or aggressive and completely lacking in emotional intelligence. This article sets out a new slant on leadership that clarifies the proper place of emotional intelligence. The bottom line is that emotional intelligence is more important for management than leadership.

What Is Leadership?

When we visualize Martin Luther King making one of his famous speeches or demonstrating against segregation on buses in Alabama, we can almost hear his brilliant oratory. But if he had used his speaking skills to sell used cars, we would never have seen him as a leader. The very reason he was a leader was that he challenged the status quo. We tend to forget that fact because we are so awestruck by his oratorical powers and their impact on us. Mahatma Gandhi also challenged the status quo by protesting British rule in India. So did Nelson Mandela with regard to white rule in South Africa. These leaders had widely different influencing styles, but they shared a passion for changing what they thought was horribly wrong.

We also think of leadership as a relationship between leaders and followers. But we overlook a more important relationship, the one between leaders and their target audiences. The three leaders mentioned above were aiming their cry for change at their respective governments and the population at large. In fact, you could say that their followers on the street actually helped them show that they were leaders, especially to their governments. For example, Martin Luther King's leadership effort in Alabama was successful when the U.S. Supreme Court ruled segregation on buses unconstitutional.

These three leaders have other things in common. None of them managed the people responsible for making the policy changes that they were promoting. They had no formal authority over their respective governments. Because

they showed leadership from the sidelines, not from an elected office, their leadership came to an end once the target audience bought their proposals. They were able to demonstrate leadership without having to manage the people who had the power to implement their proposals. Such leadership does not entail getting things done through a group of people working for or with the leader. Thus, leadership can be defined simply as the successful promotion of new directions.

Innovative Knowledge Workers as Leaders

A multitude of new business models and revolutionary products are started by young people. Think only of Google, Yahoo! and Amazon.com. But sometimes, innovators in established corporations are successful in convincing their senior management teams to move in new directions. The Sony employee who created Playstation had difficulty influencing his superiors to develop the product because they felt that Sony should not make toys. But he persisted and won them over. To realize how he did, consider the following scenario.

Bill Thompson (not his real name) is a product developer in a large software company. He was struggling to persuade his superiors of the merits of a new product his team had developed. Management resisted the innovation because it meant cannibalizing a successful, established product. After trying numerous influencing tactics ranging from a soft sell through losing his temper, he finally demonstrated a prototype of the product to a group of customers. With their support, management gave in and agreed to develop the product. Bill's leadership was bottom-up or from the sidelines, much like that of King, Gandhi and Mandela. Like them, bottom-up leaders have no authority over senior management, and they might not have anyone reporting to them. Their leadership also comes to an end once their bosses buy their new product ideas. If they demonstrate the value of their proposals with hard evidence or a convincing business case, they don't need inspirational communication skills. In fact, their presentation style might be rather quiet and self-effacing, simply factual, or even blunt and abrasive. Bill Thompson was not a very good people manager. He devoted most of his time to product development and was often short-tempered with team members who bothered him with what he saw as trivial problems. His influencing style, both upward and down, tended to be direct, factual and often aggressive. While he was not well liked, his compelling ideas often persuaded colleagues to back him.

Creativity and Leadership

Leadership, as traditionally conceived, has always been founded on the power to ascend to, and maintain, a dominant position in a group. When a "leadership position" has been attained, the leader can call the shots, make the strategic decisions that move the business forward. But it is increasingly recognized that business has become too complex and fast changing for executives to provide this type of direction. The reality is that the power to provide leadership is shifting from what it takes to dominate a group to the ability to generate profitable new products. Business has become a war of ideas. The inconvenient fact about ideas, however, is that no one can monopolize them or use them to dominate a group for long. As a result, business is now like guerrilla warfare, and leadership is more dependent on creativity. Anyone with a good idea can strive to show leadership by promoting it. Creative people, like Bill Thompson, have little emotional intelligence. Leadership conceived as simply the promotion of better ideas is an occasional act that can be shown by anyone. It is not a role. In a meeting, such leadership can shift from one person to another several times.

Managerial Leadership: Only a Special Case

Focusing exclusively on leadership shown by managers creates a distorted picture of the meaning of

leadership. As Thomas Kuhn pointed out in his epoch-shattering book, *The Structure of Scientific Revolutions*[1], accepted theories ignore anomalies because they can't explain them. Our conventional concept of leadership ignores the following inconvenient types of leadership because they fall outside the managerial framework:

- Leadership shown by outsiders such as King, Mandela and Gandhi
- Leading by example, as when a new customer service employee serves customers more effectively and colleagues soon begin to follow suit, even though there is no reporting relationship between any of them
- Leadership between companies, such as Microsoft following the lead of Apple
- Inspiration from dead leaders, as when present-day activists follow the lead of Gandhi and practice non-violence
- Sports competitors following the lead of better performers
- Bottom-up leadership, where a front-line employee, like Bill Thompson, champions new products

All of these leadership types amount to showing the way to others, nothing more. The dead leaders and the customer service employee who lead by example are not even aware of the impact they are having on their followers, let alone intentionally trying to lead anyone. Not one of these examples involves even an informal reporting relationship between leader and follower.

Why should we pay attention to such perverse instances of leadership when our real interest is in managerial leadership? There are two crucial benefits of recognizing that leadership is much broader than what managers do with their followers. First, greater weight is added to the argument that we should view bottom-up leadership as a legitimate type of leadership rather than as a mere anomaly. Second, these types of

---

[1]Kuhn, Thomas, *The Structure of Scientific Revolutions*, 1962.

leadership have only one thing in common—they move people in a new direction and give us the means to differentiate leadership from management. This is critical to understanding that emotional intelligence is critical for management, though not so for leadership.

Management is a vital function that has been wrongly cast in the rubbish bin ever since the success of the Japanese commercial invasion that began in the late seventies. At that time, everyone with a view on the subject called for an end to management, to be replaced by leadership. This was a gross error. A scapegoat was needed to blame for the failure of Western businesses to cope with Japanese competition, and management was fingered for this role. Previously, we talked of different styles of leadership or management. You could be task focused or people oriented, theory X or theory Y, transactional or transformational. But since the late seventies, management has been saddled with the bad guy side of these pairings while leadership has been conceded the good guy side. Naturally, it made sense to tack emotional intelligence onto leadership.

A very different view suggests that leadership and management are totally style-neutral functions. Leadership promotes new directions, management executes them. An inspiring leader moves us to change direction while an inspiring, transformational, people-oriented manager motivates us to work harder. Because leadership, so defined, can come from outside the organization or from the bottom up, it does not entail managing people. Executives who both lead and manage are wearing a managerial hat when they coach, empower and motivate employees to improve their performance.

The Place of Emotional Intelligence

When Daniel Goleman and others discuss the place of emotional intelligence in leadership,

they have senior executives or CEOs in mind. Occupying a role with such heavy responsibility for so many important resources, often including large numbers of people, does require integrity, emotional intelligence and other sterling character traits. For this reason, it is no surprise that established large companies usually do not have twenty-something year old chief executives. As Goleman stated: "One thing is certain: emotional intelligence increases with age. There is an old-fashioned word for the phenomenon: maturity."[2] The implication is that young technical geeks are not generally suited to be chief executives because they lack sufficient maturity to manage such heavy duties and the vast range of stakeholders that come with the territory.

This may be so, but is it necessary to be a senior executive, or even to manage people, to show leadership? Popular conceptions do imply that leaders are in charge of teams and that their purpose is to get the best out of those teams relative to certain shared goals. But, as we have seen, Martin Luther King, Gandhi and Nelson Mandela had no managerial authority over the people to whom they were striving to show leadership—their respective governments. The reality is that our vision of leadership confuses senior executives with management.

Management has a role and all roles entail responsibilities. Even a lighthouse operator who never sees anyone must be trustworthy and have sufficient emotional intelligence to communicate with users appropriately. The more responsibility people have the more they need to be trustworthy. Senior executives have a psychological contract with employees, one that calls for executives to treat employees equitably. These same executives need the emotional intelligence that enables them to sense when employees are struggling and for being able to use different approaches to motivate them.

Unlike management, however, leadership is not a role. It is an initiative or action that influences

---

[2]Goleman, Daniel, "What makes a leader?" *Harvard Business Review*, November/December 1998.

people to change direction. For example, while managers show leadership when they champion new directions, non-managers can show that same leadership as well. When people are appointed to management roles, it is often because they have shown some leadership. Once promoted, they wear two hats. When showing leadership they are effectively selling tickets for a journey; but they switch to their management hat to drive the bus to the destination. If resistance emerges en route, a further injection of leadership may be needed to resell the journey. Otherwise, getting to the destination is mainly a management task.

It is not uncommon for employees who show bottom-up leadership to be both unsuitable and uninterested in managing people. Those who are stereotypical technical geeks are only interested in their technology. They are so immersed in their own worlds that they are often quite unaware of people around them. Some even neglect their appearance or forget to eat and sleep. They not only lack the necessary emotional intelligence to manage people but often have poor organizational skills as well, making it a certainty that they would struggle to monitor performance or manage complex projects.

Because leadership divorced of managerial authority is not a role with ongoing responsibilities, there is less need for emotional intelligence. However, having interpersonal skills gives such leaders a greater number of influencing tactics. Those without such skills must rely on hard evidence and a confident delivery. Often, technical gurus are very confident, even egotistical and self-centered. Lacking emotional intelligence simply requires them to have stronger evidence for their proposals.

In short, emotional intelligence has a situational role to play in leadership. This simply means that leaders need to be sensitive only when trying to move certain audiences. Those that respond to a hard-hitting factual case or a demonstration care less about how the message is delivered. In many scientific and technical domains, such as health care for instance, the current slogan

is "evidence based practice," the idea being that hard evidence must be the primary mode of influence for prospective leaders. This trend reinforces the point that the power to lead is increasingly knowledge based and is less about personality and character. Conversely, emotional intelligence is essential for all managerial roles.

Cultivating Bottom-Up Leadership

Organizations that depend on constant innovation to prosper must cultivate bottom-up leadership. They need to recognize and encourage their Bill Thompsons. But if potential leaders are told to keep quiet until they become emotionally intelligent, they may well say good-bye before they gain the necessary maturity. The leadership shown by young knowledge workers is based on youthful rebelliousness, the desire of all young people to question authority, to make their mark and to differentiate themselves. Their impatience, zeal and negative attitude toward authority figures inclines them to be aggressive in their influencing style. But these same traits are also associated with creativity. The desire to find a better way stems from the same source as the drive to challenge the existing order. If the rough edges of such leaders are smoothed over for the sake of maturity, they might become more conservative generally—a potential disaster for organizations that depend on innovation.

To reap the benefits of bottom-up leadership, organizations need to change their cultures so that those in executive positions become more comfortable letting go of their monopoly on leadership. In addition, budding, front-line leaders need to be encouraged to express themselves freely and courageously. Empowerment so extended is very engaging and has great potential to enhance talent retention. Executives must learn to be more receptive to upward challenges to their authority if the organization's most vital leadership resource is not to be lost. This is a lot to ask of senior executives, which is all the more reason why they need emotional intelligence.

The Path–Goal Theory of Leadership

No matter what you do, the responsibility that you as a leader carry will set you apart from those you lead. You will find it from time to time a little lonely to be the boss, and sometimes a lot lonely. Do what you can to help others help you. Build personal teams, no matter whether they work directly for you or not, learn whom to trust and then use these teams and individuals and their trusted advice, personal counsel or clear views of an issue, no matter where in the world you and they may be.

—General Rick Hillier[1]

The path–goal theory of leadership is similar to the situational and contingency theories of leadership in that it prescribes appropriate leadership styles for interacting with subordinates. It is different from the situational and contingency theories in that path–goal theory adds more variables to what leaders need to consider in their relationships with employees. In essence, the path–goal theory of leadership "is about how leaders motivate subordinates to accomplish designated goals" (Northouse, 2013).

Based on expectancy theory, path–goal theory suggests that employees will be motivated if three conditions are met. These are the following: Employees believe in their ability to perform their assigned work-related tasks, they believe that their work-related efforts will lead to appropriate outcomes, and they believe that these work-related outcomes will be meaningful.

The key to understanding the path–goal theory of leadership is to think about the path that subordinates must follow to achieve their assigned goals. Subordinates are motivated by their leader to achieve these goals when leaders clearly define the goals, clarify the path to completing the goals, remove obstacles to completing the goals, and provide support to help achieve the assigned goals (Northouse, 2013). This is illustrated in Figure 7.1.

---

[1]Hillier, R. (2010, p. 290). General Rick Hillier was Canada's Chief of Defence Staff from February 2005 to July 2008.

Path–goal theory has several components that leaders need to assess if they are to create a positive association between subordinate motivation and goal achievement. Different leadership behaviors will differentially affect subordinate motivation, and this impact will depend on subordinate and task characteristics (Northouse, 2013). These four components of path–goal theory are shown in Figure 7.2.

Figure 7.1	The Basic Idea Behind Path–Goal Theory

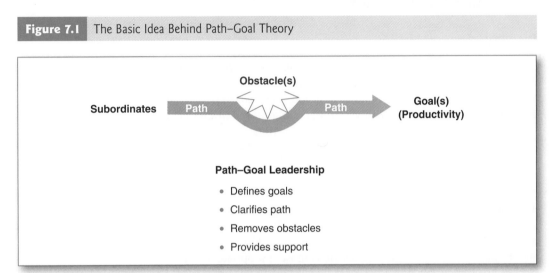

SOURCE: Based on Robert House's path-goal theory and adapted from *Leadership: Theory and Practice*, Sixth Edition, by Peter Northouse. Copyright © 2013, SAGE Publications, Inc.

Figure 7.2	Major Components of Path–Goal Theory

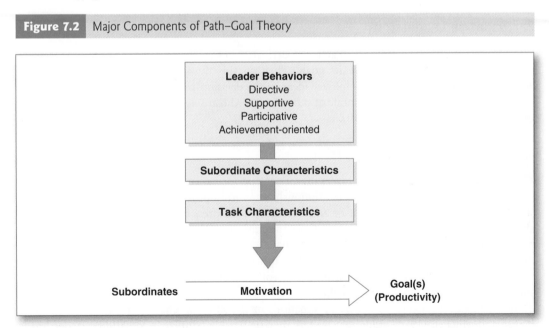

SOURCE: Based on Robert House's path-goal theory and adapted from *Leadership: Theory and Practice*, Sixth Edition, by Peter Northouse. Copyright © 2013, SAGE Publications, Inc.

Leader Behaviors

Initially, four leader behaviors were assessed but with the understanding that others would be examined as research continued. These were directive, supportive, participative, and achievement oriented (House & Mitchell, 1974; Yukl, 2012).

Directive Leadership

This leadership style emphasizes giving direction to subordinates regarding their tasks (Daft, 2011). These directions include the result expected, the manner in which the task will be accomplished, and the schedule for task completion. In addition, the leader clarifies performance expectations and explicitly outlines the required standard operating procedures, rules, and regulations (Yukl, 2012). This style increases subordinate morale when there is task ambiguity (DuBrin, 2010) and is similar to the task-oriented or initiating structure style (Daft, 2011).

Supportive Leadership

These leaders are approachable (i.e., maintain an open-door policy), friendly, and empathetic to their subordinates' needs and well-being (Yukl, 2012). They expend extra effort to ensure the workplace has an enjoyable environment, and they create an atmosphere of honor, respect, and equality for their subordinates in the workplace. This style is most appropriate for improving morale when tasks are boring, frustrating, repetitive, stressful, and dissatisfying. Subordinates who are uncertain of their capabilities, situation, and future appreciate this style more (DuBrin, 2010). In addition, this style is similar to the people-oriented or consideration style (Daft, 2011).

Participative Leadership

These leaders encourage employees to actively participate in the decision-making process that determines how the group will achieve its goals. They do this through consultation, solicitation of employee suggestions, and using employee ideas in the decision-making process (Daft, 2011). This style is most likely to enhance the morale of subordinates who are well motivated and engaged in tasks that are nonrepetitive (DuBrin, 2010).

Achievement-Oriented Leadership

This leadership style challenges employees to work at a performance level that is the best possible. The leader sets a very high standard and continuously seeks to improve performance above that initial standard (Daft, 2011). Achievement-oriented leaders also express a great deal of confidence in the abilities of employees to set and achieve very demanding goals (Yukl, 2012). This style is most appropriate for improving morale when subordinates have a high need to achieve and are working on tasks that are characterized by variety and ambiguity (DuBrin, 2010).

The path–goal theory is different from trait theory in that leaders are not constrained to a leadership style that depends on their personality. It is also different from contingency theory in that leaders do not have to be matched to particular situations or the situation changed to match leader style. House and Mitchell (1974) argue that leaders may be flexible (similar to situational leadership in

Chapter 5) and exercise all or any of the four styles described above. They suggest that it will depend on the subordinate and task characteristics. In addition, leaders may integrate styles should the situation require a blending of two or more styles (DuBrin, 2010). In the next two sections, we describe the subordinate and task characteristics on which the impact of leader behavior on subordinate motivation depends.

Subordinate Characteristics

Several characteristics determine how much satisfaction (present or future) subordinates will obtain from a leader's behavior. Four have been studied intensely. These are "subordinates' needs for affiliation, preferences for structure, desires for control, and self-perceived level of task ability" (Northouse, 2013).

Subordinates with a higher need for affiliation should prefer supportive leadership because friendly, concerned leadership will give these subordinates greater satisfaction. On the other hand, subordinates who work in uncertain situations and have a tendency to be dogmatic and authoritarian should prefer directive leadership because this type of leadership gives "psychological structure and task clarity" (Northouse, 2013).

Whether subordinates have an internal or external locus of control determines which leader behaviors give more satisfaction. Internal locus of control suggests that subordinates believe that the decisions they make affect what happens in their lives, while external locus of control suggests that subordinates believe that what happens in their lives is beyond their control. Subordinates with an internal locus of control should find participative leadership more satisfying because it gives a greater feeling of being in charge and of being an important part of the decision-making process. On the other hand, subordinates with an external locus of control should prefer directive leadership because it parallels their belief that external forces control what happens to them (Northouse, 2013).

Finally, self-perceived level of task ability is important in determining how leader behaviors affect subordinates' satisfaction and motivation. Subordinates with a higher perception of their own competence at performing specific tasks should prefer less directive leaders. As subordinates assess that they are becoming more competent, directive leadership may become superfluous and seem more controlling than necessary (Northouse, 2013).

Task Characteristics

Task characteristics also have a major effect on how leader behaviors affect subordinates' satisfaction and motivation. These characteristics include the subordinates' task design, the organization's formal authority system, and subordinates' primary work group (Northouse, 2013). For example, when there is task clarity and structure, well-established norms and customs, and a clear formal authority system, subordinates will not need leaders to provide goal clarity or coaching in how to achieve these goals. Subordinates will consider that their work is of value and that they can accomplish their tasks. Leaders in this situation may be viewed as more controlling than necessary, having little or no empathy and, therefore, unnecessary.

Other situations may need leaders to be more involved. In a context where there is goal ambiguity, leaders can provide structure. Repetitive tasks may require supportive leadership given the mechanical nature of these tasks. When there is a weak authority system, leadership may be required to provide clarity regarding rules and what is needed to accomplish assigned work. Finally, leaders may be required to encourage teamwork and acceptance of role responsibility when group norms and customs are weak.

Path–goal theory has a special focus on assisting subordinates to get around, over, under, or through obstacles that are keeping them from achieving their tasks. Obstacles may be responsible for subordinates having feelings of frustration, uncertainty, and being threatened. Path–goal theory implies that leaders should assist subordinates in getting around these obstacles or in removing the obstacles from the path to task completion. Helping subordinates in this way will increase their perceived level of task ability and their level of satisfaction and motivation.

House (1996) has reformulated path–goal theory by adding four new leader behaviors. These are facilitating subordinates' work, decision-making processes that are more group oriented, allowing work groups to network and represent themselves, and providing leader behavior that is based on values that are not focused solely on the bottom line. The essence of the reformulated theory is no different from the original—subordinates need leaders who will provide what is needed in the subordinates' environment and what is needed to make up for deficient skills, knowledge, and abilities (Northouse, 2013).

How Does Path–Goal Leadership Theory Work?

Table 7.1 suggests several possible ways the path–goal theory of leadership can integrate leader behavior with subordinate and task characteristics. While the theory is conceptually complex, it is also very pragmatic and gives direction to leaders with respect to assisting subordinates in accomplishing their work in a manner that provides them with satisfaction and motivation. The theory assumes flexibility on the part of leaders and suggests that leaders should choose leader behaviors that best suit subordinate needs and work situations. We provide some examples in the next paragraph.

First, if you as a leader see that the path is ambiguous, rules are unclear, and there is complexity and that subordinates are authoritarian and dogmatic, you should be a directive leader to provide guidance and psychological structure. Second, if the work is repetitive, not very challenging, mundane, and mechanical and if subordinates are unsatisfied, need a human touch, and have a higher need for affiliation, you should be a supportive leader to develop and provide a nurturing atmosphere. Third, when you see that the path is ambiguous, the way is unclear, the task is unstructured, and subordinates have a need for autonomy, control, and clarity, you need to be a participative leader who invites subordinates into the decision-making process. Finally, if the path is ambiguous, the task is challenging and complex, and subordinates have high expectations for what they can achieve and a higher need to excel, you need to be an achievement-oriented leader who challenges subordinates.

Of course, as we mentioned earlier, leaders may find it appropriate to exercise two leader behaviors simultaneously. It may be that the situation and subordinate characteristics call for you as a leader to be achievement oriented and supportive (DuBrin, 2010). We find that in our teaching, we set a high standard for students to challenge them to achieve, and we offer as much support as possible (without doing the work for them) to help and encourage them to achieve to the best of their abilities. There is an ethical component to this leader behavior. You have to know your students well enough to have expectations for achievement on their part that are achievable.

Leaders who are effective meet subordinates' needs. They help subordinates set goals and determine the path to take in achieving these goals. Effective leaders assist subordinates in getting around, getting through, or removing obstacles. Finally, leaders are effective when they assist subordinates in the achievement of their goals by guiding, directing, and coaching them along the right path.

Table 7.1	Path–Goal Theory: How It Works

Leader Behavior	Group Members	Task Characteristics
Directive leadership "Provides guidance and psychological structure"	Dogmatic Authoritarian	Ambiguous Unclear rules Complex
Supportive leadership "Provides nurturance"	Unsatisfied Need affiliation Need human touch	Repetitive Unchallenging Mundane and mechanical
Participative "Provides involvement"	Autonomous Need for control Need for clarity	Ambiguous Unclear Unstructured
Achievement oriented "Provides challenges"	High expectations Need to excel	Ambiguous Challenging Complex

SOURCE: Based on Robert House's path-goal theory and adapted from *Leadership: Theory and Practice*, Sixth Edition, by Peter Northouse. Copyright © 2013, SAGE Publications, Inc.

References

Daft, R. L. (2011). *The leadership experience* (5th ed.). Mason, OH: Thomson, South-Western.

DuBrin, A. (2010). *Leadership: Research findings, practice, and skills* (6th ed.). Mason, OH: South-Western/Cengage.

Hillier, R. (2010). *Leadership: 50 points of wisdom for today's leaders.* Toronto, Canada: HarperCollins.

House, R. J. (1996). Path–goal theory of leadership: Lessons, legacy, and a reformulated theory. *Leadership Quarterly, 7*(3), 323–352.

House, R. J., & Mitchell, R. R. (1974). Path–goal theory of leadership. *Journal of Contemporary Business, 3*, 81–97.

Northouse, P. G. (2013). *Leadership: Theory and practice* (6th ed.). Thousand Oaks, CA: Sage.

Yukl, G. (2012). *Leadership in organizations* (8th ed.). Upper Saddle River, NJ: Pearson/Prentice Hall.

The Cases

General Electric: From Jack Welch to Jeffrey Immelt

This case describes the leadership initiatives of two of General Electric's (GE) chief executive officers: Jack Welch and Jeffrey Immelt. Under Jack Welch's leadership, GE, one of the most admired firms in the world, began its transformation from a manufacturing conglomerate to one that focused on services. Welch's stature as a management leader grew as GE's stock price increased. Many of Welch's management practices were adopted by American and global organizations. While his changes resulted in excellent financial performance sustained over a long period of time, not all within GE agreed with his methods. Welch's departure in 2001 triggered a steep decline in GE's stock price. His successor, Jeffrey Immelt, took over the company days before the terrorist attacks in September 2001 and has spent the last few years preparing the firm for its next stage of growth.

Please Stop Working So Hard!

Matt Platt was a new production supervisor at an automobile engine plant. In that position, he has just encountered his first challenging task. He must find a way to diffuse the tension between the team of line machine operators and the team leader. Although the team leader was the hardest working individual on the team, he was repeatedly criticized for overexerting himself. This has led to workers fearing that their jobs will be in jeopardy if the team leader undertakes multiple tasks. The other team members were beginning to feel that Platt was giving the team leader special permission to break team norms and that they were being treated unfairly as a result. Team morale was deteriorating, and Platt knew that he needed to confront the team leader about this unique quandary. He wanted to figure out how best to please the team leader and the other members of the team.

The Reading

Learning Goals or Performance Goals: Is It the Journey or the Destination?

Every manager has his or her eye on the finish line, but sometimes what you do or don't do during the race is more important than winning it.

General Electric: From Jack Welch to Jeffrey Immelt

Ken Mark and Stewart Thornhill

Introduction

General Electric (GE) was a U.S. conglomerate with businesses in a wide range of industries, including aerospace, power systems, health care, commercial finance and consumer finance. In 2007, GE earned US$22.5 billion in net profit from US$170 billion in sales. In 2008, GE expected to generate US$30 billion in cash from operations. Driving GE's growth was what many commentators considered to be the "deepest bench of executive talent in U.S. business,"[1] the result of two decades of investment in its management training programs by its former chief executive officer (CEO), John F. (Jack) Welch, Jr. The current CEO, Jeffrey Immelt, took over

Version: (A) 2008-04-18

[1]Diane Brady, "Jack Welch: Management Evangelist," *Business Week*, October 25, 2004. Available at http://www.business week.com/magazine/content/04_43/b3905032_mz072.htm, accessed November 12, 2007.

from Jack Welch four days before September 11, 2001 and had spent the last few years preparing the firm for its next stage of growth.

General Electric

GE's roots could be traced back to a Menlo Park, New Jersey laboratory where Thomas Alva Edison invented the incandescent electric lamp. GE was founded when Thomson-Houston Electric and Edison General Electric merged in 1892. Its first few products included light bulbs, motors, elevators, and toasters. Growing organically and through acquisitions, GE's revenues reached $27 billion in 1981. By 2007, its businesses sold a wide variety of products such as lighting, industrial equipment and vehicles, materials, and services such as the generation and transmission of electricity, and asset finance. Its divisions included GE Industrial, GE Infrastructure, GE Healthcare, GE Commercial Finance, GE Consumer Finance, and NBC Universal.[2]

For more than 125 years, GE was a leader in management practices, "establishing its strength with the disciplined oversight of some of the world's most effective business people."[3]

When he became chairman and CEO in 1972, Reginald Jones was the seventh man to lead General Electric since Edison. Jones focused on shifting the company's attention to growth areas such as services, transportation, materials and natural resources, and away from electrical equipment and appliances. He implemented the concept of strategic planning at GE, creating 43 strategic business units to oversee strategic planning for its groups, divisions and departments. By 1977, in order to manage the information

generated by 43 strategic plans, Jones added another management layer, sectors, on top of the strategic business units. Sectors represented high level groupings of businesses: consumer products, power systems, and technical products.[4]

In the 1970s, Jones was voted CEO of the Year three times by his peers, with one leading business journal dubbing him CEO of the Decade in 1979. When he retired in 1981, the *Wall Street Journal* proclaimed Jones a "management legend." Under Jones's administration, the company's sales more than doubled ($10 billion to $27 billion) and earnings grew even faster ($572 million to $1.7 billion).[5]

Jack Welch Becomes CEO

In terms of his early working life, Welch had

> Worked for GE not much more than a year when in 1961 he abruptly quit his $10,500 job as a junior engineer in Pittsfield, Mass. He felt stifled by the company's bureaucracy, underappreciated by his boss, and offended by the civil service-style $1,000 raise he was given. Welch wanted out, and to get out he had accepted a job offer from International Minerals & Chemicals in Skokie, Ill.

> But Reuben Gutoff, then a young executive a layer up from Welch, had other ideas. He had been impressed by the young upstart and was shocked to hear of his impending departure and farewell party just two days away. Desperate to keep him, Gutoff coaxed Welch and

---

[2]http://en.wikipedia.org/wiki/General_Electric, accessed November 12, 2007.

[3]General Electric, "Our History: Our Company." Available at http://www.ge.com/company/history/index.html, accessed June 4, 2007.

[4]Christopher A. Bartlett and Meg Wozny, "GE's Two-Decade Transformation: Jack Welch's Leadership," Harvard Business School Case, May 3, 2005, pp. 1–2.

[5]Christopher A. Bartlett and Meg Wozny, "GE's Two-Decade Transformation: Jack Welch's Leadership," Harvard Business School Case, May 3, 2005, p. 2.

his wife, Carolyn, out to dinner that night. For four straight hours at the Yellow Aster in Pittsfield, he made his pitch: Gutoff swore he would prevent Welch from being entangled in GE red tape and vowed to create for him a small-company environment with big-company resources. These were themes that would later dominate Welch's own thinking as CEO.[6]

In his memoirs, Welch noted that the CEO's job was "close to 75 per cent about people and 25 per cent about other stuff."[7]

But Welch knew that his path to become CEO of GE was anything but smooth. As he recalled:

> The odds were against me. Many of my peers regarded me as the round peg in a square hole, too different for GE. I was brutally honest and outspoken. I was impatient and, to many, abrasive. My behavior wasn't the norm, especially the frequent parties at local bars to celebrate business victories, large or small.[8]

For Welch, there was a seven-person "horse race" to become CEO that was, in his words, "brutal, complicated by heavy politics and big egos, my own included. It was awful."[9] In the end, however, Welch prevailed, becoming CEO in April 1981. Later, he learned that he had been left off the short list of candidates until late into the process. Welch recalled:

> I didn't know that when the list was narrowed to ten names by 1975, I still wasn't on it. . . . One official HR [human resources] view of me stated at the time: "Not on best candidate list despite past operating success. Emerging issue is overwhelming results focus. Intimidating subordinate relationships. Seeds of company stewardship concerns. Present business adversity will severely test. Watching closely."[10]

1981 to 1987: Number One or Number Two and Delayering

Welch wanted the company to do away with its formal reporting structure and unnecessary bureaucracy. He wanted to recreate the firm along the lines of the nimble plastics organization he had come from. He stated:

> I knew the benefits of staying small, even as GE was getting bigger. The good businesses had to be sorted out from the bad ones. . . . We had to act faster and get the damn bureaucracy out of the way.[11]

Welch developed this strategy based on work by Peter Drucker, a management thinker, who asked: "If you weren't already in the business, would you enter it today? And if the answer is no, what are you going to do about it?"[12] Welch communicated his restructuring efforts by insisting that any GE business be the number one or number two business in its industry, or

---

[6]John A. Byrne, "How Jack Welch Runs GE," Business Week, June 8, 1998. Available at http://www.businessweek.com/1998/23/b3581001.htm, accessed June 4, 2007.

[7]Jack Welch, *Straight from the Gut,* Warner Books, New York, 2001, p. xii.

[8]Jack Welch, *Straight from the Gut,* Warner Books, New York, 2001, p. xii.

[9]Ibid, p. xiii.

[10]Ibid, p. 77.

[11]Ibid, p. 92.

[12]Ibid, p. 108.

be fixed, sold or closed. He illustrated this concept with the use of a three-circle tool. The businesses inside the three circles—services, high technology, and core—could attain (or had attained) top positions in their industries. The selected few included many service businesses, such as financial and information systems. Outside of the three circles were organizations in manufacturing-heavy sectors facing a high degree of competition from lower cost rivals, such as central air conditioning, housewares, small appliances and semiconductors.

Employment at GE fell from 404,000 in 1980 to 330,000 by 1984 and 292,000 by 1989. The changes prompted strong reactions from former employees and community leaders. Welch was the target of further criticism when he invested nearly $75 million into a major upgrade of Crotonville, GE's management development center.[13] Welch saw leadership training as key to GE's growth.

In addition, Welch undertook a streamlining exercise. By his estimate, GE in 1980 had too many layers of management, in some cases as many as 12 levels between the factory floor and the CEO's office. The sector level was removed, and a massive downsizing effort put into place.

Compared with the traditional norm of five to eight direct reports per manager, GE senior managers had 15 or more direct reports. Successful senior managers shrugged off their workload, indicating that Welch liberated them to behave like entrepreneurs. They argued that the extra pressure forced them to set strict priorities on how they spent their time, and to abandon many past procedures. Observers believed GE was running two main risks: having inadequate internal communication between senior managers and people who now reported to each of them; and the overwork, stress, demotivation and inefficiency on the part of managers down the line who had extra work assigned by their hard-pressed superiors. In 1989, an article in the Harvard Business Review reported "much bitter internal frustration and ill-feeling among the troops at GE."[14]

During this period, Welch earned his "Neutron Jack" moniker, a reference to a type of bomb that would kill people while leaving buildings intact. On the other hand, Welch could see that changes had to be made to make GE more competitive. He recalled:

> Truth was, we were the first big healthy and profitable company in the mainstream that took actions to get more competitive. . . . There was no stage set for us. We looked too good, too strong, too profitable, to be restructuring. . . . However, we were facing our own reality. In 1980, the U.S. economy was in a recession. Inflation was rampant. Oil sold for $30 a barrel, and some predicted it would go to $100 if we could even get it. And the Japanese, benefiting from a weak yen and good technology, were increasing their exports into many of our mainstream businesses from cars to consumer electronics.[15]

But Welch's strategy was not simply a cost-reduction effort: from 1981 to 1987, while 200 businesses were sold, 370 were acquired, for a net spend of $10 billion.

The turmoil that these changes caused earned Welch the title of "toughest boss in America," in a *Fortune* magazine survey of the 10 most hard-nosed senior executives. In tallying the votes, Welch received twice as many nominations as the runners-up. "Managers at GE used to hide out-of-favor employees from Welch's gun sights so they could keep their jobs," *Fortune* said. "According to former employees, Welch

---

[13]Ibid, p. 121.

[14]"General Electric Learns the Corporate and Human Costs of Delayering," *Financial Times*, September 25, 1989, p. 44.

[15]Jack Welch, *Straight from the Gut*, Warner Books, New York, 2001, pp. 125–126.

conducts meetings so aggressively that people tremble."[16] But Welch's credibility was bolstered by GE's stock performance:

> After years of being stuck, GE stock and the market began to take off, reinforcing the idea that we were on the right track. For many years, stock options weren't worth all that much. In 1981, when I became chairman, options gains for everyone at GE totaled only $6 million. The next year, they jumped to $38 million, and then $52 million in 1985. For the first time, people at GE were starting to feel good times in their pocketbooks. The buy-in had begun.[17]

Late 1980s: Work-Out, Boundaryless and Best Practices

Welch used GE's Crotonville facility to upgrade the level of management skills and to instill a common corporate culture. After reading comments from participants, Welch realized that many of them were frustrated when they returned to their offices because many of their superiors had discounted the Crotonville experience and worked actively to maintain the status quo. Welch wondered:

> Why can't we get the Crotonville openness everywhere? . . . We have to re-create the Crotonville Pit [a circular, tiered lecture hall at Crotonville] all over the company. . . . The Crotonville Pit was working because people felt free to speak. While I was technically their "boss," I had little or no impact on their personal careers—especially in the lower-level classes. . . . Work-Out was patterned after the traditional New

England town meetings. Groups of 40 to 100 employees were invested to share their views on the business and the bureaucracy that got in their way, particularly approvals, reports, meetings and measurements. Work-Out meant just what the words implied: taking unnecessary work out of the system.[18]

Work-Out sessions were held over two to three days. The team's manager would start the session with a presentation, after which the manager would leave the facility. Without their superior present, the remaining employees, with the help of a neutral facilitator, would list problems and develop solutions for many of the challenges in the business. Then the manager returned, listening to employees present their many ideas for change. Managers were expected to make an immediate yes-or-no decision on 75 per cent of the ideas presented. Welch was pleased with Work-Out:

> Work-Out had become a huge success. . . . Ideas were flowing faster all over the company. I was groping for a way to describe this, something that might capture the whole organization—and take idea sharing to the next level. . . . I kept talking about all the boundaries that Work-Out was breaking down. Suddenly, the word boundaryless popped into my head. . . . The boundaryless company . . . would remove all the barriers among the functions: engineering, manufacturing, marketing and the rest. It would recognize no distinction between "domestic" and "foreign" operations. . . . Boundaryless would also open us up to the best ideas and practices from other companies.[19]

---

[16]"Fortune Survey Lists Nation's Toughest Bosses," *The Washington Post*, July 19, 1984, p. B3.

[17]Jack Welch, *Straight from the Gut*, Warner Books, New York, 2001, p. 173.

[18]Jack Welch, *Straight from the Gut*, Warner Books, New York, 2001, p. 182.

[19]Ibid, pp. 185–187.

Welch's relentless pursuit of ideas to increase productivity—from both inside and outside of the company—resulted in the birth of a related movement called Best Practices. In the summer of 1988, Welch gave Michael Frazier of GE's Business Development department a simple challenge: How can we learn from other companies that are achieving higher productivity growth than GE? Frazier selected for study nine companies with different best practices, including Ford, Hewlett-Packard, Xerox and Toshiba. In addition to specific tools and practices, Frazier's team also identified several characteristics common to the successful companies: they focused more on developing effective processes than on controlling individual activities; they used customer satisfaction as their main gauge of performance; they treated their suppliers as partners and they emphasized the need for a constant stream of high-quality new products designed for efficient manufacturing. On reviewing Frazier's report, Welch became an instant convert and committed to a major new training program to introduce Best Practices thinking throughout the organization, integrating it into the ongoing agenda of Work-Out teams.[20]

To encourage employees to put extra effort into reaching their goals, Welch instituted the idea of "stretch." He was frustrated with the compromise that was occurring as work teams tried to lower targets and top management tried to raise targets. With stretch, teams were asked to develop two plans: the first reflecting what they expected to do; and the second that reflected the toughest targets they thought they had a chance of reaching. Welch explained:

> The team knows they're going to be measured against the prior year and relative performance against competitors—not against a highly negotiated internal number. Their stretch target keeps them reaching. . . . Sometimes we found cases where managers at lower levels took stretch numbers and called them budgets, punishing those who missed. I don't think it happens much anymore, but I wouldn't bet on it.[21]

1990s: Six Sigma and the Vitality Curve

One well-known program popularized by GE was process improvement, or Six Sigma. As a result of GE's Best Practices program, Welch learned from Lawrence Bossidy, a former GE executive, how AlliedSignal's Six Sigma quality program was improving quality, lowering costs and increasing productivity. Welch asked Gary Reiner, a vice-president, to lead a quality initiative for GE. On the basis of Reiner's findings, Welch announced a goal of reaching Six Sigma quality levels company-wide by the year 2000, describing the program as "the biggest opportunity for growth, increased profitability, and individual employee satisfaction in the history of our company."[22] Subsequently, every GE employee underwent at least minimal training in Six Sigma, whose terms and tools became part of the global language of GE. For example, expressions like "CTQ," were used to refer to customer requirements that were "critical to quality" in new products or services.[23]

Whereas Six Sigma was focused on process improvement, to develop GE's talent pool, Welch looked to differentiate his people. He remarked: "In manufacturing, we try to stamp out variance. With people, variance is everything." Welch knew that identifying and ranking people in a large

---

[20]Christopher A. Bartlett and Meg Wozny, "GE's Two-Decade Transformation: Jack Welch's Leadership," Harvard Business School Case, May 3 2005, p. 5.

[21]Jack Welch, *Straight from the Gut*, Warner Books, New York, 2001, p. 386.

[22]Christopher A. Bartlett and Meg Wozny, "GE's Two-Decade Transformation: Jack Welch's Leadership," Harvard Business School Case, May 3, 2005, p. 12.

[23]Matt Murray, "Can GE Find Another Conductor Like Jack Welch?" *The Wall Street Journal* Europe, April 13, 2000.

organization was not a simple task. GE began using what became known as 360-degree evaluations, in which managers and supervisors were evaluated by their subordinates and their peers as well as by their bosses. One exception was Welch. He did not get evaluated by his subordinates. "I've peaked out," he said. Nor did he evaluate the top executives immediately below him.[24]

Next, Welch put in place an assessment based on a "vitality curve," roughly shaped like a bell curve. He asked his managers to rank all their staff into the "top 20," "the Vital 70" and the "bottom 10," with the intent to force executives to differentiate their employees. The "top 20" were groomed for larger assignments, and the "bottom 10" were coached out of the organization. In addition, Welch advocated categorizing employees as "A, B or C" players. He explained that how both assessment tools worked together:

> The vitality curve is the dynamic way we sort out As, Bs, and Cs. . . . Ranking employees on a 20-70-10 grid forces managers to make tough decisions. The vitality curve doesn't perfectly translate to my A-B-C evaluation of talent. It's possible—even likely—for A players to be in the vital 70. That's because not every A player has the ambition to go further in the organization. Yet, they still want to be the best at what they do. Managers who can't differentiate soon find themselves in the C category.[25]

Welch reinforced the importance of the ranking system by matching it with an appropriate compensation structure. The A players received raises that were two to three times the increases given to Bs, and the As also received a significant portion of the stock option grants. C players received no raises or options. Welch admitted:

Dealing with the bottom 10 is tougher. . . . Some think it's cruel or brutal to remove the bottom 10 per cent of our people. It isn't. It's just the opposite. What I think is brutal and "false kindness" is keeping people around who aren't going to grow and prosper. There's no cruelty like waiting and telling people late in their careers that they don't belong.[26]

In GE's people review process, known as "Session C," managers were expected to discuss and defend their choices and rankings. During these sessions, Welch was known to challenge his managers' talent decisions aggressively, expecting them to defend their choices with passion. Welch was prone to making quick judgment calls on talent, and these snap decisions could be perceived both positively and negatively. An observer commented:

> Welch is impetuous, inclined to make lightning strikes and wage blitzkrieg. His decisions on people, assets, and strategies can be made in a heartbeat; one bad review with Jack may be the end of a long career. And the record shows that many of Welch's snap decisions have turned out to be stupendous blunders.[27]

One example was Welch's purchase of Kidder Peabody, then one of Wall Street's most prominent investment banks. Although his board of directors was opposed to the idea, Welch's persuasive arguments carried the day. But merging the two cultures proved more difficult than he imagined. Welch stated that at Kidder Peabody, "the concept of idea sharing and team play was completely foreign. If you were in investment banking or trading and your group

---

[24]Frank Swoboda, "Up Against the Walls," *The Washington Post,* February 27, 1994, p. H01.

[25]Jack Welch, *Straight from the Gut,* Warner Books, New York, 2001, p. 160.

[26]Ibid, 2001, pp. 160–162.

[27]Thomas F. Boyle, *At Any Cost,* Vintage Books, New York, 1998, pp. 11–12.

had a good year, it didn't matter what happened to the firm overall."[28] In addition, Kidder Peabody was hit by two public scandals: insider trading and fictitious trades that led to a $350 million writedown. Another example was NBC's partnership with Vince McMahon in January 2001 to launch the XFL, an alternative football league to the NFL. After losing $35 million on the venture in four months, and accompanied by falling viewership, the league shut down in May 2001.[29]

Some managers were worn down by the constantly evolving programs. A chemist who once worked for GE Power Systems stated:

> It's management by buzzword. People chant Jack's slogans without thinking intelligently about what they're doing. I've been stretched so much I feel like Gumby. All Welch understands is increasing profits. That, and getting rid of people, is what he considers a vision. Good people, tremendous people, have been let go, and it is hurting our business. I'm trying to meet the competition, but his policies aren't helping me. It's crazy, and the craziness has got to stop.[30]

Welch believed otherwise: "No one at GE loses a job because of a missed quarter, a missed year, or a mistake. That's nonsense and everyone knows it. . . . People get second chances."[31]

Over his tenure as CEO, Welch had grown GE's market capitalization by 27 times, from $18 billion to $500 billion. The company was trading 28 times forward earnings versus about 24 for the Standard & Poor's 500.[32] See Exhibit 1 for selected GE information over 25 years.

After two decades as GE's CEO, Welch retired, nominating Jeffrey Immelt as his successor. Immelt was one of three candidates shortlisted for the job. Observers noted that Immelt was "starting his tenure at the end of an unprecedented bull market and in the midst of a global economic slowdown."[33] Despite GE's consistent earnings growth even during the economic downturn, GE's stock had fallen 33 per cent from its high of about $60 per share in August 2000. Many attributed this steady drop to the anticipation surrounding Welch's departure.[34]

Immelt's first day on the job was September 7, 2001, four days before the terrorist attacks in the United States.

The Transition From Welch to Jeffrey Immelt

Immelt joined GE in 1982 and held several global leadership positions in GE's Plastics, Appliance and Medical businesses.[35] At GE Medical, his last assignment before becoming CEO, Immelt became a star by:

> persuading a growing number of cash-strapped hospitals to trade in their old-fashioned equipment for digital machines that were capable of generating more dynamic images much faster. He inked lucrative, long-term deals

---

[28]Jack Welch, *Straight from the Gut,* Warner Books, New York, 2001, p. 222.

[29]Eric Boehlert, "Why the XFL Tanked." Available at http://archive.salon.com/ent/feature/2001/05/11/xfl_demise/index.html, accessed January 11, 2008.

[30]Thomas F. Boyle, *At Any Cost: Jack Welch, General Electric, and the Pursuit of Profit,* Vintage Books, New York, 1998, p. 223.

[31]Ibid, p. 274.

[32]William Hanley, "An Eye on GE as Jack Bows Out," *National Post,* August 23, 2001, p. D01.

[33]Daniel Eisenberg and Julie Rawe, "Jack Who?" *Time,* September 10, 2001, p. 42.

[34]Ibid.

[35]"Jeff Immelt, CEO." Available at http://www.ge.com/company/leadership/ceo.html, accessed January 6, 2008.

with such hospital giants as HCA and Premier, and bought a number of smaller companies to round out his product line, all the while growing GE's market share from 25 per cent to 34 per cent and moving the company into services such as data mining.[36]

Only the ninth man to lead GE since 1896, Immelt followed in the footsteps of his predecessors by abandoning the leadership approach favored by Welch. In contrast with Welch's need to control and cajole his management, Immelt was "less a commander than a commanding presence."[37] "If you, say, missed your numbers, you wouldn't leave a meeting with him feeling beat up but more like you let your dad down," said Peter Foss, a longtime friend and colleague of Immelt's and president of GE Polymerland, part of GE's plastics business.[38] Immelt believed that leaders exhibited three traits:

> It's curiosity. It's being good with people. And it's having perseverance, hard work, thick skin. Those are the three traits that every successful person I've ever known has in common.[39]

Immelt aimed to continue GE's transition "from a low-margin manufacturer to a more lucrative services company."[40] During Welch's tenure, although revenues from services had grown from 15 per cent of revenues to 70 per cent, the majority of the revenues came from GE Capital (renamed GE Consumer Finance and GE Commercial Finance). In 2001, Immelt believed there was still room to grow services in many of its divisions, such as aircraft maintenance and monitoring contracts, and medical software and billing services.[41] There were differences in strategic approach as well. Whereas Welch had courted Wall Street by setting—and hitting—pinpoint earnings targets, Immelt gave the Street's short-term demands a back seat to long-term strategy. Whereas Welch rapidly rotated managers through different divisions to develop generalists, Immelt wanted to keep them in place longer to develop specialists. Immelt explained:

> I absolutely loathe the notion of professional management. Which is not an endorsement of unprofessional management but a statement that, for instance, the best jet engines are built by jet-engine people, not by appliance people. Rotate managers too fast, moreover, and they won't experience the fallout from their mistakes—nor will they invest in innovations that don't have an immediate payoff.[42]

By 2007, Immelt had divested GE units representing 40 per cent of revenues. To grow $20 billion a year and more, new investments were made in areas where sizeable players had an advantage. Infrastructure and infrastructure technology, according to Immelt, was "a $70 billion business that will grow 15 per cent a year for the next five years. That's a business where small people need not apply."[43] In addition, Immelt was focused on growing revenues

---

[36]Daniel Eisenberg and Julie Rawe, "Jack Who?" *Time*, September 10, 2001, p. 42.

[37]Jerry Useem, "Another Boss Another Revolution," *Fortune*, April 5, 2004, p. 112.

[38] Daniel Eisenberg and Julie Rawe, "Jack Who?" *Time*, September 10, 2001, p. 42.

[39]David Lieberman, "GE Chief Sees Growth Opportunities in 2008," *USA Today*, December 14, 2007, p. B1.

[40]Daniel Eisenberg and Julie Rawe, "Jack Who?" *Time*, September 10, 2001, p. 42.

[41]Ibid.

[42]Jerry Useem, "Another Boss Another Revolution," *Fortune*, April 5, 2004, p. 112.

[43]David Lieberman, "GE Chief Sees Growth Opportunities in 2008," *USA Today*, December 14, 2007, p. B1.

in emerging markets such as China, India, Turkey, Eastern Europe, Russia, and Latin America. Immelt believed that the international arena was where GE's future growth would come:

> In 2007, for the first time in the history of GE, we'll have more revenue outside the United States that we'll have inside

the United States. Our business outside the United States will grow between 15 per cent and 20 per cent next year. We're a $172 billion company. In 2008, with the U.S. economy growing at 1.5 per cent, we'll grow revenue by 15 per cent because we're in the right places with the right products at the right time.[44]

| Exhibit 1 | GE: Selected Information From 1981 to 2008 |

($ billions)	1981	1986	1991	1996	2001	2006
Revenues	27.2	36.7	52.3	79.2	125.9	163.4
Net Profit	1.7	2.5	2.6	7.3	14.1	20.7

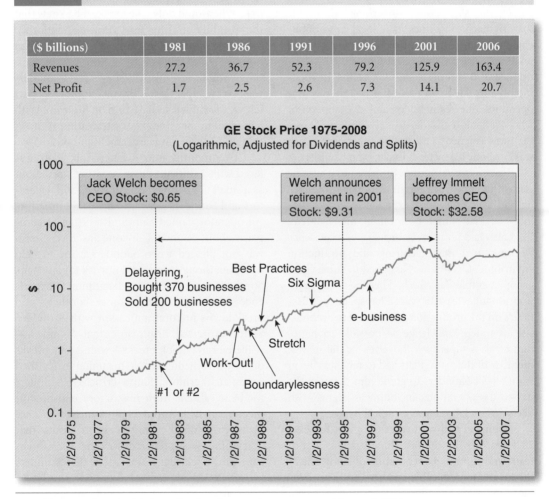

SOURCE: Case writers. Stock information from finance.yahoo.com, accessed January 5, 2008.

---

[44]Ibid.

Please Stop Working So Hard!

Seung Hwan (Mark) Lee and June Cotte

How can I punish my hardest worker? Is it really right of me to say "Please stop working so hard," "Stop working," or "Just leave"?

Matt Platt was recently hired as a production line supervisor to overlook one of the machining lines at a local automobile engine plant near his hometown. The line operated on three separate shifts (morning shift A, afternoon shift B and night shift C); each shift rotating on a weekly basis. Each shift had six machine operators, one team leader and one supervisor who overlooked the day-to-day shift operations. Platt was assigned as the C-shift supervisor, which was currently led by team leader Evan Saunders.

Platt was very young compared to everyone else on the line. As a recent university graduate, he had very little work experience; in fact, this job was Platt's first position in management. Platt also had no prior knowledge or experience working in a manufacturing and production environment, yet he was assigned to supervise a group of employees who had been with the organization for at least 15 years. Platt spent countless hours on the production floor trying to accumulate as much knowledge as possible to better himself as a supervisor; however, as the newest member of the team, Platt had to rely heavily on team leader Saunders to guide him through the day-to-day operations, including assistance with decisions on labour and technical issues.

Saunders had worked at the plant for over 29 years, serving the last three years as a shift team leader. He had a reputation of being one of the most knowledgeable and hard-working people in the plant; Saunders was very well respected by the management staff. His diligent work ethic and his willingness to go the extra mile to help out others were duly noted and appreciated by prior supervisors.

As a self-proclaimed workaholic, Saunders would sometimes skip his designated breaks and lunch times to keep the production line moving; in fact, he would only take breaks if he knew that the production line was running smoothly. Saunders would often come in at least half an hour early and stay at least an hour past his shift time without any overtime pay. Truly, Saunders was every supervisor's dream employee; Platt felt very fortunate to have him on his team. With Saunders by his side, Platt's transition into his role as supervisor was extremely smooth.

Two months into his new job, Platt was faced with a difficult dilemma: what started out as a small rift between one of the C-shift operators and Saunders grew into a volatile situation. An operator named Sam Smith began to complain about Saunders. In one instance, Smith was not pleased when Saunders came to help him even though Smith did not ask for any help. Smith also said that he was beginning to experience increasing interpersonal conflicts and breakdowns in communication with Saunders. Smith expressed displeasure that Saunders—while he rarely took breaks—would take breaks on his own schedule, not in the union-established times; furthermore, Smith criticized Saunders for being absent from mandatory end-of-shift meetings, which Saunders often missed because he was out on the line trying to ensure that everything was prepared for the subsequent shift. Smith felt that it was unfair that Saunders was given special permission to miss mandatory team meetings, and he also did not appreciate

Version: (A) 2009-12-21

how Saunders over-exerted himself each and every day at work. Smith feared that if people like Saunders worked too hard, then management would find ways to reduce the number of employees on the line or find ways to create more work for each operator.

Since the company had recently made cutbacks by laying off employees, the operators had become increasingly concerned about their job security. In the past year, the number of machine operators on the line decreased by two per shift; as a result, workload increased for every remaining operator, which led to lower morale. Ironically, it was the hardest workers in the plant who were beginning to be blamed for contributing to the recent downsizing of the plant, because they demonstrated that one person could handle a job that was meant for two.

The situation grew worse as Smith began to rally a group of individuals to support his stance. In support of Smith, other C-shift operators began to criticize Platt for treating everyone unequally, specifically in the way that he favoured Saunders over other operators. Even the operators and team leaders on the other

shifts (A and B) began to express concerns over Saunders coming in too early and staying too late without any pay, even though it was his choice to do so.

Platt needed to take action before the situation escalated any further. He knew that if he told Saunders to stop working so late and to help out less, his advice would contradict the values of hard work and doing what is best for the company. Platt was worried that Saunders might lose his motivation and his work ethic if he asked him to "Please stop working so hard!" On the other hand, if Platt did not take action, he feared that the morale of the group would sink even lower, potentially causing detrimental consequences. Smith and his group had specifically told Platt that if he did not do anything to deal with the current situation, they would file a union grievance against both himself and Saunders. As the morale of the group continued to deteriorate, Platt wanted to confront Saunders about this unique quandary. Platt needed to figure out the best way to please Saunders *and* the other operators. Platt rested on his elbows and pondered, "What now?"

Learning Goals or Performance Goals: Is It the Journey or the Destination?

Gerard H. Seijts and Gary P. Latham

While setting goals is important, setting an outcome goal—rather than a learning goal—can have a negative impact on an individual's performance. This is especially true when acquiring skills and knowledge is more important than being persistent and working harder. Instead of focusing on the end result, a learning goal focuses attention on the discovery of effective strategies to attain and sustain desired results. These authors build a compelling case for learning goals' superiority and describe the positive impact they can have on leadership, performance appraisal, and professional development.

Reprint # 9B06TC06

⊠ The Good and the Bad of Setting Goals

Nearly all executives understand the importance of goal setting. And yet, most organizations have no idea how to manage specific, challenging goals, or what are sometimes labelled "stretch goals." For example, some organizations may ask employees to double sales or reduce product-development time but fail to provide those employees with the knowledge they need to meet these goals. It is foolish and even immoral for organizations to assign employees stretch goals without equipping them with the resources to succeed—and still punish them when they fail to reach those goals. This lack of guidance often leads to stress, burnout, and in some instances, unethical behaviour.

The Lucent scandal is a compelling example of what can happen when people feel undue pressure to make the numbers. Richard McGinn, the former CEO of Lucent, prided himself for imposing "audacious" goals on his managers, believing that such a push would produce dream results. In 2000, McGinn pushed his managers to produce results they could not deliver—not, apparently, without crossing the line. The pressures that McGinn applied were described in a complaint that a former Lucent employee filed, charging that McGinn and the company had set unreachable goals that caused them to mislead the public. Empirical research supports this claim, namely that setting unrealistic performance-outcome goals sometimes causes people to engage in unacceptable or illegal behaviour.

These findings point to a fault with the type of goal that was set, namely the performance-outcome goal. Setting a learning goal, on the other hand, is likely to be far more effective in helping individuals discover radical, out-of-the-box ideas or action plans that will enable organizations to regain and sustain a competitive edge. This paper discusses both types of goals and explains why learning goals can be more effective and when it is more appropriate to use them.

⊠ Goal Mechanisms

Generally speaking, there are at least four benefits of setting goals:

1. Specific performance goals affect an employee's choice about what to focus on, or which actions are goal relevant and which are not.

2. Goals help employees adjust their effort and persistence according to the goal's level of difficulty.

3. Goals help employees persist until they have reached them.

However, these three motivational mechanisms alone are not always sufficient for attaining a goal.

4. A fourth benefit of goal setting has to do more with cognition than motivation. Specifically, it has to do with the fact that a certain type of goal, the learning goal, helps employees acquire the knowledge to understand and apply what they are doing. For complex tasks, setting goals based on one's knowledge stimulates the development of task strategies to complete those tasks. For example, the Weyerhaeuser Company discovered that unionized truck drivers who had been assigned a specific high-performance goal in terms of the number of trips per day from the logging site to the mill started to work "smarter rather than harder." After being assigned goals, truck drivers developed tactics to attain them. These included the use of radios to coordinate their efforts so that a truck would always be at the site when logs were available for loading. Performance increased because drivers drew on their existing knowledge to attain their goal. While they already knew how to use a radio, they chose to apply this knowledge in such a way that productivity increased.

Motivation or Knowledge Acquisition?

Goal setting is viewed by most executives and behavioral scientists as a motivational technique. The fact is, however, that most of the tasks that scientists have studied have been straightforward, so that the effect of a goal on an employee's choice, effort, and persistence could be easily assessed. But what happens when the task is not straightforward? Anecdotal evidence and empirical research provide a thought-provoking answer.

The ordeal of Wagner Dodge and the 15 firefighters under his command illustrates the difference between working hard (motivation) and working smart (knowledge acquisition). The ordeal is described by leadership expert Michael Useem in *The Leadership Moment*. A hellish, fast-moving forest-and-grass fire caused the group to run for their lives. With less than a minute remaining until the fire would swallow the group, Dodge discovered a way for the group to survive. He started an "escape fire" that cleared a small area of flammable prairie grass and bushes. As Useem states, Dodge survived because "he had literally burned a hole in the raging fire." However, Dodge's crew ignored his order to jump inside the expanding ring of fire and all of them died while trying to outrun the blaze. For Dodge, working smart, that is, knowledge acquisition, led to a far better result than "working hard."

In the context of running a successful business, Dell Computer Corporation CEO, Michael Dell, emphasizes the importance of information and knowledge acquisition:

> It's all about knowledge and execution. Traditionally, it was thought that lack of capital was the barrier to entry into a new competitive market. Take a look around, and you'll see that's just not true anymore. Information will increasingly become both a tool to help businesses hone their competitive edge and a weapon to protect them against the competition. Besides Dell, there are countless successful companies that are thriving now despite the fact that they started with little more than passion and a good idea. There are also many that failed, for the very same reason. The difference is that the thriving companies gathered the knowledge that gave them a substantial edge over their competition, which they then used to improve their execution, whatever their product or service. Those that didn't simply didn't make it.

In sum, a person's quest to be effective is influenced by ability and motivation, so that in the end, performance is a function of creative imagination or learning, *and* sheer effort and persistence. This is particularly true for tasks where an individual lacks the requisite knowledge or skill to master those tasks. Thus, we see that setting a performance goal can have a downside.

Performance-Outcome Goals and Their Downside

Acquiring knowledge before setting a performance-outcome goal can be critically important. On the other hand, setting a specific performance goal can damage a person's effectiveness in the early stages of learning. This is because in the early stage of learning a person's attention needs to be focused on discovering and mastering the processes required to perform well, rather than on reaching a certain level of performance.

This reality highlights the fact that the attentional demands that can be imposed on people are limited. Trying to attain a specific performance goal places additional demands on people, so much so that they are unable to devote the necessary cognitive resources to mastering the task. A performance-outcome goal often distracts attention from the discovery of task-relevant strategies. For example, focusing on a score of 95 may prevent a novice golfer from focusing on mastering the swing and weight transfer, and using the proper clubs to shoot 95. Unwittingly, the golfer has diverted the cognitive resources necessary for understanding the task to a self-regulatory activity, namely shooting 95. The golfer has focused on scoring at the expense of acquiring the skills to become a better golfer. In the process, the golfer has exposed the downside of setting a performance goal.

Learning Goals or Performance-Outcome Goals

That setting specific performance goals can sometimes actually worsen performance is at first glance astonishing in that this conclusion is at odds with the accumulated findings of over a quarter of a century of research in the behavioral sciences.

For at least three decades, this research has shown that goal setting is a powerful and effective motivational technique. Specifically, the research shows again and again that a performance goal influences choice, effort, and the persistence needed to attain it. However, it is often forgotten that performance at a high level is a function of ability as well as motivation. Consequently, we wondered what would happen if the goal of certain tasks, say those for which minimal prior learning or performance routines existed, was switched to knowledge acquisition instead of motivation. In situations where learning rather than an increase in motivation is required, setting a specific performance goal is not likely to be prudent. Perhaps a specific high-learning goal should be set instead. For example, a novice golfer should consider setting a high learning goal such as learning how to hold a club or when to use a specific iron. In short, the novice golfer must learn how to play the game before becoming concerned with attaining a challenging performance outcome (e.g. a score of 95).

To test our idea, we examined the effects of learning versus performance-outcome goals by using a complex business simulation, namely, the Cellular Industry Business Game (CIBG). The CIBG is an interactive, computer-based simulation that is based on the events that occurred in the U.S. cellular telephone industry. It uses a complex set of formulas to link the various strategic choices to performance outcomes. The CIBG consists of 13 rounds of decision making, each corresponding to one year of activity. Participants were asked to make decisions concerning ten areas of activity during each round. Examples of the strategic options are pricing, advertising, sales-force, cost containment, finance, geographic scope, and alliances with other companies. Each area of activity allowed numerous choices. For example, in the finance area, participants could raise funds by issuing bonds, public shares or dividends, or by borrowing from the bank.

The evolution of the cellular telephone industry was predetermined in the simulation. For example, during the first eight decision periods (simulating the industry's first eight years) competition was restricted by region. Following year eight, however, the telecommunications industry experienced a radical environmental change in the form of deregulation. Hence, participants in the simulation were given several warnings that deregulation was likely to occur. The strategic options that were viable before deregulation were no longer effective. Thus, to maintain or increase market share, participants now needed to discover a new set of strategies. This aspect of the CIBG simulation reflects a business environment where past success strategies are by no means a guarantee for future success.

The participants assigned a specific high-learning goal were told to identify and implement six or more strategies for increasing market share. The results revealed that

1. Performance was highest for individuals who had a specific high learning goal. Their market share was almost twice as high as those with a performance outcome goal. There was no significant difference in performance among individuals with a performance goal, or those who were simply urged to do their best.

2. Individuals who had a learning goal took the time necessary to acquire the

knowledge to perform the task effectively and to analyze the task-relevant information that was available to them.

3. Those with a learning goal were convinced that they were capable of mastering the task. This suggests that the increase in self-efficacy resulting from a learning goal occurs as a result of the discovery of appropriate strategies for task mastery. A performance goal, on the other hand, can lead to a highly unsystematic "mad scramble" for solutions.

4. Those with a learning goal had a higher commitment to their goal than did those with a performance goal. The correlation between goal commitment and performance was also significant.

These research findings are consistent with the observations of the CEOs cited throughout the paper.

⊠ Why Learning Goals?

How does a learning goal differ from a performance-outcome goal? What explains the superiority of a learning goal over a performance goal for a complex task? How can specific challenging learning goals be applied in business settings?

Learning Goals, Performance Goals and the Efficacy of the Former

The primary distinction between performance and learning goals lies in the framing of the instructions given to employees. Hence, the difference between these two types of goals is first and foremost a "mindset." The respective instructions focus attention on two different domains—motivation versus ability. A performance goal, as the name implies, frames the instructions so that an employee's focus is on task performance (e.g. attain 20 percent market share by the end of the next fiscal year). The search for information to attain the goal is

neither mentioned nor implied because knowledge and skills are considered a given for tasks that require primarily choice, effort, or persistence. Similarly, a learning goal frames the instructions in terms of knowledge or skill acquisition (e.g. discover three effective strategies to increase market share). A learning goal draws attention away from the end result to the discovery of effective task processes. Once an employee has the knowledge and skills necessary to perform the task, a specific performance goal should be set to direct attention to the exertion of effort and persistence required to achieve it. The performance goal cues individuals to use strategies or performance routines that the person knows are effective. Setting a learning goal for a task that is relatively straightforward wastes time. It is also ineffective in that the person has already mastered the requisite performance routines and is aware of the requisite job behaviors.

In short, learning goals help people progress to the point where performance-outcome goals increase one's effectiveness. The focus of a learning goal is to increase one's knowledge (ability); the focus of a performance goal is to increase one's motivation to implement that knowledge. Therefore, both learning and performance goals are needed to be successful. But, as noted earlier, our research shows that a performance goal should not be set until an employee has the knowledge to attain it.

Practical Applications of Learning Goals

Based on our findings, as well as the experiences of the CEOs we have cited, there are at least 3 areas where the application of learning goals should prove particularly helpful in improving performance—leadership, performance management and professional development.

1. Leadership

Jack Welch once stated that "An organization's ability to learn and translate that learning into action is the ultimate competitive advantage . . . I wish we'd understood all along how much leverage you can get from the flow of ideas among all business units. . . the enormous advantage we have today is that we can run GE as a laboratory for ideas."

Three examples suggest the benefits of having a leader focus employee attention on the attainment of learning goals. First, when Andy Grove was the CEO at Intel Corporation, he was obsessed with learning as much as possible about the changing environment.

In Grove's own words, "I attribute Intel's ability to sustain success to being constantly on the alert for threats, either technological or competitive in nature." Second, Sam Walton continued to refine his business strategies and discover ways for improving his stores. He never stopped learning from competitors, customers, and his own employees. He believed that there was at least one good idea he could learn, even from his worst competitor. Walton passed on this philosophy to his employees. As Kurt Bernard, a retailing consultant, noted:

> When he meets you . . . he proceeds to extract every piece of information in your possession. He always makes little notes. And he pushes on and on. After two and a half hours, he left, and I was totally drained. I wasn't sure what I had just met, but I was sure we would hear more from him.

Leaders such as Welch, Grove and Walton would increase the effectiveness of their workforce if they set specific high learning goals for sharing ideas among divisions, identifying potential threats in the environment, or extracting ideas from competitors, customers and employees.

Third, the primary use of learning goals at Goldman Sachs, as described by Steve Kerr, is to develop present and future leaders. For example, a sales manager might be asked to join or even lead a taskforce whose goal is to discover a new process for product development. People's leadership skills are developed by assigning specific

learning goals that require these people to go outside their comfort zone.

2. Performance Management

Coca Cola Foods and PricewaterhouseCoopers (PWC) are among the many companies that have incorporated goal setting into their coaching and mentoring practices. The goals are typically performance outcomes or behavioral goals that are within employees' repertory of knowledge and abilities to increase in frequency (e.g. communicate the objectives of the program to coworkers).

PWC, which recognizes that this approach is not effective for every employee, also sets learning goals. For example, like other organizations, they hire job applicants for their aptitude rather than their existing skills. New employees, therefore, benefit from mentors who actively help them discover ways to develop their competencies within the firm and who assign them specific, high learning, rather than performance, goals. Employees assigned challenging learning goals in the early stages of their job typically outperform those who are initially given specific high performance targets.

Learning goals are also appropriate for seasoned managers. For example, those who operate in global organizations find it fruitful to focus on ways to effectively manage a myriad of social identity groups so as to minimize rigidity, insensitivity, and intolerance. Newly formed work teams, especially culturally diverse teams, need time to gel. Ilya Adler observed that managers view, "the cultural issue as an additional burden to the already difficult task of making a team function effectively." Focusing on the end result before team dynamics have been ironed out can hurt the team's performance. Thus, a team leader may be well advised to focus on the discovery of 3 to 5 strategies, processes, or procedures for accelerating effective interaction and teamwork, particularly ways of fostering understanding of local customs and values and developing mutual understanding and trust. In contrast, assigning a culturally diverse work team a specific performance goal before the team's rules of conduct have become accepted is likely to lead to prolonged "storming" and "norming." Indeed, it is not uncommon to see culturally diverse teams spend more time working out their differences than doing the actual work.

3. Professional Development

Jack Welch often moved his top executives from one functional area to another. Similar to the mentoring practice at PWC, he did this to broaden their knowledge base. When this is done in any organization today, employees should be asked to come up with a specific number of ideas that would help them improve the performance of their respective businesses. Welch also introduced the Work-Out, a forum that was intended to enable management and employees to share knowledge. Facilitators of these types of sessions should be asked to set a goal of discovering a specific number of ideas or strategies that will improve organizational effectiveness.

Other executives also ensure the on-going professional development of their senior executives through job rotation. The purpose of the rotation is to "shake the executives up," provide them with opportunities to learn new perspectives, get them out of their comfort zones, and develop greater creativity. To ensure that this occurs, specific learning goals should be set to ensure that the broad perspective to which the executives are exposed actually helps the company make decisions in a cohesive fashion.

⌗ In the End, Goals Can Be Different

Today's workforce is under intense pressure to produce tangible results. Workers are perpetually in a "performance mode." This is a plus when known performance routines continue to be effective, and when the issue is fostering the conditions for a highly motivated workforce. In such instances, countless studies in the behavioral sciences support the significant motivational benefits of setting specific, challenging performance goals.

However, a high-performing workforce is a function of both high ability and motivation. This is particularly true in today's business environment in which organizations face rapidly changing technologies, information overload, escalating competitive pressures, and a host of other challenges. Hence the importance of knowing that learning goals and performance goals are different. They differ in the behavior/actions required to attain them and in their appropriateness for increasing an organization's effectiveness.

The purpose of a learning goal is to stimulate one's imagination, to engage in discovery, and to "think outside the box." The purpose of a performance goal is to choose to exert effort and to persist in the attainment of a desired objective or outcome using the knowledge one already possesses. Thus, the behavior of a person with a learning goal is to systematically search for new ideas, actively seek feedback, be reflective, and execute a specific number of ideas in order to test newly formed hypotheses. The behavior of a person with a performance goal is to focus on known ways to use the knowledge and skills that have already been mastered. When the strategy for an organization is already known and the ways to implement it have been deciphered, setting performance goals for an individual or team is appropriate. When an effective strategy requires innovation that has yet to emerge, specific high learning goals should be set.

The Leader–Member Exchange Theory of Leadership

[C]areer development has to deal with tensions between the needs of the business and the interests and aspirations of individual employees. This means talking to employees about very personal things, such as how they see themselves and what they want from work. Organizations are pretty inept at dealing with their employees as real people—it is a messy, challenging and, therefore, uncomfortable thing to do.

—Wendy Hirsch[1]

As the quote above suggests, leaders need to interact with their followers. The leader–member exchange (LMX) theory of leadership is concerned with the interactions between leaders and followers (Daft, 2011). The trait, skills, and style approaches to leadership emphasized leadership from the leader's perspective. Situational, contingency, and path–goal theories of leadership are centered on the follower and the context in which the leader and follower interact with each other. In essence, these theories are about what leaders do to each of their followers (Northouse, 2013). The focal point in LMX theory is the dyadic relationship between a leader and each of his or her followers. In other words, LMX theory is concerned with the differential nature of the relationships between leaders and each of their followers (Daft, 2011; DuBrin, 2010; Yukl, 2012). We will describe two waves of studies that have examined the LMX theory of leadership.

---

[1]Hirsh, W. (2011, p. 130).

⧖ The Early Studies

Graen and his colleagues (Dansereau, Graen, & Haga, 1975; Graen, 1976; Graen & Cashman, 1975) were the forerunners in the early studies related to LMX theory. They emphasized the vertical dyadic linkages that leaders developed with each subordinate. The relationship that a leader developed with his or her workgroup was the combination of all of these vertically dyadic relationships. This led to two broad types of relationships: those considered in-group relationships and those considered out-group relationships.

Relationships within the in-group are marked by mutual trust, respect, liking, and reciprocal influence. In-group relationships develop when leaders and followers negotiate that followers do more than required by their job description, and leaders provide more than that required by the formal hierarchy. In-group members are given more responsibility, more participation in decision making, more interesting job assignments, more tangible rewards, and more support for career advancement. In contrast, relationships within the out-group are marked by formal communication based on job descriptions (Daft, 2011; DuBrin, 2010; Yukl, 2012). In addition, in-group members communicate more, are more involved, and are more dependable than out-group members (Dansereau et al., 1975). Out-group members do what is required and no more (Yukl, 2012). They may be physically present but will only do what is necessary to retain their jobs. Mentally, they may have defected from their jobs, even though they still come to work, do enough to keep their jobs, and then go home. They will not go the extra mile that is often required to achieve higher levels of effectiveness.

⧖ The Later Studies

Whereas early studies focused on the differential nature of in-groups and out-groups, the later studies focused on enhancing organizational effectiveness. Essentially, empirically based studies have found that where there are higher-quality leader–member exchanges, there are lower employee turnover, better employee evaluations, more frequent promotions, better work assignments, more participation by employees in decision making, enhanced commitment to the organization, more favorable attitudes toward the job, and greater support and interest from the leader (Graen & Uhl-Bien, 1995; Liden, Wayne, & Stilwell, 1993; Northouse, 2013).

In essence, these studies demonstrated that leader–member exchange quality was positively related to results for leaders, their followers, the groups in which leaders and followers interacted with each other, and the organization as a whole (Graen & Uhl-Bien, 1995). This suggests that organizations where leaders develop good working relationships with each individual subordinate will outperform those organizations where the leader–member exchange reflects mostly out-group member relationships (Yukl, 2012).

⧖ Leadership Making

The later studies led to a prescriptive approach to leadership that has come to be called *leadership making*. Leadership making suggests that leaders need to form high-quality, or in-group, exchanges with nearly all of their subordinates, not just a small minority. Leadership making is also about the development of partnership networks beyond the workgroup throughout the rest of the organization.

Developing these networks should lead to better organizational performance and greater career progress for those leaders who engage in this practice (Graen & Uhl-Bien, 1995; Northouse, 2013).

There are three phases to leadership making (Graen & Uhl-Bien, 1991). They are the stranger phase, the acquaintance phase, and the partnership phase (Daft, 2011). In the stranger phase, the leader–member exchanges resemble those described earlier as out-group exchanges. In this phase, members are more concerned with their own self-interest than with what is best for the group.

In the acquaintance phase, the leader or member makes an offer to do more for the other. This is a testing period during which the leader and the subordinate are checking each other out to see if they trust each other enough to shift to in-group status or the partnership phase. During this phase, member self-interest lessens, and there is more of a focus on the group's goals and objectives.

In the mature partnership phase, leader–member exchanges are similar in quality to in-group exchanges described earlier. Leader–members who are in this stage with each other have developed a high level of "mutual trust, respect and obligation toward each other" (Northouse, 2013). Each leader–member relationship has been tested, and there is a confidence that the leader and member can count on each other. In this stage, leaders positively affect each member and are positively affected by each member. These leader–member exchanges go much farther than those previously defined as out-group exchanges in that there is a transformational nature to these exchanges that allows leaders and followers to pursue what is better for the team and the organization rather than their own self-interests (Northouse, 2013).

First Impressions

Some research (Liden et al., 1993) suggests that the leaders and members need to be aware that first impressions matter. Their results suggest that the initial expectations of leaders toward members and initial member expectations of leaders were positively associated with the leader–member exchanges 2 and 6 weeks later. In addition, initial expectations of the members toward their leader were good predictors of leader–member exchange quality 6 months into the relationship. This means that the leader–member exchange may be formed in the first days and that the old adage—you have only one chance to make a good impression—may be true (DuBrin, 2010).

How Does the LMX Theory of Leadership Work?

The LMX theory of leadership is both descriptive and prescriptive. In both cases, the heart of the LMX theory is the vertical dyadic relationship developed between a leader and each of her or his subordinates.

From a descriptive sense, LMX theory implies that we need to understand that in-groups and out-groups exist in groups and organizations and that as leaders, we participate in their development. Goal accomplishment with in-groups is substantively different than with out-groups. In-group members willingly work harder than required and are more innovative in accomplishing goals. Consequently, leaders give in-group members more opportunities, more responsibilities, more support, and more time.

Out-group members work differently than in-group members with their leaders. They work strictly within the guidelines governing organizational roles and only do the minimum necessary. Leaders are fair to these group members in that they respond to them by strictly adhering to any contractual obligations. However, they are not given any special treatment by their leaders. These out-group members receive the benefits that they are due and required based on their contract but nothing more.

From a prescriptive sense, Graen and Uhl-Bien's (1991) leadership-making model allows us to comprehend LMX theory the most. Their prescription is to develop relationships with all subordinates who are similar to those described earlier for in-group members. In other words, give all subordinates the chance to accept new responsibilities, nurture better-quality relationships with each subordinate, develop relationships based on trust and respect with all subordinates, and make the whole workgroup an in-group (Daft, 2011). Finally, leaders should form high-quality partnerships with people throughout the organization (Daft, 2011; Northouse, 2013).

Whether we view the LMX theory of leadership as descriptive or prescriptive, it works by emphasizing the dyadic relationship that both leaders and followers see as special and unique. Northouse (2013) suggests that "when these relationships are of high quality, the goals of the leader, the followers, and the organization are all advanced." Implied in this statement is that these goals are clearly defined and understood, as well as shared among all leaders and followers—this may be one of the prime responsibilities of leaders: to ensure the development of high-quality relationships between leaders and each follower. We encourage each of you to be willing to lead others but to also understand the responsibility you take on for developing special, unique relationships with each of your subordinates.

References

Daft, R. L. (2011). *The leadership experience* (5th ed.). Mason, OH: Thomson, South-Western.

Dansereau, F., Graen, G. B., & Haga, W. (1975). A vertical dyad linkage to leadership in formal organizations. *Organizational Behavior and Human Performance, 13,* 46–78.

DuBrin, A. (2010). *Leadership: Research findings, practice, and skills* (6th ed.). Mason, OH: South-Western/Cengage.

Graen, G. B. (1976). Role-making processes within complex organizations. In M. D. Dunnette (Ed.), *Handbook of industrial and organizational psychology* (pp. 1202–1245). Chicago, IL: Rand McNally.

Graen, G. B., & Cashman, J. (1975). A role-making model of leadership in formal organizations: A developmental approach. In J. G. Hunt & L. L. Larson (Eds.), *Leadership frontiers* (pp. 143–166). Kent, OH: Kent State University Press.

Graen, G. B., & Uhl-Bien, M. (1991). The transformation of professionals into self-managing and partially self-designing contributions: Toward a theory of leadership-making. *Journal of Management Systems, 3*(3), 25–39.

Graen, G. B., & Uhl-Bien, M. (1995). Relationship-based approach to leadership: Development of leader–member exchange (LMX) theory of leadership over 25 years: Applying a multi-level, multi-domain perspective. *Leadership Quarterly, 6*(2), 219–247.

Hirsh, W. (2011). In J. Storey (Ed.), *Leadership in organizations: Current issues and key trends* (2nd ed.). London, England: Routledge.

Liden, R. C., Wayne, S. J., & Stilwell, D. (1993). A longitudinal study on the early development of leader–member exchange. *Journal of Applied Psychology, 78,* 662–674.

Northouse, P. G. (2013). *Leadership: Theory and practice* (6th ed.). Thousand Oaks, CA: Sage.

Yukl, G. (2012). *Leadership in organizations* (8th ed.). Upper Saddle River, NJ: Pearson/Prentice Hall.

The Cases

Carnegie Industrial: The Leadership Development Centre

A director within the leadership development program of a large multinational organization must decide how to manage a very difficult conversation she must have with her assistant director. The assistant director, who is older and more experienced (although less educated), interviewed for the director's position and didn't get it. The assistant director has never been happy reporting to her much younger boss and has felt consistently left out of major decisions. The assistant director had confronted the director about her feelings and threatened to resign. How should the director handle this difficult conversation?

Schulich School of Medicine: Enhancing and Developing a High-Performance Culture

Dr. Jane Rylett, the newly appointed chair of the Department of Physiology and Pharmacology (department) at the Schulich School of Medicine & Dentistry, was considering the two most important issues she would face in her new role in the next 5 years. These were (a) building a cohesive department and (b) nurturing a high performance culture. She knew direction was needed, given that the department was the result of a merger between the Department of Physiology and the Department of Pharmacology & Toxicology, a much smaller department just a few years earlier. The merger had gone well; however, Dr. Rylett sensed that some of the faculty members in Pharmacology still considered that it had not been a merger but that their department had been taken over. Jane wondered how she could build a cohesive department and nurture a high performance culture.

⬚ The Reading

On Leadership: Leadership and Loyalty

Leaders expect their followers to be loyal and to be able to depend on their loyalty. Good leaders understand that there is a difference between real loyalty and a related but different concept—fealty. Smart leaders understand that fealty is demanded, whereas loyalty is earned. In this article, the author notes some things that leaders can do to earn loyalty.

Carnegie Industrial: The Leadership Development Centre

Ken Mark and Michael Sider

⬚ Introduction

Even though she knew it was coming, Shannon Copley, a director at Carnegie Industrial's Leadership Development Centre, was taken aback by her co-worker's outburst of emotion. Eleanor Galvin, the assistant director, had just issued what sounded like an ultimatum, her voice trembling with anger. Galvin was livid that she was not being considered for a full-time position in Copley's communications program.

It was May 12, 2007, and both women were standing outside Copley's office in Somerville, Massachusetts. With colleagues watching her, Copley wondered how best to respond.

Version: (A) 2008-01-03

⬚ Carnegie Industrial

Carnegie Industrial (Carnegie), headquartered in Stamford, Connecticut, was one of the biggest corporations in the United States with $125 billion in annual sales and 45,000 employees. Part of the S&P 500 since 1985, Carnegie was both a manufacturer of products for the engineering and construction industry and an industrial consulting firm, with clients primarily from the U.S. northeast. Carnegie had grown rapidly in the past decade as a result of a series of acquisitions. As a result, its workforce comprised at least four distinct cultures. In an effort to amalgamate the group, a leadership centre, patterned after General Electric's Crotonville facility, was built in Somerville, Massachusetts, in April 2001. Somerville was chosen for its location, which was central to the various Carnegie offices.

The Leadership Development Centre, or LDC, was housed in a refurbished factory, completely renovated to modern standards. A staff of 25 was led by Executive Director Elizabeth Silver and three directors. The LDC offered a menu of courses and leadership development modules. All new hires at Carnegie spent a week at the LDC as part of their orientation at the firm. The curriculum for these new hires focused on team work, financial analysis skills and the basics of project management. The leadership modules were reserved for grooming talent at the mid- and senior-level management ranks. In addition to the specialized programs in team-building, finance and project management, courses in two general areas were available: technical competency (specialized courses in engineering or science) and communications (courses in conflict resolution, negotiation, and written and oral communication).

⬚ Shannon Copley and Eleanor Galvin

Shannon Copley had been hired as director of the LDC communications program in April 2006, with a mandate to revive the program, which had foundered in the past three years as evidenced by its poor reviews. Attendees complained that the materials were either outdated or bland, and the instruction uninspiring. Although the former director had been relieved of his duties, Silver had retained the four staff members. Through an executive search firm, the LDC had interviewed several candidates for the director's position and had narrowed its search to two candidates, Copley and Galvin.

Copley, in her early 30s, had recently completed her PhD in English and Communications from a well-respected Eastern U.S. school and for the past three years had been working in the investor relations practice of a prominent Boston-based consulting firm. She was both articulate and approachable and was known for her innovative thinking and her project management skills. Copley had an informal business approach that valued results over decorum and hierarchy. Copley would arrive at work in casual clothing, wearing Birkenstocks. She encouraged her staff, all of whom were in their late 20s and early 30s, to dress in a similar manner. She disliked meetings, preferring to communicate through e-mail or personal contact. When she did gather staff for meetings, she was informal but efficient. She ran her meetings quickly, with lots of casual banter and humor, and her staff seemed to appreciate both the brevity of the meetings and Copley's enthusiasm. When clients addressed her as "Miss Copley," she would correct them with a wave of her hand. "Call me Shannon," she would say. On the other hand, Copley could be business-like when the situation called for it: when the consulting firm faced an accelerated deadline for the completion of a client project, Copley was able to work efficiently within her team setting to complete the job ahead of time. Her collaborative style was appreciated by her co-workers and superiors, and she had been recently promoted to manager level. Most recently, Copley had created an effective communications program for one of the firm's clients, and the program was winning plaudits from users. When Copley was interviewed for the position, she impressed Silver with her candor, innovative thinking and confidence:

> I've seen effective and ineffective programs. And effective programs are typically more than remedial in nature and accessible to employees throughout the business. Your previous communications program was both inaccessible and remedial. It sent the message that, if you used it, you were in need of help. When your managers sent staff to the program, the staff felt they were being criticized—that their communications skills weren't adequate. Furthermore, there were some important areas that the previous program wasn't equipped to handle, like working with the business's growing number of overseas managers whose English language skills put them at a disadvantage here in the U.S. Programs like this should be open to all associates, whether they're native English speakers or not. Everyone can benefit from improved communications. I know there's some apprehension about the costs of such a program—if we make it less remedial and open it up to lots of people as a viable part of their leadership training in the company, there would be many candidates being coached—but we shouldn't limit it to the ones who need remedial help. We should use dedicated personnel for the coaching and have learning teams from the different ranks. Junior team members can learn from seniors and vice versa. If you hire me, some of the program elements may seem avant-garde but they'd represent current thinking in the field. Don't hire me if you don't want change.

Eleanor Galvin, the other candidate for the director's position, held a master's degree in English from Oxford University and had spent 20 years in the human resources department of an international technical services firm, where she had specialized, among other things, in the leadership development of managers for whom English was a second language. Galvin was 50 years old. A conservative person by nature, Galvin preferred formal business attire at all times and dressed immaculately in expensive business suits. She was known for her attention to detail and her love of protocol and process. Galvin was reserved, cool and analytical in her business approach, but beneath the reserve was a professional respect for co-workers and clients. Galvin had been instrumental in working with her team to develop a well-regarded coaching program. Although her team of subordinates had initially envisaged a broad-reaching, high-impact (but costly) program, Galvin was able to work with them to create a more focused and thriftier version. The team never seemed to disagree with Galvin's suggestions because she was the most senior person on the team. Since joining the firm, Galvin had been promoted through four ranks from assistant manager to senior director. Her superiors praised Galvin for her no-nonsense business style. "Miss Galvin's tough but fair," quipped a junior employee. Two months earlier, Galvin left the job to be closer to her family in Somerville and was actively seeking another position.

When Galvin was interviewed for the director's job, Silver was pleased with her grasp of the objectives and her precise answers:

> We should aim to help employees who can improve the most, and we should do this in a cost-effective way. There should be clear deliverables and regular progress updates. Although we would welcome suggestions from our team members—after all, the best ideas can come from anywhere—we need to keep this program focused. The last program was very good, but the material could be refreshed. Let's not throw out the

baby with the bathwater, so to speak. Too much change can be confusing to everyone, especially before we do the required analysis of existing processes.

⊠ The "Communicate!" Program Is Created

Although Silver was impressed by both Copley and Galvin, she decided to offer Copley the director's job on the basis of her superior academic credentials and her previous experience creating a communications program, which Silver believed would bolster both Copley's credibility in the training sessions and the LDC's credibility throughout the organization. An assistant director's position was created and offered to Galvin. Silver was delighted when Galvin accepted despite the assistant director's position being only half-time. Silver strongly believed that the skills sets of the two hires were complementary and that both could work together to build an excellent program. Certainly, the two women had different approaches, but Silver believed that increased diversity of thought and personality in the workplace could lead to better results.

"I trust you to turn this program around," Silver said to Copley on her first day of work. "Here is your budget, here are your people, and you have free rein to shape this program. The only caveat is that I would like you to work closely with Eleanor Galvin."

"No problem," replied Copley, confidently. It was April 2006, and Carnegie's recruiting season was just under way. Copley knew that she had at least a month before the new hires were ready for training. In addition, mid-level and senior staff were busy completing mid-year reports and interviewing candidates. Copley called a meeting of her five team members (four from the previous director's team and Galvin) for a brainstorming session. They developed a list of priorities, then identified key action items. The sign-up web page on the intranet was updated, presentations were scheduled for each

of the business units and a curriculum outline was developed.

In the first few weeks, Copley sensed that Galvin was having trouble adjusting to her new role as the second-in-charge. On the first day, for example, Galvin had approached Copley and, shaking her hand, congratulated her on her appointment. Galvin had thanked her, assured her that she was looking forward to working with her and then said: "I'm a little confused, though, as to which office should be mine." Silver had previously asked Copley whether it was "okay with her" to share an office with Galvin for a few weeks until better offices became available for both. Copley had agreed with the arrangement and had assumed that Galvin would also have no problems with the arrangement. However, for Galvin, the lack of an office was a bigger deal than Copley had anticipated. "I just feel," said Galvin, "that it looks bad to the staff and to the whole organization to have two directors sharing an office. Can you try to find me an office of my own as soon as possible?"

Although she was a little surprised at the exchange, Copley talked to Silver, made a few telephone calls, spoke to one of her managers and found an office for Galvin. Galvin seemed delighted with the larger office, which had a window facing the park. Indeed, she spent a day at the company storage building looking for new office furniture.

Within six months, the communications program was generating positive reviews. The program's four managers—who were all in their late 20s—seemed to be excited about the new direction of the program, and they could often be seen spending time on program work after normal business hours. Copley and Galvin led training sessions for the managers once a week. Copley soon felt quite close to her managers, kindred spirits in many ways. Two of them had PhDs, and the other two had MBAs. They were young, bright, enthusiastic and incredibly quick learners. Copley often told Silver that working with them was one of the best things about her new job. These managers were the people who would help popularize the new program throughout the organization and train new program instructors—they were the core of the program—and Copley felt lucky to be able to mentor them.

Galvin, however, had some trouble with the managers. At the first training session, she seemed defensive, as if disconcerted by working with people who had the same if not more education. She spent a lot of time lecturing, used PowerPoint presentations and didn't entertain many questions. Copley, in contrast, passed out readings ahead of time and ran her sessions as small-group discussions. The managers seemed to respond with greater interest to Copley's training, but Copley felt that the difference in style between Galvin and herself was perhaps a good thing—the kind of balance that Silver was looking for in the program. Still, she noticed that the managers spent a lot of time with her and almost invariably brought any problems they encountered to her not to Galvin. Silver was worried that she was unintentionally disempowering Galvin in front of the other staff, a move that would make more work for Copley and cause Galvin obvious concern.

As time went on, Galvin, in Copley's opinion, continued to have trouble adjusting to the more collaborative, informal environment Copley wanted to create. In training sessions or when meeting with others in the organization in an attempt to sell the new program, Galvin continued to be almost rigidly methodical: she was more comfortable with one person after another speaking in turn, preferably starting with junior employees and ending with the most senior employee in the room. Her body language suggested that she had difficulty tolerating "push back" or "constructive criticism," although she had less of an issue when she was addressing the junior staff. Some managers within the company responded well to Galvin's style, however, and Copley continued to feel that Galvin, although quite different from her, was an asset to the program. Furthermore, Copley had by now found several portfolios in which Galvin's training and

her aptitude for analysis and process were benefits (the development of communications courses targeted specifically at international leaders, for example), and Copley had made sure that these portfolios kept Galvin away from the more central decision-making process in the program, and, often, away from Copley's office.

✖ Rumors and Reports

In March, 2007, one month before the new program had completed its first year of operation, a friend from her old firm called Copley to tell her that he had met Galvin at a conference the week before. According to Copley's friend, Galvin had been actively soliciting offers from other employers at the conference. He had overheard her say that she was quite unhappy with the situation at Carnegie—that she felt "secondary" and "unappreciated" and would welcome a chance to run a program of her own. Her friend had also heard her say that she did not like being subordinate to someone nearly 20 years her junior. Copley recalled that at a dinner that both she and Galvin attended, she had overheard Galvin introducing herself as "one of the two directors" of the communications program. Copley had let it go without saying anything, although her husband, who had also overheard the comment, was angry.

In April 2007, with the program's first annual review of employee performance looming, Copley tried not to let what she had heard affect her judgment. She thought she would give Galvin a "very good," one notch short of "outstanding," because Galvin had indeed attained the goals Copley had set for her, and in the demanding environment of a new initiative. However, Copley felt that Galvin was still trying too hard to lecture to the managers, and that although her guidance was sound, her tone was condescending. One manager confided to Copley that, on more than one occasion, participants had noted on their feedback forms that they found Galvin "arrogant" and "aloof." And yet program enrollment was up 100 per cent, and positive reviews had tripled during the year. Silver was clearly happy at this rapid turnaround. In addition, Copley, Galvin and their team were accomplishing this feat with a smaller budget than before. The communications team was lauded for its success in improving skills across the organization, and Copley received a steady stream of congratulatory e-mails, which she shared with her staff. Talk at the management ranks suggested promoting Copley into an operating role within a few years. Galvin wasn't a great "fit," to be sure, but Copley had to admit she was part of the program's success.

Before actually writing Galvin's review, Copley met with her to discuss the process that would be used for the review. Galvin expressed concern with the use of "360-degree" feedback that incorporated managers' reviews of their superiors. Copley argued that she felt the managers' feedback was vital, given their centrality to the program and their very strong qualifications and performance. By this time, Copley was growing weary of Galvin's constant conservatism. She seemed to be trying to protect the status quo. Galvin, however, continued to argue vociferously that only her superior should provide feedback. Finally, Copley said, "Okay, if you only want my feedback, then I'm happy to limit the appraisal to my response alone." Galvin looked shocked. "I wasn't talking about your feedback, Shannon," she said. "I was talking about direct feedback from Elizabeth." Copley, confused, told her that Galvin reported directly to her, not to Silver. Galvin insisted that, as one of the two program directors, she reported to Silver, and angrily left the office. A few minutes later, Silver phoned Copley to say that she had just met with Galvin, who was unclear about the chain of command, and that Silver had informed Galvin "in the clearest possible terms" that Galvin reported to Copley.

Two weeks after the reviews were completed, Silver approached Copley:

We're very pleased with your performance, Shannon, and we hope that you're happy with your role. We certainly want to keep you here. I want to tell you this in person because, as you know, the firm is facing difficult times and we have cutbacks across the organization. Fortunately, I made it clear that your program has my full support and, as a result, we shielded it from the cuts. The unfortunate thing is that we won't be able to expand the program as we discussed a year ago. In fact, I don't know if we'll be able to put in a budget increase in the next two years or so. I hope you understand.

Copley replied, "I can work quite well with the budget you've given us, Elizabeth. We'll make do." As she walked out of Copley's small office, Silver said, "I should also tell you that we're looking for your enrollment numbers to increase and your ratings to increase next year. This was the condition the management team asked of us, in exchange for protecting the current level of funding." Copley looked back and smiled.

▧ A Difficult Conversation

Although Copley was happy to accept the challenge of increasing program enrollment and ratings on the current budget, she knew that the decision to freeze funding would not be taken well by Galvin, who wanted a full-time position. Indeed, Copley had just met with Galvin to talk about Galvin's completed performance review. Deciding that she did not want what might be simply differences in leadership style to affect the objectivity of her review, Copley had, at the last minute, decided to give Galvin an "outstanding" rating, despite her own reservations about Galvin's performance and the equivocal feedback from the managers. However, during the meeting, Galvin had used Copley's review to suggest that she be given a full-time position. Copley had told her that funds were frozen. Galvin had suggested letting one or two of the managers go, thereby freeing funds for a full-time position. Copley had responded that her suggestion wasn't an option. Galvin had left the meeting angrily and had called in sick the next day.

On May 12, 2007, Galvin approached Copley's office, and, standing in the doorway, burst out in tears:

> It's not fair to me not to provide me with a full-time position. I've worked really hard—as hard as you—over the past year, and my contributions have been central to this program's success. But you, Shannon, have basically alienated me from the managers, and you've deliberately kept me out of the loop during some of the most important program decisions this year. You don't trust me, and this is the first place I've ever worked where I wasn't trusted. It really hurts, and I can't go on like this. You either tell me right now how you feel about me and whether you'll ever support a full-time position, or I quit.

Schulich School of Medicine: Enhancing and Developing a High-Performance Culture

Ken Mark and Murray J. Bryant

Introduction

On December 15, 2004, Dr. Jane Rylett, newly appointed chairwoman of the Department of Physiology and Pharmacology (the department) at the Schulich School of Medicine and Dentistry, was thinking about how she would approach the next five years in her new role. Rylett thought about two of the important issues she would face as chairwoman: building a cohesive department and nurturing a high-performance culture.

Rylett was taking over control of the department at a time when direction was needed. The department had been formed in June 2002 as a result of the merger between the Department of Physiology and the smaller Department of Pharmacology and Toxicology. While the merger had gone well, Rylett still sensed that some faculty members in Pharmacology felt as if their department had been taken over by the Physiology Department. In an attempt to unite both departments, an external chairperson was hired. Unfortunately, the chairperson left the department after serving only two years of a five-year term. An internal search had taken place, and Rylett was appointed as the new chairwoman.

Building a Cohesive Department

The Department of Physiology and Pharmacology was very large, with about 60 faculty members dispersed over many sites in the city, both on the main campus of Western and at its affiliated hospitals and research institutes. Faculty were associated or co-located with various groups to facilitate and promote research. Rylett wanted to find a way to bring the department's members closer together to build a strong departmental culture, but she wondered how best to accomplish this.

Version: (A) 2009-10-27

In addition, some faculty members still felt strong associations with their original departments. While these emotions were not often expressed openly, Rylett felt that internal morale could certainly be improved. She wondered whether improvement could come from encouraging members of both predecessor departments to participate in departmental decision-making and planning activities. One potential solution was to have a broad range of faculty members assume roles on an expanded executive committee. Whereas previous executive committees had been small and typically drawn from senior faculty members—some of whom had close ties to the chairperson. Rylett wanted to triple the executive committee's size and include members from all experience levels. She wondered about the positive and negative implications of this initiative.

A larger executive committee would allow Rylett to engage a wide range of faculty members from various sites. Junior faculty could potentially have their views represented. Key decisions could be made collectively or at least with the input and buy-in from various constituents. On the other hand, Rylett wondered about the trade-off in efficiency and effectiveness. Consensus-building took time, and a larger committee might result in inaction on many agenda items. Proposed changes might have to be watered down to be acceptable. It could be difficult to chart a direction for the department if decision making were dispersed broadly. And finally, a small executive committee was usually made up of faculty members with whom the chairperson could discuss important issues. With a larger executive committee, Rylett had to be careful about how she sought counsel so as not to give the impression of favoring some faculty colleagues over others. If she was seen to prefer certain advisors, then the executive committee would only be "executive" in name.

Encouraging participation in the department would have to go well beyond appointments to the executive committee. Operating a department required contributions of time by faculty members to organize lectures, training sessions or organize department meetings. Rylett's challenge was to expand the pool of volunteers beyond the current dedicated (but small) group. Growing the numbers of volunteers would ensure that more could be accomplished towards the department's goals. It would also ensure that current volunteers were not overtaxed with commitments. While it was not written into job descriptions, participation in the department's activities was strongly encouraged. However, Rylett understood that no one could be pressed into volunteering; they had to be persuaded. As a result, some faculty members had simply refused to volunteer when asked. Rylett wondered how she could link the concept of volunteerism to faculty members' interests and incentives.

Most faculty members had alternative workload arrangements that reserved 75 per cent of their time for research. In deciding whether to participate in the department's activities, faculty weighed the benefits to be gained by volunteering against the downside risk of underinvesting in their research activities. The reluctance to add on another commitment in time often stemmed from not wanting to focus on activities that would provide no support to their own research and career progression. Simply put, those who refused to volunteer were expressing their preference to focus on productive work. But a successful department depends upon members who look out for the collective interest of the group. In some cases, the choice to focus only on research—despite the alternative workload arrangements—meant that teaching commitments were viewed as secondary and as irritants. Rylett wondered whether it was appropriate to insist that teaching commitments be met when it was clear to everyone in the department that the key measure of success was research productivity.

Nurturing a High-Performance Culture

In the event of underperformance in any area, Rylett wanted to distinguish between general underperformance, which was unintentional, as the faculty member had invested effort in meeting his or her goals, and willful underperformance, which suggested a conscious effort to evade commitments in the non-research workload. The former could be remedied in part by coaching and mentorship; dealing with the latter would be more difficult.

First, research was considered by many as the No. 1 priority for the department. As long as faculty members performed well in their research activities, underperformance in other areas—such as teaching and service—was often tolerated. Second, there were no carrots being dangled to encourage faculty members to increase their performance or participation, and there was no process in place to change the behaviour of underperforming faculty members. In some cases, improvements in non-research activities occurred only during the period leading up to their performance review.

With the intent of achieving a high-performance culture, Rylett wondered what elements should be measured and how standards—if any—could be enforced. Assessing teaching would be relatively straightforward: contact hours and ratings could be tracked. But how would service and contributions to the department function be assessed? And, assuming the assessments were made, what would Rylett need to have in place to follow through on the results?

At present, it was sometimes difficult to assess an individual's performance due to a lack of documentation and to differences in the workload composition among faculty members. The current thinking was that the department had to move towards adopting best practices in their processes. Rylett wanted to look at the issue from a broader perspective. She wondered how the issue could be best framed and what a potential solution might look like.

On Leadership: Leadership and Loyalty

Jeffrey Gandz

Leaders expect their followers to be loyal and to be able to depend on their loyalty. This is why we have such a visceral reaction when a David Radler turns on a Conrad Black or an Andrew Fastow cooperates with the prosecution to give evidence against his superiors at Enron. Emotive phrases like "ratting" or "biting the hand that has fed you" find their way into otherwise sober commentary. They conjure up childhood prohibitions on snitching and sneaking.

Leaders themselves have been known to go into paroxysms of rage followed by periods of deep hurt and even depression when they find that support on which they had counted is no longer there. And individuals have paid a steep price when their leaders conclude that they are no longer loyal and cannot be trusted to do their bidding, and so find themselves marginalized in decision making and personally shunned.

Good leaders understand that there is a difference between real *loyalty* and a related but different concept—*fealty*.

⌧ Give Me Loyalty, Not Fealty

Both loyalty and fealty share some things in common; they call for allegiance, faithfulness, and fidelity. But they differ in one remarkable

Reprint# 9B07TE11

respect. Loyalty embraces the concept of allegiance to an authority to whom such faithfulness is lawfully and morally due. Fealty, on the other hand, describes the fidelity of a vassal, slave or feudal tenant to his lord and master or, in modern parlance, the unqualified fidelity of a person to his or her boss.

Fealty is dangerous in corporations as well as in other social organizations. It leads to unethical, corrupt and often illegal actions spreading to the many rather than the few, to covering up those actions sometimes to the point of obstructing justice. Loyalty, on the other hand, is a positive dimension of business since it provides a force of energy that binds people together in the pursuit of worthwhile goals.

Fealty can be coerced or bought. Consequently, when the power relationship no longer exists or a better "deal" is available elsewhere—from another employer, or a prosecutor offering a more lenient sentence—the bond of fidelity is snapped. This is not an act of disloyalty but, rather, a belated recognition that the bond was composed only of self interest. The more enlightened that self-interest, the more individuals will act in ways that are beneficial to them.

Loyalty is made of sterner stuff. It is built on sound moral foundations, of which lawfulness is one but is not the only one. People who are bound by common values and moral beliefs are not easily deterred from supporting each other. They are neither discouraged by adversity nor deflected by better offers.

It explains why many people do work for which there is little extrinsic reward, why they serve their countries or churches or other social movements as volunteers or in poorly-paid positions; why they choose to work for companies that pursue socially responsible and responsive policies; why they are attracted to companies that have reputations for treating individuals and groups with dignity and respect, who are committed to their development, who provide employees with the opportunity to speak up and speak out about things with which they disagree, who have good whistle-blowing policies and

who do not tolerate leaders who do not support these value-driven actions.

Such moral beliefs are not necessarily inconsistent with the capitalist system or the obligations of private sector managers to maximize shareholder value. Creation of economic activity leads to better lives for people, generation of profits results in investment in growth and contribution of taxes, and so on. Business can be and often is a force for good. But, sometimes, business activity does create conflict between personal morality and financially attractive activities. Ask me to be involved in a company selling tobacco products and I will say "No!" Ask me to endorse advertising approaches that deliberately mislead potential customers and, again, you cannot expect my loyalty to the company, my boss, my colleagues on the executive team to guarantee my assent to the advertising campaign. Generate profits for shareholders at the expense of environmental depredation, and you violate my sense of corporate social responsibility. Do this often, and any bonds of loyalty that might have been generated in the past erode.

Moral beliefs are not unchangeable. Not that long ago, many people had deeply held beliefs about separation of races, the evil of religions other than their own, or relationships between same-gender couples. These values were supported by the laws of those times. There are still people who hold to these beliefs, who are prepared to go to extraordinary, sometimes illegal lengths to preserve them and who willingly give their loyalty to leaders who espouse them. These time-warps are troubling to many people, yet they form part of today's operating environments for business.

Individuals' moral development is also dynamic. Some have strong foundations through family or early institutional influences while others grow up in more free-thinking environments. Some views change over time, others remain stable.

Some people are quick to realize that what they are being asked to do by their bosses is wrong, others either don't question, accepting that their boss must be doing the right thing because he or she *is* their boss, or going along with the request because they accept that "that's the way it's done in this business." Such moral naivety is not evil but it can lead to bad things.

Smart leaders understand that fealty is demanded whereas loyalty is earned. And they earn this loyalty by doing a number of things:

- They understand the values of the people they lead and try to build their business strategies, plans, processes and practices in ways that are congruent with those values. This is the acid test of the "respect for the individual" that we see in so many organizations' value statements.
- They are sensitive to and respect changes in moral values within the societies in which they operate. Occasionally this will put them at odds with prevailing societal values, and they must make difficult personal decisions either to conform or quit.
- When they see other leaders in their organizations acting in ways that are morally offensive, they speak up . . . sometimes at personal risk. They channel their dissent constructively. . . . chaining oneself to railings is not usually an effective way to challenge corporate decisions! But they seldom just go along with the decision as an act of fealty.
- They promote debate about contentious issues to ensure that there is openness and transparency and that people do not feel that expressions of doubt are interpreted as "disloyalty."

Above all else, smart leaders understand: Never, never expect or depend on fealty—earn loyalty!

9

Transformational Leadership

Transformational leaders . . . are those who stimulate and inspire followers to both achieve extraordinary outcomes and, in the process, develop their own leadership capacity. Transformational leaders help followers grow and develop into leaders by responding to individual followers' needs by empowering them and by aligning the objectives and goals of the individual followers, the leader, the group, and the organization.

—Bernard M. Bass and Ronald E. Riggio[1]

It's not about organization, structure, process or management; it's people who accomplish things, and they need to be inspired, informed, enabled and supported.

—General Rick Hillier[2]

Transformational leadership is an involved, complex process that binds leaders and followers together in the transformation or changing of followers, organizations, or even whole nations. It involves leaders interacting with followers with respect to their "emotions, values, ethics, standards, and long-term goals, and includes assessing followers' motives, satisfying their needs, and treating them as full human beings" (Northouse, 2013). While all theories of leadership involve influence, transformational leadership is about an extraordinary ability to influence that encourages followers to achieve something well above what was expected by themselves or their leaders.

Early researchers in the area of transformational leadership coined the term (Downton, 1973) and tried to integrate the responsibilities of leaders and followers (Burns, 1978). In particular, Burns (1978)

[1]Bass and Riggio (2006, p. 3)

[2]Hillier, R. (2010, p. 237)

described leaders as people who could understand the motives of followers and, therefore, be able to achieve the goals of followers and leaders. As we discussed in Chapter 1, he considered leadership different from power because leadership is a concept that cannot be separated from the needs of followers.

Burns (1978) differentiated between transactional and transformational leadership. He described transactional leadership as that which emphasizes exchanges between followers and leaders. This idea of exchange is easily seen at most levels in many different types of organizations.

He described transformational leadership as that process through which leaders engage with followers and develop a connection (one that did not previously exist) that increases the morals and motivation of the follower and the leader. Because of this process, leaders assist followers in achieving their potential to the fullest (Yukl, 2012).

Bass and colleagues (Bass, 1998; Bass & Riggio, 2006; Bass & Steidlmeier, 1999) differentiated between leadership that raised the morals of followers and that which transformed people, organizations, and nations in a negative manner. They called this *pseudotransformational* leadership, to describe leaders who are power hungry, have perverted moral values, and are exploitative. In particular, this form of leadership emphasizes the leader's self-interest in a manner that is self-aggrandizing and contrary to the interests of his or her followers (Northouse, 2013). Authentic transformational leaders put the interests of followers above their own interests and, in so doing, emphasize the collective good for leaders and followers (Howell & Avolio, 1992).

Charismatic Leadership

"Charisma is a special quality of leaders whose purposes, powers, and extraordinary determination differentiate them from others" (DuBrin, 2010, p. 68). Weber (1947) emphasized the extraordinary nature of this personality trait but also argued that followers were important in that they confirmed that their leaders had charisma (Bryman, 1992; House, 1976). The influence exercised by charismatic leaders comes from their personal power, not their position power. Their personal qualities help their personal power to transcend the influence they have from position power (Daft, 2011).

House (1976) provided a theory of charismatic leadership that linked personality characteristics to leader behaviors and, through leader behaviors, effects on followers. Weber (1947) and House (1976) both argued that these effects would be more likely to happen when followers were in stressful situations because this is when followers want deliverance from their problems. A major revision to House's conceptualization has been offered by Shamir, House, and Arthur (1993). They argue that charismatic leadership transforms how followers view themselves and strives to tie each follower's identity to the organization's collective identity (Northouse, 2013). In other words, charismatic leadership is effective because each follower's sense of identity is linked to the identity of his or her organization.

A Transformational Leadership Model

Bass and his colleagues (Avolio, 1999; Bass, 1985, 1990; Bass & Avolio, 1993, 1994) refined and expanded the models suggested by Burns (1978) and House (1976). Bass (1985) added to Burns's model by focusing more on the needs of followers than on the needs of leaders, by focusing on situations where the outcomes could be negative, and by placing transformational and transactional leadership on a single continuum as opposed to considering them independent continua. He extended House's model by emphasizing the emotional components of charisma and by arguing that while charisma may be a necessary condition for transformational leadership, it is not a sufficient condition—more than charisma is needed.

Transformational leadership inspires subordinates to achieve more than expected because (a) it increases individuals' awareness regarding the significance of task outcomes, (b) it encourages subordinates to go beyond their own self-interest to the interests of others in their team and organization, and (c) it motivates subordinates to take care of needs that operate at a higher level (Bass, 1985; Yukl, 2012).

There are eight factors in the transformational and transactional leadership model. These are separated into three types of factors: (1) transformational factors consisting of idealized influence, individualized consideration, inspirational motivation, and intellectual stimulation; (2) transactional factors consisting of contingent reward, management by exception (active), and management by exception (passive); and (3) one nontransformational/nontransactional factor, which is laissez-faire leadership (Yukl, 2012).

⊠ Transformational Leadership Factors

This form of leadership is about improving each follower's performance and helping followers develop to their highest potential (Avolio, 1999; Bass & Avolio, 1990). In addition, transformational leaders move subordinates to work for the interests of others over and above their own interests and, in so doing, cause significant, positive changes to happen for the good of the team and organization (DuBrin, 2010; Kuhnert, 1994).

Idealized Influence or Charisma

Leaders with this factor are strong role models followers want to emulate and with whom they want to identify. They generally exhibit very high moral and ethical standards of conduct and usually do the right thing when confronted with ethical and moral choices. Followers develop a deep respect for these leaders and generally have a high level of trust in them. These leaders give followers a shared vision and a strong sense of mission with which followers identify (Northouse, 2013).

Inspirational Motivation

Leaders with this factor share high expectations with followers and motivate them to share in the organization's vision with a high degree of commitment. These leaders encourage followers to achieve more in the interests of the group than they would if they tried to achieve their own self-interests. These leaders increase team spirit through coaching, encouraging, and supporting followers (Yukl, 2012).

Intellectual Stimulation

Leaders with this factor encourage subordinates to be innovative and creative. These leaders support followers as they challenge the deeply held beliefs and values of their leaders, their organizations, and themselves. This encourages followers to innovatively handle organizational problems (Yukl, 2012).

Individualized Consideration

Leaders with this factor are very supportive and take great care to listen to and understand their followers' needs. They appropriately coach and give advice to their followers and help them to achieve self-actualization. These leaders delegate to assist followers in developing through work-related challenges and care for employees in a way appropriate for each employee. If employees need nurturance, the leader will nurture; if employees need task structure, the leader will provide structure (Northouse, 2013).

Transformational leadership achieves different and more positive outcomes than transactional leadership. The latter achieves expected results while the former achieves much more than expected. The reason is that under transformational leaders, followers are inspired to work for the good of the organization and subordinate their own self-interests to those of the organization.

Transactional Leadership Factors

As suggested above, transactional leadership is different from transformational leadership in its expected outcomes. The reason is that under transactional leaders, there is no individualization of followers' needs and no emphasis on followers' personal development—these leaders treat their followers as members of a homogeneous group. These leaders develop a relationship with their followers based on the exchange of something valuable to followers for the achievement of the leader's goals and the goals of the followers. These leaders are influential because their subordinates' interests are connected to the interests of each leader (Kuhnert, 1994; Kuhnert & Lewis, 1987).

Contingent Reward

This factor describes a process whereby leaders and followers exchange effort by followers for specific rewards from leaders. This process implies agreement between leaders and followers on what needs to be accomplished and what each person in the process will receive. This agreement is usually done prior to the exchange of effort and reward.

Management by Exception (MBE)

This factor has two forms—active and passive. The former involves corrective criticism, while the latter involves negative feedback and negative reinforcement. Leaders who use MBE (active) closely monitor their subordinates to see if they are violating the rules or making mistakes. When rules are violated and/or mistakes made, these leaders take corrective action by discussing with their subordinates what they did wrong and how to do things right. Contrary to the MBE (active) way of leading, leaders who use MBE (passive) *do not closely monitor subordinates* but wait until problems occur and/ or standards are violated. Based on their poor performance, these leaders give subordinates low evaluations without discussing their performance and how to improve. Both forms of MBE use a reinforcement pattern that is more negative than the more positive pattern used by leaders using contingent reward.

The Nonleadership Factor

A third type of leadership that is further removed from transformational leadership is laissez-faire leadership. Individuals in leadership positions who exercise this type of leadership actually abdicate their leadership responsibilities. This is absentee leadership (Northouse, 2013). These leaders try to not make decisions or to delay making decisions longer than they should, provide subordinates with little or no performance feedback, and ignore the needs of subordinates. These leaders have a "what will be will be" or "hands-off, let-things-ride" approach with no effort to even exchange rewards for effort by subordinates. Leaders who do not communicate with their subordinates or have any plans for their organization exemplify this type of leadership.

⬛ Other Perspectives of Transformational Leadership

Two other streams of research contribute to our comprehension of transformational leadership: These streams are research conducted by Bennis and Nanus (1985) and Kouzes and Posner (1987, 2002). Bennis and Nanus interviewed 90 leaders and, from these leaders' answers to several questions, developed strategies that enable organizations to be transformed. Kouzes and Posner interviewed 1,300 middle- to senior-level leaders in private and public organizations. They asked each leader to tell about his or her "personal best" leader experiences. From the answers these leaders provided, Kouzes and Posner developed their version of a transformational leadership model.

The Bennis and Nanus Transformational Leadership Model

Bennis and Nanus (1985) asked questions such as the following: "What are your strengths and weaknesses? What past events most influenced your leadership approach? What were the critical points in your career?" (Northouse, 2013). The answers to these questions provided four strategies that transcend leaders or organizations in their usefulness for transforming organizations.

First, leaders need to have a clear, compelling, believable, and attractive *vision* of their organization's future. Second, they need to be *social architects* who shape the shared meanings maintained by individuals in organizations. These leaders set a direction that allows subordinates to follow new organizational values and share a new organizational identity. Third, leaders need to develop within followers a *trust* based on setting and consistently implementing a direction, even though there may be a high degree of uncertainty surrounding the vision. Fourth, leaders need to use *creative deployment of self through positive self-regard*. This means that leaders know their strengths and weaknesses and focus on their strengths, not their weaknesses. This creates feelings of confidence and positive expectations in their followers and builds a learning philosophy throughout their organizations.

The Kouzes and Posner Transformational Leadership Model

On the basis of their interviews with middle- to senior-level managers, Kouzes and Posner (1987, 2002) found five strategies through content analyzing the answers to their "personal best" leadership experiences questions.

First, leaders need to *model the way* by knowing their own voice and expressing it to their followers, peers, and superiors through verbal communication and their own behaviors. Second, leaders need to develop and *inspire a shared vision* that compels individuals to act or behave in accordance with the vision. These inspired and shared visions challenge followers, peers, and others to achieve something that goes beyond the status quo. Third, leaders need to *challenge the process*. This means having a willingness to step out into unfamiliar areas, to experiment, to innovate, and to take risks to improve their organizations. These leaders take risks one step at a time and learn as they make mistakes.

Fourth, leaders need to *enable others to act*. They collaborate and develop trust with others; they treat others with respect and dignity; they willingly listen to others' viewpoints, even if they are different from the norm; they support others in their decisions; they emphasize teamwork and cooperation; and, finally, they enable others to give to their organizations because these others feel good about their leaders, their job, their organizations, and themselves.

Fifth, leaders need to *encourage the heart*. This suggests that leaders should recognize the need inherent in people for support and recognition. This means praising people for work done well and celebrating to demonstrate appreciation when others do good work.

This model focuses on leader behaviors and is prescriptive. It describes what needs to be done to effectively lead others to embrace and willingly support organizational transformations. The model is not about people with special abilities. Kouzes and Posner (1987, 2002) argue that these five principles are available to all who willingly practice them as they lead others.

How Does the Transformational Leadership Approach Work?

This approach to leadership is a broad-based perspective that describes what leaders need to do to formulate and implement major organizational change (Daft, 2011). These transformational leaders pursue some or most of the following steps.

First, they develop an organizational culture open to change by empowering subordinates to change, encouraging transparency in conversations related to change, and supporting them in trying innovative and different ways of achieving organizational goals. Second, they provide a strong example of moral values and ethical behavior that followers want to imitate because they have developed a trust and belief in these leaders and what they stand for.

Third, they help a vision to emerge that sets a direction for the organization. This vision transcends the various interests of individuals and different groups within the organization while clearly determining the organization's identity. Fourth, they become social architects who clarify the beliefs, values, and norms that are required to accomplish organizational change. Finally, they encourage people to work together, to build trust in their leaders and each other, and to rejoice when others accomplish goals related to the vision for change (Northouse, 2013).

References

Avolio, B. J. (1999). *Leadership in organizations* (6th ed.). Upper Saddle River, NJ: Pearson/Prentice Hall.

Bass, B. M. (1985). *Leadership and performance beyond expectations*. New York, NY: Free Press.

Bass, B. M. (1990). From transactional to transformational leadership: Learning to share the vision. *Organizational Dynamics, 18*, 19–31.

Bass, B. M. (1998). The ethics of transformational leadership. In J. Ciulla (Ed.), *Ethics: The heart of leadership* (pp. 169–192). Westport, CT: Praeger.

Bass, B. M., & Avolio, B. J. (1990). The implications of transactional and transformational leadership for individual, team, and organizational development. *Research in Organizational Change and Development, 4*, 231–272.

Bass, B. M., & Avolio, B. J. (1993). Transformational leadership: A response to critiques. In M. M. Chemers & R. Ayman (Eds.), *Leadership theory and research: Perspectives and directions* (pp. 49–80). San Diego, CA: Academic Press.

Bass, B. M., & Avolio, B. J. (1994). *Improving organizational effectiveness through transformational leadership*. Thousand Oaks, CA: Sage.

Bass, B. M., & Riggio, R. E. (2006). *Transformational leadership* (2nd ed.). Mahwah, NJ: Lawrence Erlbaum.

Bass, B. M., & Steidlmeier, P. (1999). Ethics, character, and authentic transformational leadership. *Leadership Quarterly, 10*, 81–227.

Bennis, W. G., & Nanus, B. (1985). *Leaders: The strategies for taking charge.* New York, NY: Harper & Row.

Burns, J. M. (1978). *Leadership.* New York, NY: Harper & Row.

Bryman, A. (1992). *Charisma and leadership in organizations.* London, England: Sage.

Daft, R. L. (2011). *The leadership experience* (5th ed.). Mason, OH: Thomson, South-Western.

Downton, J. V. (1973). *Rebel leadership: Commitment and charisma in a revolutionary process.* New York, NY: Free Press.

DuBrin, A. (2010). *Leadership: Research findings, practice, and skills* (6th ed.). Mason, OH: South-Western/Cengage.

Hillier, R., (2010). *A soldier first: Bullets, bureaucrats and the politics of war.* Toronto, Canada: HarperCollins.

House, R. J. (1976). A 1976 theory of charismatic leadership. In J. G. Hunt & L. L. Larson (Eds.), *Leadership: The cutting edge* (pp. 189–207). Carbondale: Southern Illinois University Press.

Howell, J. M., & Avolio, B. J. (1992). The ethics of charismatic leadership: Submission or liberation? *Academy of Management Executive, 6*(2), 43–54.

Kouzes, J. M., & Posner, B. Z. (1987). *The leadership challenge: How to get extraordinary things done in organizations.* San Francisco, CA: Jossey-Bass.

Kouzes, J. M., & Posner, B. Z. (2002). *The leadership challenge* (3rd ed.). San Francisco, CA: Jossey-Bass.

Kuhnert, K. W. (1994). Transforming leadership: Developing people through delegation. In B. M. Bass & B. J. Avolio (Eds.), *Improving organizational effectiveness through transformational leadership* (pp. 10–25). Thousand Oaks, CA: Sage.

Kuhnert, K. W., & Lewis, P. (1987). Transactional and transformational leadership: A constructive/developmental analysis. *Academy of Management Review, 12*(4), 648–657.

Northouse, P. G. (2013). *Leadership: Theory and practice* (6th ed.). Thousand Oaks, CA: Sage.

Shamir, B., House, R. J., & Arthur, M. B. (1993). The motivational effects of charismatic leadership: A self-concept-based theory. *Organization Science, 4*(4), 577–594.

Weber, M. (1947). *The theory of social and economic organizations* (T. Parsons, Trans.). New York, NY: Free Press.

Yukl, G. (2012). *Leadership in organizations* (8th ed.). Upper Saddle River, NJ: Pearson/Prentice Hall.

⬚ The Cases

Douglas Fine Foods

In September 2008, Matthew Douglas, the CEO of Douglas Fine Foods, realized that a number of big decisions needed to be made. Douglas Fine Foods had been in the family for the past 80 years and Matthew knew that a different leadership style was needed, In addition, he wondered how he would pay for the buyout of his brother's share of the company, whether a major contract with a less than desirable customer should be renewed, whether to grow through acquisition, and how to transform Douglas Fine Foods, a family business, into a professionally managed, world-class business.

Spar Applied Systems—Anna's Challenge

The director of human resources must contend with internal and external pressures to make changes quickly and smoothly for the new year. She has been with the company for 6 months. In her capacity as director of human resources, she has spent her time establishing a baseline for the division so that she can then create a departmental vision and strategy for 2000. It will be one of the most interesting challenges of her career. Since joining, she has gained an understanding of the division's future direction from its leadership team. The team is under the direction of the division's new general manager.

⊠ The Reading

Culture-Driven Leadership

As the CEO of ING DIRECT USA, Arkadi Kuhlman leads his organization in what many consider to be the most competitive industry—financial services. In this article, he describes what he did, and what other leaders can do, to build a dynamic culture that is very different from other organization in the financial services industry. He argues that successful leaders are supported by a vibrant culture that engages and energizes employees. Paradoxically, in most cases, that culture has been shaped, defined, and personified by the leader.

Douglas Fine Foods

Samira Amini, Jeff Goodwin, James E. Hatch, Mary Crossan, and Gerard Seijts

⊠ Introduction

It was September 2008, and Matthew Douglas, the chief executive officer (CEO) of Douglas Fine Foods (DFF), a business that had been in his family for the past 80 years, needed to make a number of major strategic decisions. He knew he had a long weekend in front of him; on Monday he was to meet with his management team to lay out his plan.

⊠ Douglas Fine Foods[1]

The Douglas family business, Douglas Dairy, was started in 1929, by Matthew's father and grand-father as a dairy farm and one-horse delivery service just outside of Calgary, Alberta. Over the years, the business sold a number of products and services that were in demand, most of which had one common theme—food and beverage.

The family business that had spanned nearly a century, concentrated on dairy products, soft drink bottling, vending machines, tobacco and fresh foods. Through the 1970s, the company began to focus more on over the counter food services, expanding from a local vending company to a regional cafeteria food services company as DFF continued to grow and adapt to customer needs. In 1991, Matthew Douglas's two older brothers, Jason and Mark, had purchased the family business from their father in 1975. From 1992 to 2006, Matthew Douglas played a limited role in the business, but progressively helped his father and brothers, who were actively managing multiple business ventures.

In 2007, Matthew Douglas purchased one-third of the family business and became more involved in growing DFF. Later that year, he was asked to take the helm as interim CEO for a couple of months while his brother, Jason, took time for a personal sabbatical. Things ran

[1]Although this case is based on an actual situation, some financial and other details have been disguised at the request of the company.

smoothly for his trial CEO period, and Douglas made an effort not to "shake things up," never placing much effort on a strategic agenda because he knew his brother would pick up where he had left off when he arrived home. Unfortunately, no one could have prepared Douglas for what happened next. Jason arrived back in Canada rested and re-thinking his role in the business only to face the sudden passing away of the middle Douglas brother, Mark. After much consulting with his soon to retire older brother Jason, it became a moment in time when Douglas said, "I can let this crush me or use it as a catalyst." He chose the latter and, in June 2008, took the full-time reins as CEO of DFF in June of 2008.

By 2008, DFF had grown to be the largest privately held Canadian food services company. Still headquartered in Calgary, DFF provided nutritious and healthy business dining, residence and camp food services, catering, vending machine services as well as food service equipment and design. The business serviced clients in various industries, schools, sports arenas, concessions, warehouses, government offices and corporations. DFF was proud to employ 850 full-time staff and relished in the history and legacy of the company's tremendous growth story, from a $1 million business in 1991 to a $30 million business by 2008.

The business focused on creating relationships with a wide range of organizations that had a consistent need for food and beverage services. Not just a "food provider," DFF offered a broad spectrum and full array of services in nearly every aspect of the value chain, beginning with the design, construction, financing and equipping of a food service facility (e.g. a cafeteria) and extending to staffing and providing full-scale operations for delivery of the food service. In the majority of cases, the food services infrastructure was already in place, and DFF offered its expertise in working to adjust and augment the associated people, programs and operations.

DFF prided itself in its ability to offer flexible and unique services to clients. The company was able to accommodate any catering requirement from simple luncheons to elaborate high-end banquets for hundreds of guests and even outdoor events, such as corporate picnics for thousands of patrons. DFF offered several dining concepts for its institutional clients: Main Street Café for business, university and college settings; and Hero's for high schools. The company also offered the products of a number of national "brand" franchises to strengthen and support their services in large venues.

Main Street Café was DFF's own internally branded dining concept that offered product variety and menu flexibility, with a full range of healthy options. The Hero's program provided school cafeterias with excellent food quality and variety at reasonable prices and was able to compete with outside retailers. An important asset was DFF's position as an authorized franchisee for four popular national chains: Tim Hortons, Canada's largest coffee chain; Pita Pit, a retail chain specializing in healthy, fresh food; Subway, the world's largest sandwich chain and Starbucks, the world's largest coffee chain, all of which provided the necessary complement of brand recognition. In addition, DFF had its own unique blend of first-quality coffee, JOJO Stop, which was made with top-of-the-line equipment and was designed to compete with the national gourmet coffee retailers.

DFF's corporate goals provided important guidelines for decision making in the organization. Douglas felt they both provided guidance for steering the company in the right direction and embodied many of the lifelong family lessons instilled in the company's history.

Customers—To understand and contribute to their success while providing the best product and value-added service as our customers perceive it.

Employees—To attract and retain enthusiastic, knowledgeable people who will enjoy delivering top-quality food and value with courtesy and excitement.

Community—To be one of the most valued corporate citizens in the communities in which we work.

Sustainability—To engage actions, attitudes and habits that lead by example in respecting our environment.

Profitability—To obtain the most attractive bottom-line profitability for our shareholders and investors while achieving our stated customer and employee objectives.

Matthew Douglas

From a very early age, Douglas had learned about independence, hard work and integrity. As he was growing up on the family farm, his father had taught him the basics: "Be honest, work hard, treat people well and respect the land." Throughout his life, Douglas lived and breathed these principles, which were reflected in his everyday decision making. Born into a family of entrepreneurs, he started his own retail business, Douglas Waterbeds, in 1979, while attending the University of Calgary and studying criminology and law. His deep-rooted sense of entrepreneurial spirit was evident as he grew the small dorm-room venture to a four-store chain business. Subsequently, Douglas tried his hand at various other businesses: medical waterbeds, a bacteria product that eliminated grease and odor in plumbing systems, real estate ventures, coordinating provincial sailing regattas, and building one of the largest cooking stores in the Country—all before he was 30 years old. Each time, he built personal shareholder value and sold off the enterprise before moving on to a new challenge. In 1989, his two brothers bought a hotel restaurant complex, the Central Park Hotel. Douglas took a keen interest in the business and began assisting with day-to-day management activities,

helping to transform the hotel into a top-notch business and leisure lodging destination.

Douglas's personality complemented his long list of achievements. By his current age of 53, he had been a national-level athlete, had climbed Mount Kilimanjaro, had skydived, had scuba dived in the Great-Barrier Reef, had obtained his pilot's license, spent a decade acting on stage, film and TV and had published a book. His positive attitude and integrity had been transcribed into his everyday life, especially with his customers. He fostered a culture of responsibility, accountability and teamwork and consistently remarked how "employees worked in his organization because they wanted to be there—not because they were just looking for a 'job.'"

Industry

The industry was divided into commercial food service (food and beverage outlets and restaurants), which represented 79 per cent of the market, and non-commercial food service (food services non-restaurants), which represented 21 per cent of the market. See Exhibit 1 for a further breakdown of the market segments.

The food services industry in Canada was mature with a high degree of competition. Canadian food service operators were expected to face their most challenging business environment in the next decade as cutbacks on consumer and business spending were beginning to surface amid a potential economic slowdown. A Canadian Restaurant and Foodservices Association (CRFA) report[2] forecast real growth in food service sales to slip by 4.6 per cent, which equated to an industry sales forecast of nearly $59 billion for 2009. See Exhibit 2 for historical and forecast food service sales. On the basis of this economic outlook, commercial food service sales would slip 2.5 per cent in 2009, and in particular, total caterer sales were forecast to drop by 3.0 per cent due to a

---

[2]Source: CRFA's InfoStats, Statistics Canada, fsSTRATEGY Inc. and Pannell Kerr Forster.

decline in social catering and reduced contract catering spending in the business segment. Non-commercial food service was expected to see a modest increase of 2.8 per cent, and institutional food service leading the growth with a 5.8 per cent increase. See Exhibit 3 for the latest detailed forecast of food services sales by channel.

Food costs (35.4 per cent of sales) and labor costs (31.5 per cent) accounted for the two largest expenses borne by foodservice operators.[3] See Exhibit 4 for a breakdown of average industry expenses as a percentage of operating revenue. Although the average pre-tax profit was 4.3 per cent of sales, this percentage varied significantly by province (from 2 per cent to 7 per cent). Profit margins diverged even further from one sector to the next.

Competitive Landscape

DFF was vying to compete with global, regional and local players in the food services business. In Canada, only three major global competitors accounted for the majority of the food services business. These companies each had Cdn$20 billion or more in worldwide sales and tended to focus on the larger contracts. Similar to DFF, a handful of well-recognized regional Canadian competitors each had their own target clientele and levels of service in the marketplace. In addition, DFF always kept a watchful eye on local competition. With low barriers to entry, a significant number of "mom and pop" shops had opened, although these competitors tended to be smaller, niche players that only serviced local clientele. Although this atmosphere sometimes made small local contracts competitive, these undersized players did not have the scale or expertise to supply larger institutional clients.

In the food services business, the name of the game was reputation, relationships and retention. If a company was doing a good job of servicing a client, it was hard to lose the business. Typically, the larger food services contracts were tendered through a request for proposal (RFP) method and were fixed five-year contracts. The RFP required not only a formal response but usually also included presentations and product samples. It was not uncommon for a company to keep a contract well beyond its expiration date if the supplier was providing excellent service. By winning a new contract, a vendor was typically taking business from a competitor who was inadequately servicing the needs of the client.

Global Competitors

Compass Group

Compass Group[4] was founded in 1941 and was the world's largest food service company with operations in more than 60 countries. Compass Group provided hospitality and food service for a variety of businesses and public sector clients, including cultural institutions, hospitals and schools. It also offered vending services and catering and concession services for events and sports venues. Compass Group employed more than 365,000 employees worldwide. It grew to its leadership position through aggressive expansion and numerous acquisitions and was now focused primarily on streamlining operations and maximizing profits. It saw continued growth coming from its efforts to extend additional services to clients, particularly in the corporate hospitality segment. Compass was also working to expand its facilities management business. Compass Group in Canada tended to focus on health care, education (college and university), remote sites and travel concessions.

[3]Source: CRFA's Foodservice Operations Report.

[4]Source: Hoovers Company Search.

The company's total revenue and EBITDA (earnings before interest, taxes, depreciation and amortization) were US$19.1 billion and US$1.5 billion respectively for fiscal 2008.[5]

Sodexo

Sodexo[6] was the world's number-two contract food service provider with operations in 80 countries, where it employed more than 212,000 staff. Its subsidiaries offered corporate food service and hospitality services, vending services and food services for educational institutions and other public sector clients. Other operations included event concessions, health care food services and such outsourced facilities management services as cleaning, grounds keeping and laundry. Sodexo was focused on winning new clients for its outsourcing services, especially in the area of facilities management. The company had also been making targeted acquisitions to expand both its services and geographical reach. In Canada, Sodexo tended to focus more on universities, private schools, health care and camps. Sodexo's total revenue and EBITDA were US$20.4 billion and US$1.03 billion respectively for fiscal 2008.[7]

Aramark

Aramark[8] was the world's number-three contract food service provider and was also a leader in the uniform supply business. It employed 250,000 staff. Aramark offered corporate dining services and operated concessions at many sports arenas and other entertainment venues. The company also provided facilities management services and continued to look for opportunities to expand not only its client base but also the number of services it supplied to its existing customers. Aramark targeted industry segments such as correctional facilities and health care operators. Keen on international expansion, the company had recently focused on Europe and Asia, where it was the official food service provider for the 2008 Olympic Games in Beijing. Aramark in Canada focused on education (colleges, universities and private schools), health care, business dining and remote camps. Aramark's total revenue and EBITDA were US$13.29 billion and US$1.04 billion respectively for fiscal 2008.[9]

Regional Competitors

Diana Hospitality

Diana Hospitality was formed in 1988 and provided a workplace environment with quality food. The company offered hospitality programs and management services to a wide range of clients who valued fresh on-site culinary services, with a strong focus on retail food service partnerships. It had experience in the health care, education, and business and industry sectors where labor management agreements were required. Diana Hospitality's Food Consulting Services Inc. was a management advisory service specializing in innovative, resourceful solutions for clients who wanted to improve their food services.

WilliamsFoods

WilliamsFoods had built a strong reputation by providing quality food products and exceptional

---

[5]Source: Google Finance and Capital IQ.

[6]Source: Hoovers Company Search.

[7]Source: Google Finance and Capital IQ.

[8]Source: Hoovers Company Search.

[9]Source: Google Finance and Capital IQ.

customer service. The company continued to grow in size and strength and enjoyed exceptional corporate partnership with its clients. Williams-Foods offered event planning and management, culinary expertise, signature brands and cafeteria services. WilliamsFoods took care of all aspects of food service at a site, including vending with nationally branded products and their own prepared foods. WilliamsFoods also specialized in facility design from complete renovation to minor makeovers. The company provided food services to corporations, government, industrial sites, sports centres, golf clubs, educational facilities, fine dining restaurant facilities and high-profile tourism destinations. For WilliamsFoods, the choice of client was as important an issue as the choice of a food service company must be to any potential client. WilliamsFoods experience was built on quality performance and was dependent on management capability, high staff morale and the insistence that their staff show a high degree of commitment to each contract. The company believed that its staff must feel a degree of "pride and ownership" and consequently be directly accountable for all aspects of each contract.

West Coast Company (WCC)

WCC was a family-run business originating in Western Canada, now with locations across the nation. WCC had 70 major clients and primarily provided services to the education segment (secondary and college education) as well as health care. WCC had good relations with its customers and had a very similar culture and skill set to DFF.

⬚ DFF's Food Services Clients

Education

This segment consisted primarily of cafeteria services and vending machines in secondary schools, universities and colleges. The university and college sector was a mature market and was characterized by a heavy requirement for capital and high commissions. Universities, which tended to be very involved with their food service offerings, required a customized personal approach, were not always concerned about low-cost but sought good, quality service that formed a part of their on-campus offering. The college sector, although similar to the university sector, offered more emphasis on margin returns for the food service provider. High schools offered very thin margins, were primarily driven by the financial return to school boards and tended to focus less on quality. Private schools were also similar to the university and college sectors and shared their requirements for very high-quality service, but provided excellent margins. The education segment represented 29 per cent of DFF's business.

Recreation

Many recreation facilities included a "snack shop," a full-service restaurant or a concession-style service. This segment consisted of both amateur and professional venues and was associated with an upfront investment, high margins and profit sharing with partners. The professional team sector (e.g. the National Football League, the National Hockey League and Major League Baseball) was dominated by larger players in the market and offered minimal entry to mid-level players. Municipal arenas and sports complexes were abundant, and contracts tended to be awarded on shorter cycles, typically every three years. The recreation segment represented 9 per cent of DFF's business.

Health Care

Most health care facilities either operated or leased cafeteria space for staff, patients and visitors. This segment included patient food services and was characterized by high margins and adequate quality levels. Recently, health care facilities had begun to offer branded food outlets to enhance their offering. This segment represented 6 per cent of DFF's business.

Government

Similar to the education segment, government clients usually required cafeteria services and vending machines for municipal, provincial and federal facilities. Government-funded organizations tendered their food services through the RFP process. This segment represented 21 per cent of DFF's business.

Business and Industrial Clients

A large number of businesses and industrial clientele offered cafeteria services in their factories, office buildings or warehouses. These contracts offered food services to anywhere from 10 to more than 1,000 employees. Business clients focused more on quality of food for their employees. Business and industrial clients represented 35 per cent of DFF's food services business.

Services

Cafeteria and Food Services

The majority of DFF's business could be characterized as food services, which included staffing, preparing and selling high-quality cafeteria-style food. In the majority of cases, the physical infrastructure was already in place, and DFF worked to adjust and augment the people, programs, operations and food offerings. This service accounted for the majority of DFF's services revenue at 57 per cent.

Catering and Special Events

Catering and special events were typically based on relationship sales. Many of the contracts were referrals in this segment, which had been experiencing growth. The service offered high margins and had the benefit of set beginning and

end dates. This segment represented 22 per cent of revenue to DFF.

Branded Food Outlets

Branded retail offerings, such as Subway, Pizza Hut and Tim Hortons, provided high brand recognition and was a growing segment. These outlets were franchised and operated by DFF and could be provided to any segment as the sole food services provision or to complement other cafeteria services. Although the business offered lower margins, branded food was seen as a necessity to compete. Branded food outlets accounted for 11 per cent of DFF's services revenue.

Vending Sector

Vending services offered slim margins and required continuous maintenance and stocking. Although the major companies that participated in this space were profitable, vending machines sales were slowly declining. Companies looked to keep existing vending contracts and not necessarily seek out new business. Vending services accounted for 6 per cent of revenue for DFF.

Food Services Design

Another recent trend focused on adapting and enhancing existing facilities. These projects required expertise in the industry and often entailed redesigning cafeteria and food court settings (e.g. adjusting the layout, service format, equipment, physical facilities and interior design) to enhance revenue and improve efficiencies. Although most food services companies offered some form of design, only a few did it well. Food services design accounted for 4 per cent of DFF revenue.

Current Situation

In June 2008, Douglas's eldest brother announced that he would like to retire. As a result, Douglas was working on a financing arrangement to acquire all the remaining shares in the business and become the sole owner of the family enterprise.

Douglas spent his first several months as the official CEO reviewing operations, talking to employees, meeting with suppliers and discussing operational agendas with DFF's clients. After taking all this into consideration, Douglas sat back and wondered in what direction he should lead the business. After nearly every question posed to the staff, he wound up hearing the same answer: "because we've always done it that way." As the new CEO, he wondered how he would be able to change the mindset of employees who had worked in the Douglas family business their entire lives. Although the business was profitable, he wasn't sure what to do and how to prioritize his decisions.

One option Douglas had at his disposal was to position DFF for either immediate or eventual sale to a financial buyer, a private equity firm or a strategic buyer/competitor. His attitude had always been to work every day to prepare his companies for a sale. Having the good fortune to have his hand in many entrepreneurial activities in his life, Douglas understood what it took to build a successful organization, how hard it was to be profitable and how quickly the business reputation could be tarnished. DFF had achieved a positive reputation in a mature, well-established industry, which made the company a ripe acquisition target. Recently, a few of DFF's smaller competitors had been acquired by larger international players; Douglas speculated he could be next. On the other hand, he needed to make a pragmatic decision; he enjoyed the earnings and leadership role and wasn't sure how he would be perceived if he sold the business before even giving it a try as its new leader. Douglas wondered what changes could be made to make the business even healthier and more attractive to a potential buyer.

Douglas thought about where he should position the company to compete. He knew that if DFF consolidated a number of the smaller or mid-level market players, the company would have a stronger advantage against larger competitors and would have a unique, more customized approach to serve segments of the market. Because margins seemed to be tightening year after year and, except for the larger competitors, few companies had critical mass in the mid-market space, he wondered whether this situation was an attractive opportunity to take over other companies.

He was also aware that the large contracts, typically won by the bigger competitors, offered higher margins and could be won without significantly increasing the number of employees or adjusting operations. This option was advantageous because it would grow volume, achieve economies of scale and quickly grow EBITDA to position the company for a possible sale.

Another option Douglas contemplated was dedicating his efforts to growing the business organically. Plenty of opportunities were out there, and with the right focus, he felt that he could win some of these key contracts. He remarked that he already had the best employees and as a favoured author of his wrote "if you have the right people on the bus . . . you can go anywhere." Considering the maturity of the industry and the fact he wasn't exactly getting calls every day asking to buy his company, maybe consolidation really wasn't the right way to go. He considered a few approaches to organic growth and was unsure which might work best. Douglas wondered what kind of trends and product innovation DFF could capitalize on to give the company a competitive edge. Due to health issues such as obesity, diabetes and high cholesterol, more and more people were consciously choosing health and wellness as a lifestyle, and this preference was beginning to be reflected in consumer diets. Privatization and public–private partnerships by government and nonprofit organizations were also becoming standard practice; Douglas wondered how he could capitalize on this new way of securing business. He could also work on improving margins by adopting a low-cost strategy, lengthening trade payments and significantly lowering input costs. Douglas wondered whether he could grow by focusing more heavily on his existing clients. Douglas knew that some key decisions were necessary because, in this industry, you could choose to either innovate, consolidate (acquire or be acquired) or be pushed out by stiff competition of the global players.

Financial Situation

As a private business, DFF had not previously been managed to impress outside investors or hit lofty share targets but was run in the most effective manner for tax planning purposes and to meet the needs of employees. See Exhibit 5 for the latest financial statements. In the most recent year, the company had generated more than $33 million in sales, profit of $235,000 and almost $1.7 million in EBITDA. On the other hand, the company had built up a substantial amount of debt obligations.

In 2008, Douglas agreed to buy out his retiring brother's shares of the company for $1 million.[10] The company's bank had tentatively agreed to provide the company with the financing required.

Douglas knew the organization had intrinsic value for him but not necessarily for the market. In talking with various financial advisors, Douglas learned that the company needed to achieve roughly $5 million to $10 million EBITDA to successfully exit the business and position DFF as an attractive take-over target.

The Auto Decision

A major decision had to be made with respect to DFF's largest client—Canada Auto Corporation (CAC).

In 2004, DFF had received a phone call from CAC asking whether DFF would like to bid on the food services contract for an assembly plant with 5,000 employees. If DFF won the contract, it would replace one of its major competitors and heighten awareness of DFF in the automotive industry. Revenues from the contract would take the form of a management fee. A management fee was utilized in businesses in which the client wished to maintain a high degree of control and was willing to pay for that control and have a company with professional experience manage the food services division.

Initially, DFF had declined the offer to bid as it struggled with the management fee business model. Under the proposed contract, DFF would be provided with minimal financial transparency and control, yet would be expected to run the cafeteria and food services more efficiently. After lengthy negotiations with CAC, DFF decided to proceed with the RFP and subsequently was awarded the contract.

From 2004 to 2008, DFF continued to make minor improvements in food services delivery and increasingly struggled with the conflict between the contract and DFF's core values. For example, cost cutting often trumped quality. Also, retaining and motivating staff was increasingly difficult, due to poor labor relations conditions, which had a negative effect on DFF staff. The cafeteria tended to become the dumping ground for employee complaints and harassment, evidenced by an increasing trend toward conflict between members of the CAC unionized workforce and the cafeteria staff.

---

[10]Exhibit 5 does not include the money to be paid to Douglas's brother for his share of the company ($1 million), which was expected to be paid before the end of 2009.

Although the contract represented a substantial portion of EBITDA (almost 20 per cent), Douglas continued to find the contract difficult because it consumed much emotional and intellectual time. He felt he was always extinguishing small fires and was beginning to lose sight of the larger picture. On the other hand, the contract brought significant value to CAC and had transformed its dysfunctional food services operation into an effective, break-even operation by improving hours of operation, lowering costs and doing its best to enhance the atmosphere of an industry in dire straits.

By 2009, management at DFF had become somewhat reliant on the strong cash flows from the CAC contract, and many were shocked by Douglas's decision to review the agreement and discuss the merits of declining to submit a RFP for renewal of the contract. Douglas had always felt uneasy about CAC's business model and, looking ahead, he wondered whether these types of contracts were best suited for DFF's core competencies. If the company did decide to walk away from the contract, how would he replace the cash flow?

In addition, Douglas was worried about the successor liability provisions of the provincial labour code. DFF had inherited a unionized workforce when it took on the CAC contract and was worried about the liabilities it might incur if CAC went bankrupt. It was no easy decision.

▧ The Acquisition Opportunity

Douglas liked the idea of acquiring a company but wanted to ensure that any target company would be the right fit. He also wasn't sure how much he should pay for a business. He reasoned that by acquiring a competitor, he could decrease costs by achieving economies of scale and grow the top line without adding many additional staff. His criteria for selecting the appropriate target relied on strategic alignment, reputation, culture, technology, human capital, the amount of cash held by the target, key clients and market share. Before Douglas had taken over as CEO, a well-respected manager within DFF had prepared a list of potential acquisition targets on the basis of the above criteria; Douglas had narrowed the potential targets down to two.

The primary acquisition targets Douglas considered were West Coast Company (WCC) and WilliamsFoods. Both companies had approximately $8 million in sales and a cost of goods sold of $3 million. Douglas noted that WCC was facing financial stress as it had negative working capital, weak EBITDA and significant debt of $600,000. WCC was generating $150,000 EBITDA, which Douglas thought he could substantially improve, given the synergies that could be achieved; however, because acquiring WCC would be a turnaround situation, the synergies and operating improvements could be quite uncertain. He reasoned that he would be able to acquire the company for a very low price but would need to take on the debt. WilliamsFoods, on the other hand, was an attractive target because it currently had more reasonable profits, no debt and provided the opportunity for some synergies. However, this acquisition was likely to be more expensive. See Exhibit 6 for selected data on the target companies.

Douglas seriously considered this opportunity to grow his business through acquisition if the price was right. Given its good relations with DFF, the company's bank had tentatively agreed to provide the financing required to pursue an acquisition.

Douglas used an EBITDA multiple approach for valuation of the target companies. Acquisitions in the industry were typically at a price of seven to eight times EBITDA. Goodwill tended to be high in the industry because client relationships were paramount to success. To determine the company's final value, Douglas needed to keep in mind that many sellers had an emotional attachment to certain price points, and thus, his offer had to avoid disrespecting entrepreneurs who had taken their whole lives to build their business and felt that it had substantial value.

If an acquisition went through, Douglas needed to consider how the acquired company would be incorporated into DFF's existing business. Douglas needed to ensure that legacy information was maintained and that both existing clients and acquired clients were satisfied with the merger. He also had to have a financing plan in place.

From Entrepreneur to Professional Manager

Lastly and of equal importance to the many decisions that had to be made was the daunting task of how to transform the organization from an entrepreneurially oriented family business to a professionally managed multimillion-dollar company. The industry and the business world were changing. Gone were the days of lack of employment standards. Health regulations were increasingly important, business partnerships were no longer solidified on a handshake and workplace safety was at the forefront of industry news. Douglas remarked:

> In the past, relationships and verbal commitments were all you needed. In today's world clients will call and say "clause 2.2 said you'll do this—you have 30 days to comply before the contract is terminated."

Competition was tough and needed to be matched by sound management processes and strong leadership, all of which were deteriorating at DFF. Douglas knew he had his work cut out for him to transform the company into a professional setting, and he understood that the transformation needed to start from the top.

Although the industry was changing, DFF had seen little, if any, meaningful change. The physical state of their building had not changed in more than two decades, information systems were in place but utilization of such systems was barely adequate. On the people side of the business, the employees were, in general, ensnared in a culture that did not match the look and feel one would expect when dealing with a multi-million-dollar organization. Excessive tolerance for risk, use of unprofessional communication, an absence of a dress code policy and other "home grown employee habits" would be unheard of in most Canadian corporate settings. Douglas noted:

> Our employees look up to the management team . . . we know what we're doing, but we also need to look like we know what we're doing. I want to instill a sense of professionalism and passion in all of our people, including management.

Douglas noticed employees were resistant to change. For example, he had recently asked a payroll employee why he was filling out a report by hand instead of on the computer system. The employee remarked "because that is how we have always done it in the past."

DFF had frequently solicited the advice of one of the largest accounting and advisory firms in Canada with respect to employee relations. The purpose of this survey was to have employees provide recommendations for change within the organization. In a recent survey of DFF administered by the advisory firm, questions included the following:

> If I were the new CEO of DFF, the first three things I would change are. . . .

> If I were the new manager of my department, the first three things I would change are. . . .

I am held back by the following inefficiencies in the way we do business. . . .

The results had provided Douglas with ideas on how to improve the business. For example, employees felt strongly about the need to have more autonomy in their roles and in the decision-making process. Employees felt their current role limited their ability to provide recommendations.

People management was very important in the food services industry because client relationships were dependent on service delivery and professionalism on the front line. As such, DFF aimed to treat its employees well and understood that compensation was not always the most motivating factor. DFF motivated and rewarded its employees in a number of ways, including providing professional development (e.g. training and mentoring) and profit sharing.

To top it off, difficulties also existed with the senior management team, which comprised four executives. Two of the members were not pleased with Douglas taking over as CEO and would not likely support his new direction for the company; however, they held important legacy information about DFF and its clients. As a result, meetings had become increasingly difficult because members held divergent views, which created an emotional swirl. Douglas was not sure how to address this issue.

Douglas understood that change began from the top. He noted, "Culture comes from the leader and you attract people that believe in the leaders style and vision." For change to be successful in organizations, leaders need to change their own behavior first. Soon after taking over as CEO, Douglas attended a client meeting and realized that his behavior and mind space also needed to change. When the client began asking questions about the strategy of the organization and in the direction in which he wanted to take the business, Douglas had scrambled to find appropriate answers. He was stuck in the details of managing because his previous roles in the organization had always entailed some level of "doing," (e.g. preparing an RFP to bid on a new contract). He now recognized, however, that as CEO, he needed to keep his head out of the weeds and begin the transformation to become a "thinker." Thus, his responsibilities and mindset were no longer merely to manage day-to-day tasks but to worry about the strategic direction of the firm.

The Decision

Douglas knew that the Monday morning meeting would be a tough one. He was to meet with the management team and lay out his plan for DFF. Douglas hoped that the team would understand and support his vision. The problem was he was not sure what that vision would be. Should he continue to grow his business in such a mature industry? He considered pursuing an acquisition target, but didn't want to overpay because cash was already tight. Would the bank provide the financial support to implement his plans? What should he do with the CAC business? Regardless of these decisions, Douglas knew he needed a change management strategy to deal with the organizational transformation from entrepreneurial to professional. As the new CEO, Douglas had his work cut out for him.

| Exhibit I | Canadian Food Service Sales by Commercial and Non-Commercial Categories |

Commercial Foodservice (79% Market Share)

Full Service Restaurants (36%):

Includes licensed and unlicensed fine-dining, casual and family restaurants as well as restaurant-bars.

Limited Service Restaurants (32%):

Includes quick-service restaurants, cafeterias, food courts and take-out and delivery establishments.

Social and Contract Caterers (7%):

Includes contract caterers supplying food services to airlines, railways, institutions and at recreational facilities, as well as social caterers providing food services for special events.

Drinking Places (4%):

Includes bars, taverns, pubs, cocktail lounges and nightclubs primarily engaged in serving alcoholic beverages for immediate consumption. These establishments may also provide limited food service.

Non-Commercial Foodservice (21 % Market Share)

Accommodation Foodservice (9%):

Foodservice in hotels, motels and resorts.

Institutional Foodservice (6%):

Foodservice in hospitals, residential care facilities, schools, prisons, factories, remote facilities and offices. Includes patient and inmate meals.

Retail Foodservice (2%):

Department store cafeterias and restaurants.

Other Foodservice (4%):

Includes vending, sports and private clubs, movie theatres, stadiums and other seasonal or entertainment operations.

SOURCE: Canadian Restaurants and Foodservices Association, "Definitions: Foodservice Industry Segments."

Exhibit 2 Total Food Service Sales in Canada, Actual and Projected (1998–2009)

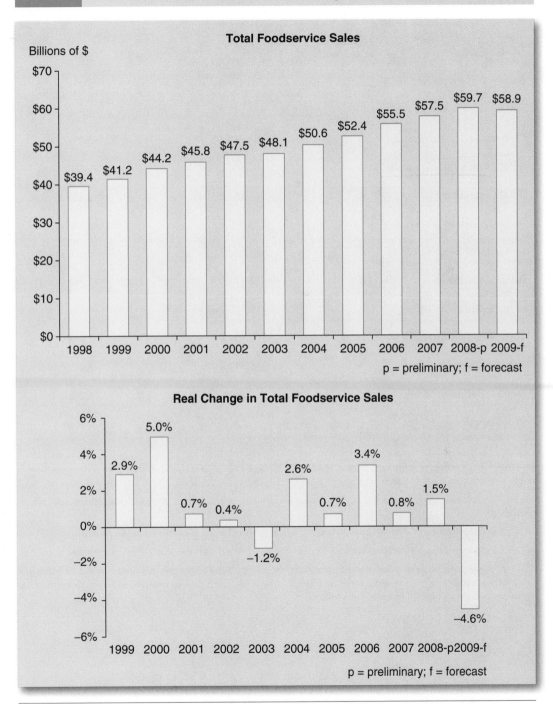

Exhibit 3	Forecast of Food Service Sales in 2009 by Category

	2009 Forecast (Millions of Dollars)	% Change '09/'08
Full-service restaurants	$20,956.5	−3.1%
Limited-service restaurants	$19,147.0	−1.8%
Contract and social caterers	$3,780.3	−3.0%
Pubs, taverns and nightclubs	$2,304.2	−2.6%
Total Commercial	**$46,188.0**	**−2.5%**
Accommodation foodservice	$5,937.0	3.5%
Institutional foodservice[1]	$3,432.4	5.8%
Retail foodservice[2]	$1,178.1	1.2%
Other foodservice[3]	$2,162.2	−2.5%
Total Non-Commercial	**$12,709.8**	**2.8%**
Total Foodservice	**$58,897.8**	**−1.4%**
Menu inflation		**3.2%**
Real Growth		**−4.6%**

SOURCE: CRFA's InfoStats, Statistics Canada, fsSTRATEGY Inc. and Pannell Kerr Forster, *CRFA's 2008 Foodservice Forecast*, http://www.crfa.ca/research/statistics/sales.asp.

NOTE 1: Includes education, transportation, health care, correctional, remote, private & public sector dining and military foodservice.

NOTE 2: Includes foodservice operated by department stores, convenience stores and other retail establishments.

NOTE 3: Includes vending, sports and private clubs, movie theatres, stadiums and other seasonal or entertainment operations.

NOTE 4: The commercial foodservice sales and units in this forecast are based on Statistics Canada's new Monthly Survey of Food Services and Drinking Places which replaces the old Monthly Restaurants, Caterers and Taverns Survey. Comparisons to previously published data must be made with caution.

Exhibit 4 Financial Operating Ratios—2006 (As a Percentage of Operating Revenue)

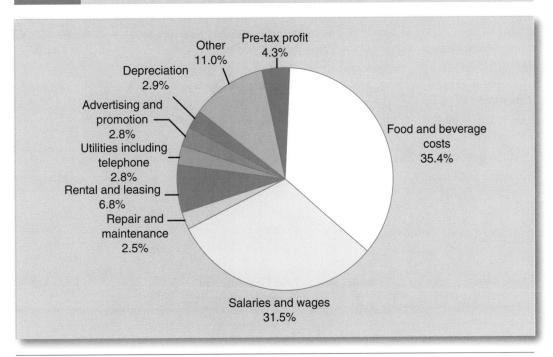

SOURCE: 2008 CRFA's Foodservice Operations Report, http://www.crfa.ca/research/2008/foodservice_profitability_ improves.asp.

Exhibit 5(a) Douglas Fine Foods Consolidated Balance Sheet as of September 30, 2008

Assets		Liabilities and Shareholders' Equity	
Current Assets		Current Liabilities	
Cash	$1,428,223	Bank Overdraft[3]	788,229
Accounts Receivable	758,804	Accounts Payable and Accrued Liabilities	3,353,883
Inventories	1,224,869	Deferred Revenue	386,571
Prepaid Expenses and Deposits	122,092	Income and Commodity Taxes Payable	66,542
Life Insurance	648,742	Current Portion of Long-Term Debt	679,418
Loan Receivable from Related Party[1]	748,361	Current Portion of Obligation Under Capital Leases	336,945
	4,931,091		5,611,588

(Continued)

Exhibit 5(a)	(Continued)

Assets		Liabilities and Shareholders' Equity	
Loan Receivable from Related Parties[1]	88,399	Long-Term Debt[4]	1,876,194
Equipment and Leasehold Improvements	14,932,117	Obligations under Capital Leases	485,089
Less: Accumulated Depreciation	11,382,671	**Shareholders' Equity**	
Net Fixed Assets	3,549,446	Share Capital	215,609
Goodwill and Intangible Assets[2]	1,044,984	Contributed Surplus	200,170
		Retained Earnings	1,225,270
			1,641,049
Total Assets	**$9,613,920**	**Total Liabilities and Shareholders' Equity**	**9,613,920**

NOTE 1: These loans are interest free and payable on demand.

NOTE 2: A large portion of goodwill arose from acquisitions.

NOTE 3: The bank automatically nets cash balances and overdrafts although these items are seen separately in the balance sheet. Interest is charged on the loan at Bank Prime plus from 35 to 225 basis points based on certain performance indicators. As of September 30, 2008 the company had a line of credit at the bank of $975,000 of which none had been utilized. The line is secured by a general security agreement over the assets of the company.

NOTE 4: The Company had a variety of loans outstanding. Interest rates varied from 6.75% to 10%. Collateral security provided varied from a general security agreement to a second mortgage on certain assets.

Exhibit 5(b)	Douglas Fine Foods Consolidated Statement of Operations for the Year Ended September 30, 2008

Sales	$33,192,512
Cost of Goods Sold	14,239,975
Gross Profit	18,952,537
Expenses and Other Income	
Operating Expenses	18,437,214
Depreciation and Amortization	978,282
Other Interest and Bank Charges	193,806

Interest on Long-Term Debt and Capital Leases	217,812
Debt Accretion Expense	67,223
Contract Management Fee Income—automotive industry	−458,700
Sundry Income	−327,248
Contract Management Fee Income—other	−447,516
	18,660,873
Earnings before Interest, Taxes & Depreciation (EBITDA)	1,681,564
Earnings (loss) before Income Taxes	291,664
Income Taxes	56,301
Net Earnings	$235,363

Exhibit 5(c)	Douglas Fine Foods Consolidated Statement of Cash Flows for the Year Ended September 30, 2008

Cash provided by:	
Operations	
Net Earnings (loss)	$235,363
Items Not Involving Cash	
Depreciation and amortization	978,282
Decrease (increase) in Cash Surrender Value of Life Insurance	−27,541
Debt Accretion Expense	67,223
Gain on Disposal of Equipment	−7,174
Loss on Disposal of Equipment	13,125
Net Change in Non-Cash Operating Working Capital	
Accounts Receivable	121,649
Inventories	−75,133
Prepaid Expenses and Deposits	−40,506

(Continued)

Exhibit 5(c) (Continued)	
Accounts Payable and Accrued Liabilities	−675,462
Deferred Revenue	−13,111
Income and Commodity Taxes Payable	−45,445
Loan Receivable from Related Party	−748,361
	−217,091
Financing	
Repayment of Long-Term Debt	−714,669
Borrowing of Long-Term Debt	400,000
Repayment of Obligations under Capital Lease	−370,411
Borrowing of Obligations under Capital Lease	329,356
Net Advances to Shareholders	−88,399
	−444,123
Investments	
Purchase of Intangible Assets	748,361
Purchase of Equipment and Leasehold Improvements	−508,991
Proceeds on Disposal of Equipment and Leasehold Improvements	48,162
	287,532
Decrease in Cash	373,682
Cash, Beginning of Year	1,013,676
Cash, End of Year	$639,994
Cash is comprised of	
Cash	1,428,223
Bank Overdraft	(788,229)
Net Cash	639,994

SOURCE: Company files.

Exhibit 6	Selected Data on Acquisition Targets (in Cdn$000)	

	WilliamsFood	**West Coast Company (WCC)**
Sales	$8,000	$8,000
Cost of Goods	3,000	3,000
EBITDA	600	150
Depreciation	20	20
Debt	–	600
Potential Synergies Leading to Increased EBITDA:		
Volume Purchases	50	50
Back-Office Expenses	200	550
Admin Expenses	200	200
	450	800

SOURCE: Company files.

Spar Applied Systems—Anna's Challenge

Laura Erksine and Jane M. Howell

It was September 1993 and Anna Solari had been with Spar Applied Systems for six months. In her capacity as director of human resources, she had spent her time establishing a baseline for the division so that she could then create a departmental vision and strategy for 2000. It would be one of the most interesting challenges of her career. Since joining, Anna had gained an understanding of the division's future direction from its leadership team. The team was under the direction of Stephen Miller, the division's new general manager. Since there was internal and external pressure to make the changes quickly and smoothly, Anna knew the vision for human resources had to be in place well before the new year.

Spar Aerospace Limited

Spar Aerospace Limited was Canada's premier space company and was a recognized leader in the space-based communications, robotics, informatics, aviation and defense industries. The company began in 1968 as a spin-off from de Havilland Aircraft and was re-organized into

Version: (A) 2010-02-03

four decentralized business segments over a period of two decades: space, communications, aviation and defense and informatics (see Exhibit 1).

The company employed approximately 2,500 people worldwide and approximately 60 per cent of Spar's sales originated outside Canada. Spar's expertise enabled Canada to become the third country in outer space, and the company continued to innovate with achievements such as communications satellites, the Canadarm, and the compression of digital communication signals.

⊠ Spar Applied Systems

Spar's Aviation and Defense area featured two distinct businesses, one of which was Applied Systems Group (ASG). ASG was born through a merger between Spar Defense Systems and the newly acquired, but bankrupt, Leigh Instruments Limited in 1990. ASG designed and supplied communication, flight safety, surveillance and navigation equipment to space, military, and aerospace organizations around the world. It also offered advanced manufacturing services for complex electronic assemblies and systems. These government contracts represented close to 100 per cent of ASG's business.

The flight safety systems products included deployable emergency locator beacons, and flight data and cockpit voice recorders that collected, monitored, and analyzed aircraft flight information to assess equipment condition and improve flight safety procedures. Communications and intelligence products included integrated shipboard naval communications systems, ground-based aircraft navigation beacons, and infrared surveillance systems. Advanced manufacturing incorporated the assembly of high quality, low volume, highly complex electronic assemblies and systems to meet stringent military and space specifications.

ASG operated out of two facilities in the Ottawa Valley (Kanata and Carleton Place), employed 340 people (43 per cent manufacturing, 20 per cent engineering and technical, 17 per cent

sales and professional, and 20 per cent other), and was the only non-unionized area of Spar. Historically, ASG's customers were primarily government-based and included Canada's Department of National Defense, the U.S. Navy and Coast Guard, as well as other international governments. For government customers, ASG had cost-plus contracts which guaranteed a minimum profit for the company, even if there were delays or occasions when the project went over budget. Customers were often told by ASG what they needed rather than delivering requirements or specifications to ASG.

Due to shrinking defense budgets, the aviation and defense industry was becoming increasingly competitive. As government contracts diminished, ASG sought more commercially oriented aviation customers who required fixed-price contracts. This meant ASG would have to finish on time and on, or under, budget in order to guarantee a profit. Time to market was becoming a critical factor in winning bids. Competition was coming from larger-scale, highly flexible, and vertically integrated companies such as Hughes Aircraft and McDonnell Douglas who were global in both strength and influence. Their capabilities, competencies, and capacities, especially related to technology and products, overshadowed those at ASG.

Applied Systems had other reasons to be concerned. More than 70 per cent of its revenues came from heritage programs that were nearing completion; it operated in too many fragmented lines of business; and a significant portion of the lines of business in their portfolio were nearing an "end-of-life" status. The Applied Systems division of Spar had just started to become profitable two years after the acquisition of the Leigh Instruments assets. In the fall of 1993, ASG made up 9.1 per cent of the revenues and 33.3 per cent of the profits of Spar Aerospace. Members of ASG's leadership were wondering how to sustain this newfound profitability.

Although the employees at ASG were among the most skilled in their fields, the company did not know how to best direct their energy. They were very comfortable working in their current environment. In the era of cost-plus contracts, they had lots of time to work on a project because deadlines were often extended. Engineers possessed the ability to dedicate themselves to designing and creating superior (sometimes over-engineered) technology, even at the expense of manufacturability. Most importantly, employees could focus on their design and manufacturing tasks because they were being directed and led by a program manager. The program manager had the responsibility of customer contact, maintaining a schedule, and looking after the "business" details. The work was very independent and narrow as specific people were asked to contribute to different phases based on their skill sets and their experience. Overall, company strategy was unimportant to ASG's engineers. Phases moved sequentially through design and manufacturing with little interaction.

Following the formation of ASG in 1990, the executive management group of Spar Aerospace Limited wanted to see the company become more firmly established in the commercial aerospace and defense industry. They felt that by adapting their military products to suit commercial aviation customers, ASG could be successful. Stephen Miller, vice-president of marketing and government relations in Spar's corporate office, was selected as general manager and joined ASG in September 1992.

◼ **Stephen Miller**

Stephen Miller, in his early 40s, had more than 20 years of experience in government and the aerospace industry. He quickly determined from his initial size-up that ASG was ill-prepared to compete in an increasingly commercial marketplace. ASG had products designed for military and government clients, had a technology rather than a customer focus, and lacked the internal attitude to move as quickly and efficiently as these new customers would require. Stephen saw an urgent need to change and established three

personal objectives. First, he wanted to change the culture at ASG so dramatically that any of his successors would be unable to revert to the way things were in the fall of 1992. Stephen wanted to change the culture from being technology-driven, reactive, internally focused, and controlling to one that would be market-driven, strategic, externally focused, and liberating. Second, he wanted the division to make money for more than six months in a row. Finally, he wanted to develop a long-term strategy that would make sense in a global context and eliminate the short-term planning with which the company was familiar. If successful, these objectives would increase both the flexibility and resiliency of the organization.

Stephen also wanted to create a culture that fostered teamwork, open communication, accountability, and recognition of performance in a skilled, challenged workforce. He strongly believed that the organization was capable of greater achievements if properly managed and motivated. He knew that the functions had to be more integrated to eliminate the functional silos currently in place. He also realized that too many changes too quickly might upset the current workforce and, although committed to his goals, Stephen was worried. ASG attracted very highly skilled employees who would be valued by competitors. Stephen was well aware that he needed the intellectual capital of ASG's employees in order to move into the commercial marketplace.

One of Stephen's first moves was to take his management team (see Exhibit 2) off-site to hammer out a mission statement and develop a strategic plan. The group achieved consensus on the following:

> Building on our heritage, we will become the market leader in informatics-based integrated digital communications and flight safety systems and services, with a particular focus on satisfying the changing needs of the global defense market. We will grow to be a fast-paced, high performance, $250 million

a year enterprise, with returns in the top 25 per cent of our industry by the year 2000.

The management team also reached consensus about a vision, later introduced and discussed with ASG employees in a series of meetings (see Exhibit 3). They also developed a three-part strategy that was intended to link organizational activities to the strategic plan. First, through business development, ASG had to capture significantly higher dollar volumes of profitable business. Second, programs had to be executed effectively (on budget, on schedule, and satisfying the customer). Third, ASG's employees needed to provide value to customers by being responsive and by delivering top quality products.

By the first quarter of 1993, Stephen was feeling confident about ASG's future ability to make progress with the initiatives, except for human resources. Unlike the present ASG and many other organizations, he wanted human resources to play a crucial role in Applied Systems' strategic plan by implementing the vision at a structural and organizational level. In order to find a leader for the new human resources role, Stephen went outside the organization to recruit Anna Solari from a high technology firm that did not compete with ASG. Anna was selected because of her strengths in integrated human resources systems, organizational development and change leadership.

⬚ Anna Solari

After receiving a Bachelor of Social Sciences in Psychology from the University of Ottawa in 1986, Anna Solari became a consultant with a large firm specializing in Human Resources consulting. From there, her 10-year career took her to two different commercial high technology firms, where she had a wide range of human resources responsibilities. Anna moved to Applied Systems in March 1993, six months after Stephen Miller had taken the role of general manager. Having recently managed the rapid growth and merger of a smaller company, she was interested in the challenges presented by a mature, relatively successful company that had to change in order to survive. When she met with Stephen, his energy and enthusiasm for radical change helped to finalize her decision to take the new job.

Just as Anna joined Applied Systems, there were a number of labor relations issues that needed to be addressed. All of Spar's divisions, with the exception of ASG, were unionized. There was regular pressure to change that situation and ASG had always maintained a labor relations component within its human resources staff to attempt to prevent a union from taking hold. The last attempt ended just as Anna arrived and was the most successful yet, where the union came close to getting the necessary 50 per cent plus one vote for certification. Reasons behind the drive were thought to be the ASG employees comparing their representation to the other Spar divisions and the difficulty that arose from attempting to mix the Leigh and Defense cultures following the acquisition. Due to closed communication paths and a lack of employee involvement, there was a feeling of "us versus them." Although the company was still not represented, the drive was so close to being successful that it was enough to give Spar management a wake-up call. Unsure of the reasons behind the drive, management breathed a sigh of relief and hoped something, anything, would end the union threat. Since then, Anna had tried to gather an understanding of the current state of affairs, a baseline, in order to create a human resources vision that would be compatible with the company's strategic direction and proactive in preventing a union drive from recurring.

⬚ The Baseline Audit

By September 1993, Anna felt she had gathered and digested a wide range of data and opinions regarding the current state of the human resources function at ASG. Given the continuing internal and external pressures to make changes,

Anna reviewed the information she had amassed in order to develop a plan for implementing needed changes quickly that could be smoothly aligned with a vision for human resources and consistent with ASG's mission.

Anna gathered the following observations during the "baseline audit" that she later shared with the case writer:

Organizational Structure

The company's leadership team had already discussed possible structures to eliminate the top-heavy pyramid in place when Anna joined. Instead of an organization revolving around program management with functional departments operating in isolation, upper management wanted a structure organized by process (winning new business, supporting the company, and delivering product) that functioned in integrated teams created for specific contracts. Their idea was that people would have a "home" based on the skills they possessed but would join one or more project teams for the length of the business contracts. Although this was a radical departure from the current structure, Stephen, Anna, and the others felt it was an important way to decrease their time to market and become more responsive to their increasing commercial customer base.

Spans of Control/ Management Responsibility

Anna recalled: "What I walked into was a very traditional, hierarchical organization with four or five layers of management. It started with the general manager/VP. Under him were director levels and those director levels may or may not have fallen within the senior management categories. If not, directors might have had senior management who then had middle level management. Middle level management might have also had entry level management or supervisors below it." (See Exhibit 4 for a departmental organization chart.) The organization was very top-heavy which

forced large spans of control at the lower levels in the company. For example, people at the very top may have only had four or five people reporting to them while entry-level supervisors were responsible for 25 or 30 people. In addition, the accountability rested with those who possessed the "manager" title whereas the real profit and loss impact resided with the general workforce.

Culture

Despite Stephen's initiatives and relationships with his management team, Anna found the culture at ASG was quite formal, hierarchical, and traditional. To a certain degree it was bureaucratic and also lived under the threat of third-party intervention. The descriptors used were: technology-driven; resource-led; tactical; reactive; "thing" (rather than people) sensitive; closed; controlling; introspective; divided; and marginal performer. Anna had conducted many focus groups of 20 to 25 employees during her baselining and these employees identified issues such as the color of the paint on the walls, poor ventilation, and questions about health and safety standards, among others. Anna started to worry:

> Because [I] wanted to make real changes in areas that impacted the bottom line and had a return on investment such as equity, behavior shifts, overtime policies and sick leave. If [the employees] were upset about paint, what would happen when we introduced things that affected their pocketbooks?

She wondered how to cope with another possible attempt at unionization without allowing that threat to overshadow any decisions that needed to be made.

Communication

There was very little face-to-face communication in ASG and the basis for information flow was formal, one-way, top-down, and written. Approval processes went up through the levels of the company, across the top, and back down again. As a result, decision making was delayed. Occasionally, the general manager would give a formal "state of the union" address to all employees that might allow for questions at the end. If you wanted to speak to someone, an appointment was made through managers' secretaries in advance. Communication seemed to Anna to be too formal and too inefficient. She vividly recalled an exchange with a member of the management team that occurred in her first weeks at ASG (see Exhibit 5).

Recruiting and Training

Recruitment was a reactive process designed to fill gaps. People leaving the organization were replaced using a position description developed many years ago and faithfully adhered to over time. The human resources department solicited resumes based on the information from a given department that an employee would be leaving or that growth required additional personnel. The target audience for filling gaps was industry.

> The organization had always targeted [the high technology defense] industry and, in fact, they broke out of the mold a little bit when they hired me. We did not focus a lot on the new [college and university] grads because experience was very important to us.

Traditional roles were defined: "a technician is a technician, a technologist is a technologist and at no point in time do those two roles meet."

The human resources department had limited involvement in the new employee orientation. New employees filled out tax and registration paperwork and received a policy manual that explained the company "rules" (absenteeism, benefits, company hours, bathroom and cigarette breaks, etc.). One striking example that stood out to Anna was the rule that employees were not permitted to sleep at their workstations during working hours. New employees then reported directly to their manager who immediately integrated them into their roles. Information about ASG and their role in the organization was picked up from their manager and their peers.

Training was also an informal process. Members of the human resources department arranged for a given employee to receive certain courses in response to a request from that employee's manager. ASG employees already possessing the necessary skills provided the specific technical courses (usually lasting a few hours) and managers could request specific "trainers." If the necessary courses were not available on site, Applied Systems reimbursed employees' tuition at a local community college. This procedure was unusual because ASG provided most courses. Training was conducted on company time and increased technical skills led to jumps in job grades and corresponding pay increases. There were 54 pay grades within ASG. Managers and employees did not need to show an immediate business need or an opportunity to use the new technical knowledge to participate in training, just a desire to learn the new skills.

Performance Appraisal and Review

Employee performance appraisals, which were conducted annually, determined merit increases for each employee. Each person's appraisal was conducted by his or her immediate manager and was based on a rating system that ranged from excellent to poor. Technical elements like quality and quantity of work were evaluated, as were factors like adherence to health and safety standards, and punctuality. Some employees indicated to Anna that they did not interact with their managers enough to be evaluated by them, while some managers complained of the time it took to complete the reviews. Merit increases were at the discretion of each manager and came from a pool of funds distributed from higher levels of the organization. As a result, Anna learned that pay equity and equality were not being maintained throughout ASG because a connection was not directly made between the performance appraisal and the amount of the merit pay.

Compensation and Benefits

Anna felt that the benefits program at Spar was one of the best that she had seen, "not only in the industry but extending into the high tech area, including software." The benefit package included everything from dental coverage to disability programs. In addition, employees at ASG were very well paid. Based on information collected by ASG from its industry hires and marketplace research, Anna found the company's compensation policy was 30 per cent above market rate. Although employee satisfaction was not a problem, Anna realized that excessively high salary levels reflected poor business practices and were inconsistent with actual divisional financial performance.

Salary administration was based on 54 job grades (secretary: 1 to 6, technician: 1 to 6, etc.) and each grade had very specific tasks that those people within it could complete. Anna described the mentality by saying:

> People knew their box and they did not want anybody stepping into their box, and, by the same token, did not want to step out of their box.

This is where the inequity was manifested. Some people with the same roles could be making salaries that differed by up to $10,000 annually because of seniority and performance appraisals.

Vision 2000

Anna, with the assistance of members of the management group and employees of ASG, wanted to design an organization that would be more competitive, more flexible, and ready to grow through mergers and acquisitions. The employees were highly skilled and very innovative in nature; however, they were demographically diverse and tended to operate within the silos fostered by the hierarchical organization. Given that ASG had created a strategy and a vision for 2000, Anna's task was to develop a vision for human resources that was compatible with Stephen Miller's strategy of capturing higher volumes of profitable business, executing effectively, and providing value to the customers. How could employee development, succession planning, and the new organizational structure be introduced and what were the best recruiting and training practices, performance evaluation process, and compensation plan? She also wondered if the labor relations component needed to change in order to prevent a successful union drive. After establishing the vision, how would the transition occur to get them there?

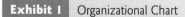

Exhibit 1   Organizational Chart

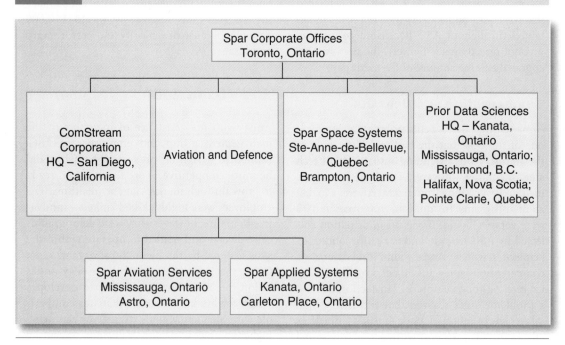

SOURCE: Company Files.

Exhibit 2   Management Team Off-Site November 1992

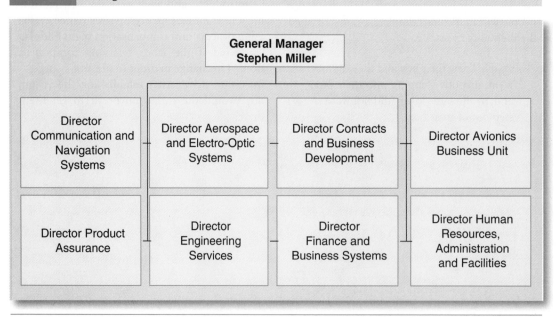

SOURCE: Company Files.

Exhibit 3 | Applied Systems Group

Vision

✓ We will grow to be a $250 million/year enterprise by the year 2000.

✓ We will attain a prominent and respected position in the new world order, climbing the systems chain, entering new markets that build on our heritage and growing those products and services that are relevant to our future.

✓ We will be recognized as being the best at what we do, on a global scale, winning consistently in excess of 70 per cent of the markets and opportunities we pursue.

✓ We will achieve total customer satisfaction by understanding their needs and through 100 per cent performance of our industry.

✓ We are mastering the concepts of teamwork and organizational growth; we will exploit its strengths to create an exciting and vibrant entity, attractive to both our customers and employees.

Exhibit 4 | Engineering Department Organization Chart February 1992

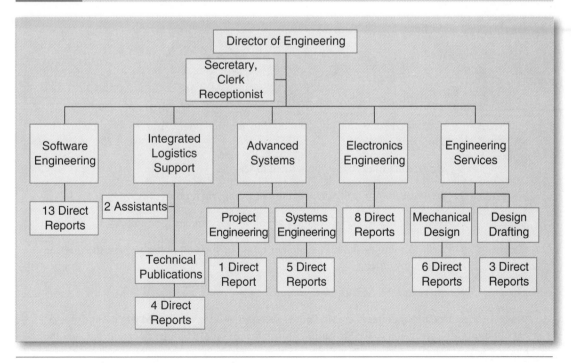

SOURCE: Company Files.

Exhibit 5	An Early Communications Example—Setting Up a Meeting

Anna's Secretary	Anna, Mr. Smith would like to set up a meeting with you. Why don't you give me your calendar so I can organize the meeting with Mr. Smith's secretary? I can also set up any other meetings you need to have without bothering you for your availability.
Anna:	Thanks for the offer but I like to keep my own schedule. Do you know where Mr. Smith's office is? I'll just walk over and talk to him right now.
Anna's Secretary:	Oh, I don't think that is a very good idea. We don't really do things like that around here.
Anna:	That's OK. If Mr. Smith needs to see me, I am free right now and I'll just walk over to see him.
Anna's Secretary:	Gives directions to a secretary's office with a closed outer door that leads into Mr. Smith's inner office (also with a closed door).

———

Anna:	Good Morning, I am here to see Mr. Smith. He wanted to speak with me.
Mr. Smith's Secretary:	Do you have an appointment?
Anna:	No, but is Mr. Smith in his office?
Mr. Smith's Secretary:	Yes, but . . .
Anna:	Is he with somebody or on the phone?
Mr. Smith's Secretary:	No, but . . . (as Anna knocked on Mr. Smith's door). You really shouldn't be doing that.
Anna:	Mr. Smith, I understand you wanted to see me.
Mr. Smith:	Yes, but I am not really prepared for a meeting right now.
Anna:	How long will it take? I can meet you in the cafeteria in 15 minutes.
Mr. Smith:	Well, 15 minutes should be enough time but I would prefer to have the meeting here in my office.
Anna:	That's fine. I'll be back in 15 minutes.

When Anna returned 15 minutes later, Mr. Smith's secretary was very surprised when Anna greeted her but didn't ask permission to see Mr. Smith. Anna knocked on Mr. Smith's door, entered, and the meeting began.

Culture-Driven Leadership

Arkadi Kuhlmann

Behind every successful leader is a vibrant culture that engages and energizes employees. In almost every case, that culture has been defined, shaped and personified by the leader. The CEO of a company in what is arguably the most competitive industry, financial services, describes the steps that he took, and that other leaders can take, to build a distinctive, dynamic culture.

Business schools spend a lot of time training students to become leaders, teaching skills and increasing knowledge aimed at turning smart, young people into effective leaders. Company training programs pick up where the schools leave off. Consider, for example, programs on workplace diversity, with their emphasis on communication and team building. A critical component of team building is culture, because if teams are to work effectively all employees must understand and embrace the culture of the particular group and business. There's no doubt that today, a leader's success depends on how he or she molds and develops that culture.

Shaping a culture is a formidable task, since many of the valuable qualities a leader might have are never taught in a classroom. They can be learned, but only from life experiences. Emotional maturity, authenticity, and a strong character are all essential if leadership in a culture-driven company is to be effective. So is an alignment among the leader's passion, the company's mission, and the corporate culture in which everything transpires. But these characteristics are developed through life experience.

My goal in this article is to lay out how to lead a culture-driven company. It is based on my experience running the consumer bank, ING DIRECT.

First, I will discuss the relationship between a successful leader and corporate culture today. I will next explain how to define a company's mission, which is central to visionary leadership, and which management professor Glenn Rowe defines as leaders who "base their decisions and actions on their beliefs and values, and try to share their understanding of a desired vision with others in the organization."[1] Finally, I will lay out how to shape the culture you want at your organization.

◪ Leading the Cause

Leadership folklore has always idolized the individual who is seen as larger than life. From the heroes of ancient Greece to the corporate raiders of the 1980s, we mythologize the chiefs who appear to be lone wolves or outsiders. Today, though, a new type of leadership is emerging – and it's just as effective as the old kind.

Today, it's possible to be in touch with anyone, anywhere, anytime. This development has had a profound impact on leadership. No one boss can be the central conduit for information about a particular company, because employees across the world are talking to colleagues and customers all the time. No one boss has all the answers, because the Internet has given us instant access to experts on any subject. The way we look at leaders has changed, and who we follow has become ever more situational. In fact, one of the reasons it seems so challenging to find successful political leaders today may be that the cultural dimensions of society have become too complex.

The great information highway has also brought us vivid images of every scandal and embarrassment that embroils our leaders in the political, corporate, and entertainment realms.

---

[1]Glenn Rowe and Mehdi Hossein Nejad, "Strategic Leadership: Short-Term Stability and Long-Term Viability," *The Ivey Business Journal*, September/October 2009.

The result is that society has become more cynical and much less tolerant and admiring of leaders. That's not necessarily fair. Most leaders today genuinely try to get things done for good and even altruistic reasons. They are nonetheless often perceived as being driven by money, materialism, and self-interest. That perception is something leaders have to deal with, by redoubling their efforts to shake off the stigma of egocentric leadership and earn trust. No one is above it all. No leader can escape this reality.

To have an impact in this new environment, a leader must be closely aligned with the culture he or she hopes to lead. That culture might be particular to one corporation, or it could be much broader, reflecting the language and nationality, or ages and interests, of employees. The leader who parachutes in from the outside is a thing of the past. A leader whose own culture is inseparable from a company's culture is likely to be much more effective.

One popular concept of the corporation paints it as a money-making machine. But when employers and employees alike see the company this way, no one is very happy or productive. When everyone is just putting in hours for a paycheck, one has to ultimately ask, "What is the point?" Who gets what share of the profit? A successful company must have a cause that is bigger and broader than the organization itself. A successful leader must truly believe in a vision and a mission that can be combined to form a cause. He or she must be identified with the cause. "Walk the talk" is the most important criteria. The best leaders are those who derive their authority from having a genuine, inspiring sense of purpose.

An effective leader of a culture-driven organization will be recognizable by several traits. When others try to describe him or her, they think of the vision first. The leader is thought of more as a person devoted to a cause than as a manager running a company. He or she articulates and spreads the values of the organization in a way that is explicit rather than implicit, and his or her personal commitment to success is obvious and frequently verbalized. The culture-driven leader constantly demonstrates passion

and energy for the work to be done and is not alone in doing so. In a culture-driven company, the style of leadership itself is emulated at all levels of the company.

So, what type of individual is cut out to lead a company that is first defined by culture and a cause? He or she possesses six fundamental attributes.

1) A calling

The leader must have a sense of purpose that is in alignment with the company's vision. At ING DIRECT, our calling is to lead Americans back to saving.

2) The guts to make the calling personal

It must come from a real place. Otherwise, authenticity is missing and no one sees the leader "walking the talk." The leader can't be an invention of the marketing department or the face of carefully scripted talking points. The leader has to be the author of the mission and feel a passion for it.

3) A powerful enemy

If there's no one to fight, there's no job for the white knight. For ING DIRECT, the enemy was the credit card companies pushing spending, with no consideration for the costs to the consumer. Having a dark force against which to fight creates a highly effective leadership goal. The thought or image of an enemy transforms competitors into dragons to be slain by all employees. You believe that you are one of the "good guys." For workers, this makes coming to work every day more heroic and more of an adventure.

4) An inner circle

Picking a core team is one of a leader's most fundamental responsibilities. Unfortunately, it's not easy to find and select people who would join a mission. The normal recruitment process does not work nor does the personal address book of colleagues. You network and search for the right people, many of whom are found in unusual places and circumstances. Character and motivation are the two qualities that separate loyal, enthusiastic, workers from mere jobholders. Lots of people can put together good-looking curriculum vitae. Often, though, the best hire is someone who has experienced failure and has something to prove to themselves and the world.

5) The possibility of failure

Working in a constant state of imminent crisis is not for the faint of heart. It can, however, create a company-wide sense that the organization and everyone in it are potential prey for an outside force. Without the risk of failure, everyone will grow complacent and corporate ego will become the silent killer. A sense of crisis keeps the enterprise in an energetic, startup frame of mind.

6) An aura of mystery

A leader can't make everything appear too mechanical. To drive the passion of your company, you have to create some mystery around you. You need to appear in some small, humble way as different as those that look to you. Team members want to follow, but they need a reason. It has to work like pixie dust.

⚅ The Mission

The most important question to ask about corporate culture is whether workers think they're in a job—or on a mission. A visionary leader is on a mission and inspires his or her employees to feel that way, too.

How do you begin to define the cause? It's a shame that the corporate mission statement went out of fashion, though it's easy to see why it happened. Too many such statements failed at their task. An effective vision has to be one that shakes up the status quo and starts a revolution. No one will ever be inspired by a puddle of ambiguity. Too many corporate mission statements were diluted into dullness by consensus and multiple levels of approval, making them utterly ineffective for rallying the troops. A mission statement, though, is the best leadership tool you can ever invent. In grassroots political organizations, the sense of being on a mission develops almost spontaneously, without central leadership, because enough people believe in the cause. A team with a purpose beats a team with a process any day.

So what makes the difference between a forgettable mission statement and one that turns workers into devotees? There are five key qualities to consider.

1) A mission statement must advocate for someone.

At ING DIRECT, we set out to champion Americans who were being preyed upon by the spending culture of consumer finance—one that encouraged high-interest debt and imposed onerous banking fees. We offered these customers a way to save, which gave them hope and confidence, and a feeling of being in control of their lives.

2) The goal in the mission statement should be nearly impossible to achieve.

At ING DIRECT we're not likely to actually turn everyone on the planet into a saver. Reaching for the goal is the inspiring and satisfying part. It's a journey. The horizon should always remain just out of reach.

3) A mission statement should read like poetry.

It should be sonorous and simple, and catchy enough that people won't be able to get it out of their heads.

4) A mission statement should be written with the leader and the most loyal followers in mind.

It should not try to please everyone. It has to matter to the people who show up every day.

5) The leader must come up with the mission statement himself or herself.

Defining the company's purpose is a leader's—and only a leader's—responsibility. Collaborating on its development or delegating the task goes against the very nature of visionary leadership. The leader must embody the company's cause and that includes being responsible for defining it.

✖ Getting the Culture Right

It is necessary to implement a feedback loop between the leader and the rest of the company as it grows. In a start up, the culture is a blank page in need of material. The leader must be aligned with the culture of the organization. At the same time, he or she is also responsible for shaping it. At ING DIRECT, we create the culture through the Orange Code. The Code and the culture it creates attract new workers who share the vision and the mission. Simplifying financial products was our tactic for helping Americans save their money. If ING DIRECT were a nation, the Code would be its constitution. If we were a political organization, it would be our manifesto.

The Orange Code doesn't measure performance. Rather, it sets out cultural principles like "We will be fair" and "We will constantly learn." The Code isn't everything, of course—job skills matter too. As a company grows, it becomes harder to ensure every hire is a cultural fit. So at ING DIRECT, we like to measure both job performance and cultural behavior. As you can see in the graph below, an individual can fall into any one of four categories, plotted here along two axes. The vertical line measures job skills, while the horizontal line measures fidelity to the Code, or culture.

Someone with topnotch job skills who fully embodies the Orange Code would fall in the top right corner of the graph. These people are the role models for the rest of the organization. They are looked to as leaders. In practice we tend to look at culture first and job skills second. We've found that someone who is a good cultural fit can learn and develop any missing job skills. The reverse is not true. Someone with great job skills but a poor cultural fit is unlikely to really embrace the Code.

It is a fact that a corporate culture will be created with or without the involvement of the leader. But it is also a fact that creating and sustaining a *healthy* corporate culture requires constant attention and active involvement. Therefore, a leader should actively shape and direct the development of the culture.

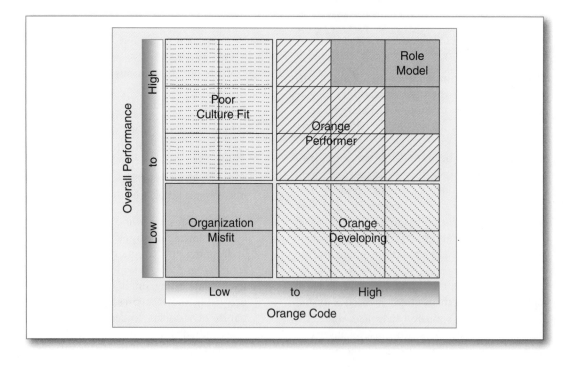

Of course, a key part of shaping the culture is hiring the right people. It may sound counterintuitive, but I believe in hiring people who have made honest mistakes, because they most likely will have learned from them. We are all the products of our experiences, good and bad. However, successful people wish to remain successful, while others will do anything to become successful. The way we weather the storms shows true character.

General Norman Schwarzkopf once said, "Leadership is a combination of strategy and character. If you must be without one, be without the strategy."

When recruiting, I tend to look outside of the banking industry and for people with broad and unusual backgrounds. People who are too narrowly educated will make the right decisions some of the time, but they won't have the breadth of knowledge and experience to make the right decisions most of the time.

Once you've made the right hire, it's essential to try to understand the personality of the person working for you. "Understanding personality has become essential for leaders of the complex, knowledge-based companies operating in the global marketplace," writes Michael Maccoby, a leadership consultant and an anthropologist.[2] Go beyond the slogans. It's the fireside chat versus the office chat. We team up for the right reason. We believe in the vision and will behave by the code that defines the company's culture. This is where a leader's true nature comes into play. If I am prepared to be completely open and honest with you, I am inviting you to be the same. That's the best chance I have as a leader to empower the culture of the organization and accomplish our mission.

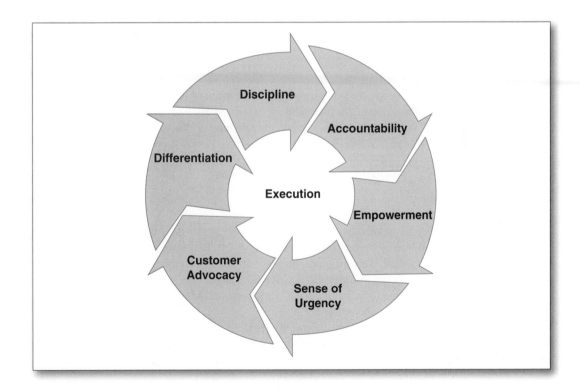

---

[2]Michael Maccoby, "To Win the Respect of Followers, Leaders Need Personality Intelligence," *The Ivey Business Journal*, January/February 2009.

Servant Leadership

The servant-leader is servant first . . . It begins with the natural feeling that one wants to serve, to serve first. Then conscious choice brings one to aspire to lead. That person is sharply different from one who is leader first, perhaps because of the need to assuage an unusual power drive or to acquire material possessions . . . The leader-first and the servant-first are two extreme types. Between them there are shadings and blends that are part of the infinite variety of human nature.

The difference manifests itself in the care taken by the servant-first to make sure that other people's highest priority needs are being served. The best test, and difficult to administer, is: Do those served grow as persons? Do they, while being served, become healthier, wiser, freer, more autonomous, more likely themselves to become servants? And, what is the effect on the least privileged in society? Will they benefit or at least not be further deprived?

—Robert K. Greenleaf[1]

The term *servant leadership* challenges our traditional beliefs about leadership. How can a leader do both: influence and serve? The traditional image of a leader does not seem to include the possibility that leaders may be servants (Northouse, 2013). However, servant leadership offers a unique and useful perspective. Servant leadership was developed based on the seminal work of Greenleaf (1970, 1972, 1991) (Daft, 2011; DuBrin, 2010; Yukl, 2012). Since then, most of the academic and nonacademic writing on the topic has described how servant leadership ought to be, rather than how it actually is in practice (van Dierendonck, 2011).

Servant leaders place the good of their followers over their own self-interests and emphasize follower development (Hale & Fields, 2007). In other words, servant leaders put their followers *first*, empower them, and help them develop their full personal capacities. Furthermore, servant leaders are

---

[1]Grennleaf (1991, pp. 13–14)

ethical and lead in ways that serve the greater good of the organization, community, and society at large. Anyone can learn how to be a servant leader (Spears, 2010). In this chapter, we treat servant leadership as a behavior, not a trait.

Spears and Lawrence (2002) identified ten characteristics in Greenleaf's writings that are central to servant leadership.

1. Listening. Servant leaders communicate by listening and acknowledging the point of view of followers.

2. Empathy. Servant leaders understand what followers are thinking and feeling and demonstrate this empathy.

3. Healing. Servant leaders care about and help improve the personal well-being of their followers.

4. Awareness. Servant leaders are attentive and responsive to their surroundings.

5. Persuasion. Servant leaders are able to convince others to change, not by using positional authority to force compliance but rather by using gentle nonjudgmental arguments.

6. Conceptualization. Servant leaders are able to see the big picture in an organization. This allows them to be visionary, provide direction, and solve complex organizational problems.

7. Foresight. Servant leaders anticipate the future and the consequences of their behaviors.

8. Stewardship. Servant leaders take responsibility for their role and manage the people and organization carefully considering the greater good of society.

9. Commitment to the growth of people. Servant leaders are committed to helping each of their followers to grow personally and professionally.

10. Building community. Servant leaders build community in organizations by making people feel safe and connected with others, while still being able to express their own individuality.

Moving beyond a list of characteristics, Liden and his colleagues (Liden, Pannaccio, Hu, & Meuser, 2012; Liden, Wayne, Zhao, & Henderson, 2008) developed a model of servant leadership, which has three main components: antecedent conditions, servant leader behaviors, and leadership outcomes. The antecedent conditions to servant leadership are context and culture, leadership attributes, and follower receptivity. These conditions represent some factors that are likely to influence the servant leadership process.

Context and Culture. Because servant leadership does not occur in a vacuum, it is impacted by both organizational context and national culture. Servant leadership is expected to differ across contexts and cultures with different norms and expectations.

Leader Attributes. Individuals differ on various attributes, such as moral development, emotional intelligence, and self-determinedness. These traits are likely to impact individuals' ability to engage in servant leadership.

Follower Receptivity. The receptivity of followers is a factor that influences the impact of servant leadership on outcomes such as personal and organizational job performance. Those who are more receptive to servant leadership will have better outcomes.

In addition to antecedents, the model comprises behaviors. Servant leader behaviors include conceptualizing, emotional healing, putting followers first, helping followers grow and succeed, behaving ethically, empowering, and creating value for the community.

Conceptualizing refers to the servant leader's thorough understanding of the organization. This ability allows servant leaders to address complex organizational problems while meeting the goals of the organization.

Emotional healing involves being sensitive to the personal concerns and well-being of others, being aware and sensitive to the problems of others, and being supportive.

Putting followers first is the defining characteristic of servant leadership. Putting followers first means demonstrating to followers that their concerns are a priority, by often placing followers' interests and success ahead of those of the leader.

Helping followers grow and succeed refers to knowing followers' professional or personal goals and helping them to accomplish those objectives. To accomplish this, servant leaders may participate in mentoring and other support activities to help individuals achieve their full potential.

Behaving ethically means doing the right thing in the right way. Servant leaders have high ethical standards and they do not compromise these standards in order to achieve success.

Empowering means to allow followers the freedom to be independent, make decisions on their own, and be self-sufficient. It is a way for leaders to share power with followers.

Creating value for the community means to purposely give back to the community. This may include volunteering and encouraging their followers to also be engaged in community service.

Although servant leadership focuses primarily on leader behaviors, it also considers the potential outcomes of these behaviors. The outcomes of servant leadership are follower performance and growth, organizational performance, and societal impact.

Follower Performance and Growth. As a result of servant leadership, followers achieve greater self-actualization and realize their full capabilities. Another outcome of servant leadership is that subordinates become more effective at accomplishing their jobs (Meuser, Liden, Wayne, & Henderson, 2011). Finally, another expected result of servant leadership is that followers themselves may become servant leaders.

Organizational Performance. Several studies have found a positive relationship between servant leadership and organizational citizenship behaviors, which are subordinate behaviors that go beyond the basic requirements of their duties and help the overall functioning of the organization (DuBrin, 2010; Liden, Wayne, et al., 2008). Servant leadership has also been found to enhance team effectiveness by increasing the members' shared confidence, improving group process and clarity (Hu & Liden, 2011).

Societal Impact. Another outcome of servant leadership is that it is likely to have a positive impact on society. This is likely to be an indirect impact in which servant leaders have a positive impact on their followers and the organization, and these healthier organizations, in turn, benefit society in the long run.

How Does Servant Leadership Work?

The servant leadership approach works differently than many of the other theories we have discussed in this book (Daft, 2011; DuBrin, 2010; Northouse, 2013; Yukl, 2012). Servant leadership focuses on the behaviors leaders should exhibit to put followers first and to support followers' personal development. Servant leadership begins when leaders commit themselves to putting their subordinates first, being honest with them, and treating them fairly. Servant leaders develop strong long-term relationships with their followers, which allow leaders to understand the abilities, needs, and goals of followers. These behaviors allow these subordinates to achieve their full potential. Servant leadership works best when leaders are selfless and are truly interested in helping others. In addition, for servant leadership to be successful, it is important that followers are receptive to this leadership style. Finally, ideally, servant leadership results in community and societal change over the long run.

Criticisms of, and Observations About, Servant Leadership

There are several criticisms that need to be noted regarding servant leadership. First, the name itself is paradoxical and whimsical. What does it mean to be a servant and a leader simultaneously? Second, what are the dimensions of servant leadership? Third, the prescriptive tones of most of the material written about servant leadership makes it seem altruistic with a utopian nature. Finally, why is conceptualizing a central characteristic of servant leadership (Northouse, 2013)?

Many elements of servant leadership have been used by such organizations as AT&T, Southwest Airlines, Starbucks, and Vanguard Group. It is more widely used than leader–member exchange (Chapter 8) and authentic leadership (Chapter 11), especially over the last 30 or so years. If one's philosophical framework includes caring for others, servant leadership prescribes a set of behaviors that can be engaged in to practically do so. These behaviors are easily comprehended and can be applied in many leadership situations (Northouse, 2013).

References

Daft, R. L. (2011). *The leadership experience* (5th ed.). Mason, OH: Thomson, South-Western.

DuBrin, A. J. (2010). *Leadership: Research findings, practice, and skills* (6th ed.). Mason, OH: South-Western/Cengage.

Greenleaf, R. K. (1970). *The servant as leader*. Westfied, IN: The Greenleaf Center for Servant Leadership.

Greenleaf, R. K. (1972). *The institution as servant*. Westfield, IN: The Greenleaf Center for Servant Leadership.

Greenleaf, R. K. (1991). *Servant leadership: A journey into the nature of legitimate power and greatness*. New York, NY: Paulist Press.

Hale, J. R., & Fields, D. L. (2007). Exploring servant leadership across cultures: A study of followers in Ghana and the USA. *Leadership, 3*, 397–417.

Hu, J., & Liden, R. C. (2011). Antecedents of team potency and team effectiveness: An examination of goal and process clarity and servant leadership. *Journal of Applied Psychology, 96*(4), 851–862.

Liden, R. C., Panaccio, A., Hu, J., & Meuser, J. D. (2012). Servant leadership: Antecedents, consequences, and contextual moderators. In D. V. Day (Ed.), *The Oxford Handbook of Leadership and Organizations*. Oxford, UK: Oxford University Press.

Liden, R. C., Wayne, S. J., Zhao, H., & Henderson, D. (2008). Servant leadership: Development of a multidimensional measure and multi-level assessment. *The Leadership Quarterly, 19*, 161–177.

Meuser, J. D, Liden, R. C., Wayne, S. J., & Henderson, D. J. (2011, August). *Is servant leadership always a good thing? The moderating influence of servant leadership prototype.* Paper presented at the meeting of the Academy of Management, San Antonio, TX.

Northouse, P. G. (2013). *Leadership: Theory and practice* (6th ed.). Thousand Oaks, CA: Sage.

Spears, L. C., & Lawrence, M. (2002). *Focus on leadership: Servant-leadership for the 21st century.* New York, NY: Wiley.

Spears, L. C. (2010). Servant leadership and Robert K. Greenleaf's legacy. In D. van Dierendonck & K. Patterson (Eds.), *Servant leadership: Developments in theory and research* (pp. 11–24). New York, NY: Palgrave Macmillan.

van Dierendonck, D. (2011). Servant leadership: A review and synthesis. *Journal of Management, 37*(4), 1228–1261.

Yukl, G. (2012). *Leadership in organizations* (8th ed.). Upper Saddle River, NJ: Prentice Hall.

⧖ The Cases

Veja: Sneakers With a Conscience

Veja is the world's first eco-sneaker company. In September 2010, the 5-year-old venture is a leader in ethical fashion and an inspiration for other eco-fashion start-ups. Like-minded large companies were approaching the two founders with acquisition in mind, but they were not yet ready to sell. Sébastien Kopp and François-Ghislain Morillion were still working toward a holistic offering that engages employees, consumers, suppliers, partners, and even artists. Kopp and Morillion wondered if the movement would be better served by large organizations who can get emerging brands such as Veja into the mainstream or by ventures such as Veja.

J.-Robert Ouimet and Tomasso Corporation

J.-Robert Ouimet (president and CEO of OCB Holding Inc.) has built a strong value set at Tomasso Corporation, a company he has led for more than 30 years. He strongly believes that, in order to manage Tomasso effectively, he has to pay as much attention to employee well-being, dignity, respect, caring, authenticity, and fairness as he pays to profit-seeking, financial discipline, focus on operational excellence, investments, and customer service. He calls this combination ISMA (Integrated Set of Management Activities) and believes that Tomasso is better able to compete with these human and economic activities combined. Ouimet is aware that the human and economic aspects of ISMA can be in conflict with each other but that they are fundamental to Tomasso's daily operations. Ouimet is wondering how to reconcile these two opposites.

⧖ The Reading

Servant-Leaders Are the Best Leaders During Times of Change

In this article, Dr. Kent M. Keith discusses why he wants to follow a servant leader during times of change. He describes the characteristics of servant leadership and contrasts these characteristics with those inherent in the power model of leadership. He concludes that one way to get more servant leaders is if followers commit to follow servant leaders and refuse to follow leaders with a power orientation.

Veja: Sneakers With a Conscience

Kim Poldner and Oana Branzei

⬚ The First Five Years

Sébastien Kopp and François-Ghislain Morillion (see Exhibit 1), recent business graduates in their twenties, had traveled the planet looking for a cool way to do business.[1] In 2005, they settled in Brazil, where they founded Veja,[2] the first ethical sneaker company in the world. The Veja sneakers were made from wild latex sourced from the Amazon River area (Amazonia) to mitigate rubber tree deforestation, from Brazilian organic cotton to enhance biodiversity and from vegetable-tanned leather to prevent water pollution. These sneakers not only made consumers look good but also prompted them to take a closer look at bigger issues, such as the use of pesticides, genetically modified crops and fair-trade labor practices.

Kopp and Morillion had designed and produced several sneaker collections, had launched brand extensions (e.g. Veja Baby and Veja Kids), had opened offices in London and had established a distinctive presence online (see Exhibit 2). In 2005, the company started off aiming to sell its sneakers—with a conscience—in conventional stores, right next to iconic brands such as Nike. By 2010, Veja was selling more than 100,000 pairs annually, in 200 stores worldwide,

including 80 in France. Customers included singer Lilly Allen and actress Angelina Jolie, whose baby had been recently photographed wearing Veja running shoes.[3] Veja sneakers had been on display at the Ethical Fashion Show (EFS) in Paris, the biggest eco fashion event that brought together 100 brands from around the world. Perhaps even more impressive, Veja had created, from scratch, a global chain that emphasized solidarity and the environment and linked small producers in Brazil to the European catwalks.

⬚ Hold or Fold?

Kopp and Morillion had been at the forefront of a rapidly changing industry. Large companies wanted a share of the rapidly increasing market that valued ecologically and socially responsible fashion. Small ethical fashion brands such as Veja were hot buys. Since 2007, several small eco-fashion pioneers had been taken over by bigger brands. These deals enjoyed great media coverage and stirred vivid debates on the future of fashion.

New ethical fashion brands were popping up in attempts to copy Veja's successful business model.[4] For example, France-based Loic Pollet,

Version: (A) 2010-10-25

[1]Their world journey is featured at the Juste Planet website; available at http://www.justeplanete.org/index.php, accessed on September 26, 2010.

[2]In Brazil, Veja means "look." For the company, "veja" symbolized looking around to develop a conscience about what is going on in the world.

[3]Ana Santi, "From Fashion to Rubber, Born in Brazil: Bringing Brazil to the UK," blog entry, posted August 22, 2010; available at http://www.borninbrazil.co.uk/2010/08/from-fashion-to-rubber.html, accessed on September 26, 2010.

[4]Eco Fashion World, "Guide"; available at http://www.ecofashionworld.com/Brands-/listA.html, accessed on September 26, 2010.

the founder of Sébola,[5] who had launched his first collection in the fall of 2008, commented "Looking at success stories like Veja, we felt inspired to start our own brand." Since 2009, Canada-based Tal Dehtiar, founder of Oliberté, had begun working with producers in Ethiopia to launch a competing eco-sneaker.[6] In March 2010, the sneaker brand Sawa shoes launched its first collection, made in Cameroon.[7] Ethical fashion companies such as Simple Shoes[8] and Patagonia[9] had also added eco-sneakers to their offerings. Multinationals such as Nike and Adidas[10] had also recently launched their own limited editions. For example, Nike's Trash Talk sneaker, co-developed with Phoenix Suns basketball star Steve Nash, was made from factories' leftover materials.[11] Veja faced even greater competition for its accessories, such as Veja's newly launched bags (see Exhibit 2). The competitors were keenly watching Veja's next move.

Ethical Fashion Deals

On December 4, 2006, Timberland acquired Howies Limited (Howies), an active sports brand created less than a decade ago to serve as "a voice and mechanism for communicating a core environmental and social conscience, to ask a different question and show the world that there is another way to do business." [12] Jeffrey Swartz, Timberland's president and chief executive officer (CEO) welcomed Howies to the family: "I want people to believe in the power of the marketplace to make things better." [13] Swartz also pledged that "Together we will leverage our complementary strengths to bring our brands to new consumers and new markets." [14] Timberland's media release commended the ethical fashion brand for innovation, authenticity and integrity. The co-founders of Howies, David and Claire Hieatt, had built a company they were proud of. They would stay onboard to help the Howies brand grow within Timberland, citing their commitment to "make better and lower impact products, to give a better service and to do more good as we go about our business. Those are our rainbows to chase. They always will be." [15]

On May 18, 2009, "the world's largest luxury conglomerate [the Louis Vuitton Group], paid an undisclosed amount to secure a minority

---

[5]Interview with Loic Pollet, October 1, 2009, used with permission; further information at http://www.sebola.fr, accessed on September 26, 2010.

[6]Oliberté Limited, "This Is Africa"; available at http://www.oliberte.com/, accessed on September 26, 2010.

[7]Sawa, available at http://www.sawashoes.com/eng/, accessed on September 26, 2010.

[8]Simple Shoes, available at http://www.simpleshoes.com/, accessed on September 26, 2010.

[9]Patagonia, Inc., available at http://www.patagonia.com/web/us/search/sneakers, accessed on September 26, 2010.

[10]Kim Poldner, "Adidas Green," *Eco Fashion World*; available at http://www.ecofashionworld.com/Trends/ADIDAS-GREEN .html, accessed on September 26, 2010.

[11]Nike, "Steve Nash and Nike Turn Garbage into Trash Talk," media release, February 13, 2008; available at http://www.nikebiz .com/media/pr/2008/02/13_Nash.html, accessed on September 26, 2010.

[12]David Hieatt, "Exciting News," December 4, 2006; available at http://www.howies.co.uk/content.php?xSecId=56&viewblog= 557, accessed on September 26, 2010.

[13]PSFK, available at http://www.psfk.com/2006/12/ethical_entrpre.html, accessed on September 26, 2010.

[14]Fibre2fashion, "USA: Timberland Acquires Howies, UK-based Active Sports Wear Brand," December 4, 2006; available at http://www.fibre2fashion.com/news/company-news/timberland-company/newsdetails.aspx?news_id=27033, accessed on September 26, 2010.

[15]David Hieatt, "Exciting News," December 4, 2006; available at http://www.howies.co.uk/content.php?xSecId=56&viewblog=557, accessed on September 26, 2010.

stake in Edun, a prominent ethical fashion line"[16] founded just four years earlier by Ali Hewson and her husband, Bono, U2's lead singer and a political activist, with designer Rogan Gregory. Edun had used "star power and edgy designs to bring worldwide attention to important ethical fashion principles."[17] Although critics wondered whether the acquisition could "green" the conglomerate, Louis Vuitton soon created a special bag for Edun (which sold for US$4,900) and agreed to donate all proceeds from the bag sales to the Conservation Cotton Initiative—an organization advocating for the development of eco-friendly, organic cotton farming to improve incomes and increase economic growth.[18] The bag was adorned with charms—distinctive bunches of ebony and bone spikes—that were produced in co-operation with Made,[19] a fair-trade brand of jewelry and accessories expertly finished by craftspeople in Kenya; these bag charms were Louis Vuitton's very first "made in Africa" product.[20] In exchange, Bono and his wife appeared in the latest Louis Vuitton campaign.[21]

On September 10, 2009, the Vivarte Group (known for such brands as Naf Naf and Kookaï) partnered with Les Fées des Bengales; Vivarte's share remained undisclosed. The ethical fashion brand Les Fées des Bengales had been founded in 2006 by two sisters, Sophie and Camille Dupuy, and their friend Elodie le Derf, after a voyage in poverty-stricken yet beautiful rural India. Sophie Dupuy recalled the trip as having been a revelation. She was captivated by the brightly colored saris and equally struck by the trying work conditions and the know-how she observed in the traditional workshops. Les Fées de Bengales was mainly set up to work with women in India.[22] Seventy per cent of its output was produced in India but the company had recently acquired new partners in Portugal, Tunisia and France to grow its output. Post-partnership, both design and production remained in the hands of the founders: "We are continuing with our strategy and now we even guarantee the eco-friendly production line."[23]

⊠ The Ethical Fashion Industry

The global apparel, accessories and luxury goods market generated total revenues of $1,334.1 billion in 2008.[24] In 2005, the industry employed approximately 26 million people and

---

[16]Ethical Style, "Louis Vuitton Buys Minority Stake in Edun," Ethical Style blog entry, May 18, 2009; available at http://ethical-style.com/2009/05/louis-vuitton-buys-minority-stake-in-edun/, accessed on September 26, 2010.

[17]Ibid.

[18]EDUN, "EDUN Launches the Conservation Cotton Initiative – Joining Forces with the Wildlife Conservation Society," news release, July 31, 2007, PR Newswire; available at http://www.prnewswire.com/news-releases/edun-launches-the-conservation-cotton-initiative---joining-forces-with-the-wildlife-conservation-society-52788817.html, accessed on September 26, 2010.

[19]Made, available at http://made.uk.com/, accessed on September 26, 2010.

[20]Trend Hunter Fashion, "Tribal Designer Bags: The Louis Vuitton for Edun Keepall 45 Duffel Is Stunning"; available at http://www.trendhunter.com/trends/louis-vuitton-for-edun, accessed on September 26, 2010.

[21]High Snobiety, "Louis Vuitton x Edun Keepall 45 Tavel Duffel Bag," September 20, 2010; available at http://www.highsnobiety.com/news/2010/09/20/louis-vuitton-x-edun-keepall-45-travel-duffle-bag/, accessed on September 26, 2010.

[22]Les Fées de Bengale, available at http://www.lesfeesdebengale.fr/v3/fr/la-marque/lhistoire, accessed on September 26, 2010.

[23]Barbara Markert, "Vivarte Partners with Les Fées de Bengale," *Sportswear International Magazine*, September 10, 2009; available at http://www.sportswearnet.com/fashionnews/pages/protected/VIVARTE-PARTNERS-WITH-LES-FES-DE-BENGALES_1877.html, accessed on September 26, 2010.

[24]*Consumer Goods: Global Industry Guide*, Datamonitor, March 2009, accessed on September 26, 2010.

contributed to 7 per cent of world exports.[25] Fierce competition and lack of supply chain transparency kept driving costs down—at a high social and environmental burden that included the use of child labor, unfair practices and disruption of natural ecosystems.

Ethical fashion was booming. Some predicted that, by 2015, certain practices, such as the use of organic cotton, would become mainstream.[26] Nearly every big label, including H&M, Guess and Banana Republic, had developed a "green" line. Nike and Adidas had integrated ethical principles into their core business, and leading retailers, such as Wal-Mart and Marks & Spencer, had made ethical sourcing a centerpiece of their new strategy.[27] For example, Wal-Mart had become the biggest buyer of organic cotton in the world. Although the quantity of organic cotton produced was still minuscule—in 2009, 175,113 metric tonnes of organic cotton were grown, representing 0.76 per cent of the cotton production[28]—the organic cotton segment was growing at an impressive 20 per cent per year.

Several established fashion brands were working together with non-governmental organizations (NGOs) to add organic fibers to their collections. For example, Vivienne Westwood[29] used her catwalk shows as platforms to campaign for less consumption and a more sustainable lifestyle. Since 2005, eco fashion designs had been shown during New York Fashion Week by such fashion brands as Versace, Martin Margiela and Donna Karan. Instead of using traditional fabrics, such as silk and cashmere, many fashion designers now preferred to use fabrics such as sasawashi (a Japanese fabric made from paper and herbs), hemp and peace silk (a silk produced in such a way that silk worms lived out their full life cycle).

In 2003, the Ethical Fashion Show (EFS) was launched in Paris. It was the first and biggest event to focus exclusively on ecological, socially responsible and environmentally friendly garment production. In 2008, EFS began expanding to other cities, from Milan to Rio de Janeiro. In April 2010, the Messe Frankfurt (also known as the Frankfurt Trade Fair)—the world's market leader in trade shows, which hosted 31 textile fairs around the world—took over the EFS. The acquisition meant that Messe Frankfurt, the combined fair and exhibition company, now covered the world's entire supply chain in the sector of textile fairs.

As the ethical fashion movement picked up,[30] it brought together like-minded stylists, activists, models, journalists, stores, celebrities and events. Eco boutiques on the web encouraged online shopping and drove change in the retail industry. Fashion schools stimulated their students to consider this issue through the introduction of special topics within the curriculum.

---

[25]HM Customs & Excise, Provided by the British Apparel & Textile Confederation (2005) provided to Defra: www.defra.gov.uk, accessed on September 26, 2010.

[26]cKinetics, *Exporting Textiles: March to Sustainability*, April 2010; available at http://www.ckinetics.com/MarchToSustainability2010/, accessed on September 26, 2010.

[27]Organic Exchange, *Organic Cotton Market Report 2007–2008*; available at www.organicexchange.org, ccessed on September 26, 2010.

[28]Organic Exchange, *Organic Cotton Farm and Fiber Report 2009*; available at www.organicexchange.org, accessed on September 26, 2010.

[29]Vivienne Westwood is a well-known fashion designer, whose four decade career remains highly influential, http://www.viviennewestwood.com/flash.php, accessed on September 29, 2010.

[30]Entrepreneurs in ethical fashion were from a variety of backgrounds. They ranged from NGO workers to business people, and only a small percentage had been trained as fashion designers. Many of them had altruistic reasons for starting their brand, such as to help a specific community in a developing country. In the beginning, the focus of these brands was often not on design, but more on survival and philanthropic goals. This focus changed as an increasing number of entrepreneurs hired professional stylists who created ever more beautiful collections.

Governments played their part by regulating destructive practices and transforming the mindset of consumers. NGOs developed systems to trace each item back to its origins. Others campaigned and lobbied to create more general awareness on ethical fashion and to help create eco fashion brands that could become successful examples of public–private partnerships.

The main actors in the ethical fashion movement, however, were the small eco-fashion brands, many of which had been born less than four years earlier. By 2010, more than 500 ethical fashion brands were in business around the globe. In the majority of the brands, the founder (and the founder's small team) worked directly with people in developing countries to source and produce socially and environmentally responsible fashion items. These ventures were no longer just designing an item to wear; they were crafting stories that signaled how individuals felt about big issues, such as poverty and deforestation. Wearing eco-fashions made a statement all right, but it was no longer just about the clothes—or shoes.

Eco-fashion was still in its infancy. Despite the financial crisis, sales of organic and ethical fashion were shooting up, growing by 50 per cent each year.[31] Although the industry was small—eco-fashion represented just 1 per cent of the sales in the broader fashion industry—it was growing momentum. Eco-fashion was particularly popular among a segment known as "cultural creatives,"[32] who were highly educated consumers who had an interest in spirituality, actively participated in society through voluntary work, advocated a conscious lifestyle and were motivated by a high need to strive for a better world. More than 50 million cultural creatives spent $230 billion on everything from yoga gear to organic apples to hybrid cars. This trend was evident not only in fashion-forward countries, such as France, the United Kingdom, Germany and the United States, but also in BRIC countries, such as Brazil, which were characterized by increasing numbers of customers seeking a green lifestyle.[33] Awareness for eco-fashion brands was growing rapidly: 18 per cent of consumers had heard of eco fashion brands, three times the number four years earlier.[34]

Business Model

Kopp and Morillion started their company without a clue about the fashion industry. After graduating from Paris business schools, Kopp and Morillion took off for a one-year journey around the world. They visited and studied sustainable development projects in different industries, from Chinese factories to South African mines to the Amazon rainforest, witnessing first-hand problems such as deforestation, exhaustion of natural resources and labor exploitation. When they returned to France, they knew they needed to act and to act now. They first tried consulting and recommended to companies such as supermarket Carrefour: "Stop charity, but instead have a close look within your company at what is wrong in the countries where you work and try to do

---

[31]Organic Trade Association, "Industry Statistics and Projected Growth," June 2010; available at http://www.ota.com/organic/mt/business.html, accessed on September 26, 2010.

[32]Cultural Creatives, available at http://www.culturalcreatives.org, accessed on September 26, 2010.

[33]Hartman Group, *The Hartman Report on Sustainability: Understanding the Consumer Perspective, 2007*; available at www.hartman-group.com, accessed on September 26, 2010. Consumers in many major markets want more green product choices. Studies show that 50 per cent of women want mass retailers to carry more green goods, and 11 per cent of these consumers see themselves as "extremely green" today, and 43 per cent say that they will be "extremely green" in five years.

[34]Forum for the Future, "Fashion Futures 2025: Global Scenarios for a Sustainable Fashion Industry," February 24, 2010; available at http://www.forumforthefuture.org.uk/projects/fashion-futures, accessed on September 26, 2010.

something positive about it."[35] Then they realized they had to do something themselves: "Let's pick a product and try to put as much sustainable development in it as we can."[36]

Both Kopp and Morillion were sneaker addicts. They knew from the start what they wanted to create: good-looking shoes that had a positive impact on both the planet and society, as opposed to the negative impacts that characterized the big sneaker manufacturers. The two friends took the path of fair trade because they felt it would be the most effective way to integrate environment and dignity into everyday products. They set out to "invent new methods of work."[37] Veja was built on three main values: using ecological inputs, using fair trade cotton and latex and respecting workers' dignity.

Getting Started

Kopp and Morillion's journey around the world had opened their eyes to the rich variety of countries and cultures. They chose to operate in Brazil. Kopp and Morillion loved Brazil, its climate, its language and culture, and they imagined themselves living in Brazil. Here, they had met many people from NGOs and social movements working collaboratively to protect the sensitive Amazonian eco-system; connecting with these players, they felt, would help them scaffold the entire value chain.

After calculating the budget needed to produce their first sneaker collection, Kopp and Morillion were able to negotiate a bank loan. They then moved to Brazil, set up their company and began producing the collection. They presented their first sneaker collection at a conventional trade fair in Paris. "Who's next?"[38] always

had extra space available to feature new designers, and Kopp and Morillion managed to secure a spot to showcase their new sneakers. They learned on the go:

> I remember running out the tradeshow to buy some paper on which we could write down the orders people placed. But then you talk to your neighbours and you pick up quickly how it works.[39]

It was a Cinderella story. Kopp and Morillion identified the stores where they wanted to place their sneakers and then invited those buyers to see their collection. People came, loved the product and started buying. Their product was so successful that the first collection sold out, and Veja was able to pay back its bank loan within a year. Veja had enough money to produce a second collection. Since then, the company grew ten-fold by following the same approach: they took little risk, produced small quantities and focused on the product. Morillion commented:

> We had a plan for the first year, then we had a plan until we presented the shoe and after that we discovered a whole world we didn't know about. We basically went learning by doing, making many mistakes.[40]

Morillion was in charge of production and finances, and Kopp ran the commercial side of the company, but they did most of the work together. "We fight every day," [Morillion] confessed. In the first few years

---

[35]Interview with François Morillion, October 2, 2009, used with permission.

[36]Ibid.

[37]Veja, "Is Another World Possible?" available at http://www.veja.fr/#/projets/VISION-26, accessed on September 26, 2010.

[38]http://www.whosnext.com/, accessed on September 29, 2010.

[39]Interview with François Morillion, October 2, 2009, used with permission.

[40]Ibid.

... every day there was a new problem because we really had no clue about the shoe business. It was definitely the biggest challenge in building Veja, to learn how to make proper shoes.[41]

Kopp and Morillion initially spent half of the year in Brazil. Then they hired a shoemaker who had all the expertise they needed and who later became the manager of the Veja team co-located in Porto Alegre, the eleventh most populous municipality in Brazil, the centre of Brazil's fourth largest metropolitan area and the capital city of the southernmost Brazilian state of Rio Grande do Sul. The Brazil-based team took care of quality, administration, logistics (e.g. shipping) and the entire raw material process of buying and paying the cotton, rubber and leather. The founders were in touch with the Brazilian team daily, via Skype, and traveled to Brazil four or five times a year to meet with their Brazilian co-workers. In addition, the team manager traveled to Paris twice a year to see the new stores where the sneakers were sold and to meet customers and colleagues in the headquarters in Paris.

Distribution Chain

Since the beginning, Veja had aimed to place its product in trendy sneaker boutiques next to other (non-ethical) brands. Veja did not see the need to promote its ethical approach to customers who were already convinced about the importance of purchasing ethical products. Instead, the company wanted to inspire customers who were accustomed to buying trendy sneakers. Veja sneakers sold in premium venues, such as the Galeries Lafayette in Paris and Rien à Cacher in Montreal. Veja sneakers were available

in selected shops across Europe and Canada, but most sneakers were sold in France, Spain and the United Kingdom.

In France, Veja collaborated with the Atelier Sans Frontières association (ASF), which facilitated work for socially marginalized people,[42] by helping them to build a new life and by promoting their social, professional and personal development. Since the founding of Veja, ASF had received all the finished sneakers from Brazil, stored them and prepared all the orders, which were dispatched to the retail stores where Veja sneakers were sold. ASF logisticians had recently started managing the functional portion of Veja's online store, the Veja Store.[43] ASF was in charge of printing, preparing, packing and sending all online orders.

Production

Veja sneakers were manufactured in a factory close to Porto Alegre. Most of the employees traced their roots to a community of German descendants who had arrived in Brazil at the end of the 19th century. All employees owned houses with running water and electricity, and 80 per cent were union members. Sixty per cent of the workers lived in the towns and villages surrounding the factory (the farthest being located 47 km away), while the remaining 40 per cent live near the factory. The factory pre-arranged coach services ensure all employees could travel safely and comfortably to work.

Veja complied with the core International Labour Organization (ILO) labor standards but felt more was needed to guarantee dignity at work. For example, Veja cared about workers' freedom to gather and uphold their rights, their standard of living and purchasing power, their social benefits and their rights of free speech.

[41]Ibid.

[42]Beyond this partnership with Veja, ASF tried to involve its employees in other tasks, such as collecting old sports material and computers and repairing them. All the work is adapted to the people depending on their skills and experience. The aim is to aid the employees in (re)building their lives and careers.

[43]Veja, http://www.veja-store.com/, accessed on September 26, 2010.

The average wage of the factory workers was approximately €238 each month, 16 per cent higher than Brazil's legal minimum wage for the shoe industry of €205 each month. In addition, Veja paid overtime and an annual bonus. The factory employees were entitled to four weeks of paid holiday, and they did not work on bank holidays. During the peak season, each employee worked a maximum of two hours extra per day, on average. Each employee contributed seven to 11 per cent of their salary to INSS (Instituto Nacional do Seguro Social, Brazil's governmental pension scheme), which provided an additional safety net for the employees.

When Kopp and Morillion were in business school, had taken internships in investment banking and consultancy companies, where they learned about hard work and earning a lot of money. Morillion commented: "In these places, we saw how people were stressed and didn't like their jobs, but just came home happy because of the money. This is definitely not our culture."[44] At Veja, employees started their work at 9:30 in the morning and left the office before 7 p.m. On Friday afternoons, everyone went home at 4:30 p.m., and the founders themselves often went out of town for the weekend. Keeping the balance between work and private life was at the core of Veja's approach of creating a company that cared about the employees.

Each year, each new member of the Veja team was given the opportunity to travel to Brazil to meet the producers. For the founders, involving their employees in the entire Veja story was essential, instead of simply letting them work in an office in the center of Paris. Morillion explained:

> We travel a lot and meet many different people, but our employees don't get that chance. If we don't involve them in the whole process, they will get bored and might want to leave the company.

[We created] different experiences for our employees and they loved it.[45]

Certification

As part of the fair trade certification process, the main shoe factory in Porto Alegre underwent two social audits. The different departments of the factory and the fabrication workshops (which housed the cutting, sewing, soles, assembling processes) were audited in 2008 and 2009, in accordance with the Fairtrade Labelling Organization–Certification (FLO-Cert) standard requirements. The auditor raised 52 non-compliances in May 2008 and 16 non-compliances in February 2009; in April 2009, the certification of the factory was officially confirmed.

While the fair trade certification was increasingly important to consumers, for it was a means to a greater end, a starting point in Kopp and Morillion's path to improve the bigger picture. Veja sought to establish higher standards and strive toward loftier social and environmental objectives. To help the farmers gain additional credibility, Kopp and Morillion supported the cooperatives in the process of obtaining certification, but their personal relationships with the farmers extended beyond certification. The founders cared about social equity, and saw their venture as one means to improve farmers' lives by supporting traditional livelihoods.

Supply Chain

Kopp and Morillion created a supply chain that was based on sustainable relationships (see Exhibit 3). They viewed the company's connection to its producers as one not just of trade but of cultural exchange. Whereas the fashion industry was accustomed to contracting new parties as soon as a factory could deliver on time or cut costs, Veja tried to improve living conditions and to work

---

[44]Interview with François Morillion, October 2, 2009, used with permission.

[45]Ibid.

cooperatively with supply chain to jointly develop the best product they could imagine. Veja bought raw materials directly from producers. The company paid a fixed price, which, though higher than the market price, was calculated by the farmers and allowed them to live in dignity. Veja was happy to pay extra. Kopp and Morillion viewed fair wages as a means of re-establishing social justice.

Cotton

The canvas for the Veja sneakers was organic cotton. With help from Esplar,[46] an NGO that had been collaborating with Brazilian farmers for 30 years, Veja started working with 150 families to grow cotton under agro-ecological principles (i.e. without the use of agro-chemicals or pesticides); Veja now sourced cotton from 400 families in the state of Ceará in northeastern Brazil.

Veja purchased 90 per cent of the organic cotton it used from ADEC, a new association of rural farmers who followed agro-ecological principles. The strong interdependence made Veja vulnerable. Changes in weather and natural disasters, such as insect plagues and violent rains, could deplete the supply of organic cotton. Production needed to adapt to the availability of organic cotton, which still varied considerably. Depending on the extent of the harvest, Veja sometimes needed to reduce the quantities of sneakers ordered by retailers.

Rubber

The Amazon was the only place on earth where rubber trees still grew in the wild. The survival of the Amazonian rainforest depended on sustainable management of its resources, including the latex extracted from rubber trees. Since the 1960s, the increasing use of synthetic rubber derived from petroleum had lowered both the demand and price for natural rubber. Thus, the inhabitants of the Amazon forest had moved from rubber tapping to more profitable activities, such as cattle-raising and wood extraction, which both required the clearing of land. As a consequence of deforestation, the soils were no longer protected by the cover of vegetation, leaving them vulnerable to accelerated erosion and desertification.

Inside the Chico Mendès Extractive Reserve, located in the Brazilian state of Acre, Veja worked with Amopreab[47] (Associação de Moradores e Produtores da Reserva Extrativista Chico Mendes de Assis Brasil), an association of seringueiros, or rubber tappers (see Exhibit 3). Beatriz Saldanha, who had lived and worked with the seringueiros for 10 years, helped Veja to make the connection. By 2010, Veja was working with 35 rubber tapper families. Paying a fairer price paid for latex not only guaranteed a better income for the rubber tappers but also provided an incentive for conserving the rubber trees.

Leather

After two seasons of relying on organic cotton and rubber, Veja started researching the qualities of leather and its impact on the environment. The typical tanning process used heavy metals, such as chrome, making leather one of the least sustainable raw materials. Chrome allowed for quick tanning, but was a dangerous product and accounted for three problems: 1) it affected the people who tanned the leather, 2) it polluted the water and 3) it was not biodegradable. Sustainable processes, however, were available. In Italy, for example, factories often used vegetal tanning techniques and worked with companies such as Gucci and Chanel. Veja searched for companies that worked with alternative tanning processes, eventually locating a factory that tanned leather the way it was done 100 years ago. At that time,

---

[46]Esplar, available at http://www.esplar.org.br/, accessed on September 26, 2010.

[47]"Portal do Meio Ambiente"; available at http://www.portaldomeioambiente.org.br/index.php?option=com_content&view=article&id=2560:vencedores-do-chico-mendes-recebem-premiacao-em-dezembro&catid=40:comunicacao-ambiental-&Itemid=733, accessed on September 26, 2010.

tanners did not work with chrome, so going back to basics helped to overcome the problem. Veja collaborated with this traditional factory to produce only eco-tanned leather created from a vegetable extract such as acacia. To obtain a consistent color without staining, Veja used conventional dying approved by Eco-Label[48]. To continuously improve the quality of the natural dyes, Veja undertook a collaboration with a Brazilian specialist in the field of vegetable and non-polluting color pigments.

Cost Structure

Veja's fabrication costs were seven to eight times higher than other footwear brands because its shoes and bags were produced in a principled way. Veja's price for organic cotton was twice the world market price. In 2009, Veja bought Brazilian wild rubber (produced according to FDL—folha desfumada liquida, or liquid smoked sheet) at €2.33 per kg. The price of planted natural rubber from São Paulo varied between €1.60 per kg to €1.90 per kg. The price of synthetic rubber, determined by the oil price, ranged between €1 per kg and €1.2 per kg.

A large part of Veja's current profits funded research and development (R&D), such as developing new applications to work with organic cotton, rubber and leather. Veja also invested in collaborations with a Brazilian dyeing specialist to help improve the vegetal tanning techniques. Veja had just started collaborating with other French-Brazilian brands, such as Envão and Tudo Bom, to work together on improving the supply chain and jointly sourcing raw material to be able to meet the quantity criteria. The Veja founders welcomed other small brands interested in sourcing from Brazil because Kopp and Morillion felt "it makes them stronger and reduces the risk for both them and their producers."[49]

Zero Ads

Generally, 70 per cent of the cost of sneakers was dedicated to marketing. Veja, however, had a "no advertising" policy. Regardless, the company's products had been endorsed by the media and appreciated by the public since the company's creation. Veja benefitted widely from media coverage, blogs, forums and word of mouth. Morillion commented:

> That is really the most rewarding thing in running this company, to see people walking down the streets on our sneakers. Last week I saw someone with a Veja bag, which is a very new product just in stores. He was not even a friend of us, but a complete stranger who had already picked up this product![50]

Zero Stock

The popularity of Veja's products paid off: most outlets had fewer Veja sneakers than they could sell. Veja did not produce extra; it produced only according to orders placed six months in advance. Veja was not about large volumes but about profitability—with a conscience.

Environmental Footprint

CO$_2$ Emissions

Veja looked at every aspect of its supply chain and adjusted the company's methods of transportation, organization, production and distribution. All Veja shoes were transported by boat from Porto Alegre, Brazil, to Le Havre in France. Upon arrival in Le Havre, the shoes traveled in barges along the canals to the Parisian suburbs. Veja's packaging was made from recycled and recyclable cardboard, and it used shoe boxes that

---

[48]http://www.eco-label.com/default.htm, accessed on September 29, 2010.

[49]Interview with François Morillion, October 2, 2009, used with permission.

[50]Ibid.

were sized down to optimize efficiency. Finally, Veja's headquarters used Enercoop (a green electricity cooperative) instead sourcing electricity from Électricité de France (EDF, the French national nuclear energy supplier).

Limitations

Veja was open, both about its limitations and its work to overcome them. Kopp and Morillion were open about the remaining shortcomings of Veja's production processes and explained how they kept working to become more sustainable. For example, because production was still low, Veja did not need many pairs of shoelaces and could thus not afford to create the laces from organic cotton. The moss used to maintain the ankle was a synthetic, oil-based product. The shoes' sole contains between 30 per cent and 40 per cent of rubber, whereas the insole contained only 5 per cent of rubber. The insole also had technical properties (i.e. comfort and resistance), which required additional components, such as synthetic rubber. The eyelets in the shoes did not contain nickel but were composed of metal whose origin was not controlled. The sneakers were shipped by boat from Brazil to France, but American and Asian stores and clients continued to be serviced by plane. Veja also aimed to recycle the sneakers, thereby further increasing their lifespan.

Message

Since day one, Veja had produced more than sneakers. It also crafted art events as a way of connecting to customers and inspiring its own employees. The company's communication team reached out, and Veja sponsored art installations made by local artists they befriended in the French and Brazilian urban art scenes.[51] For example, for the 2006 Fashion Fair "Who's next?" Veja invited the art collective Favela Chic to perform. In an example of Veja's own creativity, São Paulo's 2006 ban on advertising inspired Veja to create an installation in the window display of the Parisian store French Trotters.[52]

The most recent exhibition (in October 2009), suggestively titled "São Paulo, Mon Amour," showcased the vision of São Paulo artists on their city.[53] The pieces conveyed messages about social inequality and pollution in Brazil's capital (Brasilia) and raised awareness about these issues. The exhibition, which was held in a public space in Paris, attracted 3,000 people in two weeks' time and was jointly sponsored by the Brazilian Ministry of Culture and the Municipality of Paris. Veja chose a discreet approach to promote the event by inviting the company's contacts, who would thus associate the brand with an interesting and beautiful exhibition.

Art was also a driver in the various special collections Veja developed in collaboration with other companies and organizations. For example, in 2007, the company launched a collection designed by the young French fashion designer Christine Phung.[54] In July 2009, the Veja Kids, a line of sneakers for children, landed exclusively in Bonpoint stores around the world.[55] Using the motto "Sell your car, get a bike," the company

---

[51]Although the event was a co-production between Veja and several other parties, the company deliberately chose to not be visible in the event's promotion and publicity.

[52]Veja, "Urban Archeology," March 25, 2009; available at http://blog.veja.fr/en/site/comments/urban_archeology/, accessed on September 26, 2010.

[53]Veja, "São Paulo, Mon Amour," blog entry, posted September 9, 2009; available at http://blog.veja.fr/en/site/comments/mega-pole_insensee_mon_amour/, accessed on September 26, 2010.

[54]Curitiba 75, "Veja," video clip; available at http://www.youtube.com/watch?v=h__qANp3g8U&feature=player_embedded, accessed on September 26, 2010.

[55]Veja, "Veja and Bonpoint, One to Watch this Winter," blog entry, posted July 17, 2009; available at http://blog.veja.fr/en/site/comments/veja_and_bonpoint/, accessed on September 26, 2010.

launched the Cyclope collection in the Cyclope shop in Paris in November 2009.[56] In January 2010, the Veja + Merci became exclusively available in the Merci store, a lifestyle and fashion emporium in Paris. All proceeds from the Cyclope collection were donated to charity.[57]

⊠ The Decision

When Veja had started, Kopp and Morillion were in their mid-twenties. They had never worked for anyone else, commented Morillion:

> By now I don't think we can ever work for another company, since Veja allows us so much freedom to do what we want and to strive for our dreams.[58]

They had many ideas, but took things step by step and try to take as little risk as possible. At the moment they were focusing on their first range of accessories, like bags, wallets and computer cases. In another five to 10 years, they could save enough to open their own flagship store.

> We're always thinking about the next project, but not really about the one after. It comes as it goes.[59]

Kopp and Morillion's social change ambitions held strong. Veja's website portrayed the company as one drop in the ocean, offering the following call to action:

> Day after day, prophets of all kind are pulling the emergency cord, the entire economy is turning green and sustainable-developementising speeches are spreading around.
>
> Actions remain scarce but words abound.
>
> Beyond movies about the environment, beyond multinational companies building green windows to hide disasters, beyond the Copenhagen speeches filled with words and political promise.
>
> And despite this green-fronted economy, let's try to offer a different vision which combines fair trade and ecology and links together economy, social initiatives and the environment.
>
> A vision that proposes cultural change.[60]

Kopp and Morillion's vision for social change had already extended beyond their company. Kopp and Morillion coached new eco-fashion brands, which then started men's collections; they tried to give them direction:

> Many people call us and we meet them and give them advice. What is lacking in the ethical fashion field, is strong men's brands and this is where Veja tries to make a difference.[61]

Kopp and Morillion also aimed to influence existing brands to convert to organic and fair-trade practices. Sometimes they felt it might be easier to change existing brands because they had already create the style that people wanted to wear, whereas ethical fashion brands often lacked the right aesthetics.

---

[56]http://blog.veja.fr/fr/archive/200912, accessed on September 26, 2010.

[57]Veja, "Vega + Merci," blog entry, posted January 12, 2010; available at http://blog.veja.fr/en/site/comments/veja_merci/, accessed on September 26, 2010.

[58]Interview with François Morillion, October 2, 2009, used with permission.

[59]Ibid.

[60]Veja, "Veja Is Just a Drop in the Ocean," http://www.veja.fr/#/projets, accessed on September 26, 2010.

[61]Interview with François Morillion, October 2, 2009, used with permission.

I think the ethical fashion world is still missing a bit of fashion and that's why it doesn't grow as fast as we all hope. Our product came at the right time at the right place. If we would have done the same product without the fair-trade and organic [angle], it might have brought us the same success. It's sad, but I think it is true.

They had a lot of work ahead: "Right now I still haven't found cool ethical T-shirts and jeans and I just hope that I can wear only ethical one day."[62]

Exhibit I Veja Founders

François-Ghislain Morillion	Sébastien Kopp
Production & Finances	Sales & Marketing
Born July 25, 1978	Born July 16, 1978
MSc HEC Paris, 2002	MSc DESS, 2002
Passion: electronic music	Passion: writing

SOURCE: Prepared by the case writer on the basis of company documents and interviews. Photo credits: Veja, used with permission.

---

[62]Ibid.

Exhibit 2 Veja Collections

2005: Volley 2006: Tauá 2007: Grama 2008: The Grid 2009: SP, MA 2010: Bags, Veja+ Merci

VEJA MILESTONES

2005	2006	2007	2008	2009	2010
Feb: Launch Veja	Feb: Collaboration Agnes b.	June: launch Veja + Christine Phung	March: Launch Veja Kids	March: Launch bags+wallets	Jan: Launch Veja+Merci
Sept: Launch Veja website	July: Launch Veja blog	Sept: Veja @ Ethical Fashion Show (EFS)	Aug: London office open	Sept: Expo SP, Mon Amour	Feb: Veja+Bonpoint Merci
Nov: Launch Veja Baby	Nov: 1st rubber collection	Dec: Veja lands in Madrid	Oct: Launch online store	Nov: Launch Veja+ Cyclope	May: Snippet expo London

ETHICAL FASHION MILESTONES

2005	2006	2007	2008	2009	2010
Ethical Fashion Forum is founded in the UK	1st Esthetica in London	Organic Exchange turns 5 years old[1]	5th EFS in Paris	EFS launches in other cities like Milan	Messe Frankfurt acquires EFS
Launch of Made-By				Launch NY Greenshows and TheKey.to Berlin	

SOURCE: Prepared by the case writer on the basis of company documents and interviews.

[1]http://cogent.controlunion.com/cusi_production_files/SISI_files/FL_011210114219_Market_Report_08-_Executive_Summary.pdf, accessed September 28, 2010.

| **Exhibit 3** | Veja's Sourcing of Cotton, Rubber and Leather |

The state of Ceará in northeast Brazil has vast wealth inequalities, fragile soils and a tendency toward drought. It also works with a producers' cooperative in Paraná, a relatively more productive area located in the center of Brazil. In contrast to the predominant monoculture farming system, a group of small producers grow cotton and food plants as rotational crops. For these small-scale farmers (one hectare of land on average), farming development goes hand-in-hand with environmental protection. But there were setbacks. After a caterpillar attack, producers panicked and decided to spray pesticide to protect their harvest. Veja had committed itself to purchase the harvest and could not ask the producers to lose their entire harvest. Therefore, these 12 tons of "infected" organic and ethical cotton were used to make the shoes' lining and as a double layer for the Projet Numero Deux accessories (see http://www.veja.fr/#/projets/Coton-15 for the process). The photo at left shows the Porto Alegre team manager checking the cotton.

Seringueiros (derived from the word *seringueira*, or the rubber plant) extract natural latex directly from the trunk of the rubber tree (Hevea brasiliensis), by making small cuts in the bark. At least five hours are needed to fill a tiny container with latex, and two years must pass before new cuts can be made on the same tree. To process the liquid rubber into sheets that can be used to make rubber soles, the seringueiros use a new technology developed by Professor Floriano Pastore of the University of Brasilia, called FDL (folha desfumada liquida, or liquid smoked sheet). FDL allows the rubber tappers to transform latex into rubber sheets without any industrial intermediary processes. Once extracted, filtered and purified, the latex is stretched and "spread" in six layers onto canvas of organic cotton, and then subjected to a curing process in the open air, which allows it to dry and results in a high-quality product. To produce a pair of slabs, the seringueiros must first tap into material extracted from at least 10 rubber plants. The FDL technology permits the seringueiros to sell semi-finished products and receive a higher income. The sheets of rubber are directly sent to the factory and shaped into soles for the Veja shoes. Not only does the production of vegetable rubber represent an instrument for environmental protection, but it also provides an economic alternative for seringueiros, who wander the heart of the Amazon forest during six months a year engaged in the extraction and processing of this material. This practice safeguards the culture and traditions of autochthonous populations, who are the true guardians of the forest (see http://www.tyresonfire.com/amazonlife.com/index.php?id=60 for a clip of seringueiros at work). The photos at left show a seringueiro and Beatriz Saldanha, the woman who connected Veja with the seringueiros.

(Continued)

Exhibit 3	(Continued)

Leather is typically not made under fair trade principles because it is difficult to work directly with leather producers, and it is often difficult to confirm the leather's origin and the cattle's treatment. The breeding of cattle also requires vast fields and the relevant financial inputs. Veja chose not to marginalize leather producers but instead sought to make a positive change within this specific industry. Veja ensured that the leather it sourced did originate from the cattle from the Amazon, where cattle breeding remains a main contributor to deforestation. The company's main objective was to be knowledgeable and in control of the entire leather supply chain, from the cows' nurturing and living conditions to the tanning and dyeing process of the leather. Veja used only eco-tanned leather created with vegetable extracts such as acacia. Unlike modern tanning procedures (which use chromium and other heavy metals), ecological tanning decreases pollution in the water surrounding the tannery plant.

(See http://www.veja.fr/#/projets/Cuir-14 for a video clip of the process). The photo at left shows one step in the leather veggie-tanning process.

SOURCE: Prepared by the case writer on the basis of company documents and interviews; photos used with permission.

J.-Robert Ouimet and Tomasso Corporation

Ken Mark and Gerard Seijts

Introduction

In May 2001, Benoit Gauthier, newly appointed president of Tomasso Corporation (Tomasso), was facing several issues. Financial performance at Tomasso was suffering as a result of a downturn in the Canadian economy and customer service disruptions. Quality standards had decreased. Gauthier was also facing personnel issues due to a cutback in working hours that had followed a shift in production to a new facility in Montreal. Before his appointment as president, Gauthier had worked as a consultant to the owners of Tomasso, the Ouimet family.

Gauthier wondered what drastic changes he could suggest to turn Tomasso around. He knew that he would have to proceed carefully, because any action he initiated would be measured against the strong value set that the Ouimet family, in particular the company's CEO, J.-Robert Ouimet, espoused.

History

The Ouimet family business began in 1933, during the Great Depression, a period of extreme economic uncertainty in North America, when

Version: (A) 2009-06-29

J.-René Ouimet, a farmer's son, borrowed $20,000 to start La Maison J.-René Ouimet Ltée, a distributor of prepared foods and European cheeses in the Quebec market. Thirty years later, Ouimet merged his enterprise with Cordon Bleu Ltée, a food distribution company from Quebec, which had been started by Lucien and Aimé Faille. Cordon Bleu sold products such as canned sauces and gravies. Its flagship product was Meatball Stew, inspired by a Faille family recipe.

In 1963 and 1964, La Maison J.-René Ouimet Ltée achieved renown when the company's Cordon Bleu brand won 18 gold medals for exceptional quality at World Quality Competitions in Paris, Brussels and London. During the same period, J-René Ouimet ceded control of his company to the next generation, his three children, J.-Robert, Suzanne and Francine.

The transfer of ownership marked a new era of expansion for the firm. In 1964, J.-Robert Ouimet was promoted to executive president, and in 1965 he became the sole shareholder when he bought out his sisters' shares. Robert believed he had both the competence and the desire to lead the company, which he wanted to grow. He thus created an acquisition unit and added complementary brands such as Clark (e.g. canned beans, stews, and chilis), Paris Pâté (e.g. canned meat spreads), Esta (e.g. canned sauces), Buona Cucina (e.g. frozen meat lasagna), and Gusto Italia (e.g. frozen meat and vegetable lasagna).

With each acquisition, the company achieved savings by moving production from the predecessor firms to factories at La Maison J.-René Ouimet Ltée. The acquired companies' plants were closed and in all several hundred people lost their jobs.

In 1986, the company began to consolidate head office operations in Ville d'Anjou, east of Montreal, a process that took two years to complete.

In 1989, La Maison J.-René Ouimet Ltée acquired Tomasso Corporation, which specialized in frozen Italian meals. Tomasso had been created in 1934 by Giovanina di Tomasso, a restaurateur who owned the Piazza Tomasso restaurant in Montreal. Robert left the two Tomasso brothers, Paolo and Marco, president and vice-president of operations, respectively, to continue running Tomasso. The company was renamed Ouimet-Tomasso. Tomasso had 20 employees at the time of the purchase, but by 2000 the number had grown to 100.

Today, Tomasso is the largest manufacturer of frozen dinners in Canada. It specializes in Italian cuisine, such as lasagna and cannelloni. The client list included Sobeys, Loblaws, and A&P Canada. Tomasso competes with large firms such as Campbell's, Heinz, Maple Leaf Foods, Nestlé, and Chef Boyardee. The Canadian food industry is highly competitive. Over 65 per cent of the food products bought in Canada are imports from the United States and other countries.

The CEO's Philosophy

Robert described how, when he took over the business from his father, he encountered "a fight in my heart and in my brain, between humanity and the economics of the business. It was at this moment when my search for greatness began. I did not want to contribute to creating empty lives. I wanted to enrich people's lives."

Robert's vision was shaped by his upbringing, in which "my mother taught me the Christian faith and compassion, and my father, courage and wisdom." In his youth, Robert had been struck by a passage in the Gospel of Matthew recounting the story of a master who, before embarking on a journey, gives his servants some talents. Upon his return, the master punished the servant who failed to multiply the talents that were given to him. Within the firm, Robert saw himself as a servant, not as the master. In Robert's words, "I have received gifts I did not earn. If you receive a great deal, you must give a great deal—especially to those who have received less."

Robert began to introduce a series of spiritual and human management activities into the company in the 1970s. For example, he instituted the practice of pausing for a moment of meditative silence before executive meetings. This pause was meant to allow participants to collect their thoughts and reflect on the task at hand. A second initiative was bringing in guest speakers from all walks of life to give personal testimonies on general subjects such as mistakes made and successes. The company also allocated some work hours to volunteer work, a few times a year. It established a room for meditation and quiet reflection available to employees of all faiths. Although employees met some of these changes with skepticism, Robert was steadfast in his belief that their introduction was for the greater good of the company.

For moral support, Robert sought guidance from high-profile spiritual leaders, such as the Dalai Lama. In 1983, he travelled to Calcutta to meet with Mother Teresa, and over time she became both a friend and a trusted consultant. Mother Teresa, a Catholic nun, was the founder of the Missionaries of Charity in 1950 and worked with the poor, sick, orphaned, and the dying, in Calcutta.

When the new head office was inaugurated in 1988, Mother Teresa was there. For Robert, Mother Teresa's attendance was significant. She had inspired him with leadership and management ideas. Mother Teresa later sent Robert a letter telling him that she had "felt something special in the eyes and in the face of the humans that she met at Cordon Bleu" (see Exhibit 1).

Robert enrolled in a PhD program at the University of Fribourg in Switzerland to refine the spiritual and management activities further through academic rigor. He conducted surveys to measure the growth of 20 different values among his employees (such as dignity, brotherhood and justice), then correlated these findings with the company's balance-sheet results. This work culminated in his PhD thesis that provided scientific proof that his management tools had been successful.[1]

⊠ J.-Robert Ouimet

Robert held a Bachelor of Commerce from HEC Montréal; a Bachelor in Political and Social Sciences from the University of Fribourg, Switzerland; an MBA from Columbia University, New York; and a PhD in Economic and Social Sciences from the University of Fribourg, obtained in 1997. His motivation to pursue his PhD was straightforward: Robert wanted to put on paper what he had been doing at Tomasso and Cordon Bleu and what he and the leadership team had achieved, and then to compare the achievements with those of other organizations. It took him almost 10 years to complete the dissertation, during which time he made 36 trips to Switzerland.

In examining the changes he had made during his tenure as CEO, Robert developed a theory that valued the human aspect of management as much as a focus on profits. In his doctoral thesis, he described his views as follows:

> In essence, this thesis attempted to demonstrate that the newly discovered and tested Integrated System of Human Management Activities, can, if used properly, progressively foster in businesses profoundly human and balanced values that will slowly give a company or organization more and more heart and soul, a heart of flesh rather than a heart of stone. The thesis starts from the following premise: the market economy is by far the best economic system; it can produce a growth of material wealth for a longer time and in greater quantities than any other economic system we know. Accepting this as the major premise of the thesis, we are forced to acknowledge, especially at the beginning of the 3rd millennium, that the market economy system, and the

---

[1]Philip Preville, "For God's Sake," *Canadian Business,* June 25, 1999, p. 61.

recent globalization that results from it, not only has great strengths but also great weaknesses, which are all too well known. These include notably a lack of transparency, fraud, dishonesty, progressive dehumanization of work, growing injustice between the wealthier and the poorer—if not the indigent or impoverished—classes. All these weaknesses must be progressively reduced and if possible eliminated.

And this is where the all-new and innovative Integrated System of Human Management Activities, discovered and tested, can play a major role in the coming years. This system can foster profoundly human values in the work place and can complement the already proven strengths of the Integrated System of Economic Management Activities used in the market economy.[2]

Robert believed that it was typical for companies to focus on the economic side—serving customers, driving productivity, seeking profits—but ignore the human side—human dignity, and human well-being at work. He believed that to manage his company effectively he had to give as much attention to the human aspects as he gave to the economic aspects, defined by the Integrated System of Economic Management Activities. His MBA had prepared him for managing the economical part of the business; however, he felt he had little knowledge about the people aspect. His conviction was that people should be valued as human beings, not as cogs in the production process. Balancing the two integrated systems of management activities (ISMAs), he believed, would allow Tomasso to better compete against the big players in the industry.

Robert was convinced that the human and economic ISMAs could (and must) be reconciled in profit-oriented companies. The solution was to bring these two opposites together with a "keystone" (see Exhibit 2). The keystone reflected "transcendence." The word transcendence has multiple meanings, but to Robert, it means "the Creator."

People in the Tomasso and Cordon Bleu organizations were encouraged to interpret the value of transcendence in their own ways, for example, through reflection, meditation or prayer. Robert himself was deeply religious—he followed the motto "Pray and Work," or "Ora et Labora." He did not want to impose his own religious beliefs on others in the workplace, many of whom were of different faiths. In his thesis, Robert illustrated the integration of the two ISMAs with the image of an arch, the left column being the economic ISMA, the right column the human ISMA, and the arch being the keystone. Transcendence, he believed, should lead to inner strength, or the wisdom and courage needed in decision making.

Robert put his theory into practice at his organization. In 1997, he launched a program called "Our Project." The cornerstone of Our Project was the realization that:

> . . . all people working in the company or organization have been made by the Creator who loves them and lives in them. This includes consumers as well. The company must serve people. All people, therefore, have an inestimable value and must be respected in their lives, dignity, and personally chosen life paths.

Most organizations, in Robert's view, subscribed to the viewpoint that profits are the ultimate goal, and saw people as instruments, resources and capital. He felt that to be successful an organization had to manage the tension between the two ISMAs: it needed to practise

---

[2]J.-Robert Ouimet, "Spirituality in Management Reconciles Human Well Being—Productivity—Profits," 4th English revised edition, Holding O.C.B. Inc., Montreal, Quebec.

financial discipline, focus relentlessly on its operational performance *and* work diligently on the well-being of its employees if it wanted to prosper and grow over a long-term period.

⊠ The Values and Activities of "Our Project"

Robert's goal was to put his ideas into practice in a company that was profit-oriented. He identified a set of responsibilities, activities and values that collectively became known as Our Project. In brief, Our Project encouraged the company's stakeholders to fulfill responsibilities through a set of activities, which in turn would reinforce a set of values. Many of the ideas and activities were directly inspired by Mother Teresa.

There were six areas or "circles" of responsibility that defined Our Project (see Exhibit 3). Robert explained in detail how organizations should approach each of the six responsibilities:

1. Responsibilities toward the people who work in the company and toward their families

   - The company must recognize that work exists for man, and not man for work; the former develops people, the latter breaks them down;
   - Salaries and social benefits must be just, adequate, and at least comparable to those in other companies of similar size and activity;
   - Job enrichment must be seen to be as much a way of reducing the monotony of work as a way of contributing to people's moral and spiritual development, to their professional and technical competence, productivity, and efficiency; and
   - The company must encourage every activity that increases solidarity, brotherhood, compassion, human dignity, and people's development. Such activities must be carried out in a climate of justice, fairness, freedom,

and discipline so as to contribute to constantly growing efficiency and productivity. By their sustained efforts, all people working in the company have the primary duty of contributing to the constant and necessary growth of efficiency and productivity, for their own good, for that of their families, and for the common good.

2. Responsibilities toward the consumers of our products, toward our suppliers and customers

   - The company must listen to people when they express their needs; it must lend an ear to today's and tomorrow's consumers of its products. It must offer them products and services that have an agreeable and competitive price-quality ratio so as to ensure that the customers are better served and treated by the company than by its competitors; and
   - In order to do this, the company must manifest creativity, discipline, imagination, determination, intelligence, judgment, and wisdom. It must give primary importance to research and development; it needs to improve its productivity, to systematically review its technology and strategic orientation, and to carry out necessary investments to ensure long-term competitiveness.

3. Responsibilities of executives and managers

   - Members of management must provide the example and live themselves what they require from others;
   - The company has the responsibility of choosing its directors and managers with great care, based on the values of Our Project, so that they will help the men and women they manage to develop their inner selves, and to blossom, as well as to increase their competence and efficiency; and

- The management team members must be "the company's motors" and prefer the title "company servants" to "bosses." But above all, they must strive for excellence in the technical, scientific, professional, human, moral, and spiritual exercise of their responsibilities.

4. Responsibilities of the members of the board of directors and stockholders

   - Of all the actors in the company's life, the stockholders, administrators, and upper-level managers are by far the most privileged. This is why they must demand more of themselves, on the human, moral, and spiritual levels, than they ask of anyone else;
   - Stockholders and board members, more than others in the company, must at all times seek the happiness and the "better being" of each person working in the company as well as the satisfaction of every present and future consumer of its products and services;
   - Moreover, in regards to stockholders and other actors in the company's economic and social life, the administrators have the duty to make profits, year after year, that are at least comparable to those made by other companies of similar size and activity. This responsibility will help ensure the company's long-term existence, for the well being and happiness of all the people working in the company and of their families, for that of all present and future consumers and stockholders;
   - The administrators and stockholders have the duty to support, and communicate with, each other; to do what is necessary to increase the transparency of their decisions, to make recommendations, and to make necessary decisions in the

interest of the company's development and in line with Our Project's spirit; and
   - They have the duty to build the future by taking advantage of expansion opportunities that present themselves, by launching new products, and by building up appropriate financial reserves.

5. Responsibilities toward the society, the nation, and creation

   - The company must get involved in the community, with generosity, justice, and fairness;
   - It must participate in the pursuit of the common good by collaborating with all levels of government; and
   - It must pay its fair share of taxes and be concerned with the quality of the environment.

6. Ultimate responsibilities toward and *with* the Creator, or the Supreme Being

   - The two ultimate goals of work in a company are to contribute to the long-term growth, on the one hand, of happiness and "better being" of people and their families, and, on the other, of the company's competitive profitability;
   - The long-term, progressive, and balanced realization of these two goals over many years will be possible, however, only if there is an opening to all forms of transcendence, interpreted according to each person's convictions; and
   - Everyone in the company, therefore, has the responsibility and freedom to constantly ask for help through various forms of inner silence, reflection, renewal, meditation, and for some silent prayer.

According to Robert, as these responsibilities were fulfilled, a set of 18 values was reinforced:

Dignity	Justice	Serenity
Efficiency	Responsibility	Solidarity
Authenticity	Economic prudence	Wisdom
Faith	Hope	Brotherhood
Freedom	Love	Listening to others
Courage	Humility	Forgiveness

For a description of these 18 values, see Exhibit 4. However, he identified six core values: two humanization values (solidarity, brotherhood); two spiritualization values (faith, hope); and two values that are mixed in humanization and spiritualization (dignity, listening to others).

Robert considered it essential to "live" these core and peripheral values, and to act on them, not just endorse them. For example, to reinforce the values, Robert and his team selected directors and managers who had "a heart of flesh rather than a heart of stone." In his view, there was an abundance of people with the right set of knowledge and skills to perform well in any organization, but to succeed at Tomasso individuals also needed to have the right value set. The selection process to get people with a "brilliant brain and a heart of flesh" was therefore rigorous. For example, during the selection process, Robert and his team made it a practice to meet the candidate and his or her partner over one or more dinners. He wanted to make sure that the value set that managers brought to the job and the organization would fit with the values at Tomasso.

✎ Activities

The activities—lived out on paid time— through which the six responsibilities were fulfilled were categorized into three types of management tools.

The first kind of management tool fostered humanization and community values. These activities included:

a) A gesture (e.g. to serve a meal to homeless people);

b) The annual shared bonus, given to all employees;

c) Non-stereotyped, warm, and authentic communication; and

d) The Award of the Heart, given annually to an employee who showed compassion to someone else regardless of their hierarchical relationship.

The second kind of management tool fostered a blend of humanization and spiritualization values. These activities included:

a) The testimonial meetings (e.g. inviting people from outside Tomasso to share a personal crisis, joy, or suffering); and

b) The annual, one-on-one, non-economic meeting. This meeting gave managers an opportunity to sit down with their employees, for an hour, to discuss various topics. Employees were encouraged to vent their frustrations. Performance and salaries were not discussed during this meeting.

The third kind of management tool fostered spiritualization values. Examples included the following:

a) The availability of a meditation room (e.g. a place where employees could find some inner peace, take a time out, and have the opportunity for a silent prayer); and

b) Encouraging moments of inner silence, including at the beginning and end of board meetings, and committee meetings (e.g. Robert was inspired by Mother Teresa's belief that silence is the beginning of wisdom).

Robert believed that spirituality in life and management was essential for health and personal and organizational performance. In his words:

The spiritual is traditionally contrasted with the material, the temporal and the worldly. A perceived sense of connection forms a central defining characteristic of spirituality— connection to a metaphysical reality greater than oneself, which may include an emotional experience of religious awe and reverence, or such states as satori or Nirvana. Spirituality as a way of life concerns itself with aligning the human will and mind with the dimension of life and the universe that is harmonious and ordered. In all cases without exception when there is no spirituality . . . we all become very efficient at exploiting one another . . . we need some encouragement and guidance

from above, wherever the above is. When we have increasing wealth . . . it can make us more self-centered. What can we do to suppress our selfish desires?

He illustrated how a system of values ought to operate in a company, depicting this interplay as a feedback loop. His model is shown in Exhibit 5. Robert stated:

This illustration helps us understand the movement of values fostered by the various activities associated with the management tools. The understanding of the movement of values circulating in a feedback loop . . . is very important. In this more complex illustration . . . we see how the movement of values functions in the daily life of Our Project. We finally understood the way it works only after a long, wonderful, but often difficult experimentation process.

The feedback loops indicated that building and sustaining a core set of values was a never-ending process; the message of authenticity and caring might sound simple but it was hard work to bring these elements into the fabric of the organization. Authenticity, stated Robert, referred to the truthfulness of attributions, commitments, sincerity, devotion and intentions.

The introduction of the various activities was met with cautiousness and resistance; the room for inner silence and reflection was just one example. The experimentation at Cordon Bleu and Tomasso had been going on for more than 20 years.

Robert found great solace in the writings of Adam Smith, the father of the free market system, who wrote a number of books underlining the importance of the presence of moral and spiritual values in the economic system. For example, in his book *Wealth of Nations*, Smith wrote that:

> No benevolent man ever lost altogether the fruits of his benevolence. If he does not always gather them from the persons from whom he ought to have gathered them, he seldom fails to gather them, and with a tenfold increase, from other people. Kindness is the parent of kindness; and if to be beloved by our brethren be the great object of our ambition, the surest way of obtaining it is, by our conduct to show that we really love them.[3]

Robert felt that this quote nicely described what he and his colleagues were trying to do at Tomasso.

The responsibilities, activities and values encompassed by Our Project began when an employee was recruited and carried on even after an employee's employment was terminated. When an employee was recruited, it was important for both parties to assess if the employee would fit well within Tomasso's culture. Multiple interviews were held with the dual objectives to learn about the employee's personal values and for the employee to learn about Tomasso's values. The employee's family members were also invited to meet managers at Tomasso. This rigorous recruiting process enabled Tomasso to carefully select employees who would embrace and espouse the values shared at the firm.

If an employee were let go for any reason, Tomasso managers would take the responsibility to be in constant contact with the employee long after his or her termination. The follow-up with former employees as they transitioned to new employers was intended to demonstrate the concern Tomasso had for them. As such, it was not unusual for Tomasso managers to be in contact with ex-employees six to eight months after they had left Tomasso. In most cases, over time, ex-employees appreciated the fact that their former employer was concerned for their future well-being.

Continued Success of Our Project

Robert was convinced that five conditions had to be met to ensure the success of the integration of economic and human values within the company. These conditions were:

1. The primacy of people—focusing on the inner development of people before focusing on efficiency and profitability;

2. Freedom—having a healthy climate where people feel free to participate in the activities;

3. Leadership—support from upper management and the board of directors in words and deeds, even in the face of challenges in implementing activities;

4. Progressive implementation—accepting that progress in the implementation of activities will be slow; and

5. Support group—having a core group of people believe in Our Project, who not only work together but, within the group, share their experience with each other and even meditate together.

A Chief Spiritual Officer was appointed to the senior leadership team in 2007. The position is a part-time job. The main responsibility of the Chief Spiritual Officer is to oversee the continuous development of Our Project.

---

[3]Adam Smith, *An Inquiry Into the Nature and Causes of the Wealth of Nations*, Methuen and Co. Ltd, London, 1904.

✕ Measurement

Robert and his management team surveyed their employees every two years, to see what, if any, improvements to the system must be made. The survey focused on the activities, values, communication, degree of authenticity, working conditions, personal development and organizational climate (see Exhibit 6). The results of the survey allowed the management team to systematically identify the areas of tension and difficulties in its operations and thus to take corrective action. Outside professionals were hired to interview employees in the company. The results of the survey as well as a plan of action for improvement were subsequently submitted to the board of directors and to the employees. The company also used 360-degree evaluations to monitor how well the managers lived the values that reflect Our Project. In addition to surveys and evaluations, Robert and his management team used focus groups to better understand their workplace environment.

✕ Organizational Performance

The achievements by Tomasso can be characterized as solid. Robert pointed to a series of results to support his hypothesis that the two ISMAs can work side by side. Robert also believed that it was during times of economic difficulty that management had to work especially hard to reconcile the tension between the economic and human ISMAs by focusing on the keystone.

Robert understood that observers were skeptical about his theory and the ISMAs that he implemented. "I was a skeptic myself," he acknowledged. "But I was looking for something that could make the workplace more human, caring, spiritual, and eventually competitive." But many people still felt that while they agreed with the principles of Robert's message, the approach towards managing his company does not work for every single company, including large, publicly traded organizations. Besides . . . Robert had closed plants in the past and let people go. Was that caring? Did that demonstrate brotherhood?

✕ Implementing "Our Project" at Tomasso

By 2000, Tomasso employed more than 100 people and was selling products to Mexico and the United States. To keep up with demand, a large percentage of employees worked overtime and temporary employees were hired to work on weekends. Business was good.

As Tomasso grew rapidly, it became difficult for the two brothers to get to know the newly hired employees. Tomasso's culture began to change from that of a family-run, close-knit business, to one that was more hierarchical and structured. Conflict between management and employees began to arise as the latter complained of being overworked with no corresponding increase in reward or recognition. Employees began to see management as "too harsh" and they unionized.

The issues of conflict and lack of trust were amplified when employees were transferred to start a new factory in Baie-d'Urfé, a suburb located near the western tip of the Island of Montreal. With a modern, state-of-the-art facility, constraints on production were removed. As a consequence, the availability of overtime hours dropped. In addition, employees now had to work in damp, refrigerated conditions, with temperatures kept steady at a few degrees above zero. Although productivity was improved, customer service suffered as employees struggled with the new production machinery and computer-based ordering systems. Sales, which had been growing, dropped as some customers reduced orders or cancelled contracts.

In response, the Tomasso brothers reduced working hours to 32 a week from 40, and wage cuts resulted. This reduction occurred in May 2001, in the midst of a recession in Canada. By the end of 2001, the Tomasso brothers had left the company after tensions increased between them and Robert. The Tomasso brothers had never developed enthusiasm about Robert's values and the associated management practices; they never fully implemented them.

Robert appointed Benoit Gauthier, a consultant, as president to turn around the morale and deal with the performance problems. Gauthier was employed on an interim basis while a permanent president could be found. Some of the long-term employees at Tomasso experienced the departure of Paolo and Marco Tomasso as a significant loss.

 Decision

Robert and Benoit wondered how they should manage the various issues at Tomasso. Robert always emphasized the balance between the human and economic issues. Could they be balanced here? The two goals pulled in different directions! Combining them seemed like an impossible task. The skeptics were watching the situation closely. How would the management team act? Would their words and actions match? Were the leaders vulnerable to the perception that any action they took to address the company's economic ills could compromise the core values of the company?

Exhibit 1   Letter

LETTER FROM MOTHER TERESA
CALCUTTA, February 1995

LDM

MISSIONARIES OF CHARITY
54A ACHARYA J. CHANDRA BOSE ROAD
CALCUTTA 700016. INDIA

24 February 1995

Dear Mr. Ouimet,

Thank you for sending me the beautiful prayer you have composed for all those who work with you. I am sure that it will be a source of many blessings for all. Thank God that He is leading you to help many people to pray, for prayer gives a clean heart and a clean heart can see God. If we see God in one another, then we will want to love and serve Him in each other.

I have had one of the Sisters type your prayer at the back of this picture I was given of God the Father. There are just a few very small changes in it. In the picture God the Father is holding the world close to His Heart to show how much He loves each one of us. Let us be His own love, compassion and presence to everyone we meet.

Please also pray for our poor and for me.

God bless you,

M Teresa mc

SOURCE: J.-Robert Ouimet's dissertation.

Exhibit 2   Two ISMAs and the Keystone[1]

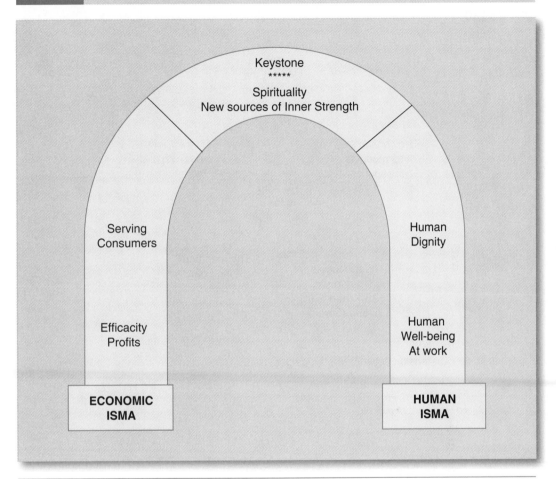

SOURCE: J.-Robert Ouimet's dissertation.

[1]All stakeholders in the company freely interpret the value of Transcendence and Spirituality of their choice. Transcendence and Spirituality are represented in the keystone. Transcendence can mean the Creator; the Higher Power; God Love; God the Father, Son, and Holy Spirit; Allah; Jehovah; Buddha; or any other opening to Transcendence. Only belief in a God of Love or in the Transcendence and Spirituality of our individual choice can help to reconcile in daily management, balance growth of human wellbeing—productivity and profits.

| Exhibit 3 | Six Circles of Responsibilities |

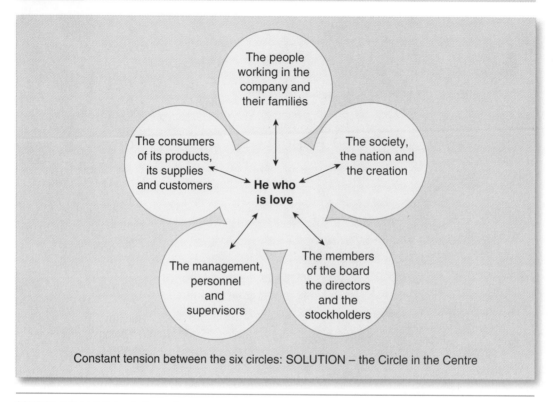

Constant tension between the six circles: SOLUTION – the Circle in the Centre

SOURCE: J.-Robert Ouimet's dissertation.

| Exhibit 4 | The Values |

DIGNITY

Dignity means the respect due to all people. It is based on the following principle: human beings are to be treated as ends in themselves, each person being unique, and not as means, instruments, or human capital.

SERENITY

Serenity is a state of the soul whose calm tranquility comes from an untroubled, moral or inner peace.

SOLIDARITY

Solidarity is the relationship between people who are aware of the community of interest that leads to the reciprocal, moral obligation to serve others.

BROTHERHOOD

Brotherhood is the quality of the link between people working in the company.

AUTHENTICITY

Authenticity is the quality of a person, of a feeling, that expresses a profound truth about the individual, not superficial attitudes or conventions.

ECONOMIC PRUDENCE

Economic prudence is the mental attitude of people who reflect on the extent and consequences of their acts, who choose appropriate means for attaining an objective, who do what is necessary to avoid errors and to refrain from everything they feel could cause harm.

WISDOM

Wisdom is a mental disposition to judge in a just, sure, and conscious way when making decisions and taking action.

LISTENING TO OTHERS

Listening to others means lending an attentive ear to the message that others communicate.

JUSTICE

Justice is the firm and long-term determination to recognize in all people their fundamental, human rights and to promote them.

FAITH

Faith is confidence and belief.

HOPE

Hope is waiting with the confidence that valued objectives will be attained.

FREEDOM

Freedom is people's capacity to initiate and to choose when they control their actions and can be held morally responsible for them.

RESPONSIBILITY

Responsibility is the capacity and the action that commit people to fulfill their duties and commitments and to repair their mistakes.

LOVE

Love is the desire for what appears to be the greatest good and to make that a reality, especially the desire to do for others what is good and right.

EFFICIENCY

Efficiency is the capacity to produce the maximum results with the minimum of effort along with the optimal use of resources.

HUMILITY

Humility is people's capacity to correctly evaluate themselves in their way of being and in relation to others and to the Absolute. It dampens pride, accepts or chooses to give up things according to circumstances, and freely matures in its way of handling tensions and conflicts. It uproots tendencies toward self-sufficiency that inhibit the recognition of the Absolute or God Love, which is present in others in their resolute commitment to serve.

SOURCE: Company files.

Exhibit 5 The Feedback Loop

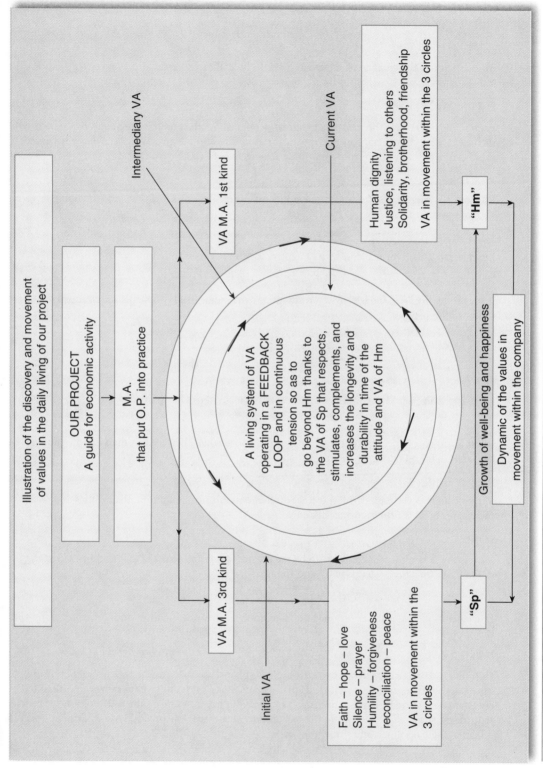

Illustration of the discovery and movement of values in the daily living of our project

OUR PROJECT
A guide for economic activity

M.A.
that put O.P. into practice

Intermediary VA

VA M.A. 1st kind

Current VA

Human dignity
Justice, listening to others
Solidarity, brotherhood, friendship
VA in movement within the 3 circles

A living system of VA operating in a FEEDBACK LOOP and in continuous tension so as to go beyond Hm thanks to the VA of Sp that respects, stimulates, complements, and increases the longevity and durability in time of the attitude and VA of Hm

"Hm"

Growth of well-being and happiness

Dynamic of the values in movement within the company

Initial VA

VA M.A. 3rd kind

Faith – hope – love
Silence – prayer
Humility – forgiveness
reconciliation – peace
VA in movement within the 3 circles

"Sp"

SOURCE: J.-Robert Ouimet's dissertation.

NOTE: M.A. —Management Activities, O.P. —Our Project, VA—Values, Sp—Spiritualization, Hm—Humanization

| **Exhibit 6** | The Survey Items |

No.	Question Asked	Main Value Measured
1	My responsibilities are generally defined, and on the whole I know what is expected of me.	Responsibility, Efficiency
2	I am properly paid for the work I do.	Justice
3	The social benefits (group insurance, etc.) that are offered to me are on the whole adequate considering the market.	Justice
4	The physical environment in which I work seems to me acceptable.	Human Dignity
5	Communication with management is on the whole adequate.	Efficiency, Listening to Others, Authenticity
6	Management knows about our problems and tries to take our suggestions into account when possible.	Listening to Others, Human Dignity
7	Communication with my immediate supervisor is normal.	Efficiency, Listening to Others, Authenticity
8	Communication with other departments is normal, and their collaboration is available when necessary.	Efficiency, Listening to Others, Authenticity
9	Communication in my work group is normal, and I have correct relations with my coworkers.	Efficiency, Listening to Others, Authenticity
10	Work is properly organized, and I can do my job correctly.	Economic Prudence, Efficiency
11	I am reasonably confident about keeping my job in my company during the coming year.	Productivity, Human Dignity
12	My chances for advancement in my company are normal.	Justice, Productivity
13	My company has normally contributed to my training and skills development.	Human Dignity, Efficiency
14	I neither agree nor disagree with the commercial objectives of my company.	Economic Prudence, Efficiency
15	I neither agree nor disagree with the non-economic objectives of my company (Our Project).	Freedom
17	In my company, the employees are treated neither better nor worse than in the other companies I know.	Dignity
18	I am satisfied working for my company; I believe that working elsewhere would not necessarily be better.	Freedom, Human Dignity
19	Since the first day I arrived at J.-R. Ouimet, I believe that my experience in the company has neither favored nor hindered my personal development and growth.	Solidarity, Brotherhood

(Continued)

Exhibit 6	(Continued)	

No.	Question Asked	Main Value Measured
20	Do you feel obligated to participate in the activities related to Our Project?	Freedom, Human Dignity
21	The possibility of freely expressing my opinions at JRO.	Freedom
22	The support, acceptance, and generosity of my colleagues regarding the difficulties I encounter at work.	Solidarity
23	The support, acceptance, and generosity of my colleagues regarding the difficulties I encounter in my personal life.	Brotherhood, Solidarity
24	The sincerity of the people that I relate to in all sorts of ways in my company.	Authenticity
25	Do you want to keep the silence and meditation room on your work site?	Freedom, Human Dignity, Faith, Hope

SOURCE: Company files.

Servant-Leaders Are the Best Leaders During Times of Change[1]

Kent M. Keith

What kind of leader do I want to follow during a time of change? I want to follow a servant-leader.

Why? Because servant-leaders do not use organizational change as the excuse for building their own power and position. They do not make changes based on personalities, factional politics, and competition between rivals. Instead, servant-leaders focus on meeting the needs of the organization and those it serves. Servant-leaders listen, consult, and analyze information so that the organization can adapt and remain relevant to changing needs. Hard decisions may have to be made, but if so, they will be made by giving

priority to the needs of employees, customers, business partners, and the communities in which the servant leaders operate.

Who is a servant-leader? A servant-leader is any leader who is focused on identifying and meeting the needs of others, rather than trying to acquire power, wealth, and fame for oneself. Servant-leaders love people, and enjoy helping them. That gives them a lot of meaning and satisfaction in their lives and their work.

One of the best things about servant-leaders is that they don't bring a lot of ego baggage with them. They don't worry about their own personal status or prestige. They just focus on the

---

[1] © Copyright Kent M. Keith 2009, Dr. Kent M. Keith is CEO of the Greenleaf Center for Servant Leadership, based in Westfield, Indiana (www.greenleaf.org). This article is based on his book, *The Case for Servant Leadership*, © Copyright Kent M. Keith 2008.

problem or opportunity at hand. That makes it a lot easier for people to work with them and follow them through the change process. There's an old saying that "it's amazing how much we get done around here when nobody cares who gets the credit." That's what servant-leaders are like. They are focused on the work, not the credit.

Fortunately, there are millions of servant-leaders around the world, quietly taking care of their families and communities, and moving their organizations forward. Sadly, there aren't enough servant-leaders in the world. That may be because the dominant model of leadership in our society is the power model. According to the power model, leadership is about acquiring and wielding power. It is about clever strategies, and how to make people do things. It is about how to attack and win.

Unfortunately, there are a lot of problems with the power model. First, the power model of leadership focuses on having power, not on using it wisely. Power is an end in itself.

Second, the power model of leadership promotes conflict between power groups or factions. People are taught that leadership is about power, so they establish themselves in power groups that compete with other power groups. These power groups become so focused on their rivalries with each other, that they can't focus on solving problems or seizing opportunities. Things don't get done.

Third, the power model defines success in terms of who gains more power, not in terms of who accomplishes the most for his or her organization or community.

There are two more problems with the power model, and that is the impact that it has on the leaders who use it. First, people who seek power often become irrelevant as leaders. They focus on what they want, instead of what other people need, and they lose touch with the people they are supposed to be serving. Second, people who seek power can never get enough of it. It becomes a kind of disease. They always want more, and more, and more. This easily results in spiritual corruption and an unhappy life of self-torment.

Servant-leaders live another model of leadership—the service model. The service model is not about acquiring power, it's about making a difference. So servant-leaders do not ask, "How can I get power? How can I make people do things?" Servant-leaders ask, "What do people need? How can I help them to get it? What does my organization need to do? How can I help my organization to do it?" Thus, rather than embarking on a quest for personal power, servant-leaders embark on a quest to identify and meet the needs of others.

One way to contrast a power-oriented leader and a service-oriented leader is this: Power-oriented leaders want to make people do things. Servant-leaders want to help people do things. That's why servant-leaders are usually facilitators, coordinators, healers, partners, and coalition-builders.

There is another big difference between the power model and the service model of leadership. The power model assumes a hierarchy. Only a few people have power— those at the top of the hierarchy—so it is assumed that only they can be leaders. In the service model, the hierarchy doesn't matter. That's because anybody in a family, organization, or community can be of service. Anybody can identify and meet the needs of others. Anybody can respond to the call to be a servant-leader.

Perhaps the simplest way to explain the difference is this: The power model is about grabbing. The service model is about giving.

Now, we live in a real world. We know that power abhors a vacuum. Somebody is going to exercise power, and it makes a difference who that somebody is. Certainly, a servant-leader can accumulate and exercise power. A servant-leader can even become angry and do battle. However, for the servant-leader, power is only a tool, one among many tools. It is only a means, not an end. So a servant-leader accumulates power or becomes angry on behalf of others. A servant-leader acts in response to the way others are treated, not in response to the way he or she is treated.

Servant-leaders can be many different types of leader, depending on their personalities and the specific circumstances. What they have in common is this. They go into a group or organization and ask, is there a gap or missing link or blockage of some kind that is making it hard for this group to achieve the change that it needs to achieve? If so, can I identify what that gap or missing link or blockage is? If I can identify it, can I do something about it? If I can't do anything about it, can I find someone who can? Since the missing link or gap or blockage will not always be the same, the servant-leader does not always perform the same role or service in each case.

The Modern Servant Leadership Movement

The modern servant leadership movement was launched by Robert K. Greenleaf, who was born and raised in Indiana. He worked for AT&T from 1926 to 1964. Toward the end of his career, he was AT&T's Director of Management Research. It was his job to figure out how leaders and managers at AT&T could become most effective.

After Greenleaf retired, he reflected and decided that there had to be a better model than the power model of leadership. In 1970 he published an essay entitled The Servant as Leader, in which he coined the phrase "servant-leader" and launched the modern servant leadership movement in America. Hundreds of thousands of people have read that essay since it was first published.

Greenleaf understood the difference between the power model and the service model. He compared leaders who are "leader first," and those who are a "servant first." Greenleaf said:

The servant-leader is servant first . . . It begins with the natural feeling that one wants to serve, to serve first. Then conscious choice brings one to aspire to lead. That person is sharply different from one who is leader first, perhaps because of the need to assuage an unusual power drive or to acquire material possessions . . . The leader-first and the servant-first are two extreme types . . .

The difference manifests itself in the care taken by the servant-first to make sure that other people's highest priority needs are being served. The best test, and difficult to administer, is: Do those served grow as persons? Do they, while being served, become healthier, wiser, freer, more autonomous, more likely themselves to become servants? And, what is the effect on the least privileged in society? Will they benefit, or at least not be further deprived?

There are a number of key practices that help servant-leaders to be effective in the daily world of work. For example, they are aware of their own strengths and weaknesses. They are good at listening to colleagues and customers, so they know what people need, and can focus on providing it. They develop their colleagues, coach and mentor them, and unleash their energy and intelligence. They have foresight, and act on that foresight, for the long-term benefit of their organizations.

Servant-leaders are sustained in their work by the personal meaning that comes from serving others. That personal meaning is an intrinsic motivator, a source of mental health, and a key to being deeply happy. These are tremendous advantages not available to other kinds of leaders.

How do we get more servant-leaders? Through education and training, and modeling the values, characteristics, and practices of servant-leaders. We will also get more servant-leaders if we, the people, are committed to following servant-leaders instead of power-oriented leaders. Greenleaf hoped that people would decide to follow servant-leaders, instead of power-oriented leaders, so that in the future, "the only truly viable institutions will be those that are predominantly servant-led." That's a future that would be very good, indeed—for all of us.

Authentic Leadership

Daina Mazutis

IMD

[L]eadership is integral to the leader as a person; leadership is the leader because it allows that person to demonstrate insight not only about the issues at hand but also about himself or herself and his or her values. Leadership is, therefore, as much internal—the way one is (in one's being and becoming identity, character and temperament)—as it is external, in the actions one takes.

—Elena Antonacopoulou and Regina Bento[1]

As a response to the seemingly pervasive ethical scandals that dominated the business headlines at the beginning of this century and during the past decade, the public demand for more honest, more trustworthy, and more genuine leadership has become increasingly animated. Both practitioners and social scientists have heeded this call and attempted to define a new approach to leadership that is based on the positive characteristics, behaviors, and capabilities of authentic leaders. Although still in its early developmental stages, the theoretical and practical approaches to understanding authentic leadership are presented in this chapter.

Authentic Leadership Defined

Authentic leadership was first defined by Luthans and Avolio (2003) as a process described as being a style:

> which results in both greater self-awareness and self-regulated positive behaviors on the part of leaders and associates, fostering positive self-development. The authentic leader is confident,

---

[1]Antonacopoulou and Bento (2011, p. 72).

hopeful, optimistic, resilient, transparent, moral/ethical, future-oriented, and gives priority
to developing associates to be leaders. (p. 243)

Since then, multiple definitions of authentic leadership have been explored, each conceived from a
unique standpoint and emphasizing different components of the theory. Intrapersonal, interpersonal,
and developmental definitions are considered below (Northouse, 2013).

Intrapersonal definitions, such as the one developed by Shamir and Eilam (2005), focus on the
leader himself or herself. In this view, authentic leaders have highly developed systems of self-
knowledge and self-regulation. They have realistic concepts of self that are rooted in strong values
and base their actions on these core values, exhibiting genuine leadership and leading from conviction (Shamir & Eilam, 2005). These values include loyalty, responsibility, trustworthiness, integrity,
accountability, respect, and fairness, in addition to attributes such as self-awareness, emotional
intelligence, and self-certainty (Michie & Gooty, 2005). This approach also stresses the importance
of the intrapersonal experiences of authentic leaders, both in the role that their personal life stories
have had in their development as well as in the role that followers play in affirming the legitimacy
of the leader and his or her behavior (Gardner, Avolio, Luthans, May, & Walumbwa, 2005; Shamir
& Eilam, 2005).

Interpersonal definitions, on the other hand, emphasize the relational aspect of authentic leadership, which is dependent on the reciprocal interactions of leaders and followers (Eagly, 2005). Here,
authentic leaders are seen not only as hopeful and optimistic, but also as builders of confidence,
hope, and trust (Avolio, Gardner, Walumbwa, Luthans, & May, 2004). Through positive modeling,
personal and social identification, emotional contagion, and positive social exchanges, authentic
leaders foster positive follower attitudes and outcomes (Avolio & Gardner, 2005; Gardner et al.,
2005). However, only if followers identify with the values of the leader will positive outcomes arise;
there must therefore be a high degree of buy-in from followers for authentic leadership to be effective (Northouse, 2013).

Developmental definitions assert that both intrapersonal characteristics and interpersonal behaviors are qualities that can be developed into authentic leadership. Several researchers, for example,
have suggested that positive psychological capabilities such as self-awareness, internalized moral
perspective, balanced processing, and relational transparency are skills that can be taught. These capabilities are thus not conceived of as static personality traits but rather as behaviors that can be nurtured and developed over time or can even be triggered by major life events. Many explorations of
authentic leadership take this explicitly developmental approach (Avolio & Gardner, 2005).

From a theoretical perspective, however, the most recent definition of authentic leadership that best
captures the intrapersonal, interpersonal, and developmental approaches is

a pattern of leader behavior that draws upon and promotes both positive psychological
capacities and a positive ethical climate, to foster greater self-awareness, an internalized
moral perspective, balanced processing of information, and relational transparency on the
part of leaders working with followers, fostering positive self-development. (Walumbwa,
Avolio, Gardner, Wernsing, & Peterson, 2008, p. 94)

Although complex, this definition includes many of the components of authentic leadership that are
currently being developed in the social science literature. This theoretical approach to authentic leadership is discussed in the next section, followed by a brief discussion of the more practical approach
that has evolved simultaneously in the popular business press.

Theoretical Approaches

Research on authentic leadership was originally spearheaded out of the University of Nebraska, where Luthans and Avolio (2003) first wrote about authentic leadership development as a model of leadership that was more ethical and more humane than what was being portrayed in the popular business press after the ethical scandals at WorldCom, Tyco, and Enron, to name a few. Although other models of leadership, such as transformational leadership, also include positive components, the meaning of authentic transformational leadership had yet to be fully explored. The related fields of ethics, positive psychology, and positive organizational scholarship were drawn upon in this foundational period (Northouse, 2013).

In addition to Luthans and Avolio's (2003) developmental perspective, different models of authentic leadership have also been proposed. As discussed above, some of these models focused on leader values and attributes (e.g., Michie & Gooty, 2005), while others have focused on the interpersonal effects of authentic leadership. For example, Ilies, Morgeson, and Nahrgang's (2005) model focused on the outcomes of authentic leadership and the positive effects on follower well-being. Similarly, both Avolio et al. (2004) and Gardner et al. (2005) argued that authentic leadership has positive effects on follower trust, hope, and positive emotions, resulting in increased meaningfulness, commitment, engagement, and workplace well-being. Empirically, authentic leadership has been shown to be a strong predictor of group-level leadership outcomes such as employee job satisfaction and performance (Walumbwa et al., 2008). Theoretically, authentic leadership has also been applied to firm-level outcomes such as organizational learning (Mazutis & Slawinski, 2008).

Recent theoretical and empirical work, however, has converged around four primary components that form the core of authentic leadership theory: self-awareness, relational transparency, internalized moral perspective, and balanced processing (Avolio & Gardner, 2005; Gardner et al., 2005; Ilies et al., 2005; Kernis, 2003; Mazutis & Slawinski, 2008; Northouse, 2013; Walumbwa et al., 2008). These four essential elements of authentic leadership are discussed in detail below.

Self-Awareness

Ilies et al. (2005) define a leader's self-awareness as "awareness of, and trust in, one's own personal characteristics, values, motives, feelings, and cognitions. Self-awareness includes knowledge of one's inherent contradictory self-aspects and the role of these contradictions in influencing one's thoughts, feelings, actions and behaviors" (p. 377). Because self-aware leaders understand their strengths and weaknesses, are tuned in to how their behavior affects others, and know who they are and what they stand for, other people perceive these leaders as more authentic (Gardner et al., 2005; Kernis, 2003).

Internalized Moral Perspective

The internalized moral perspective component of authentic leadership describes a process of self-regulation whereby "leaders align their values with their intentions and actions" (Avolio & Gardner, 2005, p. 325). Authentic leaders will resist external pressures that are contrary to their moral standards through an internal regulation process that ensures that their values are congruent with the anticipated outcomes of a behavior (Gardner et al., 2005). By aligning their values and actions and acting according to their own "true selves," leaders demonstrate consistency in what they say and what they do that translates into more authentic leadership.

Balanced Processing

Balanced processing is also referred to as *unbiased processing*. Authentic leaders are able to hear, interpret, and process both negative and positive information in an objective manner before making decisions or taking any action. This includes objectively evaluating their own words and deeds without ignoring or distorting anything that has been presented (Kernis, 2003), including interpretations of their own leadership style (Gardner et al., 2005). Balanced processing is linked to a leader's integrity and character (Ilies et al., 2005) as other perspectives are considered along with the leader's own, thus increasing attributions of authenticity.

Relational Transparency

It is not enough to be self-aware, congruent in values and actions, and objective in one's interpretations; an authentic leader must also be willing to communicate this information in an open and honest manner with others through truthful self-disclosure (Ilies et al., 2005). If it is difficult to be aware and unbiased about one's own weaknesses, it is even more difficult to expose these weaknesses to others in the organization. However, being transparent with one's feelings, motives, and inclinations builds trust and feelings of stability, fostering teamwork and cooperation (Gardner et al., 2005; Kernis, 2003). Leaders who demonstrate relational transparency will therefore be perceived as more real and more authentic.

Other Factors That Influence Authentic Leadership

Researchers have also identified several other elements that influence authentic leadership development, including (1) positive psychological capacities, (2) moral reasoning, and (3) critical life events (Northouse, 2013). First, it has been argued that authentic leaders possess the positive psychological attributes of confidence, hope, optimism, and resilience (Luthans & Avolio, 2003). These trait-like characteristics could be seen as fixed aspects of personality; however, they can also be developed through training or coaching. Confident, hopeful, optimistic, and resilient leaders welcome challenges, inspire followers, and expect favorable outcomes, yet they also adapt positively to unfavorable ones (Avolio & Gardner, 2005).

Second, moral reasoning might be an important antecedent to authentic leadership. Moral reasoning refers to the capacity to make ethical decisions. Although this develops over a lifetime, this capacity allows authentic leaders to make more balanced decisions that serve the greater good over time (Northouse, 2013).

Last, several researchers have also pointed out the role of critical life events, both positive and negative, that can act as catalysts for change, promoting individual growth, learning, and understanding and helping individuals become stronger, more authentic leaders (Luthans & Avolio, 2003; Shamir & Eilam, 2005).

◪ Practical Approaches

At the same time as a theory of authentic leadership was being developed in academia, business practitioners were also discussing the need for more honest, ethical, and accountable models of leadership. This gave rise to several practical how-to books about authentic leadership such as *Authentic Leadership: Courage in Action* by Robert Terry (1993) and *Authentic Leadership: Rediscovering the Secrets to Creating Lasting Value* by Bill George (2003). Most recently, Goffee and Jones (2006), professors and consultants at the London Business School, also published *Why Should Anyone Be Lead by You? What It Takes to Be an Authentic Leader.* These more popular practical approaches to authentic leadership are briefly described in this section.

Robert Terry's (1993) approach to authentic leadership revolves around his Authentic Action Wheel, a diagnostic tool designed to help leaders answer fundamental questions such as "What is really, *really* going on and what are we going to do about it?" Problems in the organization are categorized into six areas: meaning, mission, power, structure, resources, and existence. By locating a problem in one of these areas, leaders can then select an appropriate response that most faithfully addresses the root cause of the issue. This alignment allows leaders to base their actions on what is really happening in the organization, resulting in more authentic leadership (Northouse, 2013).

Bill George (2003), the former CEO of Medtronic and now a professor at Harvard Business School, popularized the term *authentic leadership* again a decade later by reflecting on his 30 years of business success. His approach can be seen as encompassing intrapersonal, interpersonal, and developmental aspects of authentic leaders. Specifically, authentic leadership has five core dimensions (purpose, values, relationships, self-discipline, and heart) that authentic leaders can access (or learn to access) through their behavior, passion, consistency, connectedness, and compassion. DuBrin (2010) suggests that "authenticity is about being genuine and honest about your personality, values and beliefs as well as having integrity" (p. 38). In general, authentic leaders display the following characteristics: (1) They are passionate about their purpose; (2) they have strong values and act on those values; (3) they establish trusting relationships with others; (4) they embody focus, determination, consistency, and self-discipline; and (5) they are genuinely compassionate, leading with heart.

Last, the authentic leadership approach proposed by Goffee and Jones (2006) is mostly intrapersonal, focusing on the relationship between the leader and the led. In this view, leadership is always situational, nonhierarchical, and relational and has little to do with fixed personal character traits. Here, authentic leaders are seen as particularly skilled at navigating the many tensions that are inherent in leading others, such as communicating (but not too much) and remaining true to oneself (but also conforming). The book presents some interesting insights into managing these paradoxes, providing many examples of how authentic leaders are better able to adapt their own strengths and weaknesses to the situation at hand.

How Does Authentic Leadership Work?

An empirically tested model of authentic leadership is still being developed, so important questions about its effectiveness have yet to be entirely substantiated. However, both theoretical and practical perspectives suggest that authentic leadership goes beyond a trait-based or a merely relational approach to leadership. Rather, authentic leaders may possess some key characteristics (such as confidence, hope, optimism, and resiliency) or core capabilities (such as self-awareness, relational transparency, internalized moral perspective, and balanced processing), but these abilities can also be developed over time and are enacted in relation to others. At the heart of most interpretations of authentic leadership is the notion that it is the opposite of the selfish and self-serving portrayals of corporate greed that dominated the headlines at the beginning of this century. Rather, authentic leaders have strong values upon which they act, trying to be honest with themselves and others; authentic leaders are transparent and trustworthy, striving to do what is right or good for their followers, their organizations and society as a whole. As such, authentic leadership theory provides, at minimum, some insightful questions for those seeking a more positive and more ethical approach to leadership and leadership development. Yukl (2010) stated that authentic leaders "do not seek leadership positions to gratify a need for esteem, status, and power, but rather to express and enact their values and beliefs" (p. 424).

⊠ References

Antonacopoulou, E., & Bento, R. (2011). "Learning leadership" in practice. In J. Storey (Ed.), *Leadership in Organizations: Current Issues and Trends* (2nd ed., pp. 71–92). New York, NY: Routledge.

Avolio, B. J., Gardner, W. L., Walumbwa, F. O., Luthans, F., & May, D. R. (2004). Unlocking the mask: A look at the process by which authentic leaders impact follower attitudes and behavior. *Leadership Quarterly, 15*, 801–823.

Avolio, B. J., & Gardner, W. L. (2005). Authentic leadership development: Getting to the root of positive forms of leadership. *Leadership Quarterly, 16*, 315–338.

DuBrin, A. J. (2010). *Leadership: Research findings, practice, and skills* (6th ed.). Mason, OH: South-Western/ Cengage.

Eagly, A. H. (2005). Achieving relational authenticity in leadership: Does gender matter? *Leadership Quarterly, 16*, 459–474.

Gardner, W. L., Avolio, B. J., Luthans, F., May, D. R., & Walumbwa, F. O. (2005). Can you see the real me? A self-based model of authentic leader and follower development. *Leadership Quarterly, 16*, 343–372.

George, B. (2003). *Authentic leadership: Rediscovering the secrets to creating lasting value.* San Francisco, CA: Jossey-Bass.

Goffee, R., & Jones, G. (2006). *Why should anyone be led by you? What it takes to be an authentic leader.* Boston, MA: Harvard Business School Press.

Ilies, R., Morgeson, F. P., & Nahrgang, J. D. (2005). Authentic leadership and eudaemonic well-being: Understanding leader–follower outcomes. *Leadership Quarterly, 16*, 373–394.

Kernis, M. H. (2003). Toward a conceptualization of optimal self-esteem. *Psychological Inquiry, 14*, 1–26.

Luthans, F., & Avolio, B. J. (2003). Authentic leadership development. In K. S. Cameron, J. E. Dutton, & R. E. Quinn (Eds.), *Positive organizational scholarship* (pp. 241–258). San Francisco, CA: Berrett-Koehler.

Mazutis, D., & Slawinski, N. (2008). Leading organizational learning through authentic dialogue. *Management Learning, 39*(4), 437–456.

Michie, S., & Gooty, J. (2005). Values, emotions, and authenticity: Will the real leader please stand up? *Leadership Quarterly, 16*(3), 441–457.

Northouse, P. G. (2013). *Leadership: Theory and practice* (6th ed.). Thousand Oaks, CA: Sage.

Shamir, B., & Eilam, G. (2005). What's your story? A life-stories approach to authentic leadership development. *Leadership Quarterly, 16*, 395–417.

Terry, R. W. (1993). *Authentic leadership: Courage in action.* San Francisco, CA: Jossey-Bass.

Walumbwa, F. O., Avolio, B. J., Gardner, W. L., Wernsing, T. S., & Peterson, S. J. (2008). Authentic leadership: Development and validation of a theory-based measure. *Journal of Management, 34*(1), 89–126.

Yukl, G. (2010). *Leadership in organizations* (7th ed.). Upper Saddle River, NJ: Prentice Hall.

⊠ The Cases

Goedehoop: When Social Issues Become Strategic

This case chronicles a change process to counteract the epidemic of HIV/AIDS in a coal mine in South Africa that impacts the sustainability of the organization. The case illustrates the type of leadership activities needed to deal with a compelling environmental force affecting business. It shows how a wide range of stakeholders needs to be involved and systems and practices instituted for sustainable change to be implemented. It raises the question of the role of business in society.

Organization, Founder and Clientele Transformation at VGKK

In 1994, Dr. Sudarshan, a medical professional, was awarded the Right Livelihood Award (also known as the Alternative Nobel Prize) for his efforts in changing and transforming a development organization over 30 years. Dr. Sudarshan is a social entrepreneur who led the social transformation of the BR Hills of Southern India, a nonprofit organization. Dr. Sudarshan exhibited a foundation of ethics and self-organization and the assertion of individual and human rights as he worked for tribal and forest development.

⊠ The Reading

Compelling Visions: Content, Context, Credibility and Collaboration

The "vision thing" is still with us, but while leaders insist on having a compelling vision, the fact is that many—both the leaders and the visions—leave people standing still, unmoved. A leader who engages stakeholders when developing a vision will, in the end, articulate one that resonates strongly and impels people to act.

Goedehoop: When Social Issues Become Strategic

Verity Hawarden and Margie Sutherland

Dr. Brian Brink, senior vice-president of health at Anglo American South Africa, looked across his office in Johannesburg and reflected on the success of the HIV/AIDS programme at Goedehoop Colliery. By mid-2007, the programme had been recognised and applauded internationally; HIV infections and AIDS were "under control" at the mine and Goedehoop was considered to be a role model for the corporate response to AIDS in South Africa. His predicament now was what he should do in the next three months to ensure that all the other Anglo business units were as proactive as Goedehoop (pronounced "Ghood-uh-hoorp").

Brink had been actively involved in HIV/AIDS issues since the mid-1980s and was the driving force behind Anglo American's highly admired response to the epidemic. He acknowledged that the management of HIV and AIDS was an ongoing challenge for the Anglo companies operating in countries with a high burden of HIV disease. He was all too aware that the greatest risk was in eastern and southern Africa, where it was estimated that the HIV prevalence among Anglo employees was 18 per cent at the end of June 2007.[1] While he was extremely satisfied by Goedehoop Colliery's management of the syndrome, the high prevalence statistic of the Anglo group in sub-Saharan Africa worried him.

The reality was alarming. "The global epidemic of HIV/AIDS was rapidly becoming the worst infectious-disease catastrophe in recorded history."[2]

[1]http://www.angloamerican.co.uk/static/reports/2006/rts/hc-hiv-aids.htm, accessed April 11, 2007, and meeting with Dr. Brian Brink on Oct. 8, 2007.

[2]S. Rosen, J. Simon, J.R. Vincent, W. MacLeod, M. Fox and D.M. Thea, "AIDS is your business," *Harvard Business Review*, Feb. 2003, p. 81.

South Africa was one of the most severely affected countries worldwide and the potential economic consequences were disturbing due to the fact that over five million South Africans were infected by the HI virus.[3] It was reported that the overall HIV prevalence statistic in South Africa by mid-2006 was 11.2 per cent (19.2 per cent of adults between the ages of 20 to 64 were infected).[4] South African companies faced high risks to both direct and indirect costs as AIDS killed mainly young and middle-aged adults in their most productive years. By the end of 2007, approximately 2,170,000 people had died of AIDS-related deaths in South Africa, of whom approximately 355,000 died in 2006.[5] In mid-2007, the South African population was estimated to be 47.9 million;[6] therefore, deaths from AIDS to mid-2007 equated to approximately 4.5 per cent of the total population.

Brink knew that mining companies that responded positively to the HIV/AIDS epidemic also showed the greatest productivity and profitability. Goedehoop Colliery was a case in point. While most coal mines within Anglo Coal South Africa were following suit with increasingly successful HIV/AIDS programmes, it was the Anglo companies mining other minerals in South Africa that were not responding to the syndrome at the same level as Goedehoop. Brink understood the importance of effective management leadership to ensure a successful response.

He knew that, ultimately, the productivity and profitability of Anglo American South Africa would be adversely affected if all companies within the group did not take real ownership of the HIV/AIDS problem.

Anglo and AIDS

Anglo American plc was formed in May 1999 through the combination of Anglo American Corporation of South Africa (AACSA) and Minorco. It had its primary listing on the London Stock Exchange and was majority-owned by U.K. institutions. AACSA was founded in 1917 by Sir Ernest Oppenheimer to exploit the gold mining potential of the East Rand.[7] Employing approximately 160,000 people worldwide,[8] the Anglo American Group was a global leader in mining activities, owning a diversified range of businesses covering platinum, gold, diamonds, coal, base and ferrous metals, industrial minerals, paper and packaging.[9] Anglo American plc's coal interests were held through its wholly-owned Anglo Coal business, one of the world's largest private sector coal producers and exporters. Anglo Coal had mining operations in South Africa, Australia, Colombia, China and Venezuela.[10]

Anglo Coal had a 100 per cent shareholding in Goedehoop Colliery, one of its nine South African coal mines. Goedehoop Colliery was

---

[3]Bureau for Economic Research, "The impact of HIV/AIDS on selected business sectors in South Africa, 2005," Survey conducted by the Bureau for Economic Research and funded by the South African Business Coalition on HIV and AIDS, 2005.

[4]R.E. Dorrington, D. Bradshaw, L. Johnson T. and Daniel, "The Demographic Impact of HIV/AIDS in South Africa," *National and Provincial Indicators 2006*, Centre for Actuarial Research, South African Medical Research Council, Actuarial Society of South Africa, Cape Town, 2006, http://www.mrc.ac.za/bod/DemographicImpactHIVIndicators.pdf, accessed Oct. 15, 2007.

[5]Ibid.

[6]Statistics South Africa, "Mid-year population estimates, 2007 (P0302)," 2007, http://www.statssa.gov.za/publications/P0302/P03022007.pdf, accessed Oct. 4, 2007.

[7]http://www.angloamerican.co.uk/article/?afw_source_key=19ED07F3-C5AB-427C-BACE-6DABAC9037A7, accessed April 11, 2007.

[8]Anglo American plc Annual Report 2006.

[9]http://www.angloamerican.co.uk/ourbusiness, accessed April 11, 2007.

[10]http://www.angloamerican.co.uk/ourbusiness/thebusinesses/coal/geographic locations, accessed April 11, 2007.

located 40 kilometres southeast of Witbank in the province of Mpumalanga, 180 kilometres east of Johannesburg. Employing almost 2,000 permanent staff and just under 1,000 contractors, Goedehoop (Afrikaans for the term "good hope") produced both domestic coal and high-grade thermal coal for export customers. While a small quantity of low-grade coal was produced for the domestic market, Goedehoop Colliery was one of Anglo Coal's South African export mines. In 2005, Goedehoop won an award for being the safest colliery in Anglo Coal worldwide. Goedehoop's objective for 2006 was to be "the safest and lowest cost producer of green coal in Anglo Coal."[11] All employees were constantly driven by the mantra "SHE first . . . always!" which meant a strong focus on safety, health and the environment. Employees understood that adherence to these three factors contributed towards greater production and productivity, resulting in lower costs and higher profitability.

Anglo American plc's Group HIV/AIDS policy, first introduced in 1990, stated that Anglo "recognised the human tragedy caused by the HIV/AIDS epidemic. . . we are concerned about the gravity and implications of the epidemic for our operating companies."[12] In addition, Anglo American plc became increasingly concerned over the last decade about the health and well-being of its employees, their families and the communities in which the employees lived.[13]

Dr. Jan Pienaar, chief medical officer for Anglo Coal South Africa, asserted that "Anglo Coal holds the view that holistically healthy employees are key to the long term success of Anglo Coal."[14] Brink supported the latter assertion:

> Those organisations responding to HIV/AIDS with strong leadership at the CEO level, impact assessments based on real data, negotiated HIV/AIDS policies, up-to-date strategic HIV/AIDS responses, specific HIV/AIDS performance indicators and targets, and ongoing monitoring and evaluation also happen to show the greatest productivity, the most effective cost containment and the greatest profitability. A good response to HIV/AIDS is synonymous with good management, good business and a good investment.[15]

The Business of AIDS

The impact of HIV/AIDS on life expectancy and the South African economy was profound. In 2001, South African life expectancy was 51 years.[16] Estimates from 2007 suggested that by 2010, South African life expectancy would drop to only 42 years and the epidemic would have had a marked impact on firms' costs, productivity and demand for products.[17] It had been established that the scale and speed of the epidemic was much worse than was initially expected and the demographic, social and economic consequences would have a dramatic macro economic

---

[11]Anglo Coal, "Raising the AIDS bar at Goedehoop Colliery" brochure, Exhibit C.

[12]Anglo Coal, "Raising the AIDS bar at Goedehoop Colliery" brochure, Exhibit A.

[13]GBC (Global Business Coalition) Awards for Business Excellence 2007—submission by Anglo Coal South Africa.

[14]Ibid.

[15]Bureau for Economic Research, "The impact of HIV/AIDS on selected business sectors in South Africa, 2005," Survey conducted by the Bureau for Economic Research and funded by the South African Business Coalition on HIV and AIDS, 2005, p. 37.

[16]Statistics South Africa, "Mid-year population estimates, 2005 (P0302)," 2005, http://www.statssa.gov.za/publications/P0302/P03022005.pdf, accessed Oct. 3, 2007.

[17]J.D. Lewis, "Assessing the demographic and economic impact of HIV/AIDS" in *AIDS and South Africa: The social expression of a pandemic*, Palgrave Macmillan, New York, 2005, Chapter 5.

impact.[18] Gross domestic product (GDP) is one economic indicator that enables a measurement of economic output. Research had determined that the South African GDP level in 2010 would be 17 per cent lower in an AIDS scenario than it would have been if AIDS did not exist.[19]

The macro economic impact of HIV/AIDS on business was felt as a result of several factors, specifically, a lower supply of labour, lower labour productivity through absenteeism and illness, cost pressures for companies through higher benefit payments and replacement costs, and a lower customer base as the purchasing population decreased.[20] Private sector involvement in responding to the HIV/AIDS epidemic was thus crucial due to the economic impact being experienced.[21]

The impact of the above factors on business presented a growing challenge for management to create shareholder value if, in addition, it did not take certain social issues into account. Companies were held accountable by public opinion; they wanted to be viewed as responsible corporate citizens making a positive impact in the community.[22] Business could no longer distance itself from society; the extent to which a company was socially responsible was crucial for a positive public evaluation.[23] Bearing in mind the growing demand by shareholders for companies to manage their business with a triple bottom-line focus, it became apparent that companies could not simply have a rational response to the AIDS crisis, meaning that their response was based only on a cost-benefit ratio. A reasonable response was also required; this being when the company acknowledged it had a moral duty to respond to its employees regardless of whether there was an implied cost or benefit in doing so.[24] A further challenge experienced by companies when considering a response to HIV/AIDS was the profound denial regarding the epidemic accompanied by stigma and discrimination towards infected individuals. The cultural taboo surrounding the disease had ensured that AIDS remained a silent killer.

In South Africa, the mining sector was one of the worst HIV/AIDS-affected industries, particularly as this sector employed predominantly semi-skilled and unskilled workers. Fifty five per cent of surveyed mines reported that profitability had been adversely affected by HIV/AIDS. Harmony, a significant gold mine in South Africa, estimated in 2005 that HIV/AIDS-related costs could amount to 7.5 per cent of its total labour cost for the following 15 years. The high HIV prevalence rate, especially among migrant mineworkers, was thought to be related to their long separations from regular partners/spouses, compounded by easy access to commercial sex workers.[25]

---

[18]United Nations, "General Assembly special session on HIV/AIDS," 2001, http://www.un.org/ga/aids/coverage, accessed April 18, 2006.

[19]C. Arndt and J. Lewis, "The macro-implications of HIV/AIDS in South Africa: A preliminary assessment," *South African Journal of Economics*, 68:5, Dec. 2000, pp. 856–887.

[20]K. Quattek, "The economic impact of AIDS in South Africa: A dark cloud on the horizon," Konrad Adenauer Stiftung Occasional Paper, June 2000, p. 49.

[21]C. Arndt and J. Lewis, "The macro-implications of HIV/AIDS in South Africa: A preliminary assessment," *South African Journal of Economics*, 68:5, Dec. 2000, pp. 856–887.

[22]D. Dickinson, "Corporate South Africa's response to HIV/AIDS: why so slow?" *Journal of Southern African Studies*, 30:3, Sept. 2004, pp. 627–649.

[23]A. Whiteside and C. Sunter, *AIDS: The challenge for South Africa*, Human & Rousseau (Pty) Ltd., Cape Town, 2004.

[24]N. Nattrass *The moral economy of AIDS in South Africa*, Cambridge University Press, Cambridge, 2004.

[25]Bureau for Economic Research, "The impact of HIV/AIDS on selected business sectors in South Africa, 2005," Survey conducted by the Bureau for Economic Research and funded by the South African Business Coalition on HIV and AIDS, 2005.

Leading the Way

John Standish-White had a mining engineering degree from the University of the Witwatersrand, a blasting certificate and, prior to joining Goedehoop, was the general manager at Greenside Colliery from 1999 to 2003. In his early 40s, with a relaxed and easy demeanour, Standish-White realised during these years that it was time he became involved in responding to HIV/AIDS. In 1999, a mine worker at Greenside, Sello Malefane,[26] applied to take voluntary ill-health retirement from the mine. Standish-White knew Malefane by sight and name as he consciously involved himself with his employees. He always visited staff in hospital who had been admitted either due to illness or mine accidents. Malefane was a semi-skilled mine worker and it was fairly clear to Standish-White that he was terminally ill with AIDS. Malefane opted to take early ill-health retirement and return home to Lesotho, a neighbouring country to South Africa. Standish-White offered that his personal driver take Malefane home to the rural hills of Lesotho. After a long and tiring journey, which eventually ended in painfully slow progress on tracks more suited to transport on horseback, Malefane and the driver arrived at Malefane's home. Standish-White's driver reported back to Standish-White about how shaken he had been by the despair and wailing of Malefane's family members when they first set eyes on him. Malefane was a shadow of his former self; he was unrecognisable; he was very, very ill. Not many weeks later, Malefane was dead.

Standish-White realised it was time for him to take action. In the late 1990s, HIV/AIDS was relatively unknown. People were scared to learn more about it and, as Standish-White stated, "All AIDS talks were a doom and gloom show."[27] It was time for him to show some compassion and to do something that would be proudly South African. He realised he could save lives. There was fresh ground to be explored! Anglo's head office had not yet issued specific HIV/AIDS guidelines to follow, so Standish-White simply persevered through trial and error to put in place some effective action and response programme.

Standish-White recounted how, late one afternoon, he picked up a sex worker at the cross-roads outside the mine and, in his wife's car, took her to the "usual place under the gum trees," where she explained the local sex industry to him.[28] In addition to including the sex workers, he radically restructured the Goedehoop AIDS committee on his arrival there, firing at least half of the members including all of those who did not know their own HIV status. "You need to be very tough when you start out," acknowledged Standish-White, "You need to have the courage to do the difficult and the uncomfortable."

Goedehoop Goes "Green"

Standish-White had been appointed regional general manager of Goedehoop in 2003. In August 2003, the voluntary counselling and testing (VCT) uptake was at five per cent. Standish-White and his team realised that an HIV/AIDS programme would not be successful without a structured campaign and buy-in from employees. "My main vision and drive was that with great communication you can do all sorts of things. We got the people going, got everybody aligned and raised the trust levels. We had to get our hands dirty and go and look at what AIDS was really doing to our country."[29] Goedehoop management understood that initiatives in the boardroom would have little impact at an operational level if they were not communicated and implemented in a simple, practical, user-friendly manner. By encouraging both vertical and horizontal communication at all levels, Standish-White

---

[26]Name has been changed to protect his identity.

[27]Interview with John Standish-White at Anglo Coal Head Office, Johannesburg, on May 4, 2007.

[28]Ibid.

[29]HIV and AIDS Initiatives at Anglo Coal Goedehoop Colliery DVD, Shadowy Meadows Productions.

believed he managed to change employees' sexual behaviour.[30] He asserted that the disease should be approached as a form of business risk and, whether employees were in a threatening situation deep underground in a mine shaft or whether they were in a questionable sexual situation, they should know the key questions to ask themselves when doing a risk assessment.

The 5GH approach was implemented at the Colliery and was endorsed by the Goedehoop Lekgotla team ("lekgotla" is a Tswana term for meeting place; pronounced "leh-ghort-la"). The team was made up of management and labour union leadership. The Goedehoop AIDS committee was founded and named the SIDA Shipani Committee ("SIDA" is Portuguese for AIDS and "Shipani" is an Nguni term for team).[31] It consisted of senior management, medical staff, union representatives, traditional healers and informal settlement leaders. In addition, it was assisted by a full-time AIDS coordinator and 30 work-place peer educators.

5GH was based on the following five elements:

- Status
- Education (and "qaphela!" or awareness)
- Care for our people
- Partnerships
- 100 per cent personal protective equipment (PPE)

In order for the programme to succeed, the approach had to be relevant, innovative, positive and easily understood, as South African mines were characterised by employees with very diverse home languages and varied education levels. A Confidentiality Pledge was signed on an annual basis by SIDA Shipani members, peer educators, medical personnel and Anglo Coal Highveld Hospital, which reinforced commitment to the 5GH campaign (see Exhibit 1). The above five elements and the Confidentiality Pledge encouraged great interest and allegiance to taking action against AIDS throughout the operation. In addition, they effectively communicated the benefits and importance of learning more about the HIV/AIDS pandemic. Standish-White realised it was important that the HIV/AIDS message be taken back to peoples' families.[32]

Status

Of the five elements, knowing one's status formed the foundation and main focus of the campaign. VCT was actively encouraged on an ongoing basis. Measurement of VCT uptake was evaluated annually, with the clock being set back to zero in January of each year. In 2005, the VCT uptake had increased to 96 per cent and by the end of 2006, Goedehoop had managed to achieve an uptake of 98.3 per cent. The promotion of Visible Felt Leadership at Goedehoop was constantly in place, with Sir Mark Moody-Stuart, U.K.-based Anglo American plc chairman, himself having been orally tested for HIV at Goedehoop in March 2005. Testers took the oral tests to work areas, including going underground or to night shifts, which removed excuses for non-testing.

VCT uptake had been incorporated into all bonus incentive schemes for the full workforce and a weekly departmental VCT progress report was communicated to all employees (see Exhibit 2). Goedehoop worked hard to ensure that its VCT campaign remained people-focused and did not become mechanistic and numbers-driven.[33] Simon Ndlangamandla, an orderly at Anglo Coal Highveld Hospital, was an HIV-positive man in his early 40s who stressed the importance of VCT, acknowledging that if he had not been

---

[30]Interview with John Standish-White at Anglo Coal Head Office, Johannesburg, on May 4, 2007.

[31]Anglo Coal, "Raising the AIDS bar at Goedehoop Colliery" brochure, point 3.1,

[32]HIV and AIDS Initiatives at Anglo Coal Goedehoop Colliery DVD, Shadowy Meadows Productions.

[33]Anglo Coal, "Raising the AIDS bar at Goedehoop Colliery" brochure, point 3.3.1.

tested, he "wouldn't be here today." His message to others was, "If you are negative, stay negative—if you are positive, it is not the end of the world."[34] Nursing Sister Evey Thwala asserted that "It gives one great relief if you talk about your status, especially to the people you live with and those you work with."[35]

Awareness

"To get management and everybody together to talk about one thing is not an easy job to do. So you have to convince them that actually we're talking one language," noted Sonto Mahaye, HIV/AIDS coordinator at Goedehoop.[36] The SIDA Shipani members used various tools to help raise awareness about AIDS at the mine and in the community, some examples being the Daily Safety Bulletin (see Exhibit 3), which included a weekly AIDS message and which reached everybody verbally at the beginning of each shift; a two-day Imphilo/Wellness drive, which was held at the weekly induction programme for new and ex-leave employees; weekly AIDS days every Tuesday; rural and urban AIDS tours as well as area AIDS "blitzes" by community and work place peer educators; and road shows and SAMs (shock awareness meetings). World AIDS Day on the 1st of December was celebrated with great festivity each year and placed itself on the annual calendar as the target date on which 100 per cent of the mine's employees would have received VCT for that year.

Joe Marais, a middle-aged white man and Solidarity Union Representative, admitted that "Previously we all just knew about AIDS from what we read in the papers and we all thought it was a black person's disease or a poor person's disease. As soon as the programme at Goedehoop started, I think we all were quite shocked, especially my constituency. We were quite shocked to find out that it can happen to anybody."[37]

"Khuluma" (pronounced "koo-loo-muh") means talk in isiZulu, and chat shows (khulumisanas) were regularly held to which all employees and their dependants were invited to attend. "People should be educated about this problem, even the Unions. They like the idea because it teaches people about this problem we see everyday. We at Goedehoop are happy that we are learning," stated Sixanananaxa Nizi of the National Union of Mineworkers (NUM).[38] Educational handouts were often distributed either by means of posters or attached to payslips (in English, Sotho and Zulu), one of these being the "Slippery Slope and the way back" (see Exhibit 4), an AIDS-on-one-page handout, which concisely summarised AIDS in an easily understood way.

Care, Support and Treatment

Once employees had been encouraged to know their status, it was imperative that a support system was in place to respond to those individuals who needed further treatment. Two fully equipped clinics serviced by four professional nurses, as well as easy access to the nearby local hospital, were readily available. Free antiretroviral therapy (ART) and free nutritional supplements were provided to all HIV-positive permanent employees. The success of ART was noted by the decrease in absenteeism at work. "Our employees should die of old age and not of AIDS," noted Dr. Pienaar. Viral loads and CD4 counts were monitored regularly and counselling sessions were held frequently. Support was extended to the community by peer educators who provided home-based care.

---

[34]GBC (Global Business Coalition) Awards for Business Excellence 2007—submission by Anglo Coal South Africa, p. 14.

[35]HIV and AIDS Initiatives at Anglo Coal Goedehoop Colliery DVD, Shadowy Meadows Productions.

[36]Ibid.

[37]Ibid.

[38]Ibid.

Jorge Schulz was a burly, middle-aged white man who had been working at Goedehoop for eight years as a fitter. He was HIV-positive and was the only employee who had disclosed his status to the mine management and all his colleagues. He talked emotionally about the spirit of acceptance, the lack of discrimination and about how buoyed up he was by the response from his community. He received his medication free of charge and stated that he was 90 per cent healthy and fully productive at work. Schulz acknowledged that the treatment he received from Goedehoop was "like walking into paradise; I feel at home, I feel loved."[39]

Partnerships

An important contributor to the success of the programme was the successful partnership between mine management and the three recognised unions: NUM, Solidarity and United Association of South Africa. "One of the big things is our managers information meeting—without that, you don't get your message across," noted Nick Bull of the United Association of South Africa.[40]

In addition, trust and supportive partnerships existed with Anglo Coal Highveld Hospital, Anglo American Corporate Office, schools, churches, non-governmental organisations, traditional healers and the surrounding communities. Fifty per cent of the community peer educators were sex workers themselves. "Relationship with the people is most important," stressed Sonto Mahaye. This statement was reinforced by Standish-White: "The emotional side is important; you need to start feeling it . . . you start to get to know some of your people on the mines; all the time celebrating the programme and

making it an enjoyable journey. An energy-add is what cracked the ice on our property."[41]

Protection

It was encouraged that sex was talked about openly. Standish-White believed that AIDS was everyone's problem. He even kept a wooden penis on his desk so that HIV/AIDS was "always in your face." In 2006, Goedehoop distributed about 23,000 free condoms per month to the surrounding community near the colliery (see Exhibit 5). Femidoms were freely available from both clinics. Use of protection ensured that the HIV-negative people stayed negative and the positive people protected their partners.

Achievements and Challenges

Goedehoop kept a very detailed database on all the HIV statistics, which was updated weekly. At the end of 2006, there were 362 HIV-positive employees out of the total of 2,000, of whom 129 were taking antiretrovirals. In 2005, 51 new infections were recorded. This dropped to 27 new infections in 2006, a decrease of 47 per cent. What was alarming, though, was that by the end of April 2007 (when more than half the VCT had already been completed for the year), 17 new infections had been recorded, revealing that there was still work to be done. Brink's ultimate goal was to have zero new HIV infections, zero employees and family members becoming sick or dying from AIDS, and zero babies born HIV-positive in employees' families.[42]

But the programme was not without its challenges. The colliery had to soundproof the medical sister's room to ensure that discussions within remained private. Mistakes were made. In one

[39]Ibid.

[40]Ibid.

[41]Ibid.

[42]http://www.angloamerican.co.uk/article/?afw_source_key=14052965-CC7F-43EEADCA7ED39F33ECA1&xsl_menu_parent=/cr/hivaids/ourresponse, accessed June 4, 2007.

instance, a medical vehicle arrived to collect HIV-positive employees to take them to the hospital for their monthly prescription of antiretroviral therapy. While the reason for the trip should have remained confidential, the driver announced to the crowd in a loud voice the purpose of his transfer. Needless to say, no passengers came forward for the ride. Standish-White said that they overcame the mistakes by talking about them.

Goedehoop Colliery's efforts did not go unnoticed. It won the South African weekly newspaper Mail and Guardian's "Investing in Life" Award in August 2005 for the Best Corporate Response to AIDS in South Africa. In May 2006, the Colliery was awarded a "Highly Commended" certificate at the Global Business Coalition Gala Awards banquet held in London, a function that was attended by more than 1,600 guests. Goedehoop was identified as the centre of best practice for HIV/AIDS initiatives in the Anglo American group and yet the mine was conscious of trying to continuously improve its programme.

Return on Investment

"I've been so enriched by the way Goedehoop has risen to this challenge. The support that I've had from head office has been superb and the whole mine is united in its pride. We're the number one mine on HIV/AIDS," noted Standish-White. "I know that at least I have saved one life, hopefully many more."[43]

The majority of funding for the components of the 5GH campaign was borne by Goedehoop. The annual budget allocation to the campaign was approximately R1.5m (US $220 000[44]) which excluded:

- The provision of ART, which was sponsored by Anglo American plc
- The provision of condoms, which were subsidised by the government
- The management of the two loveLife[45] centres, which were covered by a R30 million donation from Anglo American plc to loveLife
- Costs incurred for peer educators, which were sponsored by Project South Africa (PSA)[46]

Many South African industry-specific charters had been designed to assist the sectors in meeting black economic empowerment (BEE[47]) guidelines. A key component of the mining charter was the scorecard, which provided a framework for measuring the BEE process in the sector.[48] One of the recommendations in the mining scorecard was that approximately 1.5 per cent per annum of post-tax operating profit be directed towards corporate social investment. In the case of Anglo American plc, this figure easily covered all ART costs.

Goedehoop Colliery was a high-profile mine for Anglo Coal. As a flagship colliery, it

---

[43]HIV and AIDS Initiatives at Anglo Coal Goedehoop Colliery DVD, Shadowy Meadows Productions, and interview with John Standish-White at Anglo Coal Head Office, Johannesburg, May 4, 2007.

[44]South African Rand/U.S. Dollar exchange rate in Oct. 2007: approximately R6.75/$1.00 (Standard Bank).

[45]loveLife is an NGO that incorporates the lessons of more than 15 years of international HIV prevention, and a two-year process of consultation and planning—including a thorough assessment of international HIV prevention efforts and extensive focus group research with young South Africans. http://www.lovelife.org.za/corporate/research/research.html.

[46]Anglo Coal, "Raising the AIDS bar at Goedehoop Colliery" brochure, point 3.2.

[47]Black economic empowerment (BEE) is a strategy aimed at increasing black participation at all levels in South Africa's economy. It aims to redress imbalances of the past by seeking substantially and equitably to transfer ownership, management, industry and operational expertise, as well as proportionate control of South Africa's financial and economic resources, to the majority of its citizens. It also aims to ensure sustainable, broader and meaningful participation in the economy by black South Africans. http://www.southafrica.info/public_services/citizens/travelkit-bee.htm.

[48]http://www.southafrica.info/doing_business/trends/empowerment/charters.htm, accessed June 5, 2007.

made over an approximate billion Rand profit in each of the three years up to 2006. This allowed it easily to cover the cost of treatment, which in 2006 amounted to less than R400 per person per month. Standish-White agreed that the business case for responding to AIDS was a "no brainer." Ninety eight per cent of the employees who were taking ART were at work every day and they only needed a day off every six months for a CD4 cell count check-up. Labour turnover and absenteeism had noticeably decreased.[49]

The financial commitment may appear high but Brink advised that the cost of not putting a worker through the AIDS programme was $32,000 per worker.[50] Goedehoop's success was an inspiration to all Anglo American operations, more so because far fewer employees were contracting tuberculosis (TB), which is an infectious disease commonly affecting the lungs. This was a welcome side-effect of the company's efforts to tackle HIV. The number of new cases of TB had dropped by almost 75 per cent since 2001. "TB has recently taken a lower profile" said Dr. Pienaar. "It was a social problem at one time—now it has devolved into being just a medical matter."[51]

⌧ Next Steps for Brink and the Team

Sitting in his Anglo head office, Brink contemplated his main challenges. He realised that the group had not yet managed to successfully stop new HIV infections. In addition, he understood how crucial it was for infected employees to gain early access to care, support and treatment. Brink knew that these two areas could be addressed by increasing the uptake of testing. South Africa labour legislation stated that it was illegal to enforce compulsory HIV/AIDS testing in an organisation. How could Brink push the importance of testing? How could he persuade all the Anglo business units to respond optimally in the next three months to the HIV/AIDS challenge?

Furthermore, at the end of 2006 Standish-White was promoted to Anglo head office in Johannesburg to take up a position as head of underground operations. Brink wondered if the change in leadership at Goedehoop would impact the mine's 5GH programme and if Goedehoop, with new leadership in place, could attain the goal for the whole group—zero new HIV infections.

⌧ Glossary

AIDS	This is the second stage of the HI virus and is fully referred to as the acquired immunodeficiency syndrome or acquired immune deficiency syndrome.
	Acquired: the virus is not spread through casual or inadvertent contact; a person has to do something which exposes him/her to the virus.
	Immunodeficiency: the virus attacks a person's immune system and makes it less capable of fighting infections.

[49]Interview with John Standish-White at Anglo Coal Head Office, Johannesburg, on May 4, 2007.

[50]Interviews with Dr. Brian Brink at Anglo American Head Office, Johannesburg, on April 2 and 8 October 8, 2007. The figure refers to the projected lifetime cost to the company for an infected employee who does not obtain treatment (costs arriving from absenteeism, health care, early retirement, death benefits, replacement costs, etc.).

[51]http://www.angloamerican.co.uk/static/reports/2006/rts/hc-hiv-aids.htm, accessed April 11, 2007.

	<u>Syndrome</u>: AIDS is not a disease. It presents itself as a number of diseases that come about as the immune system fails; hence, a syndrome (Barnett and Whiteside, 2002). NOTE: For ease of use and due to other academic references doing the same, the term "disease" is used throughout this case.
Antiretrovirals	The name given to any class of medication which suppresses HIV and thereby slows the destruction of a person's immune system (AIDS Law Project, 2005).
Epidemic	A rate of disease that reaches unexpectedly high levels, affecting a large number of people in a relatively short time (Barnett & Whiteside, 2002).
CD4$^+$T cells	CD4 cells are vital components of the human immune system. One type of CD4 cell (which is attacked by HIV) is the CD4 positive T cell. This cell organises the body's overall immune response to foreign bodies and infections. This T helper cell is the prime target of the HI virus, the particles of which attach themselves to the CD4 cell. Once the virus has penetrated the wall of the CD4 cell, it is safe from the immune system because it copies the cell's DNA so that it cannot be identified and destroyed by the body's defence mechanisms. In a healthy person there are on average 1,200 CD4 cells per microlitre of blood. As infection progresses, the number will fall. When the CD4 cell count falls below 200, opportunistic infections begin to occur and a person is said to have AIDS (Barnett and Whiteside, 2002).
HIV	Refers to an epidemic known as the human immunodeficiency virus and is a cause of the syndrome known as AIDS. HIV attacks a particular set of cells in the human immune system known as CD4 cells. HIV can only be transmitted through contaminated body fluids in sufficient quantities. The main modes of contamination are unsafe sex; transmission from infected mother to child; use of infected blood or blood products; intravenous drug use with contaminated needles; and other blood transmission modes (bleeding wounds) (Barnett and Whiteside, 2002).
Non-governmental organisation	A community-based organisation with its own management structure; it is not part of the structure of government.
Pandemic	Epidemic of world-wide proportion (Barnett and Whiteside, 2002).
Traditional healer	A practitioner of herbal medicine and counselling in traditional African societies. The philosophy is based on a belief in ancestral spirits. Also known as a "Sangoma" in local African dialect (traditional healers were known as "witch doctors" by colonialists).
Triple bottom-line	The idea that companies can simultaneously service social and environmental goals and earn profits (Davis, 2005).

Exhibit 1	Latent Confidentiality Pledge

CONFIDENTIALITY PLEDGE

Zulu ■ Sotho

GH SIDA Shipani, Peer Educators, Medical personnel and Anglo Coal Highveld Hospital herby pledge:

- Our full time transparent and honest commitment to the 5GH campaign
- To abide by all collective agreements and legislation\To have programs in place to assist all individuals infected and affected by HIV/AIDS
- To have a programs in place to assist all individuals infected ad affected by HIV/AIDS
- To maintain 100% confidentiality & not disclose any personal information without the written consent of the person concerned

ZULU
- Ukuzibophezela, ukusebenza ngozimisela
- Ukulandela imigomo nemithetho ebekiwe
- Sizosiza kanti futhi sinakekele abaphila negciwane naba hlukunywezwe yigciwane
- Ukugqiniseka ukuthi ukugula komsebenzi kuyifihlo, ukunganikezani ngolwazi oluyifihlo ngaphandle kwemvumo.

SOTHO
- Boiponaletso ba rona bu tletseng le bonnete baho ikhokahanya ho lintlha tse hlano tsa lekhotlana la tuamiso
- Ho tsamaisana mmoho le lintlha tsohle tsali tumellano le puso
- Hoba le dlhophiso ea moralo e tsebetsong e teng ho thusa bohle ba amehang leba amiloeng ke HIV/AIDS
- Ho lokisa bocha karolo ea lekholo ea lekunutu laho boloka lekunutu la motho ka ngoliso ea motho ea amehang

Public signing: 14 June 2005 @ MIM

Dr Jan Pienaar ACHH	George Mothibi Orderly – GH Clinic	Ezekiel Lingwati Orderly – Bank Clinic 410	Lydia Makhubleo SIDA Shipani - NUM
Dr LP Louw ACHH	Janjies Motau Orderly – GH Clinic	Frank Madalane Orderly – Bank Clinic	Robert Potwana SIDA Shipani - NUM
Dr Francois Wessels ACHH	Edward Ndizimande Orderly – GH Clinic	Mzwandile Zwali Orderly – Bank Clinic	Tienie van Dyk SIDA Shipani - Solidarity
Dr Reuben Masinga ACHH	Boesman Tshehla Orderly – GH Clinic	Vusi Mathe Clerk – Bank Clinic	Johan Reiners SIDA Shipani - UASA
Sr Evey Thwala Medical Supt. – GH Clinic	Elvis Jika Orderly – GH Clinic	Sonto Mahaye AIDS Coordinator/ SIDA Shipani	Linda Sam SIDA Shipani
Sr Mary Mogashoa Medical Supt. – Bank Clinic	Selby Chawane Assistant – GH Clinic	Dup du Plooy Mine Manager	Mirriam Nyaka SIDA Shipani
Sr Stephina Thabete Sister – GH Clinic	Tembi Nguni General Assistant	Pieter Korff HR Manager/ SIDA Shipani	Collen Nhubunga SIDA Shipani – Peer Educator
Sr Regina Mahlangu Sister – Bank Clinic	Noel Mnisi Orderly – Bank Clinic	John Standish-White RGM/ SIDA Shipani	Walter Healther SIDA Shipani – Peer Educator
Steve Mokoena Orderly – Bank Clinic			Jorge Schulz SIDA Shipani

" Our passion drives us to be the best ... Viva GH!!! "

Exhibit 2 Departmental VCT Statistics

Goedehoop Colliery
SIDA SHIPANI Campaign: Element 1 = Status

VCT STATISTICS : Mine Employees per Area tested in 2006 01December 06

	Human Resources			Finance & Admin'			Technical Services''			GH Plant Processing'''		
	Act	VCT	%	Act	VCT	%	Act	VCT	%	Act	VCT	%
Officials	57	55	96%	70	65	93%	44	38	86%	11	11	100%
Snr Skilled	1	0	0%	0	0		0	0		9	9	100%
Skilled	38	37	97%	2	2	100%	25	25	100%	59	59	100%
Total	96	92	93%	72	67	93%	69	63	91%	79	79	100%

'includes Security '' includes Survey, VOHE, Geology, ''' includes Environment

	Plant 2 Processing			Plant 5 Processing			GH Plant Engineering			Plant 2 Engineering		
	Act	VCT	%	Act	VCT	%	Act	VCT	%	Act	VCT	%
Officials	9	9	100%	2	2	100%	12	12	100%	7	7	100%
Snr Skilled	9	9	100%	3	3	100%	40	40	100%	26	26	100%
Skilled	47	47	100%	26	26	100%	29	29	100%	21	21	100%
Total	65	65	100%	31	31	100%	81	81	100%	54	54	100%

	Plant 5 Engineering			Simunye # Engineering			South # Engineering			Block 5 Engineering		
	Act	VCT	%	Act	VCT	%	Act	VCT	%	Act	VCT	%
Officials	2	2	100%	10	9	90%	8	8	100%	3	3	100%
Snr Skilled	8	8	100%	33	25	76%	31	29	94%	20	20	100%
Skilled	7	7	100%	20	20	100%	19	19	100%	16	16	100%
Total	17	17	100%	63	54	86%	58	56	93%	39	39	100%

	Hope # Engineering			VL Engineering			Surface Engineering			Simunye # Mining		
	Act	VCT	%	Act	VCT	%	Act	VCT	%	Act	VCT	%
Officials	13	13	100%	10	9	90%	32	32	100%	18	18	100%
Snr Skilled	70	63	90%	57	53	93%	20	20	100%	3	2	67%
Skilled	41	39	95%	42	41	98%	77	75	97%	137	125	91%
Total	124	115	93%	109	103	94%	129	127	98%	158	145	92%

	South # Mining			Block 5 Mining			Hope # Mining			VL Mining		
	Act	VCT	%	Act	VCT	%	Act	VCT	%	Act	VCT	%
Officials	11	11	100%	13	13	100%	37	33	89%	26	24	92%
Snr Skilled	2	2	100%	1	1	100%	7	6	86%	6	6	100%
Skilled	101	100	99%	68	68	100%	238	226	95%	184	171	93%
Total	114	113	99%	82	82	100%	282	265	94%	216	201	93%

	Trainees			Men			Women			care stats		
	Act	VCT	%	Act	VCT	%	Act	VCT	%	HIV+		%
Officials	10	7	67%	361	343	95%	60	54	90%	HIV+	356	18%
Snr Skilled	11	11	100%	342	343	100%	13	13	100%	New inf	26	0.42%
Skilled				1104	1105	100%	57	50	88%	ART	131	
Total	21	18	86%	1807	1735	96%	130	117	90%			

Other VCT	
Paid by Others	46
Contractors	318
Ex Employees	24
Dependants	56
Visitors	15
Total	459

Total Employees 2006			
	Act	VCT	%
Officials	423	405	96%
Snr Skilled	355	344	97%
Skilled	1181	1146	99%
Total	1937	1895	98%

Total VCT to date	
Mine	1895
Other	459
Total	2354

Exhibit 3 Daily Safety Bulletin (DSB)

Daily Safety Bulletin DSB

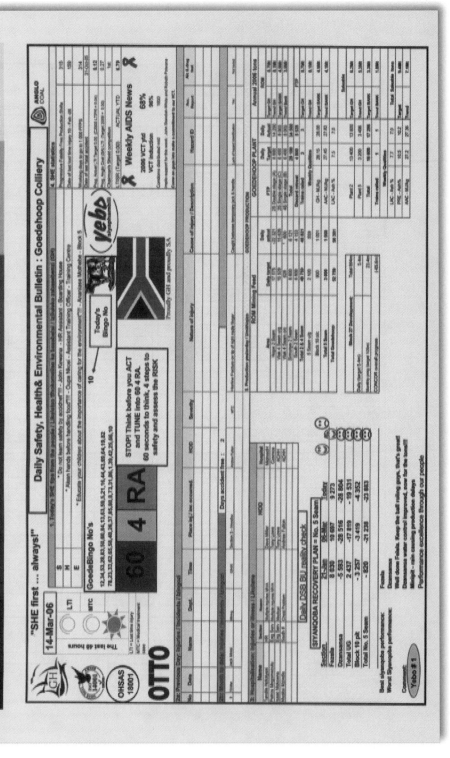

Exhibit 4   Aids-On-One-Page Handout

"AIDS-on-one-page": Slippery Slope

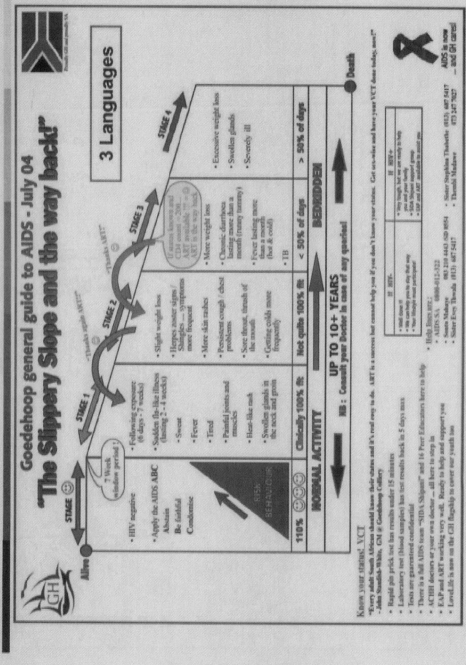

Exhibit 5 Condom Distribution Points

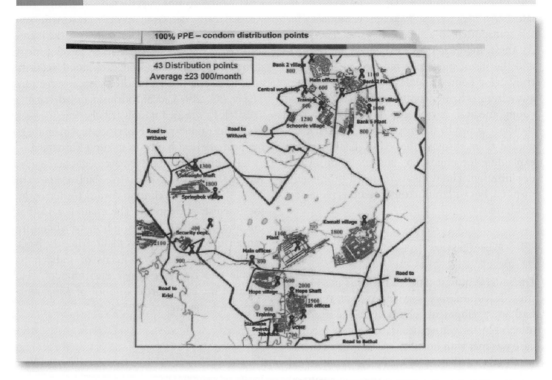

Organization, Founder and Clientele Transformation at VGKK

L. Prasad, G. Ramesh, and G.S. Goutham

▨ The Visit

The Vivekananda Girijana Kalyana Kendra (VGKK) is an organization nestled in the Biligiri Rangan region (popularly known as BR Hills), where the Western and Eastern Ghats meet in southern Karnataka, South India. It is several hundred kilometers from Bangalore, the Silicon Valley of India, and yet is far behind current standards of economic development. BR Hills is home to the Soliga tribe and is the site of one of the most inspiring indigenous socio-political interventions undertaken by a non-governmental organization (NGO) in recent history. This case is about the relentless struggle by the inhabitants and by the VGKK to enter the mainstream and to ensure the socio-economic development of the area. Closely intertwined is the story of Dr. Hanumappa Sudarshan, the founder of the VGKK, who played the catalytic role.

Some students of the Indian Institute of Management Bangalore in South India, along with

Version: (A) 2010-07-23

a couple of faculty members, went on a study tour of BR Hills and the VGKK one weekend in late 2007. They were software professionals who felt transported to a different world. The pitch darkness, the flickering, low voltage light bulbs and the insect bites they received in the forest truly drove home the point that they were miles away from urban civilization. Prashanth N.S., a young medical doctor and professional ornithologist drawn by the inspiration of Sudarshan, guided them through the VGKK headquarters, explaining the philosophy and evolution of the organization. The students returned thoroughly inspired, but with numerous questions requiring resolution.

An Overview

Dr. Sudarshan first came to BR Hills in 1979 to provide community service. At that time, he had no development agenda. Even the minimal attempt by the young idealist to provide medical care was met with hostility and suspicion by the local Soliga tribal inhabitants. He familiarized himself with the land and people, and worked hard to gain the trust of those he was trying to help. He offered cures for various illnesses of the forests, like snakebites and wild animal attacks, and treated common illnesses, such as anaemia caused by water-borne diseases.

In the following decades, he not only managed to forge a strong, trusting relationship with the tribals,[1] but spawned a self-reliant and confident institution. The VGKK became the voice and platform of the tribal population. Sudarshan always endeavored to ensure that the core identity and culture of the Soliga tribals remained intact, allowing them to chart their own course.

In the 20 years he worked with the Soligas, Sudarshan achieved what many government departments would love to accomplish. The VGKK brought down the prevalence of leprosy from 17 per 1000 people to less than 0.3. He treated

hot water epilepsy cases, which were quite prevalent, with community-based methods that stressed early detection, proper treatment and preventive health care. The VGKK worked tirelessly to achieve sustainable development through health, education, livelihood security and the promotion of biodiversity conservation. The VGKK also had an offshoot called Karuna Trust (KT) meant for non-tribals, which was a model in public-private partnership in managing primary health centres in rural Karnataka.

For his outstanding achievements, Sudarshan was awarded the Alternative Nobel Prize in 1994, the Right Livelihood Award conferred by the Swedish parliament. The citation said that this award was for "Showing how tribal culture can contribute to a process that secures the basic rights and fundamental needs of indigenous people and conserves their environment." He donated the entire prize amount of $86,000 to improving the lives of the Soligas.

The Genesis

In everyone's life, at some time, our inner fire goes out. It is then burst into flame by an encounter with another human being. We should all be thankful for those people who rekindle the inner spirit.

Albert Schweitzer

Hanumappa Sudarshan was greatly inspired by the works and example of Albert Schweitzer. Born in 1950, Sudarshan lost his father when he was barely twelve. This premature experience of loss made him want to be a doctor. In school, he had very good grades, but his admission to medical school was stalled by the rules, as he was still not sixteen.

The interim year irrevocably influenced the course of young Sudarshan's life. He took up a

---

[1]A "tribal" refers to a primitive social group or kinship.

clerical job in a flour mill while waiting for his admission to medical school. During this time, a friend took him to the Ramakrishna Ashram, a mission at Bangalore. Here, he devoured the teachings of Swami Vivekananda, which left an indelible mark on his life, philosophy and ambitions.

In 1973, he graduated from Bangalore Medical College. He joined the mission for a brief period and got an opportunity to work in Almora in the Himalayas and in the headquarters of the mission in Belur Math, West Bengal. Working as an intern, he got a hands-on perspective of the operations and ideology of a missionary service organization that dedicated itself to the poor. He then came into contact with Dr. Narasimhan, who was working among tribals in the Nilgiris district in the state of Tamil Nadu, South India. This experience inspired him to work with the tribal Soligas. Sudarshan heard about the Soligas in BR Hills for the first time when he was working with Dr. Narasimhan.

When he first came to BR Hills, it was an inaccessible hill station in the district of Chamarajanagar in Karnataka with no roads, electricity or phone lines. A visitor had to take the circuitous route through Chamarajanagar and finally trek to BR hills. Sudarshan's goal seemed simple enough at that time: perform the duties of a doctor by curing ailments and delivering health care. With this in mind, he set up a small hut as a clinic on the rocks (to avoid the elephant herd that used to frequent the area) in 1980 (see Exhibit 1). The geographical profile of BR Hills as of 2000 is shown in Exhibit 2.

◪ Getting to Know the Soligas

In the initial years, Sudarshan banked on support from some open-minded local leaders. The tribals were naturally suspicious as he was a stranger providing allopathy to an indigenous population that relied entirely on natural remedies. To overcome this suspicion, an administrator at the Biligiri Rangaswamy temple (a place of worship), Chakravarty, and non-tribal locals, like Jayakumar, helped Sudarshan gain access to podu (hamlets). They were paid Rs100 monthly. [2]

Sudarshan faced a number of obstacles in the initial years. Whenever he and his team would reach the podu with medicines, the entire podu would flee from the doctor into the forest. Even the presence of local temple authorities could not allay the fears of the tribals. He and his assistant, carrying medicines on their heads, would scope the jungles and small hideouts in search of patients.

But Sudarshan remained steadfast despite such odds. His perseverance paid off, and as he became a familiar figure in the forest, the tribe's fear gave way to its curiosity and then to acceptance. A few incidents helped gain the tribals' confidence, such as treatment of snakebites by sucking the venom out, and dressing bear attack wounds.

As more people sought his services, he shifted to promoting preventive and community medicine. There was a high prevalence of whooping cough in the forest, which made him move into preventive medicine. His experience practising community medicine made him aware that most epidemics have their root in lack of education and poverty. It was quite clear that delivering preventive, curative care alone was not sufficient to help people. He found himself diversifying into education, community-building, vocational training, etc. to empower them.

◪ The VGKK

Sudarshan founded VGKK in October 1981. He built the first VGKK building on his own by learning brick-making, foundation-laying, plastering, etc. As of 2009, the VGKK had more than 27 years of development experience with the Soligas and other tribes in the Chamarajanagar

[2] At 50 Indian rupees per U.S. dollar.

and Mysore districts of Karnataka, and had extended its expertise to tribals in other far-flung states, such as Arunachal Pradesh and the Andaman and Nicobar Islands.

Sudarshan's philosophy was, "To eliminate disease you have to remove poverty. The only way to do that, I have realized, is to organize the people for their rights." The VGKK considered its most significant achievement to be its fostering of self-organization among the people. It had a governing board of 17, out of which 10 were Soligas, and every village had its own sangha (council). Sanghas helped to fight for rights and, as a result, most of the Soligas' alienated land had now been restored to them. Soliga candidates had also done well in elections and two tribal women were chiefs of the local council.

In the early years, Sudarshan's team initially consisted of Huche Gowda, Jayadeva, the temple priest and Somasundaram. The first president of the VGKK was Made Gowda, a tribal, and the tradition of a tribal heading VGKK continued to be maintained. (Incidentally, the president in 2009 was the first student of the VGKK). The other members were tribals from other hamlets.

Initial Activities and Emerging Portfolio

The VGKK believed in an integrated approach to tribal development with health, education, livelihoods and biodiversity conservation as the means to sustainable development and empowerment. It had a formal vision and mission statement that spelled out clearly its philosophies; as well, it was visionary and artistic (see Exhibit 3).

Health

In the early days, there was no primary health centre (PHC) in the area, and the nearest centre was in Yelandur Town, which was many miles away. The Soliga tribals relied exclusively on their own traditional medicine system but critical illnesses resistant to herbal ministrations were often neglected and thought to be the product of fate. In serious cases, they turned to Lord Biligiri Ranga as their only savior.

Sudarshan was always respectful of the local culture and medical traditions. His philosophy was to help the Soligas improve their lives in their own environment rather than displacing them from their roots. Instead of fighting or repudiating traditional medicine, he studied it and tried to build upon existing practices to deliver the most effective health care possible. For example, pregnant tribal women used the squatting position for delivery. He studied this and later adopted it as the standard for pregnant tribal women. He also began to include the local midwives in his mission, as the story of Jalle Siddamma will attest (see Exhibit 4). He clearly recognized that primary health care must be based on maximum community participation, active involvement and empowerment of the people. There were interesting learnings to be picked up from them. Tribals ate some 15 to 20 green leafy vegetables as part of their daily diet, which resulted in no incidence of colonic cancer and no appendicitis. There were very few cases of heart diseases and fewer caesarian births.

Education

Sudarshan started a small, informal school, which was formalized into the first registered primary school in the area in 1982. His first class had six students, four of whom later went on to earn their master's degrees. The language of instruction was the local tribal language, Soliganudi. Every year a new grade was added and, at the end of 10 years, the school had a full-fledged grades 1 to 10 program. The growth in the number of students is given in Exhibit 5.

The syllabus was unique, filled with information on the local environment, festivals, medicinal plants, songs, dances, flora, fauna, seasons and other locally relevant topics that would resonate with the children's daily lives. Slowly, as students moved to middle school, regular Kannada (state language), English and other subjects were introduced.

⚶ Livelihood and Training

For community service to create a real impact, it needed to work on a number of levels. Health care, Sudarshan realized, would continue to figure low in the priorities of the poor, unless they moved up the income ladder. He started a number of income-generating activities to tackle the larger dimensions of poverty.

The nomadic nature and occupations of the Soligas were a major deterrent to their attaining health care and a decent standard of living. They moved from one place to another and practised shifting cultivation. Other major occupations were hunting and honey collection, and the tribals were exploited by people from the city who bought their produce. Natural honey bought at Rs6 per kilogram was sold in the market by traders at around Rs55 to 60 per kilogram. BR Hills became a reserved forest with the introduction of forest conservation policies. Even shifting cultivation became state controlled and the Forest Department introduced clear felling, where they cleared a stretch of forest where Soligas could cultivate. Once the area was abandoned, the Forest Department would undertake the replanting of trees in the area with eucalyptus, teak, etc.

This practice not only put the Soligas at the mercy of forest officials but also led to the destructive practice of monoculture. The forest officials allowed only minor forest produce (MFP) to be collected and sold by tribals. In response to these counterproductive policies, the VGKK started honey-processing units as a value-added activity to the existing forest produce and to empower the tribals. Over the years, the VGKK added more and more income-generating activities to its portfolio to address overall livelihood issues. The scaling up of the range of activities can be seen in Exhibit 6.

The VGKK also started a training institute for forest-related activities, so that tribals could be employed or become entrepreneurs in their own habitat. More than 60 per cent of Soliga people got a minimum of 300 days' employment yearly from the Forest Department and other agencies. Tribal cooperatives were set up by the VGKK, which employed 1,200 Soligas directly. The VGKK (in partnership with the Ashoka Trust for Research in Ecology and Environment) also pioneered the sustainable extraction of non-timber forest products (NTFPs) and the creation of tribal enterprises to process them.

The VGKK started a training institute for auxiliary nurse midwives (ANMs), which trained Soligas to become paramedical staff. ANMs undertook reproductive and child health activities, preventive health care programs (such as vaccine administration) and other national health programs in villages. Those who used to hide in the forests petrified at the sight of a doctor had now become confident paramedical staff.

The VGKK began educating the tribals about their rights to forest produce by creating organizations with strong tribal leadership. A tribal named Cheluvadi was made leader, which helped consolidate trust. The general impact on human development of the region on select parameters due to the efforts of the VGKK can be seen in Exhibit 7.

In voluntary services, scaling up happens in many ways, much like in corporate entities. Both expand their range of activities, spread their geographical coverage, expand membership, develop broad-based second-tier management, mobilize financial resources to reduce dependence and establish independent, related organizations. The similarities end here. The challenges are much more complex for non-profits, as membership is voluntary and there is a long gestation period for benefits to accrue or become visible. The expansion is often need-based rather than market-driven.

The VGKK observed that, once contact and interactions with the nearby plains increased, leprosy began spreading among the tribal population.

KT was instituted in 1986 as a public charitable trust affiliated to the VGKK. KT was established as a response to the prevalence of leprosy in nearby Yelandur Taluk, Chamarajnagar district. Due to the sustained efforts of KT, prevalence of leprosy dropped from 21.4 per 1000 population in 1987 to 0.28 per 1000 in 2005. KT diversified into epilepsy, mental health and tuberculosis and eventually management of the PHC at Gumballi.

KT took over the Gumballi PHC in Chamarajanagar district in Southern Karnataka in 1996 as a public-private partnership (PPP). As of 2008, KT had expanded to 26 PHCs in 23 districts of the state. KT took over the PHCs from the Karnataka government on the understanding that KT would get 90 per cent of what the government spent on these PHCs before KT took over. As a policy, primary health care was provided free of cost in India. KT managed the deficit through donations. It not only upgraded the infrastructure of the PHCs, but made a huge difference in the operations. KT assured the presence of medical doctors and the availability of medicines, which were the critical problems faced by the PHCs. These transformed PHCs were in demand by local residents and had become models for the rest of the state.

Some of the innovations that KT introduced were:

- 24-hour PHC with availability of all staff
- Gender-sensitive PHC
- Integration of community mental health in PHC
- Mainstreaming of HIV/AIDS treatment in PHC
- Essential obstetric care
- Rational drug use, essential drugs
- PHC waste management
- Community-based rehabilitation of people with disabilities

The improvement of one of the Trust-run PHCs (see Exhibit 8) was significant, and occurred within a short time. It is interesting to note that, with the same infrastructure and resources as the government-run PHCs, the Trust was able to make an impact that the government-run PHCs struggled to achieve. The impact since taking over a typical PHC is given in Exhibit 8, along with a comparison to state-level averages.

After the takeover, house surgeons of Mysore Medical College and JSS Medical College hospitals were posted to BR Hills for training. St. John's Medical College in Bangalore also sent house surgeons for brief periods. Some dedicated house surgeons stayed on even after completing their training.

KT had, over the years, expanded its geographical spread as far as Arunachal Pradesh in the extreme northeast of India and to the Andaman Islands in the middle of the Bay of Bengal.

Health Insurance

One of the important initiatives of KT was its community health insurance scheme for the poor. Studies have clearly demonstrated that a majority of tribals in remote areas with little access to proper health care have been pushed further below the poverty line as a direct result of bearing the burden of medical expenses. Most of them depend on daily wages for their most basic needs like food and a single episode of illness can wipe out their savings or assets and push them into a perpetual cycle of debt.

KT became the partner of a major initiative along with UNDP and National Insurance Company that offered community insurance. The insured paid Rs30 per annum towards the premium and would be compensated in case of illness for a wage loss at Rs50 per day up to a maximum of 25 days of hospitalization in a government PHC or a civil hospital. The insured could get an additional amount of Rs50 per day for buying medicines that were required but not available in the hospital. Reimbursement was immediate, thereby giving KT the additional resources to meet exigencies. This scheme was a successful project run by KT.

⊠ Biodiversity Conservation

The VGKK's contribution to biodiversity conservation was quite impressive. The Soligas consider themselves to be part of the biosphere and believe that damage to the elements of the biosphere directly impacts them. Hence, generations of tribals have evolved intricate and detailed practices, stories and traditions that accord protection to various elements of their environment. A huge Champaka (Michaelia) tree held in reverence by all the Soligas is an example of how sacred ideas and traditions have conservation value.

Forest fires were a major hazard for tribals and the typical Soliga response was to run away at the sight of fire. However, once the Sanghas were formed, the community decided to set up fire patrols in the dry season. The fires were then put out as soon as they were spotted and not allowed to spread. The groundwork for this was laid out by social workers, school teachers and students of VGKK School. Street theatre, skits and high school students were all used in fire-fighting promotion, which brought the locals onto a common platform to have a serious discourse on the old versus the new paradigm. Local wisdom said that localized forest fires, though destructive, also stimulated growth of the right kind of trees. Fire-fighting was often rendered dangerous because of outside poachers. Very often forest fires were deliberately started by smugglers and poachers to divert the attention of the forest department. When the VGKK staff started successfully preventing forest fires, they were threatened and warned against trying to stop sandal wood theft.

The Ashoka Trust for Research in Ecology and Environment (ATREE) was established in 1996, with a mission "to integrate rigorous natural and social sciences with policy, education and socially responsible conservation action." In collaboration with the forest department, it started participatory resource monitoring (PRM) to enable sustainable harvesting of non-timber forest produce (NTFP). BR Hills was the only forest area in the country where the collection and extraction of NTFPs was being monitored and where the local community was involved. ATREE generated detailed geographic information system (GIS) based maps for forest fire monitoring, habitat mapping and other purposes.

⊠ Finances

As of 2008, the VGKK and KT were self-managed but had still not reached the stage of financial self-sufficiency. This severely handicapped their plans for scaling up their operations. Sustainability of operations and meeting the deficit were still critical and uncertain issues that the VGKK faced every year.

The VGKK had no real business model to ensure a recurring source of revenue even though its activities were growing steadily. Its income-generating activities were caught in a scale problem, with low levels of production that never fetched sufficient revenue. Sudarshan believed that adequate money would come through goodwill and donations at appropriate times. He never really focused on the systematic generation or mobilization of funds. There was no regular funding for the first three years and he depended solely on donations.

In the early years, Sudarshan would do fundraising in his spare time. But as the scope of his work broadened, this became very difficult. Friends and relatives helped out with their own personal resources. The VGKK's first annual budget was around Rs10,000, with no government funding. Sudeep Kumar, an officer from the Indian Administrative Service who was posted in that area and who later became a member of the VGKK, helped with the construction of a new school building. Three to four years after the VGKK's establishment, the government provided some financial support to cover the VGKK's deficit. The process was tedious and full of red tape. The VGKK had to first apply by showing its accounts and deficit to the government for reimbursement, and, early on, it took at least 10 to 12 visits to government offices in Yelandur to get reimbursed. Sudarshan would get the cheque on the last day of the year and it had to be cashed the very same day. When providing this meager amount, the officials would demand bribes, which he never obliged. However, with the establishment of a formal organization, funds started flowing slowly from other sources and the VGKK gained recognition. Major help came from the Ministry of Tribal Welfare and once the ministry approved the VGKK, it became relatively easy to raise funds. The trend of finances received over the years is presented in Exhibit 9.

One activity that the VGKK still found difficult was accounting. Dr. Sudarshan himself maintained the accounts for more than 10 years. He later started training tribals to do it and was able to establish formal accounting procedures by 1994, and since then it had been working well. Another development, which came later, was the savings concept. It was slowly introduced as tribals were new to the practice of savings.

Organizational Growth— Second Line of Leadership

By 1994, Dr. Sudarshan realized that, even though the VGKK had grown to be a respected organization, it revolved around him. He played a critical part in every activity and it took his inexhaustible energy to run the organization. He knew that this was the time to disengage from the core activities of the organization, and he realized that capacity building was top priority.

Again, the solution came from within. The Soliga society had very little discrimination. It had five clans and marriage was forbidden within the same clan. Even the priest clan had no special privileges. The Soligas were headed by the head priest, Cheluvadi, president of the VGKK. Sudarshan made it mandatory that VGKK presidents would be always from the Soliga community. Since Cheluvadi was already a tribal leader, trust and respect came naturally. However, since the VGKK was a registered society, other issues

such as accounting, managing interface with the government, projecting developmental issues, conflict resolutions and crisis handling became important. It took time to build these capacities.

The political process again evolved over time. By 1984, there were podu-level Soliga Abhivruddhi Sanghas (Soliga welfare organizations). Simultaneously, the Panchayat Raj system (a system of local government) that was introduced by the government complimented the organizations' work and they got the formal status of self-governed bodies. By 1986, the Soligas became aware of their rights and started visiting government offices to demand their rights (see Exhibit 10).

Managing Growth

As of 2008, VGKK hierarchy was made up of founders and volunteers at the top, managers in the middle and coordinators at the bottom. At one time, none of the people working at the VGKK had any special financial incentives to do their job. Everybody did honorary work and took pride in it. Although the model looked good, Sudarshan slowly realized that it was not scalable.

He had to introduce the concept of formal employment. However, Sudarshan firmly believed that the nature of employment should be service oriented and so he made sure during selection that only dedicated people for whom salary was not the only consideration joined. However, he clearly recognized the need for long-term benefits and care for the family. The organization had a zero-tolerance policy for corruption at the work place.

From the beginning, the VGKK was managed by tribals, and one interesting aspect of its engagement was that the tribals could grapple with nuances of leadership, administration and even marketing, but not accounting.

With more time to spare, Sudarshan started interacting with other like-minded groups to share their best practices. Briefs in magazines put him in contact with many organizations who were working in similar areas. He could now not only try to help others with his knowledge but also chart the future course of action for the VGKK with the external insights he gained. By 1999, he was spending more time in Bangalore and got involved with the task force at the Health and Family Welfare Department of the government of Karnataka.

His periods of absence proved useful for the VGKK, which became more self-reliant and confident in management and leadership. If, in the early stages, his presence was critical for the success of the venture, later his absence became equally useful for the internal management team to develop.

Price of Development

Development came with a price. As the government doled out assistance, a dependency cycle developed. Over time, as the Soligas became less reclusive and more confident, getting money through numerous government programs and income-generation activities, their way of life began to be affected. Some of the tribal men took to an alcoholic drink, arrack, and their families suffered. It is noteworthy that by then, the women felt sufficiently empowered to participate in the activities of the VGKK and they took up this issue with courage. They held demonstrations before the district collectorate and finally were able to force the government to ban the sale of arrack/liquor in the entire BR Hills range. Soligas were used to local cannabis indicus for smoking, which was a lesser evil than tobacco. However, with greater contact with urban civilization, cigarettes and beedis took hold.

New rules and regulations brought in by the government forced individual ownership of land, which was an anathema to the community land holding of the tribals. Soligas culturally had no practice of accumulation and no institution of property rights. In one instance, when the government gave land to about 15 families, they just occupied it without caring to demarcate each other's boundaries. Soligas continued to look upon land as community property.

Looking Back

In 2006, the VGKK celebrated 25 years of existence. Sudarshan credited the achievements to openness to learning and engagement with the indigenous population right from when he first came to BR Hills. He started with a simple service mission, but as he slowly began learning the problems of the people first hand and started responding to them, the mission and method became multi-layered. He did not go to BR Hills with preexisting notions of what the tribals needed and a plan to impose solutions. The concept of rehabilitating the tribals in their homeland and in their own environment was created on site in BR Hills and the fact that the changes were brought about without any pain of dislocation was heartening to the doctor.

Looking back, Sudarshan had more than the share of struggles he bargained for when he started. Overall, the suspicious and untrained tribals were more easily convinced and supportive than the government, which should have accepted his help proactively.

He felt that he could achieve whatever he did only by going and staying where the action was. It lent him credibility in an alien space and slowly he became part of it. This philosophy was followed in the recruitment of doctors, who he instructed to stay close to the place they served. His suggestion to all prospective participants in social service was to stay with the clientele and understand them, and build institutions through them.

Sudarshan believed that the VGKK and KT symbolized two models of development. One was the evolutionary model of engagement in service, which involved hands-on work and building up trust and credibility, and the evolving process. It was replicable by any other organization but had to be built with patience. The other model was the public-private partnership that was promoted by KT, which demonstrated how an NGO and a government could come together to manage a service system.

Sudarshan never felt the need for a credit card, nor was he an income tax assessee. However, he did not want to impose his lifestyle on others. Looking back, he felt there were three kinds of leadership in the organizations he built. The first line was the leaders, who had no assets or income and whose basic needs were taken care of by the Trust. The second line was the volunteers, who worked during free time of their own volition. The third line was the highly qualified professionals who were paid honorarium, which was just around 50 to 75 per cent of market salaries. Of course, there was also a fourth layer, which was the staff for whom salary was a critical component. It was because of all these groups that the VGKK became a 20,000-people-strong organization from a mere 2000 and that KT benefitted around 500,000 people.

Sudarshan felt the VGKK was just a stepping stone for the tribals. With forest resources being scarce, he acknowledged the fact that it might not sustain all the Soligas once they were educated. So they had a choice to settle in some other place. This method, he felt, was quite natural because it rehabilitated the tribal population rather than uprooting them from their land without preparing them.

One of his contributions was providing a platform for professionals interested in community service. He prided himself on how many who had the opportunity to work with him had branched off into noble NGO activities. Some returned to work with him, such as Satyanarayana Hedge, who left after 10 years with the VGKK, only to return eight years later to manage the Integrated Learning Project. Others started their own organizations or worked in others, taking the vision and mission of the VGKK further in ways the founders would have liked.

Self-Transformation

Dr. Sudarshan got into an introspective mood in one of the interviews. He had begun as a doctor and felt initially he could make a difference by providing curative care. Then it dawned on him that curative care alone would not suffice. This led him to preventive care and then to the "development pill." The problems dawned on him one by one and he and the organization evolved to face the challenges unfolding.

After a quarter of a century of work in BR Hills, he felt that his work had brought about a change in himself resulting from a path of inner journey and inner growth. Sudarshan believed in Karma Yoga (the preaching of an ancient Indian literature), that is, realizing the divine through work. He believed that work should transform a person, whether one was in service or any other job. He had seen people getting frustrated after a decade of community service and he felt it was because these people did not understand their own personalities. He said it would do more harm than good if they continued to work in an environment in which their personalities did not mesh. One should feel inner growth along with their work. Otherwise, they need counseling to discover themselves through reflection and understanding. He felt that it took a lot of energy to do selfless service and that it was important for people to realize this before they started community service, as otherwise they would feel burnt out.

Having placed the VGKK and KT on a firm pedestal, he now played an active advocacy role. He felt his grassroots experience helped him to speak authentically. He gave no theoretical lectures. His philosophy was that theoretical lectures should be backed with hands-on experience at the grassroots level to carry credibility and that, with this credibility, confidence would automatically show in one's speeches.

He served on several government committees and played the interface role between policy and implementation, and local and central administration. He felt that the only other feedback that was available for administration was official channels, as there was no independent, third-party monitoring. He was in the Task Force of Health and once played a vigilance officer role in the anti-corruption bureau. He was vice-president of the Voluntary Health Association of India, and a member of the Independent Commission on

Health in India, the National Commission on Population, the National Nutrition Mission, the National Human Rights Commission and the Indian Planning Commission's Steering Group for the development of Scheduled Tribes. He fought against corruption as ombudsman for Health, Education & Social Welfare, Karnataka Lokayuktha. He received the Parisara (Environment) Award from the government of Karnataka (1993) and the Padma Shree Award from the president of India (2000).

Next Steps

The organization was moving forward and he felt there was still a lot to achieve. He wanted the organization to be more independent from the individuals who created it. Soliga abhivriddhi sanghas (development councils) were now independent and run by Soligas, who had become highly conscious of their rights. Fortunately, development councils received formal status with the advent of the Panchayat Raj system. They were organized into federations at the district level, which regularly met to discuss mutual problems.

Other than tribal development, Sudarshan had begun to see many urban problems troubling people such as stress, personality problem more prevalent in the middle class. He was contemplating serving this section in his future days now that VGKK and KT were self-reliant.

Sudarshan was keen to look at his service model critically. He was looking at for-profit ventures that could help cross subsidize the unviable economic and social activities. He was of the firm belief that a service-oriented mindset alone could bring about change and could be the foundation for a community organization. However, he realized that financial self-sufficiency was equally important for achieving sustainability and scalability. He wanted to create a for-profit business that would fund his community service. He still believed that the for-profit should be a separate, independent entity and

should be kept at arm's length. Its role should be only financing his services and could not dictate the service model. However, he was also strongly against using the name of services for-profit organizations to conduct business. For-profit as well as development organizations should run on their own merits and separately.

Sudarshan had been thinking of promoting low-cost drugs on a large scale, which could fund his service organization. KT was already involved in distributing low-cost drugs. It was trying to promote rational drug usage and low-cost generic drugs. Another plan was an eco-tourism project in BR Hills, which would generate income for the VGKK. The VGKK was involved in a telemedicine project, which was promoted jointly by Asia Heart Foundation, KT and Village Resource Centres. The telemedicine project was envisaged by Indian Space Research Organization (ISRO) to use space technology for the benefit of the rural poor.

The Return Journey

On the way back from BR Hills, the students had plenty of questions for Prashanth, who had been an eyewitness to the happenings of the place in recent times.

- How had the living conditions of tribals changed? Were they happy with the change?
- Were the locals a threat to the forest? How could they be organized to protect forests?
- What was an ideal educational system for them?
- Can we think of a viable health delivery system that could work in tribal areas?
- What is participatory management?
- How could the operations of the tribals be scaled up? How could their operations be made self-sustaining?
- What could be the revenue model and cross-subsidization model?

- Why did the bureaucracy always seem to be working at cross-purposes with locals and development?
- What was the role for professionals?
- What role could technology play in their lives, especially information technology?

It was an endless array of questions given that it was the first exposure for many of the students. Fresh from their experience on their journey back home, the students spent considerable time on reflection, introspection and resolution. The exposure was slowly sinking in.

Exhibit 1   The Clinic Hut: A Humble Beginning of a Great Institution

The foundation of an institution on the rocks: This hut, constructed by Sudarshan for his hospital, was built on the rocks to protect the inhabitants from elephants, frequent visitors in the early years.

Exhibit 2   BR Hills Profile

Total area of BR Hills	540 sq. km
Total number of tribal colonies within the sanctuary and its fringes	63
Total number of gram panchayats (local government)	12
Total tribal population	15,000
Population density	27.7 per sq. km

SOURCE: VGKK.

Exhibit 3 Vision, Mission and Objectives

Vision

A self-reliant and empowered tribal society rooted in its culture and tradition, living in harmony with nature.

Mission

Sustainable development of tribal people through rights-based approaches to health, education, livelihood security and biodiversity conservation.

Objectives

- To implement a comprehensive, holistic, need-based, gender & culture-sensitive, community-centred system of health care integrating indigenous health traditions.
- To establish an education system that is specific to the tribal language, culture and environment.
- To promote biodiversity conservation and sustainable harvesting of Non-Timber Forest Produce.
- To ensure livelihood security through sustainable agriculture, vocational training and value addition of forest produce.
- To empower tribal communities through sanghas (people's organizations) and women's self-help groups.

SOURCE: VGKK.

Exhibit 4 The Story of Jalle Siddamma—An Embodiment of Traditional Knowledge and Wisdom

For a long time, there was no female doctor in the VGKK hospital. A local midwife, Jallesiddamma, and her daughter, Jademadamma, assisted in all tribal births both at home and at the hospital. In all, Jallesiddamma delivered about 1,500 babies in the region, meticulously recording the date, time and case details in her record book.

Her daughter, Jademadamma, recalled a case when a baby was born but the placenta remained undelivered for many days. Jallesiddamma, with some help from her daughter and some ingenious tactics, dislodged the placenta and relieved the mother of the painful problem.

In another case, Basamma, a pregnant woman, was severely distressed because of domestic problems. Jallesiddamma counseled her and also her husband, in-laws and parents, ensuring that they realized the medical importance of a happy and peaceful state of mind in the young expectant mother. The family soon learnt to cooperate and set aside their differences.

As a competent health professional, she easily related to her patients. She also used to tell them about basic hygiene, nutrition, disease prevention and essentials of healthy living.

Jallesiddamma and the VGKK had a symbiotic relationship. She worked closely with the doctors at the VGKK hospital, referring complex cases to them for a second opinion, and the doctors returned the favor.

SOURCE: VGKK.

Exhibit 5	Enrolment and Results of School Leaving Exams at VGKK School

Year	Appeared	Passed
1989	23	5
1990	20	8
1991	17	13
1992	18	11
1993	30	18
1994	35	12
1995	27	12
2000	27	11
2005	40	38
2006	55	54
Total	524	283

SOURCE: VGKK.

Exhibit 6	Activities Promoted Through the Vocational Training Centre

Activities—Year	
Agarbathi-making unit	1981–82
Carpentry, tailoring, bakery, bee keeping, mat weaving, handicrafts, weaving, honey processing, leaf cup making	1982–83
Candle making	1985–86
Cloth printing, knitting, herbal soap nut powder	1988–89
MCR footwear	1989–90
Lacquer dolls, welding and fitting	1991–92
Silk weaving on pedal loom, medicinal herbs collection, minor forest produce processing unit, notebook section	1992–93
Polyvastra weaving unit, food processing	1993–94
Hand-made paper unit	1994–95
Khadi spinning and weaving, masala unit, screen printing, fruit and vegetable processing	1995–96

Activities—Year	
Coir ropes and mats unit	1996–97
Sambar powder unit	1998–99
Natural dyes	1999–00

SOURCE: VGKK.

Exhibit 7 Human Development Indicators—BR Hills

Indicator	1979	2005
Infant mortality rate per thousand	150	6.1
Adult literacy	Men < 40% Women < 10%	Men 65% Women 50%
Child enrolment in schools	20%	100%
Focus on female child	Close to nil	Significantly visible
Daily income	Rs10	Rs60

SOURCE: Anubhav, Karuna Trust, 2006.

Exhibit 8 Gumballi PHC and State Averages

Indicator	1997	2003	2006	State
Crude birth rate	16.1	17.7	17.5	23.3
Crude death rate	5.6	5.6	4.59	7.7
Infant mortality rate	75.7	32.6	18.5	51.5
Stillbirth rate	37.8	10.7	NA	23.3
Prenatal mortality rate	67.7	21.5	9.25	47.8
Neonatal mortality rate	70.3	13.5	13.9	37.1
Child mortality rate	12.4	5.5	4.6	18.3
Under 5 mortality rate	10.7	5.04		69.8
Maternal mortality rate	Nil	Nil	Nil	195

SOURCE: Anubhav, Karuna Trust, 2006.

Exhibit 9	Statement of Expenditure of the VGKK and Karuna Trust

Period	Amount (Rupees)
1981–82	12,953
1982–83	105,951
1983–84	838,046
1984–85	1,294,761
1985–86	1,008k914
1990–91	3,970,745
1995–96	7,106,441
2000–01	8,426,452
2001–02	13,153,739
2002–03	7,696,191
2003–04	7,066,831
2004–05	9,672,912
Total	129,217,714

SOURCE: VGKK.

Exhibit 10	Empowerment Strategy Title

Empowered: The "Three P" Strategy

The "Three P" strategy—Petition, Press and Picketing—was effectively put to use by the VGKK to demand and assert the Soligas' rights and welfare time and again. For example, in the mid-80s Soligas owned 89 tamarind trees on a land belonging to them, but the crop belonged to a politically and financially astute person from Chamarajanagar. They had signed away their yield for several years in return for a paltry loan of Rs100 or 200 ($4) each. The tamarind from each tree was worth at least Rs4000 ($80) per annum.

In 1986, the Soligas demanded back their land and rights over the tamarind produce and pro-tested against the injustice. On one day in December, 12 tribal people were arrested. On hearing this, Dr. Sudarshan went to the police station to demand their release. He himself was arrested. Despite the pleas of friends and lawyers, Sudarshan refused to apply for bail and went on a fast. When the deputy commissioner of Mysore district heard of this, he immediately visited Sudarshan in prison. He tried to coax him but he would not break his fast. As news of his fasting and incarceration spread, thousands of Soligas from various areas of the district gathered spontaneously in front of the jail at Chamarajanagar to protest. The press covered this event extensively.

The protest was a historic watershed, especially considering the fact that avoidance of any form of conflict was an integral part of the Soliga culture. They nursed a deep-seated fear of outsiders and were apprehensive of the political clout and muscle power of contractors. In spite of all these obstacles, more than 3,000 Soligas made it to Chamarajanagar that day, including men, women and children. Supporting them were all the staff and board members of the VGKK including Cheluvade Made Gowda. At the end of two days of relentless protest, their demands were met and Sudarshan was released from jail. The "Three P" strategy had worked in accomplishing the mission.

In another instance, Soliga women organized a protest. Soliga women organized themselves and blocked roads and halted buses on August 9, 2001, demanding that all the liquor licenses issued in tribal areas and temple areas be cancelled. The Excise Department had to assure them that licenses would be cancelled immediately. These are remarkable stories of the transformation of uneducated, publicity-shy people demanding their due rights.

SOURCE: VGKK.

Compelling Visions: Content, Context, Credibility and Collaboration

Jeffrey Gandz

The "vision thing" is still with us, but while leaders insist on having a compelling vision, the fact is that many— both the leaders and the visions—leave people standing still, unmoved. A leader who engages stakeholders when developing a vision will, in the end, articulate one that resonates strongly and impels people to act.

One of my favorite Peanuts cartoons shows Lucy, once again, lecturing Charlie Brown on the meaning of life:

"Charlie Brown, life is like a deck chair on a cruise ship. Passengers open up these canvas deck chairs so they can sit in the sun. Some people place their chairs facing the rear of the ship so they can see where they've been. Other people face their chairs forward—they want to see where they're going. On the cruise ship of life, which way is your deck chair facing?"

Replies Charlie, "I've never been able to get one unfolded."

Unlike Charlie Brown, leaders today must have a vision. There are many stakeholders— employees, shareholders, governments, special interest groups, and the media—who simply demand to know, "Where is this organization going and what is going to get it there?" Everyone who is a leader or wants to be a leader—of an organization, division, department or team— must be able to formulate, articulate and communicate a compelling vision if they are to engage and inspire people to follow them. They

Reprint# 9B09TB04

must also ensure that their followers find meaning in this vision, the context in which they operate. If followers can find this meaning, if they can grab on to it, hold it in their hands and make it a mental bookmark, their actions are likely to reflect and support their leader's vision.

Some visions compel people to act whereas others leave people cold or even alienate them from their leaders. This causes some leaders to give up on the visioning challenge, to let their actions rather than their words convey a sense of direction. Other leaders are simply reticent when it comes to establishing clear, directional targets for their organizations. Perhaps they don't want to be held to account for reaching or not reaching these targets; perhaps they don't want to publicly commit to some strategic direction; perhaps they think that a clear vision may appeal to one group and turn off another.

There may be many reasons for rejecting visioning as a useful exercise. Yet, as we emerge from another U.S. electoral season with a president who appears to have triumphed because his vision for America and the power with which he projected it prevailed over others, it is time to re-examine "the V word" and ask what makes one vision particularly compelling and capable of engaging people, and what makes yet another vision unsalable and essentially leaves people feeling cold.

Compelling Visions

Compelling visions that move people to action, change their behaviors, focus on key priorities, and follow the pathway that the leader lays out, have three attributes that can be summarized under the broad headings of *content, context* and *credibility*. Beyond that, they are developed as part of a *collaborative* process that engages key stakeholders.

The Content of Visions

Compelling visions are not just slogans. For example, consider General Electric's "We bring good things to life" or "Imagination at Work," Nikon's "Our Aspirations—Meeting needs. Exceeding expectations," "Honda's "How we see things" or Coca-Cola's "It's the real thing." These may all have worked well as advertising slogans or signature lines, but they didn't lay out with any degree of clarity what the leadership of these organizations wishes them to become in the future. Toronto-Dominion Bank's vision, "To be the Better Bank," is more goal-oriented, while Manulife Financial's is more specific, stating boldly that its vision "... is to be the most professional life insurance company in the world: providing the very best financial protection and investment management services tailored to customers in every market where we do business." These vision statements give a better sense of where those companies are heading. But, since they are targeted to multiple stakeholders, they also lack the specificity that some of those stakeholders would like to see.

The content or substance of a leader's vision must appeal to would-be followers as well as the leader. This appeal generally rests on the belief of followers-to-be that the leader can deliver something that they want and need— the feeling that their leader serves their needs and that they can achieve through their leader. They might assume this servant-leader role for altruistic reasons, without care for her or his own needs, or on the other hand, to satisfy their own needs through satisfying the desires of their followers.

Effective leaders are good at understanding the wide variety of physical, economic, psychosocial, and emotional needs that people have, and in their ability to tailor a "vision" so that it promises to satisfy unmet needs. The person who doesn't have a job, can't pay the rent, has a family to support and has other basic needs may be attracted to any vision that seems to promise material rewards and security. Someone who has savings, a secure pension or is near retirement age may not care too much about getting paid more, but may put a high value on the social satisfaction that they get from doing their job—the quality of interaction that they have with clients, suppliers, co-workers, and so on. Someone who has a high need for achievement may be attracted to an audacious vision; someone who has a high need for security may reject that same vision in favor of one that promises security and stability. Charismatic or transformational leaders can get followers to transcend their narrow, personal "economic" interests and embrace the leader's mission, whereas transactional leaders operate on a more material plane. Both types have to develop a content-rich vision to motivate people to follow them.

For any leader, the challenge is to figure out what will "turn people on," at least those people who will be essential for achieving the vision. The problems arise when very different, sometimes totally contradictory, things turn on the people who need to be motivated to follow. A CEO or executive team may be turned on by profit growth, especially when they have substantial stock options that vest when certain profitability targets are met. The union leader may see these profitability targets being achieved only through plant closures, loss of jobs and consequent reduction in union membership. Little surprise, then, that the union leader does not enthusiastically embrace the leadership vision. For the vision of profitable growth to be embraced by both union leaders and management, each has to see a payoff somewhere in the content of that vision. It is not essential that everyone agrees with every aspect of a vision, only that they find something in that vision which resonates with them.

Even within management teams, there may be a lack of buy-in to certain corporate visions. A risk-averse CEO who has a substantial portion of his personal wealth tied up in in-the-money options may embrace a vision that emphasizes slow and steady domestic growth. On the other hand, the head of the international division may be focused on the higher-risk strategy of entering emerging markets.

The problem with many enterprise-level visions is that they have to be crafted to appeal to multiple stakeholders or, at a minimum, so as not to create conflict among any interests that have some countervailing power. This is a high hurdle for visionaries to overcome. One vision has to appeal to shareholders, managerial and non-managerial employees, partners, customers, governments, supply-chain participants, and community activists. Such "enterprise" visions, as they are referred to, often lack the focus or an edge. Indeed, many corporations are vague about their visions, at least in public, preferring instead to focus on their broader "missions," often stated in socially progressive, non-threatening ways. Who can argue with British Petroleum's "Beyond Petroleum" in an environmentally-conscious world or Archer-Daniel-Midland's "To unlock the potential of nature to improve the quality of life"?

Vision and the Necessity for Context

If visions are to motivate, especially employees, it's essential that employees find the vision meaningful in the context of their work. A vision for an HR department may well be "to create the best employment brand of any company in our industry," or for a risk management department of a bank to embrace "the highest risk-adjusted return in our industry," or for the marketing department of a food processing company to "have 50 percent of sales in products that are less than five years old that match the lifestyles of busy people today." This means that there may be several visions within a company. All need to be aligned with the company's overall mission, though each would have a particular meaning for a selected constituency in the enterprise. Each person should have a line of sight to the firm's higher-level organizational mission and vision, and be able to see how they can contribute to its fulfillment by realizing their own visions. This means that everyone with a leadership role in an enterprise, from a team leader to department manager to business unit manager, to functional leader and CEO, must be involved in "the visioning thing." It's not just one, over-arching vision from on high that does it.

Individuals' salient wants and needs are dynamic, and vary by circumstances, time and place. Desperate people, experiencing material or psychological threats to their immediate well-being, are primed to respond to a leader who promises the hope of delivering them from their current situations.

We see this most evidently in the socio-political context. Martin Luther King drew on a deep vein of anger and frustration in the civil rights community and mobilized Afro-Americans to action. Barack Obama called for an era of change for an American population frustrated and angry with the Bush administration. Margaret Thatcher roused the British from their welfare-state torpor in the 1970s and got that country moving again, although there are still many people who would say it was in the wrong direction.

But we also see the ability of a vision to mobilize in a corporate context. Jack Welch used the powerful vision of "being number one or number two in each market we are in" to focus a number of the small, powerful business units in the conglomerate-like General Electric. He subsequently used powerful visions such as "the largest small company on earth, smart, agile, nimble" to bust the silo mentality and excessive bureaucracy that characterized the GE that he had inherited from his predecessors. The contexts for these visions were situations in which employees felt constrained, restricted and dissatisfied with the way the company operated. As well, shareholders were unhappy with results that were negatively influenced by the slow, resource-wasteful practices of the "old" GE, suppliers who found the company hard to deal with, customers who were unhappy with product and service reliability and quality, and even unions

and employees that saw the only real security in the face of free trade and Japanese competition was in superior performance.

A business leader in a turnaround situation may be able to articulate a vision that compels people to act, whereas that same vision, articulated a year earlier or later, before the enterprise has run into trouble or after it has started a recovery, may well fall on deaf ears. One who seeks to build a long-lasting institution by making long-term investments may attract few people to that vision when the stock price is low; however, such a course of action may stimulate interest when the organization is performing well. One whose vision focuses on innovation and creativity may stimulate followers to action when the basics are working well, though he or she may fail to do so when the fundamentals of the business need fixing. There are times when there are several competing visions and a leader must consider the relative power of his or her vision to move people who may be torn between competing, attractive alternatives.

Time and circumstances may compel a shift of a particular vision. As the economic slowdown of early 2008 merged with the global banking meltdown of the second half of the year, most companies had to re-think their goals in light of what was achievable over a specific time frame. As competitors succeed in reducing a market leader's advantage, that leader may have to adjust the vision. Michael Dell discovered this when Hewlett-Packard, under the leadership of Mark Hurd, achieved supply-chain economics comparable to Dell's. Dell found that the shift to notebook computers required potential buyers to have a tactile experience. This persuaded Dell to re-embrace the retail distribution channel that it had abandoned many years previously, when it switched to the Dell Direct business model.

While flexibility is required to deal with dramatically changed circumstances, constant vision changing inevitably creates confusion and consternation, a lack of faith that the leadership knows where they are heading. Vision drift is a constant danger and the "vision-du-jour" phenomenon is to be avoided at all costs. The President and CEO of TD Bank Financial Group, Ed Clark, continues to focus on creating a truly North American powerhouse in the face of an economic slowdown, a continued focus that has some critics calling for a time-out from the pursuit of this goal. But Clark is determined and very conscious of the fact that any perceived weakening of resolve could derail the achievement of a worthwhile, long-term aspiration for the Bank. This is not some innate stubbornness, but rather the resolve of a leader for whom the creation of an enduring institution is a higher-order imperative.

Credibility: Of Vision and Visionary

There are those who just have dreams and those whose dreams will inspire others to follow them. The difference may have more to do with the credibility of the visionary rather than with the content of the vision.

The leader with a good track record, who is known for having achieved what they set out to do in the past, who "knows the business" and is recognized as an expert by those they are seeking to influence, is more likely to inspire a following than one who lacks such credentials, other things being equal. Such a leader has personal credibility which, when allied with the right content and context, may provide powerful transformational leadership. Such was the case with Lou Gerstner, a former, highly successful CEO of RJR Nabisco, who was hired to turn a moribund IBM around and transform it from a product-focused company in to one that had a blend of products and services. He had an impressive track record at American Express and, importantly, was not steeped the culture of IBM, a culture that had spawned a great company in the period 1950–1990, but

was in danger of strangling it in the much faster-moving, high-technology environment of the 1990s.

But such personal credibility may not outweigh a vision that lacks substantive appeal and is credible in its own right. Has this been done before? When and where? By whom? With what resources? A vision may be appealing and the visionary may have some degree of personal credibility, but if the vision seems too fantastic, too implausible, it will not be seen as compelling, an absolute must for any successful leadership vision. When Mike Zafirovski came to Nortel Networks from Motorola, he came with high personal credibility. However, the company was in so much trouble, faced such serious financial problems, and had an innovation deficit compounded by the need to limit R&D expenditures that personal credibility could not carry the day. Individuals that might have made it possible for Nortel to succeed had defected to competitors, where they saw the resources required to be a leader in the telecommunications field. Those that remained at Nortel discovered that they did not have the resource base to compete effectively against the Cisco's and Alcatel-Lucent's of this world.

Then sometimes, we see a newcomer who, armed with words but without a history of deeds, and who may lack a degree of evidence-based credibility, can nevertheless still be persuasive. In Barack Obama's presidential campaign, we saw a leader whose oratory, command of language and personal presence in a context where people were desperate for new leadership—but one who carried a very thin resume—elected to the most powerful office on earth. This charismatic leader may inspire a following based on little except their "magnetic" force, a force that is magnified and distributed through the mass media. This charisma may exist independently of their other leadership attributes or may substantially add to them. One thinks of a Steve Jobs at Apple, Warren Buffet of Berkshire Hathaway, or Herb Kelleher of Southwest Airlines, as examples of charismatic leaders who have founded or resurrected businesses.

Collaboration: Whose Vision Is It, Anyway?

Throughout history there have been individuals who have seen something that others did not see, who were able to articulate that "something" and build followers, and manage those followers through the many changes called for by the vision. Bill Gates and Bill Allen did this with Microsoft, Steve Jobs and Steve Wozniak did it at Apple; in earlier generations there was Thomas Edison, David Sarnoff and Timothy Eaton to name just a few. But there have been many failures as well; prophets who could not change the minds of others, false messiahs, CEO's who promised the world and failed to deliver, team leaders who could not get the support of their teams and eventually were either deposed or who left under their own steam.

Several acolytes of Jack Welch failed to deliver for their organizations when they sought to "import" elements of the GE culture to their new organizations. Bob Nardelli failed to deliver at Home Depot, and Jim McNerney did not lead 3M to greater performance. Both of the organizations they joined had strong cultures and, while neither of them had sterling performance records in the years immediately before their arrival, they were not organizations that recognized that they were in trouble and in need of a savior. The visions that Nardelli and McNerney tried to impose on their new organizations were rejected by employees and failed to deliver business results that were satisfactory to shareholders.

For any new leader, the challenge is to create a vision that reflects the wants, needs and aspirations of those who will be tasked with achieving it. Such visions are borne from the dissatisfaction that people have with the current situation and their perception that there could be something better. The leader may have an important role in generating this dissatisfaction and in postulating a better way, but he or she will do so with great sensitivity to the way that people view the past and present. The challenge is to *envision* rather than to have a vision, and this is best done by engaging people in the process of developing that vision and giving them a meaningful opportunity to shape the product of this engagement. Commitment to it will develop only from this empowerment; mere involvement in a process will not result in commitment. The truly compelling vision has content, context and credibility; the process of developing it is collaborative. When people can say "That's my vision" or at least lay claim to having influenced it, it's an indication that the task of execution has started well.

This need for collaboration when framing a vision requires what Jack Welch called "aggressive-patience" on the part of a leader. While challenging the status quo, leaders must respect those who have contributed to success in the past and seek their involvement and engagement in developing the way forward. This takes time and some process skills. Leaders must approach the visioning process with an open mind, not an empty mind, one that is receptive to the concerns and inputs of those who will have a stake in the emerging vision and on whom the achievement of that vision depends. If this takes some time, if people find it necessary to develop a new vision in a gradual, iterative way, then this must be viewed as an investment in developing commitment.

Does Your Vision Compel Action?

These four characteristics of a compelling vision—content, context, credibility and collaboration—are summarized in the figure below. They suggest a set of screening questions that should be asked when any vision is being conceived, developed and articulated.

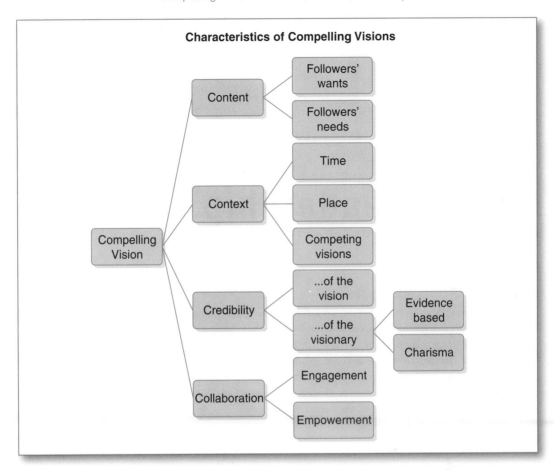

Characteristics of Compelling Visions

- Has this vision been developed in a collaborative way with those that will be responsible for its enactment?
- Does the content or substance of the vision appeal to the salient wants and needs of those you seek to inspire?
- Even if all elements of the vision do not appeal to all followers, will all those essential to making it happen see something of value for them in it?
- Is the vision articulated clearly so that followers will clearly see what's in it for them?
- Is the timing for launching the vision right or should it be delayed to the point at which potential followers will receive it better?

- Is the proposition in the vision credible to those who must embrace it?
- Are you personally credible in the role of visionary?

If the answers to all of these are "Yes" then your vision may compel action; less than that, and there is a chance that it will fall short of achieving this goal and may need rethinking or reformulating.

One of Barbra Streisand's popular songs says, "The vision ain't the solution, it's all in the execution." The emphasis on execution is important, but it must not exclude developing a compelling vision that will stimulate minds, engage passions, and move feet. The cost of launching a vision that fails to inspire is the loss of the visionary's credibility. Get it right the first time!

12

Team Leadership

Teams are everywhere: in business and industry, in government, in schools, hospitals, professional associations—indeed, almost anywhere people gather to get things done. There are executive teams, management teams, and teams within functional areas from R&D to customer service. There are also special-purpose teams, cross-functional teams, and even industry teams with members from different organizations. Indeed, the movement to collaborative teamwork has been one of the sea changes that have swept through organizations during the last two decades of the twentieth century.

—Frank LaFasto and Carl Larson[1]

Being an effective leader means understanding the nature of leadership as it applies to leading teams. Some researchers (Zaccaro, Rittman, & Marks, 2001) suggest that leadership may be the most important element in whether teams succeed or fail. Contrary to previous leadership theories, where we focused on a leader and followers, in this chapter, the leadership function can be exercised by the leader in charge of the team, shared by members of the team, or both (Daft, 2011). Some researchers refer to this shared leadership model as team leadership capacity (Day, Gronn, & Salas, 2004).

⊠ The Team Leadership Model

The team leadership model described in this chapter gives central importance to team leadership capacity in achieving team effectiveness. When the word *leadership* is used, it refers to team leadership capacity. The model itself offers a way of thinking for leaders who share the team leadership role

---

[1]LaFasto and Larson (2001, p. xi).

and should be used to determine team issues and problems as well as several alternatives to resolve these issues and problems while being cognizant of the team's resources and capabilities and the external challenges and opportunities. The word *external* could mean the organization external to the team and/or the environment external to the organization of which the team is a part. Figure 11.1 summarizes the team leadership model used in this chapter.

Effective leadership in teams assumes behavioral flexibility, problem-solving skills applicable to teams, and using discretion when determining if leader intervention is necessary. In the model in Figure 11.1, the first box suggests that leadership decisions affect team effectiveness directly and through internal and external actions that leaders can decide to take or not take.

Figure 12.1	Hill's Model for Team Leadership

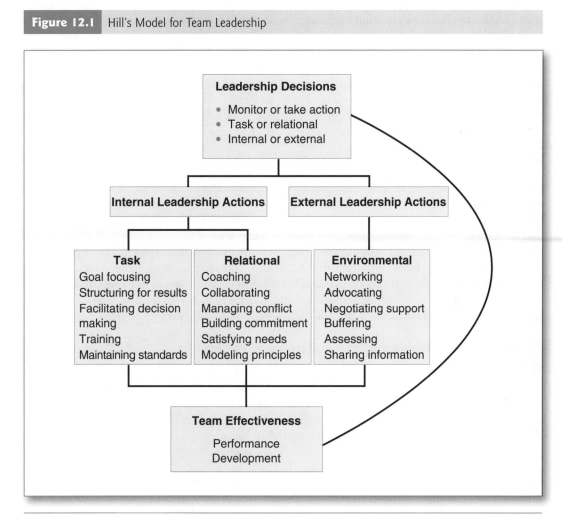

Leadership Decisions

These decisions are as follows: (1) Should I continue to monitor, or do I need to take action? (2) If I need to take action, is it task or relationship focused or both? (3) If I need to take action, do I need to intervene inside the team or in the team's external environment (the organization or the environment external to the organization)?

Should I Continue Monitoring or Take Action Now?

Knowing when to take action is a very important leadership skill to develop. Intervening too soon could be more damaging to team effectiveness than waiting. However, waiting could sometimes cause more damage than intervening immediately. This skill develops through experience (similar to most leadership skills), and leaders need to understand that sometimes they will intervene too soon or too late, but sometimes they will get it right. The ability to get it right generally increases as leaders develop more experience in a team setting. The important thing to remember is to learn from intervening too soon or too late.

To determine when to intervene, leaders need information. Gathering this information requires the ability to scan and monitor the internal team dynamics and the external environment in which the team operates. In addition, formal leaders need to let informal team leaders share this task and be open to informal team leaders coming to them with internal team problems and external environmental issues that could help or hinder the team (Barge, 1996; Fleishman et al., 1991; Kogler-Hill, 2007).

Should I Intervene to Take Care of Relational and/or Task Needs?

If team leaders decide they need to intervene, then they must determine whether intervention is necessary to improve problems and issues related to task/structure and/or whether to help improve interpersonal relations among team members, including the team leaders. Effective team leadership focuses on both task and relational issues/problems as a high level of task productivity, combined with superior intrateam relationships, leads to best team performance and development. For virtual teams, it may be necessary to focus on intrateam relationships and then work on fixing issues/problems related to getting the job or task done (Kinlaw, 1998; Pauleen, 2004). Trying to fix task-related problems first may exacerbate the intrateam relationship problems to such a degree that it may make fixing both types of problems much more difficult.

Should I Intervene Within the Team or External to the Team?

This decision is also very important. In the previous paragraph, we suggested that team leaders need to focus on task and intrateam relations. It is also important for team leaders to know when and if they need to intervene between the team and its external environment—be it within the larger organization or even external to the organization. Effective team leaders are able to balance the internal and external demands placed on their teams and to know if and when to intervene in one or in both.

Leadership Actions

The leadership decisions described above affect team performance and development through the actions team leaders take internally and externally. These actions are listed in Figure 12.1 and are based on research that discusses team performance. It is important for team leaders to assess the problem and select the right action or set of actions. The model in Figure 12.1 is a good guide for inexperienced team leaders and will become more useful as leaders gain experience that allows them to internalize the model to the point where it becomes almost tacit—that is, leaders respond to situations without even thinking about the model.

The actions listed in the model are not all inclusive, and astute team leaders will add others and maybe delete some as they gain leadership experience in a team environment. What is most important is developing the ability to discern when an intervention is needed and the appropriate action to take during the intervention.

Internal task leadership actions are used to improve a team's ability to get the job done. They include the following:

- Being focused on appropriate goals
- Having the right structure to achieve the team's goals
- Having a process that makes decision making easier
- Training team members through developmental/educational seminars
- Setting and maintaining appropriate standards for individual and team performance

Internal relational actions are those required to improve team members' interpersonal skills and intrateam relationships. They include the following:

- Coaching to improve interpersonal skills
- Encouraging collaboration among team members
- Managing conflict to allow intellectual conflict but not personal conflict
- Enhancing team commitment
- Satisfying the trust and support needs of team members
- Being fair and consistent in exercising principled behavior

External leadership actions are those required to keep the team protected from the external environment but, at the same time, to keep the team connected to the external environment. These include the following:

- Networking to form alliances and gain access to information
- Advocating for the team with those who affect its environment
- Negotiating with senior management for recognition, support, and resources
- Protecting team members from environmental diversions
- Examining external indicants of effectiveness (e.g., customer satisfaction surveys)
- Providing team members with appropriate external information

One practice that has been known to work is to have senior management speak to the team at the start of a difficult project. This is much appreciated by the team members and shows the team members that senior management supports the project.

The critical point is that team member needs, in support of the goals agreed upon, are met either by the team leader or other team members. Of course, team effectiveness will be better if team member needs are met promptly and effectively, regardless of how the needs are met (Kogler-Hill, 2007).

Team Effectiveness

Team effectiveness consists of two overarching dimensions: team performance and team development. Team performance refers to whether and how well team tasks were accomplished, and team development refers to how well the team was maintained in accomplishing the team's tasks. Several researchers have suggested criteria for assessing team effectiveness. In this casebook, we will use the Larson and LaFasto's (1989) criteria.

We will present these criteria in the form of questions to help assess team effectiveness.

- Does the team have specific, realizable, clearly articulated goals?
- Does the team have a results-oriented structure?
- Are team members capable?
- Is there unity with respect to commitment to the team's goals?
- Is there a collaborative climate among team members?
- Are there standards of excellence to guide the team?
- Is there external support and recognition for the team?
- Is team leadership effective?

These criteria are important in assessing team effectiveness. Effective team leaders will find formal and informal ways of examining themselves and their team against these criteria. Finally, team leaders must be willing to take action to correct weaknesses on any of these criteria (Kogler-Hill, 2007).

How Does the Team Leadership Model Work?

The model in this chapter is a mental map for helping team leaders constantly assess their team's effectiveness, as well as when and where the team's leaders need to intervene. If an intervention is needed, is it internal task, internal relational, or external? This constant analysis is necessary for continuous team improvement. Just as hockey general managers need to continuously assess their team coaches and players, whether winning or losing, team leaders in nonsports organizations need to continuously push for improvement and, for example, must know when it is appropriate to change the coach and/or team members. The team leadership model assists in this push for continuous improvement and helps determine weaknesses that might need an intervention on the part of a member of the team's shared leadership structure.

To continue with the sports analogy, it may be necessary for the team captain to hold a players-only meeting, it may be appropriate for the coach to change team strategy when playing different teams, and/or it might be appropriate for the general manager to change the coach and/or team players. Lou Lamoriello, the general manager of the New Jersey Devils National Hockey League team, changed his team's coach with eight games to play at the end of the 2000 season and ended up winning the Stanley Cup. Since he became the general manager in 1987, the Devils have won three Stanley Cups (he is tied with Ken Holland of the Detroit Red Wings for the most Stanley Cups won by any general manager since 1987), and Lamoriello has done this with a different coach each time whereas Ken Holland has done it with only two different coaches.

References

Barge, J. K. (1996). Leadership skills and the dialectic of leadership in group decision making. In R. Y. Hirokawa & M. S. Poole (Eds.), *Communication and group decision making* (2nd ed., pp. 301–342). Thousand Oaks, CA: Sage.

Daft, R. L. (2011). *The leadership experience* (5th ed.). Mason, OH: Thomson, South-Western.

Day, D. V., Gronn, P., & Salas, E. (2004). Leadership capacity in teams. *Leadership Quarterly, 15*, 857–880.

Fleishman, E. A., Mumford, M. D., Zaccaro, S. J., Levin, K. Y., Korotkin, A. L., & Hein, M. B. (1991). Taxonomic efforts in the description of leader behavior: A synthesis and functional interpretation. *Leadership Quarterly, 2*(4), 245–287.

Kinlaw, D. C. (1998). *Superior teams: What they are and how to develop them.* Hampshire, UK: Grove.

Kogler-Hill, S. E. (2007). Team leadership. In P. G. Northouse (Ed.), *Leadership: Theory and practice* (4th ed., pp. 207–236). Thousand Oaks, CA: Sage.

LaFasto, F., & Larson, C. (2001). *When teams work best.* Thousand Oaks, CA: Sage.

Larson, C. E., & LaFasto, F. M. J. (1989). *Teamwork: What must go right/what can go wrong.* Newbury Park, CA: Sage.

Northouse, P. G. (2013). *Leadership: Theory and practice* (6th ed.). Thousand Oaks, CA: Sage.

Pauleen, D. J. (2004). An inductively derived model of leader-initiated relationship building with virtual team members. *Journal of Management Information Systems, 20*(3), 227–256.

Zaccaro, S. J., Rittman, A. L., & Marks, M. A. (2001). Team leadership. *Leadership Quarterly, 12*, 451–483.

⬕ The Cases

The Lithium Fire

In September 2001, 24 Calgary firefighters fought a fire at a battery plant. All of them were taken to hospital with many and different ailments, e.g., throat and eye irritations, severe breathing problems, and headaches. Initially, this industrial blaze seemed to be a routine fire—just another assignment. However, a series of explosions just after they started to fight the blaze soon dispelled this notion. They were forced to withdraw, and several of their colleagues were hospitalized. The incident affected the atmosphere at the fire hall. There were comments from some that they expected better and more information. Why had they not known what was inside the plant? What had gone wrong? What could be learned for similar incidents in the future? Would this affect their teamwork?

Chuck MacKinnon

A bank supervisor must contend with various personnel problems, specifically highlighting individuals—both subordinates and superiors. His immediate supervisor said that the new group was supposed to be great, his new position fun. In the view of his boss's boss, the group had major problems. He soon discovered that he had more problems than he had anticipated. How was he to deal with a dysfunctional group when his superiors disagreed about whether or not there were problems and were also personally antagonistic?

⬕ The Reading

X-Teams: New Ways of Leading in a New World

Like a country, an organization can't be too inward looking. Over there, on the outside, lies much of the intelligence and many of the resources that it must have to innovate and lead.

The Lithium Fire[1]

Gerard Seijts

People will forever remember the response of the New York firefighters on September 11, 2001 and never forget the sacrifices they made. Many firefighters rushed into the burning twin towers in a valiant attempt to save trapped office workers.

On September 11, 2001, 343 brave, heroic, courageous firefighters perished fighting fire and taking part in rescue operations in a most courageous and fearless manner, carrying out their duties.

A little over two weeks later, 24 Calgary firefighters ended up in hospital with throat and eye irritations, severe breathing problems and headaches after fighting a fire at a battery plant. Three police officers and three civilians were also treated for minor irritations and released from hospital a short time later. Like their U.S. counterparts, Canadian firefighters and police officers risk their lives on a daily basis to protect the public.

The fire started late afternoon and continued into the evening. The management of the plant had left the facilities. The firefighters thus had limited information to incorporate in their plan to battle the flames. To the firefighters, the blaze looked like a routine fire. The men had encountered fires in commercial buildings on multiple occasions. The industrial fire was seen as just another assignment that needed to be taken care of.

Adrenaline was pumping. The bias for action that characterizes the firefighters led them to grab a hose line to back up another firefighter and to start fighting the flames with vigor. And so the firefighters began attacking the fire through windows in the garage door at the facilities. In the words of Fire Chief Wayne Morris, "Firefighters tried to drown the fire as fast as they could."

But the fire was difficult to extinguish, so the firefighters stepped up their efforts and started to pour even greater volumes of water onto the fire. These were, after all, firefighters! This line of work is about service excellence, bravery, morals, duty, camaraderie and resilience. Individuals join the Fire Service for a multitude of reasons, among them, the challenging nature of the work.

Then a series of small explosions took place. Soon after, people at the site started to complain about throat and eye irritations and severe breathing problems. The firefighters were forced to pull back and to take stock of what had just happened.

The firefighters were unaware the water they were pouring on the flames was reacting with thionyl chloride and lithium inside the building. The resulting cloud of toxic hydrogen chloride gas forced the firefighters to break off their assault. The department's hazardous materials specialists were called in to see what was happening and how to proceed. The firefighters then put out the fire using a combination of water and foam, which helped smother the flames.

In the end, 24 firefighters ended up in the hospital with respiratory distress; 12 were kept overnight. Four firefighters were kept in hospital for over a week. Two firefighters developed long-term health issues.

The working atmosphere at the fire hall was impacted. The shock and trauma in the workplace was real. Some firefighters commented that they had expected to be better looked after, that they did not have enough information about what was inside the burning plant.

Fire Chief Wayne Morris decided a thorough debriefing should be conducted. Where had things gone wrong? What mistakes had been made? What specific lessons should be carried forward? And how could these lessons be passed on to other groups that could use the knowledge to avoid future disasters?

    Version: (A) 2009-01-30

[1]This case has been written on the basis of published sources only. Consequently, the interpretation and perspectives presented in this case are not necessarily those of the Calgary Firefighters.

Chuck MacKinnon

Kate Hall-Merenda and Jane Howell

The day after his group's 1994 Christmas party, Chuck MacKinnon, a managing director with the Merchant Bank of Canada (MBC) in New York, wondered how both his group and his career had become so seriously derailed. The night before, he had witnessed the virtual disintegration of a group that he had worked diligently to mould into a fully functioning team. Chuck knew his career and his personal life, as well as the group's survival, depended on how he addressed the multitude of people problems which he thought had been resolved, but which he now knew had only been lying in wait, just below the surface. As he pondered the previous night's events as a denouement of 18 months dedicated to trying to bring his group up to speed for the changing marketplace of the 1990s, he wondered not only what he should do, but if he was the right person to do it.

Chuck MacKinnon

After graduating from Georgetown University with his Bachelor of Science in Foreign Service, Chuck MacKinnon immediately went to work for Corporate Bank International (CBI), partially because CBI offered him the opportunity to work and earn his MBA in Corporate Finance, which he received in 1980. From 1980 to 1991, he held progressively more responsible positions within CBI, including a stint in Hong Kong. Then, in 1992, following CBI's merger with the Merchant Bank of Canada, MacKinnon was offered and accepted a position managing a full service branch of MBC in Saudi Arabia.

The Saudi Arabian months, Chuck's first exposure to the MBC, were fraught with difficulties. Managing a matrix organization with many units having dotted line reporting relationships to other areas around the globe was a challenge, but the larger challenge was solving a myriad of people problems that had been left unresolved by the previous manager.

Not long after his arrival in Saudi Arabia, Chuck discovered that the senior expatriate manager in the branch frequently left the bank to lunch in a bar in the American compound and did not return, and that his predecessor had allowed it. Chuck called Pete Dimarco, his boss in the United States, advised him of the situation and wondered aloud why it had been permitted to go on for so long. He could not have anticipated that he would receive a call from Bill Perkins, yet another MBC senior manager with interests in Asia, who "went ballistic" about Chuck not calling him first. As he reflected on the situation, Chuck noted:

> Immediately I was put off by how the Bank was not dealing with these problems, seemingly allowing them to happen, and accepting it; and then even getting angry with it being surfaced.... From the beginning I was never on solid ground on how we wanted to deal with this kind of stuff. We say the right things, but the messages once you get below the surface are not the same.

And there were other problems. Chuck caught some of his staff bribing government officials; having tax refunds directed into their personal accounts; cheating on credit cards; putting foreign exchange tickets in their personal

Version: (A) 2010-01-25

desks; and having outside business interests that were in conflict with their jobs at the Bank. He resolved many of these problems by "firing a lot of people"; then he had union problems, but he persevered, trying to resolve the problems in the branch. His perseverance lasted until he started receiving death threats from a client who had bribed a Bank employee in order to get money out of the country illegally and whom Chuck had subsequently reported to the Bank of Saudi Arabia. According to Chuck:

> I thought that I had cleaned it up, that I had gotten the right people in place and that things were running fine and that maybe, after all this pain, given the cultural issues, it was time for somebody else to come in and take it to the next step.

Chuck was looking for a new lease on life when a phone call came from Eldon Frost in Montreal offering him a corporate banking job in New York City with the Merchant Bank of Canada. Eldon portrayed the New York group as "working wonderfully, making money." In fact, he said, "it's a great business, you'll have a lot of fun." Chuck, thinking of his wife and two-year-old child, jumped at the offer.

⬚ One Job, Two Mandates

In August 1993, Chuck stepped into his new position as Managing Director, Financial Institutions, with MBC in New York, looking for a fresh start. His job was to manage MBC's relationships with a multitude of financial institution clients as well as to lead a team in marketing MBC's and CBI's corporate financial services and products. His first few weeks on the job were sufficient to convince Chuck that his group had a number of people problems as well as an outdated business strategy. Yet, when he broached the subjects of adopting a new strategy to deal with changing business conditions or

making changes within the group with Eldon, Eldon's mantra was "this group is great. Hey, your group is making 10 million bucks a year; it's working wonderfully!"

Although he did support Chuck's idea of a new strategy, Eldon was unwilling to let go of the group's traditional products. He did not see the market the same way as Chuck did; he had a different perspective. Eldon's market was the world, where a shortfall in revenues in one country could be made up by strengthening revenues in another. Chuck's world, the United States, was very different; there was no "contingency" location for making up revenue shortfalls. In spite of these differences, or because of them, Eldon could not see any reason for change; he believed "our group is different, we don't need to change, we're happy, we're separate, don't worry about it."

Eldon was driven by the concept of keeping everyone happy. He had survived a major corporate downsizing and had adapted by keeping his head down and making no noise. Perhaps, Chuck speculated, that was why Eldon's attitude was, "Don't rock the boat, I'm a survivor." It did not help that Eldon had expected to be promoted into his boss's position, had been passed over, and consequently, harbored a great deal of resentment toward Margaret, who had been appointed executive vice president instead.

Margaret Mattson was two levels above Chuck in the corporate hierarchy (see Exhibit 1 for the organization chart) and Chuck met her only after he had taken up his position in New York. Unlike Eldon, Margaret was not satisfied with the Financial Institutions group or its performance. She had held Chuck's position open for a considerable length of time looking for the right person and was sure that Chuck was the person to carry out her "fix it" mandate.

In their very first face-to-face meeting, Margaret told Chuck that she was unsure if it had been the right decision to send Patrick Kinnard, one of the directors, from Montreal to New York. She was also critical of many of the staff that remained in Montreal and she wanted Chuck to fix the group by "getting rid of the weak staff." Margaret was sure that the group's current skills were not sufficient to meet the looming competitive challenges.

In their next meeting, Chuck convinced Margaret that there were also problems with the products the group had to offer and that new ones were badly needed. "That clicked for her" when Chuck showed her the numbers on price concessions the group was making on traditional products and, from that moment on, Margaret fully supported Chuck in driving the group toward a new strategy. Unlike Eldon, Margaret had worked for another investment bank during the major downsizing at MBC. Possibly because of this, Chuck speculated, "she did not have the survivor mind set," and consequently, pushed hard for him to make major changes quickly.

Chuck informed both Eldon and Margaret of their conflicting expectations of him, but it appeared to have very little impact on either of his bosses. Eldon did tell Chuck that he and Margaret had a "you leave me alone, I'll leave you alone and we'll just work together but keep our distance as best we can" type of arrangement and implied that he would have to live with it. Chuck, himself, had seen that they were like "oil and water" and that they worked very hard not ever to be present in the same room. He wondered how he could possibly fulfill both mandates.

⊠ Getting to Know the Group

When Chuck arrived in New York, his first order of business was to get to know his group (see Exhibit 2 for a profile of the group). He travelled to Los Angeles and Montreal, meeting members of his team and assessing their skills and prospects. In Los Angeles, he found a high-performing team of 50 under the deft leadership of Bruce Wilson. In Montreal, he discovered a group that felt that Patrick Kinnard, one of their number who had recently transferred to New York, "had cut a deal

for himself and deserted them to get paid in U.S. dollars." Practically all of the Montreal people wanted to join Patrick in New York. Chuck knew that Patrick's parting words to the Montreal group were that their much desired relocation would happen.

Chuck was well aware that the financial institutions banking business required that banking professionals be within easy access of their customers, not a lengthy flight away. He decided that the Montreal group had to stay in Montreal. While the group struggled with the prospect of staying in Canada (and being paid in Canadian dollars), Chuck investigated means by which they could successfully operate as a team across two countries and a continent. Technology and travel both offered solutions.

Travel was the easier of the two solutions. Chuck flew to Montreal on a varying schedule, never less than once a month, sometimes twice a week, to travel with his directors and senior relationship managers as they visited their clients. In an attempt to keep the lines of communication open, he augmented those personal visits with conference and groups calls. But, it was not enough; additional technology was required.

The Montreal group was not up to date technology wise. They didn't use e-mail or notebook computers in Canada. Chuck reflected, "possibly because of the technology lag, in Montreal they didn't see the vision" of a continent-spanning team. Chuck tried to correct the technology problem by supplying the Montreal group with notebook computers and cellular phones, primarily for use when they were travelling; but some members of the group could not, or would not, use them.

Chuck's frustration level grew. It took two days to track down one member of the group who was travelling in Europe when a client needed him; "nobody in Montreal even had an itinerary for him!" Why, he wondered, would they not use the scheduling package that he provided on their desk and laptop computers? Why did they view it as "big brother," or use it to check up on what Chuck was doing, instead of just acknowledging that it was merely a tool to make them accessible in times of need? Chuck felt that technology made it okay to have distant groups, while some of the group members said that it destroyed the camaraderie of face-to-face conversation. There was apparently not going to be a meeting of the minds.

Chuck had to admit that technology and travel could not furnish all of the answers to the group's problems. He discovered tremendous frictions within the group: Glenn Wright only worked with, and supported, Neil Forsyth, even though he was supposed to support the whole group; there was conflict between Steve Salmon, Neil and Glenn; and all of this was exacerbated when a demoted Patrick Kinnard moved to New York and began to notice that Glenn was not supporting him either. The fact that Chuck himself was an unknown to the group, except for Dale Cameron and Patrick, added to the overall tension levels. Even though the "sales people got along with everybody and they were great," they were not enough to salvage the team.

Chuck knew that something had to be done to turn his disparate and geographically dispersed group into a team and he thought maybe skill-enhancing courses might be part of the answer. He enrolled the entire group in courses to improve organizational and sales skills and to introduce them to the use of technology in sales, figuring that if they went as a group and developed skills together, it would help to build camaraderie and team spirit. In keeping with that theme, in May, Chuck and the group attended a team-building and high performance team work course that, according to Chuck, went well.

> People came out good friends. I thought there was commitment and I was positive about the whole thing.

Then, in July, Chuck hired the team-building course instructor to work as a consultant to the group.

⊠ The Strategy

Chuck had another reason for providing the group members with a minimum of 10 training days per year, even though that number exceeded the average for the Bank. His first few months in New York and Montreal convinced him that the group's business strategy was hopelessly out-of-date with the needs of the financial institutions sector and that something had to change. When he arrived, the strategy had been very much cash management-driven, dealing mostly with cash letters and lock box type accounts. There were two problems with that strategy. First, with all the U.S. mergers, the group had lost business over time because their customers were taken over and they had not always been successful in gaining the acquirer's business. Second, the trend line in the cash management and lending business was downwards, and pricing pressures had been enormous. Even though volume had been increasing, prices were declining and the revenue line had been flat. Chuck knew that "if we had just stayed doing that, there would be no bonuses, no incentive, nothing. It would have been barely treading water . . . we needed to do something else."

Something else was a new strategy that involved expanding into other product lines such as Treasury, derivative products, stock transfer, lending and trust. The group had "never talked any of those other product lines to any U.S. financial institutions." Lack of familiarity bred resistance, even though Chuck worked hard to get and keep the group involved in designing and implementing the new strategy. His people, after all, knew their customers and presumably knew what their customers needed. In Chuck's words:

> That was part of the change that I was trying to get some of these people to deal with; to get up to speed with those products and go out and market them. And that was where I ran into resistance. They would say, why these products, what we're doing now is fine. Why

change? And my feeling was that business was being commoditized and going to go away and that, in the long run, we were not going to be able to succeed with that.

He hoped by adding to their skill base and teaching them to perform as a team, their resistance to the new strategy would wither and die.

◪ The Group as Individuals

Neil Forsyth, Director

Located in Montreal, and in his mid-50s, Neil Forsyth was the first person to cause real friction for Chuck. He would say, "Why change, we cannot do this, I can't do it because I don't know how, I'm afraid, I don't see the need, I like the traditional thing and I'm good at it and it works." He was angry about the new strategy and kept agitating Chuck about it, making statements like, "You're nuts, it just won't work," while Chuck was trying to build a team. Although previously an exceptional performer, Neil received a quality contributor rating on his 1994 performance appraisal. While Neil believed that his performance ratings fell because of a personality conflict between himself and Chuck, Chuck noted that Neil's "ratings fell because he did not adopt the new strategy or provide that exceptional performance." Given the tension and disagreement between them, by late 1994, Chuck knew that he had to move Neil out of the group and he had started looking seriously for other opportunities for him within the Bank.

Glenn Wright, Associate

Also based in Montreal, during his first meeting with Chuck, Glenn told his new boss "what a great guy he was, how he was better than anyone else, and that he had been promised a directorship." Chuck, taking him at his word, promised

to look into that directorship. What he discovered was that Glenn was not always delivering exceptional service. Indeed, Chuck was receiving mixed messages about Glenn's performance from Steve Salmon and Neil; evidently, Glenn had decided he would support Neil but not Steve. Chuck decided that he would not pursue the directorship for Glenn; in fact, he told Glenn that the only way to get promoted was through exceptional performance and that he had seen no sign of such performance.

Glenn felt that he could not deliver the expected exceptional performance in a strictly support role and asked Chuck to allow him to prove himself with his own clients. Trying to be fair, Chuck gave Glenn his own portfolio. Glenn liked having his own clients and did really well with some of them; others he alienated. According to Chuck, "if he needed you, you were his best buddy; if he did not need you, he ignored you; and if you pushed him, you were an !!!!!!!!!" Many of his client relationships were strained.

Glenn displayed very poor work habits and many Monday/Friday absences. Chuck started to get "a lot of heat" about Glenn from both Margaret and Eldon. Margaret, who had initially been critical of Glenn, became even more so after she saw him playing solitaire on his computer in the office. One day Eldon saw Glenn playing solitaire and called Chuck in wonderment, asking "how can an employee play solitaire right out in the open in the office?" Glenn, for his part, did not demonstrate that he wanted to work harder or support the new strategy. His attitude was, "I think you're wrong, I don't buy into any of this, I come in at nine and I'm leaving at 4:30." The chip on his shoulder just got larger and larger.

Deitr Poehlmann, Associate

Based in New York, Deitr's initial relationship with Chuck was a good one. Chuck saw from the beginning that, for some unknown reasons, Deitr was being "grossly underpaid" and undertook to make up a $20,000 annual shortfall over a period of time. As time went on, however, Chuck noted that "Deitr's work was spotty, sometimes okay and sometimes poor," particularly when it came to verbal and written communications in English. Deitr's first language was German, and that, to him, was sufficient reason not to do anything about his English. He believed people would make allowances for his language, even though Chuck spoke with him repeatedly on the matter and told him that they would not. At one point, Deitr went so far as to find an English-speaking trainer of operational staff to attest to his fluency in the English language.

Deitr also had "tremendous problems communicating internally; he would call people liars on e-mail and send copies of the e-mail to everyone, including their bosses" (see Exhibit 3). Such behavior created seemingly endless problems for Chuck, who was called upon time and again to smooth ruffled feathers of colleagues and clients who had been offended by Deitr's rather abrupt manner of communicating and by his tactless language. Chuck attempted to counsel Deitr on both his use of English and the English he used, but to no avail. Indeed, it seemed to have the opposite effect; Deitr had, for many years, believed that the world was prejudiced against the Germans and eventually he directed those sentiments towards Chuck.

Dale Cameron, Director

Dale Cameron originally came from Corporate Bank International and started in the New York group following the 1992 merger between CBI and MBC. He had had a long standing and positive relationship with Chuck when the latter arrived in August 1993. Although Chuck did not push him, indeed, he let him slide because of more pressing issues with others; he did notice that Dale had problems with erratic work. Some of Dale's memos were totally unintelligible, while others were cogent and well written. Chuck suspected a drug or alcohol problem and suggested that Dale access the Employee Assistance Program, but Dale claimed that there was no problem. In retrospect, Chuck admitted that "I ended up protecting him a little bit, became a little co-dependent," and, in November 1994, he gave Dale a quality contribution rating on his performance appraisal, noting that Dale had both accepted, and attempted to implement, the new strategy.

Patrick Kinnard, Director

Patrick Kinnard was Chuck's predecessor, a very capable individual in the cash management business. He had developed some new product lines that were interesting and Eldon had moved him to New York from Montreal in the summer of 1993 to give him a fresh start in a new location after his demotion. Eldon publicly said that, in spite of the demotion, he thought Patrick was great at everything he did and he told Chuck that "Patrick's nose will be out of joint since you got his job, but he will come around." In the beginning, it seemed as if that might be true. Their early relationship was fine and, although Chuck had heard numerous stories about Patrick's serious drinking problem, he did not mention those stories to Patrick. Chuck had decided to reserve judgment and give Patrick a chance to prove otherwise.

Six months later, coinciding with the initiation of the new strategy, Patrick and Chuck's relationship started to deteriorate. Patrick had agreed to follow the new strategy, but felt that Chuck did not respect the traditional cash management business sufficiently. At one point, Patrick went to Eldon, complaining about the strategy and saying that they were heading for disaster. He even brought Dale along to say the same thing. Eldon's reaction was to call Chuck immediately, questioning him about what was going on in New York and demanding that they find a way to work together. Chuck's subsequent interviews with both Patrick and Dale got all of the issues out on the table and he did what could be done to address the doubts both men had about the new strategy.

Then, in the summer of 1994, Chuck received a call from Margaret inquiring about Patrick's random sick days; to her, the absences looked suspicious. Having had some experience with alcoholics and their habits and patterns, Chuck sat down with Patrick, asked him if he had a drinking problem and offered to work with him through the Alcoholics Anonymous steps. Patrick's response was that "he was dealing with it" (see Exhibit 4 for a synopsis of Patrick's absences). Chuck, who was not sure Patrick was dealing with it or that any alcoholic could deal with their alcoholism by *drinking moderately* or *keeping it under control*, suggested the Bank's Employee Assistance Program but Patrick did not take advantage of the offer. Chuck felt that he had done all that he could insofar as Patrick was concerned.

⊠ The 1994 Christmas Party

Thinking he could bring the group together and really cement the team spirit and acceptance of the new strategy that he thought was taking hold in the group, Chuck decided to hold the Christmas party in Montreal. He brought in all of the people from the New York office and some from the Los Angeles unit to join the festivities. The party was held in a fancy restaurant and they were seated out in the open. For a while, all went well, but as the evening advanced and people got progressively more "toasted," the illusion of camaraderie began to disintegrate.

The worst part came when group members rose to their feet and began to give speeches. Patrick and Glenn each gave 10-minute speeches putting down the new business direction, asking "where are we going with this strategy?" They also could not resist harping on the bitter relationships in the group. Bill Russell then gave a speech about how "we should all be getting along better." Chuck, who had been trying to sit near

those individuals who had major issues, was both embarrassed, "everyone in the place was paying attention," and angry "at the group and at individuals, for rehashing old stuff. It had been a year and a half and they weren't suggesting anything new to replace what they didn't like."

Having had enough, Chuck decided it was time for the party to break up. Passing Lynne Morris on the way out of the restaurant, Chuck could see that she was as appalled as he was and as uncomprehending of what was going on. Although he only wanted to go to sleep, the evening was not over for Chuck. In order to stop Patrick from hitting on Michelle St. Pierre, his executive secretary, he bundled Dale and Patrick into a taxi and got them to the hotel bar. In the bar, Patrick first picked a fight with Dale, and, after Chuck broke up that fight, he picked a fight with Chuck. The whole miserable evening only ended, Chuck reflected, when he finally gave up and went up to bed.

The next day Patrick was nowhere to be seen. Chuck spoke with Bill Russell to see if he could make sense out of Bill's behavior the previous evening. Bill did not really remember making the speech about everyone working together as a team, but he was embarrassed and fully apologetic and vowed it would never happen again. Chuck, for his part, was able to overlook one slip from a stellar performer—it was, after all, Christmas—but he would not overlook another one.

As Chuck reflected on the previous evening's disaster, he found some things to be thankful for. His group was not completely dysfunctional.

⊠ The Functional Group

Steve Salmon, Director

Steve Salmon was based in Montreal. He was "a good guy, an average performer, one who would never be a superstar but he supported the strategy and did his best to implement it." He was very good at his job, well liked by his clients in a portfolio that he had handled for five years and he produced consistently good results. Steve was a "solid member of the team and a pleasure to work with. He is well liked by everyone on the team."

Lynne Morris, Manager

An exceptional performer and team player, Lynne was well liked and respected by clients and team members alike. She was a delightful individual who supported the new strategy, who had made the transition into new products fairly successfully, and "she was rewarded that way with big bonuses." Chuck counted on her for fielding calls on traditional cash management issues as well as for implementing the new strategy.

Bill Russell, Manager

Bill Russell was an exceptional performer who had increased his role in the identification of sales opportunities and was taking the necessary steps to close sales. Bill was a committed team member who supported the changes taking place, who willingly brought ideas and opinions to the table, who did a lot of cross-selling of products and who had made the transition to the new products well. Like Lynne Morris, Bill was a high performer and rewarded that way and, again like Lynne, Chuck counted on him for traditional cash management inquires and problems.

Bruce Wilson

A very high performer based in Los Angeles with 50 people reporting to him, Bruce Wilson managed a quality operation with a very thin staff that dealt with a wide range of responsibilities including systems and marketing. His service levels were high and his clients were both very loyal and supportive; his employee morale was high. Bruce emerged from the 1994 Christmas

party saying, "Holy God, what the heck is going on here? Good luck to you!"

✉ Chuck's Dilemma

The previous 18 months had not been easy for Chuck. He had always been an exceptional performer but had received only a "quality contributor" rating from Eldon on his 1994 performance appraisal. Although he had tried, he could not get Eldon to explain why he considered him only "quality" and what it would take to become "exceptional" again. Eldon had only suggested that maybe the problem with the group's dynamics was partly due to Chuck's management style. At his wits end, Chuck thought maybe Eldon was right. Perhaps he "just did not get it." He thought, "This is it, I don't know what is going on around here, this isn't working" (see Exhibit 5 for an example of team conflict). But he did not have other avenues in the Bank to pursue. He had talked to people at CBI, but it was tough to get back in once you had left, and he had no network within MBC that he could tap. He felt stuck.

Chuck's growing self-doubts were reinforced by the messages he was getting from Margaret. Although he was convinced that he was pursuing the right business strategy, he wondered about his management style. Margaret's "fix it mandate" had changed; she openly wondered if Chuck's management style had been too severe, too hard. Chuck wondered if, and what, he could be doing better, if he had misunderstood the degree to which the bank was willing to change. "After all," he confessed, "when you have that many dysfunctionalities and a boss persistently saying everything is fine, the result is self-doubt."

On top of the erosion of his self-confidence in his management style, Chuck was beginning to see himself as a co-dependent in protecting Patrick and Dale. He had helped both of them with their work, redone their work and covered for them by writing memos addressing what were major problems and making light of them.

Had he been mistaken in his attempts to give everyone a fair chance to adjust to the new regime before taking action? Could some of the problems have been avoided if he had been, not softer, but tougher?

Then there was his personal life. He had been short-tempered with both his wife and children and had been feeling guilty about allowing his work stresses to spill over into his personal life. Normally, he had been adept in separating the two, but in this case, he had failed.

The day after the 1994 Christmas party found Chuck wondering what was going on. Should he be looking for work elsewhere? The messages from his boss and his boss's boss were clear: it might be his management style. Had he done something wrong? What could he, or anyone else, do to fix it now?

Exhibit 1   Financial Institutions Group Organization Chart

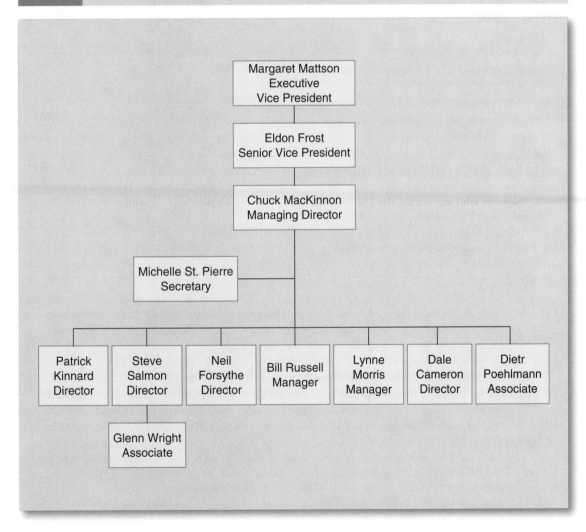

Exhibit 2	A Profile of the Financial Institutions Group

Name	Age	Years in Bank	Years in Position	PPR 1992	PPR 1993	PPR 1994
Chuck MacKinnon	39	3	1	EC	EC	QP
Patrick Kinnard	52	17	7	EC	EC	EC
Neil Forsythe	53	15	5	EC	EC	QP
Dale Cameron	40	18	1	EC	EC	QP
Glenn Wright	35	10	3	QP	QP	QP
Deitr Poehlmann	35	12	3	QP	QP	QP
Steve Salmon	50	20	7	QP	QP	QP
Lynne Morris	52	25	10	EC	EC	EC
Bill Russell	45	20	12	EC	EC	EC

PPR = Performance Planning and Review

EC = Exceptional Contribution

QP = Quality Performer

Exhibit 3	Deitr Poehlmann's Correspondence

From: Deitr Poehlmann
To: Chuck MacKinnon
CC: Bob Grange; Joe Peoples; Stan Mantrop

Chuck,

Usually people that feel threatened, weak, try to hide their weaknesses, or try to ruin one's reputation will send e-mail as Joe did (the one below). I do not know that Joe has against me. I never create conference calls unless all parties know about it and agree to it.

I spoke with Bob Grange this morning. First, he still says that he was not aware of Cory's participation. Since this view is different from mine, I suggest that we call Cory and find out his view. Bob suggested (and I agreed) that we should not have our clients get involved in this. Bob and I decided that from now on, our phone conversations will not include third parties in order to avoid one's not knowing who else is on the phone. Bob also said that Boston Mutual's situation introduced to him is very clear.

I tried to call Joe but he is already in Hong Kong. I wanted to see what was so convoluted to him as, I hope, obviously you understood my e-mail. Obviously, Joe did not. Since it is so difficult to have this thing done with Joe, I think we should just drop it and let Boston Mutual do its thing on its own (which they are as we speak).

From: Deitr Poehlmann
To: Chuck MacKinnon

Chuck, as we agreed and you asked me to do so, I am sending you this e-mail to friendly remind you that as of August 1, you were to consider giving me a merit increase in my salary. I hope that you will be generous and take into consideration all my contribution to growing revenue at International Portfolio. I hope that I am exceeding your expectations from working on reducing backlog, bringing new business, and cross-selling business to existing clients. I want to thank you for your prior recognition in the form of increases and bonus and hope that you see me as a productive member of your team. Also, as you know, my salary, in my view, is below average, although I must say that you kept your word to me about increasing it "over time" to higher level.

From: Steve Salmon
To: Chuck MacKinnon
CC: Deitr Poehlmann

Yes, and I think we'll find Lansing were unhappy as to HOW we dialogued with them, and that also had an influence. While I'm sure it was misinterpreted, I'm told Deitr Poehlmann didn't come across very well in his conversations with them.

From: Deitr Poehlmann
To: Chuck MacKinnon; Steve Salmon

Steve, if they told you that I am not surprised about the statement. There was only one person that I spoke at Lansing. She herself was rude, imposing and cancelled our (Chuck and myself) meeting with them day before we were to go to Atlanta. Their point was that we were "demanding" reciprocity business (custody) from them. I did what I was told by Chuck and Brett Davies. We did not extend the lines as they wanted and I am sorry if they did not like that. I have been dealing with them for the past 3 years without any problem until not all of their demands were met. At that point, I guess, I fell into disfavor. The only bad thing is that right now we are out of $40,000 + revenue.

(Continued)

Exhibit 3	(Continued)

Dear Merridith,

As you know, after closing USD account, Corporate Bank International still maintains Canadian Dollar account with your fine bank. With our ongoing process of reviewing all of our account relationships in an effort to process our business more efficiently and cost effectively, it has become apparent that we need to close the Canadian Dollar account that we maintain with you, as well. Therefore, we decided to close it effective May 15. The account by that time should have no balances left, however, should there be any money left on that day, please have it sent to:

Sincerely,
Deitr Poehlmann

Exhibit 4	Patrick Kinnard's Absences

From: Eldon Frost
To: Patrick Kinnard

I am writing to register my concern on your performance on June 17 as reported to me and Margaret Mattson by Peter Delottinville, VP Employee/Industrial Relations, and as related to him by the two lawyers who spoke with you by phone on Friday June 17 on matters related to a criminal court case against the Bank and where your input was requested.

As advised to me your behavior was such that you were not making sense of the information provided you, nor were you able to answer the questions posed in a coherent and understandable manner. As a result, counsel for the Bank and for Elections Canada have had to prepare a list of questions for you to answer in written form.

In addition, I understand Margaret Mattson also spoke with you by phone the morning of Friday June 17, at approximately 10 a.m., and she was of the impression you had been on calls earlier that morning with Neil Forsythe and Bill Russell. In this regard I have been informed by Neil Forsythe that neither he nor Bill Russell called on customers with you that day and that in fact you advised them that morning that you were ill and could not attend the planned meetings.

Patrick, I am very much concerned with what happened on Friday as this is not the customary behavior expected of you.

In this regard your input on the above events would be appreciated so that we may work together to overcome whatever problems may exist. Eldon Frost.

Chuck MacKinnon's log of events:

12/9 Patrick at the last minute called in to take a vacation day.

1/23 Patrick arrived at 12:00 p.m. "Drove his brother-in-law to the airport."

4/26 Sick day.

6/12 Patrick arrived at 10:00 a.m., said a cab did not show up to take him to the train, so had to drive in.

7/7 Sick Day—back was out.

7/12 Sick Day—back was out.

9/1 Vacation day, family flight delayed in returning from holidays. Called Friday morning.

9/6 Sick day, called at 8:30 a.m. with the flu.

9/25 Had lunch with Patrick today to discuss some of the concerns that he has raised previously. At the same time we discussed some of the administrative problems he has had (the audit, problems with expense claims, not getting back to Redboard on time on information he needed for a board presentation, last minute absences and vacation days, etc.). I indicated that I did not think I should be put in a position of having to cover for him on these problems. I indicated that I thought they were a possible indication of the drinking problem we had previously discussed but Patrick indicated this was not the case. He said he was just sloppy on some things and tended to procrastinate but would work on cleaning this up in the future.

9/27 Sick Day, supposed to be in Montreal after calls in Pittsburgh the prior day, had the flu, was dizzy and sick to his stomach. Had dinner with PNC the night before.

9/28 Sick day, supposed to be in New York, had the flu.

9/28 Had conversation with Eldon this afternoon. Eldon was wondering where Patrick was on Wednesday as he had an appointment to see him. I told him he was sick and Eldon wondered if he was drinking again. I don't know whether Patrick was drinking on this occasion as I did not speak to him but this is not the first time that Patrick has missed a day in Montreal after travelling and having dinner with clients the night before. I did clarify for Eldon that I had had several conversations with Patrick as a friend about the drinking and cautioned him that he could not have any repetitions of past events. When Eldon heard that Patrick continues to drink (he regularly does so with and without clients although I have never seen him drunk again) and believes that he can handle it, he was very concerned as his deal with Ken is that there can be no drinking at all. If there is, their understanding is that Patrick will no longer be allowed to be in a client marketing position as his history in Montreal indicates he cannot control his drinking. Eldon referred to this as his "smoking gun."

Exhibit 5 Team Conflict

From: Dale Cameron
To: Glenn Wright
Cc: Chuck MacKinnon

Thank you for your quick turnaround and I believe that your presentation was done well. I would add, however, that we should be careful about using words (in letters and our presentations) which tend to undermine the "relationship team" concept. Specifically and despite our clearly being more capable of answering their questions, it might have been nice to say that they could also call myself. Finally, I called Linda and Jennifer yesterday and asked for feedback. Had I known you had done so, we could have avoided the extra call and the potential of appearing that we are not coordinating with one another. I will, likewise, endeavor to do the same. I assume the reports and letters are in the centrepoint file, and will copy you on the ones for the other three visits.

From: Glenn Wright
To: Dale Cameron
Cc: Chuck MacKinnon

Dale, this is one relationship you should leave to me. I have an excellent rapport with them and I think we are starting to confuse them. They have also asked several times that the relationship be managed by me through Linda, Homer and now Jennifer, something Linda reiterated in the meeting, if you remember, and in subsequent conversations. In the end, through PPR, we will all share any rewards to be had.

Glenn

From: Dale Cameron
To: Glenn Wright
Cc: Chuck MacKinnon

I could care less about "rewards" and PPR, other than as it relates to doing the job we are expected to do in a fashion that places professionalism and client service first. For that matter, you can have 100 per cent of all the credit on anything that is done with this client. We should always do, within reason, what the client wants and as global R/M you are responsible. If you recall, I specifically said that in my intro. I do not ever remember hearing Linda say anything about this, it was never expressed that way to me by Mike or Linda on the intro call, and I would like to know what conversation you are referring to where Jennifer said this. She's your contact anyway. Finally, I haven't even heard about this request from you until today.

Chuck, your decision is needed and perhaps you should call Homer or Jennifer and ask them outright. In the meantime, as long as I am "responsible" for this specific entity, I expect to be kept appraised of what is being discussed, done and acted upon, as you would expect of me. I have done so and will continue to do so. For that matter, all other entities for which I have responsibility. Rewards—absolutely misses the point.

From: Chuck MacKinnon
To: Dale Cameron; Glenn Wright

P.S. Sounds like there is some friction here. Let's talk about this on Monday between the three of us but the client's interests must be foremost.

X-Teams: New Ways of Leading in a New World

Deborah Ancona, Elaine Backman, and Henrik Bresman

There's nothing really wrong with the way organizational teams work— except for the fact that they are inward looking. This exception is critical, since the connections that enable the firm to seize market opportunities and leverage technological breakthroughs are on the outside. X-teams are externally oriented, and enabling them will lead the organization to step up the pace of change and innovation.

Business pundits tell us that we live in a new world—a world that's flat, global, diverse, and networked.[1] In this world, information flows freely across organizational, geographic, and cultural borders. The result is a hyper-drive environment where innovation is the name of the game, rules are invented on the fly, and the challenge always is to do it better and faster or fall prey to some unknown competitor who just arrived on the playing field.

This article examines how three very different enterprises are dealing with this new reality. In doing so, the article will explore the application of two key concepts. The first is the idea of distributed leadership—a way of harnessing, aligning, and leveraging the leadership capabilities that exist all across an organization to make it more agile, responsive, and creative. The second concept is that of X-teams—teams that enable companies to practice distributed leadership and to reach beyond internal and external boundaries to accelerate the process of innovation and change.

⊠ Responding to a New World

Let's take a look at some of the ways people have reacted to the new world. Some have focused on building virtual enterprises—nimble networks of ad hoc teams leveraging new information technologies to accelerate innovation. Others have created more stable organizational structures and cultures designed for consistent and steady innovation over time. Still others have focused on strategic partnerships to spur innovative practices.

One example of the nimble-network approach is the Vehicle Design Summit, an MIT student-led international consortium formed to design a two-hundred mile per gallon car for sale in India. With over thirty-six teams on six continents, funding from major corporations, input from the best universities on the planet, the consortium has already created a working prototype. Each team works on its own part of the design and gets its own funding, while coordinating with other teams and outside individuals and companies. Coordinators—like the logistics people working on how to keep the value chain as green as possible—create rules and tools that enable the teams to reach specific targets. A management team energizes the effort, brokers conflicts, and arranges meetings where teams bring their respective parts of the car together. This is not your typical student project.

A different example is W. L. Gore[2], best known for Gore-Tex®, and which operates on a very different scale from the Vehicle Design

[1]Thomas Friedman, *The World is Flat.*

[2]Elaine's case.

Reprint# 9B08TC12

Summit. The company has been in business for 50 years, has operations in forty-five countries, and generates $2.1 billion in annual revenues. In dealing with the change sweeping across today's corporate environment, Gore has taken the approach of designing more formal organizational structures and cultures that foster innovation and change.

While the traditional role of top-level leadership is to set strategy—including choosing key products, markets, and development priorities—W. L. Gore has turned this process on its head. At Gore, employees get to spend "dabble time" on projects they see as particularly interesting and promising. They elect their own project leaders who then engage in a peer-review process to determine which projects will eventually get funded and become part of the corporate portfolio.

One of the company's engineers working on cardiac implants chose to use his "dabble time" to develop a more tone-resilient guitar string, using the polymer prominent in gore-tex fabric. Over a three-year period the engineer assembled a small team of volunteers to develop the new string and explore the market demand. The peer-review committee awarded the resources to bring the project to scale, and today the company's Elixir strings outsell their closest competitor by a two-to-one ratio.

Multiply this process many times over, add a lattice-type flat organizational structure and an elected top leadership team, and you will get an innovation hot house. Gore has leveraged its knowledge of polymers to develop thousands of products, and step out of its original textiles market into areas such as medical devices, high-tech cables, and new energy technologies.

The new world we live in has spurred even the largest firms to become more agile. One such success story is Procter & Gamble. Historically, this Fortune 50 giant relied on internal capabilities and a small set of suppliers to invent and deliver new products and services to the market. By 2000, however, the company realized that this invent-it-yourself model was not cutting it in today's more competitive environment. The result was a shift from R&D (research and development) to C&D (connect and develop)—from "7,500 individuals inside to 7,500 plus one and a half million innovators outside the company with a permeable boundary between them."[3]

In this new C&D environment, P&G cast a broad global net to find a solution to allow it write on a Pringle's potato chip. Instead of taking months to put together a product development team and charge it with creating a new technology, it found a baker in Italy who could write on a cookie. It used that technology on Pringle's. The same collaborative approach, in this case between P&G and a Japanese competitor, led to the highly successful Swiffer dusters product line.

⊠ A New Form of Leadership for a New World

Despite this shifting organizational terrain that includes everything from virtual enterprises to multi-billion-dollar global giants struggling to become "elephants that dance",[4] we cling to our old notions of leadership. We still think of leaders as those within our own organizational boundaries. We still look to the omniscient leader at the top to come up with an inspiring vision, the right strategic direction, exciting new ideas, and the answers to our most pressing problems. Leadership research and training still focuses on the individual leader—his or her traits, behaviors, charisma, character, values, and political savvy.

[3]P&G

[4]Lou Gerstner.

But the single leaders alone at the top or our organizational units cannot understand the complexity of our interdependent, information-driven world. One leader cannot manage the ever increasing levels of interconnectivity within and outside the organization. Nor can organizations afford to wait for information to be passed up to the top for decisions to be made.

In today's new world, there is a greater than ever need for leadership at all levels of the organization—what we call "distributed leadership."[5] Leadership needs to be distributed across many players, both within and across organizations, up and down the hierarchy, wherever information, expertise, vision, and new ways of working together reside. The result is a whole network of leaders who are aligned to move the organization in new directions based on market opportunities and technological breakthroughs. In this environment, influence does not just flow downward, but moves up, down, and laterally, empowering those who are best able to lead at any given time. Equally important, leadership is shared with those outside the firm who can help bring in new ideas, more efficient processes, and stronger links to outside markets and distribution channels.

But how do organizations move in this direction? How do they create the culture and structures that enable distributed leadership? How do they innovate, adapt, and execute rapidly while developing networks of leaders aligned to carry their organizations in new directions? One solution is X-teams.

◣ A New Team for a New World

X-teams are *externally* oriented teams in which team members reach across their boundaries from day one, forging dense networks of contacts inside and outside the firm. These connections enable members to keep pace with shifts in markets, technologies, cultures, and competitors. They enable team members to learn about complex problems and find innovative solutions. They help the team link upper and lower levels of the firm, so that those with the knowledge of markets and potential new products and services can align with those forging new strategic directions and change. These connections can also enable players inside and outside the firm to share expertise and create new synergies that take advantage of emergent opportunities. These external connections enable innovation and adaptation.

X-teams[6] not only reach out across their boundaries to become networked teams (see Figure 1), they also enable rapid execution by moving through three phases: explore, exploit, and export. During exploration, X-Team members act like scouts making sense of their new terrain. They try to understand their task or challenge with new eyes and new ideas—generating as many potential insights and possibilities as possible. Then, during exploitation, they shift gears and envision the one product they wish to create and move from possibilities to reality, doing rapid prototyping along the way. Finally, during exportation, they find ways to move their product, knowledge, and excitement to the rest of the organization or marketplace, assuring that their work is diffused into the broader environment.

Take a product design team at IDEO,[7] a product design firm headquartered in Palo Alto, California. Asked to design a new emergency room, team members first *explored* emergency rooms from multiple perspectives. To capture the experience of the patients they placed a camera on the head of a patient. After watching ten hours of different views of the ceiling, they *exploited* this information and decided to create a new design for the emergency room that included writing that

---

[5]Ancona, Malone, Orlikowski, Senge, In Praise of the Incomplete Leader. *Harvard Business Review*, February, 2007.

[6]Ancona and Bresman. *X-team: How to build teams that lead, innovate, and succeed.* Boston: Harvard Business School Press, 2007.

[7]Taken from a talk given at the MIT Sloan School by IDEO CEO Tom Brown.

| **Figure 1** | X-Teams Build External Networks |

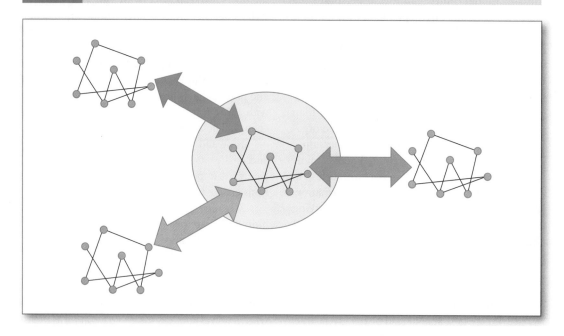

was projected on the ceiling. They tested the new design with actual patients, doctors, and hospital staff, made some additional changes, and then *exported* their design to a real hospital setting.

X-teams at VDS, W. L. Gore, and P&G are bringing to life the concept of distributed leadership in each of those very different enterprises. For example, each of the thirty-six teams of the VDS initiative operates as an X-team. The teams reach out to get expertise from surrounding companies and universities, and to secure funding from a variety of external sources. They collaborate closely with other teams, whether those teams exist within the VDS consortium or outside of it. They coordinate with the leadership team to ensure that their work is in sync with the overall plan.

Thus, each of the VDS X-teams has a rich network of connections inside and outside the consortium. Through these connections, leadership is distributed across the consortium to more effectively move the entire organization closer to its ultimate goal. Leadership is also

distributed within the teams themselves: as the teams move through the phases of explore, exploit, and export, the specific individuals taking on leadership responsibility changes.

When multiple X-teams are aligned they can be a powerful driver of change. At BP, for example, senior project leaders have been tasked with improving the company's project management capabilities. With billions spent each year on major oil and gas projects around the world, making such improvements could result in huge cost savings and strategic advantage.

Set up as X-teams, these leaders go through a BP/MIT executive program in groups of about thirty (a cadre). Melding six weeks of classroom work with their X-team work, the leaders spend a year moving through explore, exploit, and export. They reach out to benchmark other companies within the industry and those outside of it. They pull together expertise wherever they can find it. They collect data to better understand where there are problems and where there are new solutions. They communicate with top management to gain support and align with strategic goals. They invent and test new ways of managing projects, including new management systems, new modes of contracting with suppliers, and new methods of project evaluation and staffing. And then they present their ideas to top management, inspiring a whole new set of organizational initiatives that spread new programs throughout the projects community.

BP's gains as a result of this process go beyond the specific projects—although the projects have generated financial gain. More broadly, the process of embedding X-teams into the corporate mindset has created an "infrastructure of innovation" in which new ideas are emerging, knowledge is building, and the improvement in project management practices increases with each year and each new set of X-teams.

In BP's new project management model, there is no one omniscient leader at the top.

Instead, multiple leaders work within a team structure. This team creates a network of connections (See Figure 2) that carry out the leadership functions of making sense of a changing environment, creating a web of relationships that foster commitment to change, establishing a vision of what is possible in the future, and inventing new structures and processes that make the vision a reality.[8] Major change occurs as multiple teams work together over time, pulling in top-level leaders, as well as leaders outside the firm.

At organizations such as BP, VDS, W. L. Gore, P&G, and at many others, the X-Team model is an engine of distributed leadership, institutional change, and on-going innovation. As a new corporate landscape evolves, X-teams and distributed leadership will be needed to create the connectivity among these new organizational forms and to create value for employees, customers, partners, and stakeholders alike.

| **Figure 2** | Single Leaders Versus Distributed Leadership |

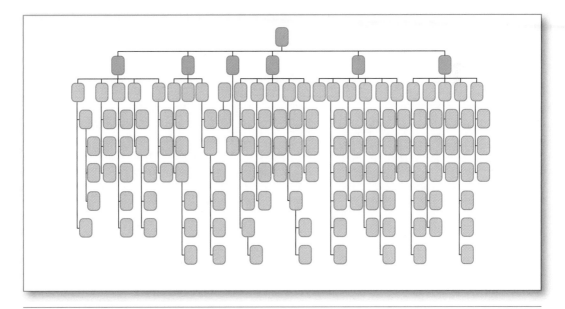

(Continued)

[8]Ancona, Malone, Orlikowski, and Senge

Figure 2 (Continued)

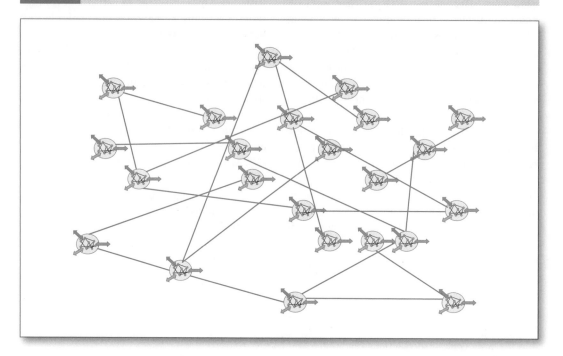

Strategic Leadership

Natalie Slawinski

Memorial University of Newfoundland

I learned that as CEO, or as any leader or manager, you must stop thinking of yourself as the only source of change. You must avoid the urge to answer every question or provide a solution to every problem. Instead, you must start asking questions, seeing others as the source of change, and transferring ownership of the organization's growth to the next generation of leaders who are closer to the value zone. Only in this way can you begin to create a company that is self-run and self-governed, one in which employees feel like the owners, are excited by their work, and constantly focus on change and disruptive innovation at the very heart of the value zone.

—Vineet Nayar[1]

I n the past 20 years, researchers have begun to pay more attention to the study of strategic leadership, which has come to be viewed by many as a critical aspect of firm success (Daft, 2011). Broadly speaking, strategic leadership refers to the study of executives who have overall responsibility for the firm and how their decisions affect organizational outcomes (Finkelstein, Hambrick, & Cannella, 2009). The focus is on top managers because they usually have decision-making responsibilities that affect the whole organization—including the other organizational members—and its overall performance (Daft, 2011). Yukl (2012) argues that the increased focus on what top executives can do to transform their organizations is reflective of what is needed to cope with societal changes,

---

[1]Nayar (2010, p. 13).

disruptive technological changes, an increase in international competition, and globalization. DuBrin (2010) states that strategic leadership "has a different focus than leadership in general" (p. 381). Rowe (2001) suggests that strategic leadership emphasizes the synergistic combination of visionary leadership and managerial leadership in a manner that ensures the long-term viability of the organization while maintaining its short-term financial success.

Strategic leaders create a sense of purpose and direction, which guides strategy formulation and implementation within the firm (Daft, 2011; Hosmer, 1982; Shrivastava & Nachman, 1989). They also interact with key stakeholders, such as customers, government agencies, and unions, especially when these relationships are critical to firm performance (House & Aditya, 1997). Organizations and the environments in which they operate are increasingly complex and ambiguous. Therefore, strategic leaders must navigate through these complexities and develop strategies that will allow their organizations to be successful, whether they are for-profit or nonprofit.

Another perspective of strategic leadership focuses on the specific activities and behaviors of strategic leaders that can improve the success of the firm (DuBrin, 2010; Ireland & Hitt, 1999; Rowe, 2001). This perspective argues that in an ever-changing complex business environment, strategic leaders may be a source of competitive advantage. Ireland and Hitt (1999) define strategic leadership as the "ability to anticipate, envision, maintain flexibility, think strategically, and work with others to initiate changes that will create a viable future for the organization" (p. 43). Given the challenges that firms face in an often turbulent and unpredictable global environment, Ireland and Hitt have identified six components of strategic leadership that will lead to enhanced organizational performance: determining the firm's purpose or vision, exploiting and maintaining core competencies, developing human capital, sustaining an effective organizational culture, emphasizing ethical practices, and establishing balanced organizational controls.

Determining the Firm's Purpose or Vision

The first component of strategic leadership consists of determining the firm's purpose or vision. This means that strategic leaders must articulate a clear and realistic statement about why the firm exists and what is distinctive about it. This statement will then empower members of the organization to develop and execute strategies that are in line with the vision of the firm.

Exploiting and Maintaining Core Competencies

Strategic leaders exploit and maintain core competencies. Core competencies are resources and capabilities that give firms an edge over their rivals. Strategic leaders need to understand which combinations of resources and capabilities are valuable, rare, costly to imitate, and difficult to substitute for, as these will allow the firm to gain a competitive advantage.

Developing Human Capital

Strategic leaders are effective at developing human capital. Human capital refers to the knowledge, skills, and abilities of the firm's employees. Because these employees are critical to the success of the organization, strategic leaders invest in them through training and mentoring.

⊠ Sustaining an Effective Organizational Culture

Strategic leaders sustain an effective organizational culture. An organization's culture is a complex combination of ideologies, symbols, and values that are shared by employees of the firm. Strategic leaders learn how to shape a firm's shared values and symbols in ways that allow the firm to be more competitive.

⊠ Emphasizing Ethical Practices

Strategic leadership involves the emphasis of ethical practices. Top managers who use honesty, trust, and integrity in their decision making are able to inspire their employees and create an organizational culture that encourages the use of ethical practices in day-to-day organizational activities.

⊠ Establishing Balanced Organizational Controls

Organizational controls refer to the formal procedures that are used in organizations to influence and guide work. These controls act as limits on what employees can and cannot do. There are two types of internal controls: strategic and financial. Strategic controls are accomplished through information exchanges that help to develop strategies, whereas financial controls are accomplished through setting objective criteria such as performance targets. Strategic controls emphasize actions, whereas financial controls emphasize outcomes. Financial controls can be especially constraining and can stifle creativity in organizations. Strategic leaders must establish balanced organizational controls by incorporating the two types in order to allow employees to remain flexible and innovative.

In addition to accomplishing the above activities, strategic leaders must balance the short-term needs of their organizations while ensuring a future competitive position. Rowe (2001) defines strategic leadership as "the ability to influence others to voluntarily make day-to-day decisions that enhance the long-term viability of the organization, while at the same time maintaining its short-term financial stability" (pp. 82–83). This type of leadership is a synergistic combination of visionary leadership, which emphasizes investing in the future, and managerial leadership, which emphasizes preserving the existing order. Strategic leaders focus on both the day-to-day operations and the long-term strategic orientation of the firm, recognizing that neither can be ignored if a firm is to be successful.

Importantly, strategic leaders have strong positive expectations of the performance they expect from their superiors, peers, subordinates, and themselves (Rowe, 2001). These expectations encourage organizational members to voluntarily make decisions that contribute to short-term stability and long-term viability of the organization. As such, strategic leaders do not have to expend as much effort on monitoring and controlling employees. It is also important that those leaders who already exhibit strategic leadership abilities encourage their development in other organizational members. In this way, strategic leadership can exist at all levels of the organization. Strategic leaders also select the next generation of leaders to ensure that the organization will continue to have strategic leadership in the long term (Boal & Hooijberg, 2000).

In addition to the above activities, DuBrin (2010) adds revolutionary and contrarian thinking. Building on Hamel's (2001) work, DuBrin suggests that organizations need strategic leaders to lead them through strategic breakthroughs or radical innovations. An example of this is the transformation of HCL Technologies after Vineet Nayar became CEO in 2005. He got HCL's employees to seek a better future by bluntly describing HCL's current situation. He opened the books, shared confidential information that other companies would not share, enabled managers and employees (including himself) to question each other, and in so doing, created a culture of trust. He inverted the pyramid by making management and the supporting functions accountable to the employees, which increased their passion for their job and their effectiveness. Finally, he changed the role of the CEO (as referred to in the quote at the beginning of the chapter) by moving the responsibility for change to the employees from HCL's senior leader—himself (Nayar, 2010).

Strategic Leadership Versus Leadership

In Chapter 1 of this casebook, leadership was defined as the process of influencing others in order to accomplish a goal. The focus was on the relationship between the leader and follower in a group context and on the process of leading in order to achieve a goal. So how is strategic leadership different from leadership? The main difference is that leadership can be accomplished at any level of the organization and can have an impact on different types of organizational goals, such as increasing the sales of a particular product line or reducing the turnover of employees.

Strategic leadership, on the other hand, is mainly concerned with, but not necessarily restricted to, the higher levels of the organization, given that executives are in a unique position to influence the direction and vision of the organization (Finkelstein, Hambrick, & Cannella, 2009). Strategic leadership has an impact on organization-wide outcomes, such as the financial performance of a small manufacturing company or the strategic change of a large multinational company. The difference can also be thought of as leadership "in" organizations versus leadership "of" organizations (Boal & Hooijberg, 2000). The leadership approaches discussed throughout this book are mainly concerned with how leaders affect followers "in" the organization, whereas strategic leadership is primarily concerned with the leadership "of" organizations by top managers. But as we saw earlier, leaders at all levels of the organization can have an impact on organizational performance. The focus of strategic leadership is often on top-level executives such as CEOs because they tend to have more power and are given responsibility for the overall performance of the firm. They are also held accountable by shareholders for the success of the firm, and poor performance can lead to their dismissal.

Positional Versus Behavioral

In contrast to some of the other theories within the realm of leadership, such as the trait approach and the skills approach, the strategic leadership perspective is not as well developed. Furthermore, there is a lack of agreement regarding what strategic leadership is. As we have seen, strategic leadership has come to have several different, but often complementary, meanings. Some (e.g., Finkelstein, Hambrick, & Cannella, 2009) view it as having to do with one's position in a company, while others (e.g., Ireland & Hitt, 1999; Rowe, 2001) view it as a set of behaviors that lead to superior performance.

The positional view argues that anyone holding the position of CEO or another top executive position is a strategic leader because of his or her decision-making power and level of responsibility. This perspective looks at the differences in psychological characteristics of strategic leaders to examine how these differences affect their organizations (Finkelstein & Hambrick, 1996). Others view strategic leadership as a set of activities that leaders must perform if they are to enhance organizational performance. For example, strategic leaders are those who sustain an effective corporate culture (Ireland & Hitt, 1999). A related perspective (Rowe, 2001) on strategic leadership views it as a leadership style that individuals may possess at any level of the organization. Rowe (2001) argues that organizations that have CEOs who are strategic leaders will create more value than those that have visionary or managerial leaders.

As we saw in the definitions above, there is no consensus on exactly what strategic leadership is, but certain themes do emerge. For instance, most of the definitions or conceptualizations of strategic leadership mention the importance of studying CEOs and other top managers to better understand why some firms outperform others. Whether it is viewed as a style of leadership, a set of activities, or a broad area of study, strategic leadership is viewed by many as critical to firm success, especially given our complex, global business environment.

Several themes emerge in the literature concerning what strategic leaders do to increase firm performance. They look after both the short-term operational side of their organization and the long-term directional aspects, such as defining the firm's purpose (Phillips & Hunt, 1992; Rowe, 2001). Strategic leaders select and develop other organizational members to ensure that these successful strategic leader abilities will exist throughout the organization, not just at the top. They influence others by behaving ethically and transparently. Strategic leaders who have overall responsibility for the firm (such as a CEO) articulate a vision that will provide the organization's members with meaning and guidance. They are also in a position to influence external constituents, such as suppliers, unions, and government agencies. Strategic leaders who incorporate these important activities can help ensure the future competitiveness of the firm.

✑ References

Boal, K. B., & Hooijberg, R. (2000). Strategic leadership research: Moving on. *Leadership Quarterly, 11*, 515–549.

Daft, R. L. (2011). *The leadership experience* (5th ed.). Mason, OH: Thomson, South-Western.

DuBrin, A. J. (2010). *Leadership: Research findings, practice, and skills* (6th ed.). Mason, OH: South-Western/Cengage.

Finkelstein, S., & Hambrick, D. C. (1996). *Strategic leadership: Top executives and their effects on organizations.* St. Paul, MN: West.

Finkelstein, S., Hambrick, D. C., & Cannella, A. A., Jr. (2009). *Strategic leadership: Theory and research on executives, top management teams, and boards.* New York, NY: Oxford University Press.

Hamel, G. (2001, May). Revolution vs. evolution: You need both. *Harvard Business Review,* 150.

Hosmer, L. T. (1982). The importance of strategic leadership. *Journal of Business Strategy, 3,* 47–57.

House, R. J., & Aditya, R. N. (1997). The social scientific study of leadership: Quo vadis? *Journal of Management, 2*(23), 409–473.

Ireland, R. D., & Hitt, M. A. (1999). Achieving and maintaining strategic competitiveness in the 21st century: The role of strategic leadership. *Academy of Management Executive, 13,* 43–57.

Nayar, V. (2010). *Employees first, customers second.* Boston, MA: Harvard Business Press.

Phillips, R. L., & Hunt, J. G. (1992). *Strategic leadership: A multi-organizational-level perspective.* London, England: Quorum Books.

Rowe, W. G. (2001). Creating wealth in organizations: The role of strategic leadership. *Academy of Management Executive, 15,* 81–94.

Shrivastava, P., & Nachman, S. A. (1989). Strategic leadership patterns. *Strategic Management Journal, 10,* 51–66.

Yukl, G. (2010). *Leadership in organizations* (7th ed.). Upper Saddle River, NJ: Prentice Hall.

▧ The Cases

Strategic Leadership at Coca-Cola: The Real Thing

Muhtar Kent had just been promoted to the CEO position in Coca-Cola. He was reflecting upon the past leadership of the company, in particular the success that Coca-Cola enjoyed during Robert Goizueta's leadership. The CEOs that had followed Goizueta were not able to have as positive an impact on the stock value. When his promotion was announced, Kent mentioned that he did not have immediate plans to change any management roles but that some fine-tuning might be necessary.

Maple Leaf Foods, Inc. (A): The Listeriosis Crisis

In the summer of 2008, Maple Leaf Foods, Inc. (MLF) learns from the Canadian Food Inspection Agency and Health Canada that they have traced an outbreak of listeriosis to a production plant owned by MLF and located in the province of Ontario. In addition, illnesses and deaths have apparently resulted from this outbreak. MLF's CEO, Michael McCain, must decide what to do today, this week, this month, as well as think about what changes need to be made to ensure the long-term viability of MLF.

▧ The Reading

Strategic Leadership: Short-Term Stability and Long-Term Viability

This brief article describes the differences among the concepts of strategic leadership, visionary leadership, and managerial leadership. In addition, it defines strategic leadership. The article suggests that strategic leaders are rare as it is very difficult to synergistically combine visionary and managerial leadership. Two CEOs, Jorgen Vig Knudstorp, CEO of LEGO, and Clive Beddoes, CEO of Westjet Airlines, are examined as to their strategic leadership style.

Strategic Leadership at Coca-Cola: The Real Thing[1]

Suhaib Riaz and W. Glenn Rowe

In recent years, The Coca-Cola Company (Coca-Cola) has seen a much lower rise in its stock price compared with the exceptional 5,800 per cent rise during the 16-year tenure of its well-known chief executive officer (CEO), Robert Goizueta. After Goizueta's untimely death from cancer in October 1997, the company witnessed some tumultuous times, and Goizueta's three immediate successors have not lasted for even half as long as his total tenure

---

Copyright © 2008, Ivey Management Services   Version: (A) 2008-10-16

[1]This case has been written on the basis of published sources only. Consequently, the interpretation and perspectives presented in this case are not necessarily those of The Coca-Cola Company or any of its employees.

(see Exhibit 1). Coca-Cola's CEO succession process was widely regarded as being ad hoc, and each succession story had its own peculiarities and intrigues. The leadership styles of CEOs at Coca-Cola differed and were often a source of interest in the media and the investment community, where many speculated on the type of leadership that was needed at the helm.

In general, leadership styles can be described as managerial, visionary or strategic.[2] In this categorization, *managerial leaders* are considered those who are risk averse, reactive and for whom goals are based on the past and on necessities, as opposed to goals arising from desires and dreams. Such leaders relate to people according to their roles in the decision-making process, see themselves as conservators and regulators of the existing order, and involve themselves in situations and contexts characteristic of day-to-day activities. They are concerned with, and are more comfortable in, functional areas of responsibility, ensuring compliance to standard operating procedures. These leaders exhibit linear thinking and are deterministic, i.e., they believe their choices are determined by their internal and external environments.

In contrast, *visionary leaders* are proactive; they shape ideas, and they change the way people think about what is desirable, possible, and necessary. They are given to risk taking. They bring fresh approaches to long-standing problems, concern themselves with ideas, and relate to people in intuitive and empathetic ways. They feel separate from their environment, working in, but not belonging to, their organizations. Such leaders are concerned with ensuring the future of the organization, especially through development and management of people. They engage in multifunctional and integrative tasks, they know less than their functional area experts, utilize non-linear thinking, and believe in strategic choice, i.e., their choices make a difference to their organizations and, through their organizations, to their environment.

Strategic leaders are a synergistic combination of managerial and visionary leadership. They oversee both operating (day-to-day) and strategic (long-term) responsibilities, apply both linear and non-linear thinking, and emphasize ethical behavior and value-based decisions. Strategic leadership is defined as the ability to influence those with whom you work to voluntarily make decisions on a day-to-day basis that enhance both the long-term viability of the organization and the organization's short-term financial stability.[3]

✉ Goizueta Is It![4]

Background

Robert Goizueta was born in Havana, Cuba, in 1931, a scion of a major sugar industry family in Cuba. Goizueta's maternal grandfather immigrated to Cuba from Spain, and, despite a lack of education beyond high school, was able to save enough money to buy a sugar refining business and some real estate during the Cuban depression. His grandfather's focus on the importance of cash made an early impression on Goizueta. After attending a Jesuit school in Cuba, Goizueta moved to a private academy in Connecticut for a year to improve his English. His outstanding performance and connections at the academy helped him gain admission to Yale University, where he majored in chemical

---

[2]W. Glenn Rowe, "Creating Wealth in Organizations: The Role of Strategic Leadership, *Academy of Management Executive*, February 2001, pp. 81–94.

[3]Ibid.

[4]Slogans used in titles retrieved from The Coca-Cola Company website, Heritage section, http://www.thecoca-colacompany .com/heritage/ourheritage.html on March 22, 2008.

engineering with an eye to a possible future in the family business.

When he returned to Cuba, he chose not to join the family business. Instead he answered a blind advertisement in a newspaper that led to a job as an entry-level chemist at The Coca-Cola Company in Havana. "It was going to be a temporary thing for me, $500 a month—my friends thought I was absolutely crazy," he recalled. However, he soon rose to become chief technical director of five Cuban bottling plants. Then, in 1959, Fidel Castro came to power and Coca-Cola's Cuban operations came under a strong threat of takeover.

The family escaped to Miami, where Goizueta, his wife, three children, and a nursemaid shared a motel room for a month. Fortunately, Goizueta landed a job with Coca-Cola in a new Miami office. His only possessions of value were 100 shares of Coca-Cola stock in a New York bank and US$40. He later recalled the importance of that experience:

> You cannot explain that experience to any person. That was ten times more important than anything else in my life. It was a shocker. All of a sudden you don't own anything, except the stock. One hundred shares! That's the only thing I had. It brings a sense of humility. It builds a feeling of not much regard for material things.[5]

After working in the Miami office, he worked as a chemist in the Bahamas for Coca-Cola's Caribbean region and later moved back to headquarters in Atlanta, Georgia. At age 35, he was promoted to vice-president, Technical Research and Development, the youngest person to hold this position. He was then promoted to head the Legal and External Affairs department in 1975 and became vice chairman in 1979.

Goizueta as CEO of Coca-Cola

Robert Woodruff, widely regarded as Coke's main power broker because he revitalized the company after taking over as CEO in 1923 and served in that position for decades, befriended Goizueta. Aided by a close relationship with Robert Woodruff, Goizueta moved up through the technical operations and became president in 1980 after J. Lucian Smith's resignation. When the chairman, J. Paul Austin retired in 1981, Goizueta became chairman and CEO. At the time, the transition was seen as messy, because Woodruff (despite being retired), used his position as the company's 90-year-old patriarch to overrule Austin's choice for successor, Donald R. Keough. Woodruff's pick, the chemical engineer from Cuba was regarded as the darkest horse in the succession process. However, Woodruff and others on the board saw Goizueta as the person needed to introduce change and improve performance.

Goizueta generously asked Keough to be his chief operating officer (COO) and president, sending the broader message that

> The day of the one-man band is gone. It would be a crime for me to try to lead the bottlers the way Don Keough can. I would look like a phony. . . . My job is to pick the people, then give them the responsibility and authority to get the job done.

Goizueta created a two-page, double-spaced document, "The Job of the Chief Executive Officer," which delineated what he could and couldn't delegate.[6] For 12 years, Goizueta and Keough complemented each other. Goizueta was known as the business philosopher, whereas Keough did more of the footwork—traveling

---

[5]Betsy Morris, "Roberto Goizueta and Jack Welch: The Wealth Builders," *Fortune*, December 11, 1995, pp. 80–94.

[6]Betsy Morris, "Roberto Goizueta and Jack Welch: The Wealth Builders," *Fortune*, December 11, 1995, pp. 80–94.

to bottlers, meeting customers and ensuring overall operations were in shape.[7]

Goizueta stated that he had viewed Coca-Cola as having become "too conservative" and revealed his desire for major changes: "It took us a little bit longer to change than it should have. The world was changing, and we were not changing with the world." At a retreat for company executives, he unveiled a "Strategy for the 80s" and emphasized that "We're going to take risks."[8]

When Goizueta took over, the company was in multiple businesses: soft drinks, wine, coffee, tea, plastics, shrimp farming, orange groves, steam generators, industrial boilers, desalting plants, and industrial water treatment. Goizueta subjected each business to a standard financial formula: Is our return on capital greater than our cost of capital? He then divested non-core businesses that did not measure up until the only business left by the late 1980s was the selling of bottled carbonated soft drinks (CSDs)—predominantly Coca-Cola and minor quantities of Sprite and Tab (a diet soft drink)—and one non-CSD beverage (i.e., Minute Maid). He stated his rule of investment: "You borrow money at a certain rate and invest it at a higher rate and pocket the difference. It's simple." He was a pioneer in promoting the idea of economic profit (i.e., after-tax operating profits in excess of capital costs) and wrote to Wall Street analysts personally about it. Today, the concept has gained ground as economic value added (EVA), a well-regarded tool for increasing shareholder wealth.

Goizueta's style was less hands-on and more intellectual. Despite the fact that Coca-Cola earned up to 80 per cent of its profits abroad, Goizueta visited only about a half-dozen countries a year and remained most comfortable defining "the character of the company" from his office at Coca-Cola's headquarters. Goizueta used rewards based on economic profit targets to motivate his management team to perform.[9] A contemporary CEO characterized Goizueta's style in the following manner: "A lot of executives can intellectualize the process, but [Goizueta] can follow through."[10]

Although Coca-Cola had never borrowed money, under Goizueta, it borrowed billions and bought out independent bottlers around the world to upgrade its own distribution systems. With Douglas Ivester as chief financial officer (CFO), the "49 per cent solution" was devised. This involved Coca-Cola buying out U.S. bottlers that were not doing well and combining them with its own bottling network. The new creation was called Coca-Cola Enterprises (CCE) and was spun off to the public, with Coca-Cola retaining a strategic 49 per cent of the stock. This arrangement helped Coca-Cola reduce its debt and divest itself of a low-return, capital intensive business.[11]

Looking back at that time, Goizueta later commented during an interview:

> We really lost focus on who our customer was. We felt our customer was the bottler as opposed to McDonald's and Wal-Mart. So consequently, we were being either cheerleaders or critics of our bottlers. But hands off; we didn't have anything to do with it—that was their job. I think the worst thing we ever had to do was to establish a sense of direction . . . so that they know where they're going. Then you can let them have a lot of freedom.[12]

---

[7]Betsy Morris, "The Real Story," *Fortune*, May 31, 2004, pp. 84–98.

[8]"Coke CEO Roberto C. Goizueta Dies at 65," *CNN Interactive News*, October 18, 1997, http://www.cnn.com/US/9710/18/goizueta.obit.9am, retrieved April 18, 2008.

[9]Patricia Sellers, "Where Coke Goes from Here," *Fortune*, October 13, 1997, pp. 88–91.

[10]Betsy Morris, "Roberto Goizueta and Jack Welch: The Wealth Builders," *Fortune*, December 11, 1995, pp. 80–94.

[11]Patricia Sellers, "How Coke Is Kicking Pepsi's Can," *Fortune*, October 28, 1996, pp. 70–84.

[12]Betsy Morris, "Roberto Goizueta and Jack Welch: The Wealth Builders," *Fortune*, December 11, 1995, pp. 80–94.

During this same interview, Goizueta emphasized the need for leaders to establish a sense of direction, so people both knew where they are going and had a lot of freedom to get there. He added that if people did not know where they were going, you do not want them to get there too fast. Finally, he encouraged people to create what can be, as opposed to what is.

Goizueta emphasized the importance of relationships. He enticed the Cisneroses (Pepsi's most venerable bottlers in Venezuela) away from Pepsi and signed the deal in the presence of three generations of the Cisneroses at Coca-Cola headquarters. "It was a very family-like gathering, to symbolize that this was to be a long-term relationship," Gustavo Cisneros recalled. "This is a people-relations business," Goizueta later said.[13]

These moves were also in line with Goizueta's overall approach of developing senior managers' intimate strategic knowledge of, and engagement in, the core business. Whereas CCE and other bottlers carried out the operational details on the ground, Goizueta focused his own role and that of other senior managers on brand building, making deals, and selling concentrate. Coca-Cola did not rotate its successful managers through jobs rapidly, in contrast to its main rival Pepsi. "If you do that, you can never see how good the people really are," Goizueta explained.

Goizueta encouraged calculated risk-taking, epitomized by his decision to put the Coca-Cola trademark on a new product, Diet Coke, in 1982, which turned into the most successful product launch of the 1980s. Traditionally, the company had never put the Coca-Cola trademark on other products. Goizueta invested outside the core business only on one occasion, to buy Columbia Pictures in 1982, after it went bust. He later sold it to Sony in 1989 for a large profit. He stated that this investment was not to hedge his bets, but to pile up earnings until he could sort out issues with the soft drinks business.

The new moves included launching New Coke. Based on a sweeter formula, it was a departure from the traditional Coke formula and was developed to counter Pepsi, which was doing better on taste tests. In Goizueta's words, the launch of New Coke was "the boldest single marketing move in the history of the consumer goods business." However, when New Coke bombed in 1985 and loyal customers demanded a return of the old formula, the old Coke was relaunched as "Classic Coke," and over time "New Coke" was allowed to die out. Coca-Cola learned a valuable lesson: its brand and marketing, not the taste of the sugar water, was its asset, and Coca-Cola marketing was consequently overhauled. "I realized what I should have before," he recalled. "That this was a most unique company with a most unique product. We have a product that people have an unusual attachment to. I had never felt so bullish about it."[14]

Goizueta encouraged speedier decision-making and kept encouraging risk-taking. At a worldwide gathering of Coca-Cola's quality assurance staff, in response to a concern about all the changes taking place, Goizueta said:

> Don't wrap the flag of Coca-Cola around you to prevent change from taking place. It is extremely important that you show some insensitivity to your past in order to show the proper respect for the future.[15]

During Goizueta's reign, the company expanded both domestically and internationally, backed by the new slogan, "Coke Is It!" Goizueta turned Coca-Cola around financially, organizationally and culturally, making it America's most admired company, against

---

[13]Patricia Sellers, "How Coke Is Kicking Pepsi's Can," *Fortune*, October 28, 1996, pp. 70–84.

[14]Ibid.

[15]Ibid.

all expectations. Coca-Cola's stock price increased 5829 percent during Goizueta's tenure (see Exhibits 1 and 2). Its market value grew 34 times, from $4.3 billion to $147 billion during Goizueta's 16-year tenure. In addition, in a *Fortune* story on Goizueta in October, 1997 describing "The Goizueta Effect" it was reported that revenues had increased from $4.8 billion to $18.5 billion, net income from $0.5 billion to $3.5 billion, and return on equity from 20 per cent to 60 per cent from 1981 to 1996 (see Exhibit 3).[16]

When asked what he looked for in a future successor, Goizueta agreed with his fellow interviewee, Jack Welch, General Electric's CEO, that his successor needed incredible energy, the ability to excite others, a defined vision, the capacity to find change fun, and the facility to be as comfortable in New Delhi as in Denver. Goizueta added that while energy is the number-one quality, two other qualities were also important—integrity and the intellectual courage to take a risk, a leap of faith, whether the leap was big or small.

Roberto Goizueta died of cancer at the age of 65 in October 1997. The 100 shares he had when he arrived in Miami were worth more than $3 million. He was a billionaire by 1997 and his belief in Coca-Cola was evidenced by the fact that in 1995 more than 99 per cent of his personal wealth was tied up in Coca-Cola stock.[17] He was replaced by heir apparent Douglas Ivester. Some said that Goizueta's strategic planning showed in his leaving behind a solid management team. Herbert Allen, a director at Coca-Cola since 1982 stated, "Roberto has filled in behind him so well. He established at least four people who can run the company . . . and behind them are ten more people who could fill their jobs."

⊠ Always Douglas Ivester

Background

In a few ways, Ivester was comparable to Goizueta. He had his own rags-to-riches story and was regarded as a dark horse who came from corporate backwaters. Ivester was the only child of conservative Southern Baptist factory workers raised with discipline and rigidity in the Georgia mill village of New Holland, 60 miles north of Atlanta. He described his parents as "strong savers, [with] very strong religious values," partly due to their being children of the Depression. They had very high expectations of him. When he got an A in school, his father would remark, "They give A-pluses, don't they?" As a child, Ivester worked after school doing odd jobs. He hardly had time for any extra-curricular activities or team sports.

"One thing I learned in Gainesville was to never let my memories be greater than my dreams," Ivester recalled. He graduated from the University of Georgia with an accounting major and worked as an accountant at Ernst & Whinney. Ivester headed the audit team for Coca-Cola and was recruited by Coca-Cola as assistant controller in 1979. Six years later, CEO Goizueta, impressed with Ivester's solutions to complex financial problems that helped maximize returns on investment, made him CFO.[18]

As CFO, Ivester was the brains behind getting Coca-Cola's low-return bottling operations and its debt off the company's books. Under Goizueta's leadership, Ivester helped create a separate bottling company, Coca-Cola Enterprises (CCE), and spun it off to shareholders while keeping 49 per cent equity for Coca-Cola to control the business. Goizueta groomed Ivester and provided opportunities for varied experiences in

[16]Patricia Sellers, "Where Coke Goes from Here," *Fortune*, October 13, 1997, pp. 88–91.

[17]Patricia Sellers, "Where Coke Goes from Here," *Fortune*, October 13, 1997, pp. 88–91; Betsy Morris, "Roberto Goizueta and Jack Welch: The Wealth Builders," *Fortune*, December 11, 1995, pp. 80–94.

[18]Patricia Sellers, "Where Coke Goes from Here," *Fortune*, October 13, 1997, pp. 88–91.

marketing and international operations. Ivester's first operations job was as president of Coca-Cola's European operations in mid-1989. When the Berlin Wall came down later that year, Ivester cut deals with bottling plants across Eastern Europe, and his opportunism saw Coca-Cola seizing control of the region that had long been dominated by Pepsi.

As president of Coca-Cola in 1990, Ivester visited overseas markets and sent out a new message. Instead of setting goals in the traditional style, he asked executives to think about what kind of growth would be possible in a market, and to figure out how to knock down the barriers to attain that growth. He also stated that, like Goizueta, he would remain focused on one business—non-alcoholic beverages. During his time as president of Coca-Cola USA, he spent every Saturday morning for a year learning marketing from Sergio Zyman, who went on to become Coca-Cola's global marketing boss. He added the position of chief learning officer and encouraged its first incumbent, Judith A. Rosenblum, to turn the company into "a learning organization." His goal was to capture all of the growth in Coca-Cola's markets.

Upon Goizueta's unexpected death due to cancer in 1997, Doug Ivester was the heir apparent and became CEO. However, it was rumored that his appointment was not supported by Don Keough.[19]

Douglas Ivester as CEO of Coca-Cola

As CEO, Ivester made some important changes in positions. His competitor for the CEO position, E. Neville Isdell, was moved to head a bottler in Britain. Carl Ware, a senior vice-president was demoted. Don Keough, who, after his retirement, had continued attending Coca-Cola board meetings as Goizueta's consultant, lost his consulting contract and his place at the boardroom table.

Ivester's personality, like Goizueta's was seen as reserved on the surface. Yet, despite wide recognition for being brilliant, Ivester seemed to lack some of Goizueta's characteristics. Ivester was known for an obsession with a rational and orderly way of operating. He was considered arrogant and insecure, blind to his own weaknesses and not forthcoming in soliciting advice. He placed less emphasis on Goizueta's tradition of having almost daily chats with directors. During his reign, Coca-Cola alienated European regulators and several executives at major customers, such as Disney and Wal-Mart. Some major bottlers, including Coca-Cola Enterprises, were also alienated. In time, he became more and more obsessed with controlling the most minor details of every operation. To make matters worse, the Asian currency crisis occurred during his reign and affected Coca-Cola's business. The U.S. dollar, which had remained weak for a long time and had contributed to Coca-Cola's earnings, strengthened during Ivester's tenure.[20]

As CEO, continuing on in his earlier approach, Douglas Ivester was known for working seven days a week and nearly all the time. On visiting Shanghai as CEO, he was known to have walked out on the streets while the "World of Coca-Cola" traveling multi-media exhibit was going on. Ivester walked into little stores and asked why Coke was not prominently displayed on shelves and noted where fountain machines were turned off. He was known to have done similar walks as president of Coca-Cola USA, going from store to store and even identifying the hairdressing salons and laundromats where Coke couldn't be found. On one Saturday morning, he drove from Atlanta to Rome, Georgia, with a video crew to identify missed opportunities along the way.[21] He

---

[19]Betsy Morris, "The Real Story," *Fortune*, May 31, 2004, pp. 84–98.

[20]Ibid.

[21]Betsy Morris, "Doug Is It," *Fortune*, May 25, 1998, pp. 71–84.

encouraged people to avoid doing things sequentially and pushed for "viral growth." As an example, he suggested if you opened offices in China, not to open them one at a time but to have each new office assist in opening several more.[22]

Ivester was known to be a CEO who communicated with people at all levels and ignored hierarchy. He wanted employees to think of themselves as knowledge workers, to think of their office as the information they carried with them, supported by technology that would allow them to work anywhere. With Ivester, business planning was not done annually, but became an ongoing discussion involving top executives. Ivester focused on getting lots of information, aided by technology, which he believed was necessary for real-time decision-making. Although past CEOs had focused on letting executives find their own solutions, Ivester involved himself in finding solutions for them. Ivester explained his involvement by stating that in such a fast and complicated world, a CEO could not run a business by sitting in an office. To many, this approach sounded like micromanaging.[23]

Jack Stahl, senior vice-president and president of Coca-Cola's North America group, reported that he often got six or seven notes a day from Ivester. And Ivester expected prompt replies to all his communications, including his voice mails. Ivester went without a number-two person for about a year, working instead with a flat structure that had 14 senior vice-presidents, including six operating heads, reporting to him directly. Ivester took less naturally to the ceremonial nature of his job, remarking to the mayor of Shanghai, "Nice place you have here," on visiting the mayor's opulent meeting room. While he delivered a message to all officials

about helping China, he was known to enjoy his time most with his troops in the trenches.[24]

Ivester's thirst for information was rarely satiated and he continued delving into every little detail of the company's worldwide operations. When an executive from Coca-Cola's biggest Mexican bottler talked about tens of thousands of mom-and-pop stores, Ivester jumped in and asked, "So which are they—moms or pops?" The bottler's COO could only muster a weak response, "I think it's more moms than pops, Doug, but I'm not sure."[25]

The downturn in overseas markets, where Coca-Cola derived about three-quarters of its profits, was met head on as an opportunity to buy bottlers, distribution, and rival brands at bargain prices. Ivester was betting that the investments would help fuel growth in the future. Whereas Goizueta had handled international operations from a distance, Ivester worked 14-hour days and stayed in contact with executives worldwide through email, voicemail, and pagers even as the business grew in size and complexity around the world.

Under Ivester, the era of exclusive contracts in the soft drink industry became very aggressive. Coca-Cola and Pepsi pursued such contracts not only in restaurant chains but in other locations, such as schools and convenience stores. A marketing consultant for Cadbury Schweppes remarked, "Coke is the No. 1 icon in the world; it has to be a good corporate citizen. They are not in a situation where they can create shareholder value by being a bully."

Whereas Goizueta had focused on stockholders, Ivester spent his energies on customers, "If you focus on the customer, the business will prosper, and if the business prospers, the stock will eventually be priced right."[26] However, when

[22]Ibid.

[23]Ibid.

[24]Ibid.

[25]"Man on the Spot," *Business Week*, May 3, 1999, pp. 142–151.

[26]Ibid.

dozens of Belgian school children fell sick after drinking Coca-Cola products, Ivester maintained silence for a week before going to Belgium to apologize. Coca-Cola ultimately recalled 65 million cans due to this incident. When he failed to promote Carl Ware, senior vice-president for African operations and Coca-Cola's top African-American executive, the doors opened for four past and current employees to sue Coca-Cola for racial discrimination.

Ivester took much of the credit for improvements in the bottler system, including the creation of CCE and technological improvements across the company. Some of these claims served to isolate Don Keough, Goizueta's erstwhile president and COO, who was also connected to two powerful Coca-Cola board members, Herbert Allen and Warren Buffet. Keough became the person all constituents, including customers, bottlers and employees, gradually started complaining to.[27]

Commenting on his earlier successes under Goizueta, Ivester had stated, "I look at the business like a chessboard. You always need to be seeing three, four, five moves ahead. Otherwise, your first move can prove fatal." His methodical approach extended to all areas, "I learned that marketing is not a black box," he stated, "Marketing can be even more logical than finance. If you ask enough questions and listen closely, you find that people are very logical."[28] He was also reported to have once said, "I know how all the levers work, and I could generate so much cash I could make everybody's head spin." However, after Ivester's more than two years as CEO, Coca-Cola's market value remained stuck at $148 billion compared with

the $147 billion market value when Goizueta had left the helm.[29]

In early December 1999, Ivester flew to Chicago for a regular meeting with McDonald's executives and during the same trip also had a private meeting with Coca-Cola's two most powerful directors, Warren Buffet and Herbert Allen. The two directors informed Ivester that they had lost faith in his leadership, and it was time for a change. Don Keough, who had been Goizueta's number-two person for 12 years as COO and president was said to have played a role in this meeting. Upon retirement in 1993, Keough had remained involved in Coca-Cola as a consultant and later rejoined as a director when Coca-Cola abolished its 74-year age limit for board membership. Keough was chairman at Allen & Co., Herbert Allen's small investment firm housed in Coca-Cola's building in New York.

At only age 52 and after just more than two years as the chairman and CEO, Ivester was pushed to retire from the position. On returning from the meeting in Chicago, Ivester publicly announced his departure from Coca-Cola, "After extensive reflection and thought, I have concluded that it is time for me to move on to the next stage of my life and, therefore, to put into place an orderly transition for this great company."[30] In reaction to the news, Coca-Cola's share price, which had already lagged the American stock market by 30 per cent over the previous two years, fell 12 per cent in two days. This drop was quite a contrast for investors who had seen the stock price rise over 5800 per cent during Goizueta's 16-year tenure.[31] During Ivester's tenure the stock price had dropped 12.3 per cent (see Exhibits 1 and 2).

---

[27]Betsy Morris, "The Real Story," *Fortune*, May 31, 2004, pp. 84–98.

[28]Patricia Sellers, "How Coke Is Kicking Pepsi's Can," *Fortune*, October 28, 1996, pp. 70–84.

[29]Betsy Morris and Patricia Sellers, "What Really Happened at Coke—Doug Ivester Was a Demon for Information," Fortune, January 10, 2000, pp. 114–116.

[30]"Coke CEO Stepping Down after Difficult Tenure," *CBC News*, December 6, 1999, http://www.cbc.ca/money/story/1999/12/06/coke991206.html, retrieved April 19, 2008.

[31]"New Doug, Old Tricks," *The Economist*, December 11, 1999, p. 55

⬚ Douglas Daft: Enjoy

Background

The next CEO of Coca-Cola, Douglas Daft, was born in 1943, in Cessnock, New South Wales, Australia. He received a bachelor of arts degree with a major in mathematics from the University of New England in Armidale, New South Wales. He later received a post-graduate degree in administration from the University of New South Wales.

Daft was a first-generation college student, being the first in his family to attend university. He later recalled that the opportunity had led him to develop a passion for lifelong learning about the world and different cultures. In an interview, he mentioned his profound respect for the differences and similarities of people and his experiences of cultural and intellectual diversity across Singapore, Tokyo, and Beijing, which shaped him for leadership roles at Coca-Cola, one of the most international companies in the world.[32]

Daft started at Coca-Cola as a planning officer in the Sydney (Australia) office in 1969. He progressed through the company, holding positions of increasing responsibility, and became vice-president of Coca-Cola Far East Ltd. in 1982. Daft was named president of the North Pacific Division and president of Coca-Cola (Japan) Co., Ltd. in 1988. In 1991, he moved to Coca-Cola's Atlanta headquarters as president of the Pacific Group with responsibilities including the Africa Group, the Middle and Far East Group, and the Schweppes Beverage Division. He was elected president and COO in December 1999.

Douglas Daft as CEO of Coca-Cola

Daft was preparing for retirement in Australia when he was brought in to replace Ivester. It was said that Daft neither aspired to, nor was groomed for, the CEO job and was "an accidental CEO."[33] Daft had spent most of his 30 years with the company in Asia, and had succeeded as president of Coca-Cola in Japan, one of the company's most difficult and largest markets outside the United States.

Daft's personality was described as low-key, unassuming, media-shy, and not communication friendly. He was known for a consensus-driven style and for avoiding conflict. He began by making changes that were seen as culturally new, such as removing flags that had traditionally flown at Atlanta headquarters: the American flag, the Georgia flag, the Coca-Cola flag, and a flag to honor the visitor of the day, generally a bottler or customer. He called upon a feng shui consultant to make interior decoration changes and to rearrange telephones so that the cords would not coil in the wrong direction. Life-sized ceramic roosters were installed in the offices of Daft and two senior executives.[34]

In his first few weeks, Daft started the process of cutting 5,200 jobs to reduce costs. However these cuts were not seen as steering the company in a clear strategic direction. Whereas Ivester's mantra had been "Think global—act local," Daft's vision leaned more toward "Think local—act local." This mindset reflected his experience away from headquarters where he had developed the idea that bureaucracy at headquarters was a problem. Daft challenged Coca-Cola's matrix system, which, created and nurtured by Goizueta, had ensured that the finance, marketing, technical, law and quality control departments at headquarters networked with and controlled the corresponding departments in other countries. Daft's approach was to get rid of corporate

---

[32]Interview with Doug Daft, Institute of International Education, IIENetwork.org http://iienetwork.org/?p=29253, accessed on June 21, 2008.

[33]Patricia Sellers, "Who's in Charge Here?" *Fortune*, December 24, 2001, pp. 76–80, 83, 86.

[34]Betsy Morris, "The Real Story," *Fortune*, May 31, 2004, pp. 84–98.

bureaucracy and give more decision-making power to the field managers.

Under Daft's tenure, Don Keough's advice and attendance at board meetings was again welcomed. Under Daft's leadership and Keough's approval, several key executives who had served under Ivester were ousted. Turnover among senior managers during Daft's tenure was severe. In just more than four years, Coca-Cola had two new marketing heads, two new European operations heads and new management in the company's human resources departments and in the North America, Asia and Latin America divisions.[35]

Daft also built the company's forays into the fast-growing area of non-carbonated drinks, including bottled water and juices,[36] exemplified by Daft's attempts to buy Quaker Oats, maker of Gatorade in 2000. Although Quaker Oats broke off talks with Pepsi and Danone, in the end the Coca-Cola board did not pass the deal. Reportedly, directors Warren Buffet and Peter Ueberroth objected, seeing the exchange of Coca-Cola's 10 per cent stock for Quaker Oats as too risky. A joint venture with Procter & Gamble Co. (P&G) was created to develop synergies between Coca-Cola's Minute Maid juices and distribution prowess with P&G's potato chip and juice brands. Ideas included developing a half-size can of P&G's Pringle's potato chips for distribution through Coca-Cola's machines and other channels. A similar deal with Nestlé was crafted to develop tea and coffee drinks using Nestlé's research and development labs. Historically, Coca-Cola had not succeeded in using its distribution and marketing to develop a presence in the high-margin premium beverage market dominated by Snapple, AriZona, SoBe and Gatorade.

These changes epitomized Daft's approach as a passionate, idea-a-minute manager, building upon intuitions from his Asia-Pacific experience.

His approach contrasted sharply with Ivester's numbers-based accountant's approach to decision making. At a retreat in San Francisco, Daft asked for new ideas from two dozen Coca-Cola executives and, on the spot, funded four of the ideas with $250,000 each. Under Daft's tenure, scientists and marketers united to build new products ranging from calcium-fortified waters to vitamin-enriched drinks bearing Disney characters' names.

Coca-Cola's advertising was also overhauled, because the "Always" campaign had "lost people, lost humanity and become clinical," according to Coca-Cola's Marketing Director, Stephen C. Jones. In a new move, Coca-Cola began to allow bottlers to customize promotions to local events. Although Ivester had opposed tie-ins with movies, Daft made a deal with Warner Bros. Entertainment Inc. to co-market movies such as the *Harry Potter* series around the world.[37]

Daft announced another major step in his restructuring when he let go president and COO, Jack L. Stahl. Steve Heyer, formerly president and COO at Turner Broadcasting, was brought in as the new president. Subsequently, Daft used this time to be out in the field to improve relations with bottlers. However, Daft remained known for making quick decisions and sometimes being unsure about them later. Coca-Cola's bottlers in Colombia had faced violence, and Daft announced at an awards dinner in Washington that he would have general counsel Deval Patrick investigate. However, the decision was abruptly reversed four months later and an announcement about Patrick's resignation leaked out. At an annual meeting, stockholders were distributed leaflets by demonstrators who shouted, "Coca-Cola, killer Cola, toxic Cola, racist Cola." None of the directors faced the crowd, and Daft, seemingly losing control, unwittingly urged a child questioner to

---

[35]Ibid.

[36]"Repairing the Coke Machine," *Business Week*, March 19, 2001, p. 86.

[37]Ibid.

"Drink Coke, Sam," later amending the line by saying "That is, if your parents let you."[38]

At the same meeting, Keough commented on Coca-Cola's succession plan saying that the company would find the best candidate for the job. A very public search was launched, which included talks with Jim Kilts, CEO of Gillette, and Jack Welch, the retired CEO of GE. During Daft's tenure as CEO, Coke's stock price increased 9.15 per cent (see Exhibits 1 and 2).

The Isdell Side of Life

Background

Coca-Cola's next CEO, Edward Neville Isdell, was born in Downpatrick, Northern Ireland, in 1943. He moved to Zambia in childhood and later completed a bachelor's degree in social science at the University of Capetown, South Africa. In 1966, Isdell joined Coca-Cola through the local bottling company in Zambia. Moving up on the bottling side of operations, in 1972 he became general manager of the Johannesburg bottler, the largest Coca-Cola bottler in Africa. In 1980, he became the regional manager for Australia, and the following year became the president of the bottling joint venture between Coca-Cola and San Miguel Corporation in the Philippines. Isdell was subsequently credited with turning around and renewing the entire Coca-Cola business in the Philippines.

Isdell's international career continued with a stint in Germany, starting in 1985 as president of the company's Central European division. He moved up the ranks of the company in 1989, when he was elected senior vice president, and concurrently became president of the Northeast Europe/Africa Group (later to become the Northeast Europe / Middle East group in 1992). During this phase, Isdell oversaw the company's expansion into new markets, such as India, Middle East, Eastern Europe and the Soviet Union. He became president of the Greater Europe Group in 1995.

Isdell subsequently moved to Great Britain in 1998 as CEO of Coca-Cola Beverages Plc in Great Britain. Under his watch, that company merged with Hellenic Bottling and resulted in the largest Coca-Cola bottler of that time, Coca-Cola Hellenic Bottling Company (HBC). He left Coca-Cola in 2001 to form his own investment company in Barbados.[39]

Isdell as CEO of Coca-Cola

Doug Daft's retirement announcement in February 2004 was followed by two months of speculation regarding his successor. Some wondered whether an outsider such as Gillette's president and CEO, James M. Kilts, might be the likely candidate. Instead, E. Neville Isdell was named the new chairman and CEO. Interestingly, Isdell had been passed over for the top job in 1997 (in favor of Douglas Ivester), despite having been Keough's preference at the time.

On accepting the position, Isdell said:

> I am both proud and humbled to be given the opportunity to help write the next chapter in this illustrious company's history. I appreciate the importance of this position and the trust placed in me by the board of directors. We are all grateful to Doug Daft for his enormous contributions and look forward to building upon the tremendous foundation he and his team have built. I am excited to get started and help shape our future.[40]

---

[38]Betsy Morris, "The Real Story," *Fortune*, May 31, 2004, pp. 84–98.

[39]The Coca-Cola Company website, http://www.thecoca-colacompany.com/ourcompany/board.html, accessed February 15, 2008.

[40]The Coca-Cola Co. 8-K report filed with SEC on 5/5/04. http://www.secinfo.com/dkrf.12f.d.htm, accessed on June 21, 2008.

During Isdell's CEO tenure, Coca-Cola's profits rose steadily, in particular from international operations. Right at the start, Isdell had laid out his plans, based on his belief in significant future growth for the Coca-Cola brand. Some growth was expected to come from new markets, such as China and India, while further growth was still possible in the United States and Europe. Keough let his confidence in Isdell be known, mentioning that it was the first time in 119 years that the company would have a CEO who had worked on both sides of the system, referring to Isdell's experience of being involved both as a bottler and concentrate person and his experience on working on five continents.[41] Under Isdell's leadership Coke's stock price increased 12.9 percent. Overall, the three CEOs who had served after Goizueta's untimely death in 1997 had increased Coke's stock price 11.6 per cent.

⊠ Epilogue

In December 2007, Isdell announced that he would step down from the CEO position in July 2008 to be replaced by Muhtar Kent, the company's COO. However, Isdell would remain chairman of the board until the company's annual meeting in 2009, splitting the position of CEO and chairman at Coca-Cola for the first time. To questions on why Isdell chose this time to announce his departure, he said, "Because it's the right time. I've been working on succession since Day 1." Although a national search had been launched when Doug Daft left, there would be no doubt as to who the next CEO would be this time.

Commenting on the news, John Sicher, a beverage industry expert remarked, "Kent understands the company and the system literally as well as anybody in the world and better than most." Deutsche Bank analyst Marc Greenberg said, "Kent has played a formative role in shaping the current course—'steady as she goes' is likely the mantra." In the position of COO, Kent saw major strategic initiatives undertaken, such as the $4.1 billion acquisition of glacéau in 2007, strengthening Coca-Cola's position with new brands, such as vitaminwater.

At the time of this announcement, Kent mentioned that he had no immediate plans to change any leadership roles but that some scope was available for fine-tuning management. He pointed out that he knew he faced challenges: "We have confidence the United States has growth left in it," he said. Regarding the bottling issues, he added, "We were at each other's throats with our bottlers a year ago—we are aligned now."[42]

As the plane headed toward Atlanta and Coca-Cola's corporate headquarters, Kent looked out at the Atlantic ocean and thought about the company's previous illustrious leaders, their times and strategies, and wondered how he would take charge and lead the company into the future.

---

[41]Betsy Morris, "The Real Story," *Fortune*, May 31, 2004, pp. 84–98.

[42]"Coca-Cola's CEO Isdell to step down," Associated Press, MSNBC, December 6, 2007; http://www.msnbc.msn.com/id/22127700/, accessed June 22, 2008.

Exhibit I	CEO Succession Timeline and Stock Price Performance at Coca-Cola

CEO	Period of Tenure	Adjusted Monthly Closing Stock Price at Beginning Month of Tenure*	Adjusted Monthly Closing Stock Price at Ending Month of Tenure*
Robert Goizueta	March 1981 to October 1997	$00.78	$46.23
Douglas Ivester	October 1997 to February 2000	$46.23	$40.54
Douglas Daft	February 2000 to February 2004	$40.54	$44.25
E. Neville Isdell	May 2004 to June 2008	$45.71	$51.61**
Muhtar Kent	July 2008 to Present		

*Closing price adjusted for dividends and stock splits
**As of June 30, 2008

Exhibit 2	Coca-Cola (KO) Stock Market Performance Compared to the Dow Jones (DJI) and Standard and Poor (GSPC) Indices

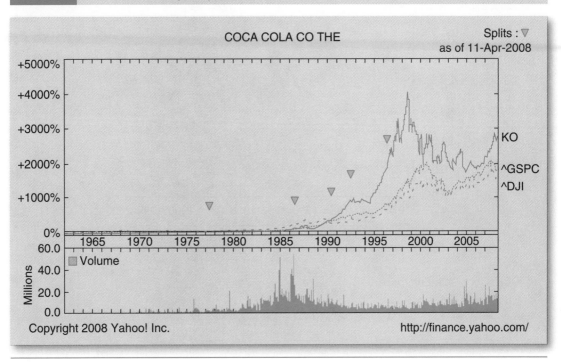

SOURCE: Yahoo Finance website, accessed April 11, 2008. Reproduced with permission of 2007 by Yahoo! Inc. YAHOO! and the YAHOO! logo are trademarks of © Yahoo! Inc. Yahoo! Inc.

| Exhibit 3 | Graphical Comparison of Net Profit/Sales and Net Profit/Equity During the Goizueta and Ivester Time Frame |

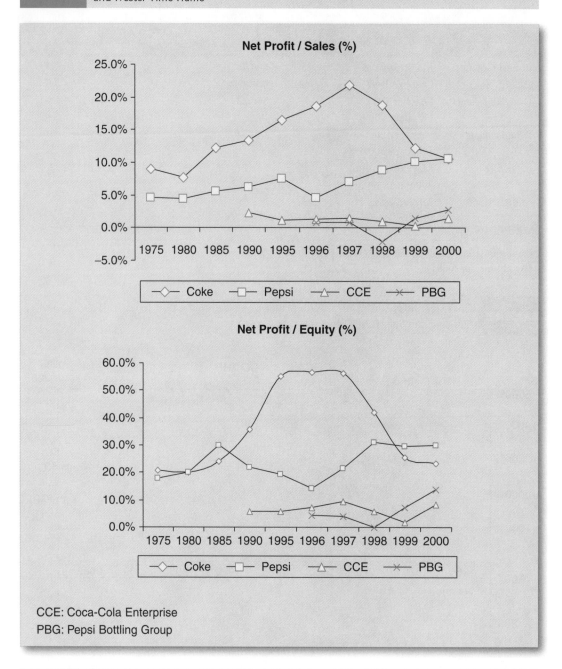

CCE: Coca-Cola Enterprise
PBG: Pepsi Bottling Group

SOURCE: David B. Yoffie, *Cola Wars Continue: Coke and Pepsi in the Twenty-First Century,* July 30, 2002, Harvard Business School, Exhibit 4, p. 19.

Maple Leaf Foods, Inc. (A): The Listeriosis Crisis

Jeffrey Gandz

Michael McCain, president and chief executive officer of Maple Leaf Foods (MLF) slowly put down the phone. The call that he had just received at 6 p.m. on August 23, 2008 was not entirely unexpected but it had still been a shock. The Canadian Food Inspection Agency (CFIA)[1] and Health Canada[2] had just advised that DNA testing had confirmed a link between a national outbreak of *Listeriosis* and two products produced at the company's Bartor Road plant in Toronto. While reported illnesses had occurred in a few dozen people, the consumption of Maple Leaf sliced deli meats had been linked to at least three deaths and there was an expectation that this death toll might rise.

In his 20 years in the food processing industry, McCain had never experienced anything like this. Food safety had been a central concern of the whole management team and employee group at MLF since the company had been formed in 1995. The company had never been involved in a recall involving Listeria or any other pathogenic bacteria. This and the company's excellent food safety record had led to the adoption of the "We Take Care" brand tag line in 2006. Now he had to face the reality that something had gone seriously wrong. As he recalled:

> My first and overriding concern was for the people and families affected and to make sure that we did everything we possibly could to minimize any further possible risk to consumers. Then, I had

to be concerned with the company— the 23,000 employees who worked in Maple Leaf's operations around the world. They would be shocked at this news. People in this company are passionate about food, and that includes the safety of the food we make. I needed to figure out what I was going to say to the board, my management team and employees, when we didn't even know the source of the problem or the extent of products affected.

And we needed a plan of action—what were we going to do to address this problem? How quickly could we find the source of contamination, fix the problem and reassure consumers?

This was uncharted territory for us. We'd never had a problem like this before—no large recall, no severe customer illness, certainly no deaths had ever been linked to Maple Leaf Food products. While we had recall procedures in place—every food processor must have these—we had never had to deal with anything of this seriousness or scale before.

Maple Leaf Foods Inc.

Maple Leaf Foods Inc. was founded in 1990 by the merger of Maple Leaf Mills Limited (flour milling and bakeries) and Canada Packers Inc.

    Version: 2011-01-07

[1]The Canadian Food Inspection Agency (CFIA) is an agency of the federal government charged with regulating and inspecting food processing companies.

[2]Health Canada is the department of the federal government responsible for public health matters.

(meat products). Maple Leaf Mills was created in 1961 through the amalgamation of the Maple Leaf Milling Company Limited, Toronto Elevators Limited and Purity Flour Mills Limited. Its origins can be traced back more than 170 years to Grantham Mills, built in 1836 in St. Catharines, Ontario. Canada Packers Inc. was formed in 1927 in Toronto, Ontario through the amalgamation of the Harris Abbatoir Company, Gunns Limited and the William Davies Company. In 1975 it was listed as the fourteenth largest company in Canada and dominated the meat processing industry in Canada.

In 1995, McCain Capital Corporation[3] and the Ontario Teachers Pension Plan[4] acquired controlling interest in the company from Hillsdown Holdings plc and continued to invest in growth primarily through acquisitions. By 2008 total Maple Leaf Foods sales were Cdn$5.2 billion[5] and the company employed more than 23,000 people in more than 100 facilities at its operations in Canada, the United States and the United Kingdom. Its business was organized into five independent operating companies: The "protein" group was made up of two leading national brands, *Maple Leaf* and *Schneiders*™, in addition to Maple Leaf *Prime Naturally*™ and a variety of household brands including *Shopsy's*™, *Mitchell's Gourmet Foods*™, *Larsen*™, *Parma*™ and *Hygrade*™. Product lines include packaged meats, wieners and hot dogs, sausage and bologna, ready-to-cook and ready-to-serve meal products and value-added fresh pork, poultry and turkey.

Fresh pork and poultry processing facilities in Alberta, Manitoba, Saskatchewan, Ontario and Nova Scotia provided high quality inputs to value-added, packaged meat and meals facilities throughout Canada. The company primarily marketed its products in Canada, the United States, Mexico and Japan through the retail trade, foodservice and industrial customers. The Maple Leaf "protein" business was highly integrated, raising hogs as well as buying them on the open market, processing them—selling fresh pork internationally and using some as raw material in its prepared meats business. By-products were wholly recycled by its rendering operations into tallow, feed additives and other products through a wholly owned subsidiary, Rothsay Rendering. It was often said "Maple Leaf Foods uses every part of the pig except the squeal."

Maple Leaf also owned nearly 90 per cent of the shares of the Canada Bread Company Limited that was founded in 1911 by the amalgamation of five separate companies. In the last 90-plus years, Canada Bread had grown to become an important manufacturer of value-added flour-based fresh and frozen bakery and fresh pasta products including familiar household brands such as *Dempster's*™, *Tenderflake*™ and *Olivieri*™.

In 2007, the meat products business (not including the raising of hogs and rendering of meat by products) accounted for 66.4 per cent of total Maple Leaf sales and 41.4 per cent of its adjusted operating earnings.[6] In total, brands marketed by Maple Leaf Foods accounted for approximately 39 per cent of the prepared meats category (bacon, sliced meats, sausages, wieners, etc.) in retail sales and a slightly larger

---

[3]McCain Capital Corporation was the holding company owned by the Wallace McCain family that included Michael McCain, Scott McCain (president and chief operating officer of the Agribusiness Group of Maple Leaf Foods) and their two sisters who are not active in the business. McCain Capital Corporation owned 31 per cent of the equity of Maple Leaf Foods as of June 2008. Its other major asset was a 33 per cent interest in McCain Foods Inc., Canada's largest privately held food processing company.

[4]The Ontario Teachers Pension Plan was the investment company managing the pension assets of schoolteachers in the province of Ontario. With more than Cdn$105 billion invested in equities and fixed income assets, OTTP's rate of return had slipped to 4.5 per cent on assets in 2007 compared with double-digit returns in the previous four years. As of June 2008, OTTP owned 33 per cent of the equity of Maple Leaf Foods, which was its seventh largest equity investment and its largest in Canada.

[5]In August 2008, Cdn$1 = US$.975.

[6]Maple Leaf Foods 2007 Annual Report.

percentage in institutional sales. Of its branded products (not including the private label sales marketed under store brands), the *Maple Leaf*™ brand accounted for 12 percentage points, the *Schneiders*™ brand for 19 percentage points and other, smaller brands, for the remainder. Seventy-two per cent of Maple Leaf Foods' prepared meats were distributed through retail stores and 28 per cent through food service and institutional outlets.[7]

This category of products was a very important one for retail stores. With margins at retail of about 30 per cent, it was among the most profitable categories carried by supermarkets. While Maple Leaf Foods was clearly the market leader in this category, competition within the category was fierce, both from other national and regional branded products such as Olymel, Maple Lodge and Lillydale as well as private label brands[8] and this was reflected on high levels of sales promotion activity by all competitors in the form of off-invoice discounts, case allowances for special displays, advertising support for special promotions and feature pricing. In some areas there had been penetration of the Canadian market by major U.S. brands including Oscar Mayer and Hebrew National. Major brands were also supported with consumer-focused advertising and promotional activities ranging from coupons to competitions.

Because it had grown primarily through acquisitions, Maple Leaf carried a lot of goodwill on its balance sheet—Cdn$856 million as of June 30, 2008 (see Exhibit 1). Its long-term debt of approximately Cdn$1 billion as of June 30, 2008 reflected a long-term strategy of relatively high leverage. This was managed very carefully and the company had never been in breach of its covenants with any lenders and had always paid a modest dividend. Its shares, always volatile on very thin trading volumes, had peaked recently at Cdn$18.24 on May 14, 2007 but had been in decline since then, standing at Cdn$10.78 on June 30, 2008 (end of Q2) and going to Cdn$9.80 on August 18, 2008.

Maple Leaf Foods Strategy[9]

In August 2008, Maple Leaf was in the midst of restructuring its protein business. This strategic renewal process had been triggered by the unprecedented increase in the value of the Canadian dollar relative to the US dollar that had taken place in the period 2003–2007 when it had gone from a low of $.64 to near-parity. This shift in currency had made Maple Leaf commodity products less attractive in previously lucrative export markets in Japan, Korea, Taiwan and other countries. It had also reduced the value of earnings in the U.S. markets when they were converted into Canadian dollars. Beyond that, a Canadian dollar at or near par made the Canadian market more attractive to U.S.-based producers such as Hormel, Oscar Mayer or Sara Lee that had considerably lower production costs than Maple Leaf. While they had not entered the Canadian market by 2008 in any meaningful way, a high Canadian dollar increased the likelihood that they would.

While it was difficult to assess, the management at Maple Leaf believed that the impact of the currency shift alone had cost the company more than Cdn$100 million in lost income over the preceding three years. The company was focusing its protein strategy on growing its value-added fresh and further processed meat and meals businesses. Through integration of its fresh and value-added further processed operations, the company's goal was to balance and optimize the value of all meats that it processes

---

[7]Maple Leaf Foods Investor Reports, 2008/2009.

[8]Products marketed under retailers own brand names although manufactured by branded products manufacturers such as Maple Leaf Foods.

[9]Maple Leaf Foods 2007 Annual Report.

by significantly increasing the proportion of the hogs that it raised and pork that it processed into its own further processing; by accelerating new product innovation; establishing a low cost manufacturing base; and reducing the scale and scope of its value chain to the size required to support its value-added meat businesses.

At the end of a multi-year process, management's intent was that all components of the protein group, including the feed, hog production and primary-processing operations would be sized to support its value-added fresh and further processed meat businesses. This would result in reducing the number of hogs processed from 7.5 million to approximately 4.3 million annually and would result in reducing the number of hogs produced from approximately 1.5 million hogs in 2006 to 750,000 hogs annually. The company was in the process of selling or exiting operations and businesses that did not support this balanced, aligned and vertically integrated model.

The goal of the restructuring was to create a simpler, more focused and profitable meat, meals and bakery company, with significantly less exposure to foreign currency fluctuations and commodity markets, building on its strengths in the higher margin, fresh and further processed meat, meals and bakery businesses through innovation, investment, and acquisitions.

In 2007 and early 2008, the company had:

- Substantially restructured its Manitoba hog production operations towards wholly owned and balanced operations concentrated in proximity to the Brandon, Manitoba, processing plant.
- Entered into transactions to sell its entire wholly owned hog investments in Alberta and most of its hog production operations in Ontario. These transactions were completed in Q1 2008.
- Sold the animal nutrition business, except for two feed mills required to meet internal hog requirements, for proceeds of $524.8 million.

- Double-shifted the front-end "kill" processing at the Brandon pork plant enabling the closure of two older facilities in Saskatoon and Winnipeg.
- Started construction of a new $12.0 million food innovation centre in Toronto, Ontario, expected to be completed in early 2009.
- Established a modern scale plant in Brampton, Ontario with capacity to support growth in value-added, packaged meats and meals, involving investment of approximately $25.0 million in 2007.
- Invested over $40.0 million in capital projects to reduce costs and add capacity in the manufacturing distribution network.
- Increased capacity utilization in the poultry and processed meats networks through closing four sub-scale facilities.
- Started to substantially reduce costs and increase margins by simplifying the organizational structure, reducing the number of independent operating companies in the protein group from eight to three, and creating a shared-services structure that would provide expert services to all operating units from a central location.

This restructuring was well underway in August 2008, but the major investments in information technology and new systems and processes were scheduled for late 2008 and 2009. These were essential to driving efficiencies and increased margins. The renewal process had already cost more than Cdn$40 million and was going to require considerable capital investment, the amount to be determined during 2008, but estimated to be several hundred million dollars. The major shareholders in the business, McCain Capital Corporation and the Ontario Teachers Pension Plan, with the complete support of the board of directors, were ready to make this investment once the details had been worked out and a financing plan had been approved. With its investment-grade balance sheet and cash-generating capability, Maple Leaf management had confidence that it was well positioned to be the dominant domestic food processing company while continuing to explore and develop global opportunities as they arose.

The Maple Leaf Culture

The leadership team at Maple Leaf had invested substantial amounts of time and money in developing a strong values framework to which all executives and the vast majority of managers had been exposed during the Maple Leaf Leadership Academy programs though which all senior and middle-level leaders had attended. There were six core values, each of which had supporting behaviors: Do what's right; Be performance driven; Have a bias for action; Continuously improve; Be externally focused; and, Dare to be transparent. These values were the basis on which people were hired, evaluated, promoted or fired at Maple Leaf and those in leadership positions were expected to live by them.

A second key element of the Maple Leaf culture was a commitment to Six Sigma methodologies for process improvement and decision-making. With a large cadre of black, green and white belts,[10] all senior and most middle-level leaders within the Maple Leaf organization were making use of Six Sigma tools and resources in the company to improve the quality of decision-making, planning and execution.

2007/08 Performance

The year 2007 had been an excellent year for Maple Leaf. Net Income of $195 million (after restructuring costs of $124 million) had translated into an EPS of $1.53 and shares of Maple Leaf had finished the year at $14.58 compared with $12.34 at the end of 2006. These excellent results had been boosted by the sale of its highly profitable animal feed business that had been deemed non-strategic but, notwithstanding this, the results had been considered satisfactory. See Exhibit 1 for 2003–2007 financial results.

However, the first half of 2008 had been a very challenging one for the company primarily because of a rapid acceleration in commodity costs. At the end of the second quarter of 2008, wheat (the major cost input in the bakery business) had increased by 116 per cent year-over-year, corn (the major cost input in raising hogs) by 67 per cent, natural gas and oil by 44 per cent and 91 per cent respectively. The share price had reflected these headwinds and reached a year-to-date low of $9.66 on July 21, 2008. Because of the large speculative elements in these increases, it was extremely uncertain as to whether these new prices reflected long-term trends or just temporary commodity bubbles. Maple Leaf's management believed that commodity prices had peaked by the summer of 2008 and would likely moderate through the rest of the year and into 2009.[11]

The impact on Maple Leaf operating performance had been substantial, putting it significantly behind the previous year's results as of the end of the second quarter (see Figure 1 and Figure 2 below). Management was confident that it would be possible to raise prices to cover the additional costs, but there was always a lag of several months between the time input costs went up for MLF and the time they could recover these costs through price increases that their customers, food retailers, wholesalers and food service operators were prepared to pass through to consumers.

---

[10]The belt colors denote the expertise in Six Sigma methodologies from white belts, the least trained, to master black belts who were at the very highest levels of proficiency.

[11]Management's discussion in Maple Leaf Food's Q2 2007 Report to Shareholders and Investor Relations Report.

Figure 1	Maple Leaf Foods Inc. Adjusted Earnings, Q2 2008

	Second Quarter		Year-To-Date	
Per Share	2008	2007	2008	2007
EPS from continuing operations	$(0.07)	$(0.05)	$(0.07)	$(0.01)
Restructuring and other related costs, net of tax[i]	$ 0.07	$ 0.18	$0.11	$ 0.26
Adjusted EPS [ii] [iii]	$(0.01)	$0.13	$0.03	$ 0.25
Discontinued operations		$0.04		$ 0.08
EPS before restructuring and other related costs[ii]	$(0.01)	$0.17	$0.03	$ 0.33

(i) Includes the per share impact of restructuring and other related costs net of tax and minority interest and includes the recognition of a tax benefit of $5.1 million in Q2 2007 related to the sale of the animal nutrition business.

(ii) These are not recognized measures under Canadian GAAP. Management believes that this is the most appropriate basis on which to evaluate results, as restructuring and other related costs are not representative of continuing operations.

(iii) Does not add due to rounding.

Figure 2	Maple Leaf Foods Inc. Earnings per Share, Q2 2008

	Second Quarter			Year-to-Date [iii]		
($ millions)	2008	2007	Change	2008	2007	Change
Meat Products Group	$ 5.7	$ 15.0	(62.0%)	$ 30.7	$ 36.5	(15.8%)
Agribusiness Group[i]	7.6	4.7	62.2%	4.8	5.5	(12.5%)
Protein Group	13.3	19.7	(32.5%)	35.5	42.0	(15.4%)
Bakery Products Group	8.7	33.4	(74.0%)	25.8	61.1	(57.7%)
Non-allocated Costs[ii]	(3.1)	(0.4)	–	(9.4)	(0.5)	–
	$ 18.9	$ 52.7	(64.1%)	$ 52.0	$ 102.5	(49.3%)

(i) Agribusiness Group excludes the results of the animal nutrition business that are reported as discontinued operations.

(ii) Non-allocated costs include costs related to the company's IT system conversion, certain shared services and consulting expenses related to restructuring initiatives. Management believes that not allocating these costs provides a more comparable assessment of segment operating results.

(iii) Table does not add due to rounding.

Maple Leaf Foods had never given guidance to the financial markets and did not forecast future sales or profitability numbers. However, in his quarterly statement to shareholders in July 2008, Michael McCain had stated:

> We fully expected the first half of 2008 to be very difficult for Maple Leaf due to the extreme inflation and volatility in commodity markets. We are focused on persevering through these unprecedented market conditions, maintaining our focus on executing the structural changes we have committed to and passing on price increases to offset the effects of commodity inflation. While the first half has been pressured, we believe the second half of 2008 will show a substantial recovery as markets stabilize and the early benefits of restructuring are realized.[12]

The balance sheet and consolidated income statement for Maple Leaf Foods Inc. at June 30, 2008 are shown in Exhibits 2 and 3.

The Bartor Road Plant

The Bartor Road plant was one of Maple Leaf's prepared meats facilities located in northwest Toronto. It was a federally registered plant and approved for export to the United States. The plant produced sliced cooked meats, bologna, and deli meats for national distribution to retail stores and food service operations. Bartor Road employed approximately 300 people, including 10 food safety and quality assurance staff, who worked on two shifts with a third shift reserved for clean-up and sanitation activities. In total, there were eleven production lines and products could be run on several different lines according to demand and capacity utilization. Formulations and packaging were specific to a brand but many different brands could be manufactured on the same line. While the original plant had been built in the early 1950s it had been updated several times and was considered a high-quality production environment.

The plant made a wide range of deli products including sliced meats (ham, bologna, other forms of sausage) as well as wieners that were packaged and shipped under several brand names including *Maple Leaf*™, *Schneiders*™, *Bittners*™, *Shopsy's*™, *Hygrade*™, *Burns*™, *Coorsh*™ and others as well as private label brands. Raw materials were received at the Bartor Road plant from a variety of sources, including Maple Leaf's own pork processing operations across the country as well as meat products bought on the open market. Hog and beef cuts were cooked, chilled and then further processed into wieners, sausages of various types and a large variety of sliced meats usually found in the "deli" departments of supermarkets and also sold through food service distribution channels to restaurants, fast-food outlets, sandwich sellers, schools, hospitals, nursing homes and others. The various products were scheduled to run on a variety of lines depending on the mix of orders and delivery requirements. While other plants in the Maple Leaf supply chain could and did manufacture some of the products made in Bartor Road, this plant was the sole supply for many of the larger brands marketed by the company.

Food Safety at Maple Leaf Foods

Maple Leaf was viewed as a good company with a high standard of food safety. The Bartor Road plant was considered to be a compliant plant in that it routinely met all the regulatory requirements under the federal Meat Inspection Act and got satisfactory marks for complying with the government's inspection and testing tasks. It was also approved by the U.S. Department of Agriculture for shipping products into the U.S. market. When Canadian Food Inspection Agency's

---

[12]Maple Leaf Foods Reports Second Quarter Results.

inspectors identified any compliance problems, the plant addressed them. Bartor Road's management maintained the necessary required records, ensured that staff training took place, and made sure its quality assurance program was completed. Much of the credit for Maple Leaf's good reputation rested with the firm's in-house safety plan. The company had introduced its own food safety procedures, which included a comprehensive HACCP[13] plan, an additional layer of food safety protection at the end of the 1990s—years earlier than was required by the regulations.[14]

Within Maple Leaf, operational responsibility for food safety was managed at the plant level and the food safety staff reported to the plant managers who, in turn, reported to divisional manufacturing executives who reported to the presidents of the operating divisions. Policies and standard operating procedures were established at the corporate level and food safety performance was monitored at the executive level and reported routinely to the Environment Health and Safety Committee (EHSC) of the board, and thence to the full board, at least three times a year. Every incident of product contamination, or consumer complaints whether from foreign objects in packaged products or bacteriological contamination had to be reported and the EHSC committee received incident-by-incident reports as well as summary statistics.

Food safety was one area of operations that was constantly being improved as new procedures and new technologies became available. Indeed, in 2006 MLF had introduced a 49-point food safety plan that the management believed was as good as any that existed in Canada. This was being rolled out throughout the Maple Leaf manufacturing plants and the Bartor Road facility had been audited against this plan and had been rated as satisfactory on all counts.

The primary route of contamination of RTE food products is from the post-lethality processing environment, where external surfaces of fully cooked products come in contact with Listeria cells present on food contact surfaces. During daily operation of the processing line, contamination might occur when cells from these protected areas are released to the processing area due to wet conditions, mechanical action of the equipment, employee traffic and other normal operating practices.

People in the food processing business live with the certain knowledge that potentially harmful bacteria exist in the environment of every processing plant. The challenge is to keep them away from contact with any surfaces that came into contact with RTE food. The kind of normal cleaning and sanitation practices that were part of standard operating procedures at the Bartor Road and other Maple Leaf Food plants had proven very effective at removing Listeria cells that may have contaminated food contact surfaces. Routinely, swabs were taken from any food surface that might come into contact with cooked products. These swabs were cultured in an on-site laboratory and if any of them proved positive as they did from time to time—a special "deep-cleaning" process was initiated until subsequent tests were shown to be negative. During that process the line would be taken out of production. In every case in the past, deep cleaning of anything that could come into contact with the meat being processed had resolved the problem and subsequent tests had proven negative.

Listeriosis

Listeria is a bacterium that can be found in soil, water and foods. There are six species of *Listeria*, but *Listeria monocytogenes* is the only one that

---

[13]Hazard Analysis Critical Control Point or HACCP is a systematic preventive approach to food safety and pharmaceutical safety that addresses physical, chemical, and biological hazards as a means of prevention rather than finished product inspection. HACCP is used in the food industry to identify potential food safety hazards, so that key actions can be taken to reduce or eliminate the risk of the hazards being realized. (Source: Wikipedia).

[14]Report of the independent investigator into the 2008 Listeriosis outbreak. Government of Canada, 2009.

causes human illness. Approximately 1 to 10 per cent of all ready-to-eat foods contain *Listeria monocytogenes.* Given that *Listeria* is everywhere, elimination is not possible and therefore risk mitigation needs to be achieved through surveillance and sanitation programs.

Listeriosis is a serious disease in humans that is primarily transmitted through ready-to-eat (RTE) foods. It is very rare, affecting one to five people out of 1,000,000 people per year and can result in death. *Listeriosis* can cause high fever, severe headache, neck stiffness and nausea. Pregnant women, the elderly and people with weakened immune systems are particularly at risk. Infected pregnant women may experience only a mild, flu-like illness, however, infections during pregnancy can lead to premature delivery, infection of the newborn, or even stillbirth. Although there is increasing evidence that low numbers of organisms are unlikely to cause illness, *Listeria monocytogenes* can grow to high numbers in RTE foods held at refrigerated temperatures.

Early Warnings

On August 7, 2008 Maple Leaf was made aware through one of their distributors, that a local public health authority in Ontario had launched an investigation into a sliced meat product. The company proactively contacted the local health authority the same day to offer assistance in tracing the product involved. The local public health authority thanked Maple Leaf for its contact but advised that no assistance was needed.

On August 8th, the Canadian Food Inspection Agency (CFIA) asked the company if three products could be traced and to investigate if they were still in inventory. This information was provided to CFIA the next day. On August 11th, the CFIA conducted a trace, and on August 12th, they informed MLF that an investigation had been launched. On August 13th, MLF notified customers in writing of the need to place three products "on hold" and not to ship or sell them. Those were Sure Slice Roast Beef, with "best before" dates of July 28th and August 9th, Sure Slice

Corned Beef, with "best before" dates of August 16th and August 23rd, and Sure Slice Black Forest Ham, with "best before" dates of August 9th and August 21st. The letter from MLF to its customers said, in part, "we are recommending that any remaining inventory of the products listed above be placed on hold as a precautionary step." This hold order was not a regulatory requirement, but a Maple Leaf best practice and the first step in protecting consumers.

The CFIA food safety specialist (Toronto region) visited the Bartor Road plant as part of her investigation. All samples taken and tested by the CFIA before that visit had been from open packages in institutions or homes with no identifiable code dates, making it more difficult to determine whether announcing a recall was the appropriate action to take. These fresh samples directly from the plant would, when tested, indicate whether a problem existed at the plant level. Such tests would normally take a couple of days to complete.

On August 14th and 15th, Maple Leaf worked internally to prepare and plan for the possibility of a recall. While no information had been received regarding the outcome of the product testing, Maple Leaf nonetheless set in motion a protocol for recall. The goal of this work was to ensure the fastest possible response in the event of positive test results for Listeria that could be traced to any Maple Leaf plant. The board of directors of MLF was advised by conference call of these actions and empowered the CEO to take any and all actions required to protect consumer health and safety.

On August 16th at 10:00 p.m., the CFIA notified Maple Leaf that tests for Listeria on one of the three products mentioned above had returned positive. Maple Leaf immediately set its recall protocol in motion. Since the products in question were sold to the food service industry, Maple Leaf targeted its efforts on contacting the distribution chain. Maple Leaf then confirmed that all affected product had been produced at the Bartor Rd. plant on lines 8 and 9. All products that had been manufactured on those lines, and that was still within the facility, were held, and subsequently destroyed.

On August 17th at 3:30 a.m., Maple Leaf issued a news release to all media in Canada with notice of the recall and product information. During the next two days, Maple Leaf worked diligently to contact 100 per cent of its food service customers.

On August 19th, Maple Leaf was made aware by the CFIA that two more tests on products produced at a different time on the same lines had come back positive. Maple Leaf voluntarily expanded the scope of the recall to include all products manufactured on lines 8 and 9 from June 2nd (the earliest affected production date). These products were predominantly food service products, but also included some retail products under the *Burns*™ and *Schneiders*™ brands.

The Situation Worsens

On August 19th, Maple Leaf was first notified that there were concerns about illness or loss of life. This information was the catalyst for the company's next sequence of actions. Even though the CFIA indicated that it had not confirmed the linkage to the Maple Leaf products by DNA pattern testing, the company proceeded with the voluntary recall. A release was issued on August 20th to all Canadian media notifying them of the expanded voluntary recall and that the plant was being closed for a comprehensive sanitization. The Maple Leaf website was updated with brand and "best before" date identifiers.

On August 22nd, the CFIA and Royal Touch Foods, a sandwich manufacturer, which was a subsidiary of Maple Leaf Foods, warned the public not to serve or consume the *Shopsy's*™ deli-fresh Classic Reuben sandwich, best before dates August 22nd and August 24th because the product might be contaminated with *Listeria monocytogenes*. This recall was initiated because the product contained sliced corned beef, one of the ready-to-eat deli meat products recalled by Maple Leaf Foods. There had been no reported illnesses associated with the consumption of these sandwiches.

On August 23rd, the CFIA and Public Health Agency of Canada concluded that the strain of *Listeria* bacteria which was linked to the illness and death of several consumers matched the *Listeria* strain identified in some Maple Leaf products and this was communicated to the company the same day.

Exhibit I	Financial Highlights				
	2007	2006	2005	2004	2003
Consolidated results					
Sales	5,210	5,325	5,555	5,425	4,187
Adjusted operating earnings [i]	199	173	201	197	83
Net earnings (loss) from continuing operations	(23)	(20)	65	68	(3)
Net earnings, as reported [ii]	207	5	94	102	30
Return on assets employed [iii]	6.7%	5.6%	7.0%	7.7%	4.3%
Financial position					
Net assets employed [iv]	2,267	2,177	2,047	1,893	1,322
Shareholders' equity	1,161	994	999	906	654
Net borrowings	855	1,213	1,063	1,046	785

	2007	2006	2005	2004	2003
Per share					
Net earnings (loss) from continuing operations	−0.18	−0.16	0.52	0.60	−0.03
Adjusted net earnings from continuing operations [i]	0.51	0.38	0.59	0.60	0.04
Net earnings, as reported [ii]	1.53	0.04	0.74	0.90	0.27
Dividends	0.16	0.16	0.16	0.16	0.16
Book value	8.96	7.82	7.82	7.24	5.78
Number of shares (millions)					
Weighted average	127.3	127.5	126.8	113.6	113.1
Outstanding at December 31	129.6	127.1	127.7	125.2	113.2

(i) Refer to non-GAAP measures on page 20 of Management's Discussion & Analysis for definition.

(ii) Includes results of discontinued operations.

(iii) After tax, but before interest, calculated on average month-end net assets employed. Excludes restructuring and other related costs.

(iv) Total assets, less cash, future tax assets, assets held for sale and non-interest bearing liabilities.

Exhibit 2 Balance Sheet, Q2 2008 (000'S Canadian Dollars, Except Earnings per Share)

	As at June 30, 2008	As at June 30, 2007	As at December 31, 2007
	(Unaudited) As restated (Note 2)	(Unaudited)	As restated (Note 2)
ASSETS			
Current assets			
Cash and cash equivalents	$ 16,419	$ 50,249	$ 28,222
Accounts receivable (Note 6)	239,596	207,449	202,285
Inventories (Note 7)	388,746	387,009	351,064
Future tax asset – current	39,886	9,415	25,409
Prepaid expenses and other assets	23,922	23,856	16,529
Assets held for sale (Note 5)	–	348,376	10,092
	708,569	1,026,354	633,601

(Continued)

Exhibit 2 (Continued)

	As at June 30, 2008	As at June 30, 2007	As at December 31, 2007
	(Unaudited) As restated (Note 2)	(Unaudited)	As restated (Note 2)
Investments in associated companies	2,656	1,068	1,207
Property and equipment	1,172,268	1,104,217	1,126,727
Other long-term assets	312,423	278,608	303,360
Future tax asset – non-current	39,011	18,270	22,837
Goodwill	856,758	802,403	817,477
Other intangibles	93,263	85,521	92,635
	$ 3,184,948	$ 3,316,441	$ 2,997,844
LIABILITIES AND SHAREHOLDERS' EQUITY			
Current liabilities			
Bank indebtedness	$ 10,092	$ 10,667	$ 9,845
Accounts payable and accrued charges	534,754	565,025	550,528
Income and other taxes payable	7,243	21,144	12,881
Current portion of long-term debt	12,251	74,787	17,945
Liabilities related to assets held for sale (Note 5)	–	61,433	–
	564,340	733,056	591,199
Long-term debt	1,089,793	1,257,611	855,281
Future tax liability – non-current	80,529	7,013	74,115
Other long-term liabilities	247,530	249,269	248,448
Minority interest	81,586	83,269	79,554
Shareholders' equity (Note 10)	1,121,170	986,223	1,149,247
	$ 3,184,948	$ 3,316,441	$ 2,997,844

The accompanying notes to the consolidated financial statements are an integral part of these statements.

Exhibit 3 Income Statement, Q2 2008 (000'S Canadian Dollars)

(Unaudited)	Three months ended June 30,		Six months ended June 30,	
	2008	2007	2008	2007
Sales	$ 1,355,301	$ 1,318,773	$ 2,558,564	$ 2,634,908
Cost of goods sold	1,204,824	1,149,931	2,252,161	2,298,703
Gross margin	$ 150,477	$ 168,842	$ 306,403	$ 336,205
Selling, general and administrative expenses	131,587	116,175	254,415	233,679
Earnings from continuing operations before restructuring and other related costs	$ 18,890	$ 52,667	$ 51,988	$ 102,526
Restructuring and other related costs (Note 9)	(11,618)	(30,715)	(19,340)	(43,425)
Earnings from continuing operations	$ 7,272	$ 21,952	$ 32,648	$ 59,101
Other income (Note 12)	1,933	1,501	1,918	1,969
Earnings from continuing operations before interest and income taxes	$ 9,205	$ 23,453	$ 34,566	$ 61,070
Interest expense	21,868	25,352	43,531	49,943
Earnings (loss) from continuing operations before income taxes	$ (12,663)	$ (1,899)	$ (8,965)	$ 11,127
Income taxes	(4,079)	1,749	(1,959)	7,965
Earnings (loss) from continuing operations before minority interest	$ (8,584)	$ (3,648)	$ (7,006)	$ 3,162
Minority interest	769	2,810	2,357	4,354
Net loss from continuing operations	$ (9,353)	$ (6,458)	$ (9,363)	$ (1,192)

(Continued)

Exhibit 3	(Continued)

	Three months ended June 30,		Six months ended June 30,	
(Unaudited)	2008	2007	2008	2007
Net earnings from discontinued operations – net of income tax (Note 4)	–	4,787	–	9,984
Net earnings (loss)	$ (9,353)	$ (1,671)	$ (9,363)	$ 8,792
Basic earnings (loss) per share (Note 13)				
from continuing operations	$ (0.07)	$ (0.05)	$ (0.07)	$ (0.01)
from discontinued operations	–	0.04	–	0.08
	$ (0.07)	$ (0.01)	$ (0.07)	$ 0.07
Diluted earnings (loss) per share (Note 13)				
from continuing operations	$ (0.07)	$ (0.05)	$ (0.07)	$ (0.01)
from discontinued operations	–	0.04	–	0.08
	$ (0.07)	$ (0.01)	$ (0.07)	$ 0.07
Weighted average number of shares (millions)	126.9	127.7	127.1	127.4

The accompanying notes to the consolidated financial statements are an integral part of these statements.

Exhibit 4	Selected Financial Data by Group

	Three months ended June 30,		Six months ended June 30,	
(Unaudited)	2008	2007	2008	2007
Sales				
Meat Products Group	**$ 856,638**	$ 878,966	**$ 1,619,183**	$ 1,774,692
Agribusiness Group	**61,567**	64,445	**120,161**	127,349
Bakery Products Group	**437,096**	375,362	**819,220**	732,867
	$ 1,355,301	$ 1,318,773	**$ 2,558,564**	$ 2,634,908

(Unaudited)	Three months ended June 30,		Six months ended June 30,	
	2008	2007	2008	2007
Earnings from continuing operations before restructuring and other related costs				
Meat Products Group	**$ 5,718**	$ 15,033	**$ 30,730**	$ 36,514
Agribusiness Group	**7,596**	4,684	**4,816**	5,505
Bakery Products Group	**8,671**	33,391	**25,828**	61,053
Non-allocated costs (Note 3(b))	**(3,095)**	(441)	**(9,386)**	(546)
	$ 18,890	$ 52,667	**$ 51,988**	$ 102,526
Capital expenditures				
Meat Products Group	**$ 38,756**	$ 24,406	**$ 71,851**	$ 61,124
Agribusiness Group	**4,077**	3,986	**6,976**	6,626
Bakery Products Group	**19,821**	30,908	**29,537**	43,975
	$ 62,654	$ 59,300	**$ 108,364**	$ 111,725
Depreciation and amortization				
Meat Products Group	**$ 19,552**	$ 17,204	**$ 37,578**	$ 34,590
Agribusiness Group	**4,333**	4,769	**8,167**	9,657
Bakery Products Group	**14,752**	12,916	**27,964**	25,735
	$ 38,637	$ 34,889	**$ 73,709**	$ 69,982

		As at June 30, 2008	As at June 30, 2007	As at December 31, 2007
		(Unaudited)	(Unaudited)	
Total assets				
Meat Products Group		**$ 1,716,978**	$ 1,603,563	$ 1,560,244
Agribusiness Group		**251,004**	652,496	302,999
Bakery Products Group		**901,740**	823,844	823,137
Non-allocated assets		**315,226**	236,538	311,464
		$ 3,184,948	$ 3,316,441	$ 2,997,844

(Continued)

| Exhibit 4 | (Continued) | | | |

		As at June 30, 2008	As at June 30, 2007	As at December 31, 2007
		(Unaudited)	(Unaudited)	
Goodwill				
Meat Products Group		**$ 450,930**	$ 450,643	$ 450,929
Agribusiness Group		**12,922**	2,042	2,058
Bakery Products Group		**392,906**	349,718	364,490
		$ 856,758	$ 802,403	$ 817.477

Strategic Leadership: Short-Term Stability and Long-Term Viability

Glenn Rowe and Mehdi Hossein Nejad

Rare is the business leader who can articulate and instill a long-term vision and manage the day-to-day operations with the requisite obsession for detail. A leader who combines both styles is what these authors call a "strategic leader," someone who, more than any other type of leader is best equipped to increase shareholder value. Leaders and potential leaders will find out what it takes when they read this article.

The business world has few leaders who have transformed their companies and the industries in which they operate. Two of the few are Jorgen Vig Knudstorp and Clive Beddoes.

When Jorgen Vig Knudstorp took over as the CEO of LEGO in 2004, things were looking bleak for this well-established, family-owned business. Over the next 5 years, he turned the company around by working on a new vision, building better relationships with employees and customers, empowering employees to make decisions at all levels of the hierarchy and, at the same time, introducing tight fiscal controls.[1]

Clive Beddoes did the same at Westjet. During his 10-year reign, he transformed a small Calgary start-up into one of the most profitable airlines in North America, with over 55 destinations in Canada, Mexico and the United States. Westjet began with just 3 aircraft, flying mostly between cities in western Canada. Beddoes expanded into eastern Canada in 2000, at a time when the air travel industry was dominated by Air Canada. As a result of Beddoes' leadership, Westjet now has 36 percent of the Canadian domestic market, compared to Air Canada's 57 percent. Westjet has maintained healthy growth and profitability during the years and has weathered a number of

Reprint# 9B09TE05

[1]O'Connell, A. (2009). Lego CEO Jorgen Vig Knudstorp on leading through survival and growth. *Harvard Business Review*, 87(1).

major economic downturns brought about by events such as the September 11th attacks and a global recession.

Knudstorp and Beddoes exercised a style of leadership called strategic leadership. They enhanced the long-term viability of their companies through the articulation of a clear vision and, at the same time, maintained a satisfactory level of short-term financial stability. And they accomplished this while maintaining relatively smooth day-to-day operations.

Strategic leadership is different than two other popular leadership styles, managerial and visionary. Managerial leaders are primarily immersed in the day-to-day activities of the organization and lack an appropriate long-term vision for growth and change. For reasons we will touch upon later, this is the most common form of leadership, especially in large, diversified organizations. Conversely, visionary leaders are primarily future-oriented, proactive and risk-taking. These leaders base their decisions and actions on their beliefs and values, and try to share their understanding of a desired vision with others in the organization.

In this article, we discuss the shortcomings of these two leadership styles and argue that sustained wealth creation, continuous growth and expansion, and a healthy financial status in the short term are more likely to occur under strategic leadership. We also argue that the demise of companies such as GM and K-Mart and the constant decline in shareholder value at these companies are, in fact, a result of leaders being too focused on day-to-day activities, to the detriment of other facets of good business practice. In other words, demise by managerial leadership.

If we accept the widely held assumption that leadership does matter, and that the function of a business leader is to increase shareholder value, it is our belief that strategic leadership is the best alternative for creating shareholder value.

Strategic Leadership Defined

While there are many different definitions of strategic leadership, we define it as the ability to influence others in your organization to voluntarily make day-to-day decisions that lead to the organization's long-term growth and survival and maintain its short-term financial health.[2]

The most important aspects of strategic leadership are shared values and a clear vision, both of which will enable and allow employees to make decisions with minimal formal monitoring or control mechanisms. With this accomplished, a leader will have more time and a greater capacity to focus on other, ad hoc issues, such as adapting the vision to a changing business environment. In addition, strategic leadership will incorporate visionary and managerial leadership by simultaneously allowing for risk-taking and rationality.

An examination of the characteristics of managerial and visionary leadership styles (presented in Table 1) will help understand strategic leadership better.

In short, managerial leaders need order and stability and need to be able to control the details of the work being performed. Mostly, these leaders have no personal attachment towards setting and using goals as motivational tools, and they may have difficulty showing empathy when dealing with employees. They will attempt to gain control through systems of rewards, punishment, and other forms of coercion. These leader/managers will be focused on the cost-benefit analysis of everyday actions and will therefore be mostly linked to the short-term financial health of the organization, as reflected in its day-to-day stock price. It is important to note that short-term gains are often a result of a least-cost approach, which might not be good for long-term viability.

[2]Rowe, W. G. (2001). Creating wealth in organizations: The role of strategic leadership. *The Academy of Management Executive*, *15*(1), 81.

Robert Milton, who was the President and CEO of Air Canada and ACE[3] for approximately 10 years, is an example of excellent managerial leadership. In 2003 and during his time in charge of Air Canada, he implemented a controversial restructuring program, which paved the way for the eventual sale of Air Canada's loyalty program, its regional carrier, Jazz, and its maintenance division.

As head of ACE, Milton sold what some believe were the most profitable arms of Air Canada, only to return the proceeds to ACE shareholders while the airline itself was in need of investment for future growth.[4] All this left Air Canada vulnerable to unexpected changes in a highly competitive industry, during a time that it also lost market share to its national rival, Westjet (see Figure 1).

While managerial leaders are focused on the past, visionary leaders are oriented to the future. Their main tool for achieving goals is their ability to influence followers, influence they use to create a shared vision and an understanding of what is to be achieved. These leaders rely heavily on their own values, and they invest in people and their network of relationships in order to ensure the viability of the organization. They articulate a compelling vision, and then empower and energize followers to move towards it.[5] The formal structures of the organization will create few constraints for these leaders, as they make decisions and

| Figure 1 | Air Canada Versus Westjet: Domestic Market Share |

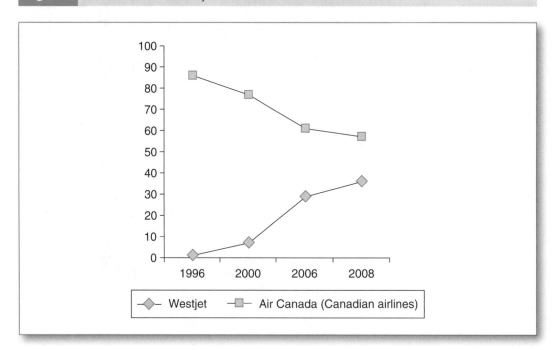

---

[3]A holding company that owns Air Canada.

[4]From Sorensen, C. (December 2008), thestar.com.

[5]Ibarra, H., & Obodaru, O. (2009). Women and the Vision Thing. *Harvard Business Review, 87*(1).

shape their vision based on their values, beliefs, and sense of identity.

According to some business scholars, the ability to envision an exciting future and create a commitment to achieving that vision is an attribute that differentiates leaders and non-leaders (or managers).[6] This may be an accurate assessment of the visionary leadership style compared to the managerial style. However, there is a major problem with most visionary leaders, namely that they tend to ignore the short-term stability and day-to-day functioning of the organization.

This shortcoming makes visionary leadership extremely risky. For this reason, most organizations tend to turn to managerial leaders, a less risky and therefore more attractive—although not more successful—alternative.

It is logical to assume that all organizations desire both short-term financial stability and long-term growth and viability. Achieving this goal calls for a combination of both the managerial and visionary leadership styles. There are two options for doing so: First, an organization could have two leaders, one a visionary and one a managerial leader, with the visionary leader in charge. Having two leaders like this requires that they trust each other implicitly and are willing to listen to each other.

Some successful combinations have been Tom Watson, Jr. and his CFO Al Williams, who subsequently became one of IBM's executive vice presidents and then president before he retired in 1966. Tom Watson Jr. credited Al Williams with helping him to grow IBM into a multi-billion dollar company—an outstanding performance at the time. At Disney, Michael Eisner and his first president/COO, Frank Wells, were another such combination of leaders. When these leaders took over in 1984, they quickly doubled profits in only two years and then went on to transform Disney into a multi-billion dollar empire. The

partnership—and period of creative initiatives associated with it—ended in 1994, with the tragic death of Wells in a helicopter crash.

As these examples indicate, some organizations can have both types of leaders working together. However, we believe that a better solution—and the second option for combining the managerial and visionary styles—is to find a strategic leader, someone from that species of leaders that can accept and manage the paradox inherent in managerial and visionary leadership—that is, one of those rare leaders who can combine managerial and visionary leadership and make that combination work.

Some scholars and practitioners believe that visionary and managerial leadership styles occupy two ends of a single continuum and thus cannot reside in one person. We disagree and suggest that, while these are two different mindsets, there are a few individuals that can well handle the paradoxical nature of managerial and visionary leadership.

⬙ The Strategic Leader Defined

We consider managerial and visionary leadership as two separate continuums (see Figure 2) and believe that individuals who are strategic leaders are more than the sum of these two styles.

Strategic leaders envision a future with the present circumstances in mind *and* pay attention to short-term financial stability, with an understanding of what is to be achieved in the long term. As the late Steven J. Ross, the former chairman and CEO of Time Warner put it, these kind of leaders come to work, dream for an hour, and then do something about those dreams for the next several hours.[7]

In terms of performance and wealth creation, it is our belief that one strategic leader can

---

[6]Kouzes, J. M., & Posner, B. Z. (2009). To Lead, Create a Shared Vision. *Harvard Business Review*, *87*(1).

[7]Loeb, M. Ross, Steven J. (1993). *Fortune*, *24*(4), quoted in Hitt et al. (2008).

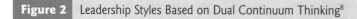

| **Figure 2** | Leadership Styles Based on Dual Continuum Thinking[8] |

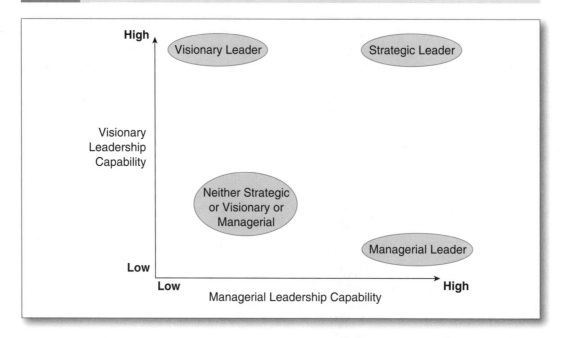

deliver better results than the previously mentioned dual leadership.

Strategic leaders encourage innovation in the face of changing environments and contexts, seeking innovation and change in moving forward. On the other hand, managerial leaders are likely to be fully occupied with the present order and stability. At the same time, strategic leaders are mindful of how the organization is functioning and, therefore, are not likely to fall into the trap of arrogant risk-taking, as might visionary leaders, who can destroy an organization's wealth even faster than a managerial leader.

The presence of a strategic leader leads to a number of outcomes for an organization that are eventually linked to share values in both the short and long term.

1. These leaders tend to pay particular attention to building their organization's

resources, capabilities and competencies in order to gain appropriate, sustained competitive advantages. Strategic leaders know that focusing on the short term and forgetting about core competencies in the face of changing circumstances and a turbulent environment are likely to lead to organizational failure.

2. Strategic leaders view human capital as an important factor in innovation and the creation of core competencies, and they expend considerable effort sustaining the health of this resource (human capital). While managerial leaders focus on the exploitation of current resources and capabilities, strategic leaders combine this focus with a search for new resources, capabilities, and core competencies, which will, when needed, be

[8]From Rowe, W. G. (2001). Creating wealth in organizations: The role of strategic leadership. *The Academy of Management Executive, 15*(1), 81.

exploited to create wealth. This dual focus on exploitation and exploration, often referred to as ambidexterity, is a prerequisite for long-term organizational success.[9] We believe that while managerial and visionary leaders are busy exploiting and exploring, strategic leaders exploit and explore in a way that maintains organizational financial stability in the short term, while building a foundation for long-term viability.

3. Organizations led by strategic leaders are more successful in learning, both at the individual and group levels. Studies have shown that both the managerial and visionary aspects of leadership are essential for organization-wide learning initiatives to succeed. While a strategic leader's articulation of a vision helps alter the institutionalized learning of an organization, his or her managerial approach helps spread and reinforce current learning initiatives.[10] This combination is necessary, since the organization always needs to learn new things and at the same time, to institutionalize newly discovered avenues of learning. Organizational learning and the creation and sharing of knowledge within an organization are important prerequisites for long-term viability and are better practiced by an organization led by a strategic leader.

The ultimate goal of a business is to create, capture and distribute wealth in a manner that is sustainable. We believe that each form of leadership will lead to a different outcome in terms of wealth creation. As illustrated in Figure 3,[11]

| **Figure 3** | The Impact of Different Leader Style on Wealth Creation |

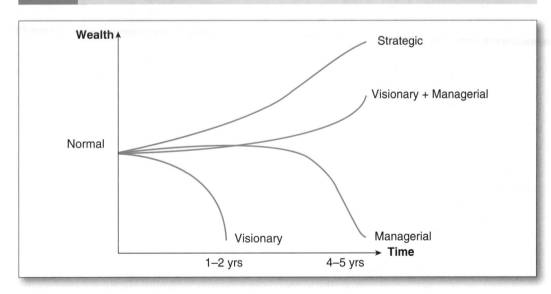

---

[9]Raisch, S., & Birkinshaw, J. (2008). Organizational Ambidexterity: Antecedents, Outcomes, and Moderators. *Journal of Management*, 34(3), 375.

[10]Vera, D., & Crossan, M. (2004). Strategic leadership and organizational learning. *The Academy of Management Review*, 29(2), 222.

[11]The years on the time axis are illustrative only.

managerial leadership will maintain the current level of wealth in the near future, or in the best-case scenario, create short-term gains.

However, based on managerial leaders' approach to innovation and change, it is highly unlikely that this trend can be maintained for long periods. As seen in Figure 3, wealth is slowly lost in the long-term. The slow decline of companies such as Air Canada and General Motors can be blamed on their lack of a long-term vision, and their lack of attention to innovation and the development of core competencies.

Visionary leaders, on the other hand, are focused mainly on the future and the direction that organization should take in that future. Such a focus is very risky, and since there is likely to be much less adherence to any type of financial control or structures, the odds of failure are extremely high. In most cases, visionary leadership results in below-normal performance faster than managerial leadership. This is because some visionary leaders lack or even reject the support of managerial leaders, making it difficult for them to keep the company in good financial health. Although these leaders do have successful stints, there is always the high probability of eventual failure. A good example is the decline of Apple during Steve Jobs' first term as CEO, where, we believe, he exercised only visionary leadership.

Although a combination of visionary and managerial leaders can yield positive results in the short and long run, there are numerous practical obstacles that can prevent such an outcome.

As illustrated in Figure 3, a strategic leader is more likely to create synergy by envisioning a desired future and growth strategy, while influencing employees to voluntarily make day-to-day decisions that will help maintain the financial stability of the organization, as well as its future viability. This was evident at GE during the years of Jack Welch, who totally transformed the company into a consistent wealth-creating, capturing and distributing entity.

⊠ Strategic Leadership Constrained

It is unfortunate that, in spite of all the benefits discussed above, many organizations still implement structures or routines that constrain and discourage strategic leadership. If strategic leadership are to emerge, an organization must offer them autonomy and protection. They need to be free to envision a future as they see it and implement growth strategies without interference. They need to be protected from the managerial leaders in the organization, who might try to impose rigid financial controls at the expense of strategic controls.

This interference is more evident in large, diversified organizations with many divisions, and which often fall into the trap of imposing highly bureaucratic controls as a result of financial restrictions, the political context and the short-term demands of the markets. Government-owned or funded organizations, for example, would constrain strategic leaders. The very fact that leadership in most democratic regimes is changed after limited terms is an incentive to use tight financial controls in order to deliver short-term results. High levels of diversification, budget deficits, political issues, and accountability for even the smallest amount of money are other factors that constrain strategic leadership in most diversified organizations.

While we acknowledge that there are many difficulties associated with finding and developing strategic leaders, we nevertheless believe that they are worth the effort. There is no safer alternative for an organization that is pursuing sustained wealth creation for its stakeholders. Creativity, innovation, competency development and continuous learning are all vital elements for growth, and a strategic leader can initiate and facilitate the development of these elements without compromising the financial health of the organization.

The fact that they are hard to find and even harder to train makes these individuals valuable and rare for their organizations.[12] An organization must try and remove as many obstacles as possible in order for these leaders to emerge in leader-development and succession programs.

Much of what we do in organizations today is, consciously or not, directed at curtailing or even eliminating ambitious thinking and innovation for some short-term gains. Managerial leaders need to be reminded that without a long-term vision, the most they'll achieve is probably a normal return for a limited time. They must be reminded that the long-term prosperity of their organizations depends on having strategic leaders at the helm.

Finally, while we acknowledge that organizations need managerial and visionary leaders, we submit that the person in charge should be a strategic leader.

Table I	Strategic, Visionary, and Managerial Leadership

Strategic Leaders

✓ synergistic combination of managerial and visionary leadership

✓ emphasis on ethical behavior and value-based decisions

✓ oversee operating (day-to-day) and strategic (long-term) responsibilities

✓ formulate and implement strategies for immediate impact and preservation of long-term goals to enhance organizational survival, growth, and long-term viability

✓ have strong, positive expectations of the performance they expect from their superiors, peers, subordinates, and themselves

✓ use strategic controls and financial controls, with emphasis on strategic controls

✓ use, and interchange, tacit and explicit knowledge on individual and organizational levels

✓ use linear and nonlinear thinking patterns

✓ believe in strategic choice, that is, their choices make a difference in their organizations and environment

Visionary Leaders	Managerial Leaders
✓ are proactive, shape ideas, change the way people think about what is desirable, possible, and necessary	✓ are reactive; adopt passive attitudes towards goals; goals arise out of necessities, not desires and dreams; goals based on past
✓ work to develop choices, fresh approaches to long standing problems; work from high-risk positions	✓ view work as an enabling process involving some combination of ideas and people interacting to establish strategies

(Continued)

---

[12]Rare means that relatively few competitors have the same resource. Few means that there are less organizations with the resource than that required for perfect competition. In the context of this paper this does not mean that organizations do not have leaders but that only a few organizations have strategic leaders.

| Table 1 | (Continued) |

<table>
<tr>
<td>

✓ are concerned with ideas, relate to people in intuitive and empathetic ways

✓ feel separate from their environment; work in, but do not belong to, organizations; sense of who they are does not depend on work

✓ influence attitudes and opinions of others within the organization

✓ concerned with insuring future of organization, especially through development and management of people

✓ more embedded in complexity, ambiguity and information overload; engage in multifunctional, integrative tasks

✓ know less than their functional area experts

✓ more likely to make decisions based on values

✓ more willing to invest in innovation, human capital, and creating and maintaining an effective culture to ensure long-term viability

✓ focus on tacit knowledge and develop strategies as communal forms of tacit knowledge that promote enactment of a vision

✓ utilize nonlinear thinking

✓ believe in strategic choice, that is, their choices make a difference in their organizations and environment

</td>
<td>

✓ relate to people according to their roles in the decision-making process

✓ see themselves as conservators and regulators of existing order; sense of who they are depends on their role in organization

✓ influence actions and decisions of those with whom they work

✓ involved in situations and contexts characteristic of day-to-day activities

✓ concerned with, and more comfortable in, functional areas of responsibilities

✓ expert in their functional area

✓ less likely to make value-based decisions

✓ engage in, and support, short-term, least-cost behavior to enhance financial performance figures

✓ focus on managing the exchange and combination of explicit knowledge and ensuring compliance to standard operating procedures

✓ utilize linear thinking

✓ believe in determinism, that is, the choices they make are determined by their internal and external environments

</td>
</tr>
</table>

Women and Leadership

Laura Guerrero

The University of Texas at El Paso

Mother Teresa was a simple woman of small stature who dressed in a plain blue and white sari, and never owned more than the people she served. Mirroring her appearance, her mission was simple—to care for the poor. From her first year on the streets of Calcutta where she tended to one dying person to her last years when thousands of people were cared for by the Missionaries of Charity, Mother Teresa stayed focused on her goal. She was a true civil servant who was simultaneously determined and fearless, and humble and spiritual. She often listened to the will of God. When criticized for her stand on abortion and women's role in the family, or her approaches to eliminating poverty, Mother Teresa responded with a strong will: she never wavered in her deep-seated human values.

—Peter G. Northouse[1]

A cademic researchers began to study gender and leadership in the 1970s. Early research asked, "Can women lead?" However, more recent research asks, "What are the differences in leadership style and effectiveness between men and women?" and "Why are women so underrepresented in executive leadership roles?" (Hoyt, 2013). This chapter looks at the differences in leadership style and effectiveness between men and women (Daft, 2011; DuBrin, 2010). It then looks at explanations for the underrepresentation of women in higher leadership positions. Finally, it discusses approaches to promoting women in leadership.

---

[1]Northouse (2009, p. 16).

⚐ Gender: Examining Leadership Style and Effectiveness

Academic researchers have not agreed on whether there are gender differences in leadership style and effectiveness between men and women. Some findings seem to indicate there are no differences, while others find small but robust differences. Eagly and Johnson (1990) found that, contrary to expectations, women were not more likely to lead in a more interpersonally oriented manner and less task-oriented manner than men. However, women were found to be more likely to lead in a participative (democratic) manner than men. Other studies have found that women are undervalued compared to men when they occupy a typically masculine leadership role and when the evaluators are men (Bartol & Butterfield, 1976). It has been suggested that women may use a more democratic leadership style to obtain more favorable evaluations (Hoyt, 2013).

Recent research has found that women's leadership style tends to be more transformational than that of men (Daft, 2011; Eagly, Johannesen-Schmidt, & van Engen, 2003). Transformational leadership includes four components: idealized influence, inspirational motivation, intellectual stimulation, and individualized consideration (see Chapter 9). All are positively related to leadership effectiveness (Lowe, Kroeck, & Sivasubramaniam, 1996). This may be one of the sources of the modern popular view that women are better leaders.

Researchers have also studied the effectiveness of female and male leaders (Yukl, 2012). A review of published research showed that men and women were equally effective overall, but women and men were more effective in leadership roles that were perceived to be congruent with their gender (Eagly, Karau, & Makhijani, 1995).

⚐ The Glass Ceiling Turned Labyrinth

Women occupy nearly half of the labor force in many countries, but they are still underrepresented in top positions in business and government. The lack of representation is unlikely to be a result of lack of women who are qualified, given that there have been several high profile women who have served as the leaders of their countries and others who have served in high level positions beyond politics. In politics, former prime ministers are Indira Gandhi (India), Margaret Thatcher (United Kingdom), Gro Marlem Brundtland (Norway), and Benazir Bhutto (Pakistan). Currently, Angela Merkel is the chancellor of Germany and Dilma Rousseff is the president of Brazil. Outside of politics, there are Indra Nooyi, the CEO of PepsiCo, Andrea Jung the CEO of Avon, Wendy Kopp, the founder of Teach for America, and Ann E. Dunwoody, a four-star general in the United States military (Hoyt, 2013).

In politics, in the United States women have 17.0% of the seats in the Senate and 16.8% in the House of Representatives. In Canada (as of November 2011), there were 36% women in the Senate and 24.7% in the House of Commons. Worldwide (as of May 10, 2010), 24 countries have 30% or more of women in their lower/single house. According to Cool (2010), the top ten countries are Rwanda (56.3%), Sweden (46.4%), South Africa (44.5%), Cuba (43.2%), Iceland (42.9%), Netherlands (42.0%), Finland (40.0%), Norway (39.6%), Mozambique (39.2%), and Angola (38.6%) tied for tenth place with Costa Rica (38.6%).

In business, women occupy more than 50% of professional and management positions and approximately 25% of CEO positions (Hoyt, 2013; U.S. Bureau of Labor Statistics, 2010). However, in larger companies, the story is less positive as women who are CEOs of Fortune 500 firms comprise less than 3%; in addition, less than 16% of board members are women, and approximately 14% to 15% are executive officers (Catalyst, 2011a, 2011b, 2011c).

The invisible barrier that prevents women from moving into top leadership positions is called the glass ceiling (Daft, 2011; Yukl, 2012). The glass ceiling can also be a barrier to other minorities. Women who are part of a racial or ethnic minority face additional challenges in the workplace. Removing barriers to advancement for women and other minorities has several benefits. First, it offers equal opportunity and, consequently, benefits society and more individuals. Second, it benefits businesses, governments, and their stakeholders by increasing the talent pool of candidates for leadership positions, which results in the availability of more qualified leaders. Third, having a more diverse profile of leaders makes institutions more representative of society. Finally, research shows that diversity is linked to group productivity (Forsyth, 2006), and gender diversity is linked to better organizational financial performance (Catalyst, 2004). Eagly and Carli (2007) have recently identified limitations with the glass ceiling metaphor. One of the limitations is that it implies that there is equal access to lower positions until all women hit this single, invisible, and impassable barrier. They propose an alternative image of a leadership labyrinth conveying the image of a journey filled with challenges along the way that can and has been successfully navigated by some women.

Explaining the Labyrinth

Human Capital Differences

One explanation for the labyrinth is that women have less human capital invested in education and work experience than men (Eagly & Carli, 2004). However, this explanation is not as convincing now that women are obtaining undergraduate (57%) and master's degrees (60%) at a higher rate than men (Hoyt, 2013; Catalyst, 2011b). In 2011, 32% of lawyers are women, but only 19% of law firm partners were women (National Association for Law Placement, 2012).

Another explanation is that women have less work experience and employment stability because they may have had to interrupt their careers to take care of their child-caring and domestic responsibilities, which are distributed unequally between genders. This explanation has some merit since it has been found that women with children are more likely to work fewer hours than women without children. In contrast, men with children are likely to work more hours than men without children (Kaufman & Uhlenberg, 2000).

Women respond to work–home challenges differentially. Some choose to attempt to excel in every role, others choose not to marry or have children, while others choose part-time employment in order to meet work and family commitments. Often, women who take time off from their careers have to reenter at lower positions than the ones they had when they left. This makes it more difficult to be promoted to higher leadership positions.

Another explanation for the existence of the leadership gap is that women choose not to pursue leadership positions for cultural reasons and instead choose to focus on raising a family. However, this argument has not found support in research (Eagly & Carli, 2004). Other explanations for the lack of representation of women in the top levels of management include women having fewer developmental opportunities, having less responsibility in the same jobs as men, having less access to mentors, and being in jobs that do not lead to top leadership positions.

Gender Differences

Other attempts to explain the leadership gap suggest that there are differences in leadership style and effectiveness between men and women. However, as mentioned earlier, research has not found evidence that women leaders are less effective or that their leadership style is a disadvantage for them. On the contrary, women are more likely to use transformational leadership, which has been positively linked to performance. Another attempt to explain the leadership gap is the alleged difference between genders in commitment and motivation to achieve leadership roles. However, research has shown that women and men show equal levels of commitment to paid employment. Both men and women view their role as workers as secondary to their roles as parents and partners (Bielby & Bielby, 1988; Thoits, 1992).

One difference researchers have found is that women are less likely than men to promote themselves for leadership positions (Bowles & McGinn, 2005). One other difference is that women are less likely than men to ask for what they want and negotiate (Babcock & Laschever, 2003). These findings may be interpreted as reluctance on the part of women to take these roles or engage in such behavior due to the social backlash that they may face if they do promote themselves or negotiate aggressively.

Prejudice

Another explanation for the leadership gap is gender bias resulting from stereotypes (or cognitive shortcuts) such as that of men as leaders and women as nurturers. These cognitive shortcuts suggest to people ways to characterize groups or group members despite different characteristics among group members (Hamilton, Stroessner, & Driscoll, 1994; Hoyt, 2013). Stereotypes are not necessarily used intentionally to harm others. However, stereotypes can lead to discrimination in the selection and promotion of women to leadership positions and, therefore, can be very harmful. Women of color face prejudice not only as a result of their gender but also because of their ethnicity or race.

Another source of bias and prejudice is the tendency of people to report more positive evaluations of those who are more similar to them. This has the potential of putting women at a disadvantage when male leaders are in charge of promoting someone to a leadership position. Research has found that women respond in one of two ways to female leadership stereotypes. They either conform to the stereotype or engage in stereotype-countering behaviors. Women who are confident are more likely to engage in stereotype resistance, and those who are less confident are more likely to assimilate to the stereotype.

▧   Navigating the Labyrinth

While there are still barriers for women in political and business leadership roles, there has been improvement in the past 20 to 30 years. Changes in organizations and in society are making it somewhat easier for women to reach top leadership positions. More organizations are starting to value flexible workers and diversity at all levels. Organizations can use career development, networking and mentoring, and work–life support programs to help ensure that women have equal opportunity to achieve top leadership roles in the workplace. There is evidence that society is also changing and that there is increasing parity in the involvement of men and women in child care and housework (Eagly & Carli, 2004). In response to the obstacles in the labyrinth, some women have opted for starting their own ventures, which allow them to have leadership positions and flexibility, rather than waiting for the business organizations to change to adapt to their needs.

☒ References

Babcock, L., & Laschever, S. (2003). *Women don't ask: Negotiation and the gender divide.* Princeton, NJ: Princeton University Press.

Bartol, K. M., & Butterfield, D. A. (1976). Sex effects in evaluating leaders. *Journal of Applied Psychology, 61,* 446–454.

Bielby, D. D., & Bielby, W. T. (1988). She works hard for the money: Household responsibilities and the allocation of work effort. *American Journal of Sociology, 93,* 1031–1059.

Bowles, H. R., & McGinn, K. L. (2005). Claiming authority: Negotiating challenges for women leaders. In D. M. Messick & R. M. Kramer (Eds.), *The psychology of leadership: New perspectives and research* (pp. 191–208). Mahwah, NJ: Lawrence Erlbaum.

Catalyst. (2004). *The bottom line: Connecting corporate performance and gender diversity.* New York, NY: Author.

Catalyst. (2011a). Statistical overview of women in the workplace. Retrieved from http://www.catalyst.org/publication/219/statistical-overview-of-women-in-the-workplace

Catalyst. (2011b). U.S. labor force, population, and education. Retrieved from http://www.catalyst.org/publication/202/us-labor-force-population-and-education

Catalyst. (2011c). U.S. women in business. Retrieved from http://www.catalyst.org/publication/132/us-women-in-business

Cool, J. (2010). *Women in parliament.* Retrieved from http://www.parl.gc.ca/content/lop/researchpublications/prb0562-e.htm

Daft, R. L. (2011). *The leadership experience* (5th ed.). Mason, OH: Thomson, South-Western.

DuBrin, A. (2010). *Leadership: Research findings, practice, and skills* (6th ed.). Mason, OH: South-Western/Cengage.

Eagly, A. H., & Carli, L. L. (2004). Women and men as leaders. In J. Antonakis, R. J. Stenberg, & A. T. Cianciolo (Eds.), *The nature of leadership* (pp. 279–301). Thousand Oaks, CA: Sage.

Eagly, A. H., & Carli, L. L. (2007). *Through the labyrinth: The truth about how women become leaders.* Boston, MA: Harvard Business School Press.

Eagly, A. H., Johannesen-Schmidt, M. C., & van Engen, M. (2003). Transformational, transactional, and laissez-faire leadership styles: A meta-analysis comparing women and men. *Psychological Bulletin, 129,* 569–591.

Eagly, A. H., & Johnson, B. T. (1990). Gender and leadership style: A meta-analysis. *Psychological Bulletin, 108*(2), 233–256.

Eagly, A. H., Karau, S. J., & Makhijani, M. G. (1995). Gender and the effectiveness of leaders: A meta-analysis. *Psychological Bulletin, 117,* 125–145.

Forsyth, D. R. (2006). *Group dynamics* (4th ed.). Pacific Grove, CA: Brooks/Cole.

Hamilton, D. L., Stroessner, S. J., & Driscoll, D. M. (1994). Social cognition and the study of stereotyping. In P. G. Devine, D. L. Hamilton, & T. M. Ostrom (Eds.), *Social cognition: Impact on social psychology* (pp. 291–321). New York, NY: Academic Press.

Hoyt, C. L. (2013). Women and leadership. In P. G. Northouse (Ed.), *Leadership: Theory and practice* (6th ed.). Thousand Oaks, CA: Sage.

Kaufman, G., & Uhlenberg, P. (2000). The influence of parenthood on work effort of married men and women. *Social Forces, 78*(3), 931–947.

Lowe, K. B., Kroeck, K. G., & Sivasubramaniam, N. (1996). Effectiveness correlates of transformational and transactional leadership: A meta-analytic review of the MLQ literature. *Leadership Quarterly, 7,* 385–425.

National Association for Law Placement. (2012). *Law Firm Diversity Wobbles: Minority Numbers Bounce Back While Women Associates Extend Two-Year Decline.* Retrieved from http://www.nalp.org/2011_law_firm_diversity

Northouse, P. G. (2009). *Introduction to leadership: Concepts and practice.* Thousand Oaks, CA: Sage.

Thoits, P. A. (1992). Identity structures and psychological well-being: Gender and marital status comparisons. *Social Psychology Quarterly, 55,* 236–256.

U.S. Bureau of Labor Statistics. (2010). Current population survey, annual averages: Household data. (Table 9: Employed persons by occupation, sex and age). Retrieved from http://www.bls.gov/cps/cpsaat9.pdf

Yukl, G. (2012). *Leadership in organizations* (8th ed.). Upper Saddle River, NJ: Pearson/Prentice Hall.

▨ The Cases

The Bank of Montreal—The Task Force on the Advancement of Women in the Bank (A)

Deborah Westman works at the Bank of Montreal (BMO) where she is a junior employee with a university degree. She is ambitious and recently finished BMO's Management Development Program. She is trying to decide whether to work in mid-market commercial account management or take a more traditional head office position. She is concerned about the "glass ceiling" but is aware that BMO has actions that are designed to eliminate barriers that limit the advancement of women. The mid-market commercial lending market has been targeted as an area for growth. But, Deborah realizes that she will be one of a very few professional females in this area. Deborah is wondering if the Task Force on the Advancement of Women can help her and whether a woman can "shatter the glass ceiling" at BMO.

Marimekko

Kirsti Paakkanen has achieved a celebrity status in Finland for her enigmatic leadership of the Finnish design company Marimekko. Purchasing the company in a state of near bankruptcy in 1991, Paakkanen took several actions to restore profitability and realize growth. As of 2006, the company has sales of €64 million (of which 80% are from Finland) and net profits of €8.4 million. Over the last few years, Paakkanen and her team have focused on growing international sales. Recently, the company has opened concept shops owned by foreign partners in Japan, United Arab Emirates, Iceland, Sweden, and the United States. In light of the international expansion, Paakkanen is wondering if any changes to Marimekko's personnel policies and/or organization structure are necessary.

▨ The Reading

Canadian Women Entrepreneurs: Pioneers of New Frontiers

Carol Stephenson (dean, Richard Ivey School of Business) gives a concise, well-articulated perspective on the state of female entrepreneurship in this reading. She suggests that being a female entrepreneur is similar to being a pioneer on the old frontier. The characteristics for success are similar: courage, know-how, and perseverance. Canada has more than 850,000 entrepreneurs; they employ more than 570,000 people and annually contribute in excess of $18 billion to the Canadian economy.

The Bank of Montreal—The Task Force on the Advancement of Women in the Bank (A)

Pamela Tebbutt and Bernard Portis

It was Monday afternoon, January 13, 1992. Deborah Westman had just completed her training through the Bank of Montreal's (BMO) Management Development Program (MDP) and had received an offer to join the Personal and Commercial Financial Services

---

    Version: (A) 2010-03-08

Group (PCFS) as a Commercial Account Manager. With MDP behind her, Deborah was considered management potential—but was she really? Deborah had become familiar with the "glass ceiling"—women's ability to see senior management ranks but not reach them. She did not want to work in a "boys' club," yet she knew that very few mid-market Commercial Account Managers were female.[1] Her decision to accept the offer instead of assuming a more "traditional" head office role would depend on her belief that change could happen—that the BMO's recently established Task Force on the Advancement of Women in the Bank would be a success.

☒ The Bank of Montreal

The Bank of Montreal, established in Montreal in 1817, is Canada's oldest chartered bank. The BMO offers personal, commercial, corporate, government and international financial services and operates across Canada and in selected centres throughout the world. United States operations are primarily carried out through a wholly owned subsidiary, Harris Bankcorp Inc. The BMO also owns 75 per cent of Nesbitt, Thomson Inc., a fully integrated Canadian investment dealer. Through Nesbitt, Thomson, the Bank offers underwriting, brokerage, advisory and investment services. Finally, specialized portfolio management services are offered through Bank of Montreal Investment Limited.

In terms of average asset base,[2] the BMO is the third largest chartered bank after the Royal Bank and the Canadian Imperial Bank of Commerce. However, based on the results of the fiscal year ended October 31, 1991, the BMO was the fastest growing of the large Canadian banks, with loan growth of 9.2 per cent to $55.1 billion and asset growth of 13 per cent to $87.4 billion. Achieving its targeted return on common equity

of 15 per cent in 1991, the BMO's profitability ranked third behind the Bank of Nova Scotia and the Royal Bank.

Two principal mandates dominated the BMO's operations in 1991. First was the challenge to maximize efficiencies and bring the expense/revenue ratio in line with the industry average of 59.4 per cent. During 1991, rationalization and the elimination of excess overhead contributed to an improvement in the expense/revenue ratio from 67.1 per cent at fiscal year end 1990 to 61.6 per cent at fiscal year end 1991. Second, the BMO strived to enhance its competitive position in 1991 by refocusing on the delivery of superior customer service at both the retail and commercial banking levels. To achieve this goal, customer service training courses were developed and offered to front-line employees. Expenditures were also made to rebuild the public image of the Bank through branch renovations, enhancements and a new advertising campaign that capitalized on the slogan "We're paying attention." For these reasons, Deborah identified the BMO as one of the more progressive Canadian banks to work for; the BMO was out to improve its image to all stakeholders, including the employees.

☒ The Glass Ceiling

The glass ceiling is an invisible barrier through which women can aspire to the more senior ranks of management, but cannot reach them. It is not exclusive to the BMO, or the Canadian banking industry. However, females accounted for 75 per cent of the Bank's employees in 1990, while only 13 per cent of senior management and six per cent of executives were women. In Deborah's opinion, this was a modest improvement since the first three female executives were appointed by the Bank in 1982. Over the past six

---

[1]Mid-market was a term that referred to commercial accounts with sales between $5 million and $500 million.

[2]Average asset base is a typical measure used to evaluate the size of a bank. Average assets is defined as beginning-of-the-year assets plus end-of-year assets, divided by two.

years, the number of senior managers at the Bank has grown by 33 per cent, while the number of female senior managers has grown by a mere one per cent per year. These statistics provided a strong argument that the glass ceiling exists.

⬚ The Task Force on the Advancement of Women in the Bank of Montreal

In response to the glass ceiling, Tony Comper, President and Chief Operating Officer, established a Task Force on the Advancement of Women in the Bank, in December 1990. Mr. Comper commented on the goals of the Task Force:

> It may well mean setting a numerical goal. But numerical targets will only be a means to our real goal. That is, to create an environment where women will meet no barriers to advancement, where there will be continuous advancement toward true equality, where both women and men can progress and enjoy rewarding careers.

Mr. Comper appointed Marnie Kinsley, Vice-President, to head the Task Force. Ms. Kinsley, a chartered accountant, joined the Bank in 1985. She had held senior positions in Corporate Audit and the Securities Service Centre in Toronto, Ontario. Ms. Kinsley reported directly to Tony Comper and was responsible for four full-time Task Force members and 11 part-time members (refer to Exhibit 1). The members represented several banking groups, geographic regions, and the gender composition of the Bank (75 per cent female and 25 per cent male). Also involved in the process was a Steering Committee, responsible for directing the activities of the Task Force, and a Consultative Group, both of which were chaired by Tony Comper. The Consultative Group, formed to provide feedback on decisions and directions of the Task Force, offered a unique perspective as it was comprised of the female executives of the Bank. As a result, the Task Force was able to benefit from the experiences of these women and use them as role models for success. Through an effective internal and external communication strategy, the Task Force had become highly visible to the employees and the media. This visibility spurred both criticism and support.

Deborah had the opportunity to meet Marnie Kinsley following a presentation by the Task Force. Ms. Kinsley had been very open with Deborah in discussing her beliefs on the issue of employment equity. She spoke of her own personal experience with the glass ceiling, as she had accepted the position as Task Force Leader amid criticism from men and women that it was a "token" role. Ms. Kinsley responded to the criticism with confidence that she had the talent and skills necessary to make change happen. This was her opportunity to become a visible change agent within the Bank. She was committed to succeed as, both in the Bank's and the public's eyes, her credibility was at stake.

The Task Force became the topic of conversation among Deborah and her co-workers on many occasions. A number of her female peers argued that real change was unlikely and that *forced* change would foster increased tokenism and rivalry between the sexes. Certain of her male colleagues did not agree that there was an equality problem; others were concerned about reverse discrimination.

During her discussion with Deborah, Ms. Kinsley described her own view of resistance as the "clay layer." Between the progressive, "blue sky" views of Matthew Barrett, Chairman and Chief Executive Officer, and Tony Comper, and the change-oriented, "grass roots" view of the more junior employees, there is the seemingly "immoveable" middle management. She attributed this resistance to change to issues such as fear of personal loss, insecurity and outright denial that a problem existed. This "clay layer" presented a substantial challenge to Ms. Kinsley, as the success of the Task Force demanded the support of all management.

The Task Force had three primary objectives: identify the barriers to advancement; recommend changes to remove the barriers; and recommend goals and methods of measurement. Advancement had been defined by the Task Force to include promotion, job enrichment and the ability to balance work and family life. Aside from the earlier statistics given on representation of females in the BMO's management ranks, the Task Force's study of work force trends identified four factors that supported the need for change.

- Women have become significant participants in the workforce. In 1951, 25 per cent of women were in the Ontario workforce. By 1990, the number reached 60 per cent.
- The province's employers are facing a "demographic crunch" due to the aging population and the declining birth rate. Specifically, Ontario workforce growth slowed from 2.8 per cent during 1956–1961 to 1.7 per cent during 1986–1991.
- Employers are facing a change in workforce values as employees are expressing concern for quality of work life and outside commitments, such as family and the community.
- With the convergence of the above, the BMO must become "an employer of choice" in order to attract and maintain a committed, satisfied human capital base.

Furthermore, proponents of the Task Force believed that the time for change was now. The BMO had undergone a dramatic shift in leadership style from the top-down approach of William Mulholland, a former Wall Street investment banker, to the teamwork-oriented, visionary styles of Matthew Barrett and Tony Comper. Matthew Barrett, considered an "icon of the caring, socially aware manager of the 1990s,"[3] had

announced to his employees his desire to "breathe new life into the Bank." The Chairman and his executive team had developed a comprehensive strategic plan for the Bank, and through a series of videos and personal visits he had taken this plan to every BMO employee. As part of the strategic plan, both Matthew Barrett and Tony Comper vowed to shatter the glass ceiling.

Initiating Change

Marnie Kinsley believed that the change process should begin with a full understanding of how employees felt about the glass ceiling and the types of barriers that women were facing in the Bank. While the issue was the Advancement of Women, the Task Force wanted the opinions of both men and women. As a first step, the Task Force met with several banking groups through employee focus sessions, open forums, presentations and interviews with executives. Marnie Kinsley, herself, did over 100 presentations across Canada. These sessions served to enhance the Task Force's understanding of the employees' concerns and the employees' awareness that change was forthcoming.

The Task Force then studied the data from the BMO's Human Resource Information System (HRIS) to develop a complete view of the Bank's employee base. The HRIS was also used to track the progress of certain key employee groups and, specifically, males versus females. The Task Force also examined the Bank's human resource policies in order to identify areas in which policies were outdated and/or lacking. Furthermore, various organizations in the financial services and other industries were visited in order to enhance the Task Force's understanding of different approaches to dealing with the glass ceiling.

From their discussions with employees, the members of the Task Force discovered a set of

---

[3] *The Financial Post*, January 6, 1992.

"conventional beliefs" among employees regarding "why women don't get promoted." The five beliefs were: women are either too young or too old; women are less committed to their work because they leave to have children; women are not as highly educated as their male peers; women don't have the right stuff to compete with men; and, time will take care of the advancement of women to senior jobs at the Bank.

The Task Force decided that a more in-depth study of the employees' concerns could be achieved through a survey. With the assistance of the consulting firm, William M. Mercer Limited (Mercer), a comprehensive 19-page survey was developed and distributed to more than 15,000 employees, or approximately 55 per cent of the Bank's staff. The survey was strictly confidential, and the questions were divided into four sections: "Your Experience at the Bank"; "Your Personal Views"; "Background Information"; and one open-ended question entitled "Your Comments." The survey was sent out in June 1991, and a 62 per cent response rate was received.

Mercer was retained to tabulate and analyze the survey responses and present the findings to the Bank. The survey revealed that women and men perceive the opportunities for women to advance differently. For example, at all management levels, at least 74 per cent of men in the Bank believe that women have the same opportunities as men to get ahead. A maximum of 33 per cent of female management share the same optimism.

Mercer also concluded that the Bank's employees saw three major barriers to the advancement of women. First, women suffer from a set of outdated assumptions and conclusions, or "conventional beliefs," held by both men and women. Second, women have not received adequate access to information regarding career opportunities and have not been encouraged by their supervisors to seek opportunities to realize their potential. Third, when employees have responded to commitments outside of the Bank (family, education or community), their commitment to their career has

been questioned. As a result, their ability to advance has been limited. The following comment, written in the survey by one of the Bank's female senior managers, reflects the type of outdated assumptions that prevailed.

> Once a woman reaches middle management, she is told she has done very well—after all, look how far you have come in the Bank. For men, however, the sky is the limit and if they aspire to be a senior vice president, more power to them! If a woman aspires to be a senior vice president, everyone snickers and wonders who she thinks she is!

The Task Force believed that the only way to "test" the conventional beliefs was through a study of the HRIS system. The data substantiated the following:

- The average age of women at the BMO (at all management and non-management levels) combined is one year younger than the average of men. Therefore, women are neither too young nor too old.
- On average, a woman's service record is one year shorter than a man's, and longer at all levels except senior management. Despite the birth of children, women are as committed to their careers as men.
- At the non-management and junior management levels, the primary feeder groups into more senior management positions, the number of females with university and college degrees outnumber the number of males with degrees by a factor of 2.64 times. Therefore, women do have the necessary education to succeed.
- At all management ranks, the percentage of females achieving the top two performance levels exceeds the percentage of males achieving these levels by seven to 14 per cent. Therefore, women can compete on performance.

- With the current pace of change, only 22 per cent of BMO senior management and 18 per cent of executives will be female by the year 2000. Therefore, time alone will not eliminate the glass ceiling.

⊠ Deborah Westman

Deborah Westman had been employed by the BMO for two years. She had joined the Commercial Banking Officer Program (CBO), a fast-track program designed to bring university graduates into the Bank. As a CBO, Deborah was responsible for analyzing the financial and operational riskiness of the BMO's corporate clients. The CBO Program was a feeder into the Bank and, more specifically, the MDP Program. Deborah was promoted into the MDP Program after 12 months as a CBO. She went on to complete her MDP training during the following year, focusing on tasks such as commercial account management and credit analysis. Because the purpose of the MDP Program was to bring young, highly educated professionals into the Bank, it consisted of solely temporary positions. As her training was complete, Deborah was required to leave the MDP Program and assume a permanent position.

Career paths beyond MDP depended on the skills and interests of the individual as well as the demands of the Bank. Since Commercial Banking had become a strategic focus of the Bank, there were Commercial Account Management positions open. However, other opportunities that Deborah faced included senior analyst positions within Corporate Banking and the Treasury Group. Deborah believed that the salary and responsibility levels offered by these positions would be very similar to Commercial Account Management. In any case, Deborah would be required to interview for these positions, as would any MDP graduate.

Deborah had been recognized by her supervisors as a strong performer. Her progress, in terms of promotions and pay increases, was indicative of that performance. Despite the competitive nature of the MDP Program, Deborah was admired by her fellow CBO/MDP peers for her degree of commitment to her job and her personal development. She had an undergraduate business degree. Despite the long hours she spent at the Bank, her personal time was used to study for part-time MBA courses.

While extremely motivated by her career progress, Deborah had two personal commitments to satisfy over the next few years. She wanted to complete her MBA and, after two years of part-time study, she felt that she would receive more from the program if she studied the final year on a full-time basis. Her motivation for doing the MBA was twofold: she enjoyed the challenge and she had been told in an initial interview at the Bank that an MBA was a requirement for "vice-president potential." For these reasons, she knew that she would be requesting an eight-month unpaid leave of absence to complete her studies. From the experience of one of her colleagues, she knew that a leave of absence was something that the BMO closely scrutinized.

Deborah was turning 30 this year and celebrating her fourth wedding anniversary. She and her husband had agreed that at age 30 they would begin thinking about a family. Deborah wanted children, but did not want to begin a family until she had completed her MBA and was well-established in her career. Her husband was more eager. Deborah did not want their plans to upset her career. She was frustrated by the notion that having children was a joint responsibility, and yet her husband's career in the investment brokerage business would likely continue unaffected.

Deborah recalled the information released by the Task Force. She had read about the survey results and, specifically, about the employees' perceptions regarding the third barrier to the advancement of women. She was concerned that her request for an unpaid leave of absence to complete her MBA and her eventual desire for maternity/child care leave would tarnish her managers' perceptions of her commitment to her job. Deborah recalled her early experiences as a

CBO. She felt that it was odd that four of the six supervisors that had moved in or out of the Program over the course of her stay were females that had just returned from maternity leave. These women had left Account Management positions to go on their maternity leaves. Deborah realized that these women may have requested a career change from Account Management to a head office/supervisory role; however; she wondered whether there were other forces at play.

Deborah was concerned that she would feel relatively isolated in the predominantly male Commercial Banking environment. She recalled the comment of one of her peers:

> Women tend to get excluded from "going to lunch groups," "going for coffee" groups and "drinks and dinner in the evenings and weekends" groups. These tend to be organized by men who feel comfortable with each other. When these groups get together, business is discussed, so women automatically miss out on useful and, at times, important information.

At the same time, the challenge of Commercial Account Management attracted her, particularly now that the executive management had targeted the commercial segment as a key area for future growth. Deborah also knew that she had the talent and skills that would allow her to do well in either a head office or Commercial Banking "line" role.

⊠ The Recommendations of the Task Force

The Task Force took eight months to fully comprehend and develop recommendations from their findings. This effort involved extensive interaction with Mr. Comper, and several executives and senior managers of various banking groups. Two full months were then spent negotiating and further refining the recommendations, with the assistance of several executives, managers,

Mr. Comper and the Steering Committee. Among the parties' considerations were the potential effect on the employees, the ease of implementation and the cost. The approval of the Bank's Board of Directors was also sought and received during a presentation by Marnie Kinsley in November 1991. This process gave rise to a final set of action plans that focused on four major strategies: *get the facts out; help all employees get ahead; reduce the stress; and make it official.* These plans are detailed below.

Get the Facts Out

The emphasis was to bridge the gap between the employees' perceptions, as revealed by the surveys, and the reality of women's abilities, career interests and degree of commitment. The Task Force recommended that all of their significant findings be communicated to the employees by way of a comprehensive 24-page "Report to Employees." Results were made public via press conferences with Tony Comper and Marnie Kinsley.

The Task Force recommended the implementation of one-day training sessions to focus on the attitudes and behaviours that contribute to the glass ceiling. The intention was to build consensus that the barriers were real and that change must occur. The sessions were to begin at the executive level, as early as February 1992.

Help All Employees Get Ahead

Improving the employees' access to information on career paths, job opportunities and career-enhancing activities was expected to benefit both genders. The Task Force recommended the implementation of a manager-training program to focus on the "coaching" and teamwork-oriented styles of leadership. The courses had been developed by the Bank's Human Resources Group and sessions were to begin in January 1992.

Access to job information was to be expanded with a pilot job vacancy notification system. The pilot was to be implemented by May 1992, and subsequently used to model a Bank-wide system for all employees at all levels.

The designation of certain management personnel as job information counsellors was recommended to increase the employees' access to career development opportunities. Individuals were to be assigned to counsellors other than their supervisors, thereby allowing them to discuss their suitability for particular jobs in complete confidence. The coaching skills developed in the manager-training sessions were expected to enhance the managers' abilities to deal with employees on a personal level. The program was to be operational by April 1992.

An Executive Advisor program was also recommended to provide senior management, male and female, with the opportunity to share ideas with executives in an informal setting. The objective of the program was to promote the level of networking among women and men in different banking groups, and ultimately to eliminate the tendency for a "boys' club." An Executive Advisor pilot was to be operational by April 1992.

The Task Force also recommended the implementation of cross-training exchanges for all employees as a means of career development. For satisfied employees not desiring increased responsibility through promotions, these activities were expected to enhance their interest in, and personal reward from, their jobs.

Finally, the Task Force recommended an increase in the participation rate of women in the Bank's commercial credit training program, CBO Program (to 50 per cent) and MDP Program (to 50 per cent). These initiatives, which were scheduled to begin immediately, were established to ensure the constant flow of talented, high-potential female candidates into the Bank's management streams.

Reduce the Stress

The focus of this strategy was to revise and/or implement policies that formally support women and men in balancing their multiple commitments to their job, family, education and communities. One of the objectives of this strategy was to revise policies in order to eliminate any discriminatory attitudes towards maternity leaves, child-care days and absences for educational purposes.

Specifically, the Task Force recommended the development of human resources policies that support flexible work arrangements such as compressed work weeks, job-sharing, part-time management positions, telecommuting (working at home via the computer) and opportunities for women to phase in their return to work following maternity leave. As an example, "People Care Days" were recommended to allow short-term leaves for employees to meet their multiple commitments. Secondly, a revision of the unpaid leave of absence policy was recommended in order to facilitate leaves for family, educational and other reasons. A "how-to" booklet on possible flexible work arrangements was to be distributed to all employees.

The Task Force also studied the concept of offering in-house daycare programs. On the basis of costs and accessibility, the study concluded that offering a daycare referral service would be a more effective means of assisting employees in finding suitable child-care providers in their own communities. This service was concurrently introduced with the report of the Task Force.

Make It Official

Lastly, and possibly most importantly, the Task Force recommended that all managers be accountable for ongoing change towards workplace equality in all job categories at all levels. The Task Force recommended that all managers be responsible for setting goals and devising action plans for the hiring, development and promotion of women. These goals, or "flexible targets," were to focus all management's efforts on eliminating barriers with true equality being the ultimate measure of success. The goal setting and planning process was scheduled to become a part of the annual business planning process, commencing in fiscal 1992.

Finally, the Task Force recommended that the rate of women's advancement in key managerial and specialty roles, including Commercial

Account Management and Credit, should be monitored on a quarterly basis. Furthermore, the whole Bank's systematic progress in advancing women was to be measured quarterly, with a report published annually to outline the progress to all employees. The reports were to include a survey and analysis of how employees were responding to the changes. The first annual report was to be published in November 1992.

Personal Decisions

Deborah sat staring at her copy of the "Report to Employees." Immediately, she identified personal gains with the proposed revisions to the leave of absence and maternity/child care policies.

But if outdated attitudes and false conclusions were also roots of the glass ceiling, were attitudes likely to change? Were the actions employed and recommendations put forth by the Task Force sufficient to change attitudes and, as a result, smash the glass ceiling? Were the recommendations regarding goal setting, monitoring and hiring likely to cause charges of reverse discrimination? With the leadership styles of Matthew Barrett and Tony Comper and the focused strategic plan of the Bank, Deborah believed that there were opportunities for a challenging and rewarding career at the BMO. Was she wrong in feeling that she could take advantage of a heightened awareness of women? Was she wrong in believing that the barriers would be removed?

Exhibit 1	The Task Force Participants

President and Chief Operating Officer

Tony Comper

Vice-President and Task Force Leader

Marnie Kinsley

Full-Time Task Force Members

Maureen Bell, Administration
Brian Bieniara, Research
Mary Lou Hukezalie, Human Resources
Terri Mabey, Communications

Part-Time Task Force Members

Judith Bonaparte, Deborah Casey, Donald Dixon, Moyna Laing, Danielle Malka, Ian Mole, Eleanor Morrison, Kathy Pack, Carl Rehel, Karen Rubin, Pamela Rueda

Consultative Group

Beverly Blucher, Yvonne Bos, Loretta Hennessey, Catherine Irwin, Kim MacNeil, Penny Chard, Deanna Rosenswig, Carol Snider, Penny Somerville, Harriet Stairs, Peggy Sum, Catharina Van Berkel, Pamela Ward, Jane Weatherbie, Linda Fitzsimmons (Harris Bankcorp), Maribeth Rahe (Harris Bankcorp), Kristine Vikmanis (Nesbitt, Thomson)

Steering Committee

Ronald Call, Tony Comper, Deanna Rosenswig, Penny Somerville, Harriet Stairs, Robert Tetley, Jane Weatherbie

Marimekko

Jordan Mitchell and Alison Konrad

Business could be called life: A good and ethical corporate culture embodies the same values as our everyday life.

—Kirsti Paakkanen, president & chief executive officer, Marimekko

⊠ Introduction

Early in the morning on May 19, 2006, Kirsti Paakkanen walked into Marimekko's head office at Puusepänkatu Road in Helsinki, Finland. The smell of coffee and blueberry cake was familiar, but today would be different. After 15 years at the helm of the legendary Finnish design firm Marimekko, Paakkanen was about to receive an honorary doctorate from the Helsinki School of Economics for her achievements in promoting Finnish design on a worldwide stage.

As Paakkanen walked to her large glass-topped desk, she thought back over the past 15 years and what she would tell the crowd about how she had restored Marimekko from a loss-making company on the verge of bankruptcy to the pride of Finnish design. As she stated:

> I feel I'm quite humble, and I feel rather inadequate in many respects. From Marimekko, there's a lot to learn. Starting with the founder, Armi Ratia, this company is a good example of being boldly different. In order to do big deeds, Marimekko had the courage to be very different

Not wanting to rest on her past successes, Paakkanen's mind quickly moved to the future.

The company was in an exciting phase of expanding internationally through exports and working with retail partners to open Marimekko-concept shops. Recently, Marimekko-concept shops had opened in Japan, the United Arab Emirates, Iceland, Sweden and the United States. Just as Marimekko had become a household name in Finland, Paakkanen was certain that its style would capture the hearts and minds of foreign customers as it had in the 1960s. At the same time, she wondered whether any changes were required to the company's personnel policies for the future. As the personnel section of Marimekko's 2005 annual report stated:

> Going international ushers in mounting challenges for Marimekko's business operations, requiring personnel to have new kinds of capabilities and to adapt themselves to changing circumstances. On the other hand, the greater diversity of tasks and operating in the international market provide employees with excellent opportunities to expand their expertise and knowledge of other cultures.[1]

⊠ Kirsti Paakkanen

Born in 1929,[2] Paakkanen grew up in the small town of Saarijärvi in the middle of Finland's forested countryside. Her early days were said to have had a profound impact on how nature was at the forefront of her values. During high school, Paakkanen worked two jobs to support herself. She entered university and earned degrees

Version: (A) 2009-09-16

[1]Marimekko Annual Report 2005, December 31, 2005, p. 22.

[2]Wikipedia, http://fi.wikipedia.org/wiki/Kirsti_Paakkanen, accessed July 28, 2006.

in Finnish studies and advertising and marketing. She began her professional career at an advertising agency in Helsinki, before breaking out on her own and establishing Womena in 1969. Paakkanen's concept was to hire only women for her advertising agency, something unheard of at the time in Finland. The name itself, aside from the overt English-language connection to the word "Women," was a poetic "Adam & Eve" connotation as "omena" means apple in Finnish.[3] Paakkanen quipped: "The first sales speech by a woman was made in the Garden of Eden when Eve persuaded Adam to eat the apple!"[4]

Paakkanen wanted to create a substantially different agency. She hired four female advertising professionals, rented a space in central Helsinki, made the office furniture herself and ensured that the scent in the office resembled that of a forest. To introduce her new agency to potential Finnish advertisers, she and her staff packaged up 600 green apples in elegant white boxes with the tag line: "Today 'omena' (apple), tomorrow 'Womena.'" Immediately, she attracted 35 customers. All business operations were financed directly through revenues.

Throughout the next 20 years, Paakkanen led the agency to become one of the most recognized names in the Finnish advertising industry. Womena was known for its all-female staff, no hierarchy among the employees and flexible job descriptions. In addition, Womena's results were often heeded by the industry—the company won over 30 national advertising awards from 1969 to 1988. As well, the agency posted profits every year. It exceeded the average European advertising agency since its operating profit before depreciation was 32.2 per cent versus the industry average of 12.8 per cent.[5] In building Womena to great acclaim, Paakkanen commented on the female-male divide and how she overcame the predominantly male culture at the time:

> At that time, women were not at all respected, and I wanted to respond in the same way to people that believed I could not do it. When men were reacting poorly to me, instead of acting poorly towards them, I acted conversely like a weak woman and threw myself at them begging for their help. It always worked—100 per cent of the time!

In 1988, Paakkanen sold Womena to The Interpublic Group of Companies, Inc./McCann Worldwide (USA). Part of the agreement was that Paakkanen would work for the group for a period of three years. When she had fulfilled that part of the deal, in March 1991, Paakkanen announced her retirement and moved to Nice in southern France. After just a couple of months, she received a phone call from Amer Group, the owners of Marimekko, to take the position of chief executive officer in the loss-making Marimekko. She turned down the offer, only to receive a counter offer to purchase the business at a nominal fee. Paakkanen agreed. She reflected back on her decision:

> First off, I'm always inspired by a strong brand. I saw that the management of Marimekko was bad, but no matter how much they abandoned it, it could not be killed off—the strength of the brand lived on. I was living in the south of France, and I suppose I was a little homesick. I have a strong sense of being Finnish, and I'm quite patriotic. I could see that Finland was going through one of its worst recessions in 1990–1991,

---

[3]Hannah Booth, "Women: Flower power," The Guardian, September 5, 2005, http://www.guardian.co.uk/g2/story/0,,1562697,00.html. accessed May 18, 2006.

[4]Profile on Kirsti Paakkanen, Internal Marimekko Publication, 2006, p. 1.

[5]Ibid., p. 2.

and I had this mission of doing my own share to save Finland. But, more than that, it was also saving a pearl within the country. To me, there's nothing more important than inspiration in the heart—I knew that it would be a tough job to turn Marimekko around, but I knew I would not and could not fail if I had inspiration in my heart.

Exhibit 1 shows some of Paakkanen's well-known quotes.

⊠ The Building of a Finnish Icon: Marimekko's History

The first step in building Marimekko was taken in 1949, when Viljo Ratia purchased Printex Oy, a company producing oilcloth and printed fabrics. Viljo's wife, Armi Ratia, an adwoman and trained textile designer, encouraged her husband not to produce common floral prints, stating: "You must print something else. You have to be different."[6] She commissioned aspiring young designers to generate prints for the company, one of which was Maija Isola, who went on to create many of the company's hallmark patterns. While the fabrics were well received by the public, many asked how they could be put to use. Armi and Viljo Ratia responded by setting up a separate company, Marimekko, in 1951. Marimekko was an amalgamation of the common female name "Mary" (spelt "Mari" in Finnish) with "mekko," meaning "dress." The concept of Marimekko was to create something radically different with beauty and longevity to give hope to the grey mood in post-war Finland. One writer described the motivation for the company in this way: "With full confidence, one can say that in its first years, Marimekko was driven forward by an idealism that involved taking personal risks and being completely indifferent to economic success."[7]

The company's dresses were known for their loose-fitting silhouettes akin to an artist's smock.[8] The garments were often described as "clothing for women who didn't want to think about clothes."[9] The company made its products available internationally in the late 1950s, in both Sweden and through the cutting-edge, Boston-based retail shop Design Research. Marimekko received a major push in 1960, when Jacqueline Kennedy, the wife of U.S. presidential candidate John F. Kennedy, purchased seven Marimekko garments from the company's U.S. distributor. She then appeared in her Marimekko dress for the cover shot of Sports Illustrated. During that time, the Kennedy-Nixon presidential campaign was in high gear, and when journalists criticized Jacqueline Kennedy for her expensive Paris-bought fashions, she quickly responded that they were inexpensive ready-to-wear garments from Finland.[10] The story spread quickly throughout the United States, and the small, relatively unknown Marimekko name was thrust into the international spotlight.

With this increased profile, press from around the world began focusing on Marimekko. However, Armi Ratia insisted that her name not be mentioned, and she encouraged the press to focus on the individual designers of each

---

[6]Judith Gura, "Marimekko: Resurgence of a Finnish Phenomenon," Scandinavian Review, Spring 2004.

[7]Edited by Pekka Suhonen, "Phenomenon Marimekko," Porvoo: WS Bookwell Oy, 2004, p. 8.

[8]Judith Gura, "Marimekko: Resurgence of a Finnish Phenomenon," Scandinavian Review, Spring 2004.

[9]Ibid.

[10]Edited by Pekka Suhonen, "Phenomenon Marimekko," Porvoo: WS Bookwell Oy, 2004, p. 23.

garment or design. Eventually, the press began focusing on Armi Ratia. Viljo stated:

> When we were creating our corporate image, I had the idea of an "entrepreneurial couple," Armi on the artistic side, me on manufacturing and management side. Once Armi had stepped into the limelight, there was no holding her back. From then on it was a solo performance. Armi was a perfect pro. Her Finnish was so original, often downright shocking, that she was much sought-after for interviews, which, at the beginning, were about Marimekko, but later about quite other subjects. . . . Interest had spread abroad and Marimekko's newly created image showed that it was not just a business but a kind of cultural phenomenon. There was a constant stream of visitors, [including] cultural personalities from Finland and abroad.[11]

Armi Ratia refused to follow Paris haute couture and avoided the word "fashion." Instead, the company talked about "dressing Finnish women or the production of functional garments."[12] Later, the company began producing men's clothing beginning with the striped "Jokapoika" (the "Everyboy" shirt) in 1956 (see Exhibit 2). The company's products, known affectionately as "marimekkos," were seen to be completely egalitarian. Armi Ratia stated:

> I don't believe in national frontiers in dressing. Dresses are often quite recklessly bold and demand an unbourgeois wearer. The purpose of a dress is to permit freedom of movement and to do justice to its wearer as an individual.

Therefore, there aren't any special models as such. They are dresses that have style. They are Finnish in the same way as are a burlap dress, a farmhorse's ear and a grey barnwall.[13]

Armi was also known for taking risks on purchasing decisions; she was guided by the principle to never say to a customer, "Sorry, we haven't got it." This led to excessive stocks and products and fabrics that needed to later be liquidated at a lower price. At the same time, designers and machinists were given freedom to make decisions, even if these decisions turned out to be unprofitable. As one designer stated: "We were encouraged to speak out like owners. Armi's order was: You have to have your own opinion!"[14]

In the late 1960s, Armi developed a plan to create the Mari village—an idyllic village community for 3,500 inhabitants. The project garnered interest from a Helsinki-based building company, but before full construction began, the building company pulled out. Marimekko was going to continue the project on its own, but, in 1967, due to a shortage of cash, the concept was terminated by the board of directors. The cash crisis forced the company to embark on a restructuring process, which took over three years and involved culling office staff by nearly 50 per cent (from 191 to 100) and factory workers by 32 per cent (from 247 to 167).[15]

From the restructuring, a new Marimekko was born. The company abandoned its plans of producing diverse products such as shippable, full-sized modern saunas, opting to focus solely on clothing and textile home products. The company contracted freelance designers including two Japanese-born individuals—Katsuji Wakisaka and Fujiwo Ishimoto—during the 1970s. See Exhibit 3 for a list of select Marimekko designers.

---

[11]Ibid. p. 24.

[12]Ibid. p. 28.

[13]Ibid. p. 49.

[14]Ibid. p. 75.

[15]Edited by Pekka Suhonen, "Phenomenon Marimekko," Porvoo: WS Bookwell Oy, 2004, p. 10.

The company expanded its printing and production capabilities in Finland with the inauguration of new plants, and it went public on the Helsinki Stock Exchange in 1974. In 1979, Armi Ratia passed away. The ownership of the company passed on to Armi Ratia's heirs. Risto Takala began as the chief executive officer (CEO) of Marimekko in 1980, and Kari Mattson lead Marimekko from 1982 for a couple of years. One design historian commented:

> Ristomatti Ratia (Armi's son) remained the company's chief image-builder, but the company never regained its lost lustre. Its image was maintained, to some degree, in licensed linen collections, and loyal retailers continued to sell the ready-to-wear to a coterie of devoted customers, but the firm generally fell "beneath the radar" of the design community, where it remained for more than a decade.[16]

In 1985, the company was suffering losses, and Amer Group, a diversified conglomerate that owned brands in sporting, plastics and other industries, purchased the company's shares. Being part of a big group, Marimekko was now managed in a centralized manner as a subsidiary through Amer Group's administration. The activities of the subsidiaries were followed mainly through reports, and special characteristics for the subsidiaries' individual business development needs were not taken into consideration. During this time, Marimekko's international sales practically disappeared, losing money every year from 1985 to 1991.

The Turnaround: Enter Kirsti Paakkanen

Paakkanen invested her own funds (generated from the sale of Womena) and took out a bank loan to finance the purchase and working capital necessary to operate Marimekko. On September 27, 1991, Paakkanen acquired Marimekko. Paakkanen commented on the business environment, "Finland was in a deep recession, the deepest Finnish business had ever experienced. Unemployment soared, and Finland's mental state was at rock bottom." Within the first few days of taking over the ownership of Marimekko, Paakkanen said to the employee base: "You possess creativity, expertise and are seasoned professionals. You have long been creating products that bear the Marimekko name. I am a newcomer to Marimekko, and to succeed in my work, I'll need every single one of you. Together we'll show them what we are made of."

Paakkanen started by eliminating hierarchy in the organization to quash bureaucratic processes. She stated:

> When I came to the organization, I found that the company had all of these boxes, and people were not communicating effectively. We had to start by bulldozing bureaucracy and turning it into a vibrant environment conducive to creativity. We had to restore the mental well-being of the employees, instill in them a belief in the future, self-confidence and enthusiasm for regeneration. We had to draw up new business strategies and write new rules of play.

In co-ordination with breaking down the bureaucratic structure, Paakkanen boosted the role of the individual designers by giving them profit responsibility on their designs. Paakkanen retrained the designers, emphasizing the profitability of their designs. She reflected: "The designers evidently found the training a novelty. But also motivating and inspiring."[17]

Paakkanen clearly stated to Marimekko's employees: "Design is now paramount throughout the organization. The entire organization serves top design." In orienting the entire company around the design function, she built state-of-the-art

---

[16]Judith Gura, "Marimekko: Resurgence of a Finnish Phenomenon," *Scandinavian Review,* Spring 2004.

[17]Kirsti Paakkanen speech, 2004, Marimekko company documents.

working facilities for the designers and gave them complete creative freedom. However, there was one condition: the designs had to be profitable. The name of each designer was placed on the inside hangtag of all garments and home products. Throughout its history, Marimekko had used a combination of in-house and freelance designers. When Paakkanen joined, there were very few in-house designers. Paakkanen opted for the freelance designer model. She sought new designers by hosting internal design competitions and working closely with both Finnish and international art and design institutes.

Paakkanen gathered existing staff to define the market position of Marimekko and determine what products to focus on. The team reached back into Marimekko's rich archives and began reproducing prints. This was before the major "retro" fashion movement in the late 1990s and before the introduction of industrial design companies. One of the first retro designs was the "Fandango" group of prints developed by Maija Isola in 1962. When the reissue sold well, Paakkanen sent a cheque to the then-retired Isola, who immediately sent it back stating in a note, "Thank you for the beautiful thought. I think you will have better use for this money than I do."[18]

The company expanded into new areas. In the early 1990s, Paakkanen put more emphasis on the development of the home interiors market, using both archived and new patterns for products such as bed comforters, curtains, tablecloths and towels (these categories had also thrived during Armi Ratia's time but had been culled in the 1980s). In the mid-1990s, the company contracted freelance designer, Ritva Falla, to design a new line of women's business wear clothing. As Falla stated:

When I came to work here at Marimekko, I didn't come to produce the "standard Marimekko" but a business range based on a concept of Kirsti Paakkanen's. Times had changed. My task was to create products that fit the spirit of the times. It hasn't been easy to convince the sales staff that the woman who typically wears Marimekko is not your '60s housewife but a busy '90s businesswoman whose wardrobe contents are determined by the demands and desires of the era.[19]

The success in Marimekko's women's business wear division caused the company to begin a men's businesswear line in 2000. Matti Seppänen was contracted as a freelance designer to lead the development of the men's line. He stated: "When I design a collection for Finnish men, I picture a guy who is a class, quality-conscious, courageous intellectual who asserts his Finnishness and knows how to play it safe with his wardrobe."[20]

In 2003, the company extended its assortment of children's wear and began expanding into more licensing agreements. One of the most notable was a deal inked with mobile phone manufacturer Nokia to license Marimekko patterns for mobile phone covers.

The expansion into new product lines was complemented by new store openings. In addition, the company set up subsidiaries in Sweden and Germany and signed a number of international distribution agreements in over 15 countries. To support the business expansion, the company went public on the Helsinki Stock Exchange in 1999 and moved to the exchange's main list in 2002. The company's financial

---

[18]Hannah Booth, "Women: Flower power," The Guardian, September 5, 2005, http://www.guardian.co.uk/g2/story/0,,1562697,00.html, accessed May 18, 2006.

[19]Tommy Tabermann, Tuija Wuori-Tabermann, "Marimekko: Spirit & Life," Porvoo: WS Bookwell Oy, 2001, p. 180.

[20]Ibid, p. 199.

situation improved year on year, from a loss of over €8 million in 1991 to a profit of €8.4 million in 2005 (see Exhibit 4).

The Marimekko Organization as of 2006

Guiding Paakkanen's management approach was her self-developed thesis, which included 11 key terms: feelings, respect, truth, enthusiasm, discipline, reward, team spirit, total responsibility, caring, fairness and social responsibility. Along with her thesis, Paakkanen openly promoted the following three components: management by emotion, doing things together, and creativity cannot be delegated. Management by emotion was based on respect for everyone in the company and the belief that all staff members were considered to have unique talents, creativity and skills. Doing things together addressed the concept that teamwork was necessary for success. Creativity cannot be delegated was a notion that permitted artistic freedom as long as it was accompanied by responsibility. See Exhibit 5 for more information on Marimekko's company principles and Paakkanen's management principles.

Marimekko's senior management team was made up of nine individuals, including Paakkanen. All of the top management was Finnish and all were female, with the exception of the recently recruited Thomas Ekström as the company's chief financial officer (CFO) (see Exhibit 6). Marimekko did not publish an organizational chart and did not have strict job definitions. Tiina Alahuhta, Marimekko's public relations manager, explained:

> For example, I'm the public relations manager, but there is no real strict job description. I also work on a number of other projects such as export and investor relations. For nearly all projects, there is a project leader and they must take responsibility and it must be clear what the objective is. We have to have good internal communication to make it work.

As of the end of 2005, the company had 377 people in total, of whom 90.9 per cent were women and 9.1 per cent were men. Approximately 90 per cent of the staff was from Finland. Staff turnover was six per cent and was attributed to retirements. The average age of the employee base was 42.

The Design Function

At the heart of Marimekko's organization was the relationship with the company's approximately 18 freelance designers. Marimekko had three main product lines—clothing, interiors and bags—each with its own product development teams. Each team was responsible for developing the context of the new line. For example, in clothing, the freelance designers worked with Marimekko's product development team, which was led by Kirsti Paakkanen and Sirpa Loukamo. In interior decoration, the product development team thoroughly examined the "soul" of a pattern after it had been created to see which types of products it could be applied to and what the pattern or product would communicate. The designers were not given any direct instructions or limitations, but they were encouraged to create their own ideas into the patterns and/or garments. When asked how this worked in practice, Paakkanen responded:

> Marimekko is principally a design house. All of the personnel are organized around the design function. Everyone in the company knows this, and everyone in the company is aware of what we're aiming at from a design standpoint—we develop and explain this constantly. In managing designers, we have to make the controls to ensure that they are well briefed about what we want. The briefing process is one of the most vital parts of what we do. And then the designers' link up into other areas of the organization and work very closely with everyone, including marketing, sales and production.

For the designer to translate the concepts into producible designs, they would work with Marimekko's internal production team to test how the designs would be manufactured. After running tests in the printing machines for color and quality, the designer would meet with Marimekko's product and retail teams to finalize the designs. Production would determine whether or not the product would be made in Marimekko's Finnish facilities or outsourced in Finland or offshore. The retail team would begin planning how the new collection would be adapted into the Marimekko shop environment. Paakkanen was a part of the discussions, offering feedback and suggestions before the goods went into production.

The rationale for having freelance designers was to access highly talented individuals who had already made or who were seeking to make their name well known in the design community. Designers were often attracted to Marimekko, not only for the aesthetic, but also due to the creative freedom and the fact that they could build their own name under the umbrella of the company. Paakkanen explained:

> We are the only company that really stresses that every product displays the name of the designer. This goes not only for apparel, but for bags and fabrics as well. By putting the names on the products, it gives the designer responsibility and it makes them proud when the items are selling well. For the designers, I tell them they have to fight for their place in the sun. By being independent from Marimekko, their sole focus is on design, and they are given free reign to be creative.

Marimekko was constantly scanning the landscape for new design talent. As Paakkanen explained: "There's a large pool of designers who want to work here. We do, however, take a proactive approach by looking at all of the design schools, and we see who are some of the best designers. We also organize our own competitions and stay abreast of what's going on with other design competitions." Marimekko typically signed contracts with new designers for a specific season or particular task. With established designers, such as the 30-year plus relationship with Fujiwo Ishimoto, Marimekko had general agreements involving stipulations on the work to be performed and on confidentiality and remuneration. Designers were paid either for an individual design, a group of designs or a complete collection. Some designer contracts included an additional financial incentive in the form of a royalty payment if the products exceeded Marimekko's internally developed targets. As Ritva Schoultz, head of personnel affairs, stated:

> The freelance contracts vary by case. Some are paid for the product that we purchase; some for a collection that we decide to buy. The basic rule of thumb is that the freelance designers present us several alternatives from which we choose the ones that we wish to purchase. The freelance contracts do not have a fixed rate. Some designers have a contract to receive royalties.

Most of the designers currently working for Marimekko were Finnish. Only Fujiwo Ishimoto (Japan), Anna Danielsson (Sweden) and Katsuji Wakisaka (Japan) were foreign. Also, American designers, such as Robert Segal and Alicia Rosauer had created some items that Marimekko still had in production. Most designers split their working time between their own studios and the Marimekko head office.

Domestic Sales

Three individuals led the sales function: Piia Rossi for Marimekko-owned retail locations; Merja Puntila for domestic wholesale; and Päivi Lonka for exports.

As of mid-2006, the company owned 24 stores in Finland, one in Stockholm, Sweden, and one in Frankfurt, Germany. Rossi's internal team was responsible for the display and training of all in-store staff. Company-owned shops were seen to be the manifestation of the Marimekko brand experience. The stores were anywhere from 150 square metres to 600 square metres in size and featured bright colors, combining raw fabric prints with men's and women's apparel, home products, bags and other licensed accessories. All staff was adorned in seasonal Marimekko co-ordinates and strove to create an energetic and spirited shop environment (see Exhibit 7).

All new staff took part in intensive training sessions, which involved presentations from Marimekko's retail and product team as well as external philosophers, psychologists and creative experts. In addition, Paakkanen herself attended a portion of each training session and spoke one-on-one with each new employee. She explained:

> A lot of people in Finland already know a little bit about Marimekko before join-ing. When we opened our last shop, we had over 300 applicants for 10 positions. In the first training session, I talk about being a creative company instead of being a bunch of bureaucrats. I then talk to everyone and I ask them about their dreams, their home life, what they want to do and what they like. I want to feel who the people are, and I want to explain my thesis to them directly. I explain how they can make the thesis their own. My intention is to set the expectations for being an employee. The purpose of this is to really explain the corporate culture as this molds the attitude of people right from the beginning.

Marimekko's domestic wholesale division was responsible for selling to approximately 140 retailers in Finland, just under one-quarter of which were Marimekko concept shops; the rest were multi-label retailers.

International Sales

Marimekko sold to approximately 1,000 shops on a worldwide basis. Since 2004, the company had been actively pursuing the Marimekko-concept shop, which were retail venues that were owned by third parties and that had Marimekko branding. In 2005, the company had opened up four new Marimekko-concept shops in the United Arab Emirates, Iceland, Sweden and the United States. Marimekko had also signed agreements with Mitsubishi and Look Inc. to open 15 Marimekko-concept shops in Japan over the next few years. Additionally, for 2006, Marimekko was planning to open concept or shop-in-shop retail points in Belgium, Portugal and Sweden to name but a few. Päivi Lonka, head of export and licensing sales, talked about selling Marimekko outside of Finland:

> Marimekko's major strength is its unique, original design. Behind each Marimekko product is a designer whose creation has earned its place in the col-lection. Furthermore, during its entire 50-year history Marimekko has always represented the most innovative designs and has managed its image within the spirit of the times.
>
> The key challenges for Marimekko's international expansion include the con-trol of the distribution and managing a consistent brand image to maintain steady growth. [Because] the Marimekko design is unique, one of our major challenges has included examining whether there is enough demand for this kind of design in a new market. The second challenge concerns introducing and increasing the awareness of a new brand with limited marketing resources. There is also a chal-lenge in maintaining a consistent brand image—without restricting the entre-preneur's freedom too much—that can still be adapted to different cultural envi-ronments. [A third challenge] is the careful examination of the products' and product ranges' ability to meet the needs of each country market.

Marimekko provided training to all third-party retail venues, although sometimes the training was done outside of Finland due to logistics and costs in transporting shop owners to Helsinki. As of 2006, the company was in the early stages of developing a training package for the concept shops located outside of Finland. Paakkanen commented on the challenge of communicating the Marimekko philosophy to all third-party operations: "I meet with all of the shop owners and explain them to the Marimekko concept. We need to carefully choose new shop owners who understand the philosophy. However, it becomes more difficult describing this to all of their employees."

Production

Production was led by Helinä Uotila and included 118 staff. Most of the company's production needs were fulfilled within the European Union (EU), which was in direct contrast to the majority of textile companies in Western Europe and North America, who opted to produce the majority of textile goods in the Far East and Latin America. Marimekko preferred to produce in Finland and the EU for reasons of control, response time and integration with the rest of the company. The company produced goods in offshore locations for reasons of expertise, such as the manufacturing of knit shirts in India and China. Helinä Uotila talked about the rationale for keeping a large portion of the production in Finland:

> We feel that the Marimekko designs in printed fabrics are so special that the best results are achieved with the co-operation of nearby designers and experienced technical personnel. This is why we think it is important to have our own textile printing factory. We intend to keep it that way.

> For the Finnish market, the origin [label] "Made in Finland" is very important. It is the same as the guarantee of good quality, and it also allows a higher price level. Moreover, Finns are very patriotic, and they want to support Finnish labor.

Marimekko's EU production was split among its own three facilities (approximately 40 per cent of domestic production) and independent contractors (the remaining 60 per cent). The company's three facilities were all located in Finland and included: a textile printing factory in Helsinki (48 employees), a clothing factory in Kitee (50 employees), and a bag factory in Sulkava (20 employees). In 2004, the company purchased a state-of-the-art printing machine for increased capabilities at the Helsinki textile printing factory. Uotila talked about Marimekko's production capacity:

> In fabrics we still have extra printing capacity. Subcontracting and sourcing from lower cost countries are also very important. In clothing and bags, we do not have any plans to increase our own production. All the growth will come from subcontracting and, at the moment, mainly from Baltic countries.

The company was constantly striving to exceed environmental regulations in its owned facilities. For example, in 2005, Marimekko began a series of studies to better utilize heat, thereby saving on energy consumption. The warehouse was located at the Helsinki complex, which housed the company's head offices.

✉ The Future

As Paakkanen reflected on Marimekko's current strength and growth prospects, she thought about the question that had often been posed by members of the press, investment analysts and other observers: "When is your retirement date?" Paakkanen responded:

> I don't have a successor right now because there's no acute need. I have no doubt that there will be the appropriate person, and I'm always keeping my eyes open. However, when I look at the future of this company, I don't see any real threats. We're fortunate to not be in a country

with earthquakes and natural catastrophes. There's nothing else that would be a threat. Originally, post-war Finland didn't have anything, and Marimekko started when the country was in a very poor state—it filled a void and it answered this need by giving beauty to everyday life. Companies that respond with genuineness to this need in the future with will be the ones that make a difference.

I don't fear big changes to anything. Together we have accepted the way we work, and I see no reason why that shouldn't continue into the future. I don't have any doubt that it will. We have great talent and a lot of new young people with great language skills who are able to deal effectively in foreign markets. In the future, the only thing I see is opportunity.

Exhibit 1	Kirsti Paakkanen Quotes

"My mother's advice: 'Each day one should work a wonder.'"

"Marimekko is so Finnish an enterprise that anything more Finnish would be difficult to find."

"Marimekko may be everyday, but it is never conventional."

"Feelings are the world's greatest natural resource."

"Whatever you're doing, be an example. Your actions speak louder than your words."

"No reward is greater than you saying to me: Thank you! Beautiful! Without pride and gratitude we would not be Marimekko."[1]

"Everyone, nearly everyone, has been imbued at birth with an extravagant force called the will to live. It moves us to go on struggling in seemingly hopeless situations and to discover in even the most trifling chaff the blossoming cherry tree. Fortunately, we know how to dream . . . Without dreams there is no life."[2]

"Marimekko has been, and remains, a way of life . . . We must create visions, see at one and the same time both near and far. Interpreting time is our most important task."[3]

On the difference between men and women in business: "Men in business start at the top, they create positions for themselves then work down. Women work from the bottom up and value their workers."[4]

On one of her mentor's: "One of the people I admire the most is Coco Chanel. She built her dynasty up when she was 70 years old. Her story has been very inspiring, and I see a lot of commonalities in her approach. I respect the way that Chanel brought a great deal of discipline to a concept—all of the Chanel stores in the world are very consistent, and each season, a new story is told maintaining the consistency of the brand."

[1]Tommy Tabermann and Tuija Wuori-Tabermann, "Spirit & Life: Marimekko," Porvoo: WS Bookwell Oy, 2001, p. 151.

[2]Ibid., pp. 22–25.

[3]Ibid., p. 217.

[4]Hannah Booth, "Women: Flower power," The Guardian, September 5, 2005, http://www.guardian.co.uk/g2/story/0,,1562697,00.html, Accessed May 18, 2006.

| Exhibit 2 | Images of Marimekko |

Maija Isola—"Kivet" 1956

Maija Isola—"Unikko" 1964

Fujiwo Ishimoto

Jokapoika "Everyboy" shirt Created 1956 by Vuokko Nurmesniemi

"Tasaraita" —Created 1968 by Annika Rimala

Mari-essu—Created by Vuokko Nurmesniemi

"Doggy" Bag from Continuing Collection 2006/07

Fall/Winter 2006/07 Women's by Ritva Falla

Fall/Winter 2006/07 Men's by Matti Seppänen

SOURCE: Company files.

Exhibit 3 List of Select Historical Marimekko Designers

Maija Isola (1927–2001): School of Applied Art, textile department 1946–1949. Maija Isola joined Printex in 1949. In 1953, she began working on printed textiles for frocks (previously she was devoted to interior textiles only). In 1979, she began designing with her daughter Kristina Isola. Her textiles were said to form the foundation for the Marimekko style, as they featured oversized geometric patterns and bright colors.

Vuokko Eskolin-Nurmesniemi (1930): School of Applied Art, ceramics, 1948–1952. She was the chief designer for Marimekko's clothing and dress fabrics from 1953 to 1960, before she established her own firm in 1964. She was most well known for the "Piccolo" brushstroke patter and the "Everyboy" shirts (1956), one of Marimekko's best selling products as of 2006.

Annika Rimala (1936): School of Applied Art, graphics. Annika Rimala was Marimekko's dress designer from 1959 to 1982. In 1982, she founded her own shop. She designed the "Even Stripe" cotton jersey t-shirt that became a symbol of the new unisex trends in fashion.

Liisa Suvanto (1910–1983): Central School of Applied Art, 1937. Designer with Marimekko from 1963 to 1975. She was known for developing woolen garments and adding a new type of flowing line to Marimekko dresses.

Fujiwo Ishimoto (Born 1941): Studied design and graphics in Tokyo, Japan. Designer at Marimekko's subsidiary Decembre from 1970 to 1974. He has worked as a designer at Marimekko since 1974.

Katsuji Wakisaka (Born 1944): Kyoto School of Art and Design. Marimekko textile designer from 1968 to 1976. He was known for the use of bright colors and the melding of Japanese sensibilities into Marimekko. One of his most successful Marimekko designs was the Bo Boo in 1975 (a pattern with colorful cars and trucks).

Pentti Rinta (Born 1946): School of Applied Art, dress design, 1964–1969. Joined Marimekko as a designer in 1969. He was known for Marimekko's shirt-dresses and was the first to design Marimekko's first full men's outfit (the Kuski).

Marja Suna (Born 1934): School of Applied Art, 1951–1954. Joined Marimekko as head designer in 1979, after having worked in the industry for 25 years. She designed a wide range of blouses, gowns and tunics with a specialty in knit wear.

Ristomatti Ratia (Born 1941): Businessmen's Commercial College, 1961–1964, Leicester Polytechnic, interior decorating 1964–1967. He worked as a designer at Marimekko from 1973 to 1977 and led Marimekko Inc. in the United States from 1977 to 1984. He was known for developing families of products.

SOURCE: Compiled from "Phenomenon Marimekko," edited by Pekka Suhonen, Porvoo, WS Bookwell Oy, 2004, pp. 118–138.

Exhibit 4	Key Indicators

In EUR 000s	2001	2002	2003	2004	2005
Net Sales	42,003	49,318	56,587	64,592	67,219
Change in Net Sales	27.1%	17.4%	14.7%	14.1%	4.1%
Operating Profit	4,720	6,450	8,849	9,129	11,413
% of Net Sales	11.2%	13.1%	15.6%	14.1%	17.0%
Financial Income	51	66	67	51	87
Financial expenses	(380)	(356)	(379)	(228)	(153)
Profit before taxes	4,391	6,160	8,537	8,952	11,347
% of Net Sales	10.4%	12.5%	15.1%	13.9%	16.9%
Taxes	1,303	1,771	2,492	2,957	2,923
Profit after taxes	3,088	4,389	6,045	5,995	8,424
Balance Sheet Total	26,119	29,271	33,592	32,735	36,302
Internet-bearing liabilities	5,238	5,515	6,004	4,912	3,738
Shareholders' equity and reserves	15,239	17,887	21,653	19,733	24,137
Return on equity (ROE) %	21.5%	26.5%	30.6%	28.9%	38.4%
Return on investment (ROI) %	23.8%	29.5%	34.6%	35.0%	43.9%
Equity ratio %	58.3%	61.1%	64.5%	60.3%	66.5%
Gearing %	25.5%	11.2%	−11.8%	−13.9%	−15.6%
Gross investments	546	626	893	2,234	1,361
% of Net Sales	1.3%	1.3%	1.6%	3.5%	2.0%
Average personnel	317	333	356	375	371
Personnel at the end of the financial year	324	344	365	355	377

SOURCE: Marimekko Annual Report, December 31, 2005, p. 62.

NOTE: Operating profit in 2004 includes a non-recurring capital loss of EUR 1.235 million on the sale of shares of Grünstein Product Oy. 2004–2005 reflects a change in accounting standard to International Financial Reporting Standards (IFRS).

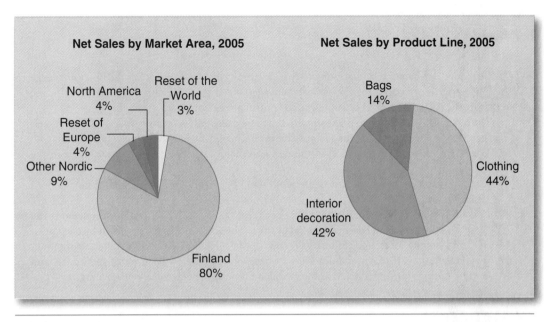

Net Sales by Market Area, 2005 — Finland 80%, Other Nordic 9%, Reset of Europe 4%, North America 4%, Reset of the World 3%

Net Sales by Product Line, 2005 — Clothing 44%, Interior decoration 42%, Bags 14%

SOURCE: Company documents.

| **Exhibit 5** | Marimekko Company Principles |

Company Principles

- Doing things together has been the most important.
- Employees are the most important capital of the company.
- Friendship has been more important than power in the working atmosphere.
- Creativity has been given the freedom, but it is also always followed by responsibility.
- One of our most important goals has been the everyday happiness of our personnel.

Kirsti Paakkanen's Management Principles

- Marimekko is an example: Whatever you do, act as an example. All your activities are followed. Your actions speak louder than your words. Today we also act as a trendsetter for our customers' consumer behavior. This is a great responsibility.
- Inspire: You must be the most enthusiastic "player" of your team. To be able to set an example to others, we need a team that pulls together. When such an exemplary group completes a project, all of its individual members and their achievements are evaluated and rewarded on the basis of the total result.

(Continued)

Exhibit 5 (Continued)

- Develop: Delegate decision-making to that organizational level which has the best knowledge and expertise required for the project. Managers need to define the direction. Trust in the team's work is necessary, but support and control are as important.
- Ascertain: It is your duty to make sure that each task that you delegate gets done. It is an excellent idea to have a team as broad as possible around you, but you always need to ascertain who is responsible for the realization of the task and make sure that it continues to move in the right direction.
- Commit yourself: When an issue is decided, stand behind it, even if you had originally been against it.
- Search: We shall look for innovation. We shall create a play with a script for every season. The script has to work from design to the retail store. The script needs to be known by everyone.
- Identify: Identify, locate and eliminate the sources of problems. Do not only cure the symptoms.
- Find out: Make sure that everybody knows where we are going. Make sure that you understand and that others understand and know at which point of the play we are proceeding.

SOURCE: Company files.

Exhibit 6 Board and Key Executives

Board of Directors

Kari Miettinen, Born 1951, B.Sc. (Econ), Authorized Public Accountant, Chairman of the Board since 1991.

Matti Kavetvuo, Born 1944, M.Sc. (Eng), B.Sc. (Econ), Member since 1997.

Kirsti Paakkanen, Born 1929, B.Sc. (Advertising/Marketing and Finnish Studies), Member since 1991.

Management Group

Kirsti Paakkanen, CEO/President. Since 1991.

Riitta Kojonen, Product Information. Employed by the company since 1986

Sirpa Loukamo, Product Development, Clothing. Employed by the company since 1973.

Piia Rossi, Retail Sales. Employed by the company since 1988.

Merja Puntila, Domestic wholesale. Employed by the company since 1970.

Päivi Lonka, Export and Licensing Sales. Employed by the company since 2004.

Helinä Uotila, Production and Purchases. Employed by the company since 1972.

Ritva Schoultz, Personnel Affairs. Employed by the company since 1982.

Marja Korkeela, Corporate Communications and Investor Relations. Employed by the company since 1999.

Thomas Ekström, Finance and Administration. Employed by the company since 2006.

SOURCE: Company files.

Exhibit 7 Marimekko Shop

Store Exterior   Store Interior

SOURCE: Company files.

Canadian Women Entrepreneurs: Pioneers of New Frontiers

Carol Stephenson

"Going into business for yourself, becoming an entrepreneur, is the modern-day equivalent of pioneering on the old frontier," according to entrepreneur and author Paula Nelson. I agree. It takes courage, know-how and perseverance to launch a business and make it succeed. Fortunately for our economy, Canada is home to more than 850,000 women entrepreneurs. Their numbers have increased more than 200 percent over the past 20 years. Today, they annually contribute more than $18 billion to our economy, employ more than 570,000 people, and continue to represent one of the fastest growing sectors. And even in these difficult economic times, they are discovering new markets, charting new territory and building new companies.

On February 17, more than 70 of these pioneers gathered at the Verity Women's Club in Toronto to share their ideas, perspectives and insights at the first Ivey Women Entrepreneurs Connect event. Designed to encourage networking and mentoring among entrepreneurs, the event recognizes that enterprising business people often uncover exciting new opportunities during an economic crisis. With the phenomenal growth

Reprint# 9B09TB13

in woman-owned businesses here in Canada, women will likely propel that trend forward.

But given their unique challenges, Canadian women entrepreneurs need inspiring role models and advisors. This special meeting provided just that with moderator Beth Wilson, Canadian Managing Partner at KPMG. Beth brought her extensive experience in advising private companies and entrepreneurs as the executive responsible for KPMG Enterprise. She was joined by three exemplary business builders on the panel.

For example, panellist and Ivey HBA graduate, Tara Longo, left her budding career as an investment banker to start up The Healthy Butcher with her partner Mario Fiorucci in 2005. In just three years, this purveyor of certified organic meat and fine gourmet foods has expanded to three locations in Toronto, gaining legions of dedicated patrons.

Panellist Mary Aitken, a "serial entrepreneur," moved to Canada from the U.K., first starting-up a courier company, then establishing an investment banking firm, and then cofounding Neo Material Technologies Inc., a high-tech company, headquartered in Toronto, that now has 1,300 employees in 16 locations across ten countries worldwide. In her latest venture, Mary took her intimate knowledge of the multi-tasking stress of most women's lives to develop the Verity Women's Club. It has since become the fastest growing private club in Toronto.

Arlene Dickinson, who is now recognized on the street through her appearances on the CBC television hit show *The Dragon's Den*, also joined the panel. Arlene built her Calgary-based marketing firm, Venture Communications, into a $40 million national company with offices in Toronto and Ottawa. Venture's core philosophy is that "marketing must deliver measurable business value." As such, marketing is about much more than advertising alone, but about the myriad of ways companies communicate with their customers. Today, Venture Communications is widely recognized as a thought leader in marketing accountability.

Arlene believes that what "drives a business forward are confidence in who you are and what you believe in and competency in terms of being able to deliver." However, many Canadian women struggle with expanding their businesses, not because they lack competency, but often because they lack the confidence and therefore the ambition to grow.

For example, Industry Canada recently reported that women-owned companies are less likely to grow beyond small- or medium-sized, when compared to companies owned by men. Research further shows that women-owned firms tend to grow slower than male owned companies, with only 37 percent of women-owned firms considered high-growth compared to 63 percent for men.

Both men and women business owners cite similar growth constraints, such as taxation, regulation and financing. However, women tend to see growth as less important, less likely and of lower value than men. And they view the personal demands related to growth as negative and stressful. Essentially, women believe that they lack the experience, family support and the peer support networks needed to grow. Consequently, 84 percent of women feel their businesses have reached a comfortable size and don't want to grow. Only 37 percent of men feel the same way.

All three panelists at the Ivey Entrepreneur event believe that networking is paramount to elevating these comfort levels. Mary says that women fail to network enough and must take the time to regularly interact with others. Arlene echoed that sentiment, emphasizing the importance of "putting yourself out there."

All the women on the panel—and several in the audience—also had stories about the difficulties of securing financing. After launching their first successful Healthy Butcher store, Tara said she and her partner wanted to expand but were seen as too small for bank financing and too risky for other investors. In the end, she and her partner funded the second and third locations completely on their own.

Despite these discussions about challenges, however, the exchanges underscored the tangible excitement of starting a new venture and being your own boss. The panellists and participants shared their insights about the best ways to engage an advisory board, the pros and cons of accessing venture capital and angel investment, and other ways to seek guidance.

Toward the end of the evening, the conversation came full circle with a vibrant discussion about mentorship. I agree with Arlene who observed: "Mentors are everywhere. I spoke with women tonight and found mentorship. You find mentorship the same way you find opportunity."

In other words, you find opportunity by consciously making an effort to discover it. And I believe that there are many new and exciting business possibilities for women entrepreneurs in the changing global economy. For example, the Internet not only offers access to new international markets, it is fundamentally transforming the practice of marketing. With the evolution from print and broadcasting media to interactive digital media, marketing is now a dialogue rather than a monologue. With digital interactivity, it has also become much more targeted and measurable.

In addition, new interactive applications are enabling companies to relate to their customers like never before. Customers are now co-creating new products and services with companies over the web. Through blogs and other social networking tools, many customers are also engaging regularly with the companies that carry their favourite brands. For enterprising women entrepreneurs, this presents a richness of innovative ways to cement customer loyalty and to capture new customers.

Today's tougher economic climate can also open up new opportunities because it is accelerating business life cycles. Firms suffering from low productivity can no longer hide their inefficiencies. There will be significant consolidation within some industries. And many established firms will be vulnerable to take-over. Entrepreneurs with their eyes open and their ears on the ground, however, will find more of the right acquisitions at the right price or new partners to strengthen their market positions.

At the same time, there are some very real impediments to growth created by our current economic crisis, particularly the credit crunch and a consumer lack of confidence. Add the mounting impact of technology and the increasing globalization of financial markets to these pressures. It's clear that a perfect storm has arrived. And like any storm, it is clearing away the old and making way for the new. But that's good news for entrepreneurs. As Peter Drucker once said: "The entrepreneur always searches for change, responds to it, and exploits it as an opportunity."

Bright new vistas resplendent in exciting opportunities are now opening up for Canadian women entrepreneurs. Ivey's goal is to help them to uncover these opportunities and exploit them to grow thriving companies. That's because we know that just like the pioneers of past centuries, Canadian women entrepreneurs can usher in a new era of prosperity for our country. And we want to encourage them to rise to that challenge like never before.

15

Culture and Leadership

Laura Guerrero

The University of Texas at El Paso

A second aspect of the India Way—holistic engagement with employees—was also readily seen in the culture of most Tata companies. The employment relationship was widely understood to be for the long term while still contingent upon satisfactory performance.

—Peter Cappelli, Harbir Singh,
Jitendra Singh, and Michael Useem[1]

Although there are no formal theories of global leadership, there are several ways in which culture affects leadership. As the trend toward globalization continues, there is increased frequency of contact between people of different cultures (Daft, 2011; DuBrin, 2010; Yukl, 2012).

Adler and Bartholomew (1992) suggest that global leaders need to develop the following cross-cultural competencies. First, leaders need to understand the business, political, and cultural environments worldwide. Second, leaders should learn to understand perspectives, tastes, trends, and technologies of many other cultures. Third, they need to learn to work with people from other cultures. Fourth, they should be able to adapt to living and communicating in other cultures. Fifth, leaders need to learn to relate to people from other cultures from a position of equality rather than a position of cultural superiority.

---

[1]Cappelli, Singh, Singh, and Useem (2010, p. 21).

✖ Culture, Diversity, Ethnocentrism, and Prejudice

Culture can be defined in several ways. Northouse (2013) defines *culture* as "the learned beliefs, values, rules, norms, symbols, and traditions that are common to a group of people" (p. 384).

Related to culture are terms such as *multicultural* and *diversity*. *Multicultural* refers to a way of seeing or doing things that takes into account more than one culture. A multicultural leader is one with the attitudes and skills to build relationships with and motivate followers who are diverse across lifestyles, social attitudes, race, ethnic background, gender, age, and education (DuBrin, 2010). *Diversity* refers to the existence of different cultures, ethnicities, socioeconomic levels, sexual orientations, or races within a group or organization (Yukl, 2012). Some people now use the term *inclusion* instead of *diversity* to highlight that organizations need to include as many diverse people as possible in organizations (DuBrin, 2010).

Related to leadership and culture are the concepts of ethnocentrism and prejudice. *Ethnocentrism* is "the tendency for individuals to place their own group (ethnic, racial, or cultural) at the center of their observations of others and the world" (Northouse, 2013, pp. 384–385). Although ethnocentrism is a natural tendency, it can act as an obstacle to effective leadership because it prevents leaders from understanding and respecting the views of others. Ethnocentrism creates challenges for minority leaders and subordinates (Daft, 2011).

Another natural tendency is that of holding prejudices. *Prejudice* can be a pejorative "attitude, belief, or emotion held by an individual about another individual or group that is based on faulty or unsubstantiated data" (Northouse, 2013, p. 385). Prejudice is often held against people or groups of people based on their race, gender, age, sexual preference, or other characteristics. Like ethnocentrism, prejudice prevents the leader from understanding and appreciating other people. Successful global leaders need to be able to recognize and minimize their own ethnocentrism and prejudice toward others, as well as manage others who may be ethnocentric or prejudiced.

✖ Cultural Dimensions

Many studies have addressed the issue of identifying the different dimensions of culture. One of the best-known studies is Hofstede's (1980, 2001). Hofstede identified five major cultural dimensions: power distance, uncertainty avoidance, individualism–collectivism, masculinity–femininity, and long-term/short-term orientation.

A more recent and comprehensive study by House et al. (2004), known as the GLOBE study, has identified nine cultural dimensions. The acronym *GLOBE* stands for Global Leadership and Organizational Behavior Effectiveness. These are the cultural dimensions identified by GLOBE researchers (Northouse, 2013; Yukl, 2012):

- *Uncertainty avoidance* refers to the degree to which a society depends on established social norms, rituals, rules, and procedures to avoid uncertainty.
- *Power distance* describes the extent to which members of society expect and are comfortable with power and wealth being distributed unequally.
- *Institutional collectivism* refers to the extent to which society encourages institutional or societal collective action as opposed to individual action.

- *In-group collectivism* refers to the extent to which individuals express pride, loyalty, and cohesiveness toward their organizations or families.
- *Gender egalitarianism* refers to the degree to which a society deemphasizes gender differences and supports gender equality.
- *Assertiveness* refers to the degree to which individuals in a society are assertive, confrontational, and aggressive in their interaction with others.
- *Future orientation* describes the extent to which individuals in a culture participate in future-oriented behaviors such as planning, investing, and delaying gratification.
- *Performance orientation* refers to the extent to which a society encourages and rewards individuals for superior performance.
- *Humane orientation* refers to the extent to which a society encourages and rewards individuals for being fair, philanthropic, generous, and kind to others.

The GLOBE study grouped the 62 countries into 10 clusters that share language, geography, religion, and historical connections. The regional clusters are as follows: Anglo, Latin Europe, Nordic Europe, Germanic Europe, Eastern Europe, Latin America, Middle East, Sub-Saharan Africa, Southern Asia, and Confucian Asia. The results of the study indicate that although scores *within a cluster* were correlated, they were unrelated to the scores in *different clusters.*

⬛ Leadership Behavior and Culture Clusters

The general purpose of the GLOBE study was to determine whether cultural differences were related to different leadership views (Yukl, 2012). GLOBE researchers used the implicit leadership theory (Lord & Maher, 1991), which states that people have implicit beliefs about the attributes and characteristics that distinguish leaders from nonleaders and effective leaders from ineffective ones. GLOBE researchers identified six global leadership behaviors (Northouse, 2013):

- Charismatic/value-based leadership is the ability to inspire, motivate, and expect superior performance from followers based on strongly held core values. This type of leadership is visionary, inspirational, self-sacrificing, trustworthy, and performance oriented.
- Team-oriented leadership places emphasis on team building and having a common purpose among members of the team. This type of leadership is collaborative, integrative, diplomatic, compassionate, and administratively competent.
- Participative leadership emphasizes the involvement of others in making and implementing decisions. This type of leadership is democratic.
- Humane-oriented leadership places emphasis on being supportive, considerate, compassionate, generous, and sensitive to other people.
- Autonomous leadership requires an independent and individualistic leadership style, which includes being self-directed and unique.
- Self-protective leadership refers to a leadership style that focuses on ensuring the safety and security of the leader and the group. This type of leadership is self-centered and interested in preserving the status of the group and the leader, even if it causes conflict with others.

The GLOBE researchers used these six global leadership behaviors to determine what leadership view each culture cluster held. Not surprisingly, it was found that different culture clusters had different leadership views. However, it was also found that certain leadership characteristics were valued across cultures, and some leadership attributes were found to be universally undesirable.

The universally desirable characteristics of an outstanding leader are trustworthiness, fairness, honesty, optimism, dynamism, dependability, intelligence, decisiveness, administrative skill, having foresight, planning ahead, being encouraging, building confidence, being motivational, being effective at bargaining, being a win-win problem solver, having communication skills, being informed, coordinating, being a team builder, and being excellence oriented (House et al., 2004).

The attributes that were found to be universally viewed as obstacles to effective leadership were noncooperativeness, irritability, ruthlessness, as well as being a loner, asocial, inexplicit, egocentric, and dictatorial (House et al., 2004).

The importance of considering culture in leadership is growing due to globalization and our increased interdependence with people of other cultures. Being aware that cultural differences affects the way people view the world and the way they act and communicate with others. It helps leaders be more effective because leaders who understand culture and its impact can adjust their leadership styles to be more effective with people of different cultural backgrounds (Daft, 2011; DuBrin, 2010; Yukl, 2012).

⬡ References

Adler, N. J., & Bartholomew, S. (1992). Managing globally competent people. *Academy of Management Executive*, 6, 52–65.

Cappelli, P., Singh, H., Singh, J., & Useem, M. (2010). *The India Way: How India's top business leaders are revolutionizing management*. Boston, MA: Harvard Business Press.

Daft, R. L. (2011). *The leadership experience* (5th ed.). Mason, OH: Thomson, South-Western.

DuBrin, A. (2010). *Leadership: Research findings, practice, and skills* (6th ed.). Mason, OH: South-Western/ Cengage.

Hofstede, G. (1980). *Culture's consequences: International differences in work-related values*. Beverly Hills, CA: Sage.

Hofstede, G. (2001). *Culture's consequences: Comparing values, behaviors, institutions, and organizations across nations*. Thousand Oaks, CA: Sage.

House, R. J., Hanges, P. J., Javidan, M., Dorfman, P. W., Gupta, V., & Associates. (2004). *Leadership, culture, and organizations: The GLOBE study of 62 societies*. Thousand Oaks, CA: Sage.

Lord, R., & Maher, K. J. (1991). *Leadership and information processing: Linking perceptions and performance*. Boston, MA: Unwin-Everyman.

Northouse, P. G. (2013). *Leadership: Theory and practice* (6th ed.). Thousand Oaks, CA: Sage.

Yukl, G. (2012). *Leadership in organizations* (8th ed.). Upper Saddle River, NJ: Pearson/Prentice Hall.

⬡ The Cases

Tata: Leadership With Trust

Tata Group is a large 140-year-old India based multinational enterprise. In fiscal year 2008–2009, Tata Group grossed approximately US$71 billion with almost 65% coming from sales outside of India. There are intricate connections between Tata's long-standing tradition of social responsibility and its profitability and competitiveness. The case explores Tata's value-creation, leadership, ethics, and sustainable development against the backdrop of rapid growth outside of India and evolving stakeholder expectations regarding Tata's involvement in corporate social responsibility initiatives.

Hebei Dawu Group: Building the First Family Business Constitution in China

Sun Dawu is the founder of Hebei Dawu Group. He has created the "Family Business Constitution" the first of its kind in China to date. The "Constitution" enabled the Group to handle several difficult challenges. Some of these were a request for a salary increase from a newly elected board member; the doubt some managers had about the "Constitution"; and suspicion from journalists and external experts concerning Dawu's elections. Sun Dawu wondered if it were possible to resolve the internal challenges he was facing and to assuage the external doubts about family business succession and governance. He wondered how he would do this in the system espoused by the "Family Business Constitution."

⌧ The Reading

Doing Business in India: Caveat Venditor

Business opportunities in India abound; but a lack of knowledge about the cultural norms and values of India can lead to less than best performance. This reading provides valuable information for doing business in India and along the way explains many cultural nuances. India is emerging as a major economic power. It is expected to rank fifth as the world's largest economy by 2025 and is the second fastest-growing economy with growth rates averaging almost 8%.

Tata: Leadership With Trust [1,2]

Oana Branzei

On February 22, 2010, Anant G. Nadkarni,[3] vice president of Group Corporate Sustainability and secretary of the Tata Council for Community Initiatives (TCCI), contemplated the past and future journey of sustainability in the Group. The Tata Group was long admired for its 140-year legacy[4] of selfless investment in the common good; some even argued that its main "business" had always been the empowerment of India's middle class.

Since Ratan N. Tata had become the chairman of the Group almost two decades back, the Group internationalized rapidly. Its financial performance stood out. The Tata Group now accounted for 5.43 per cent of the total market capitalization of the Bombay Stock Exchange

---

Version: 2011-02-14

[1]This case focuses on the sustainability strategy formulation and implementation as one part of strategic renewal of the Tata Group under the Chairmanship of Mr. Ratan Tata. A prior version of the case was featured in The Aspen Institute's 2010 Business & Society International MBA Case Competition.

[2]This case has been written on the basis of publicly available sources. The facts, interpretations and perspectives presented in this case are not necessarily those of the Tata Group, a specific Tata Company or any of its employees.

[3]Mr. Anant G. Nadkarni was the point person for the development of this case.

[4]http://www.tata.com/aboutus/sub_index.aspx?sectid=8hOk5Qq3EfQ=, accessed March 17, 2010.

and had "the distinction of having the highest market capitalisation among all business houses in [India], both in the public and private sectors."[5,6]

The Tata Group brought together 96 independent companies[7] across seven sectors: information systems and communications, engineering, materials, services, energy, consumer products and chemicals. The largest and most well-known Tata companies included Tata Steel, Tata Motors, Tata Consultancy Services (TCS), Tata Power, Tata Chemicals, Tata Tea, Indian Hotels and Tata Communications.[8] There were 24 publicly listed Tata enterprises[9] with a combined market capitalization of some $60 billion and a shareholder base of 3.5 million (see Exhibit 1). The remaining 72 were privately held.

From 2008 to 2009, Tata companies grossed US$70.8 billion in revenues (around Rs325,334 crore); 64.7 per cent of the Group's revenues came from outside India. With approximately 357,000 employees worldwide, the Group was India's largest business conglomerate—an indigenous multinational that now spanned 54 countries across six continents and exported products and services to 120 nations.[10]

The Group's stellar performance during the 2008 recession, which wreaked havoc on many exchanges and saw the stocks of many other global giants tumbling, also drew the attention of global investors. On December 29, 2009, the Tata Group topped the economic value creation charts (see Exhibits 2 and 3):

> As the market picked up the pieces from the global meltdown [. . .] thirty-one companies from the salt-to software conglomerate saw their combined market capitalization soar by more than Rs 2 lakh crore,[11] or by over 150%, in 2009 (up to December 24, 2009). The jewel in the Tata [Group] crown, Tata Consultancy Services, had a rocking year, with its M-cap trebling, by 213%.[12]

Over the next three days, 62 senior executives from 38 Tata companies would come together

---

[5]Tata group website, www.tata.com/htm/Group_Investor_GroupFinancials.htm#group, accessed March 4, 2010.

[6]On September 5, 2005, the Tata group had the highest market capitalization among Indian groups (Rs150,900 crore or US$33,212 million), followed by the Mukesh Ambani group with Rs102,400 crore (US$22,538 million), Aditya Birla Group at RS34,500 crore (US$7,593 million) and the Anil Ambani group at Rs20,600 crore (US$4,533 million), http://www.indianmba .com/Newsflash/News272/news272.html, accessed March 17, 2010.

[7]As of March 3, 2010. Each of the Tata companies was independently run and had its own board of directors and shareholders.

[8]Tata Steel became the sixth-largest steel maker in the world after it acquired Corus. Tata Motors is among the top five commercial vehicle manufacturers in the world and has recently acquired Jaguar and Land Rover. TCS is a leading global software company, with delivery centres in the United States, United Kingdom, Hungary, Brazil, Uruguay and China, besides India. Tata Tea is the second-largest branded tea company in the world, through its U.K.-based subsidiary Tetley. Tata Chemicals is the world's second largest manufacturer of soda ash and Tata Communications is one of the world's largest wholesale voice carriers. Source: www.tata.com/aboutus/sub_index.aspx?sectid=8hOk5Qq3EfQ=, accessed March 3, 2010.

[9]CMC, Indian Hotels Company, Mount Everest Mineral Water, Nelco, Rallis India, Tata Chemicals, Tata Coffee, Tata Communications, Tata Consultancy Services, Tata Elxsi, Tata Investment Corporation, Tata Metaliks, Tata Motors, Tata Power, Tata Sponge Iron, Tata Steel, Tata Tea, Tata Teleservices (Maharashtra), Tayo Rolls, Tinplate Company of India, Titan Industries, Trent, TRF, Voltas. www.tata.com/investor/inside.aspx?artid=XXajrQvzvCM=, accessed March 3, 2010.

[10]As of March 3, 2010.

[11]1 lakh=100,000; 1 Crore=10 million; the amount is equivalent to US$43,898.15 million, http://www.kshitij.com/utilities/ LnCtoMnB.shtml, accessed March 16, 2010. Current market capitalization by company is available at http://money.rediff .com/companies/market-capitalisation, last accessed March 17, 2010.

[12]"Tata group tops wealth creation charts in 2009," *The Morung Express*, December 29, 2009, www.morungexpress.com/business/ 40535.html, accessed January 27, 2010.

for the eleventh time in only nine years for a corporate sustainability workout (see Exhibit 4). This time, they would grapple with the gnawing question of whether, and how, Tata companies' sustainability-oriented values and practices might influence the Tata Group's economic success both in India and globally.

The Agenda

The February 2010 workout had an ambitious agenda: the 62 executives in attendance would discuss whether and how sustainability issues, metrics, processes and outcomes could (or should) influence the strategy of the Group in the decade ahead. Nadkarni hoped that, through deep reflection on the meaning and role of sustainability within the Group, in India, and globally, these leaders could evolve a new level of collective understanding about the relationship between purpose and profit.

The latest Group-wide working definition of CSR read:

> Corporate Sustainability (CS) is integral to value-creation in our businesses through the enhancement of human, natural and social capital complementing their economic and financial growth in order to give the enterprise an enduring future and also help create and serve a larger purpose, at all times. It facilitates accountability to all stakeholders as a systemic practice.[13]

The meaning and role of sustainability were changing, both in India and abroad. In an effort to promote both greater understanding of CSR and greater accountability and transparency, the 2010 World Economic Forum, held in Davos, Switzerland, had just unveiled second generation metrics for corporate sustainability. General Electric topped the list of the "*Global 100 Most Sustainable Corporations in the World*."[14] Starbucks placed 48th. Tata Steel, the only one in the Group to make this list, ranked 90th.[15]

Globally, investments in corporate social and environmental responsibility took a hit during the 2008–2009 global recession. A Booz & Company survey conducted in December 2008 polled 828 corporate managers—both in developed markets such as the United States and Germany and emerging markets such as Brazil and India. "At a time when many companies are fighting to stay alive, initiatives aimed at bettering the environment and local communities inevitably will be delayed, respondents said."[16] On average, 28 per cent of respondents at financially strong companies predicted that CSR agendas in their industries will be affected by the economic downturn. This percentage was higher for industrial goods manufacturing respondents (38 per cent) and consumer goods respondents (40 per cent); 47 per cent of the respondents in energy and 51 per cent of the respondents in transportation said their CSR agendas would be delayed.[17]

The Tata Group continued to support a broad range of initiatives, from emergency help and community projects to nation-building efforts. Some wondered whether the Tata

---

[13]Excerpt from the 2009 TBEM manual, Public Presentation by Anant G. Nadkarni, used with permission.

[14]The list is available at www.global100.org/annual-reviews/2010-global-100-list.html, accessed March 3, 2010.

[15]Paul Hawken, a globally-respected sustainability guru, was unimpressed: "The list does not advance sustainability because it cannot define, measure, or recognize it." Bill Baue, "Corporate Sustainability Ranking Gets a Face Lift," *Business Ethics*, February 3, 2010, http://business-ethics.com/2010/02/03/0949-corporate-sustainability-ranking-gets-a-face-lift/, accessed March 3, 2010.

[16]"Recession Response: Why Companies are Making the Wrong Moves," *Booz & Company*, www.booz.com/media/uploads/Recession_Response.pdf, accessed March 6, 2010.

[17]CSR International study, www.csrinternational.org/?p=1821, accessed March 6, 2010.

Group's profitability and competitiveness were a direct consequence of its long-standing tradition of social responsibility or a mere coincidence. Others speculated that recent economic gains might have been even greater in the absence of such a strong social mandate.

Purpose[18]

Since the creation of the Group in 1868, its purpose was clear: the Tata Group's founder Jamsetji N. Tata predicated any business activity on its payoffs to society. He stated that "In a free enterprise, the community is not just another stakeholder in business, but is in fact the very purpose of its existence."[19]

The Group had made history multiple times by spearheading several labour welfare reforms in India—all ahead of national legislation and many years before adoption in other western nations; for example, the eight-hour working day was introduced in 1912, leave with pay in 1920, maternity benefits in 1928 and the retirement gratuity in 1937 (see Exhibit 5).

The Tata name, long synonymous with India's industrialization, increasingly stood for social innovation. In India, the Group had pioneered several industries of national importance: steel, power, hospitality and airlines. Tata Consultancy Services (TCS), for example, had been India's first software company. Tata Motors had introduced India's first indigenously developed car back in 1998.

More recently, the Group had received global accolades for Tata Motors' Nano (the People's Car), a safe, low-cost and affordable transportation solution for India's middle class; electric versions of the Nano were expected to arrive both in Europe and the United States by 2012. Tata Chemicals' Swach was another remarkable example of social innovation, offering base-of-pyramid consumers a sustainable and affordable solution to the persistent problem of water born-disease, the single greatest threat to global health (see Exhibit 6).

The Tata Brand

The goodwill generated by these social initiatives helped differentiate the Tata brand refreshed and promoted through the initiatives recommended by Ratan N. Tata soon after he took over from J.R.D. Tata on March 23, 1991. This "unified brand, with a common logo"[20] came with a set of operating requirements and a code of conduct embodying the Tata Group's long standing values. Continued use and display of the Tata brand by a Tata company required that both the operating requirements and the code of conduct were upheld. Not all 96 companies used the Tata brand.

Recently valued at US$9.92 billion by Brand Finance, a U.K.-based consultancy firm, the Tata brand ranked 51st among the world's Top 100 brands.[21] In addition, *BusinessWeek* magazine ranked Tata 13th among the "25 Most Innovative Companies" list and the Reputation Institute recently rated the Group 11th on its list of the world's most reputable companies.[22]

Profits With Purpose

Growth

India's growth was driven by sectors such as mining and quarrying, manufacturing, electricity, gas and water supply, construction, trade, hotels,

---

[18]An interactive history of the group is available online at www.tata.com/htm/heritage/HeritageOption1.html, accessed March 7, 2010.

[19]Company information available at www.tata.com/aboutus/sub_index.aspx?sectid=8hOk5Qq3EfQ=, accessed March 3, 2010.

[20]R. M. Lala. *The Creation of Wealth: The Tatas from the 19th to the 21st Century,* Penguin Books India, 2004, p. 269.

[21]www.tata.com/aboutus/sub_index.aspx?sectid=8hOk5Qq3EfQ=, accessed March 3, 2010.

[22]Ibid.

transportation and communication, financing insurance, real estate and business services and community, social and personal services.[23] Tata companies ranked first or second in all these industries.

Goldman Sachs predicted that India could sustain an eight per cent growth rate until 2020—poised to overtake the United Kingdom as the world's fifth-largest economy by the middle of the next decade. India's GDP would also soon surpass Italy and France (around 2015). India's gross domestic product (GDP) had grown by 6.7 per cent from 2008 to 2009 and was estimated to grow 7.2 per cent from 2009 to 2010. At the predicted pace, the GDP per capita would quadruple from 2007 to 2020. Within 12 years, Indians would consume about five times more cars and three times more crude oil.[24]

Taking advantage of India's rapid growth required responsible leadership, as Ratan N. Tata emphasized:

> I think it is wrong for a company in India to operate in exactly the same way, without any additional responsibilities, as if it were operating in the United States, let's say . . . Companies that are not good corporate citizens— that don't hold to standards and that allow the environment and the community to suffer—are really criminals in today's world.

Unlike their western counterparts, Tata leaders felt that social responsibility was part of their job:

While today eyebrows are being raised about corporates doing social work, the Tata Group feels it is the need of the hour. Thus, where in the West companies are doubtful of spending the shareholders money and corporates are considering discontinuing Corporate Social Responsibility [. . .] which is fine for them, but not for a country like India. The governments of the western world have a strong social security net so corporates can concentrate on making profits and paying taxes regularly but in this regard India still lags behind. We are far away from reaching that phase of economic development where government is solely responsible for the basic needs of the public. We don't have a social security, adequate health and education services. So till then corporate houses should fill the gaps.[25]

Globalization

Back in 2005, Ratan N. Tata had stated that:

> One hundred years from now, I expect the Tatas to be much bigger than it is now. More importantly, I hope the Group comes to be regarded as being the best in India. . . best in the manner in which we operate, best in the products we deliver, and best in our value systems and ethics. Having said that, I hope that a hundred years from now we will spread our wings far beyond India.[26]

---

[23]"India's GDP estimated to grow by 7.2% in 2009–10," *NetIndian*, February 8, 2010, http://netindian.in/news/2010/02/08/0005237/indias-gdp-estimated-grow-72-2009-10, accessed March 7, 2010.

[24]"In 10 years, India's GDP will surpass UK's," *Rediff*, January 23, 2007, www.rediff.com/money/2007/jan/23india.htm, accessed March 7, 2010.

[25]Dr. J. J. Irani, Director of Tata Sons, www.tatainc.com/GUI/Content.aspx?Page=TataCompaniesArchives20050316A, accessed March 7, 2010.

[26]www.woopidoo.com/biography/ratan-tata/index.htm, accessed March 7, 2010.

By 2010, two-thirds of the Group's revenues came from overseas. The Group's rapid internationalization and high-profile acquisitions had improved the Tata companies' top- and bottom-lines[27] (see Exhibit 1). Tata Steel's US$11 billion acquisition of Corus in 2007 was at the time "the biggest deal ever from an emerging market."[28] In 2008, Tata Motors acquired Jaguar for US$2.5 billion. TCS acquired Citi's interest in Citigroup Global Services Limited (CGSL) for another US$2.5 billion over a period of 9.5 years.[29]

The Tata Group was now focusing on several markets of strategic importance in the years ahead—in alphabetical order: Brazil, Canada, China, the countries of the Gulf Cooperation Council (the UAE, Saudi Arabia, Oman, Bahrain, Kuwait and Qatar), Germany, the Netherlands, South Africa, Sri Lanka, Thailand, the United Kingdom, the United States and Vietnam.[30]

Some argued that global expansion could change the balance between economic returns and social responsibility. When asked back in 2007 whether the Group would extend its India-based social and environmental spending internationally, Ratan N. Tata himself was not sure. He felt that the Group could become a more conventional company—"But you would have great discontent."[31]

In the past, Group leaders had treated social initiatives as important investments, some paying off over 20 to 25 years, others taking effect across generations. But the Group's growing reliance on foreign investors, known for their emphasis on short-term returns, could change that. Some warned that globalization may even be at odds with Group's past focus on community initiatives. "In today's competitive world, the Group's community-oriented generosity seems as outmoded and unrealistic as the 'company town' paternalism of Andrew Carnegie and Henry Ford," explains Ann Graham in a review of the Group's global strategy.[32]

Leadership[33]

Competing for economic prominence in the global marketplace renewed the importance of the Group's senior executives' "two-fold ability to lead people morally and effectively"[34]:

The greatest mistake leaders can make is to assume that results alone matter, that morality and goodness do not count. On the contrary, as amorality becomes more rampant, as the heart of darkness expands, the natural human instinct is a craving towards light. We need results and we need them desperately—but with goodness and moral purpose.[35]

---

[27]Bruce Einhorn, "Jaguar Starts Making Money for Tata Motors," March 1, 2010, www.businessweek.com/globalbiz/blog/eyeonasia/archives/2010/03/jaguar_starts_m.html, accessed March 3, 2010.

[28]Tarun Khanna, "Tata-Corus: India's New Steel Giant," February 14, 2007, available at http://hbswk.hbs.edu/item/5634.html, accessed March 3, 2010.

[29]TCS press release, October 8, 2008, www.tcs.com/news_events/press_releases/Pages/TCS-To-Acquire-Citigroup-Global-Services.aspx, accessed March 3, 2010.

[30]www.tata.com/tataworldwide/index.aspx?sectid=mjDAQlgaR/s=, accessed March 7, 2010.

[31]www.strategy-business.com/article/10106?gko=74e5d, accessed March 7, 2010 (p. 11 of the printed version).

[32]Ann Graham, "Too Good to Fail," February 23, 2010, *Strategy+Business*, www.strategy-business.com/article/10106?gko=74e5d, p. 4, accessed March 10, 2010.

[33]The lives and achievements of Jamsetji Tata, J.R.D. Tata and Naval Tata are chronicled at www.tata.com/aboutus/articles/inside.aspx?artid=ud3kc0d8Nds=&sid=1d95UDdxCdM=, accessed March 7, 2010. Short tributes are available at www.tata.co.in/company/Articles/inside.aspx?artid=YJbf7uiUY0M=, accessed March 7, 2010.

[34]Ibid.

[35]Ibid.

Such dual leadership capabilities were tacit and deeply personal, inspired and rooted in the legacy of four generations of leaders. But there were few frameworks—within the Group or elsewhere—that could articulate how companies developed such capabilities, or how they could foster them moving forward.

Four Generations

In 2010, the current chairman, Ratan N. Tata was honoured "for being exemplary in corporate integrity, social consciousness and responsible capitalism—in a nutshell, for serving as the spokesperson for integrity."[36] In 2007, he had received the Carnegie Medal of Philanthropy,[37] considered the Nobel Prize of that genre. That same year, the 69 year old leader ranked 23rd in *Fortune* magazine's list of the most influential business people on earth. This recognition came, in part, for his work to restructure one of India's largest business conglomerates from a domestic player into a congregation of world-leading companies, and in part for his role model of inclusive and sustainable corporate leadership.[38]

His predecessor, J.R.D. Tata, had poignantly argued that: "[N]o success or achievement in material terms is worthwhile unless it serves the needs or interests of the country and its people and is achieved by fair and honest means."[39] All the Group leaders related back to the core value of the Group's founder: "We do not claim to be more unselfish, more generous or more philanthropic than other people. But we think we started on sound and straightforward business principles, considering the interests of the shareholders our own, and the health and welfare of the employees the sure foundation of our prosperity."[40]

Jamsetji Tata's ideals had become ingrained in the Tata culture and were stated explicitly on the company site: "Tata companies are building multinational businesses that will achieve growth through excellence and innovation, while balancing the interests of shareholders, employees and civil society."[41]

Succession

Ratan N. Tata aspired that the Tata Group would become:

> [T]he predominant business house in India, which amidst fast-eroding values, will continue to stand out as being a well-integrated, growth-oriented Group with market leadership, operating with a great level of integrity, a great value system and uncompromising in its goal to achieve results without partaking in corruption, bribery and/or political influence.[42]

But tenure was projected to end in 2012 and a formal search for a successor was already

---

[36]John Manley, former deputy prime minister and now head of the Ottawa-based Canadian Council of Chief Executives, www.thestar.com/opinion/article/771021–bata-brings-tata-to-toronto, accessed March 6, 2010.

[37]2007 Carnegie Medal of Philanthropy Winners, http://carnegie.org/publications/carnegie-reporter/single/view/article/item/209/, accessed March 6, 2010.

[38]Clay Chandler, http://money.cnn.com/galleries/2007/fortune/0711/gallery.power_25.fortune/23.html, accessed March 6, 2010.

[39]From a letter dated September 13, 1965, addressed by J.R.D. Tata to K.C.Bhansali, a schoolteacher in Calcutta. Quote from Appendix C, in R.M. Lala, *The Creation of Wealth: The Tatas from the 19th to the 21st Century*, 3rd edition, Penguin Books India, 2004, p. 277.

[40]R.M. Lala book, *The Creation of Wealth: The Tatas from the 19th to the 21st Century*, 3rd edition, Penguin Books India, 2004, p. 126.

[41]Company information available at www.tata.com/aboutus/sub_index.aspx?sectid=8hOk5Qq3EfQ=, accessed March 3, 2010.

[42]Ratan N. Tata's Epilogue to the R.M. Lala book, *The Creation of Wealth: The Tatas from the 19th to the 21st Century*, 3rd edition, Penguin Books India, 2004, pp. 271–272.

underway. When asked by the *Wall Street Journal* in November 2009 who may follow at the helm of the Group, Ratan N. Tata had answered:

> It would certainly be easier if that candidate were an Indian national. But now that 65 per cent of our revenues come from overseas, there could also be an expatriate sitting in that position with justification, now that we are a company that has global reach and global presence.[43]

Ratan Tata's also emphasized that future generations of Tata leaders ought to sustain Group's long-standing tradition of integrity and responsibility:

> I would hope that my successors would never compromise and turn to soft options to meet their ends, and never allow the Tata Group to join the growing number of companies in India which have shed their values, forgotten about their integrity and closed their eyes to maintaining ethical standards.[44]

Restructuring

Ratan N. Tata transformed the loose confederation of over 250 autonomous companies he inherited from his predecessor into a synergistic whole, with a unified direction. Under his chairmanship, the parent company began searching for a new way to harness collective synergies among the Tata companies:

> Broadly we agreed that the Tata Group should be restructured to become more competitive, to provide better returns to the shareholders, to be more nimble-footed or more proactive to the changing scene than it had been in the past. All of which would reflect positively on the fast changing scene in India—when India would be open to competition from both within and overseas—when the consumer would have far greater choice, and when the shareholder would demand a good return on his investment.[45]

He crafted a Group-level coordination structure by identifying a set of executive directors of Tata Sons who would oversee the performance of operating companies, initiate mergers and acquisitions or divestitures to strengthen the Group's market-dominance in key sectors.[46] This Group Corporate Centre (GCC) reviewed broad policy issues relating to the growth of Tata companies. The GCC also provided advisory services to Tata companies, reviewed their business portfolios when required and played a key role in protecting and promoting the Tata brand in India and across the globe.

Prompted by its rapid internationalization, which required greater professionalization and formalization,[47] the Group adopted a more systematic, unified Tata approach to CSR. The

---

[43]"My successor may be from outside India: Ratan Tata," *Business Standard*, November 19, 2009, www.business-standard.com/india/news/my-successor-may-beoutside-india-ratan-tata/376924/, accessed March 7, 2010.

[44]Ratan N. Tata's Epilogue to the R.M. Lala book, *The Creation of Wealth: The Tatas from the 19th to the 21st Century*, 3rd edition, Penguin Books India, 2004, p. 272.

[45]Ibid, p. 268.

[46]Two distinct strategic moves paved the way for Ratan Tata's steps to professionalize the management of the group. First, he introduced a mandatory retirement age for executives, which enabled the group to attract and develop new talent. Second, he increased Tata Son's personal stake in the business from 1.7 percent to 26 percent, which prevented take-overs by third parties.

[47]From an interview with Ratan Tata, describing the depth and breadth of the restructuring effort in late 1990s. Source: www.rediff.com/money/2005/mar/17inter.htm, accessed March 3, 2010.

idea of explicitly tracking social impact originated in the early 1990s, so that "future generations in Tata will recognize these traditions as
being critical to the fabric and the fundamentals
on which our Group was built and grew so successfully for over a century."[48]

Two new units were formed (see Exhibit 7):
The Tata Council for Community Initiatives
(TCCI) reported to GCC team member Kishor
Chaukar and was the steward of the Group's 140
year old commitment to the communities in
which it operated. Tata Quality Management
Services (TQMS) reported to GCC team member Dr. J.J. Irani and was the steward of the Tata
brand and the promoter of quality management
practices within the Group.[49] Both TCCI and
TQMS followed the ethical roadmap provided
by the Tata Code of Conduct,[50] which governed
the conduct and activities of all the companies
using the Tata name.

TCCI and TQMS had complementary mandates. TCCI promoted voluntary activities and
supported long-term investments in employees
and communities. TCCI's charter embraced
"social development, environmental management,
biodiversity restoration, climate change initiatives and employee volunteering."[51] TQMS
implemented and evaluated mandatory management processes, expected to drive performance
efficiencies. TQMS designed, administered and
monitored the performance of Tata companies
across seven categories: leadership; strategic planning; customer and market focus; measurement,
analysis and knowledge management; human
resource focus; process management; and business
results.[52] TCCI worked with TQMS to institutionalize sustainability practices within the Group.

Pillars

TCCI and TQMS had been systematically tracking
corporate social responsibility (CSR) for the largest companies in the Group since 2003.[53] Several
Tata companies were now voluntarily reporting
A-level compliance with the Global Reporting
Initiative (GRI) standards.[54] These two units complemented the Group's long-standing philanthropic (Tata Trusts) and its emergency relief
commitments (Tata Relief Committee).[55]

---

[48]http://www.intuitive-connections.net/2010/tata.html, accessed March 17, 2010.

[49]Since the mid-1990s, the Brand Equity and Business Promotion (BEBP) agreement, a comprehensive contract between the group and independent companies, laid down the conditions that a company had to comply with to earn the privilege of being labelled a Tata enterprise. "Companies that sign the BEBP agreement are obliged to abide by the Tata code of conduct, a set of principles that guides and governs the way a Tata enterprise runs its business. The agreement also enjoins the group to follow practices that enhance the Tata brand, and invest in building the Tata brand equity. BEBP signatories can access established group capabilities in areas such as strategic management and human resources." www.tata.com/aboutus/articles/inside .aspx?artid=FcYtZALTmz4=, accessed March 8, 2010.

[50]Tata Code of Conduct 2008, www.tatainteractive.com/pdf/TIS_TCOC.pdf, accessed March 3, 2010.

[51]"Tata Council for Community Initiatives," *www.tata.com/article.aspx?artid=lV/tF5W9eeQ=*, accessed September 6, 2008.

[52]http://www.tata.com/aboutus/articles/inside.aspx?artid=OMSlPyjJp68=#tq, accessed March 18, 2010.

[53]Oana Branzei and Anant G. Nadkarni, "The Tata Way: Evolving and Executing Sustainable Business Strategies," *Ivey Business Journal*, March/April 2008, www.iveybusinessjournal.com/article.asp?intArticle_ID=750, accessed March 3, 2010.

[54]A TCS slide presentation is available online at www.slideshare.net/nasscom/pankaj-baliga-vp-and-head-global-corporate-sustainability-tcs, accessed March 3, 2010.

[55]Since the mid-1990s, the Brand Equity and Business Promotion (BEBP) agreement, a comprehensive contract between the group and independent companies, laid down the conditions that a company had to comply with to earn the privilege of being labelled a Tata enterprise. "Companies that sign the BEBP agreement are obliged to abide by the Tata code of conduct, a set of principles that guides and governs the way a Tata enterprise runs its business. The agreement also enjoins the group to follow practices that enhance the Tata brand, and invest in building the Tata brand equity. BEBP signatories can access established group capabilities in areas such as strategic management and human resources." www.tata.com/aboutus/articles/inside .aspx?artid=FcYtZALTmz4=, accessed March 8, 2010.

Tata Trusts

Between eight and 14 per cent of the Group's net profits were distributed, annually, to social causes through the Tata trusts. Tata Group's trusteeship structure channeled about two-thirds—recently 65.8 per cent[56]—of the equity of Tata Sons (the majority stakeholder for the Group) to the Tata trusts. Over 75 per cent of the trust's funds accrued from dividends on the shares it owns in Tata Sons, one of the Tata Group's promoter companies (see Exhibit 7). The remainder came from statutory investments.[57]

The Tata trusts had laid the early foundation for indigenous scientific and technological manpower in India, funding the Tata Institute of Social Sciences in 1936, India's first cancer hospital in 1941 and the Tata Institute of Fundamental Research in 1945. Currently, there were three main trusts, each with a different focus area.

The first trust, the JN Tata Endowment, had been set up in 1892 by the founder of the Tata Group, Jamsetji Tata, to encourage young people to take up higher studies at some of the best universities in the world. When the Group founder, Jamsetji Tata, first gave grants to two female doctors to study abroad and specialize in gynecology in 1892, he famously said: "I can afford to give, but I prefer to lend,"[58] so that the money returned could thus benefit many others. With this reinvestment philosophy, by 2009, the trust had disbursed RS15.72 million (US$346 million),[59] servicing 120 scholars every year.[60]

The second trust, the Sir Ratan Tata Trust, was established in 1919. It managed Rs1,533.64 million (US$33.835 million) during 2008–09. Program grants across all five thematic areas[61] accounted for about 83 per cent, with the rest disbursed as endowments (Rs55 million) and individual grants (Rs181 million).[62]

The third trust, the Sir Dorabji Tata Trust,[63] was established in 1932. It disbursed Rs200 crore[64] (US$44 million) in 2008–2009. Sixty five per cent went to NGOs working in the fields of health, education, livelihoods, social development and natural resources management.

The Sir Dorabji Tata Trust had been working with over 700 NGOs across the country.[65] It had more partners than the Ford Foundation but had adopted a different model, which shunned the spotlight:

> . . . anybody who is anybody in the civil society NGO sector has some association with the trust. It is through these partners that our money goes far and wide, that it gets extended into the rural countryside and benefits a larger number of people. We want the NGOs we work with to get empowered, to stand on their feet and become strong

[56]www.tata.com/ourcommitment/sub_index.aspx?sectid=i6eUTkvtRos=, accessed March 4, 2010.

[57]www.dorabjitatatrust.org/about/Overview_financials.aspx, accessed March 3, 2010.

[58]R.M. Lala, *Beyond the Last Blue Mountain: A Life of J.R.D. Tata (1904–1993)*, 2nd edition, Penguin Books India, 1993, p. 301.

[59]http://www.dorabjitatatrust.org/about/pdf/08-09/Annual_Report_77.pdf, accessed March 17, 2010.

[60]http://www.tata.com/company/releases/inside.aspx?artid=NHNtCDOEih4=, accessed March 10, 2010.

[61]The five thematic areas were: rural livelihoods and communities; education; health; enhancing civil society and governance; and arts and culture. http://www.srtt.org/about_us/overview.htm, accesses March 28, 2010.

[62]www.srtt.org/about_us/ops_fin_disbursement.htm#03, accessed March 3, 2010.

[63]"Sir Dorabji Tata put all his wealth, estimated at Rs 10 million into a Trust for use, 'without any distinction of place, nationality or creed,' for the advancement of learning and research, the relief of distress, and other charitable purposes." Source: www.dorabjitatatrust.org/, accessed March 3, 2010.

[64]1 crore = 10 million.

[65]www.tata.com/ourcommitment/articles/inside.aspx?artid=nMP7URJ8ZTY=, accessed March 4, 2010.

enough to deliver with confidence. By empowering them we are actually helping the communities they are involved with, as well as ourselves.[66]

This was changing, however. Strategic philanthropy was replacing the "numerous [but] diffuse ideas coming in from partners."[67] The Sir Dorabji Tata Trust recently refocused on actively championing specific themes in order to create a critical mass in neglected but key areas, such as urban poverty.[68]

Tata Relief Committee

The Tata Relief Committee (TRC) focused on emergency charity—in India and elsewhere—by mobilizing emergency funds in response to natural and man-made catastrophes. These relief and rehabilitation activities were orchestrated as hybrids between typical emergency responses (i.e. floods, cyclones, tsunamis, earthquakes, terrorist events) and corporate-run initiatives.

TRC was often one of the first organizations to step in after natural disasters, assisting displaced people with basic supplies, and often helping communities rebuild basic infrastructure in the aftermath of disruption.[69] For example, in December 2004, TRC mobilized a 55-member team pooled from different Tata Group companies, set up a base camp at Tiruneveli, distributed relief material to nearly 4,000 families, and provided shelter to over 1,500 families affected by the Tamil Nadu tsunami.[70] Similarly, TRC coordinated donations and volunteers from Tata Steel to provide emergency assistance in the West Bengal region after cyclone Aila ravaged 54 villages, displacing 4.2 million people:

> Relief materials to the tune of 1,000 tarpaulin sheets, medicines worth Rs80,000 and 3,000 packets of consumables and other essential items were distributed. Each of these packets contained 3.5 kg of rice, 1 kg pulses, 2 kg chira, salt, candles and matchboxes. Medical aid has also been reached out to other villages, where it was deemed necessary. Bottled water was also provided to villagers. In addition, bleaching powder and other necessary items were also supplied.[71]

TRC efforts sometimes spearheaded new trusts—for example, Ratan N. Tata and the Taj Hotels set up a new trust to benefit those killed during the 2008 terrorist attacks in Mumbai.[72,73] To some outsiders, such magnanimity seemed well beyond the corporate mandate.

---

[66]Sir Dorabji Tata Trust Managing trustee A.N. Singh, www.tata.com/ourcommitment/articles/inside.aspx?artid=nMP7UR J8ZTY=, accessed March 4, 2010.

[67]Ibid.

[68]The trust invested in rural livelihoods to alleviate migration and in industrialization activities that created local jobs in rural areas.

[69]http://tata.com/company/releases/inside.aspx?artid=9gR6dMkKBuA=, accessed March 17, 2010.

[70]http://tata.com/company/releases/inside.aspx?artid=rFJRPZ2Sgbo=, accessed March 17, 2010.

[71]http://tata.com/company/Media/inside.aspx?artid=ZC0ZanBAndc=, accessed March 17, 2010.

[72]Robert Mackey, "Tracking the Mumbai Attacks," http://thelede.blogs.nytimes.com/2008/11/26/tracking-the-mumbai-attacks/, accessed March 6, 2010.

[73]"to provide immediate relief to all victims of the recent attack, including to the families of those who were killed—be it the general public, the security forces, employees of the Taj or employees of other establishments affected by the terrorists. This Trust will continue to discharge its mandate in the coming years, specifically covering relief to victims of sudden acts of violence, natural disasters, and other tragic events that inflict damage to life and property," www.sajaforum.org/2008/12/mumbai-attacks-taj-trident-reopen.html, accessed March 6, 2010.

Tata Council for Community Initiatives (TCCI)

TCCI was created in 1996 as a network-organization that brought together the chief executive officers (CEOs) of all major Tata companies to coordinate, challenge and inspire voluntary community development and environmental activities among all 96 Tata companies. The TCCI Council[74] explored the leadership capabilities that contributed to the Tata Group's longevity and prosperity.

> Social Responsibility is central to the core values we adhere[d] to in the Tata Group for over a century. Our Companies have not only been proactive on compliance to regulatory requirements but have had a far sighted vision in ensuring sustainability in business processes; restoration of biodiversity and conserving wildlife where possible. In the recent years, our Companies have marshaled these strengths together more consciously to institutionalize all this through the Tata Council for Community Initiatives (TCCI), what they have been doing for many, many years.[75]

Each company had a corporate head for social responsibility—always a senior executive. This corporate head managed a cross-functional CSR team of facilitators with specific responsibilities for community development, environmental management and volunteering. The TCCI network included over 200 facilitators and more than 11,500 registered volunteers. TCCI's periodic workouts (Exhibit 4) brought together CEOs and senior leaders across Tata companies; the 2010 workout would welcome 62.

TCCI oversaw and supported sustainability planning and reporting. TCCI was the focal point for the UN Global Compact in India, which by 2010 had 42 Tata companies as signatories—the highest number in the world from a business group. Since 2002, TCCI had worked with the Confederation of Indian Industry (CII), the United Nations Development Program (UNDP) and PricewaterhouseCooper (PwC) on the UN Global Compact (GC) and the Global Reporting Initiative (GRI). Tata companies were among the first signatories of the GC. In 2002, the crown jewels of the Group—Tata Steel, Tata Chemicals, Tata Motors, Tata Power, Tata International—had signed up. By 2010, another 10 companies under the Tata brand had signed on. Several Tata companies had also submitted GRI reports.[76]

Tata Quality Management Services (TQMS)

TQMS enabled Tata companies to become exemplars—"on business as well as ethical parameters—in their respective spheres."[77] Companies within the Tata Group that achieved or sustained scores above certain thresholds on the TBEM matrix[78] were models of excellence,

---

[74]Nadkarni had volunteered to join TCCI soon after it was created, leaving behind a successful career at Tata Motors. He soon began experimenting with a systematic way to endorse and augment Tata's generous but previously informal involvement in India's social sector. He later headed operations of the TCCI team, serving as the secretary of the council.

[75]Tata Protocol—Corporate Social Responsibility, Tata Sons Limited & Tata Services Limited, January 2007—internal circulation only. Introductory Letter, signed by Sunil Sinha, TQMS and Anant Nadkarni, TCCI. Excerpt used with permission.

[76]Tata Steel filed one in 2005; Tata Consultancy Services filed one in 2007; and Tata Tea filed one in 2008. Tata Motors reported A-level adherence with G3 standards in 2009, www.globalreporting.org/GRIReports/GRIReportsList/, accessed March 2, 2010.

[77]http://www.tata.com/aboutus/articles/inside.aspx?artid=OMSlPyjJp68=#tq, accessed March 18, 2010.

[78]The performance thresholds on TBEM are as follows: *JRD QV Award*: 600+ for the first time, *Leadership in Excellence*: 700+ for the first time, *Sustained Excellence*: 3 successive improvements beyond 600, *Active Promotion*: 500 to 600 for the first time, *Serious Adoption*: 450 to 500 for the first time, *High Delta*: High improvement in one year min 75 for under 500, *High Delta 500+*: High improvement in one year min 50, *High Delta 600+*: High improvement in one year min 25, http://www.tata.com/aboutus/articles/inside.aspx?artid=OMSlPyjJp68=, accessed March 18, 2010.

industry leadership and/or consistent improvement within their industry area. High performing companies received Group-wide recognition.

The Tata Business Excellence Model (TBEM)

Tata companies described their practices using a standardized framework, the Tata Business Excellence Model (TBEM); then, they received feedback from trained assessors, who visited the company, identified strengths and opportunities for improvement, and worked with the leadership team. TBEM identified and evaluated best practices on quality management—"leadership, strategy, customers, knowledge management, human resources, core processes and results."[79] Several areas of business performance were emphasized within the TBEM matrix: "customer-focused results; product and service results; financial and market results; human resource results; organizational effectiveness results; [and] governance and social responsibility results."[80]

TQMS selected, trained and certified the assessors. TQMS also designed and administered the assessment apparatus (matrix, process) that helped them evaluate different Tata companies.

> Every year you are assessed by trained people from [the Group's other] companies. After an exhaustive and structured assessment, assessors give their feedback, listing the company's strengths and opportunities for improvement (OFI). This makes you look at yourself

objectively. When you see that while world-class companies are at 70 per cent of the score and you are not there, it is a moment of truth.[81]

✉ Tata Group's Sustainability Journey

When a voluntary initiative spearheaded by TCCI had reached a tipping point, TQMS would step in to provide a set of mandatory guidelines and scale up and monitor implementation across the Group:

> The Tata Quality Management Services (TQMS) and the TCCI have partnered now for some time to integrate social responsibility with the business excellence process. . . . The process of experimentation and innovation continues further, wherein a Tata CSR Protocol is developed as one more step to deepen the institutionalization of social responsibility through the Internal Assessment process of the Tata Business Excellence Model (TBEM) [...] embedding CSR into the Internal Assessment process.[82]

The Tata Index for Sustainable Human Development

The Tata Index for Sustainable Human Development[83] was the very first initiative of its kind, both

---

[79]Bhushan Dewan, vice president, business excellence at TCS, http://www.tata.com/aboutus/articles/inside.aspx?artid=LNEn5 MFAEwQ=, accessed March 18, 2010.

[80]http://www.tata.com/aboutus/articles/inside.aspx?artid=OMSlPyjJp68=#tq, accessed March 18, 2010.

[81]http://www.tata.com/aboutus/articles/inside.aspx?artid=LNEn5MFAEwQ=, accessed March 18, 2010.

[82]Tata protocol—Corporate Social Responsibility, personal correspondence with TCCI, December 2007, quoted with permission.

[83]Oana Branzei and Anant G. Nadkarni, "The Tata Way: Evolving and Executing Sustainable Business Strategies," *Ivey Business Journal*, March/April 2008, www.iveybusinessjournal.com/article.asp?intArticle_ID=750, accessed September 6, 2008.

within Tata and across the world. This corporate sustainability system[84] tracked social responsibility initiatives at the company level to simultaneously promote social responsibility and drive business excellence within, and across, Tata companies.[85] The evaluation categories were as follows: human consideration, human concern, human achievement, human development and human excellence (see Exhibit 8). The Index tracked corporate progress, based on TBEM, reiterating the conviction that sustainability mattered to the success of each of the individual Tata companies, to their own success as leaders and to the Tata legacy.

The framework, originally initiated by TCCI in collaboration with the UNDP in India in 2001, had been iteratively refined with input from the CII, PwC, the ICICI Bank and the Ashoka group.[86] The Tata Index was shared with the UN Secretary General Kofi Annan and 700 CEOs and global business leaders at the UN Business Leaders' Summit, as well as to governments and businesses in Switzerland, Australia, Singapore, Bangkok, and Canada.[87]

The Index had been deployed since June 2004, with the main objective of ensuring continuous improvement in the delivery of social responsibility initiatives at the company level. By 2005, the Group averaged almost half of its intended goal—i.e., 452.95 points on a 1,000-point scale—with companies ranging from 261 (Tata International) to 712 (Tata Steel). Tata Motors achieved one of the highest scores, 663, testimony to the centrality of sustainable strategies and business practices in its business model.[88]

The Tata Protocol

The Tata Protocol for Internal Assessment, known internally as The Leadership Protocol (see Exhibit 9), was formally launched at TCCI's 2007 workout:

> Based on the three years' feedback, this Protocol offers a set of suggestions to assist a Tata Company to develop its CSR practice with a greater focus on content and specific initiatives that have been collectively agreed upon at a group level. This version is specially designed to encourage CSR Facilitators and the TBEM Internal Assessors to work together in embedding CSR into the Internal Assessment process.[89]

The 2007 workout on corporate sustainability was a significant step up in the personal engagement of the CEOs of Tata companies—Nadkarni had urged the CEOs attending the workout to reflect on what key values a Tata leader should embrace and practice, based on their shared experiences and vision for the future of the Group:

> The breakaway groups would play around with the ideas combined with the vast experience from your inventories and come to a shared "Tata" profile. This is also a good opportunity to deal with our current realities—with respect

---

[84]Oana Branzei and Anant G. Nadkarni, "The Tata Way: Evolving and Executing Sustainable Business Strategies," *Ivey Business Journal*, March/April 2008, www.iveybusinessjournal.com/article.asp?intArticle_ID=750, accessed March 3, 2010.

[85]When asked to explain the genesis of the Tata Index to outsiders, Nadkarni often emphasized the collective effort that informed the design and evolution of this voluntary framework. High-level representatives from multiple companies had come together each year to direct, measure and enhance the community work undertaken by the Tata companies themselves. They candidly shared guidelines and best practices that helped all the other Tata companies to fulfill their social responsibilities.

[86]Interview with Anant G. Nadkarni, February 2005.

[87]Ibid.

[88]Ibid.

[89]Interview with Anant G. Nadkarni, September 2006.

to real-time leadership involvement or conceptual capacity to vision or the ability to leverage collective wisdom in the organization and evolve a fairly long-term direction for CSR. One needs to examine whether our organizations have developed adequate non-business or beyond-financial goals; those that generate a higher purpose to the enterprise—such as improving quality of life. How does Leadership build a virtuous CSR cycle that inspires employees from within to match with their willingness to build that culture in the organization?[90]

Three days later, all the CEOs in attendance signed a personal pledge, punctuating an emerging collective recognition that "the sensitivities inherent in what we call 'CSR' actually give our businesses a more lasting edge."[91]

Climate Change

The most recent collaboration between TCCI and TQMS focused on the development of a Group-wide climate change policy. [92] From inception until 2007, the Group's environmental actions had always been voluntary, laced in a culture of deep commitment towards the ecosystem, as J. J. Irani explains:

> Environment and ecology are a part of the culture and ethos of the Tatas. Our companies and trusts have traditionally nurtured practices and projects that

reflect a deep concern for conservation and a conviction that the environment is not a disposable commodity.[93]

A 2007 *Harvard Business Review* article argued that "the effects of climate on companies' operations are now so tangible and certain that the issue is best addressed with the tools of the strategist."[94, 95] That same year, the Group stuck a high-level steering committee. Senior leaders, including 11 domain experts, were tasked with a broad range of climate initiatives to: a) Determine the extent of the Group's carbon footprint; b) Create awareness of the criticality of the issue; c) Make climate change a core component of corporate performance; and d) Identify new business opportunities present in the green area.

Between 2007 and 2009, TCCI workouts helped Tata companies evolve a common understanding and commitment towards environmental issues. Starting in 2009, climate change mitigation became a mandatory part of strategy for Tata companies. Implemented and monitored by TQMS, the Group-wide climate change policy was explicitly linked with the guidelines in the Tata Code of Conduct. This meant that any firms failing to abide would forego their use of the Tata brand.

The first round of implementation involved the big five companies—Tata Steel, Tata Chemicals, Tata Power, Tata Motors and TCS. By 2009, phase II had completed carbon mapping for another seven companies. Next, phase III would track the carbon footprint of another 11 more companies.[96]

---

[90]Preface to the Leadership Profile used in the 2007 Corporate Sustainability Workout, included with permission.

[91]Anant G. Nadkarni, personal communication—December 2007.

[92]Ratan N. Tata, "Climate change policy for Tata companies," www.tataquality.com/CCPolicy1_7x10.pdf, on March 3, 2010.

[93]http://www.tataquality.com/UI/APage.aspx?contentid=111009121739976266, accessed March 18, 2010.

[94]Michael E. Porter and Reinhardt Forest, "Grist: A Strategic Approach to Climate," Forethought, Harvard Business *Review* 85, no. 10, October 2007, 22–26, p. 22.

[95]In 2006, The Stern Review argued that the cost of doing nothing about climate change will require between five per cent and 20 per cent of global GDP, while prevention would cost only one per cent per year, http://www.hm-treasury.gov.uk/sternreview_index.htm, accessed March 19, 2010.

[96]http://www.tataquality.com/UI/HPage.aspx?contentid=111009144836985201, accessed March 18, 2010.

The next step was to develop abatement strategies, both for the short term and the long term. This has already been done for the companies in Phase I and II. This exercise has also helped the companies identify new business opportunities arising out of going green [such as] nano coating for glass, solar component manufacturing and solar photovoltaics, [...] bio fuels, bio diesel, eco-friendly solutions in the lighting business, setting up green buildings and smart grids.[97]

Sunil Sinha, CEO of TQMS, felt that the Group had "taken a firm stance on climate change [...] because it's the right thing to do as the environment is a shared resource. Also, it will give us competitive advantage, absolve the business of future risks in a carbon tax regime and help us explore new business opportunities.[98] He *urged Tata companies to measure their carbon footprint and strive to 1)* Be the benchmark in their segment of industry on the carbon footprint for their plants and operations; 2) Engage actively in climate change advocacy and the shaping of regulations in different business sectors; and 3) Incorporate "green" perspective in all key organisational processes.[99]

Several Tata companies had already actively contributed to the development of global standards for climate change. For example, Tata Power joined 45 other leading international companies to develop a global policy framework to combat climate change. The initiative, Combat Climate Change (3C), launched on January 11, 2007 seeks to integrate climate issues in financial markets and trading by:

Sharing a deep understanding of the industries we work in and identifying the measures with the most impact and the steps needed to gain their full effect; Working within our respective sectors to influence our colleagues and push the development of efficient technology; Working hard to reduce emissions in our businesses and to act as role models for other organizations; and Contribut[ing] our share to minimizing market failures by being transparent and by helping our customers make informed choices.[100,101]

The Decision

Pondering the past history of the Tata Group along with its current opportunities and challenges, Nadkarni wondered how the 62 leaders arriving to Mumbai for the February 2010 corporate sustainability workout envisioned the Group's sustainability strategy for the next decade. Would growth, globalization and anticipated changes in the Group's leadership loosen or tighten the link between purpose and profit? He remembered a quote that R. Gopalakrishnan, Executive Director of Tata Sons, had offered about Tata's pro-social approach to business: "We do business the way we do, not because we have clear evidence it has a better chance of success. We do it because we know no other way."[102]

---

[97]Ibid.

[98]Interview with Sunil Sinha, available at www.tataquality.com/UI/HPage.aspx?contentid=111009144836985201, accessed March 3, 2010.

[99]Ratan N. Tata, "Climate change policy for Tata companies," www.tataquality.com/CCPolicy1_7x10.pdf, on March 3, 2010.

[100]http://www.tatapower.com/combat-climate-change.aspx, accessed March 28, 2010.

[101]http://www.combatclimatechange.org, accessed March 28, 2010.

[102]www.strategy-business.com/article/10106?gko=74e5d, accessed March 7, 2010 (p. 12 of the printed version).

Exhibit I	Tata Group's Publicly Traded Companies

	Market Capitalization[1]	Current Price[2]	Operating Income[3]			
			2006	2007	2008	2009
CMC	1,936.85	1,278.45	828.81	988.91	977.19	820.45
Indian Hotels Company	7,462.62	103.15	1,084.26	1,544.63	1,764.51	1,619.57
Mount Everest Mineral Water	228.11	67.10	16.44	23.93	24.78	22.03
Nelco	243.81	106.85	117.37	61.64	197.58	340.51
Rallis India	1,558.99	1,202.5	604.19	633.04	684.61	846.65
Tata Chemicals	7,242.04	307.95	3,502.85	3,946.67	4,036.68	8,363.35
Tata Coffee	676.67	362.30	186.03	263.65	301.84	311.39
Tata Communications	8,374.73	293.85	3,780.95	4,041.83	3,283.30	3,749.43
Tata Consultancy Services	160,668.27	820.90	11,230.50	14,939.97	18,533.72	22,401.92
Tata Elxsi Ltd.	977.74	314.00	235.63	307.96	401.55	418.52
Tata Investment Corporation	2,035.39	492.25	170.24	204.26	210.07	212.33
Tata Metaliks	377.04	149.10	441.49	681.04	1,031.66	1,008.86
Tata Motors	42,627.43	783.65	20,088.63	26,664.25	28,767.91	25,660.67
Tata Power	32,241.06	1359.30	4,553.23	4,918.53	5,909.60	7,257.05
Tata Sponge Iron	573.19	372.20	193.04	285.69	456.65	609.35
Tata Steel	57,171.39	644.25	15,132.09	17,452.66	19,654.41	24,348.32
Tata Tea	5,873.24	949.75	970.76	1,055.96	1,134.70	1,361.53
Tata Teleservices (Maharashtra)	4,686.08	24.70	1,095.13	1,406.98	1,707.19	2,034.62
Tayo Rolls	137.50	134.00	162.08	193.89	213.72	167.71
Tinplate Company of India	572.07	79.35	410.34	460.82	406.39	667.90
Titan Industries	8,094.39	1,823.50	1,468.73	2,135.47	3,050.85	3,881.75
Trent	1,663.51	830.30	346.44	452.00	514.16	511.73
TRF	1,021.37	928.15	214.64	343.04	357.75	526.46
Voltas	5,722.65	172.95	1,853.14	2,400.55	3,044.54	4,033.29

SOURCE: Tata Investor Desk, http://tata.com/investor/inside.aspx?artid=XXajrQvzvCM=, accessed March 19, 2010.

[1]In Rs crores, 1 Rs crore=US$219,828.53.

[2]In Rs, 1 Rs=US$.02198.

[3]In Rs crores, 1 Rs crore=US$219,828.53.

Exhibit 2   Tata Group's Capital Market Performance

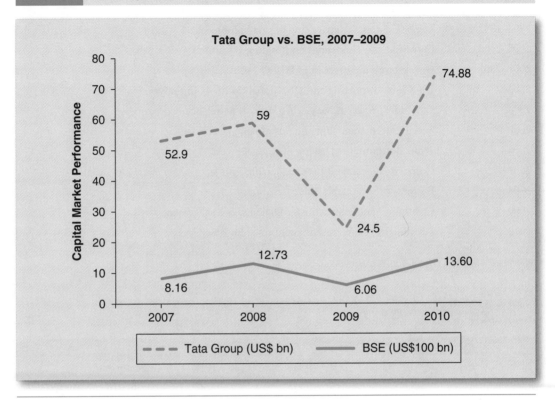

SOURCE: Adapted from www.tata.com/htm/Group_Investor_GroupFinancials.htm, accessed January 27, 2010.

Exhibit 3   Tata Group's Financials

	2007–08	2008–09	% Change
Total revenue	62.5	70.9	13.4
Sales	61.5	70.1	14
Total assets	44.1	51.7	17.2
International revenues	38.3	45.9	19.8
Net forex earnings	1.2	2.1	74.2

SOURCE: www.tata.com/htm/Group_Investor_GroupFinancials.htm, accessed January 27, 2010. Figures in US$ billion. Financial year is April-March. Revenue figures for group companies are consolidated and net of excise duty (wherever applicable). Exchange rate: US$=Rs45.92 for 2008–09 and US$=Rs40.24 for 2007–08.

Exhibit 4	Corporate Sustainability Workouts[1]
1996–1997	Regional Groups/Networking & Tata Volunteers
1998–2000	Case Studies—Guidelines on Building Community
2001–2002	Group-level Initiatives in EMS/ISO 14001
2003	UN Global Reporting and UN Global Compact Initiatives
2004	Tata Index: Towards Measuring Human Excellence
2005	Social Entrepreneurship and Sustainable Livelihoods
2006	Triple Bottom Line: Driving Business Process
2007	Corporate Sustainability & Leadership Profile
2008	Business & Sustainable Value Creation
2009	Creating Genuine Stakeholder Dialogue & Engagement
2010	Learning from the Present Economic Slowdown

[1]Presentation by Anant G. Nadkarni, used with permission.

Exhibit 5	Tata's Social Reforms

	Tata Group	Enforced by Law	Legal Measure
Eight-hour day	1912	1948	Factories Act
Free medical aid	1915	1948	Employees State Insurance Act
Establishment of Welfare Department	1917	1948	Factories Act
Schooling facilities for children	1917		
Formation of Works Committee for handling complaints concerning service conditions and grievances	1919	1947	Industrial Disputes Act
Leave with pay	1920	1948	Factories Act
Workers' Provident Fund Scheme	1920	1952	Employees Provident Fund Act
Technical Institute for Training of Apprentices, Craftsmen & Engineering Graduates	1921	1961	Apprentices Act
Maternity benefit	1928	1946	Bihar Maternity Benefit Act
Profit sharing bonus	1934	1965	Bonus Act
Retiring gratuity	1937	1972	Payment of Gratuity Act

SOURCE: Adapted from R.M. Lala, *The Creation of Wealth: The Tatas from the 19th to the 21st Century*, 3rd edition, Penguin Books India, 2004, Appendix E, pp. 284–285.

Exhibit 6 Examples of Sustainability Initiatives Within the Group[1]

Problem	Solution	Commitment
I observed families riding on two-wheelers—the father driving the scooter, his young kid standing in front of him, his wife seated behind him holding a little baby. It led me to wonder whether one could conceive of a safe, affordable, all-weather form of transport for such a family.[2]	**July 17, 2009:** First Tata Nano delivered to 100,000 customers. Unveiled on January 10, 2008, the Nano concept won the 2010 Indian Car of the Year Award, an award instituted jointly by six auto publications. It has also been individually declared as the "car of the year" by three auto publications/television channels.[3] **March 23, 2009, Tata Nano Europa** unveiled.[3] **July 6, 2009, Tata Nano in the USA** in two years. **March 4, 2010, Tata Nano EV: Launched in the** Electric Vehicle (EV) segment at the Geneva Auto Show; it will be exported from India to the European markets in another 30 months.[4]	We are happy to present the People's Car to India and we hope it brings the joy, pride and utility of owning a car to many families who need personal mobility.[5] Ravi Kant, Vice President Tata Motors: "Electrification will be an integral part of Tata Motor's initiative to launch environment-friendly vehicles. We will progressively introduce electric vehicles in all relevant markets."[6]
Water-borne disease is the single greatest threat to global health, with diarrhoea, jaundice, typhoid, cholera, polio and gastroenteritis spread by contaminated water. [...] In India, such diseases cause more than 1.5 times the deaths caused by AIDS and double the deaths caused by road accidents.[7]	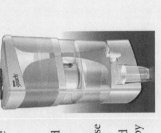 **Tata Swatch, 2009:** The replaceable filter-based product, which is entirely portable and based on low-cost natural ingredients, delivers safe drinking water at a new market benchmark of Rs30 per month for a family of five. . . . [It] produces clean and safe water without using electric power or running water, which is often not available in rural areas. The cartridge bulb is packed with a purification medium which has the capability to kill bacteria and disease-causing organisms. It can purify up to 3,000 litres of water after which the cartridge stops water flow. . . . Fourteen patents have been filed for the technology and product.[8]	R Mukundan, managing director, Tata Chemicals, said, "With the launch of Tata Swatch, we are taking a small step towards fulfilling our Chairman's vision of making safe drinking water available for all at an affordable cost. . . . with the launch of this product we are committing ourselves to work towards wiping out the curse of water-borne diseases."[9]

[1]Photos downloaded from group's media library and used with permission; www.tata.com/htm/Group_image_library_index.htm?sectid=1WG6KD86Wz0=, accessed March 8, 2010.

[2]Mr. Ratan N. Tata speaking at the unveiling ceremony at the 9th Auto Expo in New Delhi; www.tatamotors.com/our_world/press_releases.php?ID=340&action=Pull, accessed March 8, 2010.

[3]"Tata Motors unveil Tata Nano Europa," March 4, 2009http://malteshashrit.wordpress.com/2009/03/04/tata-motors-unveil-tata-nano-europa/, accessed March 8, 2010.

[4]"Geneva 2010: Tata Nano Goes Green With the Nano EV," *Nitrobahn*, March 6, 2010, www.nitrobahn.com/news/geneva-2010-tata-nano-goes-green-with-the-nano-ev/, accessed March 8, 2010.

[5]Tata media release, www.tatamotors.com/our_world/press_releases.php?ID=340&action=Pull, accessed March 8, 2010.

[6]Tata media release, www.tata.com/article.aspx?artid=gdpyclBOS8E=, accessed March 8, 2010.

[7]Tata media release, www.tata.com/media/releases/inside.aspx?artid=TtOdcdNuSRk=, accessed March 7, 2010.

[8]http://www.tata.com/media/releases/inside.aspx?artid=TtOdcdNuSRk=, last accessed March 7, 2010.

[9]Ibid.

Exhibit 7 Organizing for Sustainability

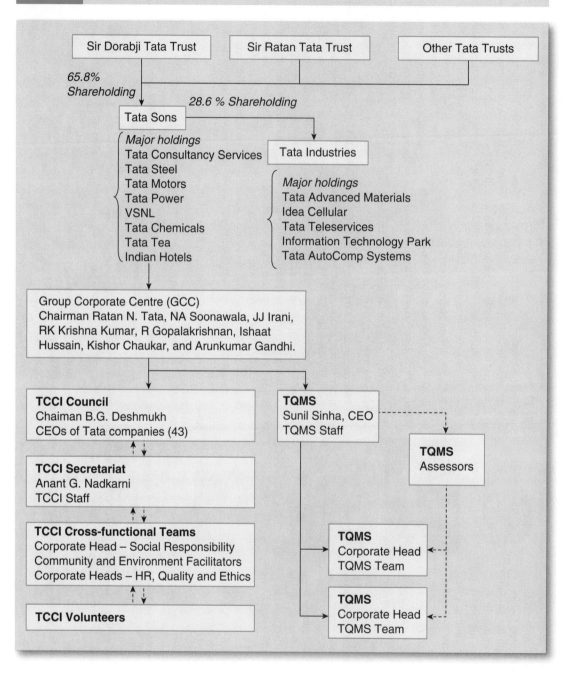

Exhibit 8 The Tata Index

Assessment Levels	Points	P+O
Systems Response: Level – I	**275**	**(150+125)**
1) Leadership Commitment and Involvement	55	(30+25)
2) Management Structure and Deployment	55	(30+25)
3) Strategy Development & Action Plan	55	(30+25)
4) Review Mechanism and Reporting	55	(30+25)
5) Communications and Awareness	55	(30+25)
People Response: Level – II	**175**	**(100+75)**
1) Selection, Career Development of key Employees and Performance Management	45	(25+20)
2) Training for Professional, Organizational, Managerial Competence and Enhancement of Role in CSR	45	(25+20)
3) Training for Leadership Development, Enrolment of other employees, Personal Learning and Development and enhancing Role in CSR	45	(25+20)
4) Volunteer Scheme and evolving degrees of Volunteering	40	(25+15)
Program Response: Level – III	**550**	**(300+250)**
1) Managing Change & Assessment of Social Impact		(35+30)
2) Felt needs of the key community related to core competencies	65	(35+30)
3) Volunteering Process in the Community	65	(35+30)
4) Social Concerns addressed through Programs	95	(55+40)
5) Improving Attitudes / government processes	65	(35+30)
6) Self-Reliance and Sustenance	65	(35+30)
7) Learning and Innovation Transfer	65	(35+30)
8) Effective Management and Good Governance	65	(35+30)
TOTAL POINTS:	**1000**	**(550+450)**

SOURCE: Tata Index for Sustainable Development, April 24, 2003, p. 17, used with permission.

(Continued)

| Exhibit 8 | (Continued) |

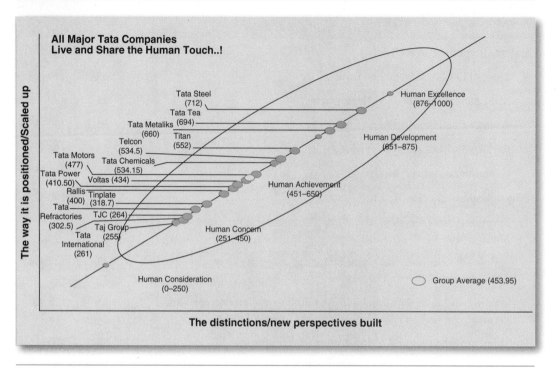

SOURCE: Anant G. Nadkani Presentation, December 2007, used with permission.

| Exhibit 9 | The Leadership Protocol |

	Values/Perspectives	Work Practices/Processes/ Methods/Systems	Behavioral Outcomes/ Demonstrable Actions
1	Leadership is not so much about "you" alone! It is more about a collective effort. Ownership in the Business Model is aimed at the prospect of creating "collective" wealth, more than individual.	Wealth created remains separate, say in a Trust, for the people. There could be other mechanisms and institutional arrangements.	Distribution pattern shows giving back of Wealth, many times over. Personal/Individual accumulation is rather restrained. Also, the concept of Wealth is not just limited to money but it is a creative way of development.

	Values/Perspectives	Work Practices/Processes/Methods/Systems	Behavioral Outcomes/Demonstrable Actions
2	Corporate Governance is based on consensus and unanimity.	Mechanisms of governance and conduct in Board Meetings show a fair degree of freedom from control. There is uncompromising commitment to ethics.	Stakeholder relationship, participatory processes at all levels are evident with low or no conflicts or retaliation.
3	The business of business is "creation of sustainable value."	Social responsibility is so central that pro-action enables account for "development costs" of venture, like labour/material. Leadership programs aim at building multiple competencies/"total intelligence"—analytical, emotional and spiritual.	Product lines are developmental in nature. Sustainability permeates in spirit and word, in procedures and protocols. Business goals go beyond making profit—to build "total value."
4	Develops alternatives to the use of authority, hierarchy coercion or force in management styles. A Leader gives more importance to the person than the product, service or an idea.	Structure is flatter, goals are evolved bottom up & genuine participatory processes are encouraged. Does not preach or force change; or seen using any form of domination. Uses creative forms of incentives with the aim to help people realize their own potential.	One set of people are not seen supervising another set. Change is a process of co-creation! Employees inculcate the habit of "serving people." They come up with radical solutions, suggestions and even innovations. Employees grow in a culture of freedom and involvement. They can contest more easily, undertake trials and feel empowered.
5	Leadership is a capacity that links inner growth with outer progress. It is about seeing the Self as the source of action and initiative.	Leadership development programmes aim at fostering different forms of learning and encourage solutions that come from the realms of deeper thought and reflection. Business processes/product features factor human consideration.	Employees and leaders relate to people better. Leaders/employees are genuinely involved in CSR-related activities. CSR sensitivities are embedded into key business functions—finance, marketing, pricing, supply chain management and so on.

(Continued)

Exhibit 9	(Continued)

	Values/Perspectives	Work Practices/Processes/Methods/Systems	Behavioral Outcomes/Demonstrable Actions
6	Believes that Leadership is about leveraging "collective wisdom" from the group, team or family. It is about: Who we are & How we are! A true Leader believes: "It is all there!"	Real time decision-making reflects "none of us is as smart as all of us." Consensus and consultation are "habitual" and "cultural." Solutions exist in the "collective intelligence."	Decisions are evolved, not prescribed. Charisma is not a precondition/qualification of leaders. Humility/Modesty are virtues, not weakness.

	Values/Perspectives	Work Practices/Processes/Methods/Systems	Related Behavioral Outcomes/Demonstrable Actions
7	The community is central to the purpose of business.	Enterprises are founded on the principles of freedom and democracy.	Selection of products and services reflect developmental goals. Structure of the company and management practice demonstrates free enterprise. "CSR" is a performance criterion and reviewed seriously.
8	"Good is the enemy of Great."	Leadership encourages to work "out of the box" and discourages complacency. Systems are in place to encourage continuous improvement.	Goal setting is more than a number game. The ultimate aim is to remain No. 1 in business or quit.
9	The Leader operates from a strong sense of "who I am" rather than "what I am."	Brand strategy emphasizes more on values than on products. CSR is the core value in the Company.	Respect diversity in products, services or social initiatives; but strives to generate a process that reflects shared values.
10	Excited by "Achievement" more than by "Opportunity."	Social challenge in the enterprise has greater attraction. Need-based thinking always supersedes flamboyance.	Business or social initiatives address felt needs of community/customers. Consultations with policy makers and people determine our action and investment— knowing it to become eventually sustainable.

	Values/Perspectives	Work Practices/Processes/ Methods/Systems	Behavioral Outcomes/ Demonstrable Actions
11	Strong sense of human purpose.	Pricing and marketing policies are based on sound social factors. Employee welfare and well-being are strongly mandated.	At Jamshedpur, for people who want to know what Tata Steel has done for its community, there is a plaque that reads: "Just look around." Credibility in the financial sector reflects it. Product pricing delivers value/is based on fairness. Smooth running of business/absence of hostility are indicators!
12	Quiet workers, interested in seeing things happen.	Social and developmental work is never over-publicized/ preached. Business and social initiatives are not confused.	Stress on action, and the satisfaction derived from it. Depth and content in the quality of work speaks for itself. Such work is done because it is the right thing to do, and good for its own sake.

SOURCE: Corporate Sustainability Workout 2007. Presentation by Anant G. Nadkarni, included with permission.

Hebei Dawu Group: Building the First Family Business Constitution in China

Yuping Du

⬚ Background

Sun Dawu, the founder of Hebei Dawu Group, smiled after the third board of directors election was successfully held on December 16, 2008. It had been witnessed by many media. The day after the election at the Dawu Hot Spring Restaurant, Chen Jianfen, a reporter from *Chinese Entrepreneur*, saw Liu Jinhu asking one of the clients to tell the chief executive officer

(CEO) that his salary and benefits were too low. Liu, a manager at Dawu Animal Feed Company, had been elected to the board of directors the day before. During the election, Sun used his preferential nomination right to nominate Sun Erwu and Liu Ping as the candidates for the positions of CEO and general manager (GM), respectively. Although those who had disagreed could vote for other candidates, both were unanimously elected. This triggered much

Version: 2011-05-16

discussion among the experts and journalists present. Facing the unexpected challenges, Sun Dawu, who was ready to retire after achieving his success in his career, pondered again about his "Family Business Constitution," the only one of its kind in China.

On June 6, 2004, Sun Dawu celebrated his 50th birthday. He wrote a poem to express his feeling: "I reflect after surviving the storm. The sun can travel in the sky because of blessings from all gods. I wonder how my fate will be. All that I can do is to pray for people who pass by!"

One year earlier, Sun had been deprived of his personal freedom because his "Grains Bank" was deemed to be involved in illegal fundraising. He spent his 49th birthday in prison. All senior executives in Dawu Group were arrested, and the government even urged the company to replace its legal representative. However, Sun was eventually released after six months. Why was he so sentimental on his 50th birthday? It seemed to be public knowledge that Sun's release was a result of an agreement among various parties. In fact, Sun's original three-year prison sentence with four-year probation indicated a somewhat relaxed policy toward private fundraising, and was also considered to be a signal of reform in China's financial industry.

Facing the unexpected imprisonment of Sun Dawu, the younger members of the Sun family including Sun Meng had decided to make some big changes to their future plans. Sun Meng was Sun Dawu's eldest son. He had recently graduated from college and had already obtained his visa to pursue further education in Australia starting in July. Yet, with his father behind bars and his mother on the run, 25-year-old Sun Meng had to assume the critical appointment of acting president. He insisted on returning the position to his father upon the latter's release, yet this idea was rejected by Sun Dawu. It seemed obvious to everyone that it would only be a matter of time before Sun Meng took over the business, as this was the convention in Chinese families. However, for Sun Meng, who

had not acquired enough working experience, managing a company worth several hundred million yuan was such a daunting task that the pressure became overwhelming. Thus, Sun Meng resigned from the position a few months later, showing his determination to acquire more front-line experience.

Sun Dawu realized that the problem was not only about his son's change in position, but also about the critical issue of selecting and developing his company successors, which was of great importance to the entire family group's sustainable development of the family business. Dawu Group had encountered major challenges in 2003 but had luckily survived. Reflecting on what he had experienced, Sun Dawu considered the succession issue and the prospects of his family business ever since 2004. Dawu Group was on the brink of a fateful revolution.

The Development of Dawu Group

Dawu Agriculture and Animal Husbandry Group Ltd. (Dawu Group) was based in Langwuzhuang Village, Xushui County, Hebei Province, 110 kilometers or a 90-minute drive from Beijing. It was a high-tech private enterprise with multiple businesses. Its founder, Sun Dawu, was from the farming and feed processing industries. As the leader of the Sun family, Sun Dawu had managed to make Dawu Group into one of the top 500 largest private enterprises in China after more than two decades of hard work. Industry authorities, including the All-China Federation of Industry and Commerce (ACFIC), rated Dawu Group as one of "China's Top 100 Most Vigorous Enterprises" for five consecutive years (from 2004 to 2008).

However, being a successful family business was not the only factor that made the Group legendary; it was also famous for its unique system, "Family Business Constitution." Sun Dawu created the system under the influence of both traditional Chinese Confucianism and Western political systems. The system had not only been functioning well, but with ongoing development and improvement had also attracted constant attention from local and international media.

Start-up Stage: From the Wife's Contracting and the Husband's Resignation to the Couple's Venture In 1970, 16-year-old Sun Dawu started his eight-year military career. He joined the Chinese Communist Party after only two years due to his outstanding performance and eventually became a battalion commander. Demobilized in 1978, Sun returned home to work in the Agricultural Bank of China and then the Rural Credit Cooperative (RCC) as a "civil servant."

In 1985, the Chinese economy was utilizing the popular "contract system." Bids were solicited for tracts of idle land. In Sun's village, the reduction of contract prices to six yuan per *mu* (about 667 square meters) had been broadcast for three months, but no one was willing to place a bid. Sun Dawu persuaded his wife, Liu Huiru, to seize the opportunity. They assumed the position of contractor under Liu Huiru's name with four other farmers as joint investment partners after collecting 10,000 yuan and raising another 20,000 yuan from loans.

Meanwhile, they set up Langwuzhuang Farm and a small feed processing plant, and hired more than 10 workers to raise 54 pigs and 1,000 chickens. The farm suffered a 16,000 yuan loss in the first year as a result of poor management. The other four shareholders decided to withdraw their money, but Sun Dawu insisted that his wife take over the business. The number of chickens on the farm steadily grew from 5,000 to 10,000, peaking at 300,000. As a consequence, not only was Liu Huiru able to repay the 20,000 yuan loan, she also earned 10,000 yuan as an initial net profit.

At the time, Sun was still working in an RCC branch. Sun decided to resign and help his wife, as he saw the business getting bigger and Liu Huiru becoming tired because of the heavy workload. Sun filed for a no-pay administrative

leave in 1989, and eventually resigned the following year. Many people around Sun thought he was behaving foolishly but Sun Dawu and his wife were determined to start their own venture.

Expansion and Rapid Development: From a Small Home Business to a Large Family Enterprise

Between January 18 and February 28, 1992, Chinese Premier Deng Xiaoping made a series of speeches in his Southern Tour, encouraging Chinese people to end the fights between the public and private sectors. Sun's business began to boom at that time. At the beginning, the couple kept their earnings of several hundred thousand yuan in a safe. When they made more money, they deposited it in banks. Over time, they became very successful. Sun Dawu's two younger brothers, in turn, also achieved local success. His younger brother, Sun Erwu, ran a prosperous small business, whereas another younger brother, Sun Zhihua, had a bright future as deputy head of Rongcheng County.

As far as Sun Dawu was concerned, the three brothers should have had bigger dreams than those minor accomplishments. He told his two brothers, "Let's work together and set up a great business! Individual wealth can never compare to prosperity in the community, so we should help all the people here to get rich as well." Sun's two brothers joined the group in July 1992. Other family members followed. Thus, Dawu Group was formed.

At this stage, Sun's business took the leap from a small home business to a rapidly developing family business. In 1994, Sun Dawu set up the Dawu Vocational School that provided free education to hone local talent, thus leading Sun to start his enterprise down a path where people who got rich earlier could help those who had not. In less than three years, more than 3,000 people received technical training in farming. In 1995, Sun Dawu was named the "the Chicken-raising Champion of Hebei Province" and chairman of the Baoding

Poultry and Egg Association. Dawu Group was ranked 224th in China's Top 500 Private High-tech Enterprises by ACFIC. Sun Dawu believed that "private businesses should not target merely at private prosperity; in fact only their form of production and management is private; what private businesses create should also be counted into social wealth." He likewise formulated his own philosophy of not aiming at profits, but at development.

Up until 1998, Dawu Vocational School had been a Provincial and Municipal Model School, National Training Base, and UNESCO's (United Nations Educational, Scientificand Cultural Organization) Corresponding Base for Research and Training Centre of Rural Education. In the same year, Dawu School was established. Within three years, the student enrolment increased from 165 to more than 1,800, and the school became a comprehensive one with a kindergarten, a primary school, a junior high school and a senior high school. Many buildings were built, including a restaurant with a 1,000 seat capacity, a cafeteria, and teaching and dormitory buildings. It was then that some media started to name the village where Dawu Group was located "Dawu Village."

Unexpected Crisis and Critical Turning Point: The Suffering and Rebirth of Dawu Group

For 18 years after its establishment in 1985, Sun Dawu's business had never suffered any financial loss. By 2002, Dawu Group had more than 1,500 employees, with fixed assets worth more than 100 million yuan and more than 9.8 million yuan in profits. On May 27, 2003, Sun Dawu was arrested and was detained for 158 days as his "Grains Bank" was suspected to have been involved in illegal fundraising.

With Sun having left, the machines ground to a halt, and the workers were forced to quit. An appalling disaster seemed to be awaiting Sun Dawu's family business. The winery and corn-starch plants had to shut down; the feed company witnessed a substantial reduction in customers.

Even worse, a significant drop in enrollment in Dawu School (with only six pupils enrolled in the first grade) led to a halt of the jointly sponsored educational projects with Canada. With the business going downhill, some workers sought other jobs. Even those who chose to stay had to accept the fact that their salaries would be greatly cut. In fact, two-thirds of the employees in each section were laid off, the construction crew was dismissed, and more than 100 workers at the winery were forced to leave their positions.

Right after the inspection, the government's liquidation and auditing report showed that Dawu Group's fixed assets were valued of 110 million yuan. Nevertheless, after Sun Dawu's arrest, his business suffered a loss of 5.84 million yuan, which was the first financial loss in its history. In total, Dawu Group suffered a loss of almost 20 million yuan. Sun Dawu's business plummeted drastically.

To revitalize his business, Sun Dawu, after his release, started to give serious thought to the firm's reform plan. Hence, Sun's long-brewing plan of "Family Business Constitution" was implemented on a trial basis in November 2004. The same year, Dawu Group's sales went up to 84 million yuan, with six million yuan in net profit. In the following year, the business successfully passed the ISO9001:2000 international quality management system certification and ranked 52nd in the selection of "China's Top 100 Most Vigorous Enterprises" held by four industry authorities, including ACFIC. Its products were named "Hebei Province Brand Name Products." More than 20 scientists and technical experts served in Dawu Group's panel tasked with the breeding of "939 Chickens." The farm raised 55,000 sets of "Dawu Jingbai 939" progenitor chickens and sold 1.5 million sets of parent chickens annually across more than 10 provinces and regions in Northern, Eastern, Southern, Northeastern and Northwestern China. In 2008, the Dawu hatchery boasted more than 100 sets of the most advanced hatching equipment in China and provided 18 million healthy commercial chickens every year. By the first half of 2007,

Dawu Breeder Company had sold 11 million "939 Breeding Stock Chickens" to 106 cities and towns in 15 provinces.

The Increase of Community Wealth: From a Rural Dream to an Urban Legend

In 2008, there were eight subsidiaries and 17 factories under the governance of Dawu Group, including Dawu Feedstuff Co. Ltd., Dawu Poultry Breeding Co. Ltd., Dawu Food Co. Ltd., Dawu Fertilizer Co. Ltd., and Dawu Crop Breeding Company, as well as Dawu School, Dawu Hot Spring Holiday Resort, and Dawu Construction Company. The Group had established a vocational school, and a hospital, and had a fleet of company cars and trucks. By 2010, Dawu Group's comprehensive services had successfully covered the primary secondary, and tertiary education industries.

Sun Dawu categorized his business strategies into four stages: 1) making profit by combining breeding, raising and processing; 2) developing by integrating poultry breeding, feed manufacturing and food companies; 3) upgrading by covering primary, secondary and tertiary education; and 4) increasing wealth for the community, that is, constructing the new homeland of Dawu City, an urban community where people could lead a peaceful and harmonious life. Sun Dawu hoped that his employees could consume in Dawu City instead of saving their money in banks. Therefore, people could turn individual wealth into community wealth shared by every member. He also wanted to attract new consumers from outside Dawu City who would substantially add to the wealth in Dawu City.

Enterprises might prosper and perish; however, it was believed that Dawu City would become a small but stable society once construction was completed. Dawu Hot Spring Holiday Resort was built in 2006. Dawu Sci-Fi Park, a 3-D cinema and a 4-D cinema had all been put into use. A dome cinema was to be completed in 2009, as well as a golf course. All the new projects

that Sun Dawu had carried out were taking him closer to his ideal society, which featured "harmony between labor and capital, the poor and the rich, government and citizens."

◎ The Family Business Succession: The "Family Business Constitution"

The idea of the "Family Business Constitution" of Dawu Group was initiated during Sun Dawu's imprisonment in 2003. At that time, Sun had been mainly engaged in farming and the feed processing business, as there was great demand for grains. However, none of the local banks was willing to grant loans to Sun due to the high-risk nature of his business. There was once a very popular saying in the Chinese banking industry: "No matter how large the family fortune, never include those with fur and feathers!" Hence, raising funds turned out to be Sun's biggest obstacle.

To resolve the feed shortage, Sun Dawu began to borrow grains from the local villagers. They called on other villagers to deposit their corn in Sun's business, which made a convenient "Grains Bank" for the local people. Sun promised the villagers that they could withdraw their grains anytime within three months, while grains still kept in the bank after three months would be turned into the Group's borrowings from villagers, for which they could gain interest. In addition, if at the time of grains deposit the market price for the grains was 1 yuan per kilogram, and after three months the price rose to 1.6 yuan per kilogram, then the withdrawal price would be calculated as 1.6 yuan per kilogram. If, after three months, the prevailing grains price fell to 0.4 yuan per kilogram, then the "Grains Bank" would still pay the price of 1 yuan per kilogram to the villagers. Lending vouchers (or IOUs) would be recognized by the People's Court as evidence for "Deposit Receipts."

As the scale of Sun's business got bigger, the workers in his firm also started to deposit their salaries and grains in the firm, thus encouraging even more villagers to come to Sun with their money, with the understanding that the money they deposited was considered as lending to Sun's business. Then, Sun Dawu decided to raise more funds through the market. The Group recruited agents and set up a few financing agencies. From January 2000 to May 2003, by offering lending rates higher than bank deposit rates, the Group issued 1,627 IOUs and raised 13,083,161 yuan in finds, involving a total of 611 people.

On May 29, 2003, as president of Dawu Group, Sun Dawu was accused of "illegally withdrawing public deposits" and was arrested by local police. The borrowing activities were later determined by the People's Court of Xushui County as withdrawing public funds in a disguised form "without the approval of People's Bank of China." The Group had issued credentials under the name of IOUs, which were in essence "Deposit Receipts." Not only did the Group provide rates higher than bank deposit rates, but it also made promises to the public that no "interest tax" would be levied. The People's Court of Xushui County made the first judgment based on provisions of the Criminal Law of the People's Republic of China. Hebei Dawu Agriculture and Animal Husbandry Group Ltd. was found to have committed the offense of "illegally drawing public deposits" and was fined 300,000 yuan; Sun Dawu was also accused of illegal fundraising and was sentenced to a three-year imprisonment with a four-year probation, as well as a fine of 100,000 yuan.

Sun never stopped worrying about the future of Dawu Group throughout the 158 days he spent in jail. At that time, all senior managers, including his two brothers, were put into prison, and the firm was temporarily taken over by the government. Three months later, however, the manager appointed by the government retired due to health problems. Sun Dawu's eldest son, Sun Meng, then only 25 years old and just graduated from college, had to take over the Group in this critical circumstance. Joining him

in the management team was Sun Meng's cousin Liu Ping (Sun Dawu's wife's niece, who was then the manager of the Breeding Stock Company).

When Sun Dawu was released half a year later, he was surprised to see that none of the members from senior management had left his Group; and when the accounts were re-opened, there were very few mistakes. Sun and his wife were deeply touched. After the downfall and the rebirth of his business, Sun realized that he had to establish a management system that fit Dawu Group better. Only this could ensure the business's prosperity in the long run. It took Sun a year to formulate the Group's future plan, including a system reform.

Tough Choice Between "Splitting" and "Completeness"

As Sun was formulating a new management system, his family members' opinions about the Group's future diverged a lot. Sun Dawu was still serving his sentence, so he could not assume his post as the Group president. He had to step down at his prime age of 49.

Being young and inexperienced, Sun Meng felt inadequate to manage such a large enterprise worth tens of millions of Renminbi. The increasing pressure eventually turned him against the idea of continuing with the position. Sun Meng tried to resign several times.

Meanwhile, Sun Dawu's brothers, together with many other veterans in the Group, all favored a joint-share system. They disagreed with Sun Dawu on keeping the enterprise private. Sun had also tried introducing such systems as the senior joint-share system and family joint-share system, but he found all of them difficult to carry out because there would always be too many conflicts between individual interests and responsibilities. Due to the requests from companies' veterans and the disputes among family members, many family joint-share systems would eventually break down once the businesses were passed down to the succeeding generations. In Sun's eyes, a joint-share system would divide the enterprise's assets, resulting in not only family alienation but also losses of many development opportunities for the Group. It would be a shame if things had to turn out this way. Sun felt that he was in a big dilemma: whether to pass the business down to his son or to other family members.

Sun's wife asked him, "Can you find a way to keep what it is now and never, ever let it be split? If our sons are capable of establishing their own businesses, then let them do it on their own. If they're not capable enough, then just let them enjoy a cozy life in the family business." The very honest words of Liu Huiru inspired Sun Dawu, which made him think further whether the business should be kept whole or run under the joint-share system.

Enlightenment From History and Reference From China and Abroad

Sun Dawu was always interested in the studies of Chinese history and, in fact, was deeply influenced by Confucianism from ancient China. The "Incident at Xuanwu Gate" story shed light on his thinking. Li Yuan, the first emperor in the Tang Dynasty, had three sons: the eldest, named Li Jiancheng, the second, Li Shimin, and the youngest, Li Yuanji. Following the Chinese tradition of passing the throne down to the eldest son, Li Yuan proclaimed Li Jiancheng the new emperor. However, Li Yuan's second son, Li Shimin, had made a great contribution to the establishment of the new empire and had gained ample support from all generals and officials. Li Shimin killed his two brothers, forcing his father to abdicate, and then ascended the throne himself.

This episode in history about the discord in the imperial family made Sun Dawu consider the situation of his family business. He viewed his family as a country: there were many things in common between a family business and an emperor's big country. Looking back at the

succession issues in many countries and families, all of them centered on whether to pass the throne to the eldest son or to the most talented. Sun regarded family businesses, especially large and medium-sized ones, as an integral part of society. Meanwhile, they also mirrored every aspect of a society. While a society was an eternal enterprise, people had to admit that a family was a miniature society. Only by getting rid of the inappropriate convention of choosing between the eldest son and the most talented executive, and combining the current social situation, could a business develop in a healthy and sustainable way.

Sun also studied carefully the "Constitutional Monarchy" in the United Kingdom, the "Separation of Powers" in the United States, and the "Central Government System of Three Councils and Six Boards" in the Sui Dynasty in ancient China. The "Constitutional Monarchy" promoted the separation of ownership and management control, imposing restrictions on imperial power and returning governance rights to the people. Meanwhile, the "Separation of Powers" practiced checks and balances among different power groups in order to maintain a stable system in administrating a country. The "Central Government System of Three Councils and Six Boards" in ancient China used a similar system of separation of powers to balance the powers of prime ministers and councils while protecting sovereignty (i.e. "Zhongshu Council" drafted the imperial edicts, "Menxia Council" reviewed the edicts, and "Shangshu Council" implemented the orders from the emperor).

Sun did a thorough study and analysis of references from historical stories and cases about the succession issue in many other companies. He also took into consideration the unique characteristics of Dawu Group. Then a brand new concept began to emerge more clearly in his mind. That was how he created and established the "Family Business Constitution" in November 2004.

⬚ The Structure and Content of the "Family Business Constitution"

The core concept of Sun Dawu's "Family Business Constitution" was separating the rights of ownership, decision-making and operations, thus creating a stable system in which the three powers could co-exist while checking and balancing each other at the same time. The constitution was the foundation of the system and was placed at the top of the "Family Business Constitution" hierarchy. The board of supervisors, board of directors and board of executives acted as the corresponding entities of the three powers. The centralization of the three powers took place under the control of the highest authority—the joint boards council. The three boards were all under this management system, each enjoying one and only one of the rights. They were also accountable for all the staff in the Group, as well as the enterprise and the society. Their rewards were closely related to the business's profitability. The Constitution could only be revised if the equity owners, the three boards, and 70 per cent of the staff with more than five years' tenure unanimously approved. Sun Dawu and his wife, Liu Huiru, jointly possessed the equity, which would be inherited by their descendants. The Constitution also covered the production management and meeting systems.

Components, Functions, Rights, Benefits and Terms of the Three Boards

Under the Constitution, the components, functions, rights, benefits and terms were formulated as follows:

The board of supervisors mainly consisted of the Sun family members, whose duty was to draft and revise general rules and regulations, as well as to monitor the board of directors and board of executives from legal, institutional and moral perspectives. The supervisors were also responsible for overseeing finance and equities. Members of the board of supervisors, as supervisors of the other two boards, could enjoy supervisor subsidies, as well as year-end bonuses and performance-based commissions. The board had ownership of the business, yet had no control over decision-making and operations. The general elections of the supervisors were held every three years. The chief supervisor (CS), vice-supervisor and other supervisors could all participate in re-elections. The CS, who had the right to draw 10 per cent of the Group's gross profit as public welfare funds, was to respect the decision-making rights of the CEO (the head of the board of directors) as well as the operational decisions of the general manager (the head of the board of executives). The administrative expense budget of the supervisors would be the same as that of the other two boards.

The board of directors was composed of directors elected by staff in the company. All directors were responsible for developing the strategic goals and direction of the Group, as well as making investment decisions of subsidiary companies. They were also responsible for selecting the top leaders for each subsidiary company, deciding on annual profit targets and making bonus allocation plans. Members of the board of directors could enjoy director subsidies as well as use both public and private cars. A CEO holding the position for more than two terms consecutively or accumulatively, and other directors holding the position for more than eight terms, would be entitled to retirement benefits. Dawu Group also encouraged the children of the directors to study abroad and to start their own businesses. Funds of 300,000 to 1,000,000 yuan were reserved for their future education and businesses. The board of directors could make administrative and strategic decisions but did not have any ownership or operational power. The directors' term was two years, whereas the CEO's was four years. All of them could participate in re-elections. In addition, the CEO could nominate several vice-directors as his assistants. The assets the CEO could deploy were not to exceed the total amount of the Group's profit plus depreciation in the past year. The CEO was monitored by the board of supervisors, and was to respect the operational decisions of the GM. The CEO had no right to dismiss the GM.

The board of executives was made up of the top leaders of subsidiary companies and office directors. All executive board members were to coordinate in raising and using funds and ensure the efficient implementation of projects and tasks, all in compliance with the decisions made by the board of directors. The executives on the board were entitled to performance-based bonuses and year-end bonuses. At retirement, a GM who had held the position for more than three terms would be able to enjoy the same benefits after his retirement. Board members who had made great contributions could also enjoy the pay level of directors. The board of executives only had power in operational issues with no ownership or administrative rights. The GM had a four-year office term and could be re-elected. He could also nominate several vice-executives as his assistants. The upper limit of funds the GM could deploy was 300,000 yuan. Signatures of two board chiefs were required if 300,000 to 1,000,000 yuan was to be used. If it was more than one million yuan, then all three board chiefs needed to give consent.

The Implementation of the "Family Business Constitution"

Of the three boards, the CEO and the GM were elected, whereas the CS was appointed according to the succession system within the Sun family. By 2008, Sun Dawu was the CS, his brother Sun Erwu was the CEO, and Liu Ping, the niece of Liu Huiru, was the GM. The Dawu Group always held its elections in December. It was in this "Dawu Election Month" that the elections of all three boards were held. As of 2008, the board of supervisors had been in charge of organizing the election meetings for the last three years.

The first election, held on February 28, 2005, adopted an equal nomination system. The Group was divided into five constituencies. Each constituency nominated its own candidates and voted separately. Fifteen people were elected to form the board of directors. In the first directors' meeting that followed, the CEO and the GM were determined. This election marked the official implementation of the "Family Business Constitution" within Dawu Group. During the directors' meeting, Sun Erwu and Liu Ping were elected the CEO and GM, respectively.

The second election, held on December 16, 2006, was conducted in three steps: public selection, representative selection and elite election. Thirteen directors, two replacement directors and seven subsidiary heads were elected from 26 candidates. (The CEO and GM were still in their office terms.) The three steps in the election ensured that top talents managed the company, which was in turn under the inspection of all staff. Jia Linnan and Li Aiming, reporters from *The Industrial and Commercial Times of China*, observed the election, and published their news report titled "Witnessing 'Family Business Constitution' of Dawu Group." In the report, they wrote, "Sun Meng, who had previously resigned, obtained 425 votes (only second to his uncle Sun Shuhua) and was thus reappointed as a member of the board of directors. Wang Caijin, chief manager of the department of power, Li Sixu, office director of the Feed Company, and Lu Huijie, office director of the Poultry Breeding Company, were elected as the youngest members of the board. The ages of member directors showed a normal distribution: the majority was between 30 and 50 years old, while there were approximately similar numbers of 25- to 30-year-olds and 50- to 60-year-olds."

The third election was held on December 16, 2008. The constituency system was also applied in this election. A total of 661 employees with more than three years' tenure in the company were eligible for voting. At the end of the election, 11 out of the 13 directors were re-elected. Another four members were elected from the 14 candidates.

They formed the new 15-person board of directors. Two replacement directors were also elected. During this election, Sun Dawu kept the nomination rights as the chief supervisor. Nine members of the board of directors, including Sun Dawu, did not vote for Sun Shuo, Sun Dawu's second son, believing that Sun Shuo should gain experience for a few more years. However, votes from the public eventually placed him on the board of directors. Only 20 people had the right to vote at the election venue of the Hot Spring Centre, which Sun Shuo was in charge of; however, it turned out that he won more than 300 votes. Most votes came from ordinary employees in other subsidiaries.

Rules for the Family Members

Sun Dawu established a set of rules for the family members, hoping to ensure the integrity of assets and properties at the time of inheritance. The rules stated that the board of supervisors was the representative and custodian of the Sun family, serving to protect the family members' legal rights and benefits, such as housing, medication, education, international travelling and entrepreneurial activities (one million yuan).

The family members were entitled to monthly subsidies as much as two to three times the average salary of the employees, even if they did not work in the company. The family members claimed this right as the owners of the assets. In addition to the subsidies, salaries were paid to the family members who worked in the Group. The female members in the Sun family, even after they were married, would be entitled to the same benefits for their entire life, but their children would not. At all times, the family members were to act as models in conforming to and implementing the Constitution. They were also encouraged to run for the CEO, GM and CS positions. The family members had the ownership of the rewards and bonuses related to the positions. All family members oversaw the CS. As to legacies, only a symbol of equity would be passed down to younger generations, which

meant that they needed to be elected to the board of directors through public elections to obtain decision-making rights. Currently, the two sons of Sun Erwu, one studying abroad and the other, starting his own business, were examples of family members getting support from the Group.

The Challenges Ahead for the "Family Business Constitution"

In 2010, it had been six years since the Constitution was first implemented, and the output of Dawu Group had doubled, with annual profits increasing rapidly at a rate of 30 per cent. Yet for Sun Dawu, expanding the business was not all that concerned him. These days, he thought about the future direction of his enterprise, as well as that of his family. As a man who held traditional values, he believed that under no circumstances should a family be separated. He once said that it was his wish to see his parents enjoy long and healthy lives, his brothers enjoy harmony among each other, and his younger generations be nurtured. However, members of the family should not rest on the enterprise's laurels. They had to gain front-line work experience and fight their way up to gradually win the support and confidence of staff and voters.

The election system also needed to be improved. The re-election for directors was held every two years, and every four years for the CEO and the GM. Re-election and re-appointment were allowed. If a director was impeached, his or her assessment report would be made public to all staff representatives. One third of the director positions would be changed every two years, and a contested election mechanism had been adopted to maintain the vitality and continuity of director positions. Sun Dawu was also considering the "withdrawal" mechanism. The tentative idea was that once a subsidiary was shut down, two director positions would be eliminated.

Should the whole business shut down, then all the director positions would automatically disappear.

Besides the unexpected internal and external challenges that emerged after the third election, some middle-level managers thought that, under the current situation, it was impossible for talented professional managers to enter the Group and that it was impossible for the Group to retain those talents; in addition, the separation of the three powers depleted the motivation to achieve sustainable growth. As Sun Dawu admitted, "Under the constitution system, the weak link would not be able to ruin the business, and it's not easy for anybody to shine either." Therefore, Sun Dawu was again concerned that the "Family Business Constitution" would not support the sustainability of his family business. Only time would tell whether the "Family Business Constitution" he created could succeed or not.

Doing Business in India: Caveat Venditor

Rajesh Kumar

Business opportunities in India may be there for the taking but not knowing the values and cultural norms can doom a western manager's or entrepreneur's best efforts. This author has written a valuable primer that will prepare a westerner for doing business in India . . . and succeeding.

China and India comprise nearly 40 percent of the world's population and their aggregate output accounts for nearly 25 percent of the global GDP. During the previous decade, China garnered the lion share of the world's attention. But that may be about to change as India emerges as a major economic power in its own right. Indeed, a vigorous debate is currently under way as to whether or not India will outperform China. Although opinion remains divided, there is now a widespread consensus that India not only has a tremendous potential, but has already begun to realize some of it. The sub-continent is expected to be the world's fifth largest economy by 2025 and is today the second fastest-growing economy in the world, with growth rates averaging nearly 8 percent during the last three years.

Liberalization has continued unabated since 1991, with India's economy more than doubling in real terms during this period. That growth is being driven by domestic consumption and the expansion of the information technology industry; both have paid handsome dividends for the country. India's consumer-goods market is already ranked among the top ten in the world and is expected to reach US$400 billion by 2010, making it the fifth largest in the world. In certain industry segments, such as aviation, the Indian market is already demonstrating tremendous potential, and causing foreign investors to look at India very seriously. Similarly, India now has over 90 million cell phone subscribers and the expectation is that within a few years India will be the second-largest market for cell phones, after China. As the Franklin Fund India manager, Sukumar Rajah notes, "Given its size and expected growth over the next few decades, an India strategy has become a must for companies across the world with global aspirations." Perhaps this may well be the reason for why AT Kearney's confidence

Reprint: 9B07TC02

index ranks India as the second most attractive FDI destination, after China. South Korea's Posco has recently decided to invest US$12 billion in the state of Orissa for the purposes of mining iron ore and manufacturing steel.

With India's emergence as an economic superpower and the increasing attraction of the country to foreign investors, many investors are having to devise an India strategy. Some companies, such as General Electric, LG of Korea, have done well, whereas others, such as Sony or Levi's, had a hard time of it when they entered India. The purpose of this article is to highlight the nature of the Indian business environment and to outline the best ways of coping with these challenges. I begin by describing the evolving economic landscape in India. In a subsequent section, I then outline some of the strategic, political, and cultural challenges that await the foreign investor. I conclude by outlining strategies that may be most appropriate in the Indian context.

India's Evolving Economic Landscape

The India of today is very different from the country which the British ruled and equally distant from the early post-independence India. Under British rule, the Indian economy stagnated, with economic growth averaging 0.8 percent between 1900 and 1950. With the population growth matching it, the per capita income was stagnant. Following independence, the Indian government embarked on an import-substitution policy that entailed extensive governmental controls on all facets of business activity. As Kumar and Anand have noted, "The underlying rationale for pursuing this policy in the Indian case was a deep sense of pessimism about increasing the country's exports, a desire to industrialize rapidly, and a romantic attachment to the fundamental tenets of Fabian Socialism . . ." It is fair to say that this policy combined the worst aspects of capitalism and socialism and significantly hampered India's ability to grow rapidly between 1950 and 1980. During this period the Indian economy grew at

a rate of 3.5 percent per annum, a rate that many analysts often came to deride as the "Hindu rate of growth."

The first steps towards reforming the Indian economy took place when Rajiv Gandhi became the Prime Minister. However, the main impetus for reform came in 1991, when the current prime minister, Manmohan Singh, and the then finance minister undertook a series of bold policy initiatives in light of the acute balance of payments crisis that the country was facing. Tariff levels were lowered, industrial licensing was eliminated, foreign investors were granted 51 percent equity in their ventures in India as a matter of routine, and the exchange rate policy was reformed.

The initiation of economic reforms has without question been widely beneficial. Poverty levels have declined by about a third and the information technology sector has grown at an impressive rate of 30 percent annually for the last five years, with India having captured 75 percent of the IT services export market. The manufacturing sector is once again growing, now at an annual rate of 9.4 percent per annum, and there is an overall shift in the composition of India's GDP, with services now accounting for 51 percent of a country's GDP and agriculture constituting only 20.5 percent. The rapid growth of the Indian economy since the economic reforms in 1991 has resulted in a growing middle class. Although it is hard to estimate its exact size, a study by the US Department of Commerce suggests that India has 20 million people with incomes greater than US$13,000, 80 million with incomes in excess of US $3,500, and 100 million people whose incomes are higher than US$2,800.

India is now also emerging as a major hub in the knowledge-based economy. This is reflected in a number of different indicators. For example, more than 225 of the Fortune 500 companies have established R&D and product design centers in India. The R&D design centers span a wide spectrum of industries. There are well over 70 companies engaged in chip design in India, of which 50 or more are located in Bangalore. General Electric has established the

John F. Welch Technology Center in Bangalore. Home to 1800 engineers, the center is responsible for carrying out fundamental research for many of GE's 13 divisions. Motorola has had facilities in India since 1991 and the R&D facilities in India have helped the company develop a US$40 cellular phone for emerging markets. Microsoft established its third international research center in India in 2005, while Intel has well over 800 engineers developing software for its global product lines. India is also emerging as a major biotechnology outsourcing destination with many multinational firms, such as the likes of Novo Nordisk, Aventis, Novartis, GlaxoSmith Kline, Eli Lilly & Pfizer, considering conducting clinical trials in India.

The rapid rise of India as a technology hub can be attributed to a number of different factors. Goldman Sachs suggests that India's R&D costs are just one-eighth of levels in western countries. The country's protection of intellectual property is also improving and it is estimated that 2000 software applications were filed in 2005 with 85 percent of them initiated by multinational firms. India also boasts an abundance of scientific and technological talent, with the country producing the second-highest number of engineering graduates in the world. Concern has been expressed, however, that the quality of these graduates is somewhat uneven, and with the relentless pressure for hiring more of the skilled graduates, a shortage may emerge in the future.

The Dynamics of Economic Reform in India

India is a vibrant, albeit fractious, democracy, in which voter turnout is often greater than that in many industrialized countries. Following India's independence in 1947, the Congress Party dominated Indian politics for 50 years, but for a brief interruption during the late 1970s. All of that began to change with the rise of the Bharatiya Janata Party, which carved out a position for itself on the basis of "Hindutva ideology," i.e., an ideology that sought to rediscover the greatness of India. These are the two parties that dominate

the national political scene, although each has had to rely on coalition governments. Coalition politics seem to have become the prevailing norm in India, at least for the foreseeable future. The Bharatiya Janata Party was ousted from power in 2004, much to its surprise and that of outside observers. The current government, the United Progressive Alliance, a 24 party alliance, is led by the Congress but relies principally on support from the Communists.

At first glance, the dominance of coalition politics may not augur well for the reform process. But appearances can be deceiving, and India is no exception to this rule. Analysts note that both of the major parties are now committed to the continuation of the economic reforms. As Zainulbhai notes, "The momentum behind reform is irreversible, for it is driven by a collective belief that India must have a strong economy to improve its standard of living, to be taken seriously by the world, and not least, to keep pace with neighbouring China." This is not to say that the reform process has always proceeded consistently or smoothly. Analysts note that second-generation reforms, such as reform of labour laws, privatization programs, or even for that matter the reduction of the government budget deficit (currently 8 to 9 percent of GDP), have still to materialize. The reform of labor laws is of particular concern to foreign investors as it has the implication that any company which employs more than 100 workers must seek state approval before making them redundant. Many of the reforms have been stifled by Leftist opposition. As Das notes, "Unfortunately, it stands rigidly against reform and for the status quo, supporting labor laws that benefit 10 percent of the workers at the expense of the other 90 percent..." Nevertheless, one of the striking things about India, as Das notes, is that "Even though the reforms, have been slow, imperfect, and incomplete, they have been consistent and in one direction." Surely this is a positive aspect and one that is likely to benefit all firms, domestic or foreign.

No discussion of economic reform can be complete without discussing the constraints of the economic infrastructure in the country. India gets a ranking of 54 out of 60 in the IMD 2005 survey. Indian and foreign businesses are often handicapped by lack of adequate and consistent power supply, inadequate port capacity, and/or insufficient number of highways. Lack of power remains one of the biggest constraints on Indian businesses and it has led many companies to set up their own generating capacity. Indian spending on infrastructure has been relatively low but there are indications that it is going to be stepped up. These problems have been magnified by an ineffective bureaucracy that as Das notes creates ". . . private benefits for those who control it." Yet, what is most remarkable about India is that notwithstanding these constraints (reform, bureaucracy, infrastructure), the Indian economy has indeed taken off. This is reflective both of the entrepreneurial spirit of the Indians as well as their resilience and creativity.

Strategic, Organizational and Cultural Challenges for the Foreign Investor

a) Strategic Challenges

Strategic adaptability is essential for success everywhere and India is no exception in this regard. The issue of adaptability is a multifaceted one and involves issues such as product adaptation/ pricing, and/or organizational adaptation. The experience of many multinationals in the Indian market suggests, that with a few exceptions, they made few adaptations on entry and were over time forced to revisit their strategies.

Consider, for example, the case of product pricing in India. Although the Indian economy is the second-fastest growing economy in the world and may have more billionaires than China, it is still a relatively poor country, with a GNP per capita of about US$480. One of the implications of this is that the Indian market is a price sensitive one and the foreign investor seeking to do business in the country must price the product accordingly.

Consider also the case of Levi's when it first entered India. The company marketed its product at a hefty price and despite the fact that the brand was much better known than its competitor, Lee, the company initially stumbled. Lee, by contrast, entered into a partnership with Arvind Group and in collaboration with it was able to introduce branded products at an affordable price. Companies in the durable goods sector have also dealt with the problem of affordability by providing financing options for the consumer. They make loans available to the purchaser expeditiously, thus facilitating the sale of their products.

Organizational adaptability deals with three key issues, namely (a) the nature of the top management team; (b) the corporate culture in the local organization; and (c) good coordination between the parent company and the subsidiary. Many multinational firms, with the exception of U.S. and U.K. firms, often relied on expatriate managers from their own units back home. Many of these companies either did not have access to expatriate Indians and/or did not recognize the importance of having them on their management team. This was a severe handicap as managing in India, as Kumar and Anand note, ". . . requires some exceptional skills including being able to develop relationships and tackle prickly unionized labor, petty bureaucrats, and people in the supply and distribution chains." The expatriate managers who did succeed in India were, as Kumar & Sethi pointed out, able to "Think Indian!" A good example of a company that has been successful in India without relying heavily on expatriate management in its parent country is the South Korean company LG Electronics. As the managing director of LG Electronics in India notes, "The expatriates are called in only when there is a problem, and they are generally seen as consultants, or advisers to the business . . . And even at the corporate level, in India every decision is made by Indian employees."

Corporate culture plays an important role in determining how an organization responds to the demands of the marketplace. Having the right spirit or ethos helps the company to more effectively execute its strategy. Many multinational firms in India are striving to create a culture that rewards performance. How successful they might be in this respect is likely to be heavily dependent on their ability to be transparent and create a culture that promotes cooperative behavior. Effective teamwork is often difficult in the Indian cultural context, but that does not by any means negate its importance. Given the fact that Indians often have a more positive perception of expatriates, it is conceivable that a skillful expatriate may be able to institutionalize these norms at the time he enters the Indian subsidiary.

Good coordination between the parent company and the local subsidiary is also essential for the effective execution of a firm's strategy. Effective execution is likely to be facilitated by a shared vision. Often enough, this is not easy, but every effort needs to be made to strive to attain this unity. It would be helpful if the parent company sent the Indian employees to corporate headquarters for training and familiarized them with the company's culture. ST Microelectronics, an Italian firm, transferred 40 engineers from India to Italy for two years to undergo training, with the objective that these employees would not only become intimately familiar with the company's technologies but would also be able to better understand the company's objectives. The top managers in the parent company must also demonstrate their commitment to the Indian market and clearly convey the message that they are in it for the longer term. Jack Welch, the former CEO of General Electric, demonstrated his commitment to the Indian market by his strong backing for GE International Capital Services, one of the biggest business process outsourcing firms in India. GE corporate headquarters was initially reluctant to proceed with this venture but the strong support that Jack Welch gave to it allowed it to become a reality.

b) Political Challenges

India is a fractious democracy and with a high degree of nationalistic sentiment the political environment can often become volatile and/or unpredictable for the multinational firm. Foreign investors in infrastructure projects, especially in the power sector, faced considerable difficulty during the mid-1990s. Many of the projects were launched with much fanfare but the end results were disappointing. Although the institutional environment in India may have been a difficult one, the foreign investors did themselves no favors by pursuing agreements that appeared to be one sided in favor of the foreign investor. Often enough contracts were negotiated and/or renegotiated in a never-ending cycle. In fairness, it needs to be pointed out that these were difficult and complex projects whose cost/benefit analysis was far from easy. But that said, it only highlights how sensitive foreign investors need to be, and especially so in the context of projects whose rationale is far from clear.

Firms in other sectors have also run into problems. For example, Coke and Pepsi were accused by a non-governmental organization in India of selling drinks that contained pesticide levels which were much higher than the EU norms. Both of these firms vociferously denied these allegations, and in independent testing, the claim of the non-governmental organization that the pesticide levels exceeded the EU margin by a range of 11-70 was decisively rejected.

How should multinational firms cope with these challenges in a volatile environment? Although each conflict may have its own specific issues that need to be dealt with on its own terms, the fundamental point is that the firm must convince the stakeholders in India that its actions, while undoubtedly benefiting itself, will also benefit India. While many foreign investors often say this routinely, the question is whether their actions are consistent with their rhetoric. A good example of a company that has gone out of its way to garner legitimacy in India is Hindustan Lever, the subsidiary of the Anglo-Dutch Giant, Unilever. The company enjoys an excellent reputation in the country, one it has attained by indigenizing its Indian operations, and helping to promote the socioeconomic objectives of the Indian government and the states in which it operates.

C) Cultural Challenges

Indian managers embody both individualistic and collective values. This implies that the Indian manager may behave differently in different situations. As an individualist, the Indian manager can be very aggressive and goal oriented. As a collectivist, the Indian manager may be sensitive to the needs and wishes of the people in his/her group. One of the implications of this cultural orientation is that the western manager may find it difficult to fully comprehend the behavior of his Indian counterpart. It does not necessarily mean, however, that the Indian manager is trying to deliberately deceive his Western counterpart. While this judgment may be tempting, it is a judgment that should not be easily rushed into. The Indian culture is also very hierarchical, which has the implication that decisions are made at the very top and the decision making process may be a slow one. The communication style of the Indians is also indirect, with many Indians reluctant to say no, even when they mean no. Indians also draw a distinction between secular and religious time and are much more sensitive to the latter than to the former. Religious time is time that is associated with the performance of rituals at a specific time and/or undertaking or not undertaking actions based on planetary configurations. The often-cited insensitivity of Indians to secular time can also be a source of frustration for the Western manager who may not be conversant with Indian cultural norms. I have also described the Indian manager as having an idealistic mind set, i.e., a way of thinking characterized by a desire to find the best possible solution to the problem. This can be both beneficial as well as detrimental. On the positive side, the high aspirations of Indians may yield high outcomes, but at the same time high aspirations may prevent the emergence of an agreement.

The Indian cultural values that I have outlined have a wide variety of implications for western managers. They affect Indian communication and leadership styles, motivation patterns, decision making processes, and/or their attitudes towards work. As such, they have wide ranging implications for a multinational firm seeking to do business in India. Outsourcing partnerships, relationships with regulatory authorities, joint venture relationships, and motivating local employees are all likely to be affected by differences in cultural values/norms. A western manager who is not consciously aware of some of the differences that set him apart from his Indian colleagues may find it difficult to cope with some of the cultural challenges that he may be confronted with. On the other hand, consider the case of Scott Bayman, President and CEO of GE India. He came to India against the objections of his wife but has lived in India for around eleven years. Both he and his wife have adapted themselves well to Indian society, with Mrs. Bayman reportedly saying "I'm nowhere ready to leave. We've lived here longer than any place. This really is home!"

In this article I have outlined the nature of the economic transformation currently under way in India and the implications that it has for foreign investors. India offers many, many advantages and opportunities to the foreign investor. The consumer sector is on the upswing, India is a key player in the knowledge based economy, and it has the most youthful demographic structure in the world with 70 percent of India's population less than 36 years old! Of course, India is still in the process of transition with institutional imperfections affecting the way in which business is done in the country. As the country evolves, many of these imperfections may be left by the wayside, but even in the interim these imperfections may not be a barrier to doing business in India, provided that the western entrepreneur is willing to transform constraints into opportunities.

Ethical Leadership

Leaders spend most of their time learning how to do their work and helping other people learn how to do theirs, yet in the end, it is the quality and character of the leader that determine the performance and results.

—Frances Hesselbein[1]

We say these are the values of the organization, and we all live them. Then, no matter what the situation, we never think, "Well, I can be slightly unethical today, but tomorrow I'll be better." It doesn't work that way. No matter how difficult the circumstances become, we stand and we act on principle.

—Frances Hesselbein[2]

This chapter presents a guide to ethical decision making in situations that will confront you as a leader and discusses several ethical perspectives that should help you make ethical decisions. There is constant debate as to where a chapter on ethics should appear in any book (e.g., textbooks, casebooks). In this book, we decided to place it last. We do this for one very specific reason. We want ethics and its intersection with leadership to be the last thing you read and consider as you finish your course on leadership. In our own teaching and research, we are struck by the number of times that what seem to be innocuous decisions can turn into very dicey ethical situations. Leaders are often presented with situations that require them to think through several ethical dimensions before making decisions. Consequently, we hope and expect that this chapter will be one you return to many times as you develop as a leader in the organization you join after you finish your current degree.

Concern regarding leaders and their ethics has been central to everyday life throughout our history. Unfortunately, it is also a very messy topic to research. Consequently, research regarding leaders

---

[1]Bunker, Hall, and Kram (2010, p. 138).

[2]Bunker et al. (2010, p. 141).

and their ethics is very sparse (Yukl, 2012). Recent research (Ciulla, 1998; Phillips, 2006) has begun to delve into these issues. Ciulla (1998) discusses how leadership theory and practices may lead to a more just and caring society. Phillips (2006) defines CEO moral capital as "the belief that the CEO justly balances the disparate interests of individual and group stakeholders to achieve positive returns that benefit the firm, its stakeholders, and the CEO."

This definition describes how CEOs and other individuals are viewed by their followers, peers, and superiors and, as Phillips (2006) argues, is based on their perception of the CEO's (or an individual's) character and behavior.

A Definition of Ethics

In the Western world, the definition of ethics dates back to Plato and Aristotle. Ethics comes from *ethos*, a Greek word meaning character, conduct, and/or customs. It is about what morals and values are found appropriate by members of society and individuals themselves. Ethics helps us decide what is right and good or wrong and bad in any given situation. With respect to leadership, ethics is about who leaders are—their character and what they do, their actions and behaviors.

Ethical Theories

As suggested above, ethical theories fall into two broad categories: those theories related to leaders' behavior and those related to leaders' character. For those theories related to conduct, there are two types: those that relate to leaders' conduct and their consequences and those that relate to the rules or duty that prescribe leaders' conduct.

Those theories related to consequences are called *teleological theories* (*telos* being a Greek word for purposes or ends). These theories emphasize whether a leader's actions, behavior, and/or conduct have positive outcomes. This means that the outcomes related to a person's behavior establish whether the behavior was ethical or unethical.

Those theories related to duty or rules are called *deontological theories* (*deos* being a Greek word for duty). These theories focus on the actions that lead to consequences and whether the actions are good or bad. Those theories related to character are described as virtue-based approaches.

Teleological Approaches

There are three approaches to assessing outcomes and whether they are viewed as ethical. First, *ethical egoism* describes the actions of leaders that are designed to obtain the greatest good for the leader. Second, *utilitarianism* refers to the actions of leaders that are designed to obtain the greatest good for the largest number of people. Third, *altruism* describes the actions of leaders that are designed to demonstrate concern for others' interests, even if these interests are contrary to the leader's self-interests.

Deontological Approach

This approach is derived from *deos*, a Greek word meaning duty. It argues that whether or not an action is ethical depends not only on its outcome but also on whether the action, behavior, or conduct is itself inherently good. Examples of actions and behaviors that are intrinsically good, irrespective of the outcomes, are "telling the truth, keeping promises, being fair, and respecting others" (Northouse, 2013). This approach emphasizes the actions of leaders *and* their ethical responsibility to do what is right.

Virtue-Based Approach

Virtue-based theories are related to leaders and who they are and are grounded in the leader's character. In addition, these virtues can be learned and retained through experience and practice. This learning occurs in an individual's family and the various communities with which an individual interacts throughout his or her lifetime. This perspective can be traced back to Plato and Aristotle. Aristotle believed that individuals could be helped to become more virtuous and that more attention should be given to telling individuals what to be as opposed to telling them what to do (Velasquez, 1992). Aristotle suggested the following virtues as exemplars of an ethical person: generosity, courage, temperance, sociability, self-control, honesty, fairness, modesty, and justice (Velasquez, 1992). Velasquez argued that organizational managers should learn and retain virtues "such as perseverance, public-spiritedness, integrity, truthfulness, fidelity, benevolence, and humility" (Northouse, 2013).

The Centrality of Ethics to Leadership

Ethics is central to leadership because of the nature of the relationship between leaders and followers. Leaders influence followers—this means they affect followers' lives either negatively or positively (Yukl, 2012). The nature of the influence depends on the leaders' character and behavior (particularly the nature and outcome of behaviors). Leaders have more power—interpersonal and/or formal hierarchical power—and therefore have a greater responsibility with respect to their impact on their followers. Leaders influence followers in the pursuit and achievement of common goals. It is in these situations that leaders need to respect their followers and treat them with dignity. In other words, leaders need to treat their followers as individuals with distinctive identities. Finally, leaders are instrumental in developing and establishing organizational values. Their own personal values determine what kind of ethical climate will develop in their organizations.

Ethical Leadership: The Perspectives of Several Leadership Scholars

In this section, we review the perspectives of two prominent leadership scholars as these perspectives relate to leadership and ethics. We focus on Heifetz (1994) and Burns (1978).

Heifetz and Ethical Leadership

Heifetz (1994) emphasized conflict and the responsibility of leaders to assist followers in dealing with conflict and effecting changes that come from conflict. He focused on the values of followers, the values of the organizations in which they work, and the values of the communities in which they live. For Heifetz, the paramount responsibility of leaders is to create a work atmosphere characterized by empathy, trust, and nurturance and to help followers to change and grow when faced with difficult situations (Northouse, 2013; Yukl, 2012).

Burns and Ethical Leadership

Like Heifetz (1994), Burns (1978) argued that leadership (especially transformational leadership, as described in Chapter 9) is about helping followers achieve higher ethical standards when differing values conflict—especially when conflict is confronted during difficult situations. He argued that the interaction of leaders and followers should raise the ethical behavior and character of both. Leaders would do this by assisting followers to emphasize values such as equality, justice, and liberty (Burns, 1978; Ciulla, 1998).

Both perspectives emphasize the relationship between leaders and followers and argue that this relationship is at the heart of ethical leadership. The ideas presented by these scholars are similar to and in agreement with Gilligan's (1982) ethic of caring. This has become a central principle in ethical leadership research and is considered of paramount importance to organizations because it is of critical importance in developing collaboration and trust among leaders and followers (Brady, 1999).

▨ Ethical Leadership Principles

In this section, we present five principles that are believed to lead to the development of ethical leadership. These are respect for others, service to others, justice for others, honesty toward others, and building community with others (DuBrin, 2010; Northouse, 2013).

Respect for Others

Ethical leaders treat others with dignity and respect. This means that they treat people as ends in themselves rather than as means to their own ends. This form of respect recognizes that followers have goals and ambitions and confirms followers as human beings who have worth and value to the organization. In addition, it leads to empathy, active listening, and tolerance for conflicting viewpoints.

Service to Others

Ethical leaders serve others. They behave in an altruistic fashion as opposed to behaving in a way that is based on ethical egoism. These leaders put followers first—their prime reason for being is to support and nurture subordinates. Service to others is exemplified through behaviors such as mentoring, building teams, and empowering (Kanungo & Mendonca, 1996).

Justice for Others

Ethical leaders ensure that justice and fairness are central parts of their decision making. This means treating all subordinates in very similar ways, except when there is a very clear need for differential treatment and there is transparency about why this need exists. In addition to being transparent, the logic for differential treatment should be morally sound and reasonable.

Honesty Toward Others

Ethical leadership requires honesty. Dishonesty destroys trust—a critical characteristic of any leader–follower relationship. On the other hand, honesty increases trust and builds the leader–follower relationship. Honesty means to be open with others by expressing our thinking and our reality as fully as we can. This means balancing openness with disclosing only what is appropriate in a given scenario. Dalla Costa (1998) says that honesty for leaders means the following:

Do not promise what you can't deliver, do not misrepresent, do not hide behind spin-doctored evasions, do not suppress obligations, do not evade accountability, do not accept that the "survival of the fittest" pressures of business release any of us from the responsibility to respect another's dignity and humanity. (p. 164)

We would argue that leaders need to ensure that *what they believe, what they think, what they say,* and *what they do* are internally consistent. This internal consistency, along with openness, will build trust among followers toward the leader.

Building Community With Others

Ethical leaders build community with others. This is crucial because leadership is about influencing others to achieve a communal goal. This means that leaders develop organizational or team goals that are appropriate for the leader and his or her followers. These goals need to excite as many people as possible, and ethical leaders achieve this by taking into account the goals of everyone in the team or organization.

⬚ How Does Ethical Leadership Work?

We are hoping that this chapter will enable you to better understand yourself as you develop your leadership skills, knowledge, and abilities. Use the thinking on ethical leadership in this chapter as a guide in making your decisions. Remember that the relationship between you and your followers is at the heart of ethical leadership and requires that you show sensitivity to others' needs, treat others in a just manner, and have a caring attitude toward others. Being an ethical leader will be easier if you entrench the following questions into your thinking (Northouse, 2013):

- Is this the right and fair thing to do?
- Is this what a good person would do?
- Am I respectful to others?
- Do I treat others generously?
- Am I honest toward others?
- Am I serving the community?

Ethical leaders must be concerned with more than running their businesses. They must be concerned with their employees, their customers, their suppliers, their communities, their shareholders, and themselves. Leadership is influencing people to achieve communal goals; ethical leadership is achieving those goals in a way that is fair and just to your employees, your customers, your suppliers, your communities, your shareholders, and yourselves (Daft, 2011; Phillips, 2006).

⬚ References

Brady, F. N. (1999). A systematic approach to teaching ethics in business. *Journal of Business Ethics, 19*(3), 309–319.

Bunker, K. A., Hall, D. T., & Kram, K. E. (2010). *Extraordinary leadership: Addressing the gaps in senior executive development.* San Francisco, CA: Jossey-Bass.

Burns, J. M. (1978). *Leadership.* New York, NY: Harper & Row.

Ciulla, J. B. (1998). *Ethics, the heart of leadership.* Westport, CT: Greenwood.

Daft, R. L. (2011). *The leadership experience* (5th ed.). Mason, OH: Thomson, South-Western.

Dalla Costa, J. (1998). *The ethical imperative: Why moral leadership is good business*. Reading, MA: Addison-Wesley.

DuBrin, A. (2010). *Leadership: Research findings, practice, and skills* (6th ed.). Mason, OH: South-Western/Cengage.

Gilligan, C. (1982). *In a different voice: Psychological theory and women's development*. Cambridge, MA: Harvard University Press.

Heifetz, R. A. (1994). *Leadership without easy answers*. Cambridge, MA: Harvard University Press.

Kanungo, R. N., & Mendonca, M. (1996). *Ethical dimensions of leadership*. Thousand Oaks, CA: Sage.

Northouse, P. G. (2013). *Leadership: Theory and practice* (6th ed.). Thousand Oaks, CA: Sage.

Phillips, J. R. (2006). *CEO moral capital*. Unpublished doctoral manuscript, University of Western Ontario, Canada.

Velasquez, M. G. (1992). *Business ethics: Concepts and cases* (3rd ed.). Englewood Cliffs, NJ: Prentice Hall.

Yukl, G. (2012). *Leadership in organizations* (8th ed.). Upper Saddle River, NJ: Pearson/Prentice Hall.

The Cases

Lee and Li, Attorneys-at-Law and the Embezzlement of NT$3 Billion by Eddie Liu (A)

Dr. C. V. Chen received news that one of Lee and Li's senior assistants had found a loophole in a power of attorney from one of the firm's clients, SanDisk Corporation (SanDisk), that had allowed him to illegally sell the client's shares in a Taiwanese company and to sneak out of Taiwan with more than NT$3 billion. Unfortunately, Lee and Li had no insurance to cover this embezzlement. Chen knew that the three senior partners needed to develop a plan of action to save the law firm, take care of the lawyers and other employees, maintain the reputation of the firm within Taiwan and abroad, do what was best for SanDisk and Lee and Li, and keep the more than 12,000 clients from deserting the firm.

A Non-Traditional Female Entrepreneur (C)

In September 2010, Jane Liu was pondering the future development of her company. As the founder CEO of New Deantronics (ND), she knew the next few years would bring major change to ND. The last couple of years had been eventful: in 2009, ND had moved to a brand new facility with three-times the space of its old location; furthermore, ND's revenue growth from 2008 to 2009 was 33%—about twice the growth from 2007 to 2008. ND was thriving even while other companies were suffering from the 2008–2009 global financial crises. The need for rapid expansion was so great that Liu knew that, within the next three months, she had to recruit around 100 good-quality employees and train them efficiently to fill ND's ever-growing influx of orders. In addition, she was expecting that she would triple revenue with no more than twice the manpower; she wanted to be a large part of fostering the development of the medical device industry in Taiwan; and she needed to develop the people who would be ND's next senior leadership team. Liu was not sure how to achieve these three goals; she had built ND on a culture of sincerity and teamwork.

The Reading

Principled Leadership: Taking the Hard Right

What makes a leader the most principled is a certain solidity at the core, a solidity founded on principles that are, essentially, points on a moral compass. Those principles are visible in the actions of some leaders, while other leaders act according to convenience. These authors lay down a blueprint that will allow a leader to be guided by principles.

Lee and Li, Attorneys-at-Law and the Embezzlement of NT$3 Billion by Eddie Liu (A)[1]

Yeong-Yuh Chiang and W. Glenn Rowe

Dr. C.V. Chen was shocked and speechless. Paul Hsu, one of Lee and Li's most senior partners, had just briefed him and Kwan-Tao Li about the actions of Eddie Liu, one of the firm's senior assistants. Liu had found a loophole in a power of attorney from one of the firm's clients that had allowed him to illegally sell the client's shares in a Taiwanese company and to sneak out of Taiwan with NT$3.09 billion (approximately US$92 million). Unfortunately, Lee and Li had no insurance to cover this embezzlement.

Many questions raced through Chen's mind: What about the firm? How would this action affect the more than 550 lawyers and employees? How would other clients react to the news of this crime? Would this breach of trust ruin the firm's reputation in Taiwan and abroad? Would the firm survive and remain financially stable? What should the firm do for the client whose shares had been used to perpetuate the fraud and theft by Liu?

Chen knew that action had to be taken quickly. The questions whirled in his head as he considered what he, Hsu and Kwan-Tao Li, the three most senior partners at Lee and Li, needed to do today, tomorrow, next week and over the next several months.

October 13, 2003 would forever be seared into Chen's memory.

⊠ The Firm: Lee and Li, Attorneys-at-Law

The firm that later became Lee and Li had been founded in Shanghai, China, in the mid-1940s.

James Lee, one of the two founders, had commenced practicing law with Allman and Kopps, and, in 1948, the firm was named Allman, Kopps and Lee. Dr. C.N. Li, the other founding partner, had also practiced in Shanghai during the 1940s. Both James Lee and C.N. Li were specialists in international legal matters.

In 1953, James Lee established his own law office in Taipei, Taiwan, and, in 1965, he was joined by C.N. Li. James Lee died in 1970, and Li renamed the firm Lee and Li. After C.N. Li died in 1973, Paul Hsu, Kwan-Tao Li (C.N. Li's son) and C.V. Chen, together with other senior partners, led the firm through extraordinary growth to become one of the largest law firms in Asia and the largest in Taiwan. Considered by many to be the top law firm in that country,[2] Lee and Li had offices in the cities of Taipei, Taichung, Hsinchu, Tainan and Kaohsiung.

Lee and Li's core values encompassed three principles: caring for people, excellence in quality and client service. A core goal was "doing well by doing good." The firm's motto "we care, we serve, we excel" was prominently displayed at the entrance to the firm's head office in Taipei. The partners and staff believed that adherence to these principles had made the firm a leader in each of its 28 practice areas. The firm was involved in the development of public policies and in promoting the rule of law in Taiwan and elsewhere, particularly in China. The firm had advised Taiwan's government on vital social and economic policies, and several firm members had helped draft new governmental legislation.

[1]This case has been written on the basis of public sources. Consequently, the interpretation and perspectives presented in this case are not necessarily those of Lee and Li or any of its partners and employees.

[2]"Plugging the Loopholes," editorial, *Taipei Times*, October 18, 2003, p. 8; Jimmy Chuang, "Fugitive Liu Wanted in Hong Kong," *Taipei Times*, June 24, 2004, p. 1.

Lee and Li lawyers had been involved in judicial reform and constitutional litigation work that were considered landmarks. Their work on pro bono cases had won them a reputation for "being a leader in public interest work in Taiwan." In 1999, the firm established the Lee and Li Foundation, a not-for-profit organization dedicated to promoting education and rule of law.

Lee and Li had several thousand clients, many of whom had been with the firm for decades. One-third of these clients were headquartered in Taiwan, and the rest were foreign firms. Companies from the United States, Europe and Japan had utilized Lee and Li's services. The firm's client list included internationally well-known firms, such as General Electric, Ford, 3M, Bank of America, City Bank, IBM, Sony, McDonald's and Siemens. Over the years, Lee and Li had represented almost all of the Fortune 500 firms and the multinational banks that were doing business in Taiwan.

Lee and Li's attorneys were globally connected, and several were fluent in English or Japanese in addition to their native tongue, Chinese. They were graduates of top law schools in countries such as Taiwan, the United States, and Japan (see Exhibit 1 for brief résumés for Chen and Li). Lee and Li's attorneys enjoyed long-standing relationships with law firms in North America, Asia and Europe. Collaboration on cross-border deals with other law firms was routine for Lee and Li attorneys. To better serve clients operating in the Greater China region, Lee and Li had established strategic alliances with Lee and Li Business Consultants (Shanghai) Ltd. and Lee and Li—Leaven IPR Agency Ltd. in Beijing.

Lee and Li had achieved a stellar reputation and received many awards for its outstanding work in the areas other than intellectual property. The firm had received several awards for its work in "managing intellectual property" (see Exhibit 2 for a list of awards, honors and recognition for Lee and Li from 1998 to 2002).

From its beginnings, the firm had developed the largest intellectual property practice in Taiwan, and in the 1970s, had been extensively involved in foreign direct investment growth into Taiwan. The firm pioneered the development of the banking and capital markets practice in the 1980s and had been pivotal in the establishment of the technology and law practice in the 1990s. Lee and Li was structured into four departments (corporate, banking and capital markets, trademark and copyright, and patent and technology) with Hsu, Chen and Li jointly managing the operations. Although the associate partners and staff worked almost exclusively for one of the four departments, they would, as a rule, engage in cross-fertilization with their colleagues in the other departments.

☒ The Client: SanDisk Corporation (NASDAQ: SNDK)

SanDisk Corporation (SanDisk) was founded in 1988 by Dr. Eli Harari, a world-renowned authority on non-volatile memory technology. Based in Sunnyvale, California, the company was the world's largest supplier of flash memory data storage card products. It designed, manufactured and marketed "industry-standard, solid-state data, digital imaging and audio storage products using its patented, high density flash memory and controller technology."[3] SanDisk was the only company that had the rights to manufacture and sell every major flash card format, including CF, SD, miniSD, SmartMedia, FlashDisk, MMC, MemoryStick Pro, xD-Picture cards and USB flash drives. The company did not operate fabrication facilities, but used a multiple-sources strategy to fluctuate its supply with changes in demand. SanDisk controlled a significant portion of its flash memory wafer manufacturing

---

[3]"SanDisk . . . Its Taiwan Law Firm," *Business Wire*, November 15, 2003, p. 1.

through its joint venture, FlashVision, and many other strategic arrangements with fabrication facility owners. These strategic and contractual partners included Toshiba, Samsung, Renasas Technology, United Microelectronic Inc. (UMC) and Tower Semiconductor Ltd. Such a multiple-sources strategy enabled SanDisk to concentrate on product designs and development of its core competency. SanDisk received a majority of its revenue from direct sales to retailers.

On September 30, 2003, SanDisk owned 147.8 million shares in UMC, one of its contractual partners in Taiwan. Twenty million of these shares were held by SanDisk with the remaining 127.8 million shares under the control of Lee and Li. SanDisk had sold 35 million UMC shares during the month of September for approximately US$30 million. The 127.8 million UMC shares controlled by Lee and Li were valued at US$83.3 million, based on cost, and were worth US$106.6 million based on trading price on the Taiwan Stock Exchange on September 30, 2003.

At SanDisk's previous fiscal year end on December 29, 2002, it reported revenues of US$541,273,000 with net income of US$36,240,000. Its diluted net income per share was US$0.26. SanDisk had working capital of US$584,450,000, total assets of US$973,579,000, long-term debt of US$150,000,000 and stockholders' equity of US$627,720,000. The company was doing well financially and was on an upward trajectory (see Exhibit 3 for the quarterly financial data as of September 28, 2003).

The Senior Partners: Hsu, Chen and Li

Paul Hsu, C.V. Chen and Kwan-Tao Li, together with other senior partners who had retired before the turn of the century, had led the firm since the deaths of the founders, James Lee and C.N. Li.

Kwan-Tao Li joined the firm in August 1969. In addition, he started teaching at Soochow University Law School and Fu Jen Catholic University that same year. Li had graduated from New York University Law School with his master's degree of law and had a master's of business administration from Kellogg/Hong Kong University of Science and Technology. Hsu had joined the firm in September 1969, preceding Chen by about four years. Chen joined in 1973 after having received his SJD (doctorate in law) from the Harvard Law School in 1972 and having taught at National Chengchi University Graduate School of Law. Together, Hsu, Chen and Li had been with Lee and Li for a combined 98 years.

The Perpetrator: Eddie Liu

Liu had graduated from National Chunghsing University with his bachelor's of law degree. He joined Lee and Li in December 1989 as a legal assistant. Liu handled non-litigation cases in the firm's corporate and investing department and was responsible for investing and mergers and acquisitions. He performed well and was considered a capable assistant. Although he was a law school graduate and a capable assistant, Liu had failed to pass the Taiwanese bar exam. On August 1, 2003, he approached the management of the firm and asked for a 12 month's leave without pay to prepare for the bar exam. Management approved his request on October 1 because the 41-year-old Liu was a trusted employee.

The Embezzlement: NT$3 Billion[4]

In 2002, SanDisk authorized Lee and Li to file an investment application with the Taiwanese

---

[4]Sheree Shiow-Ru Ma and Mei-Cyue Lee, "Internal Control and Employee's Fraudulent Behaviors," *Accounting Research Monthly*, No. 218, January 1, 2004.

government. This application was required to allow the remittance of the return on investment (the dividend) and the principle in the case of divestment to SanDisk because of the Taiwanese government's foreign exchange control. This arrangement required that SanDisk give Lee and Li a power of attorney. The power of attorney should have empowered Lee and Li only to interact with the government on SanDisk's behalf. However, it contained a clause that allowed Lee and Li to deal with the brokerage house holding SanDisk's shares in UMC. This clause meant that Lee and Li's representative could talk to the brokerage house on behalf of SanDisk. For this clause to have been included in the power of attorney was very unusual. The inclusion of the clause should have been noted by Lee and Li and deleted. The power of attorney authorized Lee and Li to make chops (signets) for SanDisk, and any transaction involving SanDisk required both these chops and those containing the name of Hsu, all of which were secured in a vault at Lee and Li.

In July 2002, Lee and Li, in its role representing SanDisk, opened a trading account in the investment firm KGI and a deposit account in Chang Hwa Bank. The proceeds from the sale of any shares acquired by SanDisk in Taiwanese firms were to be used to invest in mainland China and in Taiwan. Because of the flawed clause in the power of attorney and because of his position in the firm, Liu gained unauthorized access to the passbooks and chops for both accounts and could transact business through both accounts without any "actual" permission and/or supervision. He was not legally authorized to make any transactions but he had access to the tools that allowed him to do so.

In July 2003, SanDisk deposited 183 million UMC shares in the KGI account. Liu applied for a leave of absence on August 1 to prepare for his bar examination and immediately moved into a five-star hotel, having left his Peitou District residence in Taipei. During August, he privately opened several accounts for SanDisk at Asia Securities,

United World Chinese Commercial Bank (a branch in Taiwan and a branch in Hong Kong), Taipei Bank, Hwatai Bank, Shanghai Commercial and Savings Bank, and Chang Hwa Bank. All accounts were under the name of SanDisk Corporation except for the bank account in the Hong Kong branch of the United World Chinese Commercial Bank, which was opened in the name of "SanDisk Investing Corporation."

From August 2 to 9, Liu, having forged the authorization document required, had transferred 120.3 million UMC shares from the KGI account to the Asia Securities account. He then conspired with private investment consulting firms to bid up the price of the UMC stock. From August 6 to 28, he sold the shares and obtained NT$3.09 billion (US$92 million). During August and September, to eliminate any trace of the NT$3.09 billion, he laundered the money by buying diamonds and travelers' checks with the money he had remitted to the Hong Kong account.

During September, the Money Laundering Prevention Center (MLPC) of the Taiwanese government was informed of the huge amount of funds transfers but the information indicated that it was a routine notification of a "huge amount transfer" in excess of NT$1 million. The transaction did not appear to be illegal for two reasons: First, the information MLPC received said that "SanDisk Corporation" had transferred earnings from the sale of UMC's stock to "SanDisk Investing Corporation" in Hong Kong, not to another company or individual; second, it appeared that Liu was fully authorized by both SanDisk and Lee and Li to sell the shares and transfer the earnings. Therefore, the transaction was judged a legal transfer by the MLPC.

Around the end of September and beginning of October, Liu handed over his files to his colleagues, ostensibly in preparation for his leave without pay, and he intentionally withheld any files related to SanDisk. On October 1, Liu's leave without pay was approved; however, he continued to go to the office until Thursday,

October 9. At 2:00 p.m. on October 9, Liu left Lee and Li and proceeded directly to the airport. He bought his ticket at the airline counter using as his travel documents both his roommate's passport and his Tai Bao Zheng (a travel document required for people from Taiwan to legally enter mainland China). He then flew to Hong Kong from where it was much easier to transfer the diamonds and travelers' checks to a bank in a city within mainland China, such as Shanghai.

Lee and Li's Dilemma: What to Do?

Chen was informed of Liu's embezzlement on Monday, October 13. October 10 had been a national holiday and October 11 and 12 was the weekend. Liu's colleagues had reconciled his files early on Monday and noticed the discrepancy. This finding led to the discovery of Liu's

malfeasance, which was reported to Paul Hsu, who immediately briefed C.V. Chen and Kwan-Tao Li. The embezzlement left all of the partners in jeopardy because Lee and Li had no insurance to cover the NT$3 billion. In Taiwan, the partners in law firms shared unlimited liability, which meant that all of Lee and Li's partners faced the possibility of losing all of their personal possessions as well as their professional livelihood and standing.

Chen knew that, as the senior partners, the three of them needed to develop a plan of action that would save Lee and Li; take care of the lawyers and other employees, as well as their families; keep Lee and Li's reputation within Taiwan and abroad intact; do what was best for SanDisk and Lee and Li; and keep the more than 12,000 clients from deserting the firm. Chen knew that he, Hsu and Li had to act quickly and decisively. Liu's embezzlement would become public knowledge within hours, or the next day at the latest.

Exhibit I

Brief Résumé for C.V. Chen

Place of Birth: Yunan, China.
Nationality: Republic of China (on Taiwan).

Education

S.J.D., Harvard (1972); LL.M., Harvard (1970); LL.M., University of British Columbia (1969); LL.B., National Taiwan University (1967).

Experience

Professional: Chairman and Managing Partner, Lee and Li Attorneys-at-Law, Taipei, Taiwan; Adjunct Professor of Law, National Chengchi University Graduate School of Law, Taiwan, (1972–present); Lecture Professor of Law, Guanghua School of Management, Peking University, China; Lecture Professor of Law, School of Law, Tsinghua University, China; Chairman of Guanghua Law School Council, Zhejiang University, China; Lecturer, the Training Institute for Judges and Prosecutors, the Ministry of Justice of the Republic of China.

(Continued)

Exhibit 1 (Continued)

Pro Bono:

President, The Red Cross Society of the Republic of China (April 2000–present); Chairman, Taipei European School Foundation, Taiwan, the Republic of China (1994–present); Director, Lee and Li Foundation; Managing Director, Chinese (Taiwan) Society of International Law (Jan. 2004–present).

Honors

Honorary President, Harvard Club of Republic of China on Taiwan (1989–present); Recipient of the Order of Resplendent Banner with Special Cravat from the President of the Republic of China in 1989 for contribution to the upgrading of legal education and establishment of procurement system in the armed forces; Recipient of other medals and awards from the government of the Republic of China on Taiwan.

Publications

Numerous articles on transnational legal problems

Brief Résumé for Kwan-Tao Li

Place of Birth: Shanghai, China.
Nationality: Republic of China (on Taiwan).

Education

MBA, Kellogg-HKUST; LL.M., New York University Law School, Graduate Division; LL.B., National Taiwan University.

Experience

Chief Counsellor, Lee and Li, Attorneys-at-law; Chairman, Lee and Li Foundation; Chairman, Lee and Li Business Consultants (Shanghai), Ltd; Director, Far Eastern Medical Foundation; Director, Yen Tjing Ling Medical Foundation; Director, Far Eastern Y.Z. Hsu Science and Technology Memorial Foundation; Director, Asia Cement Corporation; Director, Far Eastern Textile Ltd; Director, Tai Yuen Textile Co., Ltd.; Supervisor, Yulon Nissan Motor Co., Ltd.; Associate Professor of Law, Chinese Culture University (1985–1998); Lecturer of Law, Soochow University Law School (1969–1999); Lecturer of Law, Soochow University Graduate Law School (1972–1985); Lecturer of Law, National Taiwan Institute of Technology (1975–1979); Lecturer of Law, Fu Jen Catholic University (1969–1971); Director, Yuan Ze University (1987–1999).

Member

Member, State Bar of New York.

Language

Mandarin, English, Cantonese, Shanghainese

Practice Area

Corporate; Entertainment; Fair Trade; Intellectual Property Rights; International Mergers and Acquisitions; Labour; Maritime; Trademarks.

Co-Author

Co-author of "A Study on Economic Contract Law of Mainland China," published by Chinese Culture University; Contributor to *Trade and Investment in Taiwan: The Legal and Economic Environment in the R.O.C.*, Published by University of Washington.

SOURCE: http://www.leeandli.com/web/e/default.htm, accessed June 8, 2008.

Exhibit 2	Awards, Honors and Recognition for Lee and Li

Managing Intellectual Property

1998	Voted No.1 Firm for Non-patent Work in Taiwan 1997
1999	Voted No.1 Firm for Trade Mark and Copyright Work in Taiwan 1998
2000	Voted No.1 Firm for Patent in Taiwan 1999
2000	Voted No.1 Firm for Trade Mark/Copyright in Taiwan 1999
2001	Voted No.1 Firm for Patent in Taiwan 2000
2001	Voted No.1 Firm for Trade Mark/Copyright in Taiwan 2000
2002	Voted No.2 Firm for Patent in Taiwan 2001
2002	Voted No.2 Firm for Trade Mark/Copyright in Taiwan 2001
2003	Voted No.2 Firm for Patent in Taiwan 2002
2003	Voted No.1 Firm for Trade Mark/Copyright in Taiwan 2002

International Financial Law Review

2001	Law Firm of the Year
2001	Pro Bono Award
2002	Regional Law Firm of the Year
2003	National Law Firm of the Year

Global Competition Review

2002	The GCR 100: A Survey of the World's Leading Competition Law Practices and Economists

SOURCE: http://www.leeandli.com/web/e/default.htm, accessed June 8, 2008.

Exhibit 3	SanDisk Corporation 2003 Supplementary Quarterly Data (In Thousands, Except per Share Data)

| | Quarters Ended | | |
	March 30	June 29	September 28
Revenues			
Product	$155,448	$214,044	$259,446
License and royalty	$19,032	$20,582	$21,954
Total revenues	$174,480	$234,626	$281,400
Gross profits	$71,591	$88,772	$113,635
Operating income	$34,686	$46,659	$66,803
Net income	$24,925	$41,326	$14,770
Net income per share			
Basic%	$0.18	$0.30	$0.11
Diluted%	$0.17	$0.26	$0.09

SOURCE: 2003, SanDisk Corporation's Annual Report on Form 10-K, 20.

A Non-Traditional Female Entrepreneur (C)

Yeh-Yun Lin and W. Glenn Rowe

In September 2010, Jane Liu—president and founder of New Deantronics (ND) was in deep thought in her new office pondering the future development of her company. Two major events had prompted her to think about ND's future development: firstly, in 2009, ND had moved to a brand new facility with three-times the space of its old location; secondly, ND's revenue growth from 2008 to 2009 was 33 per cent—about twice the growth from 2007 to 2008 (see Exhibit 1). While other companies were suffering from the 2008–2009 global financial crises, Liu's company was thriving. The need for rapid expansion was so great that she had to strategize in order to meet her short-term, mid-term and long-term goals. Within the next three months, she had to recruit around 100 good-quality employees and train them efficiently to fill ND's ever-growing influx of orders. By 2017, she expected to triple revenue with no more than twice the manpower. In the long run, she wanted to be a large part of fostering the development of the medical device industry in Taiwan. Liu was not sure how to achieve these three goals; she had built ND on a culture of sincerity and teamwork.

⬚ A Culture of Sincerity and Teamwork

Starting from scratch with the ambition to do business with major global medical device companies—and with a self-established high quality standard—Liu undertook the daunting task through her determination, sincerity and humbleness, planning to learn from whoever could and would teach her. She was fortunate that people in many major medical device companies were willing to give her an opportunity to learn and to try small orders, even though she candidly let them know that she did not yet have the relevant background. Her sincerity and confidence in her own ability to supply the best products possible won her the small orders that she needed. What was on her mind at that time was mainly that having a major customer is an efficient way to upgrade product quality, for she knew that such a company would provide technical assistance in order for her products to comply with the requested quality standards. A major U.S. medical device company—Covidien (previously named Valleylab)—sent employees to Taiwan to help ND improve its production process and enhance its product quality; afterwards, the two companies co-developed the electrosurgical pencil and became effective partners.

Through her sincere and humble attitude, Liu became friends with a key person at Olsen Surgical. At the initial stage, she often visited this gentleman for technical assistance; both parties knew that the interaction was merely for technical advice, based on their friendship. Afterwards, even though there was no need for technical assistance, Liu would drop by to have a chat when she was nearby. No business relationship was expected until one day when Olsen Surgical encountered a big problem with a supplier and needed a substitute to ensure delivery of a product; Liu was the first person this gentleman thought of, and ever since then Olsen Surgical has been a major customer of ND.

Another story often told in the industry was how Liu had settled payment when Johnson & Johnson (J&J) decided to withdraw from the electro-surgery device market and unexpectedly cancelled orders in 2003. J&J offered a full payment to compensate for ND's loss. By law, Liu could have accepted the full payment. Yet, her sincerity, empathy and firm belief of only getting what she deserved resulted in a different decision. She asked only for compensation for the materials that she had already paid for. With J&J as ND's second largest customer at that time, it was the only year in its history ND experienced negative revenue growth. However, Liu's willingness to only ask for what she had paid won ND the reputation in the U.S. market for being a supplier who could be trusted. A few years later, when J&J needed other types of medical product, ND was invited to be a certified supplier again.

Liu also believed that internal and external teamwork helped ND grow. Internally, employees were the best partners. Consequently, employee benefits were always in her mind. Caring policies included flexible working hours for pregnant women, child care, free annual health checks, free parking, work-family life balance encouragement, well-planned training, and nine more days than government regulated annual leave. As early as the late 1990s, ND had implemented a five-work day system, which was rare in Taiwan at that time. Liu also promoted an equal employment opportunity culture in terms of promotion and gender in her company. She had successfully built a family-like team culture and received a "Friendly Workplace" award from the Taiwan Bureau of

Labor Affairs in 2007, the first year such an award was conferred.

Externally, Liu invited her customers and suppliers to be her team members. Customers were her quality instructors and inspectors, and they had helped ND produce world class products. Customers had become her R&D partners as well. Further, suppliers with uncompromised quality had become ND's long-term partners.

It took Liu about 10 years to achieve her first goal—to be a premier "made in Taiwan" medical device manufacturer. It took more than 20 years for ND to advance from being an original equipment manufacturer (OEM) to being an original design manufacturer (ODM) and then to being an original brand manufacturer (OBM) with the capabilities of research and development, manufacturing, quality assurance, sterilization, and marketing. Over this 20 year period ND also became a trusted core player in the medical devices supply chain. In particular, ND was proud to have become the sole supplier of the Philip patented Auto External Defibrillator (AED).

⊠ Future Expansion

Currently, ND's sources of revenue consisted of 70 per cent from the United States and 25 per cent from Europe. Recent expansion had been targeting markets in Japan and Korea. ND had adopted a three-segment strategy in the global market. First, ND had developed several relationships with major global device companies; second, ND went into private labeling for medium size, geographically significant companies; and third, ND developed its own branded products for distribution in selected market segments. This multi-faceted global strategy provided ND with consistent revenue growth and returns.

The long-term mission of ND was to foster a medical devices industry cluster in Taiwan. Having suffered from the inability to secure requested materials and facilities locally during its growth, ND fully understood the importance of clustering. Taiwan's current metal industry and plastic industry could help grow the medical device industry in Taiwan. The clustering effect, for example high-tech industries in Hsin-Chu Science Park, would have exposure and be able to attract talented people to join the advancement of the medical device industry in Taiwan.

As Liu pondered the future of ND she wondered what strategy would achieve her goals for growth and what she would need to do to ensure the strategy was well executed. In the next three months ND needed to recruit 100 high-quality employees. These new employees would need to be trained efficiently to fill ND's ever-growing influx of orders.

In the next seven years or so, she wanted to triple ND's sales with no more than twice the number of people currently working for ND. In addition, she needed to develop the third generation leaders who would replace her and her senior management team. By 2017, she wanted to retire with ND in capable hands and with a well-entrenched culture of sincerity and teamwork.

In the longer term she wanted to be a large part of fostering the development of the medical device industry in Taiwan.

Exhibit I

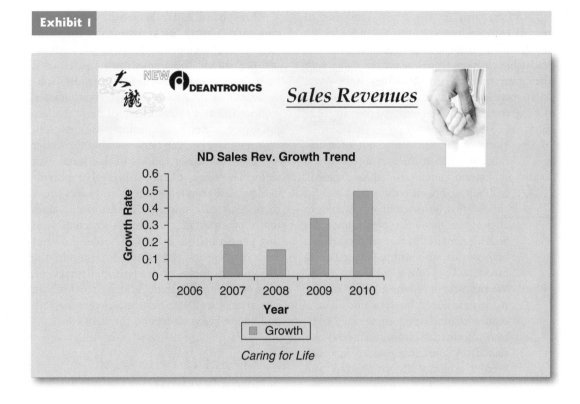

Principled Leadership: Taking the Hard Right

Gerard H. Seijts and Hon. David Kilgour

What makes a leader the most is a certain solidity at the core, a solidity founded on principles that are, essentially, points on a moral compass. Those principles are visible in the actions of some leaders, while other leaders act according to convenience. These authors lay down a blueprint that will allow a leader to be guided by principles.

On August 30, 2004, former New York City mayor Rudolph Giuliani delivered a riveting speech at the Republican National Convention. "They [the media] ridiculed Winston Churchill. They belittled Ronald Reagan," Giuliani said. "But like President Bush, they were optimists, and leaders must be optimists. Their vision was beyond the present and set on a future of real peace and true freedom. Some call it stubbornness. I call it principled leadership."

Reprint# 9B07TC05

Unfortunately, in the recent (and not so recent) past, we have seen too many leadership failures—too many examples of individuals in leadership positions who were unable to deal with the "great responsibility" that they were given. More specifically, too many so-called "leaders" did not exercise principled leadership. For example:

- Harry Stonecipher came out of retirement in 2003 to help restore Boeing's reputation after an ethics scandal. Stonecipher helped write a new code of conduct that, he indicated, would apply to all people in the Boeing organization. Yet Stonecipher violated that very code when he began an affair with a female Boeing executive. The board asked him to resign.

- WestJet Airlines admitted that its "highest management levels" were behind an elaborate scheme to steal commercially sensitive information from arch-rival Air Canada. A court case resulted in which WestJet admitted to wrongdoing and agreed to pay $5.5 million in investigation and legal bills, plus a $10 million donation to charity. On its web site, WestJet identifies nine "legendary values," among them: "we are honest, open, and keep our commitments," and "we treat everyone with respect." Did the actions of the senior leadership put a dent in the values on which WestJet was built?

- Several members of Hewlett-Packard's executive team employed a series of "disturbing" tactics (e.g., obtaining private phone record using false pretenses) in an effort to trace those board leaks. This led to the resignation of Chairman Patricia Dunn, and state and federal investigations. CEO Mark Hurd stated that the "tactics do not reflect the values of HP." Hewlett-Packard's core values include "we conduct our business with uncompromising integrity" and "we have trust and respect for individuals."

Leadership today is about winning the trust and respect of constituents, including citizens, shareholders, employees, and customers. But should these constituents place their trust (and money) in a leader's hands? Constituents take the time to evaluate the character, competence and commitment of those that are (or aspire to be) in leadership positions. And anytime there is a gap between what the leader says and does the credibility of that leader will suffer. Therefore, it is no surprise that individuals get disillusioned when their leaders prove themselves to be only mere images of the values that they espouse. It is under such conditions that people believe that their "leaders" do not show principled leadership. As a result, the dynamic currency of leadership depreciates, compromising the leader's ability to lead. In this article, we describe principled leadership and how it keeps leaders on the right course.

⊠ What Is Principled Leadership?

Alan Yuspah, senior Vice President, Ethics, Compliance and Corporate Responsibility, the Hospital Corporation of America Inc., identified three essential elements of principled leadership.

- **The articulation of certain principles or values.** Leaders need to decide what their personal or organizational values are and provide leadership consistent with these espoused or internalized values. Does the leader "live" the values in the business decisions that he or she has to make? Does the leader stick with his or her stated values no matter how difficult the business challenges prove to be? Consider the challenge that Ed Clark, the President and CEO, TD Bank Financial Group, recalled in a recent presentation to MBAs. To paraphrase him: We are trying to be an inclusive workplace, and we believe in diversity of all kinds: women, visible minorities, gays, and so forth. We are supportive of the gay community; we sponsor the Pride parade. However, I get letters from customers, that state: If you want to defy God's will then I don't want to bank with you. Clark and the TD Bank Financial Group remain committed to their diversity initiatives.

- **The principled leader is able to make tough decisions.** Principled leaders make a conscientious effort to get all the relevant information to make an informed decision and to see that their decisions are consistent with their values and those of the organization. The leadership of Flight Director Eugene Kranz during the Apollo 13 crisis is a compelling example. For years, he had championed a strong set of values: discipline, morale or confidence, toughness, competence, commitment, and teamwork. Observers of the space program have said that it was these characteristics that formed the culture that would keep Kranz's team together both in good times and, in particular, in bad times. In business settings, good leaders must be principled but also pragmatic—their principles cannot paralyze them from taking action. The principled person nearly always feels guilty that s/he cannot live up to his/her finest aspirations.
- **Principled leadership is reflected in how leaders deal with other people.** Those individuals in leadership positions should never forget that the "how" is as important as the "what." For example, humility and integrity should be part of a principled leader's behavioral repertoire. Manuel London, a management scholar and practitioner, and Director of the Center of Human Resource

Management, at the State University of New York, indicates that principled leaders always try to understand the various points of view and reach common ground without hostility, and without working over, around, or through other people. This is a key message that leaders such as Ed Clark, George Cope (President and COO, Bell Canada), Michael McCain (President and CEO, Maple Leaf Foods), and Lt.-Gen. (ret.) Romeo Dallaire keep telling our MBA students. But, as London explained, principled leaders do not ignore the tough realities of business; they have mastered the art of business diplomacy. In his words, "They work together to enhance interpersonal work relationships and are particularly valuable in making tough decisions, resolving emotional conflicts, and negotiating sensitive issues."

The 16th President of the United States, Abraham Lincoln, can inspire all of us in our own careers. For example, in *Team of Rivals: The Political Genius of Abraham Lincoln,* author Doris Kearns Goodwin writes that Lincoln was able to defeat more privileged and accomplished rivals for the Republican nomination in 1860 because his life experience had forged a character that allowed him to put himself in the place of other persons, to know what they were feeling and to understand their fears, motives and desires. This same character allowed him to bring his rivals into his cabinet and marshal their talents to preserve the Union and win the war. Goodwin wrote that Lincoln was "... plain and complex, shrewd and transparent, tender and iron-willed ... His success in dealing with the strong egos of the men in his cabinet suggests that in the hands of a truly great politician the qualities we generally associate with decency—kindness, sensitivity, compassion, honesty and empathy—can also be impressive political resources."

How to "Get" Principled Leadership?

It is foolish to believe that there is a single most important determinant of principled leadership. There are actually four determinants, and they come in to play at the individual, group, and organizational levels. We list examples in this particular order. We do not assume that our list is complete.

1. Upbringing and Life Experiences

Retired Lieutenant-General Romeo Dallaire is the former head of the United Nations Peacekeeping Force in Rwanda. He witnessed genocide. Dallaire shared the following anecdote with a group of MBAs enrolled in a leadership course. A young lieutenant and his platoon enter a small village which had been the scene of a massacre. The troops notice a ditch with women and children, several who are hacked to pieces; others are bleeding to death. There is no doubt that these people are going to die. It is hard for the soldiers to just stand by and be a witness to these people dying. What should they do? The reader should know that, before the war, over 30 per cent of Rwandans were infected with HIV or had AIDS. Soldiers do not run around with protective gear, such as rubber gloves, and have scrapes, cuts, bruises, and wounds due to the nature of their business. What should the young lieutenant order the soldiers to do? Should he order the troops not to help and to march on because of the risk of contracting the devastating disease? Or should he order the troops to console and help the women and children? The Lieutenant figures that people are dying and that the soldiers have a moral or ethical duty to assist these people in any possible way. Dallaire went to his 26 commanders and explained the dilemma. He found out that 23 commanders would order the troops *not* to go in and help; three would assist, including the Canadians. The

question then is, "For what reasons do some troops get in the ditch and assist the women and children, even with the risk involved, whereas others do not?" Dallaire believes that training has something to do with this. But perhaps more important, he articulated, it is the upbringing and the fundamental beliefs or values that Canadians espouse. Two of these beliefs are that human rights are important, and that every human is human ... one person is not more human than the other.

2. Reflection

The development of one's leadership skills requires actual leadership actions, followed by reflection or debriefing. As a principled leader, do we take the time to pause and think about how we are doing in terms of the goals we have set for ourselves? Leaders are often under intense pressure to produce results. This is a plus when the leader has mastered important skills or performance routines. But what about those behaviors that require our continued attention because the objective is to develop these behaviors? Sometimes we need to be in a learning mode. For example, leaders can focus on several questions or "tests," including a hypothetical Globe and Mail headline. Would they like to see the action they were contemplating on tomorrow's front page? Could they live with the headline? Could they explain their actions to their 10-year-old child? Seeking the advice of an executive coach who can help develop skills is becoming increasingly common for business executives.

3. Role Models

Gandhi considered modeling the moral example as the prime duty of a ruler, including the head of a family or the owner of a business. Studies have shown that people's behavior is shaped, in part, by their observation of others. For example, Albert Bandura, the David Starr Jordan Professor of Social Science in Psychology, at

Stanford University, and famous for his work on social learning, wrote:

> Learning would be exceedingly laborious, not to mention hazardous, if people had to rely solely on the effects of their own actions to inform them what to do. Fortunately, most human behavior is learned through modeling: from observing others one forms an idea of how new behaviors are manifested and perform; on later occasions this coded information serves as a guide for action.

Mentoring is consistent with Bandura's social learning theory; it involves learning in a social situation whereby a person models the behavior of a more experienced teacher or colleague. Seymour Schulich, a successful Canadian businessman and philanthropist, recently observed that, "I live the axiom that 100 years from now, it won't matter how much money you had, how big a house you lived in or what kind of car you drove. But if you are important in the life of a young person, you might make a difference. So I make time for young people and try to act as a mentor." We know that without the modeling of leadership behaviors, standards of principled leadership will be more difficult to achieve. This is because leaders help to set the tone of behavioral norms and organizational culture.

4. Code of Ethics and Communication

Organizations should have a code of ethics or a set of guiding values. Leaders should assess decisions or actions against that code. This is how the Johnson & Johnson organization was so successful in dealing with the Tylenol crisis. This is why organizations such as General Electric, Maple Leaf Foods, and TD Bank Financial Group are spending a lot of time on defining their core values and how to "live" those values. The events at Boeing discussed earlier show that a code of ethics can be effective. But a willingness to act on

the code is required. One of the main purposes of a code of ethics is to provide guidelines that help people decide what actions to take from an ethical or organizational culture point of view. The importance of values and a code of ethics must be conveyed from the top of the organization—the CEO and his or her leadership team. The leader should make values a salient aspect of the leadership agenda so that the significance of these values does in fact reach those individuals in lower-level positions.

For example, leaders can explain how a set of values guided the decision making process. Consider the following actual event. Roy Vagelos, a former senior vice-president of research at Merck, and CEO, decided to give away a drug that prevented river blindness to all those who need it and who could not afford it. Former chairman of Merck, George W. Merck, explained, "We try never to forget that medicine is for the people. It is not for the profits . . . The profits follow, and if we have remembered that, they have never failed to appear. The better we have remembered it, the larger they have been." The message? Values or guiding principles are important in making tough business decisions. Vagelos was later asked whether he would have committed his company to the costly program even without the benefits of strengthening its reputation, bolstering its recruiting, and the creation of shareholder value. He explained that he had no choice as his whole life had been dedicated to helping people.

✉ The Challenges of Principled Leadership

There can be challenges to "living the values" and a leader's principled approach to decision-making. For example, an activist group went after Ford Motor Co. and Walt Disney Co. because it believed the two companies were destroying traditional American values by supporting gay and lesbian rights. In his 2002 book *Leadership*, Giuliani recounts the events that took place in October 1995, the year in which the United Nations celebrated its 50th anniversary. The New York City Host Committee had raised money to sponsor several events, including a concert at Lincoln Center's Avery Fisher Hall. Who showed up? Yasser Arafat. Giuliani had specifically excluded the Palestinian delegation, as well as delegations from Cuba, Iraq, Iran, Libya, North Korea, Somalia, and Yugoslavia. Giuliani had special contempt for Arafat and so he had him thrown out. An international scandal was born. *The New York Times* and the Clinton administration condemned Giuliani's action. But Giuliani was convinced that he was on the right side; his core set of principles, and Arafat's ongoing terrorist activities, drove his behavior. In his words, "Some Americans are unable to face up to the fact that there really are evil people."

Sooner or later, therefore, leaders face the challenge of how to remain true to their principles, in particular, when other people put pressure on them. Most leaders operate in a fast-paced and complex world, where principles often collide. It is sometimes very difficult to do "the right thing" for both employees and shareholders, for customers and employees, for taxpayers and clients of the social welfare system. We conclude this article with five prescriptions that, we believe, will make people more receptive to principled leadership. These are the things that leaders can do to continue to "walk on water" as opposed to swimming or sinking.

1. Executives Should Be Model Citizens

John Edward Poole of Edmonton, who died recently at the age of ninety, is a hard-to-beat exemplar. On retiring as CEO of Poole Construction Ltd. (now PCL Construction Ltd.) in 1977, he and his brother George sold their majority stake to the organization's employees rather than accept the highest offer. (Today, the organization remains 100 percent owned by employees.) During the next three decades, he and his wife, Barbara, gave tens of millions of dollars, often on a sustained endowment basis, to a host of cultural, educational, social and environmental institutions in their city. The couple also led fund-raising campaigns for many good causes. *Edmonton Journal* columnist, Paula Simons, noted in a tribute, "(John Poole) believed that every man owed a duty to his fellow citizens. He understood that living in a city isn't just about occupying space—it's about participating in the life of a community. It's about taking responsibility for the future."

2. Stick to What You're Good At

How many businesses in Canada and elsewhere have been harmed or ruined by a senior leadership team that ventures into new activities or markets without enough advance study of conditions or an inadequate understanding of its own circle of competence? For example, Southwest Airlines' returns to shareholders over three decades have outdone even those of Warren Buffett's legendary Berkshire Hathaway. Southwest has no hotels, no travel businesses or real estate speculations. Both management and employees know what the airline is good at and stick to it: low-cost reliable air transportation. In an industry where profits rarely seem to last more than a year or two, Southwest continues to flourish. Contrast this approach with organizations such as K-Mart, ASDA, and Nortel that at some point struggled with strategic drift, unable to provide a clear direction in their activities. The implications for personal leadership? It is important to have a core set of convictions, or focus; without it, leaders yield to all kinds of pressures, and little gets achieved. Senator and former Democratic nominee for U.S. President John F. Kerry was seen as a mess of contradictions on various issues important to the American public. People perceived him as a flip-flopper; he lacked a clear focus. Bush won re-election, in part, because Americans wanted clear and consistent leadership.

3. An Inclusive Corporate Culture

Nucor Corporation, the out-performer in the American steel industry for many years, and one of America's most-admired organizations, is a good case study here. Its former CEO, F. Kenneth Iverson, is quoted in Jeremy J. Siegal's excellent book, *The Future for Investors*, as attributing most of the company's success to ". . . the consistency of our company and our ability to project its philosophies throughout the whole organization, enabled by our lack of layers and bureaucracy." The philosophy of "no favourites" among all members of the corporate team is demonstrated in myriad ways. Distinctions between executives and other employees are even difficult to detect. For example, there is no executive dining room at Nucor's head office. All employees of the company are listed alphabetically in the annual report, with no distinctions for titles. There are no company vehicles or aircraft and no assigned parking places. All employees receive the same amount of vacation time and insurance coverage. Ideas won't get buried in bureaucracy; the freedom to try out ideas gives Nucor a distinct advantage over other companies: a creative, get-it-done workforce. Every employee is a member of the same winning team.

4. Have Sound Whistleblower Protection or Processes for Information Flow

Sherron Watkins, the ex-Enron executive who first confronted former CEO Kenneth Lay about her suspicions of accounting improprieties, became a national "hero" when her memos to Lay were leaked to the American media. She had attempted, without success, to protest Enron's accounting practices to other executives as early as 1996, but got nowhere. The then-CFO of Enron, Andrew Fastow, wanted her fired, but senior management could find no reasonable cause.

Every organization should have policies in place to protect the Sherron Watkinses of the world and to ensure that valid concerns are acted upon with deliberate speed. "Information patriots," as Canadian whistleblowers now often prefer to be called, are still usually forced to give up their careers in the offices where they encountered and confronted wrongdoing. Consider, for example, the fate of Joseph Darby, the U.S. Army Specialist who turned in the pictures of prisoner abuse at Abu Ghraib. He was a hero to some; Caroline Kennedy and Senator Ted Kennedy gave him a Profile In Courage award in honor of President John F. Kennedy. But Darby could not return to his home because he had been threatened. Darby was supposed to remain anonymous, but former Secretary of Defense Donald Rumsfeld identified him without warning on national television, a gesture that some say was more about payback than an attempt to honor the whistleblower. There are scores of whistleblowers or information patriots that have paid a steep price for their courage to speak up. Responsible CEOs should ensure that people like Watkins and Darby are regarded as role models for all employees.

CEOs should appreciate the eyes and ears of their employees. Transparency is important; some even consider it an outright competitive weapon. Former U.S. Supreme Court Justice Louis Brandeis once said, "Sunlight is the best disinfectant." The quote refers to the benefits of openness and transparency. Some well-known organizations have made it their objective to operate in an atmosphere of avowed openness. Their leadership opines that individuals who feel a discomfort under the bright light of scrutiny may have something to hide. Those in leadership positions cannot solve problems if they don't know about them. Leaders are well-advised to create routes for their employees to express their views, so that maximum, not minimum, information is used in their decision-making.

5. Boards of Directors Should Encourage CEOs to Speak Out Responsibly on Public Issues

How many of our business leaders have had the courage to speak out from a responsible perspective against income trusts? Or take climate change, the very inconvenient and doubtless most important issue facing humanity today. Recently, the Intergovernmental Panel on Climate Change, drawing on the work of thousands of scientists around the world, reported that all of us on the planet have only a decade to reverse surging greenhouse gas emissions or risk severe climate change that would render numerous regions of the world uninhabitable. A cover story in a recent *Economist*, "The Greening of America," indicated that corporate America is now among the loudest voices calling for emission controls and other measures designed to reduce the output of carbon dioxide and greenhouse gasses. For example, the CEO of Duke Energy, James Rogers said about reductions, "It must be mandatory, so that there is no doubt about our actions ... The science of global warming is clear. We know enough to act now. We must act now." Not enough business voices appear yet have joined the parade on the issue in our own country. And for CEOs and the senior leadership team to do so effectively, they need the support of their board of directors; organizations should speak with one voice.

In her 2006 memoir titled *Tough Choices*, former Hewlett-Packard CEO, Carly Fiorina, writes about success and the importance of character. "Character was everything, and character was defined as candour, integrity, and authenticity. Candour was about speaking the truth, and about speaking up and speaking out. Integrity was about preserving your principles and action on them. Authenticity was about knowing what you believed, being who you were, and standing up for both." Fiorina explains that leaders can always choose to become something more. We suggest they can (and should) choose to work on their principled leadership, as it appears there is considerable room for improvement. A recent poll of 1,000 Canadians found that 93 per cent of respondents rated firefighters as trustworthy. In contrast, CEOs were considered trustworthy by just 21 per cent of the adult Canadians who were polled by Ipsos Reid; this number is virtually unchanged since 2002. Only union leaders (19 per cent), local politicians (12 per cent), national politicians and car salespeople (both at 7 per cent) ranked below CEOs in the "whom do we trust" survey. When asked what criteria they considered in rating the trustworthiness of people, the respondents indicated they used factors such as integrity, reliability, and commitment to promises in their ratings. These factors, of course, characterize the principled leader. But we also note that principled people sometimes cross the barrier between being right and being righteous. The first is admirable the second just alienates people.

About the Editors

W. Glenn Rowe served in the Canadian Navy for 22 years. While still in the navy, he completed his master of business administration degree at Memorial University of Newfoundland part-time (1983–1986) and taught on a part-time basis for 2 years (1986–1988) in Memorial's Faculty of Business Administration. In 1990, he retired from the navy and became a full-time lecturer in the Faculty of Business Administration at Memorial. In 1992, he began studying leadership within the context of strategic management at Texas A&M University, where he completed his PhD in 1996. He rejoined the Faculty of Business Administration at Memorial in September 1995, where he taught strategic management and strategic leadership. Professor Rowe joined the Richard Ivey School of Business as a faculty member on July 1, 2001. He served as the faculty adviser for the PhD program in general management/strategy from January 2002 to July 2009. On July 1, 2009, he became the director of Ivey's Executive MBA Program. He has taught strategy and strategic leadership to undergraduate business students and MBAs. He currently teaches strategic analysis and action to EMBAs. He serves as a reviewer for several academic journals and is active in the community. He has facilitated strategic-thinking sessions for several organizations including a couple of banks, a fish farming company, and others such as the Alliance for the Control of Tobacco (Newfoundland and Labrador), the Newfoundland and Labrador Medical Association, Fishery Products International, Gros Morne National Park, and Sir Wilfred Grenfell College. He is the coauthor of a strategic management textbook and its associated casebook, both of which are in their third edition. His research is published in journals such as the *Strategic Management Journal,* the *Journal of Management Studies,* the *Journal of Management,* the *Leadership Quarterly,* the *Journal of World Business,* and the *Journal of Management Inquiry.*

Laura Guerrero worked in retail management for 10 years in Canada, the United States, and Mexico. She has an undergraduate degree in economics from The University of Texas at El Paso. Later, she completed a master's of business administration with a concentration on management and organizational studies at Simon Fraser University in British Columbia, Canada. In 2009, she graduated with a PhD in business administration at the Richard Ivey School of Business at Western University. In addition to her interest in gender and culture as they relate to leadership, her research has focused on careers of expatriates and immigrants. In September 2009, she joined the Faculty of Business Administration at The University of Texas at El Paso as an assistant professor of management.

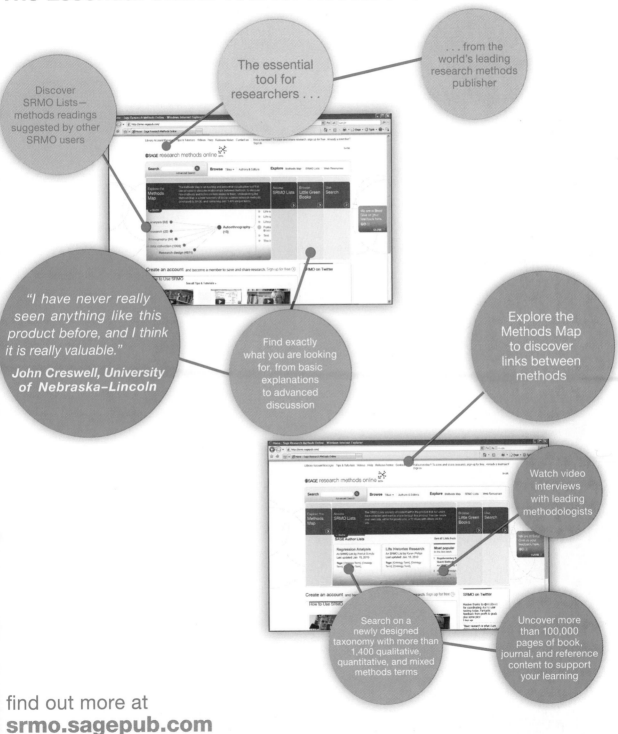

⑨SAGE research**methods**
The Essential Online Tool for Researchers

The essential tool for researchers . . .

. . . from the world's leading research methods publisher

Discover SRMO Lists— methods readings suggested by other SRMO users

"I have never really seen anything like this product before, and I think it is really valuable."

John Creswell, University of Nebraska–Lincoln

Find exactly what you are looking for, from basic explanations to advanced discussion

Explore the Methods Map to discover links between methods

Watch video interviews with leading methodologists

Search on a newly designed taxonomy with more than 1,400 qualitative, quantitative, and mixed methods terms

Uncover more than 100,000 pages of book, journal, and reference content to support your learning

find out more at
srmo.sagepub.com